THE VICTORIA HISTORY
OF THE
COUNTIES OF ENGLAND

A HISTORY OF
WILTSHIRE

VOLUME VIII

THE VICTORIA HISTORY
OF THE
COUNTIES OF ENGLAND

EDITED BY R. B. PUGH

THE UNIVERSITY OF LONDON
INSTITUTE OF
HISTORICAL RESEARCH

Oxford University Press, Amen House, London, E.C.4

GLASGOW NEW YORK TORONTO MELBOURNE WELLINGTON
BOMBAY CALCUTTA MADRAS KARACHI LAHORE DACCA
CAPE TOWN SALISBURY NAIROBI IBADAN ACCRA
KUALA LUMPUR HONG KONG

PRINTED IN THE NETHERLANDS

INSCRIBED TO THE
MEMORY OF HER LATE MAJESTY
QUEEN VICTORIA
WHO GRACIOUSLY GAVE THE TITLE TO
AND ACCEPTED THE DEDICATION
OF THIS HISTORY

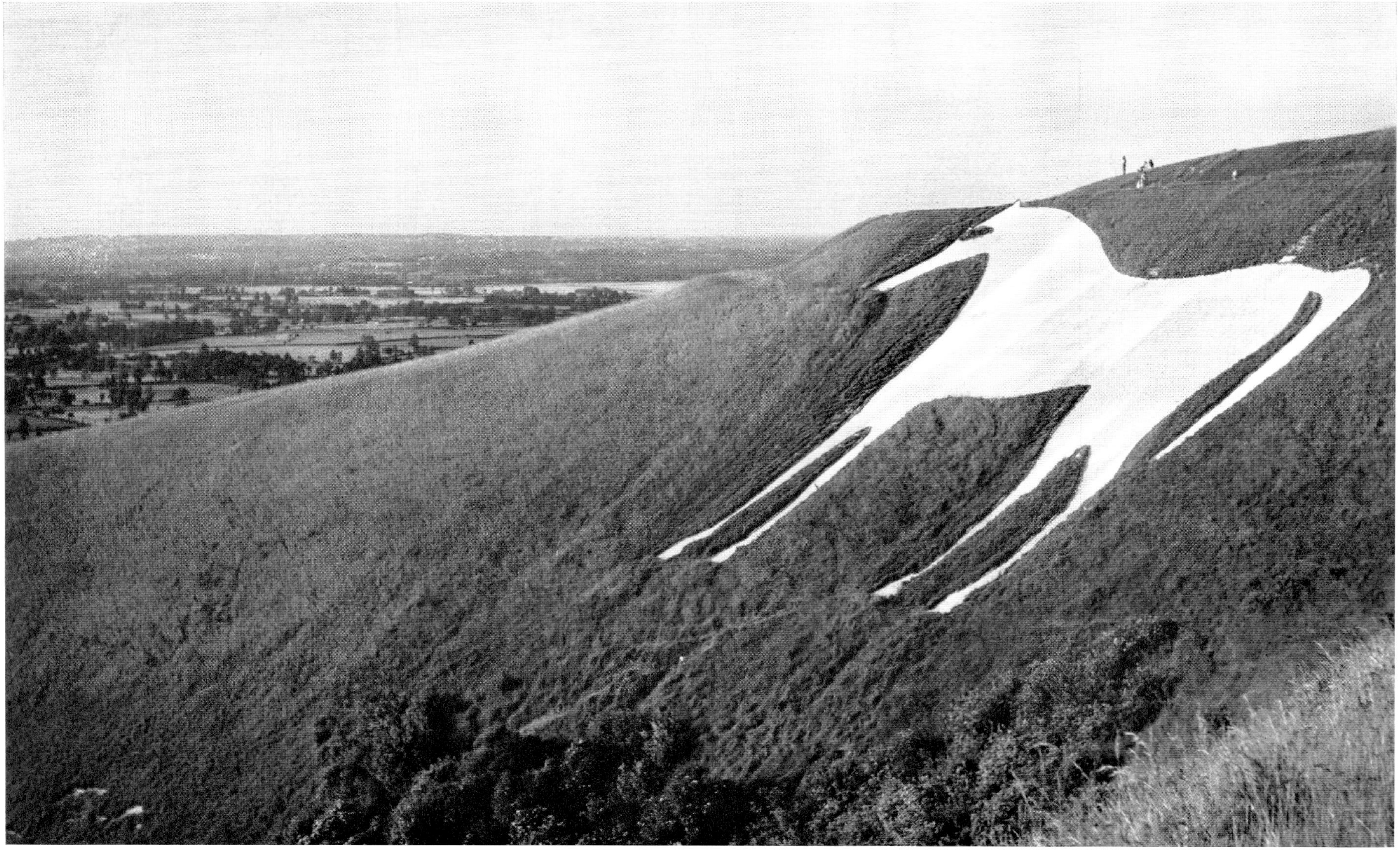

The White Horse, Bratton

A HISTORY OF
WILTSHIRE

EDITED BY ELIZABETH CRITTALL

VOLUME VIII

PUBLISHED FOR

THE INSTITUTE OF HISTORICAL RESEARCH

BY THE

OXFORD UNIVERSITY PRESS

AMEN HOUSE, LONDON

1965

CONTENTS OF VOLUME EIGHT

LIST OF ILLUSTRATIONS

Thanks are due to the following for permission to reproduce material in their possession and for the loan of prints and paintings: Wiltshire Archaeological and Natural History Society, Wiltshire Record Office, *Wiltshire Times*, Messrs. A. Laverton & Co. Ltd., Westbury, the Committee for Aerial Photography of the University of Cambridge, the Air Ministry, the Society of Antiquaries of London, the National Buildings Record, *Country Life*, Mr. H. N. Dewey, and Mr. David Robson.

LIST OF MAPS AND PLANS

All the maps were drawn by G. R. Versey of the Department of Geography, University College, London, from drafts prepared by K. H. Rogers. They are based upon the Ordnance Survey with the sanction of the Controller of H.M. Stationery Office, Crown Copyright reserved. Boundaries on the Hundred Maps are taken from the Tithe Maps of *c.* 1840.

EDITORIAL NOTE

THE present volume, the eighth in the Wiltshire series to be published, has been prepared like the previous ones under the superintendence of the Wiltshire Victoria County History Committee. That Committee, whose origin and constitution are described in the Editorial Note to the *Victoria History of Wiltshire*, Volume VII, has been good enough to continue, and indeed, to enlarge its generous grant for the support of a local editor and an assistant editor, and the University of London has thus been enabled to continue publication. The University takes pleasure in renewing its gratitude to the participating Authorities in Wiltshire for their friendly co-operation. It has to be recorded here that in May 1964 Mr. K. H. Rogers resigned from the assistant editorship, and was replaced in October 1964 by Mr. Colin Shrimpton.

Thanks are due to many persons who have helped in the compilation of the volume either by granting access to documents in their care or ownership, by examining drafts, or by offering advice. Particular mention must be made of the Clerks of the Urban District Councils of Warminster and Westbury, the Marquess of Bath and his Comptroller, Mr. R. A. Ingleton, the Earl of Pembroke and Montgomery, C.V.O., Viscount Long of Wraxall, Mr. M. G. Rathbone (County Archivist), Mr. R. E. Sandell (Hon. Librarian, Wiltshire Archaeological and Natural History Society), and Mr. Harry Ross. The late Miss D. U. Seth-Smith and the late Miss I. M. Braidwood gave much valuable help by answering questions and reading drafts. Finally it must be recorded that preliminary drafts for the accounts of the parishes in the Hundred of Whorwellsdown were, with one exception, written by Mr. W. R. Powell.

WILTSHIRE
VICTORIA COUNTY HISTORY
COMMITTEE

As at 1 March 1965

Major S. V. Christie-Miller, c.b.e., d.l., Chairman
Mr. R. K. Hedges
Sir Geoffrey Tritton, bt., c.b.e., d.l. } *Representing the Wiltshire County Council*
Sir Henry Langton, d.s.o., d.s.c.
Dr. T. R. Thomson

Councillor H. W. Gardner
Alderman A. J. Bown } *Representing the Swindon Borough Council*

Councillor E. P. Marsh *Representing the Salisbury City Council*

Mr. E. G. H. Kempson } *Representing the Wiltshire Archaeological and*
Mr. R. E. Sandell *Natural History Society*

Mr. M. J. Lansdown *Representing the Records Branch of the Wiltshire Archaeological and Natural History Society*

The Revd. Canon W. J. Cratchley *Representing the Bishop of Bristol*

Mr. R. B. Pugh *Representing the Central Committee of the Victoria County History*

Co-opted Members

Professor T. S. Ashton, f.b.a.
Professor D. C. Douglas, f.b.a.
Mr. G. E. Fussell
Professor H. J. Habakkuk
Professor C. F. C. Hawkes, f.b.a.

Mr. R. V. Lennard
Dr. J. H. P. Pafford
Professor S. Piggott, f.b.a.
Dr. G. D. Ramsay
Lady Stenton, f.b.a.
Professor R. B. Wernham

Mr. D. Murray John, o.b.e., Hon. Secretary
Mr. M. G. Rathbone, Deputy Hon. Secretary
Mr. E. Eckersley, Hon. Treasurer

LIST OF CLASSES OF DOCUMENTS IN THE PUBLIC RECORD OFFICE
USED IN THIS VOLUME
WITH THEIR CLASS NUMBERS

Chancery

	Proceedings	
C 1	Early	
C 2	Series I	
C 3	Series II	
	Six Clerks' Series	
C 6	Collins	
C 10	Whittington	
	Placita in Cancellaria	
C 44	Tower Series	
C 47	Miscellanea	
C 54	Close Rolls	
C 60	Fine Rolls	
C 66	Patent Rolls	
C 131	Extents for Debts	
	Inquisitions post mortem	
C 136	Series I, Ric. II	
C 137		Hen. IV
C 138		Hen. V
C 139		Hen. VI
C 140		Edw. IV
C 142	Series II	
C 143	Inquisitions ad quod damnum	

Court of Common Pleas

	Feet of Fines	
C.P. 25 (1)	Series I	
C.P. 25 (2)	Series II	
C.P. 40	Plea Rolls	
C.P. 43	Recovery Rolls	

Exchequer, Treasury of the Receipt

E 40 — Ancient Deeds, Series A

Exchequer, King's Remembrancer

E 134	Depositions taken by Commission
E 164	Miscellaneous Books, Series I
E 178	Special Commissions of Enquiry
E 179	Subsidy Rolls, &c.
E 210	Ancient Deeds, Series D

Exchequer, Augmentation Office

E 301	Certificates of Colleges and Chantries
E 308	Particulars for the Sale of Fee-Farm Rents
	Ancient Deeds
E 326	Series B

E 329 — Series BS

Exchequer, First Fruits and Tenths

E 347 — Writs and Miscellanea

Exchequer, Lord Treasurer's Remembrancer

E 377 — Recusant Rolls, Pipe Office Series

Home Office

H.O. 40	Disturbances, Correspondence
H.O. 67	Acreage Returns
H.O. 129	Census Papers: Ecclesiastical Returns

Justices Itinerant

J.I. 1	Assize Rolls, Eyre Rolls, &c.
J.I. 3	Gaol Delivery Rolls

Court of King's Bench (Crown Side)

K.B. 26	Curia Regis Rolls
K.B. 27	Coram Rege Rolls

Exchequer, Auditors of Land Revenue

L.R. 2	Miscellaneous Books
L.R. 14	Ancient Deeds, Series E

Court of Requests

Req. 2 — Proceedings

Special Collections

S.C. 2	Court Rolls
S.C. 6	Ministers' Accounts
S.C. 11	Rentals and Surveys (Rolls)
S.C. 12	Rentals and Surveys (Portfolios)

Court of Star Chamber

	Proceedings
Sta. Cha. 4	Mary
Sta. Cha. 8	Jas. I

State Paper Office

	State Papers Domestic
S.P. 15	Addenda Edw. VI - Jas. I
S.P. 23	Committee for Compounding with Delinquents

Court of Wards and Liveries

Wards 2 — Deeds and Evidences

NOTE ON ABBREVIATIONS

Among the abbreviations and short titles used the following may require elucidation:

C.C.C.	Corpus Christi College, Oxford.
Ch. Com.	Church Commissioners.
Char. Com.	Charity Commissioners.
D. & C. Sar.	Dean and Chapter of Salisbury.
G.R.O.	General Register Office.
Hants R.O.	Hampshire Record Office.
Sar. Corp. MSS.	Salisbury Corporation MSS.
Sar. Dioc. R.O.	Salisbury Diocesan Record Office.
W.A.S.	Wiltshire Archaeological and Natural History Society.
W.A.S. Libr., Devizes	Library of W.A.S. in the Museum, Devizes.
W.A.S. Rec. Brch.	Records Branch of W.A.S.
W.C.M.	Winchester College Muniments.
Wilts. Cuttings	Volumes of Wiltshire newspaper cuttings in W.A.S. Libr., Devizes.
Wilts. Tracts	Collection of pamphlets and papers in W.A.S. Libr., Devizes.
W.R.O.	Wiltshire Record Office.
Andrews and Dury, Map (W.A.S. Rec. Brch.)	Crittall, Elizabeth (ed.) *Andrews' and Dury's Map of Wiltshire 1773* (W.A.S. Rec. Brch. viii).
Bounds of Wilts.	Lord Fitzmaurice and W. L. Bown, *Boundaries of the Administrative County of Wilts.* (1918).
Cal. Feet of F. Wilts. 1195–1272, ed. Fry	Fry, E. A. (ed.) *Calendar of Feet of Fines Wilts.* 1195–1272 (W.A.S. Devizes, 1930).
Cart. Sax. ed. Birch	Birch, W. de Gray (ed.) *Cartularium Saxonicum.*
Crockford	Crockford's *Clerical Directory.*
Crown Pleas Wilts. Eyre, 1249 (W.A.S. Rec. Brch.)	Meekings, C. A. F. (ed.) *Crown Pleas of the Wiltshire Eyre, 1249* (W.A.S. Rec. Brch. xvi).
Dugdale, *Mon.*	Dugdale, W. *Monasticon Anglicanum* (edn. 1817–30).
Early Stuart Tradesmen (W.A.S. Rec. Brch.)	Williams, N. J. (ed.) *Tradesmen in Early-Stuart Wiltshire* (W.A.S. Rec Brch. xv).
Endowed Char. Wilts. (1908)	*Endowed Charities of Wilts.* H.C. 273–1 (1908), lxxxi.
Feet of F. Wilts. 1272–1327 (W.A.S. Rec. Brch.)	Pugh, R. B. (ed.) *Abstracts of Feet of Fines Wilts. for reigns of Edw. I and Edw. II* (W.A.S. Rec. Brch. i).
First Pembroke Survey, ed. Straton	Straton, C. R. (ed.) *Survey of Lands of William, First Earl of Pembroke* (Roxburghe Club, 1909).
Halliday, Information	Information about Warminster, MS. compiled *c.* 1820–40 by J. E. Halliday (1963 *penes* Mr. H. N. Dewey, Warminster).
Hoare, *Mod. Wilts.*	Hoare, Sir Richard Colt, *Modern Wiltshire* (1822–37).
Jones, *Fasti Eccl. Sar.*	Jones, W. H. *Fasti Ecclesiae Sarisberiensis* (Salisbury and London, 1879).
Leland, *Itin.* ed. Toulmin Smith	Toulmin Smith, Lucy (ed.) *Itinerary of John Leland.*
Manley, Regional Survey	Regional Survey of Warminster, MS. by C. V. Manley (1963 *penes* Warminster U.D.C.).
Nightingale, *Wilts. Plate*	Nightingale, J. E. *The Church Plate of Wiltshire* (Salisbury, 1891).

P.N. Wilts. (E.P.N.S.)	*The Place-Names of Wiltshire* (English Place-Name Society).
Pembroke Manors 1631–2 (W.A.S. Rec. Brch.)	Kerridge, E. (ed.) *Surveys of the Manors of Philip, First Earl of Pembroke and Montgomery* (W.A.S. Rec. Brch. ix).
Pevsner, *Wilts.*	Pevsner, N. *The Buildings of England: Wiltshire* (1963).
Phillipps, *Wilts. Inst.*	Phillipps, Sir Thomas (ed.) *Institutiones Clericorum in Comitatu Wiltoniae* (priv. printed, 1825).
Phillipps, *Wilts. M.I.*	Phillipps, Sir Thomas, *Monumental Inscriptions of Wiltshire* (1821).
Q. Sess. and Ass. 1736 (W.A.S. Rec. Brch.)	Fowle, J. P. M. (ed.) *Wiltshire Quarter Sessions and Assizes, 1736* (W.A.S. Rec. Brch. xi).
Ramsay, *Wilts. Woollen Industry*	Ramsay, G. D. *Wiltshire Woollen Industry in the 16th and 17th Centuries.*
Reg. Ghent (Cant. and York Soc.)	Flower, C. T. and Dawes, M. C. B. (ed.) *Registrum Simonis de Gandavo* (Canterbury and York Society).
Reg. Martival (Cant. and York Soc.)	Edwards, K. (ed.) *Registers of Roger Martival, Bishop of Salisbury, 1315–30* (Canterbury and York Society).
Reg. St. Osmund (Rolls Ser.)	Jones, W. H. Rich- (ed.) *Vetus Registrum Sarisberiense alias dictum Registrum S. Osmundi Episcopi* (Rolls Series lxxviii).
Sar. Chart. and Doc. (Rolls Ser.)	Jones, W. H. Rich- (ed.) and Dunn Macray, W. (ed.) *Charters and Documents illustrating the History of Salisbury* (Rolls Series xcvii).
Sess. Mins. (W.A.S. Rec. Brch.)	Johnson, H. C. (ed.) *Minutes of Proceedings in Sessions, 1563, 1574–92* (W.A.S. Rec. Brch. iv).
Taxation Lists (W.A.S. Rec. Brch.)	Ramsay, G. D. (ed.) *Two Sixteenth-Century Taxation Lists, 1545 and 1576* (W.A.S. Rec. Brch. x).
Tropenell Cart. ed. Davies	Davies, J. S. (ed.) *Tropenell Cartulary* (W.A.S. Devizes, 1908).
Walters, *Wilts. Bells*	Walters, H. B. *The Church Bells of Wiltshire* (Devizes, 1927).
W.A.M.	*Wiltshire Archaeological and Natural History Magazine.*
Wilts. Inq. p.m. 1242–1326 (Index Libr.)	Fry, E. A. (ed.) *Abstracts of Wilts. Inq. p.m.* 1242–1326 (Index Library xxxvii).
Wilts. Inq. p.m. 1327–77 (Index Libr.)	Stokes, Ethel (ed.) *Abstracts of Wilts. Inq. p.m.* 1327–77 (Index Library xlviii).
Wilts. Inq. p.m. 1625–49 (Index Libr.)	Fry, G. S. and Fry, E. A. (ed.) *Abstracts of Wilts. Inq. p.m. for reign of Chas. I* (Index Library xxiii).
W.N. & Q.	*Wiltshire Notes and Queries.*
Wilts. Q. Sess. Rec. ed. Cunnington	Cunnington, B. H. (ed.) *Extracts from the Quarter Sessions Great Rolls of the 17th Century* (Devizes, 1932).

THE HUNDRED OF
WARMINSTER

THE main part of the hundred of Warminster lies on the western edge of the county surrounding the town from which it takes its name. One small detached piece, the southern half of the parish of Pertwood, lies just beyond the southern end of the main part of the hundred; another detached piece, consisting of the parishes of Fisherton de la Mere, Teffont Magna, and Dinton, lies about 4½ miles south-east of its eastern border. A large part of the hundred thus lies in the valley of the Wylye, and the northernmost part of it, Upton Scudamore parish, lies on the watershed between the Wylye and the Biss, a tributary of the Bristol Avon, and so between the English and Bristol Channels. To the west Corsley is drained by tributaries of the Frome, while in the south Teffont Magna and Dinton lie in the valley of the Nadder. All the parishes are geologically dominated by the chalk with its associated outcrops of greensand. In several of them the outcrops are extensive, providing level stretches of good arable land, while water meadows could be made in the valley bottoms. From the late Middle Ages until the present century the typical sheep and corn husbandry of South Wiltshire was carried on throughout the hundred. Warminster was a celebrated corn market until the late 19th century, and had a large trade in malting. The woollen industry also flourished there in a modest way, and some mills in the district around the town were used by clothiers, chiefly in the 16th and 17th centuries. Agriculture, however, has always been foremost in the region, as it is today. Warminster, although its clothing trade has gone, and its market and malting have very much declined, retains its position as the shopping centre for the surrounding villages and provides employment in light industries and in the military establishments in and near it.

In 1084 Warminster hundred included the royal manor from which it took its name and estates in Dinton, Fisherton de la Mere, Bishopstrow, Norton Bavant, Sutton Veny, and Upton Scudamore.[1] Reasons are given below for assuming that Warminster then included Corsley and Dinton included Teffont Magna.[2] These places and Upper Pertwood were in any case in the hundred by 1249.[3] Pertwood is not mentioned by the Geld Rolls as being in another hundred, so that it is likely that in 1084 the hundred contained all the places which were reckoned to be in it in 1831.[4]

The hundred always appears to have been appurtenant to the manor of Warminster, and followed the same descent.[5] The jurisdiction did not exclude the sheriff, who held two tourns yearly for the hundred.[6] Some of the lords within it claimed liberties which might properly have belonged to the sheriff. Thus in the 13th century the Mauduits claimed a gallows at Warminster,[7] the Prioress of Studley view of frankpledge, a gallows, and assize of bread and ale at Corsley,[8] and the Clares assize of bread

---

[1] *V.C.H. Wilts.* ii, pp. 188–9.
[2] See pp. 15, 76.
[3] *Crown Pleas Wilts. Eyre,* 1249 (W.A.S. Rec. Brch.), 211–3.
[4] *V.C.H. Wilts.* iv. 330.
[5] See p. 96.
[6] *W.A.M.* xiii. 114; S.C. 2/208/29; Hoare, *Mod. Wilts.* Warminster, 11.
[7] See p. 128.
[8] *Rot. Hund.* (Rec. Com.), ii. 277; J.I. 1/1006 m. 55d.

and ale at Smallbrook.[9] The Abbey of Lacock claimed extensive liberties in Bishops-trow,[10] and in fact that tithing paid nothing at the sheriff's tourn, and did not appear at the other hundred courts in later times.[11] Corsley was still reckoned a liberty in the early 14th century, and the bailiff of the hundred held separate views of frankpledge there.[12] The Prebendaries of Warminster claimed exemption for their tithing in the 13th century,[13] but it is not clear with what success. Whitbourne was said to be exempt in 1288-9, and does not appear as a tithing in later times.[14]

In 1348-9 the lords of the hundred were holding a three-weekly hundred court and two courts leet a year.[15] Profits from them often amounted to £12 or £15 a year in the later Middle Ages.[16] The same courts were held in 1652, but then it was said that few presentments were made or amercements imposed.[17] This statement is borne out by surviving records of courts in the 17th and 18th centuries. The few presentments made generally concerned highways or the customs of commons, and there seem to have been no suits between parties. The only real business was the collection of the dues of tithing silver or certain money, and mill fine, which amounted to £2 or £3 a year.[18] The curious practice of appointing the manorial officers of Little Sutton in the hundred court should also be mentioned. Yearly courts were still held in the 1830's.[19]

In 1195 the hundred was divided into home and foreign parts,[20] or as they were later called, in- and out-hundreds. In 1427 the tithings of Great Sutton, Little Sutton, Upton Scudamore, Norridge, Thoulstone, Dinton, Teffont Magna, Fisherton de la Mere, Bapton, Pertwood, Norton Bavant, Corsley, and Avenel's Fee appeared at the out-hundred court.[21] All still did so in the 18th century except Avenel's Fee which was generally reckoned in the in-hundred, with Boreham and Warminster.[22] The courts of the in-hundred, or town and liberty, are described below.[23]

Before his death c. 1264 William Mauduit had granted the bedelry of the hundred to Walter Bernard. Later in the century Walter's son John had a life interest in it which he conveyed to Richard Sculy.[24] By 1311 Sculy's interest had apparently passed to John Goscelyn, who then quitclaimed his right in the bailiwick of the hundred to Thomas Mauduit, the lord. This transaction was probably on the death of John Bernard, for Mauduit already had seisin of the bailiwick.[25] Soon after this it was granted in fee to Robert le Bore.[26] His interest passed to John Mauger, apparently by 1324,[27] although le Bore was still exercising the office in 1336.[28] Some dispute between Mauger and John Mauduit, lord of the hundred, was ended in 1349 by a quitclaim from Mauger's son to Mauduit.[29] Perquisites for that year were accounted for by a paid bailiff.[30] The bailiwick appears to have been sometimes let at farm and sometimes held by salaried officers in the 14th and 15th centuries.[31] It was mentioned as appurt-enant to the manor of Portway in 1499,[32] but nothing more is known of such a con-nexion. In 1508 it was at farm,[33] and this seems to have been the practice throughout the 16th century.[34] By 1652, however, the foreign bailiwick had evidently been

[9] J.I. 1/1006 m. 55d.
[10] Ibid.
[11] e.g. *W.A.M.* xiii. 114; Hoare, *Mod. Wilts.* War-minster, 11; Longleat MSS. Court Proceedings *passim.*
[12] J.I. 3/130 mm. 14, 15d., 93.
[13] *Close R.* 1231-4, 134; J.I. 1/1006 m. 55d.
[14] J.I. 1/1006 m. 55d.
[15] Longleat MSS. Parcel XXVII, Acct. Roll, 1348-9.
[16] Ibid. Acct. Rolls *passim.*
[17] Hoare, *Mod. Wilts.* Warminster, 10.
[18] Longleat MSS. Court Proceedings *passim.*
[19] Hoare, *Mod. Wilts.* Warminster, 85
[20] *Pipe R.* 1195 (P.R.S. n.s. vi), 140.
[21] Longleat MSS. Parcel XXVIII, Hundred Court

Roll, 1427.
[22] Ibid. Court Proceedings *passim.*
[23] See pp. 128-9.
[24] Longleat MS. 8900.
[25] Ibid. 9117.
[26] *Cal. Pat.* 1317-21, 491.
[27] *Cal. Close,* 1323-7, 61.
[28] J.I. 3/130 m. 14.
[29] Longleat MS. 9159; C 44/1/24.
[30] Longleat MSS. Parcel XXVIII, Acct. Roll, 1348-9.
[31] Ibid. Acct. Rolls *passim.*
[32] C.P. 25(1)/257/66/25, 27.
[33] Longleat MSS. Parcel XXVII, Rental, 1508.
[34] Ibid. 9445 and Parcel XXVIII, Rental, 1578.

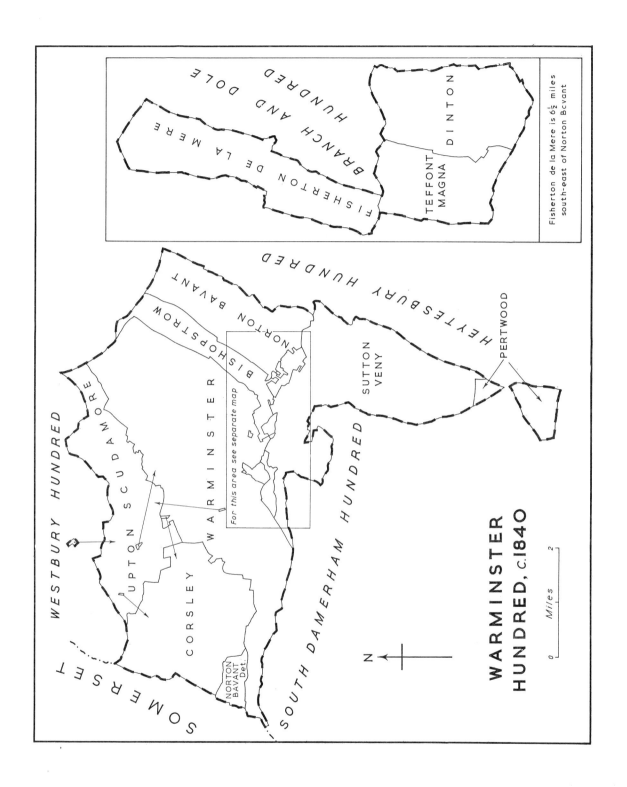

WARMINSTER HUNDRED, c.1840

N

Miles
0   1   2

WESTBURY HUNDRED

SOMERSET

UPTON SCUDAMORE

CORSLEY

WARMINSTER

NORTON BAVANT Det.

SOUTH DAMERHAM HUNDRED

BISHOPSTROW

NORTON BAVANT

For this area see separate map

SUTTON VENY

HEYTESBURY HUNDRED

PERTWOOD

BRANCH AND DOLE HUNDRED

FISHERTON DE LA MERE

TEFFONT MAGNA

DINTON

Fisherton de la Mere is 6½ miles
south-east of Norton Bavant

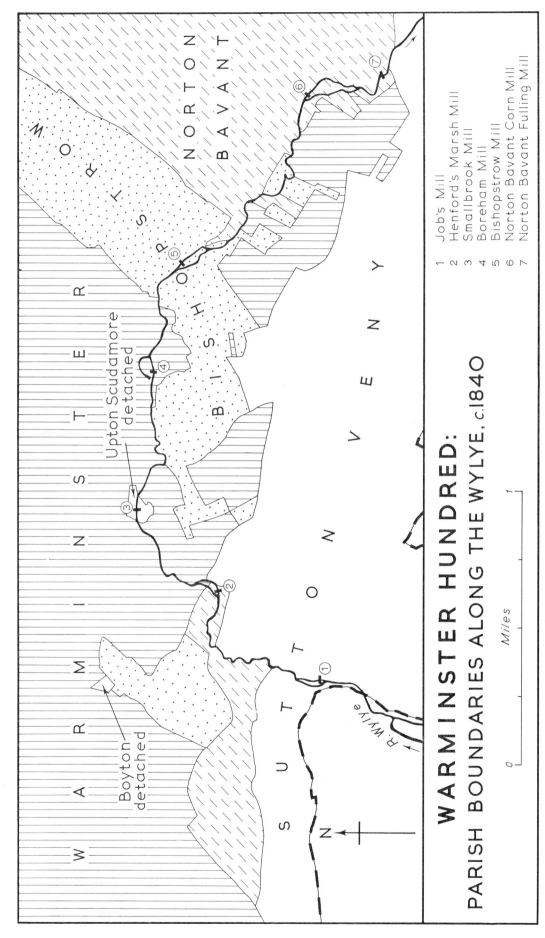

WARMINSTER HUNDRED:
PARISH BOUNDARIES ALONG THE WYLYE, c.1840

1   Job's Mill
2   Henford's Marsh Mill
3   Smallbrook Mill
4   Boreham Mill
5   Bishopstrow Mill
6   Norton Bavant Corn Mill
7   Norton Bavant Fulling Mill

Boyton detached

Upton Scudamore detached

WARMINSTER

BISHOPSTROW

NORTON BAVANT

SUTTON VENY

R. Wylye

N

Miles

united with the bailiwick of Warminster town,[35] and is not again heard of. There were two high constables in 1620,[36] probably one for each part of the hundred, but in later times the out-hundred does not seem to have had officers separate from those of the town.

In 1439 the sheriff's tourn for the hundreds of Warminster and Heytesbury was held at 'Ilegh', later called Iley Oak, a great tree which stood probably in Southleigh or Eastleigh Woods between Sutton Veny and Longbridge Deverill.[37] It was still the meeting place of the tourns in 1652.[38] Nothing is known of the meeting place of the other hundred courts until 1831, when they met in the Town Hall at Warminster.[39] The name Moot Hill, applied to the low mound across the Wylye south-west of Norton Bavant village, which was formerly a detached part of Warminster parish,[40] may indicate that the early meeting place of the hundred was there.

[35] Hoare, *Mod. Wilts.* Warminster, 10.
[36] *Early Stuart Tradesmen* (W.A.S. Rec. Brch.), 8.
[37] *W.A.M.* xiii. 107–8; *P.N. Wilts.* (E.P.N.S.), 154–5.
[38] Hoare, *Mod. Wilts.* Warminster, 85.

[39] W. Daniell, *Warminster Common*, 192.
[40] W.R.O. Warminster Inclosure Award. It is clearly shown, although not named, on *Andrews and Dury, Map* (W.A.S. Rec. Brch.), pl. 7.

BISHOPSTROW

THE small parish of Bishopstrow adjoins the Urban District of Warminster, running the length of its south-eastern boundary in a strip some $3\frac{1}{2}$ miles long and about $\frac{1}{2}$ mile wide.[1] The modern civil parish differs from the ancient parish by the addition to it in 1884 of Eastleigh Farm house and the fields near it, and of a small piece of land in the village, both formerly detached pieces of Warminster. At the same time lands formerly called Hillwoods, a detached piece of Bishopstrow near Warminster Common, were transferred to Warminster.[2] The parts of Pit Mead which belonged to Bishopstrow were added to Sutton Veny.[3] The area of the parish was thus reduced from 1,045 to 999 a.[4]

The same geological sequence of greensand valley and chalk down occurs here as in the next parish of Norton Bavant.[5] The village lies south of the Warminster-Salisbury road, which crosses the parish from west to east. The way in which this road ran north of Boreham and the present site of Bishopstrow House in the early 18th century is described below.[6] In 1773 the turnpike road from Warminster followed the present line of the main road through Boreham as far the bend near the entrance to the house; there it turned sharply to the north-east for a short way, and then again at right angles to rejoin the present line of road near the parish boundary. The road had been straightened by 1808.[7] The main part of the village lies along a road which branches south from the main road at Boreham and continues south to Sutton Veny. West of it the large houses called Eastleigh Court and Draytons (formerly The Buries) stand in extensive grounds. The Buries takes its name from a large earthwork from which excavations carried out by Hoare yielded much Roman material.[8] Further off is Eastleigh Farm, on its own near the parish boundary. East of the village street the church and former rectory are at the end of a lane, from which a path and footbridge lead across the river to the mill and so back to the main road. North of the road are only Bishopstrow House[9] and Bishopstrow Farm. The village street consists chiefly of continuous terraces of early 19th-century cottages. The similarity of their design, particularly in the wooden drip-moulds above the doors and windows, probably indicates that they were built by the lord of the manor. Some were formerly thatched, but all now have tiled roofs. When the parish was inclosed in 1808, the surveyor did not include these houses on the map, possibly because they were then being rebuilt. At the north end of the village, the house called Shirley House was formerly a timber-framed house consisting of a central hall and two cross wings. Between the hall and the cross wing part of a cruck truss survives; the house has been refaced in stone and brick, and the former thatched roof replaced by tiles.

In 1377 there were 87 poll-tax payers in Bishopstrow.[10] The population of the parish was 227 in 1801, and had grown to 296 by 1841. Since then it has declined intermittently to 153 in 1951.[11] The closeness of the village to Warminster has not affected it, and there has been little recent building apart from a few council houses. Agriculture has always been the chief pursuit carried on in the village, although there was some activity in the cloth trade from the 16th to the 18th century, which is described below.[12]

MANOR. Edred held *BISHOPSTROW* before the Conquest, but by 1086 it had passed to Edward of Salisbury.[13] It was part of the lands, later known as the honor of Trowbridge, which were given by Edward to Humphrey (I) de Bohun, husband of his daughter Maud. It descended in the Bohuns, later Earls of Hereford, until the division of the honor in 1229, when Bishopstrow was one of the demesne manors allotted to Ela, Countess of Salisbury.[14] In 1236 Ela made an agreement with her son William Longespée, which enabled her to give the manor to the nunnery of Lacock which she had founded a few years before.[15] It remained in the possession of Lacock until the Dissolution. In 1550 it was granted by the Crown to Thomas Temmes,[16] brother of Joan, the last abbess.[17] After his death in 1575[18] his son John, who had moved to Sussex, sold Bishopstrow in 1577 to John Middlecott, reserving a rent of £50 on it. Eight years later Middlecott, who had also left Bishopstrow, for Somerset, sold the manor to George, Lord Audley, later Earl of Castlehaven (d. 1617). In the following year the manor was let to James Gayner of Salisbury for 31 years.[19] On the execution of Mervin, Lord Castlehaven, in 1631 his property was forfeited to the Crown, but regranted to his son two years later.[20] In 1635 he sold Bishopstrow to William Temple, in whose family it remained for 300 years.[21] Temple's son Peter re-

[1] The maps used in this account were the same as those mentioned on p. 47, n. 1.

[2] *Bounds of Wilts.*; *Census* 1891.

[3] See p. 610.

[4] *Census*, 1881, 1891.

[5] See p. 47.

[6] See p. 93.

[7] *Andrews and Dury, Map* (W.A.S. Rec. Brch.), pl. 7; W.R.O. Inclosure Award.

[8] Hoare, *Ancient Wilts.* ii, Roman Aera, 108; for the houses, see below, p. 7.

[9] See p. 7.

[10] *V.C.H. Wilts.* iv. 311.

[11] Ibid. 341.

[12] See p. 10.

[13] *V.C.H. Wilts.* ii, p. 137.

[14] Ibid. pp. 108–10, and vii. 128; I. J. Sanders, *English Baronies*, 91.

[15] W. G. Clarke–Maxwell, 'Earliest Charters of Lacock', *W.A.M.* xxxv, 193–6, 203–5.

[16] W.R.O. 132, Deeds of Manor.

[17] *Genealogist* N.S. xiii. 24; *W.N & Q.* vi. 554-62.

[18] C 142/172/160.

[19] W.R.O. 132, Deeds of Manor. Previous sales of the manor and farm by Middlecott referred to in C 66/1252 m. 26 and C 66/1298 m. 13 were for mortgage: E 134/9 Chas. I/East. 14.

[20] C 66/2619 no. 7.

[21] W.R.O. 132, Deeds of Manor.

deemed the £50 rent, which had passed through various hands, in 1690.[22] Peter's son Samuel had two sons, of whom the elder, Peter, died unmarried in 1755. The younger, William, left, by his third wife, a son William who was born shortly before his father's death in 1781, and died in 1875. He was succeeded by his grandson Vere de Lone Temple, who died unmarried in 1893, when the manor passed to his brother Grenville Newton Temple (d. 1949).[23] In 1950 the house and parkland were sold to W. Keith Neale, but in 1962 the Temple family still retained much property in the parish.[24]

In 1533 the manor house and farm of Bishopstrow were let for 99 years to Robert Abath, who had married a sister of Joan Temmes, the last Abbess of Lacock. In 1592 Clement Abath assigned the lease to Geoffrey Hawkins of Bishopstrow, clothier, and in 1613 Hawkins's widow and her second husband assigned it to John Temple of Kingston Deverill, whose son bought the freehold of the property.[25]

Until the early 19th century the manor house of Bishopstrow lay between the Salisbury road and the Wylye, just above Bishopstrow Mill.[26] In 1736 it was apparently only a small house with a hall, two parlours and four main chambers.[27] It may have been added to later in the 18th century, when the garden was expensively beautified. A small circular temple is dated 1770, and there are a summer-house and a boat-house of rather later date. A late 17th-century brick building with stone-mullioned windows and quoins also remains on the site; it may have been an outbuilding of the former house. William Temple seems to have decided to build a new house north of the Salisbury road soon after the inclosure of the parish. In 1815 he made a tunnel under the road with a brick vault and elaborately decorated entrances of vermiculated stone. The new house was begun in 1817 to the design of John Pinch the elder of Bath.[28] It is a square two-storied building of ashlar with very fine joints; the plain design is relieved by a door set in a recess and decorated with Ionic columns on the main (east) front, and by a semi-circular bay on the south front.

LESSER ESTATES. About 1120 Humphrey (II) de Bohun gave land at Bishopstrow to the Priory of Lewes (Suss.), intending it as a partial endowment of the proposed daughter house at Farleigh.[29] It was transferred to Monkton Farleigh on its foundation, the gift being confirmed in the foundation charter of Humphrey (III) de Bohun[30] and by Henry I.[31] It was evidently the practice of the monks to lease out this small estate for long terms. In 1249 they appear to have obtained a surrender of such a lease in return for an annuity of 40s.,[32] and in 1294 it was let at farm for the same amount. At that time it was called Horsepool.[33] In the earlier 14th century John of Bradford, Rector of Bishopstrow, held a life estate in the property,[34] the reversion of which was granted to Robert Hungerford.[35] In 1501 it was held by Maud Walrond on a 30-year lease,[36] and in 1518 it was granted to John Benet for his life.[37] After the Dissolution the hide of land called Buryshott and Horsepool was granted in 1543 to Richard Andrews and Nicholas Temple,[38] who immediately sold it to Sir John Thynne of Longleat.[39] In 1571 Thynne conveyed it, with other lands, to Thomas Gifford of Boreham, in exchange for land in Longbridge Deverill.[40] From that time it descended in the same way as the other property of the Gifford family,[41] to Sir John Dugdale Astley, who sold the lands, then called the Eastleigh estate, to Capt. Arthur Howard Southey in 1884.[42] He died in 1915 and his son J. A. Southey in 1956;[43] the land was then sold to Major J. C. Walker of Sutton Veny.

The farmhouse of this estate was perhaps that called in 1963 The Cottage, which has a brick front of the 18th century but is somewhat older at the back. By 1808 a larger brick house had been built in more extensive grounds nearby.[44] It was called Bury Cottage, and in 1822 was the home of William Temple,[45] who perhaps occupied it while Bishopstrow House was being rebuilt. In 1841 it was the home of F. D. Astley.[46] It was much added to later in the century, and in 1963 was used as a preparatory school. There was no house on the site of Eastleigh Court, which later became the chief house of the estate, in 1830.[47] In 1837 F. P. B. Martin lived in Eastleigh Lodge, no doubt recently built there.[48] By 1849 it had passed to the Astleys,[49] and, as Eastleigh Court, was sold with the lands to Capt. Southey in 1884.[50] Most of the large brick house in a plain Tudor style dates from after the sale, but some walling at the back, the outbuildings, and the gate piers are probably relics of the earlier house.

Among several small properties acquired by the nuns of Lacock after they had received the capital manor was one also described as in Horsepool. In the earlier part of the 13th century it had been held by Walter the physician; Godfrey Waspail, lord

[22] Ibid. Deeds of Rent.
[23] Hoare, *Mod. Wilts*, Warminster, 73; Burke, *Land. Gent.* (1952), where the date of G. N. Temple's death is incorrect.
[24] Ex inf. Mr. W. Keith Neale.
[25] W.R.O. 132, Deeds of Farm; C 2 Eliz. I./H. 10/56.
[26] *Andrews and Dury, Map* (W.A.S. Rec. Brch.), pl. 7.
[27] W.R.O. 132, Inv. of Peter Temple, 1736.
[28] Ex inf. Mr. W. Keith Neale.
[29] *Lewes Cartulary, Wilts. &c. portion* (Suss. Rec. Soc.), 22.
[30] Dugdale, *Mon.* v. 26.
[31] *Regesta Regum Anglo-Normannorum*, ed. Johnson and Cronne, ii. 382.
[32] C.P. 25 (1)/251/15/1.
[33] Dugdale, *Mon.* v. 29.
[34] *Cal. Close*, 1318–23, 599; *Cal. Pat.* 1330–34, 81; *Cal. Inq. Misc.* 1307–49, 300.
[35] *Year Bk.* 1345 (Rolls Ser.), 58–65.

[36] S.C. 6/Hen. VIII/3957; this acct. must be of Hen. VII's reign because of the prior's name.
[37] Longleat MSS. Thynne Papers, Bk. 63, p. 27; C 1/620/4.
[38] *L. & P. Hen. VIII*, xviii (1), p. 530.
[39] Longleat MSS. Thynne Papers, Bk. 64, p. 16.
[40] Longleat MS. 8283.
[41] See p. 103.
[42] Inf. supplied by Capt. Southey, 1908.
[43] M.I.'s in church.
[44] O.S. Map Wilts. 1″ sheet 14, 1st edn.
[45] Hoare, *Mod. Wilts*. Warminster, pl. opp. p. 91; *Paterson's Roads* (1822).
[46] W.R.O. Tithe Award.
[47] Hoare, op. cit. pl. opp. p. 91.
[48] W.R.O. 132, Covt. to produce Deeds, 1837.
[49] Ibid. 160a, Astley Settlement, 1849.
[50] Parish Records, Eastleigh Estate Sale Catalogue.

of Smallbrook (fl. *c.* 1250), gave it to his daughter Agnes, who gave it to the nuns in 1261. It consisted of a house and about 20 a. of land.[51] The gift of the mill of Bishopstrow to the abbey is described below.[52] In 1321 William le Bole was licensed to grant a house and 10 a. in Bishopstrow to Lacock.[53]

Several small free tenancies had been created in the Lacock manor by *c.* 1260. The largest was one of two virgates held then, and still twenty years later, by Walter Swoting.[54] He had a son Robert, who had land in Bishopstrow in 1327.[55] It was probably the same two virgates which were by 1403 held by Thomas Felawe in right of Agnes his wife.[56] In 1414 Hugh de la Lynde held the estate by grant of Felawe.[57] Soon after this time it must have passed to John Leverich (or Loverige); he left a daughter and heir Agnes who married into a family called Stalbridge. Her grandson Richard Stalbridge left two daughters and heirs, Agnes, wife of John Collins, and Katharine, wife of Richard Penyll. In the early 16th century they were engaged in a lawsuit with Roger Uffenham over the property,[58] in which Uffenham must have been successful, for his son Richard held it in 1539.[59] Early in Elizabeth I's reign Richard's daughter Emma and her second husband John Maggs were dealing with land in Bishopstrow.[60] In 1582 Maggs sold the estate to William Middlecott;[61] Middlecott's brother John included it when he sold the manor three years later, and although it was the subject of a lawsuit in the reign of Charles I, it probably descended with the manor from 1585.[62]

Two freeholds which had existed *c.* 1260 were held at the Dissolution by Thomas Gifford. One was of 1½ virgate, held by Jocelin *c.* 1260 and Robert Goscelyn his son *c.* 1280.[63] Robert left a son John who was of Bishopstrow in 1311.[64] Osbert Goscelyn lived there in 1319.[65] Thereafter the descent is unknown until at the Dissolution Thomas Gifford held it by descent from his father Maurice.[66] The second estate, of one virgate, was held by Adam Serle *c.* 1260 and Andrew de Lye *c.* 1280.[67] At the Dissolution Thomas Gifford held a virgate called Lythis, once of John Taylor, and late of John Bennett.[68] These two estates, held at rents of 13*s.* each in 1539, made up the lands in Bishopstrow held under the lords of the manor by John Gifford at his death in 1601; the rent was then said to be 26*s.* 4*d.*[69] Their subsequent descent was like the rest of the Gifford estate.[70]

In 1731 the Gifford estate in Bishopstrow consisted only of the former Lacock Abbey property and of Knapp Farm.[71] That farm must therefore have consisted chiefly of these 2½ virgates formerly held under the abbey. It descended with the rest of the property until 1808, when all the arable land and downs, some 104 a., were sold by F. D. Astley to William Temple.[72] It was probably at the same time that the remainder of the farm was sold to William Munday. In 1841 he or a descendant of the same name held a farm of 48 a.[73] The early-19th-century farmhouse stands north of the Salisbury road near the drive into Bishopstrow House.

When the manor of Bishopstrow was sold to William Temple in 1636, the lands he bought were only charged with 33*s.* 5*d.* out of the 53*s.* 0½*d.* fee-farm rent to the Crown payable out of the whole manor.[74] At least one other estate was therefore probably sold by Lord Audley at about the same time. This was perhaps the farm called Hoggetts, which in 1713 was the largest estate in the parish except for the Temple and Gifford holdings.[75] In the late 18th century Hoggetts was held by the Bayly family;[76] in 1836 James Bayly left it to his grandson F. W. Bayly[77]. In 1841 the farm had an area of 93 a.[78] The house stood south of the Salisbury road, on the west corner of the lane and footbridge leading down to the church. It was sold to William Temple separately from the lands in 1868.[79]

ECONOMIC HISTORY. In 1086 there was land for six ploughs in Bishopstrow; half was in demesne, with 4 serfs, and the remainder was held by 9 villeins, 6 bordars, and 2 cottars. There were small quantities of meadow and wood, and the pasture was 5 furlongs long and 3 broad.[80] A detailed survey and custumal of the mid-13th century[81] lists 9 holders of one virgate each and 6 of 4 a. each, and there can be little doubt that their holdings were those of the villeins and bordars of 1086. There were in addition freeholders who held lands amounting to over 4½ virgates, and some 60 or 70 a. of land in the west of the parish had been given to Monkton Farleigh Priory and so was not included in the survey.[82] Since it is unlikely that the area of the demesne farm had been much reduced, there is clear indication of a considerable expansion of cultivated area between 1086 and *c.* 1250. As in other places,[83] this expansion was accompanied by a growth in population. Compared with the recorded 21 tenants of 1086, there were 57 at the later date, of whom 37 held only houses or very small amounts of land. They included a smith, two shepherds, two millers, a capper and several widows; many of the remainder must have earned a living working on the demesne or the larger free

[51] Lacock Abbey MSS. Newer Cartulary, ff. 69v.–71v.
[52] See p. 10.
[53] *Cal. Pat.* 1317–21, 535.
[54] W. G. Clark–Maxwell, 'Customs of Four Manors of the Abbey of Lacock', *W.A.M.* xxxii. 311–46.
[55] B.M. Add. Ch. 26703–4, 26706, 26711.
[56] C.P. 25 (1)/256/56/20.
[57] C 131/59/5.
[58] C 1/129/29.
[59] S.C. 6/Hen. VIII/3985 m. 28d.; C 1/1080/1–2.
[60] *W.N. & Q.* vi. 354, 551; *Genealogist* N.S. xiii, 26.
[61] C.P. 25 (1)/240/24 Eliz. I Hil.
[62] E 134/9 Chas. I/East. 14; W.R.O. 132, Deeds of Manor.
[63] *W.A.M.* xxxii. 320, 323; B.M. Add. Ch. 26703–4.
[64] Longleat MS. 9115.
[65] Hist. MSS. Com. *Hastings*, i. 220.
[66] S.C. 6/Hen. VIII/3985 m. 28d.

[67] *W.A.M.* xxxii. 320, 323.
[68] S.C. 6/Hen. VIII/3985 m. 28d.
[69] C 142/271/157.
[70] See p. 103.
[71] W.R.O. 132, Settlement 5 Oct. 1731.
[72] Ibid. Deed of Exchange, 1808.
[73] W.R.O. Land Tax Assessments and Tithe Award.
[74] Ibid. 132, Deeds of Manor.
[75] Ibid. 621, Poor Rate in Parish Register.
[76] Ibid. Land Tax Assessments.
[77] Ibid. 132, Will of Jas. Bayly.
[78] Ibid. Tithe Award.
[79] Ibid. 132, Deed Bayly to Temple, 1868.
[80] *V.C.H. Wilts.* ii, p. 137.
[81] *W.A.M.* xxxii. 320–4.
[82] See p. 7.
[83] See *V.C.H. Wilts.* iv. 9–10.

or bond holdings. The virgaters themselves were obliged to work five days a week on the demesne farm from Midsummer to Michaelmas, and every second day for the rest of the year, while the holders of 4 a. worked every day through the first period and the same as the virgaters for the rest of the year. Some of the cottars had to do boon-work at haytime and harvest. Allowance seems to have been made for the tenants to redeem at least some of their works by the payment of larger rents, but it may be that this represents former customs, for on many Wiltshire manors such options were being withdrawn by this time.[84]

Although the 13th-century survey reveals little of the lay-out of the fields and meadows of the manor, the topography of the parish makes it certain that the larger part of the open-field land lay north-east of the village on the greensand levels which lie on either side of Middle Hill. The further of these must be 'Cinuba on the north side of Hirthbir' ' from which five loads had to be carried daily in harvest, and the nearer the 'midles', from which seven loads were required. Some land which was apparently arable, or at least lying in acres, lay on the lower ground near the village.[85] More lay to the south-west, in the area round the present Eastleigh Farm, which was called Old Field in the early 13th century; here, however, there were already inclosed crofts.[86] Of the meadows named c. 1250, Tunmead lay along the Wylye near the mill, and 'Beuemede' was no doubt nearby. Little is known of the farming of the land at this time, although sheep were evidently kept in some numbers, for in 1249 the Abbess of Lacock obtained a grant of pasture for 200 of her flock on land belonging to William Mauduit, lord of Warminster.[87] Some years earlier she had granted two of her free tenants rights to run their sheep on her own pasture.[88]

No more is known of agriculture in Bishopstrow until the 16th century. The first known lessee of demesne was William Cabell in the early 16th century,[89] although the practice of leasing was probably much older. The nine bond virgates of 300 years before can still be discerned in 1539, when they were held by five tenants, four of whom held two each.[90] A flock of 320 sheep was kept on the demesne farm,[91] and there is no doubt that the sheep and corn husbandry typical of the district was carried on, based on the commonable open fields and meadows and the downland pastures. What changes there were consisted of the inclosure of open land and the consolidation of holdings. There is no indication of extensive inclosure; even west of the village what appears to have been open field arable still existed in Elizabeth I's reign,[92] although it was perhaps not subject to a common

field course, for about 1550 it had been sown in three successive years with oats, barley, and wheat.[93] In this part of the parish ground called Shuttles-borrow and a coppice of 10 a. in the detached part of the parish at Hillwood had recently been inclosed in 1636.[94] After the Dissolution the large copyholds seem to have been obtained by the lords and added to the demesne farm, for by 1636 all the holdings except the farm were very small.[95] It is possible, however, that they formed a freehold estate separate from the manor.[96]

The way in which the fields and commons were managed in the 17th century is only partially known. In 1631 the rectorial glebe lay in the field next to Boreham, the field over the hill, and the middle field south of the hill. Later terriers indicate that there was no glebe in the first middle field,[97] so that there seem to have been four fields, which in 1801 were evidently in a four-year course.[98] It was the custom to hain the land on which the corn had been cut from Michaelmas to Martinmas; during that time the tenants' cattle were in the field destined for winter sowing, and were presumably moved to the fallow field at Martinmas. Pit Mead and other common meadows were available for the tenants' stock from the carrying of the hay until Candlemas, first for cattle and, after St. Thomas's day, for sheep as well. On the Cow Down the tenants had common for cattle from 3 May until Martinmas, but it was several to the tenant of the farm for the remainder of the year.[99] The tenants were clearly very dependent in this parish on their pasture rights in the common fields and meadows, because for much of the year they had no other feed available. As late as 1801 a quarter of the arable land in the parish was uncultivated annually because of manorial rights, 'to the great detriment of agriculture'.[1] In these circumstances improvement was perhaps slower than elsewhere, and confined to the large manor farm. At least some of its arable land was in a separate Farm Field by 1631,[2] and there were water meadows belonging to it by 1662.[3] The first known rack lease of the farm, with newly-built farmhouse, was made in 1719.[4] Later in the century the several Farm Down of 205 a. surrounded the smaller Cow Down in which the tenants still had summer and autumn pasture. The tenants' sheep could, however, feed the fallow Farm Field from Lady Day to Michaelmas, a serious drawback to improvement.[5] In 1764 the loss of common pasture by the inclosing of 3 a. of land had to be made good by bounding out 3 a. of the Farm Field adjoining the Tenantry Field.[6] The final parliamentary inclosure of the parish took place in 1811 when the chief allottees were William Temple (642 a.), James Bayly for Hoggetts Farm (85 a.), and William Munday (40 a.).[7] The lands

[84] Ibid. 8.
[85] Lacock Abbey MSS. Older Cartulary, f. 32.
[86] Ibid. Newer Cartulary, ff. 69v., 70v.
[87] Ibid. f. 73.
[88] Ibid. f. 72v.
[89] C 1/502/48.
[90] S.C. 6/Hen. VIII/2985 m. 28d.
[91] W.R.O. 132, Lease Lacock Abbey to Abath.
[92] E 134/17 and 18 Eliz. I/Mich. 1; W.R.O. 132, Deed Middlecott to Audley, 1585.
[93] E 134/17 and 18 Eliz. I/Mich. 1.
[94] W.R.O. 132, Deed Audley to Temple, 1636.
[95] Ibid.

[96] See p. 8.
[97] Sar. Dioc. R.O. Glebe Terrier, 1631.
[98] H.O. 67/23.
[99] W.R.O. 132, Court Papers.
[1] H.O. 67/23.
[2] Sar. Dioc. R.O. Glebe Terrier, 1631.
[3] Ibid. Chwdns' Pres. 1662; W.R.O. 132, Agreement Temple and Rector, 1680.
[4] Ibid. Lease Temple to Hooper, 1719.
[5] Ibid. Court Papers.
[6] Ibid.
[7] W.R.O. Inclosure Award, made under 48 Geo. III, c. 44 (Priv. Act).

of the Astley, formerly Gifford, estate west of the village were all old inclosures, probably of long standing.

Almost all the allotments made to William Temple were held by his tenant of Bishopstrow Farm. In 1769 it consisted of 41 a. of inclosed meadow land, 216 a. arable and 205 a. of several down.[8] In 1808 Temple added to it 104 a. of arable land formerly belonging to Knapp Farm, which he had obtained by exchange from the Astley estate.[9] and in 1814 it was let at a rent of £600.[10] It was probably about this time that the farmhouse and buildings, which had previously been near the old manor house, were moved to their present site near the Salisbury road. In 1833 it consisted of 29 a. of pasture, 40 a. meadow, 318 a. arable land and 286 a. downland; in that year the farmhouse was destroyed by fire.[11] In 1851 a further 124 a., part of Morgan's Farm in Boreham, were added, so that the farm expanded to 772 a. of which 140 were in Warminster.[12] As on many farms at this time, the arable area was increased; in 1849 43 a. of downland were broken up.[13] There were only two other farms of any size in the parish. In 1838 Hoggett's Farm, the property of the Bayly family, contained 93 a.;[14] Bury Farm or Old Field Farm (now Eastleigh Farm), part of the Astley estate, was of 349 a. in 1849, much of which was in Sutton Veny parish.[15] When it was sold in 1884 Old Field Farm was described as an excellent sheep and corn farm, let at £340 a year.[16] These were, however, the last days of the old sheep and corn husbandry of the chalk country. In 1839 about half the parish had been arable and much of the rest downland,[17] but before the end of the century Bishopstrow Farm was held by S. W. Farmer, a partner in the firm of Frank Stratton & Co., which began the large-scale production of milk for the London market on chalk farms.[18]

The first clothier known to have worked in Bishopstrow is Richard Middlecott. He was quite highly assessed in the benevolence of 1545,[19] and in 1562 was able to pay over £600 for a grant of Crown lands in several counties.[20] He acquired much property in Warminster and founded a family fortune which lasted until the 19th century.[21] His son John, also a Bishopstrow clothier, acquired the manor of Bishopstrow in 1578.[22] A third rich clothier of this period was Geoffrey Hawkins, who bought the lease of Bishopstrow Farm for £632

in 1592;[23] this included the mill, which had been in use as a fulling mill for at least 60 years.[24] The names of a number of clothiers and cloth-workers who lived in the village in the 17th and 18th centuries have survived,[25] but little is known of their businesses or prosperity. Richard Short, a clothier who died c. 1684, left assets worth £1,662.[26] Peter Temple, a younger son of the lord of the manor, carried on business as a clothier between 1734 and 1745, when he went bankrupt.[27]

MILL. A mill worth 15s. belonged to the manor in 1086.[28] It was apparently held in fee in the middle of the 13th century by Elias Serle, but c. 1259 several parties who had obtained an interest in it after his death released it to the nuns of Lacock.[29] Thereafter it seems to have remained part of the manor. In 1533 it formed part of the property let to Robert Abath; it was then described as a fulling mill, gig mill, and grist mill.[30] It was still a fulling mill in 1636,[31] but in 1734 it was described as a grist mill and wood mill for grinding dyestuff.[32] In 1747 the lease was assigned to a Heytesbury clothier,[33] but from 1778 to 1837 it was let with Bishopstrow Farm and was presumably used as a grist mill.[34] After that time it was held separately by a succession of millers.[35] The mill was burnt down in 1873.[36] The present three-storied building of brick was built to replace the one destroyed; by 1885 steam power was used in addition to water.[37] Since about 1936 the mill has been used by W. A. King and Co. as a provender mill; water and electric power are used.[38]

CHURCH. Bishopstrow, 'the bishop's tree', has been connected with the 'Biscepes truue' mentioned by William of Malmesbury[39] as the place where St. Aldhelm's staff miraculously grew into an ash tree.[40] The suggestion is plausible, for the dedication of the church of Bishopstrow to St. Aldhelm is recorded as early as the 13th century,[41] and there is a possibility, discussed below, that a church of the Saxon period stood here until the 18th century. When the church is first mentioned c. 1120[42] it had, therefore, probably long stood on a site used for Christian teaching since the early 8th century. It has remained the only Anglican place of worship in the ancient parish. In 1957, however, St. John's Church, Warminster, which had previously been a chapel-of-ease to Warminster parish church, was

[8] W.R.O. 132, Lease Temple to Miell.
[9] Ibid. Deeds of exchange Astley and Temple.
[10] Ibid. Lease Temple to Munday.
[11] Ibid. Valuation of Farm.
[12] Ibid. Leases, Temple to Murton.
[13] Ibid. Misc. Papers.
[14] W.R.O. Tithe Award.
[15] W.R.O. 160a. Astley Settlement, 1849.
[16] Bishopstrow Parish Records, Eastleigh Estate Sale Catalogue.
[17] W.R.O. Tithe Award.
[18] W.A.M. xliii, 494; V.C.H. Wilts. iv. 106–7.
[19] Taxation Lists (W.A.S. Rec. Brch.), 36.
[20] Cal. Pat. 1560–3, 234.
[21] See pp. 93, 103.
[22] See p. 6.
[23] W.R.O. 132, Assignment Abath to Hawkins.
[24] See below.
[25] W.R.O. 132, Deeds passim: W.A.M. xxxviii. 575; Wilts. Apprentices (W.A.S. Rec. Brch.), p. 47.
[26] Hist. MSS. Com. 15th Rep. App. II, 324.
[27] W.R.O. 132, Lease Temple to Temple, and Assign-

ment, 1747; Gent. Mag. 1745, xv. 389.
[28] V.C.H. Wilts. ii, p. 137.
[29] Lacock Abbey MSS. Newer Cart., ff. 67v.–69, 74v.; Close R. 1256–9, 281; J.I. 1/996 m. 14d.
[30] W.R.O. 132, Lease Lacock to Abath; see above, p. 7.
[31] Ibid. Deed Audley to Temple.
[32] Ibid. Lease Temple to Temple.
[33] Ibid. Assignment Langley to Everett.
[34] Ibid. Leases of Bishopstrow Farm and Particular, 1833; Pigot, Nat. Com. Dir. (1830).
[35] P.O. Dirs. Wilts. and Kelly's Dirs. Wilts.
[36] Warminster Herald, 3 Jan. 1874.
[37] Kelly's Dir. Wilts. (1885).
[38] Ex inf. W. A. King and Co.
[39] Gest. Pont. (Rolls Ser.), 384.
[40] P.N. Wilts. (E.P.N.S.), 151; J. U. Powell, 'Early History of the Upper Wylye Valley', W.A.M. xxxiii. 116–9.
[41] Lacock Abbey MSS. Newer Cart. f. 72.
[42] Lewes Cartulary, Wilts. etc. portion (Suss. Rec. Soc.), 22.

transferred to the charge of the Rector of Bishopstrow, and a new ecclesiastical parish of Bishopstrow and Boreham was founded.[43]

The church formed part of the endowment provided by the de Bohun family for Monkton Farleigh priory,[44] and the advowson was held by the monks there until the Dissolution. During part of the 14th century the patronage was exercised by the king as belonging to an alien priory;[45] in 1343 and 1346 Robert Hungerford contested this because he held a life estate of the prior, but was unsuccessful.[46] In 1472 and 1531 laymen presented to the living by grant of the prior.[47] After the Dissolution the advowson was held by successive owners of the former estate of the priory in Bishopstrow,[48] except twice in the 17th century when the Bisse family presented by grant of the then owners, the Giffords.[49] In 1962 it was held by Major J. C. Walker of Sutton Veny.

The monks only appropriated the tithes of their own estate, but charged the rectory with a yearly payment of 40s.[50] This payment was retained by the Crown at the Dissolution, but redeemed in the late 18th century by William Buckler, who released the rectory from it.[51] Beside this charge, the rectory was valued at £10 in 1291[52] and at just over £14 in 1535.[53]

In the mid-16th century the rectory was held by Sir John Thynne, presumably because of his tenure of the Monkton Farleigh estate, and by agreement with the incumbents. Humphrey Roberts, described as curate, collected the tithes for Thynne c. 1550 and referred to him as his master,[54] and an 18th-century rector had heard that William Kidley, who held the living later in the 16th century, received only £8 a year from Thynne.[55] The tithes seem to have been restored to the rectors after the living passed into the ownership of the Gifford family. In 1652 the rectory was let for a year at £150,[56] and was augmented by £10 in 1655.[57] In 1820 the tithes and glebe were valued at just over £300;[58] this was perhaps a gross figure, for in 1835 the average income was said to be £220.[59] In 1884 the rectory was worth 'rather over £240'.[60] In 1820 the rector owned the great and small tithes of 943 a. of the parish, which were worth £262.[61] The tithes of the estate called the Buries, containing 78 a. were impropriate to the monks of Farleigh, and belonged to the later

owners,[62] although the rector claimed the tithes of the lands in 1631, and the tithes of the whole parish in 1783.[63] In the 19th century they were regarded as tithe free. The rector's tithes were commuted in 1838 for £228 10s.[64] In 1341 the rector's glebe consisted of 8 a. of arable land, 2 a. of meadow, and a house. In 1631 it was reckoned at 9 a. of arable land, a close and gardens of 2 a. adjoining the parsonage, and a small close near Henford's Marsh in Warminster.[65] At the inclosure of the parish an allotment of 8½ a. was made to the rector in lieu of his open-field land, and he received 1 a. in Pit Mead.[66] In 1828 an exchange was made of some 4 a. of land lying north and south of the rectory to Joseph Everett of Heytesbury; the rector received in return about 6 a. lying south of the church on either side of Pit Mead Drove.[67] The total area in 1838 was 11a. [68] In 1949 ½ a. was sold for building council houses.[69]

In 1304 the Rector of Bishopstrow was given leave to study for 3 years on appointing a chaplain.[70] In 1322 another rector was a rebel against Edward II.[71] Two 15th-century rectors, Thomas Frome (1411–20) and John Hody (1420–5) held prebends and offices elsewhere, [72] and are unlikely to have resided. Thomas Lock was deprived in 1555;[73] in the following year several of the chief parishioners were said to have sold the church goods.[74] Lock's successor held the living through the changes under Elizabeth I until his death in 1571.[75] In 1583 William Kidley, the rector, was accused of 'using hunting, but very seldom', of churching women on working days, and of not wearing the regulation square cap.[76] Walter Bisse, rector from 1619, had his living sequestrated in 1646 and in the following year it was given to Thomas Pace. Bisse subsequently became Vicar of Alvediston, but was restored to Bishopstrow in 1660,[77] where he was succeeded by his son Thomas four years later.[78] Incumbencies during the 17th and 18th centuries were relatively long. There is no evidence of nonresidence until 1782 when Thomas Fisher, who was also vicar of Norton Bavant but had resided at Bishopstrow since 1767, was forced by gout to retire to Bath for the winter.[79] Since he is known to have employed a curate later,[80] it may be that his absence became permanent. In Fisher's time services were held twice on Sundays, with a sermon in the afternoon, and the sacrament was adminis-

[43] Ex inf. Revd. P. F. Tambling.

[44] *Lewes Cartulary, Wilts. &c. portion* (Suss. Rec. Soc.), 22.

[45] *Cal. Pat.* 1343–5, 141, 510; 1345–8, 225, 445; 1348–50, 477; 1370–74, 261.

[46] Phillipps, *Wilts. Inst.* i. 38, 41; *Cal. Pat.* 1343–5, 510; *Year Bk.* 1345 (Rolls Ser.), 58–61.

[47] Phillipps, op. cit. i. 161, 202.

[48] See p. 7.

[49] Phillipps, *Wilts. Inst.* ii. 10, 27.

[50] *Tax Eccl.* (Rec. Com.), 181; S.C. 6/Hen. VIII/3957; *Valor Eccl.* (Rec. Com.), ii. 104, 143.

[51] W.R.O. 132, Will of Wm. Buckler, 1790.

[52] *Tax Eccl.* (Rec. Com.), 181.

[53] *Valor Eccl.* (Rec. Com.), ii. 104.

[54] E 134/17 and 18 Eliz. I/Mich. 1.

[55] W.R.O. 413, Answers to Parochial Queries c. 1705.

[56] *Walker Revised*, ed. Matthews, 370.

[57] W. A. Shaw, *Hist. Eng. Church*, 1640–60, ii. 512.

[58] Parish Records, Valuation, 1820.

[59] *Rep. Com. Eccl. Revenues*, H.C. 54, pp. 824–5 (1835), xxii.

[60] Parish Records, Eastleigh Estate Sale Catalogue.

[61] Ibid. Valuation, 1820.

[62] W.R.O. 413, Answers to Parochial Queries c. 1705.

[63] Sar. Dioc. R.O. Glebe Terrier, 1783.

[64] W.R.O. Tithe Award.

[65] Sar. Dioc. R.O. Glebe Terrier, 1631.

[66] W.R.O. Inclosure Award.

[67] Ibid. 132, Deed of Exchange, 1828.

[68] Ibid. Tithe Award.

[69] Parish Records.

[70] *Reg. Simon de Gandavo* (Cant. & York Soc.), 866.

[71] S.C. 6/1145/12.

[72] Emden, *Biog. Reg. Oxon.* ii. 731, 941.

[73] Phillipps, *Wilts. Inst.* i. 218.

[74] Sar. Dioc. R.O. Ep. Vis. 1556.

[75] Phillipps, *Wilts. Inst.* i. 225.

[76] Sar. Dioc. R.O. Ep. Vis. 1583.

[77] *Walker Revised*, ed. Matthews, 370; *Calamy Revised*, ed. Matthews, 378.

[78] *Misc. Gen. et Her.* 2nd. ser. i. 379, and 4th ser. ii. 337.

[79] Sar. Dioc. R.O. Vis. Queries, 1783; Phillipps, *Wilts. Inst.* ii. 82, 97.

[80] W.R.O. 132, Will of Wm. Buckler.

tered four times a year to about 14 people.[81] Fisher's successor, William Williams, was a Warminster man and resided on the benefice.[82] J. G. D. Thring, 1830–45, was also of a Warminster family, but held a Somerset living in plurality and resided there; at Bishopstrow he employed a curate whose salary was £62 a year in 1835.[83] J. W. Griffith, 1846–59 held the rectory of Pertwood in plurality.[84] In his time services were held morning and afternoon on Sundays; attendance was about 120 and there was a Sunday School of about 35.[85] J. H. A. Walsh, 1859–71, administered the sacrament twelve times a year to about 45 people; for his Sunday services the church was generally well filled.[86]

The church of *ST. ALDHELM* lies in flat meadowland a short distance east of the village street, and consists of nave, chancel and western tower with spire. Although reasons have been given above for thinking that a church stood on the site in Saxon times, little is certainly known about the building before the 18th century.[87] An inscription records its 'restoration from the lowest foundations' in 1757. This clearly involved a remodelling of the nave in the classical style. It was widened by about 2ft. 6 ins. and round-headed windows were inserted; the only entrance was under the tower. W. S. Champion, who restored the church in 1876, believed that the nave so renovated was of the 14th century. Early masonry at the west end on either side of the tower shows its former width. The 15th-century tower and spire were left untouched in 1757, but it is not clear what was done at the east end of the church. Hoare's plan of *c.* 1830 shows a semi-circular apse lighted by small windows to the north-east and south-east. This feature has been interpreted as a remnant of a Saxon church,[88] but it is not known whether the apse was rebuilt in, or even dated from, 1757, or whether any early masonry survived in Hoare's time. In 1840 the apse was replaced by a square chancel extending further east and providing 50 extra seats; this was paid for by William Temple.[89] The next year the stone tiles which covered the nave were replaced by slates.[90] The church was again restored in 1876 under the direction of W. S. Champion of London. The chancel of 1840 was already in decay, and was rebuilt with an open roof of oak in place of its plaster ceiling, and a floor of glazed tiles. The 'circular apology' for a chancel arch was replaced by one more correct in style. In the nave the old roof, which Champion believed was partly medieval, was opened out and restored, and traceried windows in the style of the 14th century replaced those of

1757. The west gallery was removed, and the organ placed in a new chamber adjoining the chancel. Oak stalls were placed in the chancel and pitch-pine benches in the nave, and a new font and pulpit were given. In the western face of the tower advantage was taken of an old bearing arch to insert a window incorporated in the door head. In 1931 the spire was rebuilt.[91]

There were three bells at Bishopstrow in 1553. Some bells were said to have been taken from there to Norton Bavant,[92] and in 1783 there was only one.[93] This was recast by Wells of Aldbourne in 1785.[94] A second bell was added in 1902; it was given by J. M. Benett-Stanford, who had it cast for use at Pythouse but found it too heavy.[95] There was a clock in the church in 1799.[96] The present one was fitted as a thank-offering for the return of various parishioners from the S. African War.[97]

In 1553 17 oz. of silver were taken for the king and a 13-oz. cup was left for the parish.[98] In 1783 there were a cup, a flagon, and a very thin plate, all of silver and uninscribed.[99] The plate consists in 1962 of a set of two chalices and patens of 1797 and a chalice of 1929.[1] The parish registers are complete from 1676.[2]

In 1783 the rectory house was built partly of stone and partly of brick; one part was tiled and the other thatched and it contained 2 parlours, 5 bedrooms, and 2 garrets.[3] Much of this building still remains in the present Old Rectory, which was much enlarged in the 19th century. It was sold in 1954.[4] Payments for the maintenance of a thatched church house were made by the churchwardens between 1770 and 1825.[5]

NONCONFORMITY. In 1583 John Middlecott, lord of the manor, and his household were presented for not receiving the sacrament,[6] and in 1662 William Temple, lord of the manor, and his wife were among seven inhabitants who did not attend church.[7] Members of both these rich families were for many years prominent in the Old Meeting at Warminster,[8] but no congregation of dissenters was ever permanently established in Bishopstrow. In 1864 there were about five avowed dissenters in the village; a bakehouse was fitted up for worship but not regularly used.[9]

PARISH GOVERNMENT. Poor rates were being raised in Bishopstrow in 1585[10] but little is known about the management of the poor until the years immediately preceding the amendment of the law

---

[81] Sar. Dioc. R.O. Vis. Queries, 1783.
[82] Foster, *Alumn. Oxon.* 2nd ser. iv. 1573; H.O. 67/23.
[83] *Retn. of Eccl. Revenues,* H.C. 54, pp. 824–5 (1835), xxii; Venn, *Alumn. Cantab.* 2nd ser. vi. 184.
[84] Foster, *Alumn. Oxon.* 2nd ser. ii. 569; *Clergy List,* 1859.
[85] H.O. 129/10/260.
[86] Sar. Dioc. R.O. Vis. Queries, 1864.
[87] The acct. of the church is largely based on Hoare, *Mod. Wilts.* Warminster, 74; notes by C. E. Ponting in *W.A.M.* xxvii. 268 and by Sir S. Glynne, ibid. xlii 174; W.A.S. Libr. Devizes, drawing by Buckler; Parish Records, Architect's Report, 1876 and newspaper cutting on re-opening, 1877.
[88] e.g. *W.A.M.* xx. 126 and xxxiii. 116–9.
[89] W.R.O. 132, Faculty.
[90] Parish Records, Vestry Min. Bk. 1837–1922.
[91] *Kelly's Dir. Wilts.* (1939).

[92] *W.A.M.* xxvii. 267–8, but cf. below, p. 57.
[93] Sar. Dioc. R.O. Glebe Terrier, 1783.
[94] W.R.O. 621, Chwdns'. Acct. Bk. 1768–1914.
[95] Ibid. Note in 1st Register.
[96] Ibid. Chwdns.' Acct. Bk. 1768–1914.
[97] Ibid. Note in 1st Register.
[98] Nightingale, *Wilts. Plate,* 81.
[99] Sar. Dioc. R.O. Glebe Terrier, 1783.
[1] Ex inf. Revd. P. F. Tambling.
[2] Those older than 1812 are in W.R.O. 621.
[3] Sar. Dioc. R.O. Glebe Terrier, 1783.
[4] Char. Com. File 112918.
[5] W.R.O. 621, Chwdns.' Acct. Bk. 1768–1914.
[6] Sar. Dioc. R.O. Ep. Vis. 1583.
[7] Ibid. Chwdns.' Pres. 1662.
[8] See p. 125.
[9] Sar. Dioc. R.O. Vis. Queries, 1864.
[10] Sar. Dioc. R.O. Ep. Vis. 1585.

in 1834. The parish owned a poor house in 1812.[11] A newly built one was conveyed to the parish in 1828.[12] Expenditure on the poor between 1816 and 1824 varied between £173, in 1821, and £412, in 1818.[13] Between 1830 and 1835 it was between £250 and £375. Regular payments were made to some 20 or 25 recipients, no doubt aged or infirm people, and to the maintenance of bastard children. Extraordinary payments to unemployed labourers varied considerably; they were particularly high, some £135, in the winter of 1833–4.[14]

SCHOOL. In 1808 there was a school in Bishopstrow where 12 poor girls attended,[15] no doubt the same one at which in 1818 the girls of the parish were taught knitting and straw plaiting at the expense of the lady of the manor. Some children went to schools in Warminster.[16] In 1833 18 boys and 21 girls were taught in a school at the expense of their parents, and William Temple, lord of the manor, paid for the schooling of 15 boys.[17] In 1842 it was described as a National School for girls.[18] A school building of two rooms was erected in 1848, providing accommodation for 60 children.[19] About ten years later it was still chiefly maintained by Temple, and attended by 40 or 50 children.[20] In 1864 boys left the school at the age of 9 or 10, and girls at about 12; a successful evening school was held in winter.[21] In 1871 only 10 boys attended the school compared with 36 girls.[22] Average attendance in 1919 was only 27,[23] and two years later the school was closed.[24] The small one-story building on the west side of the village street still stood, derelict, in 1962.

CHARITIES. None known.

CORSLEY

AT the making of Domesday Book most of Corsley was included within the great royal manor of Warminster, and even after it had been granted away by Henry II the church of Corsley was parochially dependent on Warminster until the 15th century.[1] The common fields of Cley and Chedlanger were shared by the tenants of Corsley and Warminster until their inclosure in 1783,[2] while the rectorial tithes of Corsley, which formed the endowment of a prebend in Wells Cathedral, included those of lands in Thoulstone in Upton Scudamore and Bugley in Warminster.[3] The parocial affiliations of Thoulstone and Norridge were not firmly made with Upton Scudamore until the 16th century, and even then certain parts of Norridge were regarded as extra-parochial.[4] In agriculture and manorial custom Little Corsley and Norridge were closely linked.[5] It is thus not surprising that the eastern boundary of Corsley was not formally defined until the inclosure of 1783.[6] The other boundaries were presumably already ancient; that to the north existed in 1235, when Corsley included Chapmanslade 'under the road'.[7]

The ancient parish as finally defined in 1783 was an irregular rectangle, its western boundary being also the county boundary with Somerset. Three small detached pieces of Corsley, two locally in Warminster near the Bath road, and one containing the buildings of Thoulstone Farm in Upton Scudamore, were added to the parishes which surrounded them under the Divided Parishes Act of 1882. The detached part of Norton Bavant adjoining Corsley on the south was added to the parish at the same time, so that its area was increased from 2,580 a. to 3,056 a.[8] In 1934 the northern part of the parish was united with parts of Dilton Marsh and Upton Scudamore to form the civil parish of Chapmanslade. At the same time Corsley received a large addition on the south by the transfer to it of the northern part of Longleat park and woods, previously in Warminster. These changes increased the area of the parish to 3,585 a.[9]

The parish occupies the western part of a shelf of greensand which extends from the north-western scarp of Salisbury Plain near Warminster across the Somerset border to the valley of the Frome. The shelf is generally some 400 ft. above sea level, but is diversified here by the prominent chalk outlier of Cley Hill, rising to 784 ft., in the south-west corner of the parish. On it are two barrows and a univallate hill-fort.[10] Adjoining Cley Hill to the north is Little Cley Hill; this has given rise to the traditional rhyme,

> 'Big Cley Hill do wear a hat
> Little Cley Hill do laugh at that'.[11]

Two small streams rise in the lower slopes of Cley Hill and cross the parish from east to west. Rodden Brook, the northernmost of the two, runs in a fairly broad valley to join the River Frome, but the other, which gave its name to the hamlets of Whitbourne, has a narrower valley. Corsley lay within the bounds of Selwood Forest in the Middle Ages,[12] and much of the parish must have consisted of woodland which was only gradually cleared. This has left its mark on the pattern of

[11] W.R.O. 621, Chwdns.' Acct. Bk. 1768–1914.
[12] Parish Records, Vestry Min. Bk. 1837–1922.
[13] *App. Rep. Sel. Cttee. on Poor Rate Retns.* H.C. 556, p. 190 (1822), v; ibid. H.C. 334, p. 230 (1825), iv.
[14] W.R.O. 621, Overseers' Accts. 1830–36.
[15] Lambeth Palace Libr. MS. 1732.
[16] *Digest of Returns to Cttee. on Educ. of Poor*, H.C. 224 (1819), ix(2).
[17] *Educ. Enquiry Abstract*, H.C. 62 (1835), xliii.
[18] Pigot, *Nat. Com. Dir.* (1842).
[19] *Kelly's Dir. Wilts.* (1885).
[20] *Acct. of Wilts. Schools*, H.C. 27 (1859 Sess. 1), xxi (2).
[21] Sar. Dioc. R.O. Vis. Queries, 1864.
[22] *Return relating to Elem. Educ.* H.C. 201 (1871), lv.

[23] *Bd. of Educ. List* 21, 1919.
[24] Ibid. 1922.
[1] See pp. 15, 21.
[2] See p. 19.   [3] See p. 21.
[4] See p. 79.
[5] See p. 19.
[6] W.R.O. Inclosure Award.
[7] Hist. MSS. Com. *Wells*, i. 435–6.
[8] *Census*, 1881, 1891.
[9] Ibid. 1951.
[10] *V.C.H. Wilts.* i (1). 169, 264. See pl. facing p. 14.
[11] J. U. Powell, 'Folklore Notes from South-west Wilts.', *Folklore*, xii, 78.
[12] *V.C.H. Wilts.* iv. 415.

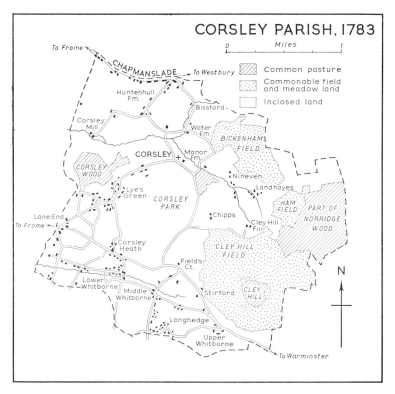

This map is based on the inclosure award map

settlement. Apart from the village of Chapmanslade, of which the southern side of the street lay in Corsley until the boundary changes of 1934,[13] the parish contains only small hamlets and isolated farms. Some of the hamlets, such as Huntenhull, Corsley, and the three Whitbournes,[14] are of early origin, while Longhedge, Corsley Heath and Lane End are all groups of cottages built on former common land, probably from the 16th century onwards.[15] In spite of this Corsley was clearly well populated in the 14th century. In 1334 the assessment of the vill was 130s., higher than any other in the hundred except Warminster, while a further 26s. 8d. was assessed on Whitbourne.[16] In 1377 there were 128 poll-tax payers in Corsley, the third largest number in the hundred, and 49 at Whitbourne.[17] In the 16th century the parish was apparently well-populated and prosperous.[18] The population of 1,412 in 1801 increased to 1,729 by 1831, in spite of the emigration of 200 people to America since 1821. After that it declined steadily, owing to the decay of the cloth industry and to the increasing preponderance of dairy-farming, to 729 in 1931. In 1934 194 people lived in the part of Corsley transferred to the new parish of Chapmanslade, while only 49 lived in the area gained from Warminster. In spite of that the population had risen to 745 by 1951.[19]

The road from Westbury to Frome formed the northern boundary of the parish until 1934, and that from Warminster to Frome passes across the south of the parish. A network of minor roads and

lanes links the various hamlets and farms together. The hamlet of Corsley itself stands halfway between the main roads; it consists only of the church, the school, and Manor Farm. The farmhouse represents the remains of a larger house, built or remodelled by Sir John Thynne about 1563, and occupied by him for 5 years during the rebuilding of Longleat after the fire of 1567.[20] A deer park was made to the south of the house in the 1570's. In 1606 the building had a hall, some 40 bedchambers, 8 living-chambers, a clockhouse and 4 lodges; it was alleged that Dame Dorothy Raleigh, Sir John's widow, had let it fall into decay when she held it in dower.[21] The present house, set behind a forecourt, has a 4-gabled front and two wings projecting to the rear. Possibly in Thynne's time the forecourt was completely inclosed with buildings. The walls are mainly of brick, but stone rubble at the front and in the wings may have survived from an even earlier house. The main block contains a hall with a cross passage at its west end and a massive stone chimney at the rear. Some at least of the square-headed stone-mullioned windows were supplied in 1563 and were similar to those made for Longleat before the fire. It has been suggested that the stone gateway to the present forecourt is of the same date and was formerly part of a hall porch. It bears the lion rampant from the Thynne arms, and the advanced style of its classical ornament may be explained by the fact that it was the work of the Longleat masons.[22]

Corsley House stands on its own just north of

[13] For Chapmanslade, see p. 147.
[14] See pp. 15–17.
[15] Maud Davies, *Life in an English Village*, 6–9.
[16] *V.C.H. Wilts.* iv. 302.
[17] Ibid. 311.

[18] *Taxation Lists* (W.A.S. Rec. Brch.), 36, 146–8.
[19] *V.C.H. Wilts.* iv. 318, 321, 322, 345.
[20] *Arch. Jnl.* cxvi. 207, 212, 217.
[21] Longleat MSS. 6797, 6816, 6942, 6957.
[22] *Arch. Jnl.* cxvi. 207, 212, and pl. xxv.

CLEY HILL, CORSLEY

Air view of Iron Age hill-fort from the east

CORSLEY HOUSE, *c.* 1863

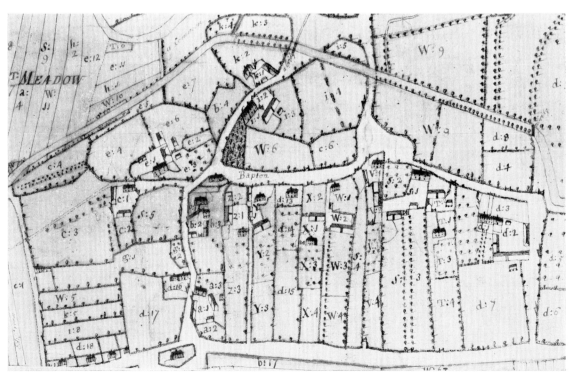

PART OF FISHERTON DE LA MERE, 1742

the Frome-Warminster road.[23] It was begun in 1814 and is an elegantly-designed building showing the Greek influence of the period. The stone ashlar front is of two stories and five bays, with a segmentally-arched Doric porch. The south end of the front range is bowed, and the house has pilasters decorated with incised line ornament. This also appears on the gate piers, and there are contemporary iron railings. Another large house of the early 19th century is Sturford Mead. Other than these the parish contains only farmhouses and cottages, none of which appears externally to be older than the 17th century.

Corsley has always looked to both Frome and Warminster as market towns. Much of its soil is suitable for either arable or pastoral farming, and the amount given to each has varied considerably.[24] The cloth trade flourished chiefly in the 18th century but survived until the 1840's.[25] An elaborate picture of the social and economic life of the parish in the opening years of the present century is to be found in Maud Davies's *Life in An English Village*, published in 1909. The work was prepared at the instance of Sidney and Beatrice Webb, and gives a detailed account of the character, circumstances, and daily life of each family in the parish. It revealed that the large majority of people there were comparatively affluent, and only about one eighth of households had an income insufficient to provide necessary food and clothing. This relative prosperity was largely due to the good gardens attached to the cottages, the abundance of allotment land, and the number of smallholdings in the parish.

James Dodsley Cuff, a numismatist of some note was born in Corsley in 1780, the son of a yeoman.[26]

MANORS. The only estate at Corsley mentioned in Domesday Book was very small,[27] and most of the land there formed part of the royal manor of Warminster until Henry II gave it to Henry Dodeman, a Norman.[28] He was no doubt the Henry of Corsley who paid a mark to the sheriff in 1166–7.[29] In John's reign Thomas FitzHenry held Corsley[30]; the wardship of his land and the marriage of his heir were granted to John Russel in 1215.[31] The heir was perhaps a daughter, and may have been married to Thomas de Biseleg, whose wardship was held by Godfrey de Craucumbe c. 1226.[32] Thomas probably died under age, for in 1232 the manor was granted to Godfrey to hold until the king should restore it to the right heir.[33] Three years later William FitzRichard, a Norman, nephew and heir of Thomas FitzHenry, surrendered his interest, and the grant to Godfrey de

Craucumbe was made absolute.[34] About 1245 Godfrey gave the manor to the Benedictine nuns of Studley (Oxon.) to found a chantry of two priests celebrating for his soul in their church.[35] The priory held Corsley until 1536, when it was granted, apparently before the final dissolution of the house, to Sir Edward Seymour,[36] later Duke of Somerset. On his attainder and execution in 1552 it reverted to the Crown. In 1560 it was granted to Sir John Thynne of Longleat,[37] who had held it since 1547 by lease from the duke.[38] After Thynne's death in 1580 his widow had a life estate in the manor.[39] She married Carew Raleigh as her second husband, and held it until her death.[40] The manor then descended with the Longleat estate.[41]

In 1086 Azor held one hide in Corsley.[42] He also held land at Barley in Bradford-on-Avon, which was later associated with the Husee family.[43] As the Husees were also lords of the manor of *LITTLE CORSLEY*, or as it was later called, *CORSLEY KINGSTON*, there can be little doubt that Azor's holding formed part of that manor. It was perhaps not the whole, however, for the overlordship was not the same as that of Barley. In 1242–3 Little Corsley was said to be held of Reynold de Mohun of the honor of Dunster,[44] and the same tenancy was mentioned in the 15th century.[45] How it came to be part of the Mohun inheritance is not known.

Although members of the Husee family held lands in Wiltshire in the 12th century,[46] the first who certainly held the land in Corsley was Geoffrey Husee who died c. 1219. Henry Husee, his heir, was son of William Husee whose relationship to Geoffrey is not clear. In 1227 he confirmed dower in lands in Corsley and elsewhere to Geoffrey's widow, who had remarried Geoffrey le Savage.[47] From Henry, Corsley seems to have descended in a different way from the rest of Geoffrey's property. In 1242–3 Robert of Whatley held it of Henry Husee;[48] in 1260 Walter of Roddenhurst, who may have succeeded Whatley, released 2 carucates in Corsley to Henry.[49] A certain William FitzHenry of Warminster then had some claim, but subsequently released it to Hubert Husee,[50] presumably Henry Husee's son. Hubert was dead by 1277,[51] leaving three daughters and coheirs.[52] One of them, Maud, died unmarried c. 1285. Of the other two, Margaret married Henry Sturmy[53] and Isabel was probably wife of Robert de Lucy.

At his death c. 1323 Nicholas de Kingston held lands in Corsley of Sturmy and Lucy.[54] His heir was his brother John, who forfeited his lands as a rebel.[55] They had been restored by 1329, when

[23] Davies, *English Village*, passim.
[24] See p. 19.
[25] See p. 20.
[26] *D.N.B.*
[27] *V.C.H. Wilts.* ii, p. 161.
[28] *Rot. Hund.* (Rec. Com.), ii. 276.
[29] *Pipe R.* 1167 (P.R.S. xi), 131.
[30] *Red. Bk. Exch.* (Rolls Ser.), 482; *Cur. Reg. R.* 1205–6, 247.
[31] *Rot. de Ob. et Fin.* (Rec. Com.), 566.
[32] *Bk. of Fees*, 381; *Rot. Litt. Claus.* (Rec. Com.), ii. 63.
[33] *Cal. Chart. R.* 1226–57, 148; *Close R.* 1231–4, 25.
[34] *Cal. Chart. R.* 1226–57, 190.
[35] Ibid. 283; for Studley see *V.C.H. Oxon.* ii. 77–9.
[36] *L. & P. Hen. VIII*, x, p. 526; *V.C.H. Oxon.* ii. 79.
[37] *Cal. Pat.* 1558–60, 469; Longleat MS. 6831.
[38] Longleat MS. 6884.
[39] C 142/195/118; C 66/1283 m. 36.

[40] Longleat MSS. 6836–8.
[41] The Manor Farm is described above, p. 14.
[42] *V.C.H. Wilts.* ii, p. 161.
[43] Ibid. vii. 18.
[44] *Bk. of Fees*, 728.
[45] *Feud. Aids*, v. 274.
[46] Dugdale, *Baronage*, i. 622–3.
[47] C.P. 25(1)/250/5/31; Dugdale, op. cit. i. 623; *Wilts. Inq. p.m.* 1242–1326 (Index Libr.), 69.
[48] *Bk. of Fees*, 728.
[49] C.P. 25(1)/251/20/5.
[50] J.I. 1/998 m. 10d.
[51] C.P. 40/18 rot. 6d.
[52] *Wilts. Inq. p.m.* 1242–1326 (Index Libr.), 160.
[53] Ibid. 160–1.
[54] Ibid. 433.
[55] *Cal. Fine R.* 1319–27, 330.

they were settled on John, his son Thomas, and Maud, Thomas's wife.[56] Thomas and Maud left a son and heir John[57], probably the John de Kingston who held Corsley in 1412.[58] He died soon after this leaving a son Thomas, who was dead by 1428; the lands were then held by William Fynderne, presumably the second husband of Thomas's widow.[59] Thomas's son Thomas succeeded him and died c. 1505.[60] His son John died before him, and the heir was John's son, another John.[61] He and his brother Nicholas both died under age, and the estate passed to their sister Mary, wife of Thomas Lisle.[62] She died without issue in 1539 and her heirs were the descendants of her father's sisters, Margaret Gorffyn and Katharine Mallory.[63] In the division of the estate Little Corsley fell to Margaret, granddaughter of Katharine, and wife of Thomas Boughton of Cawston (Warws.). In 1579 their son Edward sold the manor to Sir Walter Hungerford.[64]

Little Corsley descended in the Hungerford family of Farleigh Castle until 1674, when Sir Edward Hungerford sold it to Thomas Thynne of Longleat. The farm of the manor was then occupied by John A'Court of Rodden (Som.), under a lease of 1662.[65] In the 18th century his descendants held the farm and claimed manorial rights. This was presumably by purchase from the Thynnes, but it is not known when, or whether, the sale comprised all the lands of the manor or only the farm. John A'Court died in 1692; his great grandson Pierce A'Court, later called A'Court Ashe,[66] held Little Corsley in 1733 and still in 1751.[67] It was probably soon after 1751 that the property was sold to the Jesser family. William Jesser, late citizen of London, was buried at Corsley in 1762, and his widow the following year.[68] They were succeeded by a family called Coope. John Coope and Elizabeth Jesser held the estate when the parish was inclosed in 1783,[69] and William Jesser Coope and John Coope in 1828.[70] Later in the 19th century it belonged to the Barton family of Corsley House.[71]

The farm of Little Corsley, now Cley Hill Farm, was held by the Carr family by c. 1545.[72] In 1631 Thomas Carr had lost a lawsuit about it, and the sheriff was ordered to put Hopton Haynes in possession. Carr, assisted by 'a multitude of base persons', held the house by force; the sheriff could not persuade local gentry to help him, and had to send for ordnance and gunners from Bristol to batter the house.[73]

The origin of the manor of *HUNTENHULL* is to be found in a grant of land by Godfrey de Craucumbe, lord of Corsley, to William of Idmiston, made before he gave Corsley to the nuns of Studley c. 1245. In the 17th century 'ancient evidences' were still extant which showed that it consisted of land which John Huntenhull and Peter Huntenhull had formerly held, a grange called Dallymore, and lands in Chapmanslade.[74] Somewhat later the Prioress of Studley gave lands which William de la Forde and Adam le Porter had formerly held to Daniel, son of Thomas of Idmiston.[75] These must have been added to the manor, for in 1604 it included a tenement called Ford's and several closes called Porter's.[76] These two grants to Idmiston had passed by the early 14th century to a family called Lye; William de Lye held the advowson of Corsley, which had also been given to William of Idmiston, in 1309,[77] and must have held the manor then. A previous holder was perhaps James de Lye who held 2 virgates freely of the Prioress of Studley in 1285.[78] William de Lye was said after his death to be of Huntenhull.[79] A son John evidently succeeded him[80] and was followed by Thomas,[81] whose son Robert occurs between 1370 and 1412.[82] Richard, son of Robert, occurs between 1425 and 1441.[83] Another Robert was dead by 1465,[84] leaving a son Robert who survived until the early 16th century. He left two daughters and coheirs, Elizabeth Stanter and Anne Beckett;[85] they probably sold the manor to Richard Powton, who held the advowson of Corsley, which was appurtenant to Huntenhull, by 1524.[86] He was succeeded by William Powton, who in 1545 mortgaged the manor to John Mill of Southampton.[87] Powton probably released his right the following year[88]; Mill certainly held Huntenhull by 1549, when he let the whole manor to William Moggridge of Salisbury for 70 years.[89] In 1563 Thomas Mill sold the reversion of Huntenhull to Sir John Thynne,[90] and from that time it descended with the Longleat estate.

The property of the priory of Maiden Bradley in Corsley and Warminster, known as the manor of *WHITBOURNE AND BUGLEY* was acquired by a series of gifts of varying size. One of the earliest gifts was of land and rent in Whitbourne

[56] *Cal. Pat.* 1377–81, 490.
[57] C 47/84/12/336.
[58] *Feud. Aids*, vi. 538.
[59] Ibid. v. 274.
[60] *V.C.H. Berks.* iv. 350.
[61] *Cal. Inq. p.m. Hen. VII*, i. 557–8.
[62] *L. & P. Hen. VIII*, i, pp. 465, 1329; C 142/30/44.
[63] C 142/65/33; C 142/67/152; C 142/94/51. Certain woods in Corsley passed in the same way as Little Sutton manor to the Marquess of Winchester, and were sold by him to Boughton in 1553: C 54/493.
[64] C 54/1068; W.R.O. 490, List of deeds, 1651.
[65] C 54/4425; Longleat MS. 6885; ibid. 6893 is a renewal of 1677.
[66] Hoare, *Mod. Wilts.* Heytesbury, 119–21.
[67] C.P. 43/600 rot. 153; C.P. 43/672 rot. 266.
[68] Hoare, *Mod. Wilts.* Warminster, 65.
[69] W.R.O. Inclosure Award.
[70] C.P. 43/980 rot. 159.
[71] Soc. Antiq. Jackson MSS. s.v. Corsley.
[72] C 1/1154/20.
[73] *Cal. S.P. Dom.* 1631–3, 157, 168, 170, 192–3, 194,

251–2.
[74] Longleat MS. 6830. A field called Dallemores belonged to Huntenhull Farm in 1682: ibid. 10648.
[75] B.M. Add. Ch. 40029, of c. 1251–8.
[76] Longleat MS. 6795.
[77] Davies, *English Village*, 299; see below, p. 21.
[78] *Feet of F.* 1272–1327 (W.A.S. Rec. Brch.), 24.
[79] C.P. 25(1)/255/46/15.
[80] Davies, *English Village*, 299; Longleat MSS. 9152, 9216.
[81] Hoare, *Mod. Wilts.* Frustfield, 83–4, where a pedigree is given which is borne out by the evidence cited here; Longleat MSS. 9162–3, 9168.
[82] Davies, *English Village*, 299; *Feud. Aids*, vi. 532.
[83] Davies, *English Village*, 299.
[84] P.C.C. 8 Godyn.
[85] Hoare, *Mod. Wilts.* Frustfield, 84.
[86] Davies, *English Village*, 299.
[87] Longleat MS. 6785.
[88] C.P. 25(2)/52/381.
[89] Longleat MS. 6786.
[90] C 54/634.

which Godfrey de Craucumbe gave to William de Stanton and his wife,[91] and which they gave to the priory.[92] Other gifts probably of the 13th century were made by Juliane Corp[93] and William of Corsley[94] in Corsley, while several small pieces of land, houses, and rents were given in Warminster.[95] In 1337 William of Littleton was licensed to grant a house and about 80 a. in Corsley and Warminster to the brethren,[96] and a further licence was given to John of Marshton and John of Homington for land in Whitbourne and Corsley in 1363.[97] After the Dissolution the property of the house in Warminster and Corsley was granted in 1544 to Richard Andrews and John Howe,[98] who sold it to Sir John Thynne in the same year.[99] It then descended with the Longleat estate.

The manor of *WHITBOURNE TEMPLE*, which was held in the later Middle Ages by the Hospital of St. John at Wilton, must have formerly belonged to the Knights Templar of Templecombe (Som.). At the Dissolution the Knights Hospitaller of Templecombe, who succeeded to the Templar property there in 1309,[1] were receiving a rent of 6s. 8d. from their Whitbourne property[2], which was paid by the master of the hospital.[3] It is not known when the Templars acquired Whitbourne; they do not seem to have had it in 1185, but members of the Husee family were then mentioned as benefactors, and may have given part of their fee of Little Corsley after that time.[4] Nor is it known when the Templars alienated their land to the hospital in return for the rent of 6s. 8d. The hospital is first known to have held land in Whitbourne in 1270,[5] and enjoyed the estate until the 16th century.[6] Although St. John's survived the dissolution of chantries and hospitals,[7] part of Whitbourne Temple was for some reason regarded as confiscated land, and several tenements in it were granted to Sir John Thynne in 1548.[8] Thynne obtained a release from the master of the hospital,[9] but does not seem to have regarded his title as good. When the hospital leased the Whitbourne property to John Middlecott for 99 years in 1571, Thynne obtained the whole of it by various assignments,[10] and his descendants seem to have enjoyed it as leaseholders until 1636. In that year Giles Thornburgh, the new master, attempted to take control

of the property and brought a chancery suit against Sir Thomas Thynne.[11] This was apparently unsuccessful for the Thynnes continued to hold the whole manor by lease until the 19th century.[12]

LESSER ESTATES. In 1369 Isabel, widow of John atte Bergh, died holding his estates, which included a rent of £4 at Corsley and Whitbourne.[13] Christine, widow of their son and heir John, died holding land there in 1396,[14] and another John held them in 1412.[15] It was probably the same John who settled his lands on Drew atte Bergh and Ann his wife in 1431.[16] Drew must have been the ancestor of the family of Abarrow of North Charford (Hants),[17] to which belonged Edward Abarrow of Salisbury who held the Corsley lands in 1585.[18] By 1613 the holding belonged to Leonard Bilson; it was described as land called Field's Court, held of the manor of Corsley freely by a rent of 7s. and ½lb. pepper.[19] Bilson was evidently a relative of Thomas Bilson, Bishop of Winchester, and Field's Court descended in the bishop's family to Leonard Bilson who died in 1715.[20] Before his death he sold it to Mary Halliday of Frome, widow, who in 1741 sold it to Robert Meares of Corsley, clothier. It then consisted of the house called Field's Court or Vine's Court, four small closes, and 12½ a. of field land.[21] The Meares family retained it for at least a century.[22] By 1887 the house had been pulled down.[23] It stood on the north side of the Frome road south of Corsley House.

A small estate in Corsley belonged to the Horton family of Westwood in the 16th century. Edward Horton held it in 1580,[24] Jeremy Horton in 1599,[25] and Toby Horton in 1613. It was then described as lying in 'Sloe Street', and contained 33 a., held of the manor of Corsley by a rent of 4s. 1d. and ¾lb. pepper.[26] Toby Horton sold it in 1618 to his cousin Sir John Horton of Broughton Gifford, who still held it in 1643.[27] No more is known of the property until 1736, when Robert Eyres of Chapmanslade held it.[28] He still had it in 1750,[29] but by 1773 it belonged to John Barter. It was then called the Water House,[30] and is probably to be identified with the present Water Farm.

In 1317 certain lands in Corsley were settled on Thomas, son of Walter le Vake, when he married

[91] E 210/3391.
[92] E 210/7187.
[93] E 210/2061. For another possible gift, see E 210/7077, dated 1283.
[94] Hoare, *Mod. Wilts.* Mere, 105, 106. Hoare prints (p. 100) a confirmation of Henry III dated 1227 which includes the gifts of Wm. de Stanton and Wm. of Corsley, but they are not in the enrolment of it (*Cal. Chart. R.* 1226–57, 41–2) and it seems possible that they were inserted before the inspeximus of 1285. Stanton's gift is not likely to be so early as 1227, as Craucumbe did not hold Corsley then.
[95] E 210/1830, 5676, 6494,7202.
[96] *Cal. Pat.* 1334–8, 540; *Wilts. Inq. p.m.* 1327–77 (Index Libr.), 126.
[97] *Cal. Pat.* 1361–4, 394–5.
[98] *L. & P. Hen. VIII*, xix(1), p. 630.
[99] Longleat MSS. Thynne Papers, Bk. 64, p. 7.
[1] *V.C.H. Som.* ii. 146–7.
[2] *Valor Eccl.* (Rec. Com.), i. 202; *Cal. Pat.* 1557–8, 317.
[3] *Valor Eccl.* (Rec. Com.), ii. 100.
[4] B. A. Lees (ed.) *Records of the Templars in England* (Brit. Acad.), 53, 200.
[5] *V.C.H. Wilts.* iii. 366; see also C.P. 40/181 (1277).
[6] Hoare, *Mod. Wilts.* Branch and Dole, 128–9.
[7] *V.C.H. Wilts.* iii. 366.

[8] *Cal. Pat.* 1548–9, 52.
[9] Longleat MS. 6987.
[10] Ibid. 6832, 6988.
[11] Ibid. 7013.
[12] Ibid. Title Deeds, Schedule I; *Endowed Char. Wilts.* (1908), p. 849.
[13] *Wilts. Inq. p.m.* 1327–77 (Index Libr.), 356–7.
[14] C 136/91/13.
[15] *Feud. Aids*, vi. 532.
[16] C.P. 25 (1)/257/62/19.
[17] *Visitation of Hants* (Harl. Soc. lxiv), 202.
[18] C.P. 25 (2)/241/27 and 28 Eliz. I Mich. For other lands of this family, see p. 69.
[19] Longleat MS. 6931.
[20] *V.C.H. Hants*, iii. 89; *Genealogists' Mag.* ix. 501-2.
[21] Longleat MSS. Title Deeds, Schedule IV, Bundle 3.
[22] Ibid.; W.R.O. Land Tax Assessments.
[23] O.S. Map 1/2,500 Wilts. LI. 6 (1st edn.).
[24] Longleat MS. 6942.
[25] *W.A.M.* xli. 244.
[26] Longleat MSS. 6931, 10647.
[27] *W.A.M.* xli. 252, 256.
[28] Longleat MS. 6881; *Wilts. Q.S. and Ass.* 1736 (W.A.S. Rec. Brch.), 147.
[29] Longleat MSS. Rental 1750.
[30] Ibid. 1775; W.R.O. Land Tax Assessments.

Edith atte Punde of Bugley.[31] Thomas had been succeeded by his son John by 1348,[32] who apparently still held the land in 1376.[33] Another John Vake held it in 1425;[34] he was perhaps the John Vake of Chard (Som.) who in 1440 granted it to his nephew John, son of his brother Thomas Vake of Bugley.[35] Later that year the younger John granted the estate to his father-in-law, Andrew Woodhouse of Warminster.[36] Woodhouse only held it as a trustee, and after some litigation in the late 15th century it passed to Edward Forrest *alias* Philpott, whose wife Ellen was John Vake's neice.[37] In 1508 Philpott sold it to John FitzJames, so that it was probably intended to be part of the endowment of the grammar school at Bruton (Som.). If so the intention never took effect, perhaps because the acquisition of parts of the manor of Furnax in Warminster soon afterwards made it unnecessary.[38] It may have been sold to Richard Poole; in 1555 a division was made of his lands between his daughter Elizabeth Rossiter of Longbridge Deverill, widow, and her sister's son, William Thomas of Rode (Som.). The estate included a ruinous house called Vake's Hayes, and land at Ballhayes and elsewhere.[39] Elizabeth Rossiter subsequently acquired Thomas's share.[40] William Hooper held it by 1572 when he exchanged 'Vage's Close' in Corsley Park for land near his own at Ballhayes.[41] In 1636 Robert Hooper sold a tenement called Ballhayes to Sir Thomas Thynne.[42]

In 1569 John Trapp settled a tenement called Trapp's Place in Well Street on his daughter Avice when she married William Trolloppe[43] of Horningsham; Trapp's son and heir Thomas released his right in 1582.[44] Trolloppe's son Allen Trolloppe sold the tenement to Sir Thomas Thynne in 1636.[45] It consisted of a house, 3 closes adjoining, and 3 a. of field land, and was held of the manor of Little Corsley.[46]

In the early 18th century Stephen Williams, a clothier of Whitbourne, left his freehold property to his son Stephen. In 1708 the younger Stephen sold land there to Samuel Adlam,[47] already a leaseholder there under the Longleat estate.[48] Two years later William Down obtained the leasehold[49] part of Adlam's estate and also a lease of his freehold land; before his death in 1743 he had bought a half of the rest of Stephen Williams's land from one of his coheirs, Mary, wife of John Smith of Friggle Street in Frome. Down's son John bought the other half of Williams's land from his grandson William Greenhill, son of the other daughter Elizabeth. John Down died *c.* 1783 and left two daughters. Margaret married John Carpenter who died in 1812,[50] leaving a daughter who married H. A. Fussell. Ann, John Down's other daughter, never married, and left her share to the Fussells. H. A. Fussell built Sturford Mead on part of his estate, but in 1854 the house and land were sold to Lord Bath.

The Barton family first appear as prosperous inhabitants of Corsley in the earlier 18th century. William Barton held a large copyhold called Lamb's or Nineveh in 1736,[51] and by 1743 held the tithes of the Prebend of Luxfield.[52] He was succeeded in both by his son John,[53] who died in 1784. John's son Nathaniel practised as an attorney in Warminster, and sat in Parliament for Westbury.[54] He built Corsley House.[55] At his death in 1828 he was succeeded by his son Nathaniel, whose only son N. F. Barton died without issue in 1899.[56]

In 1235 the forester of Selwood was ordered not to molest the men of Hubert Husee for inclosing Norridge Wood.[57] In 1241 Hubert made an agreement with the coheirs of Roger of Bugley about their common rights in his wood of Norridge, by which they gave up their claim to the northern half and allowed Hubert to inclose it.[58] At the death of James Husee in 1249 it was said that he held an assart in Norridge Wood of the king, but that Henry Husee claimed it as belonging to his manor of Stapleford.[59] James left a son Hubert[60] from whom Godfrey Scudamore bought part of the wood.[61] This part evidently descended with the manor of Upton Scudamore until it was in the hands of Edward VI, who in 1549 granted it to Richard Fulmerston of Thetford.[62] From him it was bought by Sir John Thynne in 1549.[63] Another part of Norridge Wood must have passed to Hubert Hussee's daughter Margaret, wife of Henry Sturmy,[64] who sold it *c.* 1318 to John de Kingston.[65] It descended with Kingston's manor of Little Corsley, for in 1582 Norridge Wood was divided between Sir John Thynne and the lords of Little Corsley. Six coppices then belonged to Little Corsley.[66] In 1682 nine coppices, amounting to 172 a., belonged to the Longleat estate.[67]

ECONOMIC HISTORY. Some of the woodland 2 leagues long and 2 leagues broad which in 1086

31 Longleat MSS. 6803-4; they were probably descendants of Ralph le Vake, fl. 1280: *Cal. Close*, 1279-88, 43; E 210/3991.
32 Longleat MS. 9216.
33 Ibid. 9175.
34 Ibid. 9214.
35 Ibid. 6808.
36 Ibid. 6807.
37 Ibid. 6805; C 1/141/81-2.
38 See p. 101.
39 Longleat MS. 6812.
40 Ibid. 11260.
41 Ibid. 6816.
42 Ibid. 6921.
43 Ibid. 6944-5.
44 Ibid. 6949.
45 Ibid. 6967-8.
46 Ibid. 6980.
47 Ibid. Title Deeds, Schedule IV, Bundle 1-2, on which this paragraph is chiefly based.
48 Ibid. 7065-6.
49 Ibid. 7115-6.

50 Hoare, *Mod. Wilts.* Warminster, 65.
51 *Q. Sess. and Ass.* 1736 (W.A.S. Rec. Brch.), 147. For the previous history of the holding see e.g. W.R.O. 442/1; Longleat MS. 6973; C3/400/35.
52 Longleat MS. 7179.
53 Ibid. 7241, 7245.
54 *W.N. & Q.* vii. 96.
55 See p. 14.
56 *W.N. & Q.* vii. 96; *Wilts. Times*, 9 Feb. 1902.
57 *Close R.* 1234-37, 88.
58 C.P. 25 (1)/251/13/54.
59 *Wilts. Inq. p.m.* 1242-1326 (Index Libr.), 6.
60 *Ex. e Rot. Fin.* (Rec. Com.), ii. 338.
61 *Visitation of Hunts.* (Camd. Soc. 1st ser. xliii), 82.
62 *Cal. Pat.* 1548-9, 299.
63 Longleat MSS. Thynne Papers, Bk. 64, p. 37.
64 *Cal. Fine R.* 1272-1307, 227.
65 *Cal. Pat.* 1317-21, 187; see also *Cal. Chart. R.* 1300-26, 450.
66 W.R.O. 442/1.
67 Longleat MS. 10652.

belonged to the royal manor of Warminster[68] probably lay within the area later occupied by the parish of Corsley. The only estate then recorded at Corsley consisted of land for only one plough, and had woodland measuring a furlong by a half-furlong.[69] The valleys of the two streams which cross the parish were probably wooded. A close called Millwood near Corsley Mill and a considerable area of land called Corsley Wood in the 18th century,[70] north-west of Lye's Green, indicate part of the area covered. Further up the Rodden Brook the surviving names Sandhayes, Landhayes, and Trussenhayes all contain the Old English element *haeg*, woodland inclosure,[71] and other instances of its occurrence have been noted in names now lost.[72] Between the streams Corsley Heath lay uninclosed until the 18th century. The only land suitable for open-field farming was on the eastern fringes of the parish, where the common fields lay until the inclosure of 1783. Bickenham Field, mentioned early in the 14th century,[73] was between the upper stretches of Rodden Brook and the Upton Scudamore boundary. Cley Hill Field[74] lay west of Cley Hill and Ham Field north-east of it, while Chedlanger Field, south of Norridge Wood, was shared with Warminster.[75] Beyond their existence, however, nothing is known of the fields in the Middle Ages.

The clearing of the wooded parts of the parish was probably accomplished slowly throughout the Middle Ages, each newly-cleared piece being inclosed to form a 'croft'. Thus Southcroft, a name which still exists near Chapmanslade, was adjoined by two other crofts in the mid-13th century,[76] and four inclosed crofts called Heathcrofts lay in Whitbourne in 1367.[77] In 1364 the farm of the manor of Whitbourne belonging to Maiden Bradley included, beside 57 a. of field land, 34 a. inclosed in 7 crofts.[78] Nothing is known of demesne farming on any of the manors. At the Dissolution the whole of the Prioress of Studley's manor was held at farm under a lease of 1504, and the Prior of Maiden Bradley had let the farm of Whitbourne for 70 years from 1532.[79] Similar leases had probably been made for many years previously.

The amount of inclosed land in the parish becomes clearer in the 16th century. In 1589 the farm of Little Corsley, later called Cley Hill Farm, included 56 a. of inclosed meadow and 75 a. of inclosed pasture. Beside this some of its 218 a. of arable land lay in closes which were several to the farmer for part of the year; these included 50 a. in two closes which lay between Norridge Wood and Clear Wood. Other holdings of the manor contained similar or larger proportions of inclosed land.[80] In the early 17th century the customary holdings of the manor of Corsley contained some 150 a. of arable land, 280 a. of pasture and 50 a. of meadow; most if not all of the two latter categories was inclosed.[81] In 1608 the rector's glebe consisted of 23½ a. in closes and 3½ a. of open-field arable.[82] In 1604 the customary holdings of the manor of Huntenhull consisted almost entirely of inclosed land.[83] There were by that time several large farms in the parish. Cley Hill Farm consisted in 1589 of the demesne of the manor of Little Corsley and three former customary holdings, and amounted in all to about 350 a., while another farm of about 70 a. also belonged to the manor.[84] Whitbourne Farm was of over 90 a. at the Dissolution.[85] The farm of Corsley let in 1654 at a rack rent of £170.[86] It included the park south of the manor house, which had been made by Sir John Thynne (d. 1580).[87] There is, however, little sign of the consolidation of copyholds here. In the early 17th century only one out of over 50 customary tenements of the manor of Corsley contained more than 40 a., and most were under 20.[88] Whitbourne, Whitbourne Temple, and Huntenhull also consisted chiefly of small holdings.[89]

There is little evidence of agricultural change in Corsley before the 18th century. Presentments of the two-year course of the fields occur as late as 1701,[90] although it is not clear how the course was worked. Little of the Thynne estate was let at rack before the inclosure of the common fields; the chief exception was the manor farm, which was making £230 in 1775.[91] Whitbourne Farm of about 114 a., and Huntenhull Farm, about 125 a., were still held on lives at the end of the 18th century.[92] With Corsley Farm, of 300 a., and Cley Hill Farm, 186 a., they were the largest holdings in the parish at the inclosure of 1783. After centuries of piecemeal encroachment the final inclosure of the parish began in 1741, when what was left of Corsley Heath was inclosed by agreement, and divided between 27 tenants.[93] In 1783 the common fields of the parish, which had not been greatly affected by inclosure, were inclosed by Act of Parliament, and also the remaining common pasture land in the parish, Corsley Wood and Trussenhayes Green.

The effect of the inclosure on Corsley seems to have been to turn it more toward arable farming, perhaps a tendency which had existed before 1783. By 1828 there were over 1,500 a. of arable land in the parish compared with 466 a. of pasture and meadow, and 88 a. of water meadow.[94] The Barton family practised conventional sheep and corn husbandry typical of the downland districts, and kept hardly any dairy cattle.[95] In spite of this Corsley

[68] *V.C.H. Wilts.* ii, p. 116.
[69] Ibid. p. 161.
[70] W.R.O. Inclosure Award, hereafter used in this section without references.
[71] *P.N. Wilts.* (E.P.N.S.), 433.
[72] See e.g. W.R.O. 442/1; Longleat MSS. 10647-8.
[73] Longleat MS. 9089.
[74] 'The field of Cly': E 210/2061 (13th cent.).
[75] See p. 106.
[76] E 326/11087
[77] E 210/3991.
[78] Davies, *English Village*, 293.
[79] Longleat MSS. Thynne Papers, Bk. 63, pp. 18, 21.
[80] W.R.O. 442/1.
[81] Longleat MS. 10647.

[82] Sar. Dioc. R.O. Glebe Terrier, 1608.
[83] Longleat MS. 6795.
[84] W.R.O. 442/1.
[85] Longleat MS. 11260.
[86] Ibid. 6980.
[87] Ibid. 6816-7, 6942.
[88] Ibid. 10647.
[89] Ibid. 6795, 10647.
[90] Ibid. 6981.
[91] Ibid. Rental, 1775.
[92] Ibid. 1798.
[93] Davies, *English Village*, 32. For previous encroachment on the heath, see Longleat MS. 6957 (1619).
[94] Davies, *English Village*, 53-4.
[95] Ibid. 54-5.

was said in 1834 to consist chiefly of small farms.[96] The preponderance of corn-growing over dairy-farming continued until about 1870; between then and the end of the century much of the parish reverted to grass. The difficulty of letting the larger farms increased so much that some were broken up and let in small-holdings.[97] In 1904 only about 500 a. of the parish was arable land, most of which was on the large farms. Only the largest of all, 454 a., then depended chiefly on corn crops; many of the dairy farms made their own cheese and butter, but some were already sending milk to the factory at Frome.[98]

In contrast to the parishes of the Wylye valley, Corsley was apparently not affected by the blossoming of the Wiltshire cloth trade in the 15th and 16th centuries. A weaver lived in the parish in the early 17th century,[99] but it was not until the second half of that century that clothiers were associated with it. George Carey of Corsley issued a token bearing the clothworkers' arms in 1666.[1] He was succeeded in the trade by Thomas Carey in 1712, and he by George Carey in 1734.[2] Samuel Adlam was a clothier in Corsley in 1688,[3] and Stephen Williams at Whitbourne soon afterwards. The way in which their property at Sturford passed to William Down, a dyer, has been described above.[4] Down was succeeded in business by his son John, a blue and medley dyer, and he by his son-in-law John Carpenter, also an 'eminent dyer', who died in 1812.[5] Carpenter in turn was succeeded by his son-in-law H. A. Fussell, who carried on an extensive business as a dyer in the early 19th century, probably depending on work from the factories at Frome.[6]

The business, begun by William Down and probably typical of Corsley because it was fairly small, was carried on by several generations of one family, and was concerned as much with dyeing as with making cloth. A similar one was probably that of James Cockell, who was a dyer at Bissford in 1746.[7] James and Nicholas Cockell occupied a dyehouse there in 1770,[8] and John and James Cockell in 1783.[9] A few years later John, James, and Nicholas were all described as superfine clothiers.[10] A third business of long standing was perhaps begun by Ebenezer Coombs, who was a clothier at Whitbourne Temple in 1756;[11] in 1783 he was described as a 'second and livery clothier'.[12] A later member of the family in the 19th century turned to the silk trade and had a 'factory' at Whitbourne Moor.[13]

Several other clothiers and dyers flourished in Corsley in the 18th century. In 1736 George Prowse took a lease of a dyehouse at Whitbourne Moor which he had just spent £400 to build.[14] It belonged to Thomas Singer in 1783.[15] Robert Meares, a dyer, was a considerable free-holder in the mid-18th century.[16] It is also clear that a considerable part of the population of Corsley derived all or part of its livelihood from the cloth trade in the 18th and early 19th centuries. Thus in 1811 and 1821 about half the families in the parish were supported by manufacture and handicraft, but by 1831 the proportion had fallen considerably.[17] Many weavers and other craftsmen, who were either employed by local clothiers or those from nearby towns, also engaged in small farming or gardening.[18]

The end of the cloth industry at Corsley probably came in the decade 1840–50, rather later than in many villages, probably because of its nearness to Frome.[19] In the 1830's there seem to have been at least three concerns still working: the Fussell dyeworks at Sturford, the Coombs silk factory at Whitbourne Moore, and the woollen factory of a Mr. Taunton at Corsley Mill.[20] The latter was probably the mill at Corsley which had a 4 h.p. wheel and employed 3 men and 10 women in 1838.[21] In addition there was a mill just across the Somerset border in Rodden, which in 1838 employed 122 people, many of whom must have come from Corsley.[22] This was destroyed by fire shortly before 1851,[23] marking the end of the woollen trade in Corsley.

In 1232 Godfrey de Craucumbe was granted a weekly market in Corsley on Fridays and a yearly fair on the feast of St. Margaret (20 July).[24] Nothing is known of a market being held in the village, and a fair is not again mentioned until 1770, when one was held on Corsley Heath on the first Monday in August for the sale of cattle, horses, and cheese.[25] It was still held in the later 19th century on 'Cock Heap', a large artificial mound on Corsley Heath, for the sale of cheese and horses. The date was then 27 July. Another fair was held at Whitsuntide, probably for amusement only, in the early 19th century. By 1909 both had entirely ceased.[26]

MILLS. One of the seven mills which belonged to the manor of Warminster in 1086[27] was probably in the area which later formed the manor of Corsley, but in fact no mention of a mill belonging to Corsley has been found before the 16th century.[28] From

---

[96] *App. Rep. Com. Poor Law, Rural Queries*, H.L. 8c, p. 571a (1834), v.
[97] Davies, *English Village*, 87.
[98] Ibid. 110–1.
[99] Longleat MS. 6790.
[1] *W.A.M.* xxvi. 396.
[2] Davies, *English Village*, 25–6.
[3] Longleat MSS. 7065–6.
[4] See p. 18.
[5] Bailey, *Brit. Dir.* (1783); Hoare, *Mod. Wilts.* Warminster, 65.
[6] Davies, *English Village*, 42–3.
[7] Longleat MS. 6853.
[8] Davies, *English Village*, 43.
[9] W.R.O. Inclosure Award.
[10] *Univ. Brit. Dir.* iii. 137.
[11] Longleat MS. 6989.
[12] Bailey, *Brit. Dir.* (1783).
[13] Davies, *English Village*, 85; *App. Rep. Com. Poor*

Law, Rural Queries (1834), p. 571 a.
[14] Longleat MSS. 7165–6.
[15] W.R.O. Inclosure Award.
[16] Longleat MS. 7183; see above, p. 17.
[17] *Census*, 1811, 1821, 1831.
[18] Davies, *English Village*, 32–4, 41–5.
[19] *V.C.H. Wilts.* iv. 172.
[20] Davies, *English Village*, 41, 45, 85.
[21] *Retn. of Mills and Factories*, H.C. 41, pp. 158–9 (1839), xlii.
[22] Ibid.; for this mill, occupied by G.W.B. and G. Sheppard of Frome, see Longleat Estate Office, Survey 1743, s.v. Lullington.
[23] Davies, *English Village*, 85–6; *V.C.H. Wilts.* iv. 321.
[24] *Cal. Chart. R.* 1226–57, 148.
[25] *Traveller's Pocket Book* (1770), 293.
[26] Davies, *English Village*, 95–6.
[27] *V.C.H. Wilts.* ii, p. 116.
[28] *Cal. Pat.* 1558–60, 469.

that time a water mill is regularly mentioned as a leasehold or copyhold tenement of the manor.[29] The long tenure of the Carr family, between 1594[30] and 1691,[31] gave it the alternative name of Carr's Mill. The Carrs were followed by the Rimell family who still held the mill in the 1750's.[32] In 1775 it was held with a considerable amount of land at rack rent.[33] This was probably the beginning of Mill Farm, occupied in the early 19th century by a Mr. Taunton, who used the mill both as a grist mill and for the clothing trade.[34] He probably built the present mill, a five-bay building of brick with segmental-headed stone-mullioned windows typical of the period. It was formerly of three stories with a mansard roof, but in 1963 had been recently reduced to two. Nearby is the late 17th-century mill-house, of brick with stone-mullioned and transomed windows and central doorway with curved hood above.

A mill belonged to the manor of Little Corsley in 1086,[35] and was still working in the early 14th century.[36] By 1589 it had long since disappeared, and a cottage had been built on the 'pleck' of ground it had occupied, 'between Medgmead and Couchmead'.[37] Its site was apparently at Bissford.[38]

CHURCHES. There was a parson of Corsley in the mid-13th century.[39] The church there was referred to as the chapel of the manor of Corsley in 1245,[40] but evidently assumed some parochial functions because of the distance to the mother church of the parish at Warminster. In the 17th century it was described as a chapel-of-ease 'anciently founded within the parish of Warminster' because Corsley people were often hindered from getting there 'by the inundation of waters'.[41] In 1341 the Vicar of Warminster had mortuaries and small tithes worth 40s. within the bounds of Corsley,[42] and it was not until 1415 that the incumbent of Corsley became fully independent of Warminster when he obtained the right of burying the inhabitants in the churchyard of the village.[43] An agreement probably made in the early 16th century gave all the small tithes, oblations, and mortuaries to the incumbent of Corsley, and charged him with the payment of 26s. 8d. a year to the Vicar of Warminster.[44] This payment was still made in the 19th century.[45] The church built in 1867 at Chapmanslade, just outside the ancient parish boundary, was at first a chapel-of-ease to Dilton Marsh, but since 1924 has been held with Corsley.[46] The church of St. Mary at Whitbourne

Temple, built in 1903, is a chapel-of-ease to Corsley parish church.[47] Two free chapels which existed in the parish in the Middle Ages are mentioned below.

The disputes over the advowson of Warminster in the 12th and early 13th centuries[48] were ended in 1235 by an agreement which assigned to a prebend in the cathedral church of Wells the great tithes of Great Corsley, Whitbourne, Bugley, Thoulstone, Chapmanslade 'under the road', and Little Corsley.[49] From that time until the 19th century the Prebendary of Warminster *alias* Luxfield was impropriator of the rectory of Corsley and of certain great tithes in the two neighbouring parishes. In spite of that the incumbent of Corsley has always been styled rector.[50]

When Godfrey de Craucumbe gave the manor of Corsley to the nuns of Studley *c.* 1245 he had already given the advowson of 'the chapel of the manor' to William of Idmiston.[51] The first recorded presentation, in 1306, was made by the Prioress of Studley;[52] the reason for this is not known, for otherwise the advowson descended from Idmiston in the same way as the manor of Huntenhull.[53] In 1946 it was transferred to the Diocesan Board of Patronage.[54]

The prebend of Warminster *alias* Luxfield was valued at £6 13s. 4d. in 1291[55] and at £13 8s. gross in 1535.[56] Sir John Thynne held the tithes and glebe belonging to it on lease before 1580,[57] and successive owners of Longleat held as leaseholders until the 19th century, paying a fixed rent of £11 6s. 8d. to the prebendary.[58] In 1598 the tithes were underlet for £15,[59] and in the mid-18th century to John Barton for £104. At that time the glebe of the prebend consisted of a close called Broom Close, a small coppice adjoining it, and a piece of land with a house on it.[60] Most of the tithes in Warminster and Corsley were commuted at the inclosure of 1783, either for land or fixed money payments. After that the prebend consisted of 205 a. of land and a fixed money payment of about £46. There were besides 9 a. in Warminster, 21 a. in Corsley, and 92 a. in Upton Scudamore still subject to the payment of tithes in kind.[61] In the early 19th century the value of the whole was reckoned at £440.[62] The remaining tithes were commuted by the parish awards at about £2 in Warminster, £3 in Corsley, and £35 in Upton Scudamore.[63] In 1847 the whole prebend was transferred to the Ecclesiastical Commissioners,[64] and in 1866 it was sold, with most of the rectory of

[29] Longleat MSS. 5678 (1560), 10647 (1612), 10648 (1682); 18th cent. Rentals *passim*.
[30] Longleat MS. 6730.
[31] Ibid. 10648.
[32] Ibid. 7192.
[33] Ibid. Rental 1775.
[34] Davies, *English Village*, 85, 92–3; see above, p. 20.
[35] *V.C.H. Wilts.* ii, p. 161.
[36] *Cal. Fine R.* 1319–27, 330.
[37] W.R.O. 442/1.
[38] Ibid.
[39] *Sar. Chart. and Doc.* (Rolls Ser.), 319.
[40] *Cal. Chart. R.* 1226–57, 283.
[41] Longleat MS. 6830.
[42] *Inq. Non.* (Rec. Com.), 170.
[43] *Cal. Papal Regs.* vi. 491.
[44] W.R.O. 490, Hungerford Cart. f. 110A; Davies, *English Village*, 294–5.
[45] Daniell, *Warminster*, 152.
[46] *Crockford*, 1926.

[47] See below.
[48] See pp. 117–18.
[49] Hist. MSS. Com. *Wells*, i. 435–6.
[50] e.g. *Inq. Non.* (Rec. Com.), 170; Longleat MS. 6830; *Crockford, passim*.
[51] *Cal. Chart. R.* 1226–57, 283.
[52] Phillipps, *Wilts. Inst.* i. 6.
[53] Ibid. *passim*; see above, p. 16.
[54] Sar. Dioc. Regy. Patronage Register.
[55] *Tax. Eccl.* (Rec. Com.), 200.
[56] *Valor Eccl.* (Rec. Com.), ii. 102.
[57] Longleat MS. 6834.
[58] Ibid. 6830; Hist. MSS. Com. *Wells*, ii. 437; Longleat MSS. Rentals, *passim*; Ch. Com. 5344–6.
[59] Longleat MS. 8105.
[60] Ch. Com. 5347.
[61] Ibid.; W.R.O. Inclosure Award.
[62] Ch. Com. 5347.
[63] W.R.O. Tithe Awards.
[64] *Lond. Gaz.* 1847, p. 45.

Warminster, to the Marquess of Bath in exchange for the rectory of Imber.[65]

In 1341 the Rector of Corsley had a house and land tithes worth 30s. and oblations worth 50s.[66] The small tithes then belonged to the Vicar of Warminster, and were probably first allotted to the Rector of Corsley in the early 16th century.[67] In 1535 the benefice was worth £11 0s. 10d. clear,[68] and in 1704 it was said to be only worth £28.[69] In 1709 the 1st Viscount Weymouth endowed it with £20 a year payable out of lands in Herefordshire.[70] It was discharged from the payment of first fruits and tenths by Queen Anne's Bounty, and in 1745 was reckoned worth £60 a year.[71] In 1835 the incumbent reckoned his clear income at £215,[72] but his successor in 1851 returned his income as £183.[73]

The Rector of Corsley was letting his small tithes c. 1574.[74] In 1704 the tithes and other profits of the rectory apart from the glebe were only worth £8.[75] In 1783 the rector received an allotment of 66 a. in lieu of the small tithes of most of the parish, and a fixed payment of about £28 from other lands, while some 21a. remained titheable in kind.[76] These last tithes were commuted for £2 in 1841.[77] In 1608 the rector's glebe consisted of a little house and garden, 8 closes amounting to 23½ a., 1 a. in Bristol Mead, and 3½ a. of field land.[78] This land was worth £20 a year in 1704.[79] At the commutation of the tithes in 1783 66 a. were added to it.[80] The whole glebe was worth £120 a year in 1851[81] and £155 in 1887, when it amounted to 96 a.[82]

Nothing is known of the religious life of Corsley before the 16th century. Rectors resigned c. 1555 and c. 1563[83] but it is not known whether it was because of the religious changes of the times. John Cutler, 1579–1608, had, it was said in 1583, allowed the clerk to say service in his absence, and had quarrelled with a parishioner over a seat in the church.[84] Nothing is known of changes under the Commonwealth, but a new rector was appointed in 1660.[85] Such a small benefice was not attractive. Richard Jenkins had only just taken his degree when he was appointed to Corsley in 1667,[86] and his successor, Thomas Aylesbury, was apparently only 17 on his appointment in 1668.[87] He held the living for 56 years; from 1682 he was also perpetual curate of Horningsham, but continued to reside at Corsley.[88] Two 18th-century incumbents, Lionel

Seaman, 1736–8, and William Slade, 1774–83, were of local land-owning families in Upton Scudamore and Warminster respectively.[89] Millington Massey (later Massey-Jackson), 1768–74, held Kingston Deverill in plurality from 1770.[90] Thomas Huntingford, 1783–7, was headmaster of Lord Weymouth's School in Warminster, and only resided at Corsley for two months of the year. When he took the living, services had only been held once on Sunday, alternately morning and afternoon, for many years. He began to hold them twice, and also began extra services in Lent and monthly celebrations of the sacrament. His brother and successor, George Isaac Huntingford, evidently continued the more frequent services,[91] and began a Sunday School in 1788.[92] He was subsequently Bishop of Gloucester and then of Hereford.[93] R. C. Griffith, 1816–45, was a pluralist, holding the rectory of Fifield Bavant, where he employed a curate.[94]

In 1851 two services were held each Sunday; average attendance was 250 in the morning and 400 in the afternoon, and there was in addition a Sunday School 140 strong.[95]

The church of ST. MARGARET stands near the former manor house, at the junction of three minor roads which cross the parish from north to south, but remote from its chief centres of population. The dedication was to St. James in the earlier 16th century,[96] and was still mentioned in the 18th.[97] The present dedication has not been met with before 1786.[98] The old church consisted of nave, north aisle, chancel, south porch, and western embattled tower. The tower was probably of the 15th century, while the low nave with north aisle which joined it was perhaps older.[99] In 1636 the parishioners complained to Archbishop Laud that the chancel was 'quite taken away'. When Laud complained to Sir Thomas Thynne that his family had removed it, Thynne replied that the oldest man living there could not remember it, and that either there never was one, or that 'it fell of itself, the parish being then very poor'.[1] There was perhaps some truth in the charge, however, for it was said a few years later that there stood near the middle of Dartford Wood 'a little coney lodge, sometime said to be the chancel of Corsley'.[2] The outcome of the dispute is not known, but a simple

[65] Ch. Com. 125663.
[66] Inq. Non. (Rec. Com.), 170.
[67] W.R.O. 490, Hungerford Cart. f. 110A; Davies, English Village, 294–5.
[68] Valor Eccl. (Rec. Com.), ii. 102.
[69] Sar. Dioc. R.O. Glebe Terrier, 1704.
[70] Endowed Char. Wilts. (1908), pp. 1007–8.
[71] Clergyman's Intelligencer (1745), 215.
[72] Rep. Com. Eccl. Revenues, H.C. 54, pp. 830–1 (1835), xxii.
[73] H.O. 129/10/260.
[74] C 3/152/40.
[75] Sar. Dioc. R.O. Glebe Terrier, 1704.
[76] Ibid. 1784; W.R.O. Inclosure Award.
[77] W.R.O. Tithe Award.
[78] Sar. Dioc. R.O. Glebe Terrier, 1608.
[79] Ibid. 1704.
[80] W.R.O. Inclosure Award.
[81] H.O. 129/10/260.
[82] Retn. of Glebe, H.C. 307, p. 163 (1887), lxiv.
[83] Phillipps, Wilts. Inst. i. 219, 221.
[84] Sar. Dioc. R.O. Ep. Vis. 1583.
[85] Phillipps, Wilts. Inst. ii. 22.

[86] Ibid. 29; Foster, Alumn. Oxon. 1st ser. ii. 808.
[87] Foster, op. cit. i. 47; Hoare, Mod. Wilts. Warminster, 65.
[88] Sar. Dioc. R.O. Chwdns.' Pres. 1689; Hoare, Mod. Wilts. Heytesbury, 275.
[89] Foster, Alumn. Oxon. 2nd ser. iv. 1270, 1305.
[90] Phillipps, Wilts. Inst. ii. 85, 106.
[91] Sar. Dioc. R.O. Vis. Queries, 1783; Davies, English Village, 58.
[92] Davies, op. cit. 59.
[93] D.N.B.
[94] Rep. Com. Eccl. Revenues (1835), pp. 830–1.
[95] H.O. 129/10/260.
[96] Davies, English Village, 294; Phillipps, Wilts. Inst. i. 208.
[97] Ecton, Thesaurus (1763), 398.
[98] Bacon, Thesaurus (1786), 901.
[99] The only authorities for the old church are the plan in Hoare, Mod. Wilts. Warminster, 64, a view by Buckler (See pl. facing p. 60) and another reproduced in Davies, English Village, pl. opp. p. 60.
[1] Longleat MS. 6830.
[2] L.R. 2/301, f. 223.

chancel was added to the church; this was probably done before 1662, for no complaint was made then about the state of the church.[3]

In 1830 the church was in a bad state and insufficient for the needs of the parish, and the vestry decided to rebuild it.[4] The present church was then built to the design of John Leachman.[5] It consists only of nave and western embattled tower. The nave is very wide with a low pitched roof of slate, and tall narrow windows with forking tracery. There is no chancel. Entrance is from doors flanking the tower at the west end, which open into vestibules from which access is also gained to the western gallery. On the gallery is a royal achievement probably made when the church was built.[6] The only furnishings which survive from the old church are the plain pulpit of c. 1700, and three painted benefaction boards given to the parish in the 17th century. There are also a number of monuments from the old church. They include a wall tablet of 1724 to Thomas Aylesbury, a rector, and an elaborate monument in the Greek style to various members of the Barton family. The pews and other furnishings date from 1890, when the church was renovated and altered under the direction of F. W. Hunt. At that time galleries down the sides of the church were taken away.[7] A barrel-organ given by Nathaniel Barton was placed in the old church c. 1825. It probably replaced an orchestra, for a clarionet was bought for the singers in 1817.[8] The present organ is of 1874, by W. C. Vowles of Bristol.

There were 3 bells at Corsley in 1553. By 1783 there were 6; of these 3 had been cast in 1732 and 2 in 1746, all by William Cockey of Frome, and the remaining bell was recast by William Bilbie of Chew Stoke (Som.) in 1779. Two of Cockey's bells were recast in 1903; the other 18th-century bells still remain.[9] A clock was provided by the bequest of Robert Moody, butler at Corsley House, c. 1885.[10] In 1553 the Commissioners took 20 oz. of silver for the king and left only 7½ oz. Of the plate they left, a silver-gilt paten of c. 1510 still survives. The chalice which they left was remodelled in the 1570's. A flagon was given by John Minty in 1700, and an almsdish is of 1742. A second set of plate was given by J. H. Waugh, rector 1845–86.[11]

In 1783 the parish was allotted 1 a. of land under the inclosure award. The small income it produced was applied to the repair of the church until 1957 when it was sold for £60, and the proceeds invested for the same purpose.[12]

In 1784 the parsonage house was of stone with a slate roof; it had two rooms on the ground floor, one with a dirt floor, four chambers, and two garrets.[13] The present rectory is of the mid-19th century.

At her death in 1899 Mary Barton of Corsley House left £10,000 to buy a piece of land at Whitbourne Temple and build a chapel-of-ease in memory of her husband, Nathaniel Barton, and son, Nathaniel Fletcher Barton. The church of ST. MARY was designed by W. H. Stanley of Trowbridge and opened in 1903. It is a small brick building comprising nave, chancel, and polygonal bell turret with spire at the east end, all in the Perpendicular style. The remainder of the money, amounting to over £5,000, was invested for the maintenance of services there by the Rector of Corsley.[14]

There was a chapel at Little Corsley in 1277 when Margaret, widow of Hubert Hussee, claimed the advowson of it on behalf of his heirs. The Prior of the Hospital of St. John at Wilton said that he held the chapel by Hubert's gift, and Margaret's claim was dismissed.[15] Services may have continued there until the reformation; in 1589 it was said that the farmer of Little Corsley paid 1 a. of corn a year to the prebendary of Warminster alias Luxfield, which was formerly for him to come to the chapel and say 24 masses and 4 sermons a year.[16] In 1544 the Master of St. John's Hospital let the chapel called Kingston Court chapel with the tithes belonging to it to John Holwey for 41 years.[17] At that time the hospital claimed all the tithes of corn and hay from Kingston Court Farm, and half the tithe of wool and lambs from it, the other half belonging to the Prebend of Luxfield.[18] In 1571 John Middlecott, lessee of all the hospital's Whitbourne property, underlet the chapel to William Middlecott, with its tithes and a small amount of land.[19] The chapel passed by assignment to John Thynne in 1589;[20] a few years later he was engaged in a lawsuit with the lessee of the rectory of Warminster to determine what land owed tithe to it. Deponents said that there were in fact two chapels at Little Corsley, one in the farmhouse and one nearby, and that certain land in Warminster and Corsley owed tithe to them.[21] There were still some remains of a chapel at Cley Hill Farm, the site of the manor of Little Corsley, in 1831,[22] but no more is known of the impropriate tithes belonging to it. The distinction between them and those payable to the prebend of Luxfield may have been lost because all were held by the Thynne family.

St. John's Hospital, Wilton, also owned another chapel at Whitbourne, which c. 1657 was let to John Rawlings.[23] According to deponents in 1598 it was dedicated to St. Joan and had tithes belonging to it.[24] In 1635 it was described as a toft called the Temple, 5 a. of pasture, and certain tithes,[25] but no more is known of it.

NONCONFORMITY. There were 24 sectaries

[3] Sar. Dioc. R.O. Chwdns.' Pres. 1662.
[4] Davies, English Village, 60.
[5] Colvin, Biog. Dict. Eng. Architects, 358.
[6] W.A.M. xlviii. 106.
[7] Colvin, Biog. Dict. Eng. Architects, 358; Kelly's Dir. Wilts. (1939); Wilts. Times, 21 April 1888.
[8] Davies, English Village, 59.
[9] Walters, Wilts. Bells, 65–6; Sar. Dioc. R.O. Glebe Terrier, 1783; Davies, English Village, 61.
[10] Endowed Char. Wilts. (1908), p. 131; Davies, op. cit., 94–5.
[11] Nightingale, Wilts. Plate, 82–4.
[12] Endowed Char. Wilts. (1908), pp. 126, 129; Char. Com. file 138488; Wilts. Times, 8 Feb. 1902.
[13] Sar. Dioc. R.O. Glebe Terrier, 1784.
[14] Char. Com. File 110268.
[15] C.P. 40/18 rot. 6d.
[16] W.R.O. 442/1.
[17] Longleat MS. 6934.
[18] C 1/1154/20.
[19] Longleat MS. 6832.
[20] Ibid. 7013.
[21] Ibid. 6346.
[22] Hoare, Mod. Wilts. Warminster, 64.
[23] Longleat MS. 7013; C 3/152/40.
[24] Longleat MS. 6346.
[25] Ibid. 7013.

in Corsley in 1662[26] and 50 in 1676.[27] No organized congregation is known to have existed in the village in the 17th century, and it has been suggested that villagers probably belonged to the Baptist church at Crockerton.[28] Several houses were licensed for worship in the earlier 18th century; that of James Coombs in 1700, that of John Meares in 1724, and two in 1738.[29] None of these licences can be certainly connected with any permanent congregation, and probably the first society to establish itself in the parish was of Methodists. Corsley was 'a new place' with 31 members in 1769. The following year it had increased to 46, and Wesley preached in the parish in 1772.[30] A building was registered for worship in 1773;[31] it was at Lane End,[32] where a Wesleyan Methodist congregation has continued until the present (1963). In 1829 there were 150 attenders.[33] The plain chapel of brick with stone dressings is dated 1849. In 1851 three services were held each Sunday, and there was a Sunday School of some 30 pupils.[34]

Other dissenters in Corsley must have attended the Independent and Baptist causes which began just outside the parish boundary at Chapmanslade in the 1770's.[35] It was probably there that the 30 'Presbyterians' who lived in the parish in 1783 went. There was, however, at that time a Baptist congregation within the parish, with 20 adult members, a licensed house, and a preacher named Parrot.[36] A building which must have housed it stood at Whitbourne Temple,[37] and may perhaps have been the subject of one of the early licences mentioned above. By the first years of the 19th century the cause was apparently reduced to 2 or 3 people, and owed its revival to Richard Parsons of Chapmanslade. After he had preached there for several years, numbers had so increased that a chapel was built and opened in 1811. To raise the £700 needed to pay for it, Parsons visited not only neighbouring towns but also Bristol and London, walking all the way to save money; in London he is said to have walked 40 miles daily for a month. He remained pastor until his death in 1853.[38] There were 250 attenders in 1829.[39] In 1851 three services were held each Sunday; average attendance at the morning one was 130, and there was a Sunday School 60 strong.[40] In 1890 there were 44 members.[41] Some years after it was built the whole chapel was raised several feet and it was probably then that side and end galleries were fitted. In 1882 the interior was almost all renewed. The organ came from Longleat House.[42] Externally the building, of stone rubble with brick dressings and a brick front, is much as it was in Parsons's time.

A room was licensed for Primitive Methodists in 1848.[43] A congregation of 30 met in it in 1851,[44] but had apparently ceased to exist four years later.[45]

PARISH GOVERNMENT. The earliest surviving volume of accounts of the overseers of Corsley dates from 1729 to 1755.[46] During that period the parish regularly maintained a number of impotent poor, widows, and children, and also provided occasional assistance to tide the able-bodied over hard times. The parish took a lease of a cottage, no doubt to house homeless paupers, in 1757. In 1769 it was decided that a workhouse should be provided, and four years later a thatched building was put up at Upper Whitbourne. Not all the paupers were moved into it, but it is possible that all the regular ones had to go in. Between then and 1802 a salaried master was employed whose duty it was to keep the inmates at work. In the house the manufacture of linsey, carding and spinning wool, knitting, netting, and shoemaking were carried on; vegetables were grown and pigs kept, both for the supply of the house and for sale. From 1786 inmates were hired out for varied purposes to employers in the parish. Although the workhouse was never apparently self-supporting, it made some money, and probably led to a fall in expenditure in the late 1770's, when about 30 inmates and 20 others were relieved for about £250 a year. In the later years of the century the numbers requiring relief increased, until in 1801 they probably included most of the inhabitants. In 1802 £1,640 was spent; all attempts to keep the in-paupers at work were abandoned, and a salaried assistant overseer appointed. There was soon a considerable improvement, and expenditure did not apparently again exceed £1,000 until the late 1820's.[47] From 1828 there was a good deal of emigration from Corsley, and two years later the parish paid for 66 people to go to Canada.

SCHOOLS. In 1662 the churchwardens of Corsley presented that Richard Carpenter was a fit person to be a schoolmaster there.[48] In 1783 a dissenting minister from a congregation outside the parish ran a school in it.[49] In the earlier 19th century there were several small private and dame schools in different parts of the parish.[50] In 1846 a subscription was raised to establish a National School; grants were made by the National Society and the government, and the school, near Corsley church, was opened in 1847.[51] Twelve years later the buildings were described as 'excellent and picturesque'. About 80 children were taught in one large room

[26] Sar. Dioc. R.O. Chwdns.' Pres. 1662.
[27] *W.N. & Q.* iii. 537; the total of conformists (3,000) is a wild exaggeration, so the no. of nonconformists may be too.
[28] *V.C.H. Wilts.* iii. 111–2.
[29] W.R.O. Certs. of Dissenters' Meeting Houses.
[30] Davies, *English Village*, 56–7.
[31] G.R.O. Retns. of Regns.
[32] W.R.O. Inclosure Award.
[33] Ibid. Retns. of Nonconformist Meetings, 1829.
[34] H.O. 129/10/260.   [35] See p. 183.
[36] Sar. Dioc. R.O. Vis. Queries, 1783.
[37] W.R.O. Inclosure Award.
[38] W. Doel, *Twenty Golden Candlesticks!*, 178–9; J. D. Parsons, *Memoir of Richard Parsons*, 1854 (copy in Wilts. Tracts, 41).

[39] W.R.O. Retns. of Nonconformist Meetings, 1829.
[40] H.O. 129/10/260.
[41] W. Doel, *Twenty Golden Candlesticks!*, 180.
[42] Ibid. 180.
[43] G.R.O. Retns. of Regns.
[44] H.O. 129/10/260.
[45] *P.O. Dir. Wilts.* (1855).
[46] This section is based, unless otherwise stated, on the full account of poor relief in Davies, *English Village*.
[47] *App. Sel. Cttee. on Poor Rate Retns.* 1821, H.C. 556, p. 190 (1822), v; ibid. 1825, H.C. 334, p. 230 (1825), iv.
[48] Sar. Dioc. R.O. Chwdns.' Pres. 1662.
[49] Ibid. Vis. Queries, 1783.
[50] Davies, *English Village*, 89–90; *Educ. Enq. Abstract*, H.C. 62 (1835), xliii.
[51] Davies, op. cit. 90; Nat. Soc. File.

by a master and sewing mistress, with some help from the rector.[52] When Lord Bath gave the site of the school to the parish in 1861 it was said that 535 children had passed through it since 1847. In 1870 83 children attended, while 11 more went to a National School at Chapmanslade. Five other schools in the parish provided for a further 70 children, and only a few children between 5 and 12 were receiving no education.[53] Since the opening of the Avenue School at Warminster, Corsley has been a junior mixed and infants' school. It became an aided school under the Act of 1944.

By his will dated 1703 Henry Frederick Thynne left £3,000 for charitable purposes. His trustees invested it in lands, and charged them with certain annuities, of which one of £10 was to provide for the education of 10 poor children of Corsley and 15 of Frome. In 1820 it was said that this had been regularly done, but no details were given of its application. In 1854 the annuity was increased to £75 which was paid to the school at Frome East Woodlands. In 1903 only a few Corsley children from the hamlet of Stalls Brickyard attended there.[54]

CHARITIES. In the 16th and 17th centuries a number of donors left or gave small sums of money to the poor of Corsley.[55] The first detailed account surviving, for 1751, shows that the stock, then amounting to £118, was lent out at interest, and the proceeds were distributed to the poor not receiving relief, with small sums to the sacrament, minister,

clerk, and bells. In 1773 the parish borrowed the capital toward the building of the new workhouse, and paid £5 17s. a year interest. Most of this was in the early 19th century spent on bread, which was added to the 100 loaves and a fat bullock always given by the Marquesses of Bath at Christmas. In 1839 the parish's interest in the workhouse was sold for £117, and the money put into a bank and used for the same purpose.[56]

Samuel Adlam (d. c. 1730) charged his property at Sturford with 42s. 6d. a year, of which 40s. was to be distributed annually to 8 poor men and 8 poor women not receiving relief.[57] This was regularly paid until 1920, when the charge was redeemed for £85 stock.[58]

James Sainsbury of Sturford Cottage, a corn dealer, d. c. 1845, left £1,000 to the parish, but owing to an ambiguity in his will, only £130 was received. He directed that the interest should be distributed to twelve poor people.[59] William Knight, d. c. 1880, left £100, the interest of which was to be paid to deserving poor people who were natives of Corsley.[60] Robert Moody, d. c. 1885, butler at Corsley House, left £300 to provide clothes for poor parishioners.[61]

In 1934 all these charities were consolidated into the Corsley Parochial Charities for the general benefit of poor people in the parish. The interest from about £690 stock is distributed by the trustees who are the rector and churchwardens and 3 members of the parish council.[62]

DINTON

THE parish of Dinton lies in and to the north of the valley of the Nadder. It contains 3,403 a. and extends about 3 miles from north to south and 2 miles from east to west. The River Nadder forms the southern boundary and the Grovely Grim's Ditch the northern.[1] Until the 19th century Teffont Magna, adjoining on the west, was a chapelry of Dinton, and ecclesiastically it remained a chapelry until 1922. In 1934 the Dinton parish boundary was extended on the east to take in the entire ancient parish of Baverstock (836 a.).[2]

About two-thirds of the parish lie on the southern slope of the chalk downs which divide the valleys of the Nadder and the Wylye. On the top of the downs, in the extreme north of the parish, the land rises to over 600 ft. It then drops southwards towards the Nadder, but where the chalk gives way to the sands and clays of the valley, it rises steeply again to form a sandy ridge or escarpment.[3] Between this ridge and the river lies the village at a height of about 300 ft. The western end of Grovely Wood, a part of the former Grovely Forest, occupies the northernmost part of the

parish. In the mid-16th century the part of Grovely in Dinton was known as Rigly Wood and covered about 180 a. Nearer the village, Marshwood comprised, at the same date, about 100 a.[4] The parish was still well wooded in 1962 with a belt of trees along the southern slope of the sandy ridge and the finely-wooded park of Dinton House, as well as Grovely Wood.

Neolithic and Bronze Age implements have been found on the downs north of the village and at Dinton Beeches. Wick Ball Camp, on the sandy ridge behind Dinton House, is a univallate Iron Age hill-fort.[5] Until the 20th century the chalk lands of the parish were used almost exclusively for corn and sheep farming. After the practice of floating water-meadows was begun in the 17th century, there was more fodder for dairy cattle and in the 20th century there has been large-scale mixed farming on the downlands.[6] Nearly all the meadows along the river are scored with traces of early irrigation channels, and some meadows were still being artificially flooded in 1962. Between down and water-meadow the strip of greensand

---

[52] *Acct of Wilts. Schools*, H.C. 27 (1859 Sess. 1), xxi (2).
[53] Davies, *English Village*, 90–1.
[54] *Endowed Char. Wilts.* (1908), p. 129.
[55] Hoare, *Mod. Wilts.* Warminster, 66.
[56] *Endowed Char. Wilts.* (1908), pp. 123–5, 128.
[57] Ibid. pp. 123, 128; for the Sturford estate, see above, p. 18.
[58] Char. Com. Corr. File.
[59] *Endowed Char. Wilts.* (1908), p. 130; Davies, *English Village*, 93.   [60] *Endowed Char. Wilts.* (1908), p. 130.

[61] Ibid. p. 131; Davies, *English Village*, 94–5.
[62] Char. Com. Corr. File G. 14.
[1] O.S. Map 1/25,000 sheets 41/03, 31/93.
[2] *V.C.H. Wilts.* iv. 347.
[3] For some account of the geology of the region see Fry, *Wilts. Land Utilization*, 156, 234.
[4] *Survey of the Lands of William, First Earl of Pembroke*, ed. C. R. Straton (Roxburghe Club 1909), i. 230.
[5] *V.C.H. Wilts.* i (1), p. 63.
[6] See p. 30.

provides a soil pre-eminently suited to market gardening, and in the 18th and 19th centuries there were numerous orchards strung out along this part of the parish.[7]

The presence of two burgesses at Dinton in 1086 may imply some degree of urbanization, but it is likely that they were in fact appurtenant to Warminster.[8] Little can be said about the size or importance of Dinton in the Middle Ages. John Britton claimed that Shaftesbury Abbey had a cell for six nuns there.[9] No evidence for this has been found, although it is known that the abbess's capital messuage had a chapel attached to it.[10] In 1334 Dinton's contribution to the 15ths was the fifth highest out of the 21 places separately assessed to the tax in the hundred of Warminster,[11] and in 1377 the number of poll-tax payers was second only to that of Warminster.[12] To the benevolence of 1545 Dinton had the third largest number of contributors in the hundred, and to the subsidy of 1576 the fourth.[13] Between 1801 and 1841 the population rose from 421 to 565. After 1841 it declined, except for a slight rise in 1911, until 1931, when it was 389. In 1951, after the addition of the ancient parish of Baverstock, the population was 458.[14]

The Roman road from the Mendip lead mines to Old Salisbury ran through Grovely Wood in the north of the parish. Just south of the wood the Ox Drove crosses the parish about a mile north of the village. This green track, probably of great antiquity, was used for driving cattle to Wilton and Salisbury markets. Two of the milestones placed along it in 1750 lie within the parish. In 1773 there was an inn called the New Inn beside the track just before it left the parish on the east.[15] This disappeared early in the 19th century. Its site was excavated in 1962.[16] Until the beginning of the 19th century the main road from Salisbury to Hindon followed the course of the road which runs along the top of the sandy ridge behind the village to Teffont Magna. This was turnpiked in c. 1760.[17] By 1837 this had become the 'old turnpike road' and the present (1962) main road had become the 'new turnpike road'.[18] By 1746 the western part of the present main road was called Ranger's Lane and was gated where it left Dinton for Teffont Magna. The road leading south from the church to join Ranger's Lane was called Forster's Lane, and the continuation of Ranger's Lane east beyond this junction was called Rosemary Lane. The junction was called Four Corners. Except for a footbridge by the mill,[19] the Nadder is crossed by only one bridge in the parish. This is Catherine Bridge, built of faced blocks of Chilmark stone, and carrying the road from Dinton to Fovant.[20] The railway line from Salisbury to Exeter, opened in 1859,[21] runs through the south of the parish between the Nadder and the main road. Dinton station is about ½ mile from the centre of the village.

The oldest part of the village lies along the road that branches off from the present main road and runs north past the church. Most of the houses in this part of the village are built of local stone, and a number still in 1962 retained their thatched roofs. There are a notable number of small farmhouses of 17th-century date in the village, all built of stone. Speargate Cottage, Cotterells, Jesse's Farm, and Lawes Cottage afford good examples of these. Lawes Cottage was given to the National Trust by the widow of George Engleheart in 1940.[22] Little Clarendon, a rather larger house adjoining Lawes Cottage, probably dates from c. 1500 and is also National Trust property.[23] The Manor Farm, the farmhouse of Lord Pembroke's manor, and presumably standing on or near the site of the abbess's capital messuage,[24] lies in the extreme east of the parish nearly ¾ mile from the church. Dinton Park and House lie behind the church and Rectory on the opposite side of the parish.[25]

About ¾ mile north of the church, in a valley running east and west between the sandy escarpment and the chalk downs, stands Marshwood House. The central part of the present house is thought to have been built by a Mr. Gwynne early in the 18th century. Edward Whatmore (d. 1787) added the two flanking wings.[26] The house was part of Lord Pembroke's manor, but was leased to members of the Wyndham family after Whatmore's death.[27] By the Inclosure Award of 1837 Lord Pembroke exchanged the house and grounds with William Wyndham for property elsewhere in Dinton.[28]

There was no piped water in the village until 1904 when Lord Pembroke built a reservoir to supply his tenants with water.[29] This was the only piped water supply until 1958 when mains water was installed.[30] Most of the 20th-century building has taken place along the present main road which virtually by-passes the older part of the village. Since the Second World War blocks of Council houses have been built along the road leading south from the church, and others, of slightly earlier date, lie on both sides of the road leading to the station. Since the Second World War an Admiralty Gunnery Equipment sub-depot has occupied a site between the railway and the main road.

Edward Hyde, future Lord Chancellor, and first Earl of Clarendon, was born at Dinton in 1609 and was baptized in the church there.[31] His father, Henry Hyde, had apparently leased the rectory and advowson of Dinton from his brother Sir Lawrence Hyde, the lay rector.[32] Edward and

[7] B.M. Map 5710 (52).
[8] *V.C.H. Wilts.* ii, pp. 20–21, 128.
[9] John Britton, *Beauties of Wilts.* iii. 327.
[10] *First Pembroke Survey*, i. 228.
[11] *V.C.H. Wilts.* iv. 302.   [12] Ibid. 311.
[13] *Taxation Lists* (W.A.S. Rec. Brch.), 35–6, 145.
[14] *V.C.H. Wilts.* iv. 347.
[15] *Andrews and Dury, Map* (W.A.S. Rec. Brch.), pl. 5.
[16] Ex inf. Hon. Sec. Southern Command Corps of Signals Archaeological Soc.
[17] *V.C.H. Wilts.* iv. 262.
[18] W.R.O. Inclosure Award.
[19] Map by W. Wapshare of west end of Dinton 1746 at Little Clarendon, Dinton, and copy at Som. Rec. Off.

[20] E. Jervoise, *Ancient Bridges of South Eng.* 69.
[21] *V.C.H. Wilts.* iv. 281.
[22] *W.A.M.* l. 294.   [23] See p. 29.
[24] See p. 27.
[25] For Dinton House see p. 28 and pl. facing p. 76, and for the Rectory see p. 29.
[26] *W.N. & Q.* i. 147–9. There is a map of the estate dated 1787 in W.R.O.
[27] B.M. Maps 5710 (52), 5710 (26).
[28] W.R.O. Inclosure Award.
[29] Dinton W. I. Scrapbk.
[30] Local information.
[31] *D.N.B.*; Dinton Ch. reg. 1558–1653.
[32] See p. 31; Clarendon, *Life* (1761 edn.), 6.

eight other children of Henry Hyde and his wife, Mary Langford, were born at Dinton,[33] presumably in a house on or near the site of the present Rectory House.[34] Until he went to Oxford at the age of 13, Edward Hyde was educated by the Vicar of Dinton.[35] Some time between 1623 and 1625 Henry Hyde left Dinton for Purton.[36] The mother of the musicians William and Henry Lawes came from Dinton and Henry, the younger brother, was baptized there in 1596.[37] Henry (d. 1662) wrote the music for 'Comus' and composed the anthem 'Zadok the Priest' for the coronation of Charles II.[38] Roger Ludlow, the deputy–governor of Connecticut in 1639, who helped to draft the constitution of Connecticut, was the son of Thomas Ludlow of Dinton.[39] His younger brother, George, who became a prominent member of the council in Massachusetts, was baptized at Dinton in 1596.[40] Edward Whatmore of Marshwood House (d. 1787) patented a movable fire-escape which could also be used for picking fruit.[41] George Herbert Engleheart (d. 1936) was universally known among horticulturists for the work he did in his garden at Little Clarendon on the cultivation of daffodils.[42]

MANOR. By the time of the Domesday Survey *DINTON* belonged to Shaftesbury Abbey.[43] The 20 hides at which it was assessed almost certainly included the whole of Teffont Magna, another Shaftesbury manor, and not separately mentioned in the survey.[44] Later evidence shows that the two manors were jointly administered by the abbey, and for some time after the Dissolution, by Lord Pembroke. How and when Shaftesbury acquired Dinton is unknown, but there are two charters of the 8th and 9th centuries respectively in the abbey's cartulary relating to land in Teffont.[45] In 1086 there was also a two-hide estate in Dinton held by Gunfrid, whose predecessor in the time of King Edward had been unable to detach it from the abbey.[46] If Gunfrid is Gunfrid Maldoith, who held land elsewhere in Wiltshire in 1086, and from whom a branch of the Mauduit family is thought to have descended,[47] then these 2 hides could represent the freehold estate held by the Mauduits in Dinton in the 12th and 13th centuries.

Dinton remained among the possessions of Shaftesbury Abbey until the Dissolution.[48] In 1540 the site with the chief messuage of the manor was granted to Sir Thomas Arundell (d. 1552),[49] who immediately obtained licence to alienate it to Matthew Colthurst.[50] Colthurst in turn obtained

licence to convey it to William Green of Heale, in Woodford.[51] What these transactions achieved, if anything, is not known, and in 1547 the entire manor was granted to Sir William Herbert, later Earl of Pembroke (d. 1570).[52] Thenceforward Dinton descended with the Pembroke title until 1918 when, as an outlying part of the Wilton estate, it was sold in lots.[53]

In 1552 the demesne farm including the demesne lands of Teffont Magna was leased to William Mellowes for 21 years and before then it had been occupied by John Reave.[54] In 1610 Roger Earth was the lessee,[55] and in 1634 the lessees were Prudence and Joseph Earth.[56] In 1649, for the first time, the Dinton demesne farm was leased without the lands in Teffont Magna, which from this date formed a separate estate.[57] The lease of 1649 of the Dinton farm was to John Low. In 1658 the lessee was Nicholas Daniels, and the farm continued to be leased by members of the Daniels family until 1717 when the lease was acquired by Wadham Wyndham (d. 1736), a younger brother of William Wyndham, of Dinton Park.[58] The demesne farm was leased under Lord Pembroke by Wadham's son, Henry (d. 1788), and by his grandson, Henry Penruddock Wyndham.[59] But, on the death of Henry Penruddock Wyndham in 1819, Lord Pembroke granted the lease to Walter Baily who held it until *c.* 1850.[60] The manor farm was then leased by a number of persons until 1902 when D. Coombes became the lessee, and on the sale of Lord Pembroke's lands in Dinton in 1918 Mr. Coombes bought the farm.[61]

In 1567 the demesne farmhouse was tiled and contained a hall, parlour, kitchen, and other rooms necessary for occupation by a tenant farmer. There was also a chapel, and, among the farm buildings, a large barn of 15 bays with 2 porches, and a dovecot.[62] All these were stone-tiled. In 1963 Manor Farm had an early 19th-century front range, with an older range behind. This had been much altered in the 19th and 20th centuries and contained no features which could be accurately dated. In 1952 it was alleged that a dovecot still existed on this farm,[63] and this is perhaps to be identified with the rectangular stone outbuilding standing to the north of the farmhouse. Across the road from the farm is a range of three cottages which may originally have formed a single house dating from the 16th century or earlier. The two central bays at least have a roof with raised cruck trusses and curved wind-braces, and the walls, now mainly of stone, were formerly timber-framed on a high stone base.

[33] *W.A.M.* ix. 287.
[34] See p. 29.
[35] Clarendon, *Life* (1761 edn.), 6.
[36] *W.A.M.* liv. 394; Clarendon, op. cit. 8.
[37] *D.N.B.*; *W.A.M.* liv. 395. No evidence has been found for connecting the family with any particular house in Dinton, although Lawes Cottage was named after it in the present century.
[38] *D.N.B.*
[39] Ibid.; *W.N. & Q.* ii. 295.
[40] *D.N.B.* (under Ludlow, Roger).
[41] *W.N. & Q.* i. 5; *Gent Mag.* lvii. 640.
[42] *W.A.M.* xlvii. 426–7.
[43] *V.C.H. Wilts.* ii. p. 128.
[44] Ibid. p. 95.
[45] See p. 76.
[46] *V.C.H. Wilts.* ii. p. 128.
[47] *Dom. Bk. Wilts.* ed. Jones, 237; *V.C.H. Wilts.* ii, p. 157 n. 62: see below, p. 28.
[48] *Valor Eccl.* (Rec. Com.), i. 277.

[49] *L. & P Hen. VIII*, xv. p. 412.
[50] Ibid. p. 475.
[51] Ibid. xviii (1), p. 450; for Wm. Green see *V.C.H. Wilts.* vi. 224.
[52] *Cal. Pat.* 1547–48. 112.
[53] W.A.S. Libr., Devizes, Sale Cat.
[54] *First Pembroke Survey*, ed. Straton, 228.
[55] *Pembroke Manors* (W.A.S. Rec. Brch.), 28.
[56] Wilton House MSS. Surveys of Manors, vol iii. 283.
[57] Ibid. For Teffont Magna, see p. 76.
[58] Wilton House MSS. Surveys of Manors, vol. iii. 283. For Wadham Wyndham, see H. A. Wyndham, *Family Hist.* 1688–1837, p.x. For William Wyndham see below p. 28.
[59] Wilton House MSS. Surveys of Manors, vol. iii. 283; Survey Bk. No. 6.
[60] Ibid. Survey Bk. No. 6; Rent Rolls.
[61] Ibid. Rent Rolls and Audit Bk.
[62] *First Pembroke Survey*, ed. Straton, 228.
[63] *W.A.M.* liv. 399.

LESSER ESTATES. In the 14th century the family of Cole had an estate in Dinton. In 1316 Robert Cole acquired land there from Walter of Langford,[64] and about ten years later he, or another of the same name, was deprived of his estate in Dinton for his adherence to the Lancastrian cause.[65] From an agreement made in the second quarter of the same century it appears that the Coles held their land in return for keeping the abbess's woods of Rigly and Marshwood, both within her manor of Dinton.[66] This duty and presumably the land that went with it, passed at an unknown date to the family of Lambert.[67] Edmund Lambert died in 1493 holding the same amount of land as the Cole family had held.[68] This passed to Edmund's son, William, who died in 1504 and was succeeded by his brother Thomas.[69] Thomas was followed in 1510 by his son William.[70] In 1567 William Lambert was a freeholder on Lord Pembroke's manor of Dinton holding his lands in return for his services as keeper of Rigly and Marshwood.[71] No subsequent reference to the Lambert family in Dinton has been found and it is not known to whom their estate passed.

Another freehold estate was held by Henry Mayhew in 1567.[72] This had presumably come to him from John Mayhew, a free tenant on the manor.[73] Henry, a recusant, died excommunicate in 1587.[74] His sons, Henry and Edward, went into exile overseas and the estate was conveyed in 1591 by Henry Mayhew, the younger, to his uncle, John Mayhew.[75] In 1616 John Mayhew settled the property upon himself for life with remainder to his daughter Dorothy, then about to marry Thomas Blake.[76] John Mayhew and Thomas Blake sold the estate in 1625, described as 'their manor, lordship, and capital messuage of Dinton and Teffont' to William Rolfe and five years later Rolfe sold it to Richard South, who already had a freehold estate in Dinton and Teffont.[77]

The estate of the South family may originate in the holding of the Mauduits in Dinton. In the mid-12th century Ancelin Mauduit, who may have been a descendant of the Gunfrid of the Domesday Survey, held 2 hides on the manor,[78] and in 1242 three mesne tenants held land in Dinton of Joanna Mauduit, who held of the Abbess of Shaftesbury.[79] In 1567 the freehold estate of Thomas South included lands called Mauduits, Wick, Gerrards, and Uptons, then occupied by William Dunne.[80] Ten years later Thomas South settled 'the manor or farm of Dinton called Mauduit's' upon Thomas

his son on his marriage with Martha Goldston.[81] The younger Thomas died in 1606 and the 'manor of Dinton Mauduits' passed to his son Edward.[82] Edward was succeeded by Richard South, probably his son, who in 1630 acquired from William Rolfe the property which Rolfe had acquired five years earlier from John Mayhew and Thomas Blake.[83] In 1689 George South, grandson of Richard, sold his estate to William Wyndham, second surviving son of Sir Wadham Wyndham of Norrington and Salisbury.[84] Thus the estate acquired by the Wyndhams, later called the Dinton Park estate, included the freehold estate of the Souths, situated in Dinton and Teffont,[85] and that of the Mayhews which had passed to the Souths in 1630 (see above).

The Dinton Park estate was much enlarged in the 18th and early 19th centuries by acquisitions of land in Dinton and Teffont Magna.[86] Among these acquisitions, was the estate known as Dalwood, which Lord Pembroke conveyed to William Wyndham in 1802 in exchange for land elsewhere in the parish.[87] The Dinton Park estate descended from father to eldest son in the Wyndham family until 1916 when William Wyndham sold it to Bertram Erasmus Philipps.[88] In c. 1940 B. E. Philipps let the house on a long lease to the Y.W.C.A. as a holiday home, and in 1943 he gave the house and park, comprising some 200 a., to the National Trust.[89]

Dinton House (also called since 1943 Philipps House) was designed by Jeffry Wyatt (later Sir Jeffry Wyatville) at the beginning of the 19th century to replace the earlier house on almost the same site, which until then had been the home of the Wyndhams. The new house was completed in 1816. Built of Chilmark stone, it is a two-storied house with symmetrically set chimney stacks and central lantern. The south front has nine bays with an Ionic portico. The architect is believed to have based his design upon Pythouse, Tisbury, some seven miles away. Inside the house, the rooms are planned round a spacious square hall. It was one of the earliest houses to have a central heating system installed. This was achieved by pumping hot air from a boiler in the basement into the stair well.[90]

Another freehold estate in Dinton at the time of the Inclosure Award was one of about 30 a. belonging to William Maslem Barnes and known as Hayters.[91] The early history of this has not been traced. It was acquired by Henry Hayter of Clarendon Park in 1697 and from the Hayters

[64] *Feet of F. Wilts.* 1272–1327 (W.A.S. Rec. Brch.), 93.
[65] S.C. 6/1148/24.
[66] B.M. Harl. MS. 61, f. 110d.
[67] B.M. Eg. MS. 3098, f. 10.
[68] *Cal. Inq. Hen. VII*, i, p. 404.
[69] Ibid. ii, p. 541.
[70] C 142/25/4.
[71] *First Pembroke Survey*, ed. Straton, 216.
[72] Ibid.
[73] B.M. Add. Ch. 24440.
[74] C 142/231/69; E 178/2445.
[75] E 178/2445; Som. Rec. Off. DD/WY Box 97.
[76] Som. Rec. Off. DD/WY Box 97; Hoare, *Mod. Wilts.* Dunworth, 102–3.
[77] Hoare, op. cit. 103. All the deeds relating to these transactions are in Som. Rec. Off. DD/WY Box 97.
[78] B.M. Harl. MS. 61, f. 74v. For Gunfrid see p. 27.
[79] *Bk. of Fees*, ii, p. 734.
[80] *First Pembroke Survey*, ed. Straton, 217.

[81] *Antrobus D. before* 1625 (W.A.S. Rec. Brch.), pp. 55, 57.
[82] C 142/291/144; *Wilts. Visitation* 1623 (Harl. Soc. cv–cvi), 187.
[83] Hoare, *Mod. Wilts.* Dunworth, 103; the deeds relating to this transaction are in Som. Rec. Off. DD/WY Box 97.
[84] Hoare, op. cit. 103, 108, and Som. Rec. Off. DD/WY Box 97; H. A. Wyndham, *Family Hist.* 1688–1837, p. x.
[85] See p. 76.
[86] For these acquisitions see Som. Rec. Off. DD/WY Boxes 83, 93, 100, 101, 104.
[87] Som. Rec. Off. Box 102. Copy of Agreement as to Inclosure Award.
[88] H. A. Wyndham, *Family Hist.* 1688–1837, p. x; *W.A.M.* liv. 398.
[89] James Lee-Milne, 'Dinton, Wilts.' *Country Life*, 17 Dec. 1943, 1082; *The Times*, 30 Apr. 1943.
[90] *Country Life*, 17 Dec. 1943, 1082.
[91] W.R.O. Inclosure Award.

passed to John Barnes in 1797. It passed to John's brother, William Maslem Barnes, in 1822. During the 19th century the property changed hands a number of times, and in 1901 was bought by George Engleheart.[92] Engleheart died in 1936[93] and in 1940 his widow gave the former farmhouse of the estate, by then called Little Clarendon, to the National Trust.[94]

Little Clarendon[95] is a stone farmhouse probably dating from the late 15th or early 16th century. The two-storied porch and mullioned windows are of slightly later date. The gable front of the south-east wing appears to have been added, or re-built, in c. 1900. In the angle between this wing and the main block is a stair turret containing a stone newel staircase. The house was completely restored by George Engleheart at the time that he bought it when it was sometimes called Steps.[96]

The rectors of Dinton held a small estate in the parish. This passed with the rectory upon the Dissolution to Sir Thomas Arundell and thenceforth descended like the rectory and advowson[97] until the 1920's when it was sold. In 1567 the rectorial estate included 14 a. of arable divided between three fields on the east side of the manor and 16 a. of arable divided between three fields on the west side of the manor. There was also some 2 a. of meadow and grazing rights for 60 sheep and other beasts.[98] A parsonage house existed at least as early as 1249.[99] In 1567 the house belonging to the rectory estate had a tiled roof, a dovecot, outhouses, and about 2 a. of garden and orchard.[1] The land belonging to the rector was assessed at 49 a. in 1837.[2] It was sold in lots during the 1920's.[3] The Rectory House was sold to B. E. Philipps in 1924,[4] and was re-named Hyde's House. It was given by Mr. Philipps in 1943 with Dinton House to the National Trust.[5]

The Rectory House has some walls and windows of Tudor date, but it was re-fronted on the south side early in the 18th century. This front, built of Chilmark stone, is of 5 bays, the central 3 projecting slightly and being surmounted by a pediment. The central door is also pedimented. Edward Hyde, first Earl Clarendon (d. 1674), who was born in Dinton in 1609 was probably born in what was then the Rectory House.[6] Detached from the house, is a large dovecot dating from the 15th century.[7]

ECONOMIC HISTORY. Domesday Book records 20 a. of meadowland, the same of woodland, and pasture a league long by half a league broad. Of the 20 hides making up the manor, undoubtedly including Teffont Magna, 7 were in demesne, and 2 held by Gunfrid, leaving 11 hides for tenant farming. There were 2 ploughs and 4 serfs on the demesne, and on the rest of the manor there were 21 villeins, and 10 bordars with 11 ploughs.[8] A survey of the manor, which has been dated c. 1160,[9] reckons Dinton at only 10 hides, an estimation which possibly excluded the demesne lands. This survey, which again includes Teffont as but a part of Dinton, begins with a list of some 50 tenant holdings. Of these, 29 were holdings of 1 virgate. The rest, except for one of 1½ virgate, were all smaller, many of only one acre. The rents and services due from holders of a virgate are meticulously set out, and included, besides ploughing, reaping, and harvesting, thatching houses, and making malt and carrying it to Shaftesbury. After these 50 holdings and their tenants, 15 cotsetlers are named, often with holdings of 4 acres, and all owing rent and services. Among them were a shepherd, an oxherd, and a smith, who held their few acres in return for special services.[10] Finally there were 9 franklins, most of whom had holdings larger than one virgate. They owed rent only, and in some cases, suit at the shire and hundred courts, as well as at the manor court. The parson of Dinton appears in the list of franklins. Almost nothing is known about the agrarian economy of the manor during the next 400 years. As on the other Wiltshire estates of Shaftesbury Abbey, both the abbess and her tenants had sheep on the downland of the parish. At the beginning of the 13th century the number of sheep kept by 36 tenants from Dinton and Teffont Magna outnumbered the flock belonging to the abbey.[11]

From at least as early as 1535 the demesne lands were leased out for an annual rent.[12] In 1535 the perquisites of the manorial court were worth £2 and rents nearly £29.[13] Immediately after the Dissolution these rents were made up of £3 from the free-tenants and some £26 from customary tenants.[14] A survey made in 1567, 20 years after the manor had passed into William Herbert's hands, shows that Dinton and Teffont Magna were still farmed as one estate but that the two places had their own sets of common fields. Of the demesne arable 129 a. lay in the three open fields of Dinton, and 82 a. in Teffont's three fields.[15] There were some 44 a. of pasture mostly inclosed in small meadows, but there were also 5 a. in the common meadow. On Dinton Downs there were 120 a. of inclosed grazing for the demesne flock of 400 sheep, and on Teffont Downs there was common pasture for another 300 sheep. On the rest of the manor there were 11 freeholders, some with land in both Dinton and Teffont, and 32 customary tenants holding by copy of court roll. Nearly all tenants had pasture rights which, if exercised, would have allowed for

[92] H. F. Chettle, 'Dinton and Little Clarendon', W.A.M. liv. 400–03.
[93] W.A.M. xlvii. 426–27.
[94] Ibid. liv. 403.
[95] For some suggestions as to the origin of this name see W.A.M. liv. 403.
[96] For brief illustrated description see Country Life, 17 Dec. 1943. [97] See pp. 31–32.
[98] First Pembroke Survey, ed. Straton, 231.
[99] Crown Pleas Wilts. Eyre 1249 (W.A.S. Rec. Brch.), 214.
[1] First Pembroke Survey, ed. Straton, 231.
[2] W.R.O. Inclosure Award.
[3] Ex. inf. the Estates Bursar, Magdalen Coll. Oxford.
[4] Ibid.

[5] Country Life, 17 Dec. 1943, 1080.
[6] See p. 26.
[7] For a description of the house see Country Life, 17 Dec. 1943, 1081.
[8] V.C.H. Wilts. ii. p. 128.
[9] In an unpublished study of 'The early economic history of Shaftesbury Abbey', by Lydia M. Marshall. Thanks are due to Miss Marshall for lending the TS.
[10] B.M. Harl. MS. 61, ff. 72d–74d.
[11] E 179/242/47.
[12] Valor Eccl. (Rec. Com.), i. 277, and see above, p. 27.
[13] Valor Eccl. (Rec. Com.), i. 277.
[14] Dugdale, Mon. ii. 486.
[15] First Pembroke Survey, ed. Straton, i. 216–32.

a combined flock of about 1,300 sheep on the downs. Inclosure of common for arable was evidently in progress at this date, and, to offset the consequent loss of common grazing, tenants were permitted for every yardland they held to inclose 12 a. of pasture.[16] Much of the grassland along the river was thus divided up into small inclosed meadows. There are frequent references in the 1567 survey to these recently made closes, and the manor court at about the same date was dealing with tenants who failed to maintain the hedges just planted between their lands in 'the marsh'.[17]

Another survey made in 1631 reveals the progress at Dinton of the current changes in husbandry which were taking place throughout the region.[18] All the demesne arable situated in Dinton had been consolidated into a single field of some 120 a., although the demesne arable lying in Teffont was still distributed among the three fields there. All the demesne meadow lay in small closes. Dinton Down was said to be so barren that down and fields together could only support about 300 sheep in spite of the provision of 20 loads of hay as extra fodder. The number of sheep which could be maintained at Teffont had similarly declined, and here the reason was specifically attributed to inclosure. The number of freeholders on the manor at this date is not given. Two of the customary tenants held by lease from Lord Pembroke and the remaining 33 were copyholders. By this date nearly all tenants, in addition to their inclosed meadows, had closes of arable as well as their holdings in the common arable fields, and it is clear that in many cases these arable closes had been made from the formerly open downland. The pattern of the three common arable fields was also undergoing some modification at this time. New fields had either been created, or the old ones subdivided into more convenient units. The encroachment of arable upon the downs may not, however, have resulted in any drastic reduction in the numbers of sheep on the manor. The sheep grazing rights of the tenants were in fact slightly higher in 1631 than they were in 1576, and the loss of downland to the plough may have been offset by the greatly increased feeding provided by the water-meadows which began to be made at Dinton in the first quarter of the 17th century.[19]

In 1650, for the first time, the demesne lands lying in Teffont were leased as a separate estate[20] and thenceforward the Dinton demesne farm lands lay in Dinton only. A map of 1800 shows the demesne arable as a compact block of land extending along the east side of the parish, north of the Manor Farm. Two common arable fields divided into strips are discernible above the village but the process of consolidation was advancing here too, and three or four farmers held compact blocks of

land within these fields.[21] This process of consolidation was completed by an Inclosure Award of 1837. After the early 17th century nearly all the fields along the river were floated as water-meadows, and the earlier grazing and bigger hay-crop thus afforded resulted in an increase in dairy farming in the parish. At the end of the 19th century considerable flocks of sheep were still kept on the downs,[22] but in the 20th century much of the chalkland was converted into arable, and since the Second World War chicken farming has been carried on on a large scale in this part of the parish. In 1903 there were four farms in Dinton.[23] In 1919 Manor Farm comprised 564 a., East Farm 377 a., Jesse's Farm 132 a., and Fitz's Farm 84 a. All were mixed farms and all had their fields lying partly on the downs to the north of the village, and partly on the clay and loam land to the south.[24] In 1931 there were three farms farming over 150 a.,[25] and in 1962 there were two.

In spite of being an entirely agricultural community and lying in a region where there was much unrest, Dinton remained peaceful throughout the disturbances of the 1830's. Agricultural machinery was broken at Wilton, Barford St. Martin, and Tisbury, all close by, but no incidents occurred at Dinton.[26] This has been attributed to the firm action taken by William Wyndham of Dinton Park,[27] who by that date owned, or farmed, nearly half the parish. Several of the Wyndhams played important parts in the economic history of the parish. William Wyndham (d. 1785) was a pioneer in agricultural improvement,[28] and his great-grandson, another William Wyndham, installed an extensive land drainage system.[29] The fox-hunting activities of the family also provided a certain amount of employment in the 19th century, for the kennels of the South and West Wilts. Hunt were at Dinton Park for a time.[30]

The greensand strip running through the parish between the chalk and clay provides a soil particularly well suited to market gardening. At the end of the 18th century there were extensive orchards in and around the village and a traveller remarked that when these were in bloom a stranger might suppose he were in Devon or Herefordshire.[31] Early 20th-century directories include apples among the chief crops of the parish, but in 1962 there was no large-scale market gardening and there were no commercial orchards. In 1910 a successful tobacco-crop was grown in the parish probably for one of the Salisbury tobacco manufacturers.[32]

Agriculture has always been predominant in the economic life of the parish. In 1831 of the 111 families in Dinton 76 were employed in agriculture. Of the 131 men over 20 years of age 9 were farmers employing labourers, and 73 were agricultura workers.[33] Besides occupations ancillary to agri-

[16] E 178/2445.
[17] B.M. Add. Ch. 24440, 24441.
[18] Pembroke Manors (W.A.S. Rec. Brch.), 28.
[19] For an account of the history of the water-meadows, see E. Kerridge, 'The floating of the Wilts. Watermeadows', W.A.M. lv. 113.
[20] Wilton House MSS. Surveys of Manors, vol. iii. 282. For subsequent history of the Teffont lands see p. 76.
[21] B.M. Map 5710 (52).
[22] Dinton W. I. Scrapbk.
[23] Kelly's Dir. Wilts. (1903).

[24] W.A.S. Libr., Devizes, Sale Cat.
[25] Kelly's Dir. Wilts. (1931).
[26] Charlotte M. Wright, Extracts from the Dinton-Dalwood Letters 1827–53 (priv. printed), 67.
[27] H. A. Wyndham, A Family History, 352.
[28] Ibid., 181
[29] V.C.H. Wilts. iv. 90; W.R.O. 135, Plan of Drainage System.
[30] V.C.H. Wilts. iv. 372.   [31] Gent. Mag. 1795, 997.
[32] V.C.H. Wilts. iv. 241.
[33] Census, 1831, occupational tables.

culture, and positions as servants at Dinton Park, there was almost no employment, other than agricultural, available in the parish. The coming of the railway in 1859 brought some new opportunities.[34] Dinton station was used extensively by farmers from neighbouring parishes who came there to complete their journey to Salisbury market by train. The nearby 'Wyndham (later Nadder) Arms' had to make special stabling arrangements for their horses.[35] There was a post office in the village by 1842 and at the turn of the century the village shop was rebuilt by the lord of the manor.[36] In the first half of the 20th century there was a brick, tile, and pottery works south-east of the village where there is a bed of suitable clay. In 1918 this included, besides the pottery works, three large brick kilns.[37] The Admiralty Gunnery Equipment Depot established just south of the village since the Second World War has provided but little civilian employment. In 1963 a smithy was still operating in the village. Since the Second World War many retired people have made their homes in Dinton.

MILLS. In 1086 there were two mills at Dinton.[38] These were probably the two mills later known as Dalwood Mill, and Cole's, or Dinton, Mill. Two millers are named in the 12th-century survey of the manor. One, probably at Dalwood, had to grind the corn from Teffont Magna, and the other was entitled to eat with the abbess's household when the abbess visited her manor.[39] Dalwood Mill was acquired by Sir Thomas Hungerford in 1337,[40] and in 1389 it was held with a meadow and messuage of the Abbess of Wilton by Roger de Karentham.[41] No more is known of Dalwood Mill, and all trace of it is gone, although its site on the Nadder, south of Dalwood Farm, is known.

Cole's Mill was called after the family of that name who were presumably at one time millers under the Abbess of Shaftesbury.[42] In 1249 Thomas Cole was killed by the inner wheel of the mill.[43] In 1631 about 5 a. of land went with the mill and all tenants of the manor were obliged to grind their corn there.[44] In the later 18th century the miller was involved in disputes over water rights which were complicated by the many demands for channels to irrigate the water-meadows.[45] In 1775 the reversion of the lease of the mill was granted by Lord Pembroke to Charles Penruddock of Compton Chamberlayne, and the mill continued to be leased by the Penruddocks until 1930 when Lord Pembroke sold it to Captain G. W. Penrud-

dock.[46] The mill ceased to work in c. 1900.[47]

The present mill building probably dates from the 18th century. The mill house which adjoins it was a late 19th-century addition.

CHURCH. The first reference found to a church at Dinton is a mention of Ivo the parson there in c. 1160[48], and it is likely that there was a church at Dinton even earlier. Traces of Saxon work have been found in the church of Teffont Magna[49] and it is probable that from earliest times the church there was attached to the church of Dinton. Throughout the Middle Ages Teffont Magna was a chapelry of Dinton and remained so until 1922 when it became instead a chapelry of Teffont Evias.[50] In 1924 the church of Dinton was united with that of Baverstock, but in 1952 the two churches were disunited, and since then the livings of Dinton and Teffont (including the chapelry of Teffont Magna) have been held in plurality.[51]

Dinton was one of the churches attached to the conventual church of Shaftesbury as a prebend.[52] The rectors, or prebendaries, of Dinton, often, but not always, canons of Salisbury, were appointed by the abbesses of Shaftesbury for the services they could render the abbey.[53] In return for these services the rectors enjoyed the profits and perquisites of the rectory which was not appropriated to Shaftesbury, and which included a small estate with a rectory house and the patronage of the church of Dinton.[54] The abbesses of Shaftesbury presented to the rectory, or prebend, of Dinton until the Dissolution, except in 1354 when the Bishop of Salisbury presented, in 1530 when the Abbess of Wilton presented, and in 1394 when the king was patron during an abbatial vacancy.[55]

After the Dissolution the rectory with advowson of the church were included in the grant of the manor to Sir Thomas Arundell (d. 1552), and were conveyed by him with the capital messuage to Matthew Colthurst.[56] In 1548 they were sold 'at the desire of Matthew Colthurst' to William Herbert, later Earl of Pembroke (d. 1570), who had acquired the manor the previous year.[57] In 1585 Henry, Earl of Pembroke (d. 1601), sold rectory and advowson to Lawrence (I) Hyde of West Hatch (d. 1590).[58] Robert (I) Hyde, eldest son of Lawrence (I) sold them in 1594 to his brother Sir Lawrence (II) Hyde (d. 1641).[59] From Sir Lawrence, they passed to his son, Sir Robert (II) Hyde, Chief Justice of Common Pleas (d. 1665). Sir Robert (II) Hyde died without surviving issue and rectory and advowson

[34] See p. 26.
[35] Dinton W.I. Scrapbk.
[36] Ibid.
[37] W.A.S. Libr., Devizes, Sale Cat.
[38] V.C.H. Wilts. ii, p. 128.
[39] B.M. Harl. MS. 61, f. 73.
[40] W.A.M. liv. 391.
[41] Cal. Inq. p.m. Edw. I, ii, p. 451.
[42] See p. 28.
[43] Crown Pleas Wilts. Eyre 1249 (W.A.S. Rec. Brch.), 211.
[44] Pembroke Manors (W.A.S. Rec. Brch.), 29.
[45] W.R.O. 332, Correspondence arising out of disputes, 1779–1883.
[46] Wilton House MSS. Surveys of Manors, vol. iii. 305, 306; Dinton and Teffont Tithe Apportionment, Collected Ref. (added notes).
[47] Dinton W.I. Scrapbk.

[48] BM. Harl.MS. 61, f. 74v.
[49] See. p. 78.
[50] Ibid.
[51] Orders in Council 12 Aug. 1924; 22 Feb. 1952; 18 July 1952.
[52] For an essay on prebends in nunnery churches see A. Hamilton Thompson in the 'Abp. of Canterbury's Cttee. on the Ministry of Women', App. viii.
[53] Phillipps, Wilts. Inst.; Jones, Fasti Eccl. Sar. A canon of Chichester was prebendary in 1268: Cal. Pat. 1266–72, 300.
[54] See p. 29.
[55] Phillipps, Wilts. Inst. under these dates.
[56] See p. 27.
[57] Magdalen Coll., Oxford, Macray Cal. Dinton nos. 2 and 3, see above p. 27.
[58] Magdalen Coll., Oxford, Macray Cal. Dinton no. 9.
[59] Ibid. no. 14.

passed to his nephew, Robert (III) Hyde, son of Alexander Hyde, Bishop of Salisbury.[60] Robert (III) Hyde died childless in 1722, and rectory and advowson passed by his will to his cousin Dr. Robert (IV) Hyde.[61] Dr. Hyde was a Fellow of Magdalen College, Oxford, and on his death in 1723, he devised rectory and advowson to his college.[62] Magdalen College retained the advowson until 1950 when it was transferred to the Bishop of Salisbury.[63]

After the Dissolution both rectory and advowson were occasionally leased for terms of years. Robert Grove, who leased the rectory from the Earl of Pembroke for 21 years in 1553, presented to the church in 1544, 1555, and 1556.[64] William Blanchard and Giles Clutterbuck, also lessees, presented in 1664.[65] Henry Hyde, father of the First Earl of Clarendon, and brother of Sir Lawrence (II) Hyde, appears also to have presented on at least one occasion.[66]

The church of Dinton was assessed for the taxation of Pope Nicholas in 1291 at £16 13s. 4d.[67] In 1320 and 1428 it was valued at the same sum.[68] In 1535 the rectory with all its appurtenances was valued by the rector at £17 gross. Out of this he paid 10s. 9d. in synodals, and £1 6s. 2d. to the Vicar of Dinton.[69] The great tithes were said to be worth only 16 marks in 1341 because, among other reasons, of the impoverished state of the parish.[70] In 1732 Magdalen College leased the rectorial great tithes to the vicar and thenceforth they were farmed by him.[71] In 1835 the vicar was unable to give a separate annual value for the vicarage as distinct from the rectory.[72] The tithes were commuted in 1843 for £397.[73] Magdalen College gave permission for the tithe barn to be pulled down in 1842.[74]

The earliest presentation found of a vicar to the church of Dinton is in 1306.[75] In 1336 a vicarage was ordained.[76] This was valued by the vicar in 1535 at nearly £6 including, presumably, the allowance from the rector.[77] The vicarial tithes were commuted in 1843 for £374 10s.,[78] and after 1732 the vicar also leased the rectorial tithes.[79] Some glebe belonged to the vicar as distinct from the estate belonging to the rectory. This lay mainly at Four Corners, in the angle formed by the junction of Ranger's and Foster's Lanes.[80] In 1608 the vicar had a house which at that date had a hall, buttery, and chamber.[81] It is mentioned again in

1661 and 1705[82] but from time to time the vicar probably occupied the Rectory House, as he is known to have done in 1783.[83] In 1746 the vicarage stood north of the Rectory House,[84] but it was subsequently demolished and its foundations were uncovered by a plough in 1951.[85]

Some time before 1291 a portion of the tithes of Dinton, valued at £5, was allotted to the Rectory of Iwerne Minster (Dors.), another prebend of Shaftesbury Abbey church.[86] In 1480 the church of Iwerne Minster was appropriated to the dean and canons of St. George's Chapel, Windsor, who thus acquired the portion of Dinton's tithes.[87] From at least as early as 1537 the dean and canons leased out these tithes, and in 1661 they were leased to Sir Robert (II) Hyde, lay rector of Dinton.[88] Leases continued to be made to the Hydes, and when the rectory was devised to Magdalen College, Oxford, in 1723, leases were made to the college.[89] When the tithes of Dinton were commuted in 1843 those due to the dean and canons of Windsor, still being leased by Magdalen, were valued at £81.[90]

As prebendaries of the conventual church the rectors of Dinton had special responsibilities towards the community at Shaftesbury, and in this capacity the rector was required by the bishop in 1298 to enjoin penance upon some delinquent nuns.[91] In the 16th century the rector had to pay 10s. a year to a chaplain celebrating mass daily in the abbess's chapel. It is not clear which chapel this was, but possibly it was the one in the demesne farmhouse.[92] The abbess provided her chaplain with some supplies in kind and a rent-free house. The rector supplied candles for the chapel.[93] In 1535 he also made an allowance to the Vicar of Dinton and was probably responsible for maintaining, or partly maintaining, a chaplain for Teffont Magna although he paid no salary to one that year.[94] It is not known how often a chaplain was appointed for Teffont Magna, nor, until the end of the 18th century, how often services were held in the church there. The inhabitants of the chapelry contributed towards the upkeep of Dinton church, and in 1674 their chapelwardens and sidesmen were presented for not bringing their contribution which was a third of any sum spent upon repairs.[95] In 1783 there was no curate for Teffont and the Vicar of Dinton held services there every third Sunday afternoon. Morning and evening services, with a sermon in the mornings,

[60] Hoare, *Mod. Wilts.* Underditch, 145.
[61] P.C.C. Marlbro 158.
[62] Magdalen Coll., Oxford, Macray Cal. no. 23; ibid. J. R. Bloxham, 'Bk. of Benefices', p. 122.
[63] Order in Council 8 Dec. 1950.
[64] *First Pembroke Survey*, ed. Straton, 230; Phillipps, *Wilts. Inst.*
[65] Phillipps, *Wilts. Inst.*
[66] Clarendon, *Life* (1761), 8; see above p. 26.
[67] *Tax. Eccl.* (Rec. Com.), 181.
[68] *Reg. Martival* (Cant. and York Soc.), i. 142–6; *Feudal Aids*, v. 294.
[69] *Valor Eccl.* (Rec. Com.), ii. 105.
[70] *Inq. Non.* (Rec. Com.), 170.
[71] Magdalen Coll., Oxford, J. R. Bloxham, 'Bk. of Benefices', p. 122.
[72] *Rep. Com. Eccl. Revs.* H.C. 54, p. 832, (1835), xxii.
[73] W.R.O. Tithe Award.
[74] W. D. Macray, *Reg. Magdalen Coll.* vi. 18.
[75] *Reg. Ghent* (Cant. and York Soc.), ii. 682.
[76] Sar. Dioc. Regy. Reg. Wyvil, i, f. 34.

[77] *Valor Eccl.* (Rec. Com.), ii. 107.
[78] W.R.O. Tithe Award.
[79] See above.
[80] Map by W. Wapshare at Little Clarendon.
[81] Sar. Dioc. R.O. Glebe Terrier, 1608.
[82] Ibid.
[83] Sar. Dioc. R.O. Vis. Queries, 1783. For the Rectory House see p. 29.
[84] Map by W. Wapshare at Little Clarendon.
[85] *W.A.M.* liv. 395.
[86] *Tax. Eccl.* (Rec. Com.), 181; *V.C.H. Dors*, iii. 553.
[87] *Cal. Pat.* 1476–85, 222.
[88] *MSS of St. George's Chapel, Windsor*, ed. J. N. Dalton, p. 430.
[89] Ibid.
[90] W.R.O. Tithe Award.
[91] *Reg. Ghent* (Cant. and York Soc.), i. 14.
[92] See p. 27.
[93] *First Pembroke Survey*, ed. Straton, 231.
[94] *Valor Eccl.* (Rec. Com.), ii. 105.
[95] Sar. Dioc. R.O. Chwdns. Pres. 1674.

were held at Dinton every Sunday. At Holy Communion, celebrated four times a year at Dinton, there were usually 10 or 12 communicants.[96] By 1864 a curate assisted the vicar. Morning service was held every Sunday at Teffont Magna and the transepts of Dinton church, which had been reserved for the congregation from Teffont, were occupied by the poor of Dinton as free-sittings. The congregation at Dinton averaged between 150 and 200, and there were 120 communicants in the parish. The congregation at Teffont was said to have decreased at that date owing to the activities of the Methodists, at that time referred to as 'ranters'.[97]

Philip Pinckney, a signatory to the Presbyterian Testimony, was Vicar of Dinton in 1608.[98] He subsequently became Rector of Fugglestone,[99] but apparently returned to Dinton where he died *c.* 1661.[1] His son, John, followed him at Dinton and was later ejected from the living at Longstock (Hants).[2]

The church of *ST. MARY THE VIRGIN* is cruciform with nave, crossing, and transepts dating from the early 13th century. The north doorway and square font of purbeck marble are of the same period. The nave windows were apparently inserted in the 14th century. Later in the same century the chancel was rebuilt on a grand scale. It is of ashlar masonry externally and on both north and south sides has three uniform windows with reticulated tracery. Two of these contain original stained glass. The large east window has interlacing tracery of the same date. The two upper stages of the tower were added, or rebuilt, together with the vault above the crossing about the middle of the 15th century. At the same time the south wall of the south transept was rebuilt, and the north wall of the north transept repaired and a new window inserted. An octagonal stair turret in the angle between the nave and north transept is surmounted by a conical roof below the level of the belfry and is connected to the tower by a short passage. Much restoration was carried out during the later 19th century under the direction of William Butterfield.[3] The royal arms of George II hang on the south wall of the nave. In 1553 a chalice weighing 9½ oz. was left for the parish and 22 oz. taken for the king's use. The church has an Elizabethan cup with paten.[4] There are 6 bells. Numbers 1 to 5 are all of 17th-century date. Number 6 may have been cast in Dorset in the 14th century.[5] There are the remains of the steps and socket of a medieval stone cross in the churchyard.

The registers date from 1558 and are complete.

ROMAN CATHOLICISM. Henry Mayhew, holder of a freehold estate, died excommunicated as a papist in 1587.[6] According to a nearly contemporary local report, he was buried in the churchyard at Teffont Magna, which was not normally used as a burial ground.[7] His two sons, Henry and Edward, left the country and entered the English College of Douai, then at Rheims.[8] Between *c.* 1595 and 1613 Edward worked in England as a secular priest, possibly in the Dinton neighbourhood.[9] He later entered the Benedictine Order and became prior of the monastery of St. Lawrence at Dieulouard (Lorraine). He died in 1625.[10] The churchwardens presented 5 persons as papists in 1668 and 6 in 1676.[11] In 1783 there was said to be none.[12]

In 1921 Maude Isabel Engleheart, wife of George Engleheart, converted and furnished an outbuilding at Little Clarendon, her home in Dinton, as a Roman Catholic chapel dedicated to Our Lady of Pity.[13] In 1962 this was served from Tisbury and Mass was celebrated every Sunday.[14]

PROTESTANT NONCONFORMITY. Three families were presented as dissenters in 1668,[15] and the following year there were said to be groups of Anabaptists and Quakers in the parish, although their numbers were uncertain.[16] William Bate (1661–89), one of the few General Baptist leaders in the country, was a Dinton labourer, and probably worked among the Anabaptists there for a short time.[17] The Dinton Quakers may have come under the influence of the outstanding Quaker centre at Fovant which flourished *c.* 1661.[18] In 1683 and 1686 among some 15 persons presented for not attending church, were members of the Jesse and Sheppard families,[19] and in 1702 Sarah Sheppard's house was licensed as a meeting-place for Quakers.[20] There were, however, said to be no dissenters in the parish in 1783.[21] In 1821 Alexander Ware certified his house in Dinton as a nonconformist meeting place.[22] In 1864 a group of Primitive Methodists, who were influential in Teffont Magna, held meetings in the summer on Sundays outside Dinton church, and thereby interrupted the service.[23]

A Primitive Methodist chapel was built in 1895.[24]

PARISH GOVERNMENT. Court rolls of the manor court survive for 1558–9, 1566–7, and 1584,[25] and there are court books for the period 1724–1899.[26] These records show that one court for Dinton and Teffont Magna was held annually by Lord Pembroke's steward, and at this Dinton and Teffont were represented by separate homages.

[69] Ibid. Vis. Queries, 1783.
[97] Ibid. 1864.
[98] *W.A.M.* xxxiv. 184.
[99] *V.C.H. Wilts.* vi. 48.
[1] Phillipps, *Wilts. Inst.* ii. 23.
[2] Mathews, *Calamy Revised*, 390.
[3] There are N.W. and S.E. views of the church in 1804 by John Buckler: W.A.S. Libr. Devizes, vol. ii. 12.
[4] Nightingale, *Wilts. Plate*, 50.
[5] Walters, *Wilts. Bells*, 75 and illustration facing.
[6] See p. 28.
[7] E 178/2445.
[8] Ibid.; *D.N.B.*
[9] *V.C.H. Wilts.* iii. 88.
[10] *D.N.B.*
[11] Sar. Dioc. R. O. Chwdns'. Pres. and Lists of Papists.
[12] Sar. Dioc. R.O ʹ s. Queries, 1783.

[13] *V.C.H. Wilts.* iii. 96; ex inf. Mrs. Streader, Little Clarendon.
[14] *Cath. Dir.* 1962.
[15] Sar. Dioc. R.O. Chwdns'. Pres. 1668.
[16] G. Lyon Turner, *Orig. Rec. Early Nonconformity*, i. 118.
[17] W. T. Whitley, *Mins. Gen. Assembly of Gen. Bapt. Churches*, i, p. xliii; *V.C.H. Wilts.* iii. 121.
[18] *V.C.H. Wilts.* iii. 112.
[19] Sar. Dioc. R.O. Chwdns' Pres. 1683, 1686.
[20] W.R.O. Certs. of Dissenters' Meeting Houses.
[21] Sar. Dioc. R.O. Vis. Queries, 1783.
[22] G.R.O. Rtns. of Regns.
[23] Sar. Dioc. R.O. Vis. Queries, 1864.
[24] Inscription on building.
[25] B.M. Add. Ch. 24440, 24441, 24718.
[26] Wilton House MSS. Ct. Bks. 1724–1770, 1743–1899.

The 16th-century courts were concerned with the maintenance of hedges and ditches, encroachments upon the waste, the admission of tenants, and particularly with the payment of heriots. The records of the 18th-century courts consist to a large extent of a recital of manorial customs, but tenants, were still presented for encroachments and for other similar offences. In 1743, for example, the tenants of Teffont Magna were required to fill in the holes made when trees were uprooted on the common. Dinton was apparently divided for certain purposes into a West and an East End. In 1749 a tenant was presented for driving his sheep over the down belonging to the West End tenants, and in 1760 a right of way through fields belonging to the East End tenants was denied to the tenant of the Manor Farm. The court also regularly ordained an annual perambulation of the manor boundaries. As late as 1800 the court appointed a hayward, but no record has been noted of the appointment of any other manorial officers. Very little can be said about the government of the parish in the 19th century. Apart from the registers, a vestry book for 1834–1928 is the only surviving parish record and this is a mere list of small disbursements.[27] The first meeting of the parish council took place in the old schoolroom in 1894.[28]

SCHOOLS. There was a public school for boys and girls in Dinton in 1783 then said to be very well regulated.[29] In 1818 some 80 children attended the school kept by the parish clerk with the assistance of three women. It was claimed that at that date nearly every child in the parish went to school and that many were paid for by the wealthier inhabitants.[30] The children of Teffont Magna also attended the Dinton school.[31] In 1845 the school was conducted in some outbuildings close to the Rectory House which had been converted into one large schoolroom.[32] This still stood in 1962. In 1859 about 60 children, including those from Teffont Magna and Baverstock, were taught there by a mistress, assisted in the mornings by a master.[33] A bequest of £100 was made to the school in the will of Thomas Barnes, proved in 1864.[34] By 1871 a school had been opened in Teffont Magna,[35] and in 1872 the Dinton school moved to a new building. This was built with financial aid from the State, the National Society, and Magdalen College, Oxford, on the south side of the main Salisbury-Hindon road.[36] In 1936 the school at Teffont Magna was closed, and the younger children from there again attended the Dinton school, by then a junior mixed and infants' school.[37] The school was given controlled status in 1950, and in 1962 there were 3 teachers and 75 children.[38]

There were two private schools in the parish in 1833, but in 1859 only one is recorded, and was then attended by a few farmers' children.[39] This was possibly the school which in 1865 was run by Harriet Doughty and took boarders, and continued under her management until 1870.[40] There was another private school in the parish in 1893.[41] In 1864 the vicar conducted a night school in the parish which he reported to be fairly well attended.[42]

CHARITY. By his will proved in 1865 William Maslem Barnes bequeathed £100 for the benefit of the poor of the parish. The annual income from this, which was about £2, was to be distributed at the beginning of every year among the 13 oldest and most deserving parishioners.[43] In 1958 the income from the investment was unchanged and the sums distributed amounted to just over 4s.[44]

FISHERTON DE LA MERE

THE ancient parish of Fisherton de la Mere formed, with Dinton and Teffont Magna, a detached part of the hundred.[1] It lay on the River Wylye and consisted of two villages, Fisherton proper and Bapton. Its life was extinguished in 1934, when Fisherton, which accounted for 1,660 of its 2,834 acres, was transferred to Wylye, and Bapton to Stockton.[2]

In shape it was a rather narrow oblong.[3] On the north-east its boundary ran along the old road, now largely grass-grown, that connected Chitterne with Serrington, in Stapleford; on the south it coincided with Grovely Grim's Dyke. The other boundaries followed no geographical feature, either natural or artificial. The area that the former boundaries enclosed runs roughly north and south up into the down on either side the river. Each slope descends from an altitude of 550–600ft., but the north slope is rather steeper than the south one. The southern extremity forms a plateau, extending into Wylye and called by 1838 the Bake.[4] To the south-west the boundary cuts through a combe called Roakham Bottom. Both slopes of the valley are chalk; the valley itself is gravel and

[27] penes the parish clerk.
[28] Dinton W. I. Scrapbk.
[29] Sar. Dioc. R.O. Vis. Queries, 1783.
[30] Digest Rtns. to Cttee. of Educ. of Poor, H.C. 224 (1819), ix (2).   [31] Ibid.
[32] Magdalen Coll. Oxford, J. R. Bloxham, 'Bk of Beneficies', p. 118.
[33] Acct. of Wilts. Schools, H. C. 27 (1859 Sess. 1), xxi (2); Nat. Soc. File.
[34] Char. Com. Wilts. (1908), p. 138.
[35] Rtn. relating to Elem. Educ. H.C. 201 (1871), lv.
[36] Nat. Soc. File; W. D. Macray, Regs. Magdalen Coll.. vi. 65.
[37] Bd. of Educ. List 21, 1938; Teffont W.I. scrapbk.
[38] Ex. inf. the head teacher.

[39] Educ. Enq. Abstract, H.C. 62 (1835), xliii; Acct. of Wilts. Schools (1859 Sess. 1), xxi (2).
[40] P.O. Dir. Wilts. (1865); Dinton W.I. Scrapbk.
[41] Dinton W. I. Scrapbk.
[42] Sar. Dioc. R.O. Vis. Queries, 1864.
[43] Endowed Char. Wilts. (1908), p. 138.
[44] Char. Com. File 13083 and Accts. File G. 15.
[1] This article was written in 1963. Its author is grateful to Lt.-Col. F. W. N. Jeans and to Mr. R. S. Newall for some help in its compilation.
[2] V.C.H Wilts. iv. 361; Census 1931, Pt. II.
[3] The boundaries are incorrectly drawn in Andrews and Dury, Map (W.A.S. Rec. Brch.), pl. 5 and on the map at p. 4 of V.C.H. Wilts. v.
[4] W.R.O. Tithe Award.

alluvium.[5] It is upon the gravel, perforated by many wells,[6] that Bapton is built. The area of the former parish has always been devoted to husbandry. Of Fisherton an estate agent declared in 1898 that the village was 'so picturesque that artists often resort there when wishing to paint truly beautiful and real country scenery'.[7]

In 1086 12 a. of wood were attributed to Fisherton.[8] Presumably these lay in the south of the ancient parish, where in 1742,[9] as to this day, the western edge of Stockton Wood extended across the southern slope of the Bake into Wylye. The tithe award of 1838 is accordingly misleading when it declares that the parish was without woodland. In the 19th century small plantations began to appear on the north slope of the valley. By 1817 one had been set on the down just south of Parry's Field Barn. By 1881 there was a rather larger one to the east of this, called Gilbert's Plantation in 1889, strips to the north and west of the barn, and 3 small spinneys towards the northern parish boundary. By 1898 there had been a further increase, so that by that time some dozen plantations could be numbered.[10] All these still existed in 1963.

Fisherton, which is first mentioned in 1086,[11] takes its suffix from the de la Mere family, who held the manor in the later 14th century.[12] Bapton is first mentioned in a document that cannot be earlier than 1216.[13] Each settlement was reckoned a township in 1249.[14] Fisherton lies just south of the present main road from Warminster to Salisbury, hereinafter called the Codford-Deptford road. Bapton is strung along a minor road, hereinafter called the Stockton-Wylye road, running to the south of, and parallel with the other. In 1838 the boundary between the two villages ran eastwards along the main stream of the Wylye to a point just south of Bapton Manor House, then south almost to the Stockton-Wylye road, and then east to the boundary with Wylye, taking Little Bapton in.[15] The north-south line, but not the rest, can be traced from 1742.[16] The area between the roads is traversed by the river and by several artificial water-carriages which already existed in 1742.[17] Many drainage ditches have subsequently been added.

Of the appearance of the villages we know nothing until 1742, when Fisherton manor (including Bapton) was first mapped and surveyed.[18] At that time Fisherton extended along a street, Fisherton Street, running a little south of the Codford-Deptford road. At its east end, which was not built up, Fisherton Street debouched upon that road at two points. One of these was close to what is now called The Old Vicarage.[19]

The other, which was further to the east, was at what was once known as Black Gate.[20] The west end of Fisherton Street was blind, as it is today. A little to the west of the church, which stands near the west end of the street, a lane curved up hill to join the Codford-Deptford road at a point where that road made a dog's leg bend in its onward course to the west. This lane originally traversed what is now the village green. The green, however, is now completely grass-grown and a newer road leaves Fisherton Street a little further to the west at right angles to it. The kink in the Codford-Deptford road was later straightened out, presumably when the road was turnpiked in 1760–2.[21] There is some reason to believe that before 1742 the street had not taken a northward direction at its eastern end but had continued eastwards in a gentle curve to Deptford. A line of trees or bushes which existed in 1742 could well mark that former course, and it could be that a house lying on the parish boundary at a point where this hedge touches it was once accessible from the street. North of the street an L-shaped road, called Church Lane, led eastwards and then northwards from the east end of the church into the Codford-Deptford road. It was then called Church Lane but was known in the present century as Gilbert's Lane, no doubt after the local family of that name.[22]

Between 1807 and 1838 the course of Fisherton Street was changed.[23] The eastern section disappeared, together with the houses that flanked it. The north-south section was severed from the rest and became simply a lane leading into the fields, as it is today. The middle section, east of the church, fused itself into the east-west branch of Church Lane, which henceforth replaced Fisherton Street as the means of access to the houses that had once fronted upon that street. The back gardens of those houses were cut off and converted into orchards. The houses along Church Lane declined in number between 1838 and 1881 and have since become less numerous still.[24]

In 1742 Bapton lay a little to the north of the Stockton-Wylye road.[25] A lane ran northward and westward from that road and returned to it in a southward direction. It was, no doubt, this curving road which was called Bapton Street in the 16th and 17th centuries.[26] From it a track and footpath led northward across a tree-fringed water-carriage to Fisherton and terminated there in a roadway called Mill Way.[27] This route was still open in 1838,[28] but since 1889 at least[29] its southern end has lain further to the east. Between 1742 and 1838 the east-west branch of the lane that in the mid-18th century had run round the

[5] O.S. Drift Geol. Map 1″ CCXCVIII.
[6] O.S. Map 6″ Wilts. LIX (1st edn.) marks 9.
[7] W.A.S. Libr., Devizes, Sale Cat.
[8] V.C.H. Wilts. ii, p. 154.
[9] W.R.O. 628, Survey of Fisherton manor.
[10] O.S. Map 1″, sheet 17 (1st edn.); 6″ Wilts. LIII, LIX (1st edn.); W.A.S. Libr., Devizes, Sale Cat. For the barn, see p. 36.
[11] V.C.H. Wilts. ii, p. 154.
[12] See. p. 38.   [13] See p. 41.
[14] Crown Pleas Wilts. Eyre, 1249 (W.A.S. Rec. Brch.), p. 211.
[15] W.R.O. Tithe Award.
[16] W.R.O. 628, Survey of Fisherton manor.

[17] Ibid.
[18] Ibid. See pl. facing p. 15 for small part of map.
[19] See p. 45.
[20] Ex inf. Mr. R.S. Newall.
[21] V.C.H. Wilts. iv. 261–2.
[22] Ex inf. Mr. R. S. Newall. For the Gilberts, see p. 42.
[23] W.R.O. Inclosure and Tithe Awards.
[24] W.A.S. Libr., Devizes, Sale Cat. The map shows clearly a fragment of the old street, at its W. end.
[25] W.R.O. 628, Survey of Fisherton manor.
[26] Sar. Dioc. R.O. Glebe Terriers.
[27] W.R.O. 628, Survey of Fisherton manor
[28] W.R.O. Tithe Award.
[29] O.S. Map 6″ Wilts. LIX (1st edn.).

village was cut short about half way in its course, so that there was no longer any means of access from the more easterly of the two north-south lanes to the east-west lane. Since 1838 what remains of the east-west lane has become a foot-path and the eastern north-south lane has been brought into the grounds of Bapton Manor House. The houses of Bapton, like those of Fisherton, are less numerous than they were in 1742 and even in 1838.

East of Bapton, and connected with it by a line of beeches, lies a small group of houses, three of which are thatched. The houses are marked on the maps of 1742[30] and 1838,[31] and since 1889[32] have been called Little Bapton.

Apart from Fisherton House,[33] the Manor,[34] The Old Vicarage,[35] and Bapton Manor,[36] there are no houses of any size. A few yeomen's houses still exist and there are one or two 18th- and 19th-century cottages. Of the yeomen's houses in Fisherton mention may be made of two that stand at the west end of Fisherton Street. The more southerly of these, an L-shaped building, much altered, may date in part from the 17th century. It was Joseph Rebbeck's house and malthouse in 1742[37] and by 1881 had become the dairy of Fisherton farm.[38] The other, a thatched building of 2 stories, with attic, was in 1742 one of four farms occupied by William Ingram.[39] No. 3 Watermeadow Lane, Bapton, still thatched, may date from the early 17th century. It was John Rebbeck's house in 1742.[40] Another house (The Laurels), in the same lane, which has had its roof raised, is rather later. It was in the nominal occupation of George Slade in 1742.[41] All these four were private houses in 1963. The T-shaped Dairy House, to the north-west of Bapton Manor, occupied by Edward Green in 1742,[42] was built at various times in the later 16th or earlier 17th century. It has stone-mullioned windows with drip moulds and a thatched roof. The dairy itself was added on the east side, after 1838.[43] It is now fitted up as a hostel for farm workers, but is not so used.[44] The parish does not contain, and probably never has contained, any inns.[45] A recreation room in Bapton, on the Stockton-Wylye road, existed by 1923.[46]

Outside Fisherton village, about ¾ mile due north of the church, there was built some time between 1817[47] and 1838[48] a house with farm buildings and yard. The buildings have been called Parry's Field Barn since 1889,[49] and since 1881 have included dwellings.[50]

Access to the parish in 1742[51] was chiefly gained by means of the Codford-Deptford and Stockton-Wylye roads. In addition there was a road running

north-westward and then northward from near Fisherton Manor House to join the ancient road from Chitterne to Serrington. This road, which is still passable, connected at the northern tip of the parish with other downland roads to Maddington, Tilshead, and Codford. On the south a road led out of Bapton to join the Wylye-Hindon (now the Wylye-Mere) road. This road is now only open at its northern end.

Poll-tax payers in Fisherton and Bapton together numbered 142 in 1377—a total divided almost equally between the two villages and exceeding that of any other place in the hundred apart from Dinton (156) and Warminster. If the taxation tithings be grouped together in such a way as to form parishes, this figure implies that Fisherton with Bapton was fifth in population among the ten parishes in the hundred for which receipts survive. Among the seven parishes in this part of the Wylye valley it was fourth.[52] In 1801 the population of the parish was 270. It had fallen to 195 in 1931. In the intervening decades it reached its highest point in 1851 when it was 373. The average between 1801 and 1931 was 283.[53]

Fisherton House was the home of Mrs. Josephine Mary Newall (d. 1923), a distinguished embroideress, who taught cripples to embroider in it.[54] At Bapton Manor lived Sir Cecil Chubb, Bt. (d. 1934), who, in 1905, bought Stonehenge and presented it to the public.[55] The parish is otherwise undistinguished and of its form of government virtually nothing is known. It is indeed almost a classic example of the happiness that comes from an absence of annals. In 1621 the tithingmen presented that they had 'no popish recusants', no absentees from church, 'no inns or alehouses licensed or unlicensed, no unlawful weights or measures, no neglect of hues and cries, no roads out of repair, no wandering rogues or vagabonds, and no inmates of whom they desire reformation'; and they added 'thanks be to Almighty God therefor'.[56]

MANORS. The manor of *FISHERTON DE LA MERE* was held before the Conquest by Bondi, a Scandinavian.[57] After the Conquest it passed to Roger de Courcelles,[58] a large landowner in Somerset, though in Wiltshire he held this manor only.[59] He was succeeded here as in nearly all his other manors by the Malets, who, Round thought, obtained Roger's possessions by a fresh grant, rather than by descent.[60] The manor descended in the Malet family until 1216 when William Malet II died leaving two daughters, one of whom, Mabel, married Hugh de Vivon,[61] and the other, Helewise, Hugh Pointz.[62] Pointz was dead by 1220,[63] and his

[30] W.R.O. 628, Survey of Fisherton manor.
[31] W.R.O. Tithe Award.
[32] O.S. Map 6″ Wilts. LIX (1st edn.).
[33] See p. 39.
[34] Ibid.
[35] See p. 45.
[36] See p. 40.
[37] W.R.O. 628, Survey of Fisherton manor.
[38] W.A.S. Libr., Devizes, Sale Cat.
[39] W.R.O. 628, Survey of Fisherton manor.
[40] Ibid.
[41] Ibid.
[42] Ibid.
[43] Not marked on Tithe Map.
[44] Ex inf. Major R. H. Heywood-Lonsdale.
[45] W.R.O. Aleho. Recogs.; *Kelly's Dirs. Wilts.*
[46] O.S. Map 6″ Wilts. LIX (3rd edn.).

[47] O.S. Map 1″, sheet 17 (1st edn.).
[48] W.R.O. Tithe Award.
[49] O.S. Map 6″ Wilts. LIX (1st edn.).
[50] W.A.S. Libr., Devizes, Sale Cat.
[51] W.R.O. 628, Survey of Fisherton manor.
[52] *V.C.H. Wilts.* iv. 306–11.
[53] Ibid. 348.
[54] *Wilts. Gaz.* 23 May 1918; *W.A.M.* xlii, 510.
[55] *W.A.M.* xlvii. 130.
[56] Hist. MSS. Com. *Var. Coll.* i. 93.
[57] *V.C.H. Wilts* ii, pp. 68, 154.
[58] Ibid. p. 154.
[59] Ibid. p. 104-5.
[60] *V.C.H. Som.* i. 413.
[61] *Ex. e Rot. Fin.* (Rec. Com.), i. 109.
[62] *Rot. Litt. Claus.* (Rec. Com.), i. 30
[63] *Ex. e Rot. Fin.* (Rec. Com.), i. 45. 2.

relict married Robert de Muscegros by 1221.[64] Muscegros seems to have obtained through her the honor of Curry Mallet and a moiety of Fisherton manor, rated at ½ fee.[65] After his death in 1253–4[66] this moiety passed to Nicholas Pointz, his step-son, by which time the other moiety belonged to William Forz,[67] to whom it had passed on the death of his father, Hugh de Vivon, c. 1249.[68] By 1274–5 Nicholas had acquired both moieties, rated as a whole fee.[69] Thereafter the overlordship descended in the Pointz family until 1358, when it was sold with Curry Mallet by Sir Nicholas Pointz to Matthew de Gurney.[70] It passed from the Gurneys to the Crown about the middle of the 15th century, and in 1492 belonged to Arthur, Prince of Wales,[71] to whom the Crown had presumably assigned it. It was stated in 1346 that the service due from the manor was that of inclosing part of Curry Mallet park with a hedge.[72] While the foregoing correctly states the formal position, there was a period in the 14th century when the Crown successfully deprived the Pointzes of their rights. In 1325 the Crown seized the wardship of the heir to one of the shares of the under-tenancy[73] and in 1326–8 and 1351 presented to the rectory, then annexed to the manor, during similar minorities.[74].

The overlords subinfeudated the manor at an early date, but the history of the tenure in demesne is hard to unravel. By 1193–4 Godfrey de St. Martin held an estate in Fisherton ('Fisserton Godefridi de S. Martino') which was then being administered as an escheat, perhaps because of its lord's adhesion to Count John.[75] In 1194–5 Wandrille de Courcelles, presumably a descendant of Roger the former overlord, was trying to secure a judgment against Godfrey and one Constance, daughter of Robert de la Stane.[76] Godfrey appears to have married Constance by 1210[77] and to have died by c. 1232, when Constance gave land in Fisherton to Maiden Bradley priory.[78] By 1200 Fisherton is called a 'manor'[79] and by 1201 Wandrille was pursuing his claim to it against Godfrey and Constance by writ of 'mort d'ancestor'.[80] The judgment, if any, is not known, but by 1223 Ralph FitzBernard and his wife Eleanor were claiming the manor, as Eleanor's right, against John de la

Stane,[81] and in 1227 the joint overlords were claiming it against the same John by novel disseisin.[82] The presumption is that a Courcelles overlord had died about 1194–5, that Wandrille tried to repossess himself in demesne of the manor which his ancestor had subinfeudated, but that he and his successors in the overlordship were frustrated by the terre tenants and their heirs. Whatever may be the precise explanation, John de la Stane was holding in demesne ½ knight's fee in Fisherton and Bapton in 1242–3.[83]

Between 1249 and 1253 John de la Stane's tenement was being claimed against him by William Braunche and Joan his wife, in Joan's right. Joan's mother's name was Eleanor and she may be the same as Eleanor the wife of Ralph FitzBernard.[84] The suit was unsuccessful, for in 1274–5 Peter de la Stane was holding Fisherton, then rated as a whole fee.[85]

Peter de la Stane died ante 7 Feb. 1312[86] leaving three daughters, Elizabeth, who married Sir James de Norton, Margery, who married William Saffrey (otherwise Reed or Rude), and Christine, who married Anthony Bydik.[87] Dower was assigned to Christine de la Stane, who died ante 1 March 1319.[88] Elizabeth de Norton died in or before 1315–16,[89] having borne her husband two sons, Peter, who died vivente patre,[90] and Thomas. James de Norton died ante 27 Jan. 1330 and was succeeded in his third share by Thomas,[91] who died, a knight, in 1346.[92] A third of Thomas's share was given in dower to his wife, Margaret,[93] who later married Robert de la Puylle.[94] The remaining two-thirds were assigned to the custody of Peter de Brewes until Ralph, Thomas's son, should come of age.[95]

William Saffrey died ante 13 May 1325, leaving a minor son Brian,[96] whose wardship, despite the protests of Hugh Pointz as overlord,[97] was granted by the Crown to Brian de Papworth, Rector of Great Houghton (Northants).[98] In 1331 the wardship was transferred to Master Henry de Clif, a canon of Salisbury,[99] who sold it in 1332 to John de Leicester.[1] By 1345 the Bydik third had passed from Anthony and Christine to John Bydik, who appears to have granted it to a Dorset priest called

[64] Ibid. 61.
[65] Bk. of Fees, 718, 731.
[66] Cal. Inq. p.m. i, p. 82.
[67] Close R. 1251–3, 440.
[68] Ex. e Rot. Fin. (Rec. Com.), ii. 62.
[69] Rot. Hund. (Rec. Com.), ii. 277.
[70] Pedes Finium . . . for . . . Somerset, 1347–99 (Som. Rec. Soc.), 39.
[71] Cal. Inq. p.m. Hen. VII, i, p. 353.
[72] Cal. Inq. p.m. viii, p. 467.
[73] See below.
[74] See pp. 43–44.
[75] Pipe R. 1194 (P.R.S. N.S. v.), 18.
[76] Pipe R. 1195 (P.R.S. N.S. vi), 233 (entered under Somerset and Dorset, nova promissa). The entry is repeated in Pipe R. 1196 (P.R.S. N.S. vii), 217. See also B.M. Stowe MS. 925, ff. 91 v.–92.
[77] Curia Regis R. i. 374.
[78] See p. 40. The grant states Godfrey was buried in the priory ch.
[79] Curia Regis R. i. 208.
[80] Ibid. 374.
[81] Ibid. xi. 158.
[82] Ibid. xiii. 87.
[83] Bk. of Fees, 718, 731.
[84] J.I. 1/996 m. 10; Close R. 1151–3, 440; G. Wrottesley,

Pedigrees from the Plea R. 497 (1259).
[85] Rot. Hund. (Rec. Com.), ii. 276.
[86] I.p.m. on Nicholas Pointz: Cal. Inq. p.m. v, p. 195. Pointz's ½ fee in Fisherton and Bapton was then said to be shared between James de Norton and William Saffrey only. This was repeated in 1315: Cal. Close, 1313–18, 168.
[87] Cal. Inq. p.m. vi, p. 94. For the name of Norton's first wife see ibid. vii, p. 163. For Saffrey's aliases see C 60/144 mm. 1 and 3 (where he is called Rude) and Rot. Parl. i. 429 (where he is called Reed).
[88] Cal. Inq. p.m. vi, p. 94.
[89] By this year Norton had married a woman called Margaret: C 143/114/17.
[90] Inferred from the ultimate descent to Thos. For his name see Cal. Inq. p.m. vi, p. 94.
[91] Ibid. vii, pp. 162–3.
[92] Ibid. viii, pp. 466–7.
[93] Cal. Close, 1346–9, 95.
[94] C.P. 25(1)/288/46/559.
[95] Cal. Close, 1346–9, 95.
[96] Cal. Inq. p.m. vi, p. 361.
[97] Rot. Parl. i. 429. Brian's mother is here called Elizabeth, evidently in error.
[98] Cal. Fine R. 1319–27, 346.
[99] Cal. Close, 1330–3, 302.
[1] Cal. Pat. 1330–4, 314.

37

John of Tilshead. In that year the third was claimed by Sir John de la Mere and Henry Russell,[2] but the outcome is unknown.

Margaret de la Puylle was still holding dower in the Norton third in 1359. In that year Ralph de Norton settled the remainder of this share upon himself with reversion, in default of heirs, to one John de Erdington, the elder.[3] By stages that are uncertain this third and the Saffreys' third became vested in Sir John de la Mere, of Nunney (Som.), who in 1375 settled two-thirds of the manor and advowson in trust.[4] In 1381 Godfrey Bydik sold him the remaining third.[5] Sir Philip de la Mere, son of John, held the whole manor in 1390.[6] Sir Ellis de la Mere, who was probably Philip's son,[7] was apparently seised of the manor by 1412.[8] He died, without issue, some time between September 1414[9] and 14 March 1428,[10] and was succeeded by his nephew Sir John Paulet (I), son of his sister Eleanor.[11] He was succeeded by his son another John (II), who in 1460 settled it upon himself and his wife Eleanor.[12] He died in 1492 and was succeeded by his son John (III),[13] who on his death in 1525 was succeeded by his son William, Lord St. John,[14] created Marquess of Winchester in 1551.[15] The manor descended in the line of the marquesses of Winchester until after the fall of Basing House (Hants) in 1645. John, 5th marquess, was then imprisoned and declared a traitor and his lands forfeited by Act of Parliament (1651).[16] Fisherton appears to have been sold by the Treason Trustees to Lt.-General Charles Fleetwood and four others in 1652.[17] Successful efforts were, however, made to keep it in the family,[18] and in 1655 the marquess's son, Charles Paulet, Lord St. John of Basing, was conveying lands in Fisherton to a Thomas Jaques.[19] These conflicts in the evidence are at present unresolved. In 1660 all the marquess's estates were restored to him. The marquess died in 1675 and Charles became Duke of Bolton in 1689. Thereafter the lands descended with the dukedom until the death of Charles, Duke of Bolton, in 1765.[20] It was then settled by Chancery decree that the trusts established by the will should be discharged,[21] and the manor sold to enable certain liabilities on the estate to be met. It was sold accordingly to Edward Whatmore, who occupied land in Fisherton

in 1780–7.[22] He was, however, exonerated from the purchase by mutual agreement, and by order of the court the manor was resold in 1789 to James Graham, of Lincoln's Inn. He, in turn, in 1790 sold it, with statutory authority, to Edward Seymour, Duke of Somerset (d. 1792).[23] Edward Augustus, Duke of Somerset (d. 1880), the late Duke's nephew, who had succeeded to the manor, sold it, together with the rectory and advowson to a trustee to the use of the brothers John (d. 1840) and Thomas (d. 1816) Davis. The Davises, who had for some time held much of the land on lease, determined between themselves what each should hold. John took lands in Bapton and William the manor of Fisherton and lands there.[24] On John's death, John (d. 1860), his nephew, acquired all the property, and in 1841 the legal estate,[25] and from him it passed to his sons John (d. 1878) and William.[26] The manor and farm lands, which had been mortgaged in 1877, were then sold, without the then manor house, to William and John Parry,[27] who had been farming the land since 1872.[28] The manor was then owned successively by W. H. Pettey (1895, 1899), F. R. Hunt (1903), William McMinnies (1907), John Young (1911, 1915), M. R. C. Young (1920), and Dr. C. H. Brookes (1923).[29] In 1929 it was bought by Lt.-Col. F. W. N. Jeans,[30] who was lord in 1963.[31]

Fisherton farm, presumably with the manor house annexed, was leased in 1574 by Lord Winchester to Thomas Topp and Alexander and John Topp sons of John Topp of Stockton.[32] Thomas was one of the Topps of Stockton—a *familia generosa* according to a near-contemporary account.[33] He died in 1586 and left the farm in trust until his son Alexander should come of age.[34] Alexander was Hugh Broughton's companion on his continental travels.[35] The lease was still in being in 1597,[36] and a Topp still the most highly-taxed inhabitant in 1648.[37] After the death of Alexander Topp in 1663 it was jointly leased to William Ingram and Thomas Kellow.[38] Ingram occupied the house in 1742.[39] A lease of Ingram's moiety in reversion was granted by the Duke of Bolton to John Davis (d. 1791) in 1769.[40] The other moiety seems to have belonged to the Bowles family who leased it to John Davis (d. 1840),

² C.P. 40/344 rot. 462.
³ C.P. 25(1)/288/559 and /567.
⁴ *Cal. Close*, 1374–7, 323.
⁵ C.P. 25(1)/289/53/54.
⁶ *Cal. Pat.* 1388–92, 335.
⁷ Hoare, *Mod. Wilts.* Heytesbury, 255.
⁸ *Feud. Aids*, vi. 532.
⁹ He was sheriff 1413–14: *P.R.O. List of Sheriffs.*
¹⁰ *Cal. Close*, 1429–35, 66.
¹¹ Ibid.
¹² *Cal. Inq. p.m. Hen. VII*, i. p. 353.   ¹³ Ibid.
¹⁴ C142/44/94.
¹⁵ *Complete Peerage.*
¹⁶ Ibid.; *Acts and Ords. of Interr.* ed. Firth and Rait, ii. 520.
¹⁷ S.P. 23/18 f. 754.
¹⁸ Hants R.O. 11 M 49/230 (acct. of Daniel Witcharley, the purchaser of part of the Paulet estates, 'to prevent the sale thereof to strangers' 1651–4); C.P. 43/278 rot. 113–113d. (conveyance by 3 Paulets to Witcharley and another, 1652). It seems, however, that a doc. once existed whereby Fisherton was conveyed in 1653 by the marquess and 5 others to Robt. Smith of Upton (Essex): Soc. Antiq. Jackson MSS. vol. vii.
¹⁹ C.P. 25(2)/609/1655 East.
²⁰ *Complete Peerage.*

²¹ W.R.O. 628, Abstract of Title, 1870; 30 Geo. III, c. 37 (priv. act).
²² W.R.O. Land Tax Assessments.
²³ W.R.O. 628, Abstract of Title, 1870; 30 Geo. III, c. 37 (priv. act).
²⁴ W.R.O. 628, Abstract of Title, 1870 and Note on the Descent, 1840.
²⁵ At any rate the legal estate in the advowson passed in this year: W.R.O. 628, Note on Advowson, 1877.
²⁶ W.R.O. 628, Wills of John Davis (d. 1860) and John Davis (d. 1878).
²⁷ W.R.O. 628, Docs. about sale of Fisherton Estate.
²⁸ W.R.O. 628, Assignment of the interest of the former lessee by his administrator.
²⁹ *Kelly's Dirs. Wilts.*
³⁰ H. J. S. Banks, *Ch. of . . . Fisherton Delamare*, 7.
³¹ Ex inf. Lt.-Col. Jeans.
³² C 54/1027.
³³ W.R.O. Parish Records, Burial Reg.
³⁴ P.C.C. 13 Spencer.
³⁵ *D.N.B. s.v.* Broughton, Hugh.
³⁶ C3/373/2.
³⁷ *W.A.M.* xxxvii. 369.
³⁸ Hants R.O. 11 M 49/458.
³⁹ W.R.O. 628, Survey of Fisherton manor.
⁴⁰ W.R.O. 628, Lease.

probably not for the first time, in 1798 and again in 1817.[41] It is not known in what circumstances the freehold was eventually acquired by the Davises. The farm land was leased to Thomas Compton in 1865.[42]

The house, which since at least 1876 has been called Fisherton Delamere House,[43] lies to the north of the church, apparently on the site of the medieval manor house.[44] It was a small building in 1742[45] but had been much enlarged by 1838.[46] Extensive works were done upon it in 1863[47] and in 1865. More recent alterations made about the middle of the 20th century have preserved the Georgian style of the original house. John Davis (d. 1878), who had by that time moved to Richmond (Surr.), leased it to Mrs. Alice Everett.[48] From 1871 it was leased by Laurence Birch, a former House of Lords clerk.[49] When the manor was sold to the Parrys in 1881 Birch purchased the house, with its park of 17 a.,[50] and lived there until his death in 1895.[51] It was then sold to G. R. Ryder, a former M. P. for Salisbury, on whose death in 1901 it was bought by Arthur Newall.[52] In 1955 it was sold by Arthur's son, Mr. R. S. Newall, to Col. H. Blake-Tyler.[53]

After the former manor house had been detached from the manor at the sale of 1881, the lords of the manor lived in what had previously been called Fisherton Delamere Farm. Since 1889[54] it has been called officially, if not popularly, The Manor. It is a stone building, and is the only house in the former parish to lie north of the Codford-Deptford road. A map of 1773 marks no house on the site, nor does the tithe map of 1838,[55] and the house appears to date from the second quarter of the 19th century. Additions made in the 1920's include a Georgian porch, french windows on the south front, and many internal fittings.

Court rolls or books survive for 1662,[56] 1686,[57] 1700–54 and 1771–89.[58] In addition to these there are transcripts of proceedings for 1684 and for some years between 1801 and 1841.[59] So far as has been established, courts baron were held throughout the period. On various occasions between 1804 and 1825 customary courts also sat.[60]

At some time, probably in the early 14th century, Baldwin de Bellany gave lands in Boulsbury in South Damerham (Hants) and $\frac{1}{5}$ virgate in Fisherton, which his brother William held, to Hugh Wake, lord of Winterbourne Stoke. They were to be a marriage portion for Joan, his daughter.[61] About 1329 Joan died seised of 5 virgates in Bapton and Fisherton of which the $\frac{1}{5}$ virgate mentioned above very possibly formed a part. Her son, Thomas, was her heir,[62] and in 1384 was dealing with lands in both places.[63] He died after 1398–9 and was succeeded by his cousin and heir, Thomas Poynings, Lord St. John (d. 1429), who in 1426–7 conveyed the lands to Sir Walter Hungerford, later Lord Hungerford (d. 1449). From him they descended in the Hungerford line to Mary, Lady Hungerford, who married Edward, Lord Hastings, in 1481.[64] They were called the manor of *BAPTON* in 1487.[65] Edward and Mary Hastings transmitted them to their son George Hastings, Earl of Hundingdon (d. 1545), who held them in 1532 by the name of the manors of Fisherton and Bapton.[66] In 1537 he granted them to William Paulet, Lord St. John, and thereupon they became an integral part of the capital manor.[67]

The ownership of an estate in *BAPTON*, then claimed as a 'manor', was contested in the early 16th century between members of the Kellaway family and other suitors. Some time between 1486 and 1493 or between 1504 and 1505 a Thomas Hymerford claimed to have been seised of the 'manor', but to have been deprived of the deeds by Thomas Kellaway,[68] and in the period 1532–44 Edmund, son of Thomas Estcourt, laid a similar charge against Robert Kellaway.[69] In 1545 a John Kellaway was living in Bapton,[70] and it was no doubt he who in 1566 bought out Edmund Estcourt's interests in Fisherton and other places[71] and who died in 1568 seised of a capital messuage and lands in Bapton and Tisbury, held of the Marquess of Winchester as of Fisherton manor.[72] There is some reason to think that Robert and Thomas Kellaway, mentioned above, were respectively his father and grandfather.[73] If this is so, then John's great-grandfather was called William

[41] W.R.O. 467/3 and /5. A tenement belonging to Wm. Bowles was occupied by John Davis in 1785: W.R.O. Land Tax Assessments. For the concentration of estates in the hands of the Davises, see p. 43.
[42] W.R.O. 628, Lease.
[43] Ibid.; *Kelly's Dirs. Wilts.* It was called Fisherton House in 1867: *Kelly's Dir. Wilts.*
[44] Hoare, *Mod. Wilts.* Heytesbury, 259.
[45] W.R.O. 628, Survey of Fisherton manor.
[46] W.R.O. Tithe Award.
[47] W.R.O. 628, Building Accts.
[48] W.R.O. 628, Lease.   [49] Ibid.
[50] W.R.O. 628, Docs. about sale.
[51] *Kelly's Dirs. Wilts.*; Wilts. Cuttings, xvi. 170.
[52] *Wilts. County Mirror*, 9 Aug. 1901 (Wilts. Cuttings, vii, 242); ex. inf. Mr. R. S. Newall.
[53] Ex inf. Mr. R. S. Newall.
[54] O.S. Map 6″, Wilts. LIX (1st edn.) calls it Fisherton Delamere Farm, but *Kelly's Dir. Wilts.* gives it its new title.
[55] *Andrews and Dury, Map* (W.A.S. Rec. Brch.), pl. 5; W.R.O. Tithe Award.
[56] Hants R.O. 11 M 49/9 (homage only).
[57] Dors. R.O. 10936.
[58] Ibid. D45.
[59] W.R.O. 467/2; ibid. 628, Papers about Court. For most years between 1716 and 1740 there are presentments: Hants R.O. 11 M 49/356.

[60] W.R.O. 628, Papers about Court.
[61] W.R.O. 490, Hungerford Cart. f. 30. Hugh was married by 1308 (*Feet of F. Wilts.* 1272–1327 (W.A.S. Rec. Brch.), 71). and was dead by 1314 (*Wilts. Inq. p.m.* 1242–1326 (Index Libr.), 394). The witnesses make the date 1308–1314 a possible one. 'Balleborne', mentioned in the grant, can only conjecturally be identified with Boulsbury.
[62] *Cal. Inq. p.m.* vii, p. 241 (1331). There is an earlier and defective inquisition of 1329 (ibid. p. 165) which tells substantially the same story, but misrepresents the facts about the overlordship.
[63] *Cal. Close,* 1381–5, 565.
[64] Hoare, *Mod. Wilts.* Addenda, 34–35.
[65] *Cal. Close,* 1485–1500, 48.
[66] Hist. MSS. Com. *Hastings,* i. 309.
[67] E40/12751.
[68] C1/139/27.
[69] C1/785/20.
[70] *Taxation Lists* (W.A.S. Rec. Brch.), 36.
[71] C.P. 24 (1)/2/ 8 Eliz. I Hil.
[72] C 142/152/171.
[73] Hutchins (*Hist. Dors.* iv. 194) prints a pedigree. This branch of the Kellaways came from Dors. but intermarried with Wilts. families. Robt. Kellaway, when conveying Bapton in 1625, was described as late of Lillington (Dors.). Robt. Keilway, the law reporter (*D.N.B.*), was presumably a member of this family.

Kellaway. William married a Joan Barret, and in 1413 a John Barret was holding land in Bapton, Tisbury, and other nearby places, which he acquired from his cousin, Thomas Payne, who, in his turn, had acquired them from his father-in-law, John Ellis. This Ellis had another son-in-law, called Walter Estcott—presumably the same as Estcourt.[74] It is possible that it was through the gift of John Payne to John Barret that the Kellaway lands in Bapton were first acquired and the claim to those lands by Edmund Estcourt first set up.

John Kellaway was succeeded in the capital messuage by his son Henry.[75] He and his son Robert leased the property to Joan Hibberd and Henry Hoskins, her son, in succession, and in 1599 this lease was renewed to Hoskins alone. This second lease took effect about 1620.[76] In 1625 Robert Kellaway, his son Robert, and a third person sold the freehold, under the name of Bapton Farm, to Sir Edward Wardour,[77] who by 1627 had also acquired the interest in the lease of 1599.[78] Wardour, in turn, sold it in 1627 to John Davis, a yeoman from North Wraxall,[79] who in 1626 had married Joan Hoskins (d. c. 1654),[80] presumably Henry's relict. The property remained in the Davis family, who eventually acquired Fisherton manor and almost all the land in Fisherton and Bapton,[81] until 1871. It was then sold, with the rest of the Davis property in Bapton, to Joseph Deans Willis, the tenant.[82] Willis (d. 1895) left all his property to his sons Joseph Deane Willis (d. 1942) and J. G. D. Willis, between whom it was settled in 1897 that the former should own Bapton absolutely.[83] He remained owner, and reputed lord of the manor, until about 1927 when the property was acquired by Sir Cecil Chubb, Bt. (d. 1934).[84] In 1939 it was sold by the Chubb family to Alfred Douglas Hamilton, Duke of Hamilton and Brandon (d. 1940), whose representatives sold it in 1946 to Mr. E. Leigh Pearson. In 1959 it was bought by Major R. H. Heywood-Lonsdale, the present owner and occupier.[85]

John Davis (d. 1840) appears to have lived in the house until his death and farmed most of the 1,059-acre estate.[86] In 1841 the house and farm were leased to George Fleetwood, and in 1866 to the elder Willis.[87] In 1927 Major Dunbar Kelly, Chubb's agent, was living in the house.[88] During the Second World War it was in military occupation.[89]

The earliest part of the stone-built house, now called Bapton Manor, is the east end, which seems to date from the 17th century if not from an earlier time. To the west of this is a block, dating from the 1730's with a symmetrical ashlar front of 5 bays and a broken central pediment.[90] In the later 19th century various extensions were made on the north. In 1742 a garden abutted the house to the south and an avenue of trees connected it with a large field on that side. An orchard, paddocks, and, on the east, farm buildings adjoined, and there was also a way in, perhaps the front entrance, from the north.[91] By 1838 the surrounding paddocks had been much altered.[92] The road northwards of the house having been closed,[93] the north entrance naturally ceased to have any justification, and access was gained by two drives across the southern fields. The adjacent farm buildings have now (1963) been pulled down, though some boundary walls remain in the garden. The modern farm buildings are to the west and replace a large barn burnt in 1958.[94]

LESSER ESTATES. In the 16th century the Mompesson family held an estate in Fisherton and Bapton under the Paulets,[95] as of the manor of Fisherton. It had descended to them from the Lamberts, who had interests there in the early 15th century.[96] John Mompesson died in 1500 seised of 3 houses and 3 virgates in Bapton and ½ virgate in Fisherton.[97] His grandson John, son of Drew Mompesson, succeeded, and died seised in 1511.[98] He left an infant son, Edmund, on whose death in 1553, without male issue, the lands were divided between his three sisters Anne, wife of William Weyt, Elizabeth, wife of Richard Perkyns, and Susan Mompesson, and his nephew, Gilbert, son of Mary Wells.[99] In the earlier years of the century the Mompessons appear to have claimed that villeins were regardant to this estate.[1]

In or shortly before 1232 Constance, daughter of Robert de la Stane, gave a hide of land in Fisherton to Bradenstoke priory in free alms.[2] It was valued at 30 s. in 1291[3] and is no doubt the messuage and 4 virgates which the priory leased in 1528 to William Snelgar at a little above that sum.[4] In 1539 it was granted to Sir William Paulet, Lord St. John.[5] A virgate and a *rusticus* in Bapton (Babigton) were given by a William Malet to Warminster church in settlement of a dispute over 1½ hide of land.[6] The conveyance cannot have been earlier than 1156 or

---

[74] B.M. Add. Ch. 26777.
[75] C142/152/171.
[76] W.R.O. 628, Bargain and Sale, 1627.
[77] W.R.O. 467/13.
[78] W.R.O. 628, Bargain and Sale, 1627.   [79] Ibid.
[80] W.R.O. Parish Records, Marriage Reg., where Davis is described as of S. Wraxall. For Joan's will, see P.C.C. 175 Alchin.   [81] See pp. 38–39, 43.
[82] W.R.O. 628, Papers about sale. Willis leased the property from 1866: W.R.O. 628, Lease.
[83] W.R.O. 628, Copy of Willis's will, 1895, and deed of partition, 1897.
[84] *Kelly's Dirs. Wilts.* (1923, 1927).
[85] Ex inf. Major Heywood-Lonsdale.
[86] So estimated when leased in 1841. The lessor was then in occupation of 1,013 a.: W.R.O. 628, Lease to Geo. Fleetwood. John Davis's whole estate in Bapton was, however, estimated at 1,081 a. in 1840: W.R.O. 628, Note on the Davis estate in Fisherton and Bapton.
[87] W.R.O. 628, Leases to Fleetwood and Willis.
[88] *Kelly's Dir. Wilts.* (1927); ex inf. Mr. R. S. Newall.
[89] Ex inf. Major Heywood-Lonsdale.

[90] Ex inf. Major Heywood-Lonsdale, who states that the last figure of the date stone is illegible.
[91] W.R.O. 628, Survey of Fisherton manor.
[92] W.R.O. Tithe Award.   [93] See pp. 35–36.
[94] Ex inf. Major Heywood-Lonsdale.
[95] *Cal. Inq. p.m. Hen. VII*, ii, p. 317.
[96] Req. 2/4/327. John, son of Edmund Lambert, of Bapton, quitclaimed land in Fisherton to Thomas Bonham in 1409: *Cal. Close, 1405–9*, 530.
[97] *Cal. Inq. p.m. Hen. VII*, ii, p. 317.
[98] C 142/26/127.
[99] C 142/104/123.
[1] C1/567/52 (1518–29); Req. 2/4/327 (temp. Hen. VII or Hen. VIII).
[2] B. M. Stowe MS. 925, ff. 91v.–92; royal confirmation in *Cal. Chart. R.* i. 160. A Robt. de la Stane held land in Dors. and Som. in 1167–8: *Pipe R.* 1168 (Pipe R. Soc. xii), 135.
[3] *V.C.H. Wilts.* iii. 282.
[4] S.C. 6/Hen. VIII/3985 m. 57.
[5] *L. & P. Hen. VIII*, xiv (1), p. 421.
[6] Hist. MSS. Com. *Wells*, i. 59.

later than *c.* 1216.[7] In 1221 Robert Goyon (Guiun) gave a hide in Bapton to Thomas of Bapton (Babinton)[8]. Nothing further is known of either of these estates.

ECONOMIC HISTORY. Fisherton presumably owes its origin to fishing. In 1086 it was assessed at 10 hides of which 5½ were in demesne. There were 10 ploughlands, 3 of them in demesne, 12 a. of meadow, and pasture ½ league square. There were 16 villeins, 12 bordars, and 14 cottars.[9] Bapton is not named in the Survey.

Fisherton with Bapton was rated at £9 to the fifteenth and tenth of 1334. Compared with other places in the hundred and in the vale of Wylye this figure is a high one. Within the hundred only Warminster with Boreham, Bugley, and Small-brook (£9 18s.) was more highly rated, though Upton Scudamore, with Norridge and Thoulstone (£8 18s.), ran it pretty close. No contiguous vale parish attained so high a rating; the nearest was Steeple Langford, with Bathampton and Hanging Langford (£7 1s. 4d.).[10] The conclusion must, therefore, be either that Fisherton was unexpectedly prosperous or that its boundaries were more extensive than they are today. In the 16th century, if taxation assessments be any guide, this pre-eminence was not maintained. In 1576 Fisherton with Bapton was eighth among the ten parishes of the hundred, and, apart from Sherrington, the least prosperous of the adjacent valley parishes.[11]

The only extents of the capital manor, surviving from medieval times, are dated 1319,[12] 1325,[13] 1330,[14] and 1346.[15] They relate to fractions and consequently give no reliable picture of that manor as a whole. It is clear from them, however, that the manor was peopled by bond tenants or virgaters, who might hold either a virgate or half a virgate, and by cottars. The extent of 1330 also mentions free tenants. It was also then said that the virgaters and cottars were bound to mow and carry the meadow, and that the meadow could be mown each year before Lammas and that after mowing it lay in common until Candlemas. In 1346 it was remarked that a part of the meadow, lying next Salisbury Plain, could not be mown in a dry summer.

In 1415–6 the Hungerford manor in Fisherton played its part in the system for exchanging stock between the different estates belonging to that family. Cart-horses, lambs, and pigs of varying ages were exported from the manor in that year, and 160 sheep and one or two beeves received in return, together with some corn.[16]

In 1600 the common of pasture appurtenant to a yardland was for 30 sheep, 4 rother beasts, a yearling, and a horse.[17] The yardland, however, which formed the main constituent of the glebe, was said from 1605 to 1807 to be fit to be stocked with 60 sheep, 3 horses, 3 beasts, and a 'rearer'.[18]

A lack of surveys makes it impossible to draw any satisfactory picture of the husbandry practised in the village in the 16th and 17th centuries. A study of a number of surviving wills and inventories, however, leads to the following tentative conclusions.[19] Between 1500 and 1660 barley and wheat were the staple crops, barley preponderating. From the late 16th century small quantities of vetches and peas were grown and in the 17th century of oats as well. In 1617 a woman had a stock of woad.[20] Naturally many sheep were reared. In the period 1546–98 Thomas Topp seems to have owned over 700 at his death, but it does not follow that all of them were folded in Fisherton parish.[21] Most flocks were much smaller but in the 1640's two testators left over 200 each.[22] William Merywether, of Bapton (d. 1580), employed a shepherd.[23] The crops and livestock are such as we should expect at this time in the Wiltshire chalk country.[24]

The land seems to have been divided among small family farmers. Of those with a long connexion with the parish mention may be made first of the family of Snelgar, one member of which, William, apparently in the early 16th century, purchased his land from John Mompesson to extinguish any claim to servile obligations that might be thought to inhere in it.[25] Another—or perhaps the same—William farmed the rectorial estate in 1530–6.[26] What appears to be the last Snelgar was living in 1720.[27] Other such families were those of Kellaway (16th cent.),[28] Foster (1545–1648),[29] Rebbeck (1576–1805),[30] Wansborough (1546–1745),[31] Eyles or Hicks (1573–1730),[32] Topp (1574–1783),[33] and

[7] Wm. Malet I fl. *c.* 1156, d. 1169; Wm. Malet II succeeded 1194, d. 1216: Sanders, *English Baronies*, 38.
[8] C.P. 25(1)/250/4/10.
[9] *V.C.H Wilts.* ii, p. 154.
[10] Ibid. iv. 297, 299, 302.
[11] *Taxation Lists* (W.A.S. Rec. Brch.), 145–9. In order to arrive at these conclusions the ratings of the several taxation tithings have been assembled as far as possible according to the boundaries of the several 'ancient' parishes.
[12] *Wilts. Inq. p.m.* 1242–1326 (Index Libr.), 418.
[13] Ibid. 440.
[14] Ibid. 1327–77, 43.
[15] Ibid. 171.
[16] S.C. 6/1053/15. Cf. *V.C.H. Wilts.* iv. 19.
[17] C 2/Eliz. I/R. 7/15.
[18] Sar. Dioc. R.O. Glebe Terriers; W.R.O. Inclosure Award.
[19] The wills and inventories examined comprise those of testators and intestates, with Fisherton and Bapton addresses, whose wills were proved or estates administered in the P.C.C., the Bp.'s Consistory Ct., and the Archdeacon of Sarum's Ct.
[20] W.R.O. Arch. Sar., Inv. of Eliz. Doughty.

[21] He had a house in Wilton and probably interests in the Codfords, Stockton, and Wylye: P.C.C. 13 Spencer.
[22] W.R.O. Arch. Sar., Invs. of John Ingram (1646) and Hen. Rebbeck (1641).
[23] Ibid. Bk. 6, f. 2.
[24] *V.C.H. Wilts.* iv. 45, 54–55.
[25] C 1/567/52. The bill may be assigned to 1518–29.
[26] E 210/5653; S.C. 6/Hen. VIII/3969 m. 6. A Thos. Snelgar was presented to the living in 1530: Phillipps, *Wilts. Inst.* i. 201.
[27] Hants R.O. 11 M 49/356.
[28] See p. 39.
[29] *Taxation Lists* (W.A.S. Rec. Brch.), 36; *W.A.M.* xxxvii. 369.
[30] *Taxation Lists* (W.A.S. Rec. Brch.), 146; W.R.O. Land Tax Assessments. He was still an owner, though not an occupier in 1831, as the Land Tax Assessments show.
[31] W.R.O. Arch. Sar., Bk. 2, f. 41; W.R.O. 628, Marriage Settlement of Eliz. Wansborough, relict of Wm.
[32] W.R.O. Arch. Sar., Bk. 5, f. 142; Hants R.O. 11 M 49/356.
[33] W.R.O. Parish Regs., and see p. 38. There is some reason to feel that by the 18th cent. the Topps had come down in the world.

Ingram (1549–1809).[34] Families originating apparently in the 17th century include those of Doughty (1610–1838),[35] Pashion, Patient, or Patience (1610–1785),[36] and Davis (1627–1878),[37] though the last was not of much account until the later 17th century. The Gilberts,[38] the Slades, and the Bowleses do not become prominent until the 18th century, although a Bowles was buried in 1597.[39]

In 1742 the manor of Fisherton, with Bapton, was carefully surveyed and minutely described.[40] It consisted, according to contemporary measurement, of 2,724 statute acres. Of this total Fisherton proper amounted to 1,676 a., and to this portion belonged 3 fields all lying N. of the Codford-Deptford road. These were North Field, East Field to the S. of it, and West Field to the W. of both. N. of North Field lay Fisherton Sheep Down (252 a.). S. of the Codford-Deptford road lay a substantial area of meadow, all by this time held in severalty, together with orchards and gardens.

The Bapton portion was divided into West, Middle, Greenland, and East Fields.[41] S. of these lay the large area of Bapton Sheep Down. Beyond this, still further southward, were Bapton Cow Down on the W. and the Furze ('Fuzey') on the E. S. of the Furze lay another part of the Sheep Down. These pastures totalled some 480 a. N. of Bapton village were the meadows and orchards belonging to Bapton. Some of these were several, but on the N.W. there lay Bapton Common Meadow, and, to the E. of it, two stretches of common land, devoted to pasture. The lay-out of the two villages makes it obvious that there had once been two distinct village communities — in fact two manors — but that they had been fused in consequence of a long-standing common lordship.

In the Fisherton portion there were at this time 20 separate tenements, held by 16 tenants. To most of these a house was annexed and most tenants held strips in the common fields together with parcels of the downland. These 'down pieces' were said to represent what the tenants had purchased for 4-year terms, after the expiration of which their plots were again laid down as downland. The average holding was a little under 85 a., the largest that of Mr. Bowles, who held 521 a. The whole of the W. side of this portion, called the Field Lands, was made up of newly-broken ground, divided into large compact fields and shared between Bowles himself and William Ingram. In the Bapton portion there were 17 tenants and tenements, apart from cottage holdings of 7 a. and below. These were a mixture of freeholds and copyholds. The average holding was about 60 a., the largest

apparently John Davis's (d. 1743) of 120 a. Of the area of the whole manor (Fisherton with Bapton) 740 a. were pasture, 164 a. meadow, 10 a. gardens and orchards, and 2 a. oziers. There were also 5 a. described as 'waste', which included 11 empty houses.

A valuer, reporting apparently at the time of the sale by the Duke of Somerset in 1790, describes the meadow ground of the manor as in general 'of a very deep black soil rather too much inclinable to the moor or swampy kind'. This he considered reduced its value, which he set at £2 an acre. He found the quality of the arable very variable, 'that in the bottoms being much better than that on the hills, except it be the flinty parts' which were as good as the bottoms. In particular the arable in Bapton fields was much better than that in Fisherton fields and was capable of growing fine barley.[42] The crop returns of 1801 showed an equal acreage of wheat and barley, 250 in each case, with 40 a. of oats, and 20 each of peas and root crops.[43]

Some information survives about the manorial economy in the century before inclosure. Five times between 1722 and 1728 the manorial tenants were forbidden to put cattle in Bapton common meadow until the furlong of corn 'opposite' to it had been gathered in. In 1730 this regulation was altered, so that the meadow was out of bounds to cattle until two furlongs, one each side of the Stockton-Wylye road, had been harvested. The regulation was constantly reiterated in the same form between 1771 and 1805. Many times between 1701 and 1805 the tenants in Bapton, and latterly in the whole manor, were forbidden to graze cattle on the lands' ends or 'meres' of the common fields before the corn harvest. The cutting of bushes on Bapton Down was forbidden in 1708, 1711, 1732, and 1733. Between 1700 and 1745 and between 1771 and 1787 the tenants in both villages, but those in Bapton the oftener, were repeatedly directed to meet, usually in the early summer, and set or repair the boundary stones or boundaries in the common fields. Perambulations either at Rogationtide or on Maundy Thursday were ordered in 1724, 1732, and 1739, and after 1751 were often combined with the foregoing operation. Haywards, one for each village, were appointed in 1739, and in 1704, 1724, and 1727 two men were chosen to number the sheep, so that the common might not be surcharged. In 1738 the number of sheep to a yardland was limited to 42. In 1801 and 1805 it was declared to be the custom that only sheep should be fed in the summer fields.[44]

Fisherton was inclosed in 1807 and Bapton in 1810, in each instance by private agreement.[45]

[34] W.R.O. Arch. Sar., Bk. 5, f. 63; W.R.O. 628, Label on bdle. of conveyances from Ingram to Davis. Edw. Ingram was said to have made a conveyance in 1548–9: C 2/Eliz. I/R. 7/15.
[35] W.R.O. Arch. Sar., Bk. 8, f. 195; ibid. Tithe Award. The first Doughty (Joel, d. 1610) was vicar of the parish.
[36] W.R.O. Arch. Sar., Bk. 8, f. 116; ibid. Land Tax Assessments, 1785, though at that time the man in question, Wm. Patient, was not an occupier.   [37] See p. 40.
[38] W.R.O. 628, Survey of Fisherton manor.
[39] W.R.O. Parish Reg.
[40] W.R.O. 628, Survey of Fisherton manor.
[41] The W. field of Bapton is mentioned in 1569 (W.R.O. Arch. Sar., Bk. 5, f. 63); the E. field in 1620 (ibid. Bk. 8, f. 182).
[42] W.R.O. 628. The report is undated, but a reference

to Wm. Bowles as the tenant of half Fisherton Farm (see p. 38), together with the presumption that a sale was impending, give a sufficiently exact indication of the period.   [43] H.O. 67/23.
[44] Hants R.O. 11 M/356; E.R.O. 628, Papers about Fisherton manor ct.
[45] W.R.O. Fisherton and Bapton Inclosure Awards. To the former a map of some of the parcels of land is annexed. In W.R.O. 628 is a list of deeds relating to the Davis estate, one entry in which reads: '3 Dec. 1784. Agreement by John Davies and others, owners of the common fields and downs in Bapton, for dividing, allotting, and enclosing them'. The original has not been found, but the presumption is that there was an abortive attempt to inclose Bapton 36 years before inclosure was achieved.

In Fisherton there were only three allottees apart from the two Davises, in Bapton only two. Of these the chief beneficiary was John Gilbert who received 105 a.

Such an uncomplicated settlement was possible because, for a generation or more, the Davis family had been engrossing the land. Many leases testify to the extent to which the family had acquired parcels of land as tenants in the 18th century,[46] but the stages of accumulation are made clearer by the land tax assessments. In 1740 John and William Davis together occupied 9 out of 33 tenements assessed, in 1800 14, and in 1810 25. In 1820 and 1830 the two John Davises occupied 29 out of 34 assessed tenements. Viewed from another standpoint there were 13 separate occupiers in 1780 and only 6 in 1830.[47] In 1838 the Davis family occupied all but 124 a. of the parish,[48] and by 1840 they owned everything except the glebe.[49] Thus a parish which in 1640 and 1740 was a community of small farmers had by 1840 been monopolized by one. In 1838 942 a. were reckoned to be meadow or pasture of which 792 were downland.[50]

During the 19th century the Davises and their tenants improved their property both as an agricultural and a sporting estate, building houses, cottages, and barns, and planting woodlands.[51] A surveyor, reporting on Fisherton Farm in 1877, after Bapton had been sold off,[52] said that it made 'a fine holding of average quality' and that it was 'in the hands of good and apparently substantial tenants', who kept 'a fair dairy of cows and an exceptionally fine breeding stock of sheep'.[53] Sale particulars of 1898 declared that the land then carried nearly 2,000 Hampshire Downs sheep and 100 milch cows.[54] Bapton became the home of shorthorn breeding. A herd was established there about 1854 by J. Deans Willis (d. 1895), the tenant, and continued by his son J. Deane Willis (d. 1942) and by Sir Cecil Chubb. It has been said that at one time, presumably in the early 20th century, it was 'second to none in the kingdom'.[55] In 1905 the whole parish contained 1,415 a. of arable, 545 a. of permanent grass, and 60 a. of woodland.[56]

There was a mill at Fisherton in 1086.[57] It is not expressly mentioned again until 1375, when it was annexed to the ⅔ of the manor and was declared to have formerly belonged to Walter de Freynes.[58] There was a miller in 1439.[59] In Elizabeth I's reign John Ember held mills in Fisherton as a lessee. By

his will dated 1582 he bequeathed the lease to John Slade, his grandson. On the death of the former, about 1588–9, a disagreement about the lease arose between Slade and John Barnaby, another of Ember's grandsons.[60] Evidently Barnaby was worsted, for, in 1594, Slade, then called 'miller', sold all his rights in the mills to John Topp, of Stockton.[61] Presumably these mills (or mill) were owned by Lord Winchester. At all events in 1646 he, with others, let a corn mill at Fisherton to Nicholas Whitehart, of Wylye. Whitehart's interest descended to William Clare, of Heytesbury, who in 1697 assigned his interest to John Ingram of Bapton.[62] By 1771 Ingram's interest had descended to John Davis (d. 1791), who next year acquired from the Duke of Bolton an extension in his own right.[63] The ownership of the mill was included in the grant of the manor to John Davis[64] and was sold with the Fisherton estate in 1881.[65] The mill was no doubt often let. In 1867 it was in the hands of Thomas Compton, but in 1895 Pettey, the lord of the manor, was himself described as a miller. From 1911 to 1931 Charles Carpenter occupied the mill, and in 1935 Charles Carpenter & Sons.[66] The Carpenters remained in occupation until c. 1956,[6] since when the mill has fallen out of use. In 1898 the mill not only ground corn but drove pumps that supplied water to the estate.[68]

Thomas Moore (or More), of Bapton, a millwright, died in 1640, leaving a 'working-house' full of tools.[69] He was apparently descended from the Ingrams through the female line and had once been a farmer.[70] A youth was apprenticed to a Fisherton maltster in 1720[71] and two malthouses existed in Fisherton in 1742.[72] William Wansborough, described as a husbandman in 1701, was an 'edgetool-maker' in 1708 and 1710.[73].

CHURCH. Although its masonry attests its 12th-century origin, the church of Fisherton is not mentioned until 1291,[74] and the rector not until 1314.[75] In 1326 the advowson was the subject of a dispute between Sir James de Norton and the king, as guardian of William Saffrey's heir. A writ of *ne admittatis* was issued in January of that year, pending a settlement of the dispute,[76] but in December, before any settlement was reached, Norton and Edward II, as guardian, presented rival clerks.[77] Edward III, on his accession, renewed his father's presentation.[78] A vacancy, however, seems to have

[46] These are in W.R.O. 628 and W.R.O. 467. See also Hackwood Hall, Hants, Lease Bk. ff. 153–67, which shows that between 1761 and 1788 10 separate leases were granted by the Boltons to members of this family.
[47] In W.R.O.
[48] W.R.O. Tithe Award. The award states the area of the parish as both 2,861 and 2,865 a. Hence the lands occupied by the Davises may be variously reckoned as 124 or 128 a.
[49] W.R.O. 628, Note dated 1840 and Abstract of Title.
[50] W.R.O. Tithe Award.
[51] See p. 35.   [52] See p. 40.
[53] W.R.O. 628, Messrs. Bailey, Norman & Brown's report, 1877.
[54] W.A.S. Libr., Devizes, Sale Cat.
[55] *W.A.M.* xlv. 339; xlvii. 130.
[56] Statistics supplied by the then Bd. of Agriculture.
[57] *V.C.H. Wilts.* ii, p. 154.
[58] *Cal. Close*, 1374–7, 323.
[59] *W.A.M.* xiii. 114.
[60] Req. 2/35/100.
[61] Bristol Univ. Libr., MS. W. 282 (extracted from TS.

list in Inst. Hist. Research).
[62] W.R.O. 467/8.   [63] W.R.O. 467/8 and /14.
[64] W.R.O. 467/1.
[65] W.R.O. 628, Sale Cat.; W.A.S. Libr., Devizes, Sale Cat.
[66] *Kelly's Dirs. Wilts.*
[67] Ex inf. Major J. G. Cassels.
[68] *Devizes Gaz.* 23 June 1898.
[69] W.R.O. Arch. Sar., Inv.
[70] C 2 Eliz. I/R. 7/15.
[71] *Wilts. Apprentices* (W.A.S. Rec. Brch.), 8.
[72] W.R.O. 628, Survey of Fisherton manor.
[73] W.R.O. 628, Deeds and Abstract of Title to Davis estates.
[74] *Tax Eccl.* (Rec. Com.), 181.
[75] B.M. Add. Ch. 13014. He was Wm. de Beloney, perhaps a relative of Baldwin de Bellany (see p. 39).
[76] *Reg. Martival* (Cant. and York Soc.), i. 379.
[77] Ibid. 367–8.
[78] Ibid. 370; *Cal. Pat.* 1327–30, 15. The entry of a presentation by the Crown of a different clerk on the same day is presumably an error: ibid. 11.

occurred shortly after, for in October 1327 the bishop collated by devolution.[79] Next year the king recovered the presentation,[80] presented a new clerk,[81] and successfully issued process against the bishop to enforce institution.[82] He presented again in 1351 during the minority of a Norton.[83] In 1381 Sir Ralph de Norton presented.[84] It appears from these facts that from at least 1326 the advowson was appurtenant to the manor, and was exercised in turn by those who owned shares in it. In 1314 a rector and vicar coexisted[85] and on six occasions between 1329 and 1398 the rector presented a vicar.[86]

In 1390 Philip son of Sir John de la Mere, with the assent of Sir Matthew Gurney as overlord, granted the advowson, with an acre of land, to Maiden Bradley priory.[87] The priory, which also appropriated the rectory, exercised the patronage until the Dissolution, except in 1448 when, for unknown reasons, the Abbess of Shaftesbury presented, and in 1530 when the prior granted it to Thomas Mayo of Maiden Bradley.[88] After the priory was dissolved in 1536, the Crown granted both rectory and advowson, in 1539, to Sir William Paulet, Lord St. John.[89] Both descended with the manor until 1804. In 1637, however, John Foyle, of Kimpton (Hants), presented by grant from Lord Winchester, and in 1673, Charles, Lord St. John of Basing.[90] Presumably this was because the marquess, as a Roman Catholic, could not present. In 1778 the bishop collated by lapse.[91]

In 1804 the Duke of Somerset conveyed the rectory and advowson, with the manor, in trust to John and William Davis, who agreed to exercise the patronage in turn.[92] John Davis (d. 1840) presented in 1820 and John Davis (d. 1860), his nephew, in 1830 as legatee of his father's turn. In 1840 this John acquired both turns and presented in 1854 and 1868.[93] The advowson was mortgaged with the manor in 1877 and sold in 1881 to William Chapman.[94] He sold it in 1883 to Mrs. Mary Davies,[95] who presented twice in 1884.[96] The Revd. T. Ratcliffe presented in 1885, the bishop collated by lapse in 1893, and Athelstan Riley presented in 1898.[97] In 1929 the benefice was united with Wylye.[98] An attempt made in 1649–50 to unite Deptford and Great Bathampton Farm, both in Wylye, with Fisherton, and to detach Bapton

and unite it with Stockton, was frustrated.[99]

Notwithstanding a statement by Hoare[1], repeated by Jackson,[2] there is no evidence of any chantry having been established in the church.

The rectory was valued at £6 13s. 4d. in 1291.[3] Between 1445 and 1535 its gross revenues were charged with small payments to the Bishop, the Archdeacon, and the Chapter of Salisbury, and with £6 13s. 4d. which formed a pension for a chaplain at Nunney.[4] The pension had been granted by Philip de la Mere in 1394 in return for the advowson and the acre of land referred to above and he in turn had used it to endow a family chantry.[5] After the Dissolution of chantries it was settled on William, Marquess of Winchester, in 1561.[6] In 1445–52 the rectory was farmed for £14 13s. 4d.[7] Its letting value then declined to £12 in 1466–7[8] and £10 16s. 8d. in 1530.[9] In 1535 it was said to be let for only £2 2s. 7d.[10] In 1605 the lay rector owned half the tithes of hay.[11] A parsonage house existed in 1445–6.[12] There was still a 'parsonage' in 1742,[13] doubtless the lay rector's home, but it was empty.

The vicarage was valued at £8 7s. 10d. net in 1535.[14] It is not appraised again for many generations, but it is known to have been let for £30 in 1705[15] and to have been let again, without the house, in 1806 for £135.[16] In 1783 it was described as 'of small value'.[17] In 1831 its capital value was augmented by £400, of which Queen Anne's Bounty paid a half,[18] and four years later its mean income was set at £135.[19] A valuation made c. 1883, apparently with care, set it at £197 gross and £158 net.[20]

A late 16th-century terrier describes the nature of the benefice income. Glebe consisted of a yardland (29½ a. of arable), 1 a. of common, and 1 a. of several meadows. Tithe arose from the following sources: half the hay of the common meadows of Fisherton and Bapton and of 'Banmead' in Norton Bavant; from all the hay of the 'hamlets' below Fisherton Street, the 'hamlets' and closes in Bapton, the orchards and gardens in both villages, 3 hams between the Common (or Moor) and Bapton Street, most of the closes, 'hamlets', and orchards west of the Hindon road,[21] and Brimble Close (just north of Bapton Manor House); from corn from 1½ yard above Bapton village; from 12 bz. of corn of the

[79] Reg. Martival (Cant. and York Soc.), i. 379.
[80] Ibid.
[81] Cal. Pat. 1327–30, 310.
[82] Reg. Martival (Cant. and York Soc.), i. 379.
[83] Phillipps, Wilts. Inst. i. 50.
[84] Ibid. 65.
[85] B.M. Add. Ch. 13014.
[86] Phillipps, Wilts. Inst. i. 25, 50, 52, 73, 79, 84.
[87] Cal. Pat. 1388–92, 335; B.M. Eg. Ch. 587.
[88] Phillipps, Wilts. Inst. i. 140, 201.
[89] L. & P. Hen. VIII, xiv (i), p. 421.
[90] Phillipps, Wilts. Inst. ii, 19, 32.
[91] Ibid. 89.
[92] W.R.O. 628, Note on Advowson.
[93] Ibid.; Sar. Dioc. Regy. Bp.'s Regs.
[94] W.R.O. 628, Papers about Advowson.
[95] Ibid.
[96] Sar. Dioc. Regy. Bp.'s Regs.
[97] Ibid.
[98] Order in Council, 17 Dec. 1929.
[99] W.A.M. xl. 299.
[1] Hoare, Mod. Wilts. Heytesbury, 255-56.
[2] W.A.M. x. 282.
[3] Tax. Eccl. (Rec. Com.), 181.
[4] S.C. 6/1054/11, /12, /14; S.C. 6/1108/20; S.C. 6/

Hen. VIII/3969 m. 6.
[5] Cal. Pat. 1391–6, 370. Cf. V.C.H Wilts. iii. 298–9, where it is incorrectly stated that the pension was exchanged for Fisherton manor.
[6] Cal. Pat. 1560–3, 50.
[7] S.C. 6/1054/11, /12; S.C. 6/1108/20.
[8] S.C. 6/1054/14.
[9] E 210/5653.
[10] Valor Eccl. (Rec. Com.), ii. 98.
[11] Sar. Dioc. R.O. Glebe Terrier.
[12] S.C. 6/1108/20.
[13] W.R.O. 628, Survey of Fisherton manor.
[14] Valor Eccl. (Rec. Com.), ii. 103; S.C. 6/Hen. VIII/3969 m. 6.
[15] Sar. Dioc. R.O. Glebe Terrier.
[16] W.R.O. 467/7.
[17] Sar. Dioc. R.O. Vis. Queries, 1783.
[18] Hodgson, Queen Anne's Bounty, p. cccxxxv.
[19] Rep. Com. Eccl. Revenues, H.C. 54, pp. 834–5 (1835), xxii.
[20] W.R.O. 628, printed Advertisement for sale of advowson.
[21] Presumably this means the road (now a track) that leads S. from the Stockton-Wylye road just opposite Bapton Manor Ho.

mill; and from 24 pigeons. In 1605 2 a. of ground in the Marsh had been added to the glebe, and common of pasture was expressly declared to be appurtenant to the yardland. Tithe arose as before, except that corn might now be taken from 2½ yards in Bapton field. The area of glebe remained virtually unchanged until the inclosure of Fisherton in 1807. In 1680 and 1705 the tithe hay was said to come from grounds lying north and west of Bapton Street and south of Fisherton Street. By 1807 hay was no longer taken from these home grounds and corn and pigeons were no longer tithed. Otherwise the system was much as in 1605.[22] At inclosure the glebe was consolidated into an estate of 20 a. on the east edge of Fisherton village.[23] It was undiminished in 1883.[24] In 1838 tithe was commuted for £143.[25]

A vicarage house existed in 1605.[26] In 1742 it stood in Fisherton Street, well to the east of the church.[27] At inclosure a plot of land was allotted to the vicar, at the extreme east edge of the parish on the Codford-Deptford road, in lieu of this house.[28] It was promptly let to John and William Davis,[29] and, with the glebe, was still on lease in 1838.[30] Its fate thereafter is uncertain. There was no house in 1835,[31] but at that time a new one is said to have been built to replace the 'miserable cottage inhabited by a pauper' that was then the nominal vicarage.[32] This new vicarage, now called The Old Vicarage, still stands in the Codford-Deptford road and is a substantial stone building of 7 bays.

The Protestant inclinations of the vicar in Mary's reign may perhaps be deduced from his failure, when Pole's legatine visitation took place in 1556, to reerect the altar.[33] He was also presented at the same time for living 'incontinently' with a woman[34] —possibly his lawful wife. Thomas Crockford (1613–34)[35] kept the registers in florid Latin and noted in them many personal details about his parishioners. He died, a happy instance of a 'reading' clergyman, possessed of 338 books.[36] The views of Interregnum vicars, whose names are not known, may possibly be deduced from the fact that in 1662 the church possessed no book of homilies, no copy of Jewell's *Apology*, and no surplice.[37] In 1783 service was held but once on Sundays and had never been held more frequently

within living memory. Communion was administered at Easter, Whitsun, and Christmas to about 16 persons. Services were conducted by a curate, who was also curate at Codford St. Mary.[38] A curate signed the crop returns of 1801.[39] The vicar presented in 1829 was also Rector of Sutton Veny and employed a curate to serve Fisherton.[40] It was a curate who made the return to the Ecclesiastical Census of 1851.[41]

On census day 85 attended morning and 102 evening service. The figures for Sunday school attendance were respectively 48 and 44.[42] The average morning and evening congregations were said to be 85 and 102 respectively. In 1864 services were held twice on Sundays and there were also services on Wednesdays and Fridays in Lent, Christmas Day, Good Friday, and Ash Wednesday. Communion was administered on the three great festivals and on the first Sunday in each month to from 17 to 30 people.[43] In 1881 also there were two Sunday services.[44]

The church of *ST. NICHOLAS*, which already bore that dedication in 1326,[45] consists of chancel, nave with west and south doors, north transept, vestry, and south porch with tower above.[46] The earliest work in the church dates from the late 12th century and from that period survive the responds of the chancel arch with their carved capitals, several voussoirs with chevron ornament built into the south wall of the nave, and two detached capitals. The chancel itself appears to have been completed by the mid-13th century and, although rebuilt in 1861, retains most of its original features. These include narrow lancet windows, buttresses, and corbel tables to both north and south walls. Twin lancets at the east end have moulded rear arches with attached shafts and a quatrefoil pierced in the spandrel between them. In the 14th century 2-light windows were inserted in the nave and also near the east end of the chancel. The north transept is probably of this date; a drawing of c. 1804[47] shows it as a low gabled projection with a blocked door or window of 14th-century character in its north wall. In the 15th or 16th century a low tower was built on the south side of the nave. Serious dilapidations were reported in 1583 and 1585,[48] and in 1595 money seems to have been collected for the repair of the fabric.[49] In 1662 attention was

[22] Sar. Dioc. R.O. Glebe Terriers of late 16th cent., 1605, 1671, 1680.
[23] W.R.O. Inclosure Award.
[24] W.R.O. 628, Printed Advertisement for sale of advowson.
[25] W.R.O. Tithe Award.
[26] Sar. Dioc. R.O. Glebe Terrier.
[27] W.R.O. 628, Survey of Fisherton manor.
[28] W.R.O. Inclosure Award. The plot is numbered 9 in the award but no such number can be found on the map.
[29] W.R.O. 628, Lease.
[30] W.R.O. Tithe Award.
[31] *Rep. Com. Eccl. Revenues* (1835), pp. 834–5.
[32] H. J. S. Banks, *Ch. of St. Nicholas, Fisherton Delamere* [?1962]. Mr. R. S. Newall reports the belief that the 'miserable cottage' was a cottage still standing to the W. of the ch. in the lane running N. into the Codford-Deptford road, just S. of the farm-yard belonging to Fisherton Delamere House.
[33] *V.C.H. Wilts.* iii. 31.
[34] Sar. Dioc. R.O. Ep. Vis.
[35] *W.A.M.* xii. 210.   [36] W.R.O. Consist. Ct. Wills.

[37] Sar. Dioc. R.O. Ep. Vis.
[38] Ibid. Vis. Queries, 1783.
[39] H.O. 67/23.
[40] *Rep. Com. Eccl. Revenues* (1835), pp. 834–5.
[41] H.O. 129/10/265.
[42] Ibid.
[43] Sar. Dioc. R.O. Vis. Queries, 1864.
[44] W.R.O. 628, Sale Cat. 1881.
[45] Phillipps, *Wilts. Inst.* i. 23.
[46] For the building before its restoration in 1833, see B.M. Add. MS. 36391, ff. 125, 125b, which appear to be sketches for water-colours among the Buckler drawings (iii. 29) in W.A.S. Libr., Devizes. The water-colours are dated 1804. See also Hoare, *Mod. Wilts.* Heytesbury (1822), 257 with plan. For the building after this but before the restoration of the chancel in 1861 see Soc. Antiq. Jackson MSS. vol. vii, which includes a description of the church written in Aug. 1856. See also Banks, *Fisherton Delamere Church*, which contains a plan *ut nunc*.
[47] B.M. Add. MS. 36391, f. 125.
[48] Sar. Dioc. R.O. Ep. Vis.
[49] W.R.O. Arch. Sar., Will of Phil. Williams.

drawn to further decay.[50] It has been thought[51] that it was after this report that the masonry of the tower was extended above the string-course and capped with a wooden belfry, and the chancel arch raised and remodelled above the imposts. It was perhaps in the 18th century that the east wall was strengthened with angle buttresses and the west wall with a pilaster buttress.[52] Hoare's plan of c. 1822 shows a north door to the nave, immediately opposite the existing south doorway; no access, either from the outside or from the nave, is shown to the north transept. Hoare commented that though the chancel was 'early', the rest of the building seemed to have been 'rebuilt out of the ruins of the former church'.[53]

In 1833 John Davis (d. 1840) restored and altered the building.[54] He appears to have rebuilt the nave and transept, raising the walls by 2 ft. and consequently altering the pitch of the roofs, changed the fenestration, inserted a west door, closed the north door, built a vestry east of the transept, and replaced the wooden belfry, then used as a pigeon house,[55] by a 'Perpendicular' tower of stone. In 1861 John Davis (d. 1878) had the chancel taken down and carefully rebuilt under the superintendence of W. Hardwick, a Warminster surveyor.[56] The only important alteration then made was the elimination of the 'Decorated' windows in favour of lancets, 3 new ones being added to the 3 already existing. A heating system was introduced in 1905 and in 1912 the church was again restored.[57] Since 1856 at least the church has been equipped with a west gallery and has been ceiled.[58]

The font is of the 12th or 13th century. The achievement of Royal Arms dates from 1801–16.[59] The altar was given by Bishop Wordsworth in 1868. The Jacobean pulpit, fitted with a new stem and base, was brought from an unknown East Anglian church in the early 20th century. The pews, inserted in 1912, replace deal pews dating from the 1833 rebuilding, which in turn replaced box pews.[60] Of these earlier pews vestiges remain. The screen was provided in 1914, apparently by Athelstan Riley.[61] The chief monument[62] within the church, formerly on the north-east buttress,[63] commemorates, in a florid inscription, two infant children of Thomas Crockford, vicar 1613–34. There are several monuments to members of the Davis family.

A chalice (11 oz.) was left for the use of the church by the commissioners of 1553, and 2½ oz. silver taken for the king. There is also a chalice, dated

1631, a paten and flagon given in 1842 by John Davis (d. 1860), and an almsdish given by him in 1851.[64] There were 3 bells in 1553. Of the present 5, 2 were cast by James Burrough, of Devizes, in 1745, and 3, cast by C & G. Mears, of London, were given by John Davis (d. 1860) in 1844.[65] The registers of baptisms date from 1561, of marriages from 1566, and of burials from 1567. The baptisms are complete. Marriages are wanting between 1708 and 1744 and burials between 1638 and 1677.

NONCONFORMITY. The tithingmen declared in 1621 that the parish was free of every kind of recusancy.[66] Seven persons failed to attend church in 1662 and 2 in 1674.[67] They may not have been professed dissenters; one of them in the former year refused to pay the church rate. In 1676 there were said to be 3 Protestant dissenters and no papists.[68] William Fowels's house was registered, for Independent worship, in 1799,[69] and James Titford's house in Bapton, for worship by an unspecified congregation, in 1813.[70] There is no other evidence of nonconformity.

SCHOOLS. In 1808 there was no school,[71] but in 1840 about 40 very young children were receiving some form of schooling. It was said then that as soon as they were old enough they were sent to work in the fields.[72] In c. 1858 between 30 and 40 children and 15 infants were taught by a mistress in two rooms in a cottage lent by 'the squire'.[73] Presumably it was not long after this that the present building, which abuts a house standing to the west of the church, was erected. By 1871, when the building was settled in trust,[74] grants towards the school had been made by the state and the National Society.[75] At this time there was also a private school in the parish.[76] In 1919 average attendance at the church school was only 18,[77] and in 1922 it was closed.[78]

CHARITIES. In 1449–50 6s. 8d.[79] and in 1466–7 3s. 4d.[80] were paid by the farmer of Fisherton parsonage to the poor. Since, on the second occasion, this was said to be done ex antiqua consuetudine, the payments may be said to bear some resemblance to an endowed charity. It was reported at a manor court held in 1705 that the inhabitants, largely at their own cost, had erected seven houses within the manor for the use of the poor. The homage declared it to be its wish that these houses should be permanently consecrated to that use.[81] Otherwise no charities are known.

50 Sar. Dioc. R.O. Ep. Vis.
51 Banks, op. cit.
52 Ibid.
53 Hoare, Mod. Wilts. Heytesbury, 257.
54 Inscription on tower.
55 Hoare, op. cit. 257.
56 W.R.O. 628, Faculty and Building Accts.
57 Wilts. Times, 23 Nov. 1912 (Wilts. Cuttings, xiii. 273).
58 Soc. Antiq. Jackson MSS. vol. vii.
59 W.A.M. xlviii. 108.
60 Banks, Fisherton Delamere Church.
61 Ibid.; Wilts. Times, 23 Nov. 1921.
62 For M. Is. see Soc. Antiq. Jackson MSS. vol. vii, and, for those in the chyd., W.A.S. M.Is. viii.
63 B.M. Add. MS. 36391, f. 125; Hoare, Mod. Wilts. Heytesbury, 257.
64 Nightingale, Wilts. Plate, 70.
65 Walters, Wilts. Bells, 87.
66 Hist. MSS. Com. Var. Coll. i. 93.
67 Sar. Dioc. R.O. Chwdns'. Pres. 1662, 1674.
68 W.N.&Q. iii. 537.
69 G.R.O. Retns. of Regns.
70 W.R.O. Certs. of Dissenters' Meeting Houses.
71 Lambeth Palace Libr. MS. 1732.
72 Digest of Returns to Cttee. of Educ. of Poor, H.C. 224 (1819), ix (2).
73 Acct. of Wilts. Schools, H.C. 27 (1859 Sess. 1), xxi (2).
74 W.R.O. 628, Draft of Trust Deed.
75 Return Relating to Elem. Educ. H.C. 201 (1871), lv; Nat. Soc. files.
76 Acct. of Wilts. Schools (1859).
77 Bd. of Educ. List 21, 1919.
78 Ibid. 1922.
79 S.C.6/1054/11.
80 S.C. 6/1054/14.
81 Dors. R.O. D45.

NORTON BAVANT

Until the 19th century Norton Bavant parish was in three pieces.[1] The main part of the parish, which forms the present civil parish, lies north of the Wylye between Bishopstrow and Heytesbury. The smaller of the detached parts consisted of about 115 a. straddling the road from Warminster to Crockerton, south of Warminster Common and some two miles from Norton village, while the larger, about 246 a. on the Somerset border between Corsley and Longleat Park, lay six miles from Norton. This more distant part probably included the considerable amount of woodland belonging to the manor in 1086;[2] the smaller part probably also belonged to Norton then, as it certainly did by the mid-13th century.[3] The larger detached part was transferred to Corsley civil parish and the smaller to Warminster in 1884.[4] At the same time a small piece of Pit Mead which belonged to Norton was added to Sutton Veny.[5] This reduced the acreage of the parish to 1,856.[6]

In the main part of the parish a greensand level runs from the Wylye to a steep scarp of chalk north of the Salisbury road. The scarp runs across the parish from Middle Hill on the Bishopstrow boundary by Scratchbury to Cotley Hill on the Heytesbury boundary. Scratchbury and Cotley Hill are both over 600 ft. high. On the former is a univallate hill-fort, and on the latter a circular enclosure with an inner ditch. Beyond these heights the ground drops again to a broad valley of greensand, watered by a streamlet which runs into the Wylye at Heytesbury. North of this again are the high downs of the higher chalk of Salisbury Plain. There are many barrows in the parish, and Bronze age and Roman remains have been found.[7] The detached parts of the parish contain both greensand and clay. The village lies low beside the Wylye, secluded both from the Warminster-Salisbury road and from a minor road which leaves it for Sutton Veny. Norton Bavant House, with the vicarage and the church within its park, stands at the north-west end of the village. About 1775 the farm yard of the manor farm stood between the house and the churchyard, but the farmer occupied the house now called South Farm. This is an 18th-century house of 5 bays, of stone with tiled roof. The extensive range of thatched outbuildings adjoining it occupies what was c. 1775 the void site of a house. They were no doubt built when the park was enlarged so that the church was within it, and the old farm buildings cleared away. This was presumably done at inclosure. The rest of the houses are small and informally scattered about several roads and lanes. Middleton Farm lies north of the Salisbury road near the boundary with Bishopstrow, and North

Farm is over the first ridge of hills north-east of Scratchbury. Butler's Coombe Farm lies in the former part of the parish south of Warminster, while in the other former detached part are Mad Doctor's Farm and a few cottages. A small village lay at Middleton in the Middle Ages. In 1377 there were 18 poll-tax payers there.[8] Twelve small closes where houses had stood were empty by 1538, and only two houses remained beside the farmhouse.[9]

There were 94 poll-tax payers in the parish in 1377.[10] In 1676 there were apparently 196 adults there.[11] Nothing more is known of its population until 1801, when it was 264. Between then and 1881 it varies intermittently between 250 and 290. The boundary changes of 1884 resulted in a loss of some 36 people and took place in a decade of considerable decline, due no doubt to agricultural changes. In 1891 there were only 163 people in the parish compared with 264 ten years before. Since then it has declined further to 128 in 1951.[12] Agriculture has always been the chief occupation of the inhabitants, although there was some clothing activity associated with the water mills on the Wylye between the 15th and 18th centuries.[13] In the 1860's Mr. Thomas Foreman's bathing and general pleasure grounds at Henford's Marsh were a summer attraction for the townsfolk of Warminster, and a brass band attended on Wednesday evenings.[14]

Cobbett had a high opinion of Norton Bavant and Bishopstrow. He was especially impressed by Middleton Farm when he passed this way in 1826, noting the fine trees surrounding the farm yard, which had 22 ricks in it, the turnpike road running through the arable land with great flocks on the downs on one side, and cattle 'up to their eyes in grass in the meadows' on the other. The air, he said, must be of the best in the world, and the country 'singularly bright and beautiful'.[15]

MANORS. Alfred of Marlborough held *NORTON* in 1086.[16] Like most of his Wiltshire fief it formed part of the honor of Ewyas in the 13th century, the overlordship descending in the same way as that of Upton Scudamore.[17] Unlike Upton no undertenant was mentioned at Norton in 1086; it was probably among the Wiltshire fees of the honor held by the Scudamores in the 12th century, but its certain connexion with the family has not been established before 1216, when it had been forfeited by Peter Scudamore.[18] It descended in the same way as Upton[19] to another Peter Scudamore who died in 1293 leaving as heir to most of his Wiltshire estates except Upton, a daughter Alice, wife of Adam Bavant.[20] She was a widow then or soon after-

[1] The following maps were used: O.S. Maps 1/25,000, ST 84, 94 (Provisional edn.); 6″ Wilts. LII (1st and later edns.); W.R.O. Inclosure and Tithe Awards.
[2] *V.C.H. Wilts.* ii, p. 142.
[3] See p. 50.
[4] See p. 90.
[5] *Bounds of Wilts.* 16.
[6] *Census*, 1881, 1891.
[7] *V.C.H. Wilts.* i(1), 93, 142, 185, 210, 257, 268, 277.
[8] Ibid. iv. 311.
[9] Eton College MSS. Survey 1538.
[10] *V.C.H. Wilts.* iv. 311.

[11] *W.N. & Q.* iii. 537.
[12] *V.C.H. Wilts.* iv. 354.
[13] See p. 54.
[14] *Warminster Miscellany*, June 1862.
[15] *Rural Rides*, ed. G. D. H. Cole, ii. 389–90.
[16] *V.C.H. Wilts.* ii, p. 142.   [17] See p. 80.
[18] *Rot. Litt. Claus.* (Rec. Com.), i. 285.
[19] See p. 81.
[20] *Wilts Inq. p.m.* 1242–1326 (Index Libr.), 194; *Coll. Top. et Gen.* vii. 152; for a small estate retained by the Scudamores in Norton, see Hist. MSS. Com. *Hastings*, i. 223, 245.

wards, and her son Roger was still a minor in 1306.[21] He had been succeeded by his son, another Roger, by 1338. [22] Six years later the younger Roger granted almost all his estates in Wiltshire and elsewhere to the king.[23] The reason for his doing this is not fully clear, but there are indications that he was estranged from his wife Hawise. Certain feoffees successfully reclaimed the Wiltshire lands in 1344 because Roger had previously granted them an estate for the life of Hawise, to pay her and her children an allowance.[24] Roger died in 1355.[25] After his death Hawise alleged that in fact the property was entailed upon her and her issue, but the claim was apparently backed by a deed sealed with a forged seal which Roger had disclaimed before he died, and on her son and heir John leaving for Italy to become a Franciscan friar, she withdrew it.[26]

In 1358 the king granted Norton to William Thorpe and William Peek for their lives, and they ensured an annuity to Hawise; after their deaths it was to go to the Dominican nuns of Dartford in Kent.[27] Thorpe was connected with that house[28] and probably acting for it, for the nuns immediately began to exercise their rights at Norton.[29] Hawise finally surrendered all her right in 1361.[30] The last claimants to the Bavant inheritance were Joan, daughter of Roger and Hawise, and Sir John Dauntsey, her husband, who finally relinquished their right in 1373 in return for a grant of the manor of Marden.[31] From then on the nuns of Dartford held Norton Bavant unmolested until the Dissolution.

When Norton passed to the Crown, the lease of the manor farm was held by the Benett family, which had been prosperous in the village since the late 14th century. John Benett claimed to hold land there in 1390.[32] Another John, a clothier, died in 1461,[33] and a third John, also a clothier, flourished in the late 15th century.[34] He had apparently been succeeded by a son John in 1509.[35] Thomas Benett is mentioned in the family pedigree[36] as father of John, presumably the one who died c. 1543,[37] but in 1519 the nuns of Dartford let the farm to a William Benett.[38] This or another William obtained a renewal of the lease in 1544.[39] He died c.

1566,[40] and was succeeded by another William, who left the farm to his second son William at his death c. 1574.[41] The lease was renewed again on lives in 1583.[42] Seven years later William Benett bought in a 50-year lease in reversion of his own which had been granted to Sir Henry Woodrington.[43] Finally in 1609 the whole manor except certain leaseholds was granted in fee to George Salter and John Williams.[44] Two years later, sixteen tenants of the manor joined together to buy the freehold of their holdings. Of the purchase price of £1,842 10s., £1,069 was paid by William Benett, and it was agreed that he should hold the manorial rights with the farm.[45]

From that time Norton remained in the Benett family until the 19th century. William died in 1618.[46] His son Thomas died in 1653, and left Norton to his wife and then to the issue of his second marriage.[47] The eldest son John died without surviving issue in 1706; his brother William married Patience Bishop, heir to the Benetts of Pythouse in Tisbury. Their son Thomas bought back Pythouse, which had been sold in 1669, in 1725, and from that time the family was chiefly seated there. Thomas died in 1754 and was succeeded by his grandson William, who died without issue in 1781 and left all his estates to his widow.[48] This provoked a lawsuit in chancery which led to the manor being put up for sale in 1788.[49] It was bought by Catherine Benett, spinster daughter of Thomas (d. 1754).[50] At her death it passed back to her nephew John, son of Thomas Benett (d. 1797), to whom Pythouse had been left by will. He died in 1852 having outlived both his sons, and the estate passed to his grandson, John Edward Benett, who died unmarried in 1856.[51] The next heir was another grandson, Vere, son of John Benett's eldest daughter Lucy Harriet by the Revd. Arthur Fane. He assumed the surname of Benett, and, on his marriage to the daughter and heir of William Stanford, that of Stanford in addition. At his death in 1894 he was succeeded by his son, John Montagu Fane-Benett-Stanford,[52] who died in 1947 having outlived both his children.[53] Most of the Norton Bavant property north of the railway had been sold to the War Office in 1930,[54] and the

---

[21] *Rot. Parl.* i. 202; *Cal. Pat.* 1292–1301, 561.
[22] Wrottesley, *Pedigrees from the Plea Rolls*, 37.
[23] *Cat. Anct. D.* v. A 11962; *Cal. Close*, 1343–6, 451.
[24] *Cal. Close*, 1343–6, 456; *Wilts. Inq. p.m.* 1327–77 (Index Libr.), 166; *Cal. Pat.* 1343–5, 440, 543; 1345–8, 125; *Cal. Close*, 1346–9, 92.
[25] *Cal. Inq. p.m.* x, p. 314.
[26] *Cal. Close*, 1369–74, 421–2; the reference to a son Roger in *Wilts. Inq. p.m.* 1327–77, 196, is probably an error.
[27] *Cal. Pat.* 1358–61, 126, 187.
[28] *V.C.H. Kent*, ii. 181, where an account of the house will be found.
[29] *Cal. Pat.* 1358–61, 245.
[30] *Cal. Close*, 1360–4, 383.
[31] K.B. 27/421 rot. 137d.; *Cal. Close*, 1369–74, 518; *Cal. Pat.* 1370–4, 370.
[32] *Cal. Close*, 1389–92, 241.
[33] M.I. in church.
[34] *Cal. Close*, 1485–1500, 172; S.C. 6/Hen. VIII/1757 mm. 28d–29.
[35] *L. & P. Hen. VIII*, i(1), p. 224.
[36] *Genealogist*, N.S. xi. 249–50.
[37] P.C.C. 26 Spert.
[38] S.C. 6/Hen. VIII/1757 m. 29.

[39] *L. & P. Hen. VIII*, xx(1), p. 684; W.R.O. 413, Copy of Letters Patent.
[40] P.C.C. *Admons.* 1559–71, ed. Glencross, 66; cf. W.R.O. 413, where there is a will dated 1558.
[41] *W.N. & Q.* vi. 184.
[42] W.R.O. 413, Letters Patent.
[43] C 66/1342 m.1; W.R.O. 413, Assignment Woodrington to Benett.
[44] C 66/1822 m. 19.
[45] W.R.O. 413, Deed of Sale, Salter and Williams to Benett and Turner, and Arts. of Agreement between tenants, 1611.   [46] C142/375/142.
[47] W.R.O. 413, Will of Thos. Benett.
[48] Hoare, *Mod. Wilts.* Warminster, ped. opp. p. 78.
[49] *Salisbury and Winchester Jnl.* 24 March 1788; *Lond. Gaz.* 1788, p. 125.
[50] W.R.O. 413, Deed Parry and others to Benett, 25 March 1789.
[51] Ibid. Papers in Chancery suit, Benett v. Wyndham and others; cf. Burke, *Land. Gent.* (1937), which does not mention J. E. Benett.
[52] Burke, *Land. Gent.* (1937).
[53] *W.A.M.* lii. 132–3.
[54] W.A.S. Libr. Devizes, TS. History of Norton Bavant by J. M. Benett-Stanford.

remainder was sold after 1947. The house was bought by Sir Kenneth Nicolson, who in 1963 still occupied it.[55]

In the early 17th century the house called the farmhouse of Norton Bavant was ruinous, but the farmers of the demesnes had long occupied another house which was in good order.[56] This was no doubt the house which in 1618 consisted, beside domestic offices and servants' quarters, of only a hall, a parlour, and four chambers.[57] In 1641 Thomas Benett made a contract with John Tommes of Andover, bricklayer, to build a house in a meadow called the West Garden adjoining the previous house. Its dimensions were to be 65 ft. by 24 ft., which agrees well with the present north range of the house, as far back as a massive wall which separates the rooms on that side from the rest. This building was, however, probably added to another which is represented by the present east wing, for this retains several internal features of the earlier 17th century.[58] In 1654, moreover, the house contained hall, parlour, dining chamber, domestic offices and ten chambers,[59] probably more than could be contained only in the house specified in the contract. About 1700 the house was completely remodelled. The 'decent gable ends' of 1641 were replaced by a hipped tiled roof with dormers to the attics, and a west wing was added to make the house U-shaped. The mullioned and transomed windows and the shell hood on carved brackets over the north door are of this date, as are many internal features. In the late 18th century the space between the two projecting wings was filled in; the flat lead roof of this addition is dated 1774. Behind the house are detached outbuildings, one of brick with stone dressings and one of flint and stone chequer-work. The former is probably the separate brewhouse mentioned in the contract of 1641.

After Pythouse was bought in 1725, Norton House was not favoured by the family because of its low and damp position.[60] For many years in the 19th century it was the home of Etheldred and Anna Maria, maiden sisters of John Benett, M. P. Etheldred was noted for her skill in geology. She supplied a catalogue of fossils for Hoare's *Modern Wiltshire*, and is said to have been given a doctorate in Civil Law by St. Petersburg in the mistaken idea that she was a man.[61] After the death of the last sister in 1858, the house was let to a succession of tenants.

Domno held an estate in *MIDDLETON* before the Conquest. By 1086 it had passed to Osbern Gifford, and was held of him by the church of St. Stephen of Fontenay in Normandy (dèp. Calvados).[62] In 1242–3 it was said that the Abbot of Fontenay held one hide there in free alms by gift of the ancestor of Elias Gifford,[63] and in 1274 the estate was said to be held by the abbot of John Gifford as part of the barony of Brimpsfield (Glos.).[64] In 1293 it was taken into the king's hands as a possession of an alien house.[65] When this happened again in 1325, it was reckoned as part of the lands of the priory of Brimpsfield, which was a cell to Fontenay.[66] It remained in the possession of Brimpsfield, with intervals of confiscation during French wars,[67] until the priory was finally seized in 1414.[68] In 1428 it was held at farm of the king.[69] In 1441 Brimpsfield and its possessions were given by Henry VI to his newly-founded college at Eton.[70] They were resumed by Edward IV in 1461,[71] but restored to the college in 1467.[72] In spite of this various pensions were paid out of the property to royal servants and the royal household for much of the remainder of the 15th century.[73]

Eton College had let the Middleton estate at farm to John Dew by 1491.[74] Richard Dew held it early in the 16th century, but by 1538 it was held by William Benett[75] who also farmed the manor of Norton Bavant. It was probably the same William who died *c.* 1566 and left it to his younger son John.[76] He died at about the same time,[77] and it passed to his son William.[78] It was renewed to his trustees in 1566. By *c.* 1600 Augustine Poore held the farm. It was renewed to Thomas Robins of Ilfracombe in 1605 and 1611, and to Adam Poore of Longstock (Hants) in 1624 and 1633. In 1641 it was let to Margaret, widow of the John Turner, who acquired the freehold part of Middleton.[79] Ten years later a new lease was made to John Toogood of Norton. In 1666 and 1672 leases were made to John Slade the younger of Norton.[80] Slade still evidently held the farm from Eton in 1697, when he confirmed an under-lease to Nathaniel Houlton in 1689.[81] Houlton left his interest to his daughter Mary Woolley in 1714.[82] In 1708 John Summers evidently occupied both freehold and leasehold parts of the farm; a Mr. Warren held them in 1714 and 1720,[83] but both must have been tenants to the lessees under the college. By 1733 a Mr. Bayly held both parts.[84] He died about 1747, and

[55] Ex. inf. Sir Anthony Rumbold and Sir Kenneth Nicolson.
[56] Longleat MS. 8829.
[57] W.R.O. 413, Inv. of Wm. Benett, 1618.
[58] Ibid. Contract, 1641.
[59] Ibid. Inv. of Thos. Benett, 1654.
[60] W.A.S. Libr. Devizes, TS. History of Norton Bavant by J. M. Benett-Stanford.
[61] Walters, *Wilts. Bells*, 95.
[62] *V.C.H. Wilts.* ii, p. 154.
[63] *Bk. of Fees*, 743.
[64] *Rot. Hund.* (Rec. Com.), ii. 276.
[65] B.M. Add. MS. 6164, f. 38.
[66] S.C. 6/1127/11.
[67] *Cal. Fine R.* 1369–77, 362; 1377–83, 22, 36.
[68] *V.C.H. Glos.* ii. 102–3, where St. Stephen of Fontenay in the diocese of Bayeux is mistakenly confused with St. Wandrille (Fontenelle) in Rouen diocese; *Gallia Christiana* (1874), xi. 155, 413.
[69] *Feud. Aids*, v. 274.

[70] Dugdale, *Mon.* vi. 1436; *Rot. Parl.* v. 81.
[71] *V.C.H. Bucks.* ii. 170.
[72] *Cal. Pat.* 1467–77, 63.
[73] Ibid. 1461–67, 435, 532; 1467–77, 266; 1485–94, 26; *Cal. Fine R.* 1461–71, 149; 1471–85, 27, 31, 75; *Cal. Close*, 1461–8, 345; 1476–85, 371; *Rot. Parl.* vi. 303, 304, 500.
[74] S.C. 6/Hen. VII/1473.
[75] Eton College MSS. Survey. Thanks are due to Mr. H. N. Blakiston for guidance and access to the College MSS.
[76] W.R.O. 413, Will dated 1558; see above, p. 48, n. 40
[77] P.C.C. *Admons.* 1559–71, ed. Glencross, 67.
[78] C 3/179/57; C 2/Eliz. I/85/30.
[79] Eton College MSS. Deeds; see below.
[80] Eton College MSS. Deeds.
[81] C. P. 25 (2)/889/9 Wm. III Mich.
[82] *W.N. & Q.* vi. 167.
[83] W.R.O. 413, Ch. Rates, 1708, 1710, 1714, 1720.
[84] Ibid. Land Tax Assessment, 1733.

was succeeded by his nephew William Bayly, a War-minster maltster, to whom leases were made in 1755 and 1770. He was succeeded by his widow Mary and then by his son James. James died c. 1836 and left the whole farm both freehold and leasehold to his grandson James Buckler Osborne Bayly, who held the farm until the 1860's.[85] The Eton College estate was sold to V. F. Benett-Stanford c. 1887,[86] and added to his Norton Bavant manor estate.

In 1086 Edward of Salisbury held 3 virgates of land in *MIDDLETON* which before the Conquest had belonged to Lewin and Alric.[87] A holding there under the Earls of Salisbury is regularly mentioned until the 15th century.[88] In 1242–3 it had been subinfeudated twice, to John de Strode, and under him to Edward of Middleton.[89] Edward was a juror for Warminster hundred in 1274,[90] and witness to a Bishopstrow deed,[91] which indicates that this is the Middleton where the fee held under Salisbury lay. Nothing more is heard of the tenants of this holding until the 15th century, when in 1467 John Barly and Margaret his wife, daughter and heir of John Bronker, conveyed the manor of Middleton to Sir Roger Tocotes.[92] Like the rest of Tocotes's property it was forfeited in 1484[93] but restored by Henry VII. In 1508 a chief rent of 2s. 2½d. for lands late of Robert Tocotes in Middleton was paid to the manor of Warminster;[94] this was for land in Sambourne which belonged to the manor.[95] In 1535 Sir Roger Tocotes sold it with much other Wiltshire property to William Stump.[96] Not long after this it had passed to the Button family of Alton Barnes. William Button was a free tenant of the manor of Norton Bavant for a cottage and certain pasture rights c. 1550[97] and certainly held Middleton by 1572.[98] It descended in his family to Sir William Button, the first baronet,[99] who sold it to John Turner of Norton before 1633. Turner died in that year leaving a son and heir John,[1] who died in 1645.[2] The descent of the property is not known from that time until Nathaniel Houlton held it in 1692.[3] From that time it descended in the same way as the leasehold interest under Eton College,[4] and was probably acquired by the Benett-Stanfords in the late 19th century.

In 1609 it was supposed that the Eton College estate and the other part of Middleton should be equal in all respects, although then the Eton estate was slightly smaller and had less pasture rights and no buildings.[5] In 1769 they were believed to have been formerly one estate, and no one living knew what belonged to one and what to the other because they had been occupied together for so long.[6] The house and buildings at Middleton were built by J. B. O. Bayly c. 1857.[7]

LESSER ESTATES. In 1252 William le Fevere of Norton acknowledged that he held a free tenement and land in 'Rodhurst' and Norton of Godfrey Scudamore by rent and ward of the castle of Ewyas Harold.[8] His holding was that called in later times Butler's Coombe, formerly in the detached part of Norton near Warminster Common and now in Warminster. It takes its name from a family which had probably succeeded le Fevere before the end of the 13th century. Robert le Boteler, living in 1270,[9] was perhaps the father of John le Boteler who flourished between 1279 and 1300,[10] and was dead by 1319.[11] Edward le Boteler and Christine his wife were mentioned in the following year,[12] and in 1337 were described as of 'Rodhurst'.[13] In 1346 they let all their estate to their son John on condition that he should maintain them.[14] John left a son John who had apparently succeeded by 1375,[15] and was pardoned for a murder in 1393.[16] He left a sister and heir Maud Hartshorn, who in 1408 sold her brother's property to Sir Walter Hungerford. It lay in 'Rodhurst', and consisted chiefly of 64 a. of arable land and 300 a. of pasture.[17] John's wife Helen was still living in 1421, when the demesne lands of the holding were let to John King.[18] In 1451 the estate was let to William Middleton at a nominal rent.[19] By 1464 it was held by John Mervyn of Fonthill Gifford, who seems to have married a Hungerford, and soon afterwards the freehold of the property was granted to him.[20] It may then more certainly be identified with Butler's Coombe, for it was said to lie in Norton Bavant and near Crockerton.

Nothing more is known of the farm until the 17th century. Anthony Long was one of the most prosperous men in the parish in 1648,[21] and probably held the farm then, as he or a successor of the

[85] Eton College MSS. Deeds and Letters; W.R.O. 132, Will of Jas. Bayly 1836.
[86] Eton College MSS. Various papers; W.A.S. Libr. Devizes, TS. History of Norton Bavant by J. M. Benett-Stanford.
[87] *V.C.H. Wilts.* ii, p. 137.
[88] e.g. *Bk. of Fees*, 719; *Cal. Close*, 1405–9, 458.
[89] *Bk. of Fees*, 719.
[90] *Rot. Hund.* (Rec. Com.), ii. 239.
[91] B.M. Add. Ch. 26703.
[92] C.P. 25(1)/257/65/12; the property was still remembered as Bronker's lands c. 1500: Eton College MSS. Copy Survey c. 1500.
[93] *Cal. Pat.* 1476–85, 501.
[94] Longleat MSS. Parcel XXVII, Rental 1508.
[95] Eton College MSS. Survey of Middleton Brimpsfield, 1609.
[96] W.R.O. 88, Deed Tocotes to Stump, 1535.
[97] W.R.O. 413, Free Rental temp. Edw. VI.
[98] *W.N. & Q.* vii. 212.
[99] *Wilts. Visitation Pedigrees*, 1623 (Harl. Soc. cv-vi), 33–4; *Complete Baronetage*, i. 193.
[1] *Wilts. Inq. p.m.* 1625–49 (Index Libr.), 179–80.
[2] Hoare, *Mod. Wilts.* Warminster, 80.
[3] W.R.O. 413, Church Rate, 1692.   [4] See above.

[5] Eton College MSS. Survey 1609.
[6] Ibid. Letter from Wm. Bayly 1769.
[7] Ibid. correspondence from J. B. O. Bayly.
[8] C.P. 25(1)/251/17/20.
[9] Longleat MS. 9078.
[10] Ibid. 9090; B.M. Add. Ch. 26696; *Cal. Close*, 1288–96, 112; *Wilts. Inq. p.m.* 1242–1326 (Index Libr.), 250.
[11] Longleat MS. 9129.
[12] Ibid. 9131.
[13] Ibid. 9143.
[14] Ibid. 9153.
[15] Ibid. 9172–3.
[16] *Cal. Pat.* 1391–3, 303.
[17] C.P. 25(1)/256/59/16.
[18] S.C. 6/1061/23.
[19] S.C. 6/1061/24.
[20] S.C. 6/1061/25; *Cal. Close*, 1461–8, 272; 1468–76, 59; Hoare, *Mod. Wilts.* Dunworth, ped. opp. p. 20. Cf. Sir W. R. Drake, *Fasciculus Mervinensis*, 7.
[21] *W.A.M.* xxxvii. 367; W.R.O. 413, Church Rate 1651; Robert and Henry Long of 'Botlars' are mentioned in the will of Thos. Long of Trowbridge, dated 1555 (P.C.C. 12 Chayre), but no Longs were taxed in the parish in 1545 or 1576.

same name certainly did by 1683. At his death about two years later it passed to his son, another Anthony, who in turn left it to his son Robert in 1712. It was probably another Robert who died without issue *c.* 1785, leaving the farm to trustees to be sold. It was bought by John Gawen of Westbury, who died *c.* 1801, and in 1803 his trustees sold it to Lord Bath.[22] About 1820 the part of the farm east of the Crockerton road, which included the house, was conveyed to the Astleys of Boreham and remained in their possession until their estate was sold in 1884.[23]

The sale of the manorial lands to the tenants in 1611 made Norton a parish of many freeholds, most of which were eventually absorbed into the Benett estate. The largest of them consisted principally of a house called the Church House lying at the Cross in Norton, and 4 virgates of land. At the Dissolution this was held from the nuns of Dartford by Thomas Moore under a lease for 50 years granted in 1538.[24] It passed at his death to his son William.[25] A new Crown lease was made in 1582, which was assigned to Moore in the same year. In 1599 he assigned it to John Turner, who in the previous year had acquired a 40-year reversion.[26] At the sale of the manorial lands Turner bought both this and several other small holdings.[27] Before his death in 1633 he also acquired a virgate called Matthews's which Thomas Matthews bought in 1611.[28] Like Middleton Farm these lands descended to his son John who died in 1645.[29] After this their history is somewhat obscure; they did not descend in the same way as Middleton, but are almost certainly to be identified with the freehold estate held by John Marven by 1678.[30] By 1708 Thomas Benett had added it to his estate.[31]

Dartford Wood, the detached part of Norton Bavant near Corsley, was probably part of the manor in 1086,[32] and remained so until the Dissolution. In 1549 it was granted to William, Lord Grey of Wilton, in fee-farm.[33] He sold it to Sir John Thynne in the following year,[34] and it has remained part of the Longleat estate until the present day. After the Benetts obtained the manor, they asserted a claim to the land, but were unsuccessful in several lawsuits between 1637 and 1672.[35]

ECONOMIC HISTORY. The topography of the main part of the parish of Norton Bavant makes the lay-out of its pre-inclosure farming clear. Meadow-land lay along the bank of the Wylye, while open field arable lay both on the greensand levels south of the chalk scarp joining Scratchbury Hill to Cotley Hill and in the trough of greensand between those hills and the high chalk of Salisbury Plain in the north of the parish. The chalk hills provided pasture land. The parish remained in open fields until 1809, and the history of its agriculture before then is largely of the change from demesne farming to leasing, and then the gradual consolidation of the smaller customary holdings with the farm.

In 1086 there were eight ploughs in the manor, of which two were on the demesne and six were held by 12 villeins and 8 bordars. It is not known why the value of the manor had fallen from £24 to £14 since 1066.[36] No more is known until the manor was extended in 1362, when the demesne consisted of 400 a. of arable land, 10 a. of several meadow, and another 20 a. of meadow, which was several only while the grass grew and was cut, and lay common for the rest of the year. There were then 24 bond tenants.[37] It is quite likely that the nuns of Dartford never farmed the demesne. The practice of letting the demesne must certainly have been of long standing when it is first met with in the early 16th century. Thomas Dew and John Dew are mentioned as former farmers in the series of leases to the Benett family from 1519.[38]

The first detailed picture of the agriculture of the manor is provided by a survey of 1604.[39] Although a number of free tenants paid rents, they were chiefly from former Bavant property in Tisbury and elsewhere, and apart from Middleton, which was manorially and agriculturally separate and is dealt with below, almost the whole of the main part of the parish was leasehold and copyhold land of the manor.[40] Thirteen copyholders held lands which were reckoned at 7 virgates and 11 small lands, as the half-virgates were called in this manor. Ten of them held either a single virgate or a small land, while the other three held totals of 1½, 2, and 2½ virgates respectively. In addition five tenants held by lease; one of them only held a small land, but two others held 2 virgates each and a third held the tenement called the Church House and 4 virgates. The fifth leasehold comprised the demesnes and 3 virgates and a small land. Thus by 1604 18 virgates and 13 small lands were divided between 18 tenants, of whom 7 held more than a single virgate. These holdings consisted almost entirely of open field arable land; the copyholds contained 261¼ a. of arable out of a total of 278½ a., and on the leaseholds, apart from the Benett holding, the proportion was 234¾ a. out of 247¼. The Benett leasehold contained 250 a. of arable land. The land lay in Home Field, evidently south of Scratchbury and Cotley Hill, and North Field, beyond them. More detailed accounts of land in strips show that the Home Field was divided into East and West Fields.[41]

[22] Longleat MSS. Title Deeds of Butler's Coombe.
[23] W.R.O. Land Tax Assessments and Tithe Award; Bishopstrow Parish Records, Eastleigh Estate Sale Catalogue, 1884.
[24] C 3/120/68; C 3/129/58.
[25] Req. 2/98/23.
[26] W.R.O. 413, Survey of Manor, 1604.
[27] Ibid. Agreement, Benett and Turner and other tens., 1611.
[28] Ibid.; ibid. Survey of Manor, 1604; *Wilts. Inq. p.m.* 1625–49 (Index Libr.), 179–80.
[29] See p. 50.
[30] Sar. Dioc. R.O. Glebe Terriers, 1609, 1678; W.R.O. 413, Church Rate, 1692.

[31] W.R.O. 413, Church Rate 1708; Marven was still living in 1709: Eton College MSS. Survey, 1709.
[32] See p. 47.   [33] *Cal. Pat.* 1549–51, 70.
[34] W.R.O. 413, Papers in Benett *v.* Thynne.
[35] Ibid.; C3/396/30; L.R. 2/301, f. 223f; Longleat MS. 7345.
[36] *V.C.H. Wilts.* ii, p. 142.
[37] *Wilts. Inq. p.m.* 1327–77 (Index Libr.), 319–22.
[38] See p. 48.
[39] W.R.O. 413, Survey of Manor, 1604.
[40] The biggest exceptions were probably the vicarial and rectorial glebe.
[41] e.g. Hoare, *Mod. Wilts.* Warminster, 81–2; *Wilts. Inq. p.m.* 1625–49 (Index Libr.), 179–80.

Common meadows called Longham, Heathfield, Elsham, and Drowsen belonged to the demesne farm but the tenants probably had some hay from them beside the winter common which the survey mentioned. Two small several meadows also belonged to the farm, and most tenants had small closes near their houses. The downs provided common pasture for sheep, cows, and oxen. The stint of sheep for a small land varied between 9 and 16, and for a virgate was 40, making a tenant flock of about 700. These had pasture in the tenants' downs on Scratchbury and Cotley Hill and in the fields. The farm flock of 600 sheep had pasture in a several down of 120 a. and also winter pasture in the Cow Down and on Cotley Hill. It is likely that the winter pasture was shared with the tenant flock. The stint of other beasts for a small land was two or three and for a virgate four; the farm had 40, making a possible herd of about 130 head, which had pasture on the Cow Down in summer and in the fields and meadows in winter.

About this time it was reckoned that 518 a. of arable land were sown yearly; since, including Middleton, there must have been over 1,000 a. of field land in the parish, it is clear that a two-year course was followed. This land was said to produce from 280 to 350 quarters of wheat and about 400 quarters of barley, beside peas and vetches.[42]

Apart from mentioning two new closes at 'the Gore', the 1604 survey shows no sign of agricultural change. The vicarial glebe lay in many small pieces in 1609, but the abuttals, mentioning the 9 acres and the 40 acres of the farm land, show that the farm lands had been at least partly consolidated.[43] The Benetts were letting the farm at rack rent by 1611; it then included a several ground of 8 a. called New Leaze near the vicarage which had formerly been arable land. The sheep pasture was excluded from the lease, and the tenant was allowed the fold of his landlord's flock.[44] This practice of the landlord keeping the sheep himself was still followed in 1675; a lease for 4 years made then was in the form of an agreement for the tenants to sow the arable land 'thirds and tenths'. Since they agreed to carry the thirds and tenths into the landlord's barns, this was evidently a rent in kind, in which the lessee paid $\frac{1}{3}$ of the produce beside the tithes.[45] By 1680 there were water meadows in Norton, and a reference to sowing the hookland no doubt means that some part of the fallow field was being cultivated.[46]

The sale of the manorial lands to the tenants in 1611 opened the way for the accumulation of the small freeholds created then into larger farms. It is likely that some smaller tenants had difficulty in raising the money, and quickly mortgaged their lands. In 1611 John Turner bought the freehold of his leasehold Church House and 4 virgates and also

of a small land held by Ambrose Malyn in 1604.[47] Before his death in 1633 he had added to the holding another small land, and a virgate formerly held by the Matthews family.[48] The Benetts must have added to their estate in the same way; probably the acquisition from William Dew in 1703 of holdings in Norton which had once belonged to Richard Flower and John Whatley was by no means the first addition.[49] At about the same time they acquired the large estate formerly of John Turner called Marven's.[50] By 1733 Middleton Farm was the only estate of any size in the parish which did not belong to the Benetts.[51] At least some of the additions were probably let with the farm. In 1788 it contained 717 a., and the other leaseholds under the Benetts were insignificant by comparison.[52] In 1797 about 70 a. acquired from James Bayly in return for the great tithes of Middleton were added to the estate.[53]

A map of c. 1775 reveals the course of change since the early 17th century. The arable land still lay in two great stretches north and south of the scarp of the downs. Each of these was divided into three fields, East, Middle, and West near the village and Castle, Middle, and South beyond the scarp. Careful provision was made for the route of the village herd to and from the Cow Down, presumably so that it could keep to fallow land. This route followed a four-year cycle, so that the fields must have been in a four-year course. The strips of the farm land had been consolidated into larger pieces, generally between 5 a. and 30 a., but little of this had been done on other holdings. The Cow Down, of 196 a., provided pasture for as many black cattle as each holding could winter; adjoining it was the Farm Down solely for the farm flock, while Scratchbury, Cotley Hill, and the downs between them provided 230 a. of pasture for flocks belonging to other holdings. Common meadows stretched along the Wylye on either side of the Sutton Veny road.[54]

Little further change was made before the Inclosure Act of 1805.[55] One large inclosure in the North Field was ignored by the commissioners, presumably because it was still commonable.[56] In 1801 212 a. each were sown with wheat and barley and 163 a. with oats. There were small acreages of potatoes, peas, beans, turnips, and rye[57]. At the inclosure occupiers were ordered to allow new allottees to sow in $1\frac{1}{2}$ bushel of grass seeds to the acre in the North Field, and $\frac{1}{2}$ bushel grass seed and 10 lbs. of clover in the Home Field.[58] Allotments were made to Benett in respect of the farm (595 a.), Marven's (200 a.), the tenantry lands (380 a.) and the rectorial glebe (83 a.). Only the vicar (39 a.) and one other freeholder (27 a.) were allotted any significant amount of land beside Benett.[59] Although the separate allotment for the

---

42 Longleat MS. 8830.　　43 Hoare, op. cit. 81–2.
44 W.R.O. 413, Lease Benett to Chambers, 1611.
45 Ibid. Lease Benett to Knight, 1675; the practice of leasing land in this way is mentioned in Longleat MS. 8830, c. 1590–1600.
46 W.R.O. 413, Letter Long to Benett, 1680.
47 Ibid. Survey of Manor, 1604, and Agreement Benett and Turner and tenants, 1611.
48 Wilts. Inq. p.m. 1625–49 (Index Libr.), 179–80.
49 W.R.O. 130, Deeds Dew to Benett, 1703; earlier deeds relating to both properties are in W.R.O. 413. Whatley and Flower were the grantees in 1611.

50 See p. 51.
51 W.R.O. 413, Land Tax Assessment, 1733.
52 Ibid. Sale Particular, 1788.
53 Ibid. Deed of Exchange Benett and Bayly, 1797. They had been acquired from the families of Edwards and Chambers, both among the grantees in 1611.
54 Map penes Sir Kenneth Nicolson.
55 45 Geo. III, c. 74 (Priv. Act).
56 W.R.O. 135, Draft Inclosure Map.
57 H.O. 67/23.
58 W.R.O. 256, Minutes of Inclosure Commissioners.
59 W.R.O. Inclosure Award.

tenantry was made, it seems that most of it was already in hand and let with the remainder of the estate as one or two farms.[60] North Farm was built by 1805, [61] although it had not existed in 1773.[62] The two farms were held together by J. M. Sidford from c. 1827.[63] In 1842 he only held North Farm, and South Farm was held by William Hayward.[64] Soon after that time William Melsome, a member of a well-known farming family, took both farms, comprising some 1,200 a. held at a rent of about £1,800.[65] He went bankrupt in the depression of the 1870's,[66] and was succeeded by Robert Coles who farmed much of Boreham, Bishopstrow, Middleton, and Norton.[67] A successful sheep-breeder, Coles was the last of the old sheep and corn farmers at Norton, for at his death Stratton and Co. took North Farm for part of their great dairying business.[68]

The small estates at Middleton contained together land for three ploughs in 1086, with small amounts of meadow, pasture, and wood, and one villein, two bordars, and a serf.[69] Middleton Brimpsfield had a demesne of 100 a. of arable land and 3 a. of meadow in 1294, and free and villein tenants paid 40s.[70] By 1538 all the villein tenements except two had been allowed to decay, and rents amounting to 66s. 8d. which had formerly been paid to Eton College were in default. The lands belonging to them were evidently let with the farm, and in the earliest surviving lease, of 1566, that sum was added to the rent of 26s. 8d. which had been charged in 1491.[71] A survey of c. 1500 mentions fields called North Middles, Brook Furlong, Burn Furlong, and Ash Furlong.[72] In 1609 arable land lay in Brook Furlong in South or Home Field, a field adjoining it, North Field, and Henchcombe. It amounted to 118 a., while 124 a. belonged to Sir William Button's farm; by this time these were the only two properties in Middleton.[73] From the late 17th century at least, one farmer occupied both farms, and it became difficult to tell what belonged to each owner.[74]

In 1770 the arable land belonging to the farm was conventionally divided into North Field, between the farm house and the down, and South Field, from the house down to the Wylye. This land was in four-year course, the fourth being a summer fallow. About 200 a. of field-land had had some 20 or 30 a. of downland broken up and added to it. About 40 a. more downland had been broken up some years previously but had by then gone back to grass, although it was still very coarse. The down supported a flock of some 250 sheep during the summer months. The farm was badly lacking in meadow land; it only had some 7 a. in the common meadows of Norton, all subject to winter common rights, and farmers had to rent other land to make enough hay.[75] Since the farm was all one tenancy and not subject to common rights, it was not included in the parish inclosure. More downland, of little value for sheep pasture, was broken up to grow turnips in 1853.[76]

The two detached parts of the parish differ from the main part in physical characteristics, which has much affected their agricultural history. Butler's Coombe lies at the edge of broken country, largely common until the 18th century and later part of Longleat Park. In 1252 a good deal of the estate was evidently 'the heath called Rod-hurst',[77] and in 1408 it was conventionally described as 64 a. of arable land and 300 a. of pasture,[78] which was no doubt heathland. In the 18th century the farm consisted of 8 closes of land around the house, amounting to about 50 a. and probably used chiefly as meadow and pasture. About 1760 Robert Long, the owner of the property, inclosed 106 a. of heath land into four closes and cleared them for pasture;[79] they no doubt lay on the rising ground to the west of the Crockerton road. After the division of the estate in the early 19th century,[80] this western part remained part of the Longleat estate. The larger part of it was in 1842 called Heath Farm, farmed from the house now called Bore Hill Farm.[81] The old farmlands and the house which passed to the Astleys were let with lands in Bishopstrow, Warminster, and Sutton Veny amounting to well over 100 a.[82]

The woodland ½ league long and 4 furlongs broad, which belonged to Norton manor in 1086, probably covered the detached part of the parish adjoining Corsley.[83] In this part lay in 1362 the hamlet of Emwell where there were 10 a. of pasture and 60 a. of wood, the latter lying common.[84] The pasture and a grove called Emwell Coppice were let at farm at the Dissolution.[85] A piece of land at the north-west corner of the wood had been newly inclosed in 1549 while the rest of the tract consisted of Emwell Coppice and Dartford Wood.[86] A newly-built cottage in the south-west corner near Timbers Hill was let in 1588.[87] In the early 17th century the main part of Dartford Wood contained 170 a. well planted with trees, in which the tenants of Norton Bavant had common for their cattle; inclosures made from it comprised the 18 a. of Emwell Coppice 'anciently inclosed', 12 a. called Newleaze, no doubt the inclosure of c. 1549, and 8 a. 'of late times'.[88] In the mid-17th century much timber was cut down in the wood, and a survey of

[60] Ibid. Land Tax Assessments.
[61] Ibid. Inclosure Award.
[62] *Andrews and Dury, Map* (W.A.S. Rec. Brch.), pl. 7.
[63] W.R.O. Land Tax Assessments.
[64] Ibid. Tithe Award.
[65] W.R.O. 413, Rentals 1852–70; *W.A.M.* xlv. 338.
[66] W.A.S. Libr. Devizes, TS. History of Norton Bavant by J. M. Benett-Stanford.
[67] Ibid.; *W.A.M.* xlv. 339.
[68] *W.A.M.* xlv. 340.
[69] *V.C.H. Wilts.* ii, pp. 137–8, 155.
[70] B.M. Add. MS. 6164, f. 38.
[71] Eton College MSS. Survey, 1538, and Deeds; S.C. 6/Hen. VII/1473.
[72] Eton College MSS. Copy Survey, c. 1500.
[73] Ibid. Survey, 1538.

[74] Ibid. Survey, 1709 and Correspondence.
[75] Ibid. Survey and Map, 1770.
[76] Ibid. Correspondence.
[77] C.P. 25(1)/251/17/20.
[78] C.P. 25(1)/256/59/16.
[79] Longleat MSS. Title Deeds of Butler's Coombe.
[80] See p. 51.
[81] W.R.O. Tithe Award.
[82] W.R.O. 160a Astley Settlement, 1849; Bishopstrow Parish Records, Eastleigh Estate Sale Catalogue, 1884.
[83] *V.C.H. Wilts.* ii, p. 142.
[84] *Wilts. Inq. p.m.* 1327–77 (Index Libr.), 319–22.
[85] S.C. 6/Hen. VIII/1757 m. 28d.
[86] *Cal. Pat.* 1549–51, 70.
[87] Longleat MS. 7343.
[88] W.R.O. 413, Custom of Manor of Norton Bavant.

1651 shows that land was being cleared for agriculture. Much of the western fringe of the wood consisted of closes of pasture and arable land with several cottages, while Emwell Coppice in the northeast and Tubb's Coppice in the south-west had been partly cut and sold by Sir James Thynne. The uninclosed part was then reckoned at 178 a., partly wood and partly a rabbit warren which had been mostly destroyed in the Civil War. The tenants of Norton made little use of their common rights because they lived too far away.[89] In the late 17th century Tubb's Coppice was let to be ploughed, the rent being respited while the tenants cleared the ground.[90] The wood was probably reduced to its present size in the 18th century. Mad Doctor's Farm stood at the north end in 1773.[91]In 1841 Dartford Wood and Ragland Coppice together contained 64 a. The remainder of the district consisted of the 89-acre Mad Doctor's Farm and several smaller holdings, all mixed arable and pasture land.[92] Almost all the district is now grazing land for dairy cattle, although the areas of woodland still remain.

The cloth trade in Norton is chiefly associated with the water mills on the Wylye.[93] Both mills in the main part of the parish were used as fulling mills in the 16th century. Among clothiers who occupied them may be mentioned some early members of the Benett family,[94] Geoffrey Hawkins, who moved to Bishopstrow later in the 16th century,[95] and the Everetts of Heytesbury in the late 18th and early 19th centuries.[96] Robert Long, described as a clothier in 1753,[97] is probably to be identified with the owner of Butler's Coombe Farm. Weavers who lived in the village in the 17th and 18th centuries[98] must have worked either for the local clothiers or for masters in Warminster. A dyehouse adjoining Longbridge Fulling Mill was let in 1751.[99]

A field south of Mad Doctor's Farm adjoining Redford Water was called Brick Kiln Piece in 1842,[1] and the place where the earth was excavated can still be seen, but it is not known when it was worked. Stone quarries were worked in the late 18th century on the top of the downs north-east of the point where the Salisbury road now crosses the railway. A platform of chalk projecting at the top of the scarp and a channel extending from it down to the foot of the hill can still be seen. They were used for letting stone down, presumably by means of a winch.[2]

MILLS. There were two mills at Norton in 1086.[3] A water mill belonged to the demesne of the manor in 1362;[4] it was probably the same mill which was let as a fulling mill to John Benett in 1486,[5] and was held with the demesne farm in the 16th century.[6] It passed with the farm to the Benett family, and descended with the manor until the 19th century. It was described both as a fulling mill and a corn mill in 1573, when it was held by a Bratton fuller,[7] but in 1625 it was described specifically as 'the grist mill'.[8] In 1788 it had recently been rebuilt and was used only as a corn mill, let at a rack rent of £42.[9] It continued in use as a corn mill until early in the present century.[10] The building is in 1963 used as a store house; it still contains its undershot wheel and much of its machinery.

Another fulling and corn mill in Norton was let by the Priory of Dartford in 1533 to Richard Bath alias Whitaker for 80 years.[11] The lease was assigned to John Benett, younger son of William (d. c. 1558), in 1560.[12] John's widow and her second husband underlet the mill to Geoffrey Hawkins of Norton, who 'planted himself there in the art of clothing'.[13] John's son William was able to buy in a reversion of the lease which was granted by the Crown in 1594, and he still held the mill in the early 17th century.[14] In 1609 the mill and a fishery in the river near it were granted to Edward Ferrers and Francis Philips at fee farm.[15] In 1611 William Benett of Norton made an agreement with William Benett of London that the latter should procure him a grant of the same mill,[16] and it is possible that it passed to him soon afterwards, although it is not certainly known to have belonged to the Benetts before the early 18th century.[17] In 1625 it was called Thresher's Mill from its occupier, Anthony Thresher.[18] In 1788 it was held on lives by Joseph Everett,[19] and it was still occupied by the Everett family in 1830.[20] It stood just above the bridge which carries the Sutton Veny road over the Wylye, where remains of the pond can still be seen.

A fee farm rent of 70s. 10d., the same as had been reserved on the lease of the mill in 1533, was charged by the Crown on it in 1609.[21] It subsequently passed into private hands; it belonged to William Levinz and his wife Anne in 1711.[22] In 1715 they conveyed it to Thomas Bennet of Salthrop in Wroughton.[23] Elizabeth Bennet, probably his widow, made the rent part of the endowment for the charity she founded at Broad Hinton and

[89] L.R. 2/301, f. 223.
[90] Longleat MS. 10652.
[91] Andrews and Dury, Map (W.A.S. Rec. Brch.), pl. 7.
[92] W.R.O. Tithe Award.
[93] See below.
[94] See p. 48.
[95] Sess. Mins. 1563–92 (W.A.S. Rec. Brch.), 61, 62; see above, p. 10.
[96] Univ. Brit. Dir. (1798), iii. 262; Pigot, Nat. Com. Dir. (1830).
[97] Wilts. Apprentices (W.A.S. Rec. Brch.), p. 169.
[98] Sar. Dioc. R.O. Chwdns'. Pres. 1662; Wilts. Apprentices (W.A.S. Rec. Brch.), pp. 39, 103.
[99] W.R.O. 413, Abstract of leases.
[1] W.R.O. Tithe Award.
[2] Map penes Sir Kenneth Nicolson.
[3] V.C.H. Wilts. ii, p. 142.
[4] Wilts. Inq. p.m. 1327–77 (Index Libr.), 319–22.
[5] S.C. 6/Hen. VIII/1757 m. 28d.
[6] See p. 48.
[7] W.R.O. 413, Bond Benett to Whatley.

[8] Longleat MSS. Parcel XXI, Hundred presentment, 1625.
[9] W.R.O. 413, Sale Particular, 1788.
[10] Warminster Miscellany, 25 March and 13 June, 1868; Kelly's Dir. Wilts. (1911).
[11] S.C. 6/Hen. VIII/1757 m. 29.
[12] W.R.O. 413, Survey of Manor, 1604.
[13] C 2/Eliz. I/B. 5/30.
[14] W.R.O. 413, Survey of Manor, 1604.
[15] C 66/1821 m. 1.
[16] W.R.O. 413, Agreement 6 Feb. 1611.
[17] C.P. 43/547 rot. 95.
[18] Longleat MSS. Parcel XXI, Hundred presentment, 1625.
[19] W.R.O. 413, Sale Particular, 1788.
[20] C.P. 43/990 rot. 5.
[21] C 66/1821 m. 1.
[22] C.P. 25(2)/980/10 Anne Trin.; probably Wm. Levinz, M. P. for Nottingham 1710–14: N. & Q. 2nd ser. iii. 515.
[23] C.P. 25(2)/1077/1 Geo. I Trin.; W.R.O. 413, Accounts Benett and Bennet, 1722–32.

it was still paid to the trustees of that charity in the early 20th century.[24]

A mill at Henford's Marsh in the detached part of Norton Bavant south of Warminster is first heard of in 1332, when Robert Swoting assured it to Thomas of Helmesford and Joan his wife.[25] It subsequently passed to the Hungerford family; in 1421 the fulling mill called 'Wysshele' was let to Henry Tucker,[26] and in 1441 a chief rent of 2s. was paid to John Whissheley for 'Helmesffordesmull'.[27] By 1465 the 2s. rent belonged to Richard Page.[28] The mill seems to have passed from the possession of the Hungerfords by the mid-16th century.[29] Cecily Blake paid a chief rent of 22s. 6d. to the manor of Norton Bavant c. 1550 for closes near Henford's Marsh called Mill Mead and Westleyes (no doubt named from John Whissheley), and may well have occupied the mill itself.[30] John Blake paid the same rent in 1604.[31] Soon after this the mill belonged to Tristram Watts, who c. 1623 sold it to Francis Shergold.[32] In 1637 Shergold let the mill, which had been in ruins for many years to Joshua Abath, who rebuilt it and enlarged the watercourse to it.[33] It was used as a grist mill in 1678.[34] Edward Shergold owned the mill in 1691.[35] In 1733 John Gibbs paid the land tax for Shergold's mill,[36] and in 1773 it was owned by a Mrs. Halliday. It passed to the Astleys of Boreham c. 1796[37] and remained part of their estate until it was broken up in 1884. It was then described as having been recently erected, and had five floors and modern machinery.[38] It remained in use until the early years of the present century,[39] and was pulled down just before the Second World War.[40]

CHURCH. There was no doubt a church at Norton Bavant in the mid-12th century, when Edward the priest of Norton was twice mentioned.[41] Part of a Norman font which was found re-used in the tower in 1894 also points to the existence of a church at that time.[42] The advowson was annexed to the lordship of the manor until the Dissolution;[43] it was reserved by the Crown when the rectory was granted away, and was exercised by the sovereign or the Lord Chancellor until 1955, when it was transferred to the Bishop of

Salisbury.[44] Since 1956 the living has been held in plurality with Sutton Veny, where the vicar lives.[45]

The church was valued at £13 6s. 8d. in 1291.[46] In 1373 the nuns of Dartford were licensed to appropriate the rectory.[47] At the Dissolution it was held on lease by Thomas Lovell of Stretton (Herts.) for 40 years at a rent of £12 16s.; it had previously been held by John Dew.[48] Further leases were made to Ralph Smethers in 1563,[49] John Middlecott in 1576,[50] Robert Whitwood in 1585,[51] and George Lazenby in 1593.[52] In the late 16th century the tithes were underlet at £50 a year.[53] In 1607 the rectory was granted in fee to Richard Roberts and George Tyte;[54] they subsequently sold it to Francis Phillips and Richard Moore, who surrendered it and obtained a new Crown grant in 1612.[55] Phillips and Moore sold it in the same year to James Spark of Horningsham,[56] who already held the leasehold interest in the rectory granted to Lazenby.[57] In 1614 Christopher Spark, son and heir of James, sold the rectory to Richard Pearce of Elm (Som.),[58] who bought a moiety for himself and a moiety on behalf of Simon Sloper of Warminster.[59] The rectory descended in moieties in the Pearce and Sloper families until 1681 when John Pearce of Elm and others conveyed their share to William Benett, lord of the manor.[60] Benett bought the remainder from Simon Sloper of Bath in the following year,[61] and from that time it descended in the same way as the manor.

Not all the great tithes of the parish belonged to the rectory. In 1842 Dartford Wood and all other lands in the detached part of Norton Bavant near Corsley were exempt from all tithes, while the other detached part south of Warminster paid all tithes, both great and small, to the vicar.[62] This arrangement, which was in force by 1609,[63] may date from the first endowment of the vicarage. The vicar also claimed tithes of hay throughout the rest of the parish except from the demesne farm in 1609; in 1842 he owned the tithe of hay from 46 a., presumably all the meadow-land in the parish,[64] which was perhaps also part of his original endowment. The tithes of the demesne farm were a cause of much controversy in the 17th century. Sixteenth-century leases of it to the Benett family included

[24] Endowed Char. Wilts. (1908), pp. 557, 559.
[25] C.P. 25(1)/254/42/15.
[26] S.C. 6/1061/23.
[27] S.C. 6/1061/11.
[28] Tropenell Cart. ed. Davies, ii. 67.
[29] S.C. 6/Hen. VIII/3918.
[30] W.R.O. 413, Copy of Free Rental, Edw. VI.
[31] Ibid. Survey of Manor, 1604.
[32] C 2/Chas. I/S. 109/51.
[33] C 6/154/113; W.R.O. 413, Lease Benett to Abath, 1637.
[34] Sar. Dioc. R.O. Glebe Terrier, 1678.
[35] C.P. 43/431 rot. 58.
[36] W.R.O. 413, Land Tax Assessment, 1733
[37] W.R.O. Land Tax Assessments.
[38] Ibid.; W.R.O. 160a, Settlements 1849 and 1873; Bishopstrow Parish Records, Eastleigh Estate Sale Catalogue.
[39] Kelly's Dir. Wilts. (1903).
[40] Ex inf. the owner of Henford's Marsh Farm (1962).
[41] Reg. St. Osmund (Rolls Ser.), i. 340, 349.
[42] W.N. & Q. i. 475.
[43] Phillipps, Wilts. Inst. passim.
[44] Ibid.; Crockford; Sar. Dioc. Regy. Patronage Reg.
[45] Ex. inf. Revd. D. V. Evening.
[46] Tax. Eccl. (Rec. Com.), 181.

[47] Cal. Pat. 1370–74, 327; Cal. Pap. Let. iv. 517.
[48] S.C. 6/Hen. VIII/1757; E 321/4/14.
[49] Cal. Pat. 1560–3, 493; it is unlikely that this grant took effect; it included the lease of the Church House which Smethers never enjoyed: see above, p. 51.
[50] C 66/1156.
[51] C 66/1285 m. 12; Req. 2/89/52.
[52] C 66/1404; Lazenby subsequently assigned his interest, which was still reversionary: W.R.O. 413, Watson to Reason, 1593; ibid. Pleadings in Sloper and Pearce v. Benett; C 2/Jas.I/S.14/22.
[53] Longleat MS. 8830.
[54] C 66/1719 no. 2.
[55] W.R.O. 413, Pleadings in Sloper and Pearce v. Benett; C 66/1900 no. 8.   [56] C 54/2112 no. 13.
[57] Moulton's 1930 Catalogue, 243.
[58] W.R.O 413, Pleadings in Sloper and Pearce v. Benett.
[59] W.R.O. 130, Agreements Sloper and Pearce, 1618, 1619, 1626; Moulton's 1930 Catalogue, 244.
[60] W.R.O. 413, Deed Pearce to Benett; the Pearces seem to have claimed some right in the rectory as late as 1720: C.P. 25(2)/1088/6. Gco. I East.
[61] W.R.O. 413, Deed Sloper to Benett.
[62] W.R.O. Tithe Award.
[63] Hoare, Mod. Wilts. Warminster, 81–2.
[64] Ibid.; W.R.O. Tithe Award.

all tithes arising from it, but the owners of the rectory alleged that this leasehold interest was not conveyed with the freehold of the farm. They were unable to make their claim good in several trials between 1674 and 1679.[65] In 1797 Thomas Benett conveyed the great tithes of Middleton Farm to James Bayly, the owner and lessee, in return for some lands in Norton.[66] By the time of the commutation of tithes the Benetts were evidently letting most of their property free of all tithes which belonged to them, and the award confirmed this arrangement. John Benett was awarded £12 for the great tithes of a small freehold belonging to James Knight, and £13 for some from his own lands. J.B.O. Bayly was awarded £60 for the tithe of corn and most of the tithe of hay of Middleton Farm.[67]

Nothing is known of any glebe land which belonged to the rectory before the 16th century. When it was let to Thomas Lovell in 1538 it included, beside the tithes, a tenement and 48 a. of land which had been held by John Dew, the previous lessee, and 6 a. of land called Marvens.[68] These lands were regularly mentioned as appurtenant to the rectory from then on,[69] and, whatever their origin, were generally described as glebe. In the late 16th century they were reckoned at 66 a., let at £23 a year.[70] At the inclosure of the parish in 1809 John Benett was awarded 38 a. of arable land and 45 a. of down for the rectory.[71] From the later 18th century the glebe was generally let with the farm.[72] The house belonging to the rectory and two barns were burnt down in the late 16th century, and the house had not been rebuilt some years later.[73] It was perhaps never replaced, for c. 1775 the parsonage yard contained only a barn. It stood south-east of the church on the side of the present road from the park gates to the main road.[74]

The vicarage was valued at £6 0s. 8d. in 1535.[75] It was discharged from the payment of first fruits on the foundation of Queen Anne's Bounty; its value then was reckoned at £40 a year, but later in the century was said to be £50 or £60.[76] In 1783 the living was worth £63 or £64 a year.[77] The net income was £150 in 1835.[78] Three years later the living was endowed with £200 by Queen Anne's Bounty to meet benefactions of £200 by Edward Eliot, the vicar, and another £200 by trustees.[79] This and the commutation of the tithes raised the income to £228 by 1851.[80]

In 1609 the vicar claimed all tithes of the part of Norton near Warminster, and the small tithes and tithe of hay of all lands in the main part of the parish except the farm and certain new leazes taken out of the fields.[81] He collected his tithes in kind in 1770.[82] At the commutation the vicar was awarded £89 for tithes of hay, £44 for all tithes of the lands near Warminster, £15 for all the tithes of his own glebe, and £5 for the small tithes of the rectorial glebe.[83] In 1609 the vicar reckoned his glebe at 32 a.[84] and the terrier of 1783 records a similar amount.[85] At the inclosure the vicar was allotted 39 a. of field land in addition to the garden and pasture near the house.[86] It was let for £85 in 1851[87] and for £96 in 1887.[88] J. M. Benett-Stanford bought the vicarial glebe in 1934 and added it to his estate.[89]

Little is known of any of the medieval vicars of Norton. Roger Lovell, instituted in 1531, survived the changes of religion into Mary's reign; it was said in 1556 that he had two benefices, but he was able to produce permission for this. The church was then without the necessary ornaments.[90] Nothing is known of any ejection in Elizabeth I's reign or during the Interregnum. John Berjew, vicar from 1638, was approved as a preacher by the Long Parliament in 1642,[91] and held Norton until 1662, when he was succeeded by his son of the same name.[92] William Wroughton, vicar 1736–49, was a pluralist, holding Norton as a second benefice to Westbury.[93] Thomas Fisher, 1765–94, held the living of Bishopstrow, where he resided, and performed one service on Sundays at Norton. The sacrament was administered four times a year to 7 or 8 people.[94] His successor, George Smith, held the perpetual curacy of Hill Deverill from 1798.[95] In 1851 the average congregation at morning and afternoon services was about 60, and there was a Sunday School of 30 children.[96]

There was a chantry at the altar of St. Thomas the Martyr in the church in the mid-14th century; it belonged to the manor, but nothing is known of it after the lordship passed to the nuns of Dartford.[97] A chapel dedicated to St. Stephen stood in the buildings belonging to the Priory of Brimpsfield at Middleton. The oblations belonged to the Vicar of Norton. In 1443 the small thatched building was partly ruinous, and no more is known of it.[98]

The church of *ALL SAINTS'*, a dedication

[65] W.R.O. 413, Pleadings in Sloper and Pearce v. Benett; *W.N. & Q.* i. 540.
[66] W.R.O. 413, Deed of exchange, Benett and Bayly.
[67] W.R.O. Tithe Award.
[68] S.C. 6/Hen. VIII/1757; E 321/4/14.
[69] e.g. W.R.O. 413, Deed Stockman and Good to Spark, 1612.
[70] Longleat MS. 8830.
[71] W.R.O. Inclosure Award.
[72] Ibid. Land Tax Assessments and Tithe Award.
[73] Longleat MS. 8829.
[74] Map of Norton Bavant *penes* Sir K. Nicolson.
[75] *Valor Eccl.* (Rec. Com.), ii. 103.
[76] Ecton, *Thesaurus*, various edns.
[77] Sar. Dioc. R.O. Visitation Queries, 1783.
[78] *Rep. Com. Eccl. Revenues*, H.C. 54, pp. 842–3 (1835), xxii.
[79] Hodgson, *Queen Anne's Bounty*, pp. ccxxiv, ccxxxvi.
[80] H.O. 129/10/260.
[81] Hoare, *Mod. Wilts.* Warminster, 81–2.
[82] Eton College MSS. Survey and Map, 1770.

[83] W.R.O. Tithe Award.
[84] Hoare, *Mod. Wilts.* Warminster, 81–2; apparently statute acres, for the no. of field acres is over 40.
[85] Sar. Dioc. R.O. Glebe Terrier, 1783.
[86] W.R.O. Inclosure Award.
[87] H.O. 129/10/260.
[88] *Retn. of Glebe*, H.C. 307, p. 166 (1887), lxiv.
[89] W.A.S. Libr. Devizes, TS. History of Norton Bavant by J. M. Benett-Stanford.
[90] Sar. Dioc. R.O. Ep. Vis. 1556.
[91] Shaw, *Hist. Eng. Ch.* 1640–60, ii. 302.
[92] Foster, *Alumn. Oxon.* 1st ser. i. 112; cf. *W.A.M.* xxxiv. 175, where father and son are confused.
[93] Venn, *Alumn. Cantab.* 1st ser. iv. 480.
[94] Sar. Dioc. R.O. Vis. Queries, 1783.
[95] *Rep. Com. Eccl. Revenues* (1835), pp. 842–3; Hoare, *Mod. Wilts.* Heytesbury, 273.
[96] H.O. 129/10/260.
[97] *Cal. Pat.* 1358–61, 129; 1364–7, 1; *Wilts. Inq. p.m.* 1327–77 (Index Libr.), 319–22.
[98] Eton College MSS. Surveys, 1443, 1538.

mentioned in 1364,[99] stands now just inside the park gates of Norton Bavant house. It consists of a nave and chancel, south chapel off the middle of the nave, north porch and vestry, and western tower; of these only the tower and the arch into the chapel date from before 1838–40, when the rest of the church was rebuilt by William Walker of Shaftesbury.[1] The old church was on the same plan as the present, which was, however, 'somewhat enlarged'.[2] The arch into the chapel is of the 14th century,[3] and there can be little doubt that the chapel itself housed the chantry mentioned above. A piscina survived in it until the rebuilding.[4] The two lower stages of the tower are also of the 14th century; the upper of them has a moulded fireplace, the flue of which was blocked when a third stage was rebuilt or added *c.* 1500. The whole is surmounted by a moulded string course, with angle gargoyles and a battlemented parapet. At the north-east angle of the tower is a stair turret projecting to the north. It is carried well above the top stage of the tower, and has its own string course and battlements, crowned with a small stone spire.[5] The remainder of the church is of ashlar from Tisbury, in a vaguely Perpendicular style. It was built between 1838 and 1840, partly by church rates but mainly by subscription; John Benett, the lay rector, provided for the chancel and the chapel, while his sisters gave largely toward the remainder.[6] It was restored at the cost of John Torrance in 1868, while his widow restored the tower in 1894.[7]

The most noteworthy internal feature is the pair of 17th-century wrought-iron gates at the entrance to the chapel. In the chapel are many monuments of the Benett family from 1653 to the present century. Brasses of male and female figures with kneeling children below occupy an indented stone in which only the two upper shields survived at the beginning of the 19th century. One of the shields bears a merchant's mark and the initials W.B., and the other two pairs of shears.[8] In spite of this the present brass has an inscription to John Benett (d. 1461); this was mentioned by Hoare, who is not clear about the state of the brass in his day.[9] The font in use dates from the rebuilding of the church. Part of a Norman one was found re-used upside down as the lowest of the tower steps in 1894.[10]

There were three bells at Norton in 1553. One of them still remains, inscribed 'Sancte Tome Ora Pro Nobis'; it is thought to have been cast at Bristol in the late 14th century, and forms the third of the present peal of five. The first was added to the

peal in 1894; the second is a re-casting of that date of a bell formerly dated 1656; the fourth is by Edward Lott, the Warminster founder, dated 1711, and the fifth is of 1656.[11] A tradition that the bells were taken to Norton from Bishopstrow seems to be unfounded,[12] at least for the bells dated 1656 and 1711, for each bears the name of a churchwarden who certainly lived in Norton.[13] There were four bells in the church by 1783.[14]

In 1553 Edward VI's Commissioners left a 9-oz. chalice at Norton and took 2 oz. of silver away. The plate in 1783 included a chalice dated 1576, but this has been replaced by one given by Anna Maria Benett in 1849. There are also three patens and a flagon, all given by members of the Benett family in the 18th century. A bowl, hall-marked 1696, and given by Etheldred Benett for use as an alms-dish in 1824, was originally made for letting blood.[15] The organ is by W. Sweetland of Bath, dated 1876.

In 1783 the vicarage was part brick and part stone covered with thatch, and contained a parlour, a kitchen, and two good and two smaller chambers.[16]

NONCONFORMITY. There were six sectaries in Norton Bavant in 1662.[17] Three Anabaptists and a Quaker were presented in 1674 with three others who did not attend church,[18] and two years later there were eight who refused to conform.[19] Houses were registered for worship by Independents in 1788, 1811, and 1832,[20] probably as stations of the New Meeting at Warminster, but no permanent congregation has ever been established in the village.[21]

SCHOOL. In 1808 the employment of children in agriculture prevented a full time school, but in the winter evenings they were instructed in reading and the catechism.[22] In 1818 it was reported that the poorer children of the parish were generally taught to read, and that those unable to pay were instructed at the expense of certain individuals.[23] There was a school in 1833 for between 20 and 30 children supported partly by subscriptions and partly by payments from parents.[24] In 1843 grants were made by the state and the National Society towards converting a building as a school for about 40 pupils.[25] A cottage was conveyed as an endowment for the school in 1857,[26] and in *c.* 1858 the school was said to have an endowment of £400.[27] In 1871 it provided accommodation for 38 children; of the 24 who attended only 5 were boys.[28] Average

[99] *Cal. Pat.* 1364–7, 1.
[1] Pevsner, *Wilts.* (Buildings of England), 323.
[2] Hoare, *Mod. Wilts.* Warminster, 79, and Addenda, 58.
[3] C. E. Ponting, 'Notes on the Churches in the Neighbourhood of Warminster', *W.A.M.* xxvii. 266–8.
[4] Hoare *Mod. Wilts.* Warminster, 79.
[5] *W.A.M.* xxvii, 266–8.
[6] Hoare, *Mod. Wilts.* Addenda, 58.
[7] *Kelly's Dir. Wilts.* (1903).
[8] *W.A.M.* xxxix. 400–1.
[9] Hoare, *Mod. Wilts.* Warminster, 79.
[10] *W.N. & Q.* i. 475.
[11] Walters, *Wilts. Bells,* 147–8; *W.A.M.* xxvii. 267–8.
[12] *W.A.M.* xxvii. 268.
[13] e.g. 1656 bell, Walter Chambers: *W.A.M.* xxxvi. 367; 1711 bell, Geo. Knight: W.R.O. 413, Land Tax Assessment 1708. A Geo. Knight also appears on the 1656 bell, and the surname regularly occurs in the village in the 17th century.

[14] Sar. Dioc. R.O. Glebe Terrier, 1783.
[15] Nightingale, *Wilts. Plate,* 94–5; Sar. Dioc. R.O. Glebe Terrier, 1783.
[16] Sar. Dioc. R.O. Glebe Terrier, 1783.
[17] Sar. Dioc. R.O. Chwdns.' Pres. 1662.
[18] Ibid. 1674.
[19] *W.N. & Q.* iii. 537.
[20] G.R.O. Retns. of Regns.
[21] W.R.O. Retns. of Nonconformist Meetings, 1829; H.O. 129/10/260.
[22] Lambeth Palace Libr. MS. 1732.
[23] *Digest of Returns to Cttee. of Educ. of Poor,* H.C. 224 (1819), ix (2).
[24] *Educ. Enq. Abstract,* H.C. 62 (1835), xliii.
[25] Nat. Soc. files.
[26] *Return of Non-Provided Schools,* H.C. 178 (1906), lxxxviii.
[27] *Acct. of Wilts. Schools,* H.C. 27 (1859 Sess. 1), xxi (2).
[28] *Return relating to Elem. Educ.* H.C. 201 (1871), lv.

attendance in 1919 was 27,[29] and in 1921 the school was closed.[30]

CHARITIES. Catherine Mompesson at an unknown date left £20, the interest of which was to provide the poor with linen for shirts and shifts. The management of the charity was taken over by the Benett family in the mid-18th century. In 1841 Etheldred and Anna Maria Benett added £20 to

the principal sum. By his will dated 1811 John Knight left £50 to provide payments for poor widows and orphans. George Smith, Rector of Norton from 1794, left £20 to provide blankets to be given away at Christmas to the deserving poor. Etheldred and Anna Maria Benett added £20 to it in 1841.[31] The income from all these three charities, which amounted in 1952–5 to £2 11s. a year, is distributed to needy people in the parish.[32]

PERTWOOD

The ancient parish of Pertwood lay on the summit of the downs about 3½ miles north from East Knoyle and the same distance south from Sutton Veny.[1] It comprised 450 a.[2] and since the 16th century consisted of a single farm. The parish was made up of two separate, roughly triangular shaped pieces of land, the apex of the northern, and smaller, triangle pointing towards, but not quite touching the apex of the southern, and larger, triangle.[3] Tracks running over the top of the downs formed the eastern and western boundaries of both parts of the parish.[4] The northern boundary of the northern part of the parish ran just north of Pertwood Wood, and the southern boundary of the southern part across Bockerly Hill just south of Upper Pertwood Bushes.[5] The church of St. Peter,[6] and Upper Pertwood Farm, comprising the farm house, called (in 1962) the Manor House, four or five farm cottages, and the farm buildings, form the only settlement within the area of the ancient parish. This fairly compact group of buildings lies in the southern portion of the former parish towards the top of the down and is approached by a drive from the main road. In 1885 all the southern portion of Pertwood was taken into the civil parish of East Knoyle and the whole of the northern portion into that of Sutton Veny.[7]

The entire ancient parish lay upon the Upper Chalk which in this region is capped with clay-with-flints.[8] In the northern part of the parish the land rises to about 700 ft., and in the southern part falls to about 550 ft. John Aubrey, writing towards the end of the 17th century, remarked that in spite of its high, and apparently bracing, situation, Pertwood was frequently enveloped in mist and was not a healthy place.[9] In 1962 there were two woods in the northern part of the former parish but many of the trees of Pertwood Wood (sometimes called Wylye Wood) had been cut. In both parts there were plantations of very large beech trees forming windbreaks. Such plantations stretched along the former northern and southern parish boundaries and another sheltered the church and farm from the west.

On Pertwood Down, to the west of the ancient

parish, there are numerous barrows and clear traces of Celtic field systems, but none of these lies within the area of the ancient parish. In 1962 the main road from Shaftesbury to Warminster in the extreme south-west corner was the only road within the former parish. But the point between the apexes of the two triangles of land comprising the former parish is the meeting place of a number of tracks running over the downs, and through this junction ran the Roman road from the Mendip lead mines in the west to Old Salisbury in the east. In 1962 a footpath led from the farm to Chicklade, the nearest village, about 2 miles away.

No evidence has been found to suggest that there was ever a much larger settlement at Pertwood. It was assessed at 28s. to the 15th of 1334 when 5 hamlets in the hundred of Warminster had lower assessments.[10] No poll-tax payers were returned for Pertwood in 1377,[11] and in 1428 it was among those places not assessed for taxation because they had fewer than 10 householders.[12] When the Census figures begin in 1801 there were 15 inhabitants and the largest number ever returned for the ancient parish was 38 in 1881.[13]

Pertwood Manor stands facing east about 100 yds. from the church. It presumably stands upon the site of an earlier house, which was the home of the Mervyns in the 16th century, and possibly of earlier lords of the manor. John Mervyn in his will, proved in 1601, bequeathed to his brother, Philip, the right to live at Pertwood for life 'if he will take it, and orderly and quietly behave himself in the same'.[14] The present (1962) house dates from the 18th century but has been altered in the 19th and 20th centuries, so that what was a quite modest farmhouse has become a more sophisticated residence. It is a stone house of two stories with attic. The east, and main, front of 3 bays has 4-pane sash windows with drip moulds, and a half-glazed double door in the centre.

MANOR. The manor of *PERTWOOD* was held before the Conquest by Wlward, but by the time of the Domesday Survey it had passed to Geoffrey de Mowbray, Bishop of Coutances.[15] Like Wing-

[29] *Bd. of Educ. List* 21, 1919.
[30] Ibid. 1922.
[31] *Endowed Char. Wilts.* (1908), pp. 355–6.
[32] Char. Com. Accts. File G. 31; ex. inf. Revd. D. V. Evening.
[1] O.S. Maps 1/25,000, 31/83, 31/93; 6″ Wilts. lvii and lviii (1st and later edns.); 1/2,500 Wilts. lvii and lviii.
[2] *Census*, 1881.
[3] W.R.O. Tithe Map.
[4] O.S. Map 1/25,000, 31/83, 31/93. A map of 1773 marks these tracks clearly but draws the boundary of the ancient parish incorrectly: *Andrews and Dury Map*

1773 (W.A.S. Rec. Brch.), pl. 4.
[5] W.R.O. Tithe Map.
[6] See p. 60.
[7] *Kelly Dir. Wilts.* (1939), and see p. 61.
[8] Fry, *Land Utilization Wilts.* 162.
[9] John Aubrey, *Nat. Hist. Wilts.* (1847), 15.
[10] *V.C.H. Wilts.* iv. 302.
[11] Ibid. 311.
[12] Ibid. 314.
[13] Ibid. 355.
[14] P.C.C. 82 Woodhall.
[15] *V.C.H. Wilts.* ii, p. 122.

field, another estate of the bishop in 1086,[16] Pertwood passed to the Earls of Gloucester and an estate in Pertwood belonged to the honor of Gloucester until the beginning of the 15th century.[17]

The Pertwood estate of the Earls of Gloucester was held of them by the St. Quintins. It may have formed part of the fee in Wiltshire held of the honor of Gloucester by Herbert St. Quintin in 1210–12.[18] In 1242–3, 1299, and 1324 a John St. Quintin held ⅓ fee there of the honor.[19] After the last date no further trace has been found of the St. Quintin interest in the manor.

By the middle of the 13th century the Mortimers, later Earls of March, had also acquired an estate in Pertwood. In 1242–3 Richard of Pertwood (Pertewurth) held ⅕ fee there of Brian de Brampton, who held of Ralph de Mortimer, and Thomas de Caveresworth held ¼ fee there of the same Ralph.[20] The overlordship of the Earls of March lasted presumably until this honor was merged in the Crown upon the accession of Edward, Duke of York, as Edward IV in 1460. It was among the possessions of Edward's great-uncle, Edmund, Earl of March (d. 1425).[21]

In 1242–3 the estate in Pertwood held of the honor of Gloucester by the St. Quintins (see above) had been further subinfeudated and was held by Roger de Trowe and Robert Gentil.[22] At the same date Roger de Trowe also held 2 hides of James de Trowe who held them of Hugh de Vivon.[23] This 2-hide estate may also have been held of the honor of Gloucester, for in 1401 Roger de Trowe held a 2-hide estate there of that honor.[24]

Lack of evidence makes it impossible to trace satisfactorily the subsequent descent of these various holdings. In 1267 Alexander de Pertwood (Purchewort) and Agnes, his wife, conveyed a messuage and ½ virgate of land in Pertwood to Christine de Pertwood (Purcewort), who may have been the widow of the Richard de Pertwood of 1242–3 (see above).[25] Robert de Hoppegras and Alice, his wife, possibly descendants of the Pertwoods, conveyed a messuage, a carucate of land, and the advowson of the church of Pertwood in 1294 to Walter de Sutton.[26] Walter settled this estate in 1320 upon himself and his wife Joan and their issue with remainder to John Styward of Upton Scudamore.[27] In 1330 Richard, son of James de Trowe, conveyed his estate at Pertwood, part of which was then held by his sister, Joan, to William de Northo and Christine his wife with remainder

to William's son, another William, and Denise his wife.[28] Sir William Sutton appears to have been lord of the manor in 1333, for he presented to the living of Pertwood that year,[29] and in 1365–6 John Joye and Christine his wife, sold the manor, which they held in right of Christine, to John Amberlegh.[30] John presented to the rectory in 1376 and 1379.[31]

Even less is known of the descent of the manor during the 15th and earlier 16th centuries. If the manor descended with the advowson, as is probable, it was from 1400 until 1419 in the possession of John Britte, or Brut, of Hindon; in 1433 of William Elys, and in 1450 of John Elys.[32] Towards the end of the 15th century William Fletcher became possessed of the manor, apparently in right of his wife Joan, daughter of John Brother of Pertwood.[33] William died early in the 16th century, leaving as his heirs two daughters, Agnes, wife of John Maton, and Margaret, wife of John Ingram.[34] Margaret seems to have married, as a second husband, William Mervyn[35] and before 1539 her share of the manor had passed to her son John Mervyn.[36] The moiety belonging to Agnes Maton had by then passed to Robert Temmys and Joan his wife, who was probably Agnes's daughter.[37] This part of the manor subsequently passed to George Ludlow, who sold it in 1553 to John Mervyn who thus became possessed of the whole.[38] John Mervyn was succeeded by his son, also John, who died in 1601, when the manor passed to his son Thomas.[39] Thomas died without issue and Pertwood passed to his brother George.[40] It then descended in the Mervyn family until 1692 when John Mervyn, grandson of George, sold it to Sir James Howe.[41] Sir James died without issue in 1736 and left the estate to his nephew Henry Lee, commonly called Lee Warner.[42] On Lee Warner's death in 1804 the estate passed to his nephew James Woodward, who assumed the name of Lee Warner,[43] and sold Pertwood in 1805 to John Benett of Pythouse.[44] Benett sold it in 1810 to Richard Ricward of Longbridge Deverill.[45] Before 1838 it passed to Henry Seymour, and from Seymour's son, Alfred, it was bought in 1877 by the Hon. Percy Scawen Wyndham.[46] In 1919 Guy Richard Charles Wyndham, grandson of Percy Scawen Wyndham, sold the estate to Arthur Mitchell, who in c. 1939 sold it to Paul Weldon.[47] In 1945 it was bought from Paul Weldon by Col. Scrope Egerton who owned it in 1962.[48]

[16] Ibid. vii. 70.
[17] Feudal Aids, vi. 629.
[18] Red Bk. Exch. (Rolls Ser.), 489.
[19] Bk. of Fees, ii. 723; E 179/196/6; Feudal Aids, v. 217.
[20] Bk. of Fees, ii. 729.
[21] Complete Peerage, Mortimer and March; C 139/18/1.
[22] Bk. of Fees, ii. 723.
[23] Ibid. 718.
[24] Feudal Aids, vi. 629.
[25] Cal. Feet of F. Wilts. 1195–1272, ed. Fry, p. 56.
[26] Feet of F. Wilts. 1272–1327 (W.A.S. Rec. Brch.), p. 40.
[27] Ibid. p. 107.
[28] C.P. 25(1)/254/41/6.
[29] Phillipps, Wilts. Inst. 28.
[30] C.P. 25(1)/255/51/4.
[31] Phillipps, Wilts. Inst. 61, 63.
[32] Ibid. 86, 108, 124, 142.
[33] Wilts. Visitation Pedigrees 1623 (Harl. Soc. cv–cvi), 124; Phillipps, Wilts. Inst. 161; Hoare, Mod. Wilts. Mere, 179.
[34] Phillipps, Wilts. Inst. 193.

[35] Hoare, op. cit. 180. Wm. Mervyn was grandson of John Mervyn who acquired the manor of Fonthil. Gifford in the 15th cent.: Misc. Gen. et Her. (N.S. i), 358l
[36] Phillipps, Wilts. Inst. 208.   [37] Ibid.
[38] W.N. & Q. iv. 159.
[39] C 142/264/115; P.C.C. 82 Woodhall.
[40] Hoare, Mod. Wilts. Mere 180; Phillipps, Wilts. Inst. ii. 19.
[41] Hoare, op. cit.; C.P. 43/438 m. 7.
[42] Hoare, Mod. Wilts. Dunworth, 3.
[43] Ibid.; C.P. 43/887 rot. 354.
[44] W.R.O. 413, Deed D. H. Lee Warner and John Benett, 1809; Hoare, Mod. Wilts. Dunworth, 3, Mere, 179.
[45] W.R.O. 413, Conveyances D. Lee Warner to John Benett and John Benett to Ric. Ricward; Hoare, Mod. Wilts. Mere, 179.
[46] Letter dated 2 June 1908 from P. S. Wyndham penes General Ed. V.C.H.
[47] W.A.S. Libr., Devizes, Benett-Stanford papers.
[48] Ex inf. Miss Katharine Egerton.

CHURCH. The earliest reference found to a church at Pertwood is in 1333 when a rector was instituted to replace another.[49] The living was a rectory and the advowson belonged to the lords of the manor who, so far as is known, always exercised their patronage except in 1469 when the 'abbot of St. Saviour, Syon' presented.[50] Rectors seem to have been instituted fairly regularly until 1899 when the church was annexed to that of Chicklade as a chapel-of-ease.[51] It was then served by the Rector of Chicklade until 1921, when Chicklade with Pertwood were united to the church of Hindon, and since this date all three churches have been served by the Vicar of Hindon.[52]

The living was discharged in the 18th century when it was valued at £28,[53] and a grant of £6 10s. a year was made from Queen Anne's Bounty.[54] There were approximately 10 a. of glebe. In 1677 the glebe arable was distributed between the East, Middle, and West Fields and there was a close of meadow.[55] The tithe map of 1838 shows the glebe lying in two lots of roughly equal size in the southern part of the parish just below the farmstead.[56] All tithes were paid to the rector and were commuted in 1838 for a rent charge of £74.[57] In 1677 there was a rectory, or parsonage, house with barn and stable adjoining.[58] This is not mentioned in the glebe terrier of 1704[59] and at the end of the 18th century the rector lived in Hindon.[60] In 1835 the house was still there but was said to be uninhabitable.[61] It was, however, later restored and in 1919 was let, with the glebe lands, to the tenant of Pertwood Farm.[62] In 1962 a small farm cottage stood on the site of the former parsonage house just to the south-east of Pertwood Manor.

Little is known about the church. In c. 1361 William le Frend of New Salisbury left 40d. in his will to it.[63] Richard Mervyn, probably a brother of the lord of the manor, was instituted as rector in 1631 and held the living for 7 years.[64] Lancelot Morehouse, scholar and mathematician, and a friend of John Aubrey, was rector in c. 1660.[65] In 1676 the congregation seems to have amounted to no more than 8 persons.[66] A service was held at 1 o'clock on every other Sunday and at no other times in 1783. Communion was not administered and the family living in the farmhouse usually went to church in Hindon. The incumbent at this date also served the church at Hindon, then a chapel-of-ease of East Knoyle.[67] In 1863 the rector lived at Chicklade, but Pertwood was his only benefice. Services were held on every Sunday, either in the morning or in the afternoon, and a sermon was preached at every service. There was also a service on Christmas Day,

and on Good Friday, and Communion was celebrated at Christmas, Easter, and Whitsun. There were 4 regular communicants, but the congregation sometimes numbered 40 and was said to have much increased of late. Fairly substantial numbers came from Brixton Deverill to attend the services. In that year there was one baptism within the church and one burial in the churchyard.[68] In 1919 a service was held on one afternoon a week, and in 1962 about once a month and at the time of the Harvest Festival.[69]

Until the beginning of the 19th century, the church of *ST. PETER* was a small, stone, 12th-century building with a round-headed door on the south side.[70] It was restored in c. 1812 by the lord of the manor, and in 1822 there was said to be no feature of antiquity left except a holy-water stoop to the south of the altar. The chancel at the later date was separated from the nave by a round-headed arch.[71] Late in the 19th century the church was completely rebuilt in flint with stone dressings. It comprises nave, chancel, and small north aisle. In spite of their long connexion with the manor there are only two memorials to the Mervyn family: one to Sheldon Mervyn (d. 1734), the other to his sister Mrs. Mary Pouldon (d. 1747). There is a wall tablet to Richard Ricward, lord of the manor after 1810 who restored the church. In 1908 the bowl of a 14th-century font was discovered buried in a nearby copse and was restored to the church at the expense of the then lord of the manor, Percy Scawen Wyndham.[72] In 1553 there were two bells. In 1963 there was but one small bell probably of late 13th-century date.[73] In 1553 a chalice weighing 2 oz. was left for the parish and ½ oz. silver taken for the king. In 1963 there was a silver-gilt chalice with an indistinct hall-mark date, thought to be 1676 and a paten probably of the same date.[74] The oldest surviving register begins in 1811.

ECONOMIC HISTORY. In 1086 Pertwood comprised 2 hides. Of these, 1½ was demesne on which there was one plough, leaving ½ hide for tenant farming. There were 2 villeins and 3 bordars with 1 plough. At that time there were 20 a. of pasture and 4 a. of woodland.[75] Situated entirely on chalk downland, the land of Pertwood for most of its history has been used for corn growing and sheep rearing. Since the middle of the 16th century, when John Mervyn acquired the whole manor,[76] the parish has comprised but a single farm. Almost nothing can be said about its agrarian economy before the 19th century. John Mervyn, who died in 1601, bequeathed 100 sheep each to

[49] Phillipps, *Wilts. Inst.* 28.
[50] For lords of the manor see pp. 58-59; Phillipps, *Wilts. Inst.* 159 and *passim* (for index see *W.A.M.* xxviii. 227). The abbey of St. Saviour must be Syon, a house of the order of St. Bridget, with both male and female religious, although it did not have an abbott.
[51] *Crockford*, 1907.
[52] Ibid. 1926 and list of incumbents in Chicklade Ch.
[53] Ecton, *Thesaurus*, 398.
[54] Sar. Dioc. R.O. Vis. Queries, 1864.
[55] Sar Dioc. R.O. Glebe Terrier, 1677.
[56] W.R.O. Tithe Map.
[57] Ibid. Tithe Award.
[58] Sar. Dioc. R.O. Glebe Terrier, 1677.
[59] Ibid. 1704.
[60] Sar. Dioc. R.O. Vis. Queries, 1783.
[61] *Eccl. Revenues Inquiry Com.* H.C. 54, pp. 844-5

(1835), xxii.
[62] W.A.S. Libr., Devizes, Sale Cat.
[63] Sar. Corp. MSS. Swayne Scrapbk.
[64] Phillipps, *Wilts. Inst.* ii. 16, 19.
[65] John Aubrey, *Nat. Hist. Wilts.* (1847), 15.
[66] *W.N. & Q.* iii. 537.
[67] Sar. Dioc. R.O. Vis. Queries, 1783.
[68] Ibid. 1863.
[69] W.A.S. Libr., Devizes, Sale Cat.
[70] There is a S. W. view of the church in 1804 by John Buckler: (see facing pl.).
[71] Hoare, *Mod. Wilts.* Mere, 180.
[72] *Sar. Dioc. Gaz.* Apr. 1908.
[73] Walters, *Wilts. Bells*, 156.
[74] Nightingale, *Wilts. Plate*, 96.
[75] *V.C.H. Wilts.* ii, p. 122.
[76] See p. 59.

PERTWOOD CHURCH in 1804, rebuilt in the later 19th century

CORSLEY CHURCH in 1804, rebuilt in 1832

St. Leonard's church in 1804, abandoned 1868

St. Leonard's church interior, 1866

Polebridge House, showing hall roof

SUTTON VENY

two of his younger sons, presumably over and above his main stock which went with the manor to his eldest son.[77] This son, Thomas Mervyn, had a warren at Pertwood, which was plundered by two of his neighbours from Sutton Veny and their servants.[78]

In 1838 of the land subject to tithe 203 a. were arable, 181 a. down, 8 a. pasture, and 30 a. wood. Oats were the largest crop then produced, followed by barley, followed by wheat. At this date in the southern portion of the parish there were 2 large arable fields, namely West Field and Middle Field, and 3 smaller arable fields, two of them apparently

subdivisions of Middle Field, and the third possibly made from the down at a fairly late date. In the northern portion of the parish, much of which was woodland, there were 2 fairly small arable fields.[79] In 1857 a sale notice mentions 800 sheep, and 23 horses, but no other stock on the farm.[80] In 1919 the arable was described as some of the best corn-growing land in the district. New dairy buildings had recently been erected. About 188 a. of the former parish were then pasture and 148 a. arable.[81] In 1962 the land was used mainly for cereal crops but there was also a herd of pedigree cows.

SUTTON VENY

THE village of Sutton Veny is situated about three miles south-east from the centre of Warminster and about a mile south-west from Heytesbury. In 1881 the area of the parish was 3,580 a. of land and inland water, but within the next decade changes in the parish boundary enlarged the area to 4, 111 a.[1] In 1884 land in Southleigh Wood, formerly a detached part of Heytesbury parish, and Pit Mead, a stretch of meadowland south of the Wylye, previously divided between Warminster, Bishopstrow, and Norton Bavant, were brought within the parish boundary. Two years later the whole of the northern part of the ancient parish of Pertwood was transferred to Sutton Veny. The acreage of the parish (4, 111 a.) then remained unchanged until 1934 when 151 a., representing a narrow tongue of land stretching westwards and taking in part of the hamlet of Crockerton, were detached from Sutton Veny and added to Longbridge Deverill.[2]

No further boundary changes have been made so that in 1963 the parish contained 3,960 a. It is long and rather narrow in shape with an extension at the north-west corner taking in Southleigh and Eastleigh Woods.[3] The western boundary of this extension is the River Wylye, here flowing from south to north. The Wylye, having turned eastwards also forms a part of the north-eastern boundary.[4] A strip of upper greensand runs through the north-western half of the parish[5] and on this lie the extensive Southleigh and Eastleigh Woods once part of Selwood Forest.[6] The woods are situated at a height of over 400 ft. and beyond them, towards the west, the land falls steeply to the Wylye. The northern part of the parish, also bounded by the Wylye, is flat and, in parts, marshy, and it is this marshy land which gave Sutton the descriptive part of its name, i.e. Fenny, once pronounced and later spelt, Venny or Veny.[7] All the southern half of the parish lies on the chalk downs which sweep

up to a height of over 700 ft. In the extreme south, formerly part of the ancient parish of Pertwood, there is some woodland, and a windbreak of beech trees, characteristic of that parish.[8] The downs have in the past supported large flocks of sheep, and the land of the parish has always been devoted to farming, pasture and downland grazing predominating over arable, although since 1939 much downland has been ploughed.[9]

There are numerous barrows in the southern part of the parish, and there are three on the outskirts of the village to the north and east. Robin Hood's Bower, in the middle of Southleigh Wood, is an Iron-Age earthwork. In Pit Mead, quite close to the Wylye, there are the sites of two Roman villas.[10]

By 1249 there were two townships within the parish, namely Great and Little Sutton, and by the early 14th century Newnham is mentioned as a third distinct area of settlement and was separately assessed for taxation.[11] All three places lay along the road running south of, and roughly parallel to, the Wylye. Little Sutton remains in 1963 a small, separate hamlet lying against the eastern boundary of the parish. Great Sutton was the area around the church of St. Leonard, and with Newnham, which lay just beyond it to the north-west, corresponds with what is called in 1963 the village of Sutton Veny. By the 16th century Newnham was sometimes included with Great Sutton for purposes of taxation,[12] but it retained its separate identity until the end of the 19th century and is marked on maps of that date.[13] A few houses belonging to the hamlet of Crockerton lay, until 1934, in the extreme west of the parish of Sutton Veny. But since the greater part of the hamlet lies in Longbridge Deverill, its history is reserved for treatment with that parish.

The parish may have been of some importance in the late 13th century, for in 1298 the lord of the

[77] P.C.C. 82 Woodhall.
[78] Sta. Ch. 8/216/23.
[79] W.R.O. Tithe Award.
[80] *Warminster Miscellany*, Sept. 1857.
[81] W.A.S. Libr., Devizes, *Sale Cat.*
[1] This and subsequent acreages from *Census*.
[2] *Bounds of Wilts.* (1918); *Census*, 1891.
[3] According to the Inclosure Map of 1808 the greater part of Southleigh Wood then lay outside the parish boundary. Part of it was a detached part of Heytesbury parish and the rest seems to have been extra-parochial.
[4] O.S. Maps 1/25,000, 31/83, 84, 93, 94; 1/2,500 Wilts.

LI, LII, LVIII (1st and later edns.).
[5] A.H. Fry, *Land Utilization Wilts.*
[6] *V.C.H. Wilts.* iv. 415–16.
[7] *P.N. Wilts.* (E.P.N.S.), pp. xxi, 154.
[8] See p. 58.
[9] See p. 68.
[10] *V.C.H. Wilts.* i (1). 192, 270, 110.
[11] *Crown Pleas Wilts. Eyre* (W.A.S. Rec. Brch.), 202; Land at Newnham is named in a number of 14th-century deeds: *W.A.M.* xxxvii. 38 sqq.
[12] *Taxation Lists* (W.A.S. Rec. Brch.), 35, 146.
[13] O.S. Map 6″ Wilts. LII (1st edn.).

manor of Little Sutton was granted a weekly market and an annual fair to be held on his land within the tithing of Great Sutton.[14] It is not known, however, whether these were ever established. To the 15ths of 1334 Newnham contributed 16s., Little Sutton 50s., and Great Sutton 80s.[15] In 1377 there were 33 poll-tax payers in Newnham, 36 in Little Sutton, and 82 in Great Sutton.[16] To the benevolence of 1545 Little Sutton had one subscriber, Great Sutton two,[17] and to the subsidy of 1576 there were 5 subscribers in Little Sutton, and 20 in Great Sutton.[18] On both occasions residents in Newnham were taxed with those in Great Sutton. When the Census figures begin in 1801 the population of the parish was 622. Thereafter it rose, except for a slight drop in 1861, to 881 in 1871. But ten years later it had dropped to 715. In 1911 it was down to 566, and although it was rather above 600 in 1921 and 1931, it was down to 568 in 1951.[19] These fluctuations cannot be attributed to changes in the parish boundaries.

No main roads enter the parish, and apart from two secondary roads which cross at the north-west end of the village, the only other road is a minor one leading through Southleigh Wood, across the Wylye, and out of the parish to join the main Warminster-Shaftesbury road. The railway line between Warminster and Salisbury, opened in 1856,[20] just crosses the extreme north-east corner of the parish, and Heytesbury station is less than ¼ mile outside the eastern boundary. During the First World War a railway line, 3½ miles long, was constructed by the War Department from Heytesbury station to the military camp in Sutton Veny. It was closed soon after the end of the war.[21]

The oldest part of the village seems to be its south-east end, which was once the separate tithing of Great Sutton. The parish church, the rectory, and, after 1850, the village school, all lay here until towards the end of the 19th century.[22] Here, too, on either side of the lane leading to the church, were Church and Polebridge farms, which were possibly the demesne farms of the two manors of Great, or Fenny, Sutton, dismembered in the 17th century.[23] After both farms were acquired at the beginning of the 20th century by the Hon. W. P. Alexander, the dwelling-house of Church farm became his residence, and has since been called Polebridge House. The central block on the north side of the house can be identified as a medieval great hall, later divided into two stories, the timbers of the fine open roof being apparently of 14th-century date.[24] The house has been much altered and extended, notably in 1902 when the west wing, with that date inscribed upon it, was added. The Glebe farm also lies not far away, close to the road as it leaves the former tithing of Great Sutton for Little Sutton.[25] It has an 18th-century farmhouse with 19th-century additions.

In 1963 the main part of the village lay along the secondary road from Warminster which forms the village street for about ¾ of a mile and runs through the former tithing of Newnham. The new parish church, the school, and the Congregational chapel were all built on the north-east side of this street in the later 19th century.[26] Many of the houses along the street date from the early 19th century and are of coursed rubble with red-brick dressings. A few houses are, however, earlier, being of stone ashlar with mullioned windows, and on the south-west side of the street there is a row of four cottages, originally one building, which has exposed timber-framing. The brick gutters running along either side of the road were constructed to replace earlier unpaved ditches in 1868 when the vestry was particularly concerned with the insanitary state of the parish.[27] A number of the cottages flank the road so closely that at that date dirt and damp from these ditches sometimes seeped through their walls.[28]

Many of the buildings at the north-west end of the village bear witness to the position of the Everett family in the parish in the later 19th century. In 1850 Joseph Everett acquired the Greenhill estate, formerly the home of the Hinton family,[29] and in 1856 he enlarged and embellished the house.[30] In 1963 this house was called Sutton Veny House. Before J. E. Everett sold the property in 1898 he built in a Tudor style the Greenhill farm buildings and estate houses which lie along the road to Norton Bavant.[31] Much of the 20th-century building in the parish has also been at this end of the village, along the road from Longbridge Deverill to Norton Bavant.

At the extreme east end of the parish, in the hamlet of Little Sutton, there are Sutton Farm, called in 1963 Pond's Farm, an early 19th-century house, and Little Sutton Farm, which may have been the demesne farm of the Kingston manor of Little Sutton.[32] But in 1963 the house belonging to this farm was no longer occupied as a farmhouse and was called Sutton Parva House. It is a timber-framed house of 17th century, or earlier, date, re-fronted in stone in c. 1700. Further east still, where Little Sutton adjoins Tytherington, there was once another farm. A brick dovecot, with the inscription 'R.L. 1810', and some other farm buildings of coursed rubble with brick dressings of probably the same date remain. A ruined, rustic summerhouse in a nearby garden suggests that there was once a house of some standing here which has been demolished. Between 1919 and 1927 the kennels of the Wylye Valley Hunt were at Little Sutton, and between c. 1830 and 1918 those of the South and West Wilts. Hunt were at Greenhill (see above).[33]

Eastleigh Wood is thought to be the place, spelt *Iglea*, which King Alfred reached on the second

[14] See p. 65.
[15] *V.C.H. Wilts.* iv. 302.
[16] Ibid. 311.
[17] *Taxation Lists* (W.A.S. Rec. Brch.), 35–36.
[18] Ibid. 146.
[19] *V.C.H. Wilts.* iv. 358.
[20] Ibid. 284.
[21] Ibid. 292.
[22] See pp. 71, 72, 73.
[23] See p. 65.
[24] See pl. facing p. 61. No architectural investigation of the house ever seems to have been made.

[25] See p. 67.
[26] See pp. 71, 72, 73.
[27] See p. 73.
[28] *Rep. to Medical Dept. Local Govt. Bd. 1–3 Feb. 1872* (Copy in W.R.O.).
[29] W.A.S. Libr., Devizes, Everett MSS. Memoranda Bk. 65; ibid. vol. ii. 99, 103.
[30] Ibid. vol. ii. 99.
[31] Ibid. 103; Sale Cat.
[32] See p. 65.
[33] *V.C.H. Wilts.* iv. 372–3, 376.

day after entering Wiltshire in 878.[34] A wood called Elywood, perhaps the same, formed part of William Button's estate in *c.* 1589.[35] Iley Oak, sometimes called Hundred Oak, the meeting-place of Warminster Hundred, was somewhere in, or near, this wood. In 1651 the sheriff's tourns were held there.[36]

MANORS. An estate of 4 hides at Sutton Veny was held before the Conquest by Spirtes the priest. At the time of the Domesday Survey it was held of Niel (Nigellus) the physician, by the abbey of St. Mary de Monteburg (dép. Manche).[37] It may have passed soon afterwards from Niel to Hamelin de Ballon, for Round suggests that the church of Sutton was among Hamelin's gifts made about the beginning of the 12th century to the abbey of St. Vincent at Le Mans (dép. Sarthe) for the endowment of a dependent priory at Abergavenny.[38] In the reign of Henry II Hamelin's lands, which included part of Sutton Veny, later to become the manor of *GREAT SUTTON*, were divided between Reynold de Ballon and Geoffrey FitzAce and his wife Agnes,[39] and by 1210 the manor of Sutton was held by Reynold's son, John de Ballon.[40] In 1215 Nicholas de Limesy was granted the land of Thomas de Ballon in Sutton during the king's pleasure,[41] but this appears to have been restored to the de Ballons shortly afterwards. In 1226 Margery Limesy, widow of Nicholas, Richard of Cromhale, and William of London were holding lands in Sutton which were said to have descended to them from Hamelin de Ballon.[42] Their holdings may, perhaps, represent the share of Geoffrey and Agnes FitzAce who shared Hamelin's lands with Reynold de Ballon in the time of Henry II. The overlordship, however, must upon this division have gone to Reynold, for Margery, Richard, and William were holding of Reynold's son, John, in 1226.[43] In 1242–3 the manor was held of John's son, another John, as of the honor of Much Marcle (Herefs.).[44] John was again recognized as overlord in 1274–5 but this is the last mention of the de Ballon overlordship.[45]

In 1242 Margery de Limesy had been succeeded in her holding by Walter de Limesy, presumably her son, and the other two tenants were, as in 1226, Richard of Cromhale, and William of London.[46] The next year William of London conveyed all his holding in both Great and Little Sutton to Roger of Cromhale, presumably Richard's son,[47]

but in 1274–5 the manor was still held under John de Ballon by three mesne tenants, namely John of Cromhale, Roger's son, John de Kingston, and Joan de Wauton.[48] John de Kingston's holding presumably became merged with his manor in Little Sutton[49] and by 1325 William de Wauton was holding the other two parts of the manor,[50] presumably that held by Joan de Wauton in 1274 and that held at the same date by John of Cromhale whose kinsman William was.[51] A William de Wauton died some time before 1350 seised of lands in Sutton, but from his son William they passed in a way that is no longer clear to Elias Daubeny and his wife Agnes. Elias and Agnes then conveyed a life interest in the lands to William's brother, Thomas, in return for the manor of Cromhale (Gloucs.).[52] Two years later Elias and Agnes granted the reversion of the Sutton property after the death of Thomas to Nicholas Chamberlain,[53] and in 1359 they conveyed the manor to Thomas Hungerford (d. 1397).[54] Thomas was succeeded by his son, Walter, who died seised of the manor in 1449 and whose heir was his son, Robert (d. 1459).[55] Robert's son, also called Robert, was attainted in 1461 and executed in 1464, but as the manor had been settled upon his mother, Margaret Botreaux, it was not among the possessions which were forfeited.[56] In 1469 the manor appears to have been held by Robert's daughter, Frideswide,[57] but when Margaret Botreaux died in 1477 it was among her estates.[58] Margaret's heir was her great-granddaughter Mary, daughter of Sir Thomas Hungerford (d. 1469), and later wife of Sir Edward Hastings. Great Sutton, however, was among the estates which Margaret directed by her will to remain in the male line of the family.[59] It passed, therefore, to Walter Hungerford (d. 1516), second son of Robert (d. 1464), who was in possession in 1510.[60] The manor, like that of Upton Scudamore, then descended in this line of the Hungerford family. After the execution of Walter, Lord Hungerford in 1540 it passed to his son Sir Walter Hungerford (d. 1596) and descended in the family until 1684–5 when Edward Hungerford, the 'spendthrift' (d. 1711), sold it to Sir Stephen Fox.[61] With the other manor in Sutton Veny formerly belonging to the Hungerfords, namely Fenny Sutton, Great Sutton was immediately split up by Sir Stephen Fox and was sold in parcels.[62] A few facts about the subsequent descent of some of these parcels are given below with the manor of Fenny Sutton.

[34] Ibid. ii, p. 6.
[35] W.R.O. 442/1, Survey of Manor, 1582.
[36] *W.A.M.* xiii. 108, and see p. 5.
[37] *V.C.H. Wilts.* ii. p. 157.
[38] J. H. Round, *Studies in Peerage and Family Hist.* 192.
[39] *Rot. de Ob. et Fin.* (Rec. Com.), 382.
[40] *Pipe R.* 1210 (P.R.S. N.S. xxvi), 76. For relationship of Reynold de Ballon to Hamelin, see J. H. Round, *Peerage and Family Hist.* 198–206.
[41] *Rot. Litt. Claus.* (Rec. Com.), i. 240b. Thos. seems to be a mistake for John.
[42] C.P. 25(1)/250/5/19.
[43] Ibid.
[44] *Bk. of Fees*, ii. 731. John succeeded his father in *c.* 1235: *Ex. e Rot. Fin.* (Rec. Com.), i. 276. For Much Marcle, the head of the Ballon Barony, see Round, *Peerage and Family Hist.* 200, 204.
[45] *Rot. Hund.* (Rec. Com.), ii. 276.
[46] *Bk. of Fees*, ii. 731.
[47] C.P. 25(1)/251/14/17.

[48] *Rot. Hund.* (Rec. Com.), ii. 276; B.M. Add. Ch. 26708.
[49] See p. 65.
[50] *Feet of Fines* 1272–77 (W.A.S. Rec. Brch.), 133.
[51] B.M. Add. Ch. 26710.
[52] *Cal. Close*, 1349–54, 238, 512. For some notes on these members of the de Wauton family, see John Smyth, *Berkeley MSS.* iii. 162.
[53] C.P. 25(1)/255/48/22.
[54] C.P. 25(1)/255/49/35.
[55] C 139/135/30; *Complete Peerage*, Hungerford.
[56] *Cal. Close*, 1354–61, 440; C 140/320/56.
[57] *Cal. Close*, 1468–76, 62.   [58] C 140/67/40.
[59] Hoare, *Mod. Wilts.* Heytesbury, 98.
[60] S.C. 2/208/28.
[61] C.P. 25(2)/747/36 Chas. II Trin.; for descent of Hungerford estates from Walt. Hungerford (d. 1516) to Edw. Hungerford (d. 1711) see *Complete Peerage*, Hungerford, p. 626, *n.*c.
[62] Hoare, *Mod. Wilts.* Warminster, 86.

The names of some of the lessees of the demesne farm of the manor of Great Sutton under the Hungerfords are known. Between *c.* 1417 and *c.* 1435 it was John Claydon, who was stock-keeper of the Hungerford flock.[63] In 1439 it was Robert Vincent, and between 1454 and 1472 there were four tenants, namely John Osborn, John Cosyn, John Locke, and William Snell.[64] In *c.* 1574 a lease of the demesne lands and the mansion house by Sir Walter Hungerford to John Boland was renewed.[65] By 1582 Boland had been succeeded as tenant by John Elderton[66] who still leased the farm in 1609,[67] but had been succeeded as lessee in 1621 by his widow Jane.[68]

Another estate in Sutton Veny was held T.R.E., by Alwold and his sister and had passed by 1086 to William son of Guy (filius Widonis).[69] As was the estate held in 1086 of Niel the physician,[70] William's estate was later usually called Fenny or Great Sutton. In the 14th century it was sometimes called Northcourt,[71] and in the 15th century was known as Sutton Morton. Throughout this article, however, it will be called *FENNY SUTTON*, while the manor held of Niel in 1086 has been called Great Sutton.

Fenny Sutton passed, probably in the same way as William son of Guy's Somerset manor of Horsington,[72] to Henry de Newmarch who paid $\frac{1}{2}$ mark for land in Sutton Veny in 1166–7.[73] Henry was succeeded in 1204 by his brother, James,[74] whose heirs were his two daughters Isabel, wife of Ralph Russell, and Hawise, first the wife of John Botreaux and then of Nicholas de Moels (d.*c.* 1264).[75] The overlordship of the land in Sutton Veny was assigned to Hawise and the manor was said to be held of her second husband in the mid-13th century as $\frac{1}{2}$ a knight's fee.[76] The overlordship descended in the Moels family until the death of the last of the male line, John de Moels, in 1337.[77] In 1428 the overlords were still said to be the heirs of Nicholas de Moels. But this was probably inaccurate, since in 1340 the manor was said to be held of Sir John Haudlo,[78] in 1384 of Nicholas Burnell, Sir John's son,[79] and in 1433 of the king of the honor of Trowbridge.[80] In 1473 the same estate was said to be held of the dowager Countess of Wiltshire as of her manor of Warminster.[81]

No record has been found of any mesne tenants before the mid-13th century when Maud, daughter of Nicholas de Moels, married Richard Lorty.[82]

The fee simple of the manor appears to have formed part of Maud's dower, for in 1242 Richard Lorty held it of Nicholas de Moels.[83] Richard was succeeded by his son, Henry Lorty,[84] who in 1309 settled the manor upon himself and his wife Sibyl.[85] Henry and Sibyl were followed by their son, John Lorty, who before 1340, conveyed the manor to Sir Ralph de Middleney and his wife Elizabeth, whose son, John, married Sibyl Lorty, John Lorty's daughter.[86] Sibyl released her claim in the manor in 1341.[87]

The descent of the manor over the next decade or so is obscure. In 1380 Sir Robert Ashton, who may have been the second husband of Elizabeth de Middleney, was said to hold three manors in Sutton Veny, one of which was possibly Little Sutton.[88] The reversion of a manor called Fenny Sutton was conveyed by Sir Robert to trustees for Alice Perers, mistress of Edward III, and wife of William of Windsor.[89] Alice's interest was subsequently transferred to her husband, and after the death of Sir Robert Ashton in 1384, William entered the manor without licence.[90] The heirs of John and Sibyl Middleney were their daughters Maud, wife of John Langrich, and Elizabeth, wife of John Gunter, and in 1385–6 they were claiming the manor in the court of Common Pleas.[91] In 1390 John of Windsor, presumably William's son, John Langrich, and John Gunter bound themselves to abide by the award of the arbitrators,[92] and in 1392 seisin was given to John Langrich and John Gunter.[93] Before 1394 John Langrich was dead and his widow, Maud, had married William Horslegh.[94] Maud died without issue and her share in the manor passed to her sister, Elizabeth, who married John Andrews as her second husband.[95] Elizabeth died in 1422 seised of the manor, then called Northcourt in Fenny Sutton, and was succeeded by her son by her first marriage, Roger Gunter.[96] Before 1469 Roger was succeeded by his son, John,[97] who died seised of the manor in 1473 and was succeeded by his brother, William.[98] William, by order of the king, assigned the manor in 1483 to Thomas Oxenbridge and William Weston,[99] and in 1484 and 1485 his nephews, Thomas and Edmund, sons of his brother Giles Gunter, assigned their interest in the manor to the grantees.[1] Oxenbridge and Weston appear to have conveyed the manor to John Morton, Bishop of Ely (later Archbishop of Canterbury), and to Robert Morton,[2] and in 1504

[63] R. C. Payne, 'Agrarian Conditions on Estates of Duchy of Lancaster, the Lords Hungerford, and Bprc.,' of Winchester 13th–15th cents.' Ph. D. (Econ.), London, thesis, 1940, see below, p. 67, n. 97.
[64] Ibid.
[65] Req. 2/130/55.
[66] W.R.O. 442/1, Survey of Manor, 1582.
[67] Ibid. 442/2, Survey of Manor, 1609.
[68] Ibid. 490/7, Survey of Manor, 1621.
[69] *V.C.H. Wilts.* ii. p. 152.
[70] See p. 65.
[71] B.M. Harl. Ch. 58 D 9.
[72] Collinson, *Hist. Som.* ii. 371.
[73] *Pipe R.* 1166–67 (P.R.S. xi), 131.
[74] *Rot. de Ob. et Fin.* (Rec. Com.), 205; *Red Bk. of Exchequer*, ii. 482.
[75] Burke, *Extinct Peerages*, 401; *Complete Peerage*, Moels.
[76] *Bk. of Fees*, ii. 142.
[77] *Cal. Inq. p.m.* viii, p. 83.
[78] *Wilts. Inq. p.m.* 1327–77 (Index Libr.), p. 137.
[79] C 136/30/5.
[80] C 139/1/22.

[81] C 140/47/61.
[82] *Ex. e Rot. Fin.* (Rec. Com.), ii. 295; *Complete Peerage*, Lorty.
[83] *Bk. of Fees*. ii. 735.
[84] *Rot. Hund.* (Rec. Com.), ii. 276.
[85] C 143/78/15.
[86] *Cal. Close*, 1339–41, 564; *Wilts. Inq. p.m.* 1327–77 (Index Libr.), 137; *Complete Peerage*, Lorty.
[87] C.P. 25(1)/287/40/11; B. M. Harl. Ch. 58 G. 5.
[88] *Cal. Pat.* 1377–81, 503; see p. 65.
[89] C 136/30/5.
[90] Ibid.; *Cal Pat.* 1381–85, 386.
[91] C.P. 40/499 rot. 346.
[92] B.M. Harl. Ch. 58 D. 8.
[93] Ibid. 49 G. 13.
[94] C.P. 40/533 rot. 78.
[95] C 138/27/40.
[96] C 139/1/22.
[97] B.M. Harl. Ch. 51 A. 26.
[98] C 140/47/61.
[99] C.P. 40/898 rot. 537.
[1] B.M. Harl. Ch. 51 A. 24, 30.
[2] C.P. 40/898 rot. 537.

it was in the possession of Agnes Morton, widow of Robert,[3] who in 1507 released her claim to Thomas Morton.[4] Robert Morton was lord of the manor in 1536 and 1555.[5] He died in 1559 having devised the manor to his wife, Dorothy.[6] His grandson and heir, George Morton, sold it in 1572–3 to Sir Walter Hungerford (d. 1596) and his halfbrother, Edward Hungerford (d. 1607), lords of the manor of Great Sutton.[7] Under the name of the manor of Sutton Morton[8] the estate then descended with that of Great Sutton, and was sold with Great Sutton by Edward Hungerford (d. 1711) in 1684–5 to Sir Stephen Fox.[9] Fox then almost immediately sold the two manors off in lots and all manorial rights became extinct.

Under the Hungerfords the manor of Fenny Sutton was leased to Elizabeth and Daniel Franklin who succeeded Robert Chamberlayne as tenants.[10] In 1609 and 1621[11] Daniel Franklin was tenant.[12]

It has not been possible to trace the descent of all the various lands and tenements, which Sir Stephen Fox sold in c. 1686. One estate was conveyed to Farwell Perry, who with his wife Anne, conveyed it in 1706 to Sir Walter Long of Whaddon (d. 1710).[13] This subsequently passed as Whaddon to Walter Long of South Wraxall (d. 1807),[14] and thereafter as South Wraxall to the Longs of Rood Ashton,[15] who seem to have sold it towards the end of the 19th century.[16] Among the property which Sir Walter Long acquired in 1706 was Polebridge Farm and in 1788 his son, also Sir Walter Long, claimed unsuccessfully the lordship of the manor of Sutton Veny.[17] The manorial rights he was claiming may have been those of the former manor of Fenny Sutton, for in 1535 a tenement called Polebridge was held of Robert Morton, lord of the manor of Fenny Sutton.[18] From the Longs the Polebridge farmlands passed to James Nowlson Parham. Parham died in 1904 and the property was bought by the Hon. Walter Philip Alexander (d. 1934).[19]

Another estate was conveyed by Sir Stephen Fox in 1689 to Thomas Buckler.[20] This had formerly been part of one of the Hungerford manors in Sutton Veny. This estate passed to Thomas Buckler's grandson, also called Thomas,[21] who in 1741 was seised of a farm called Sutton Farm.[22] By 1783 Thomas was succeeded by his son William.[23] In 1804 Sutton Farm belonged to Francis Dugdale Astley,[24] who had married William Buckler's daugh-

ter. But not long after it was acquired by Worthy Beaven, described as the late owner in 1837.[25] Towards the end of the 19th century, by which time it was called Church Farm, the property was acquired by William Henry Laverton of Westbury.[26] Laverton sold it in 1889 to John Julius Estridge,[27] who sold it in 1901 to the Hon. Walter Philip Alexander.[28] W. P. Alexander thus became owner of both Polebridge and Church farms and amalgamated the two properties.[29]

The 5-hide estate of *LITTLE SUTTON* was held T.R.E. by Colo. By the time of the Domesday Survey it was held of William de Mohun by Walter Husee.[30] The overlordship of the de Mohuns descended with their honor of Dunster and the last mention found of it is in 1285.[31]

In 1242–3 Henry Husee, undoubtedly a descendant of the Walter Husee of 1086, held Little Sutton of Reynold de Mohun, and under Henry the manor was divided between Walter de Limesy, Richard of Cromhale, and William of London, the same three as were holding the manor of Great Sutton under John de Ballon.[32] In 1243 William of London conveyed his share in the manor to Roger of Cromhale, as he did in Great Sutton, and by 1274, again as in Great Sutton, John of Cromhale, son of Roger, had his father's holding, and the former Limesy holding was apparently divided between John de Kingston and Joan de Wauton.[33] The de Wauton land in Little Sutton then probably passed like the family's property in Great Sutton to Thomas Hungerford (d. 1397).[34]

John de Kingston's holding seems to have comprised the manor of Little Sutton. In 1284–5 he held his fee there directly of John de Mohun, the overlord,[35] and between 1312 and 1333 he presented to the free chapel of the manor.[36] The lands belonging to this manor, like that of the other manors in the parish, lay in both Great and Little Sutton,[37] and when in 1298 John de Kingston was granted a weekly market and an annual fair on his manor, these were apparently held in the tithing of Great Sutton, while the accompanying grant of free warren was for his demesne lands in both tithings.[38] By 1322 John de Kingston had forfeited his lands,[39] and in 1325 Little Sutton was granted to Hugh le Despenser.[40] The following year it was in the custody of Robert Hungerford,[41] but by 1329–30 it had been restored to Sir John de King-

³ C.P. 40/971 rot. 343.
⁴ B.M. Harl. Ch. 53 G. 41.
⁵ Ibid. 53 F. 51; 53 G. 35.
⁶ C 142/128/70.
⁷ C.P. 25(2)/239/15 Eliz. Trin.
⁸ C.P. 43/166 m. 13; C.P. 25(2)/616/1650 Mich.
⁹ See p. 63.
¹⁰ W.R.O. 442/1, Survey of Manor 1582.
¹¹ Ibid 442/2, Survey of Manor 1609.
¹² Ibid. 490, Survey of Manor 1621.
¹³ C.P. 25(2)/979/5 Anne Mich.
¹⁴ *V.C.H. Wilts.* vii. 173.   ¹⁵ Ibid. 22.
¹⁶ W.A.S. Libr., Devizes, Everett MSS. Large Folder quoting the Revd. E. C. Long.
¹⁷ Ibid. vol. vi. 53 quoting extract from Summer Assizes at Salisbury 1788.
¹⁸ B.M. Harl. Ch. 53 F. 51.
¹⁹ W.A.S. Libr., Devizes, Everett MSS. vol. i quoting deeds in possession of Miss Alexander of Polebridge.
²⁰ W.A.S. Libr., Devizes, Everett MSS. v. 32–3 quoting deed contained in abstract of title of Mr. Sam. Long of Newnham to an estate in Sutton Veny, 1809 in

Long family papers.
²¹ C 12/1215/47.
²² E 112/1309/111.
²³ Sar. Dioc. R.O. Glebe Terrier, 1783; W.A.S. Libr., Devizes, Everett MSS. Large Folder.
²⁴ W.R.O. Inclosure Award.
²⁵ *Salisbury and Winchester Jnl.* 12 June, 1837.
²⁶ W.A.S. Libr., Devizes, Everett MSS. Large Folder.
²⁷ Ibid.
²⁸ Ibid. and Sale Cat.; *W.A.M.* xlvii. 131.
²⁹ See p. 62.
³⁰ *V.C.H. Wilts.* ii, p. 150.
³¹ *Cal. Inq. Edw. I,* ii, p. 353.
³² *Bk. of Fees,* ii. 718; see p. 63.
³³ See p. 63.
³⁴ Ibid.
³⁵ *Cal. Inq. Edw. I,* ii, p. 353.
³⁶ See p. 69.
³⁷ See p. 61.
³⁸ *Cal. Chart. R.* 1257–1300, 474.
³⁹ S.C. 6/1145 m. 12.
⁴⁰ S.C. 6/1148 m. 24.   ⁴¹ S.C. 6/1148 m. 19.

ston, who that year settled it upon his son Thomas and Maud, Thomas's wife. [42] In 1363 Thomas de Kingston conveyed the manor of Little Sutton, with other lands in Sutton Veny, to Peter Piperd for life.[43] In 1380 the manor was said to be held by John Pecche, a citizen of London, at the time of his death in right of Mary his wife, who thus seems to have been a Kingston.[44] Two years later Sir Robert Ashton presented to the free chapel of Little Sutton and it is possible that he held this manor for a short time as well as that of Fenny Sutton.[45]

Sir Thomas de Kingston was succeeded by his son, John, who settled the manor upon himself and his wife Elizabeth in 1414–15.[46] Elizabeth survived her husband and held the manor until her death in 1463, when it passed to her grandson, Sir Thomas de Kingston.[47] Sir Thomas conveyed it in 1488 to his son John, and John's wife Eleanor,[48] and John died seised of the manor in 1496.[49] His heir, John de Kingston, was at that date a minor, but livery of the manor was made to him in 1511.[50] John died without issue three years later and was succeeded by his brother Nicholas.[51] Nicholas also died childless and was succeeded by his sister, Mary wife of Sir Thomas Lisle.[52] In 1521 the manor was among the lands conveyed as dower by Sir Thomas Lisle to Susan, widow of John de Kingston.[53] Mary Lisle died without issue in 1539 and the heirs to the lands which had come to her from her brother, Nicholas, were four cousins, namely William Gorffyn, of Reading, Margery, wife of John Cope, of Canons Ashby (Northants.), Katherine, wife of Thomas Andrews of Charlton (Northants.), and Margaret, wife of Thomas Boughton.[54] Little Sutton apparently passed to William Gorffyn on whose death without issue in 1547,[55] it was divided between his sister, Alice Gorffyn, and Margaret Boughton who is called one of his heirs.[56] Alice conveyed her share in the manor in 1551 to Thomas and Katherine Andrews,[57] who forthwith conveyed it to William Paulet, Earl of Wiltshire, that year created Marquess of Winchester, and Chidiock Paulet his son.[58] In the following year Thomas and Margaret Boughton conveyed their share to Lord Winchester,[59] and in 1563 Chidiock Paulet conveyed the whole estate to Sir John Thynne.[60] The manor then descended in the Thynne family to the Marquesses of Bath. In 1810 the Marquess of Bath conveyed the larger part of his lands in Sutton Veny to Francis Dugdale Astley in exchange for

land elsewhere.[61] The manorial rights were not apparently, however, included in the conveyance and manor courts for Little Sutton continued to be held by Lord Bath until about the middle of the 19th century.[62]

Besides the manor held by the Kingstons in *LITTLE SUTTON* which eventually passed to the Thynnes in the middle of the 16th century, another manor there, passed to the Hungerfords, who were lords of the manor of Great Sutton after 1359.[63] This was probably the estate held by Joan de Wauton in Little Sutton in 1274 and may have passed to Thomas Hungerford (d. 1397) in the same way and at the same time as the de Wauton land in Great Sutton.[64] It apparently retained its separate identity, and in the 16th century while its courts were sometimes held with those of Great Sutton, they were more usually held separately although on the same day.[65] The manor apparently passed like Great Sutton after the death of Margaret Botreaux, Lady Hungerford, in 1477 to the male line of the family,[66] but after the forfeiture of Walter, Lord Hungerford's possessions in 1540, it did not descend with Great Sutton to Lord Hungerford's son, Sir Walter Hungerford (d. 1596).[67] In 1545, with the advowson of the church of Sutton Veny, the Little Sutton estate was granted to James Tutt and Nicholas Hame.[68] Their rights, including the advowson, were apparently almost immediately conveyed to William Button who died seised of the manor of Little Sutton in 1547 leaving as his heir his son William.[69] The estate thenceforward descended as the advowson until 1796 when the Button freehold in Great and Little Sutton was sold to Mary Long by John Walker Heneage.[70] As far as is known all manorial rights were by then extinct and the estate is last called a manor in 1715.[71]

LESSER ESTATES. In 1265 Edith and Mabel, daughters of Hereward of Newnham, granted to the priory of Maiden Bradley land in Newnham called 'le Battedeaker' in 'le Battelond' to hold for the space of twelve harvests.[72] Two years later Geoffrey le 'Chamberlain' granted 32 a. in Great Sutton to the priory.[73] Maiden Bradley had an estate in Newnham until the house was dissolved in 1536.[74]

In 1532 the capital messuage and lands belonging to this estate were leased to Thomas Hinton, and John and Stephen his sons, on the understanding that they should rebuild the house with 3 bays of

[42] *Cal. Pat.* 1377–81, 490.
[43] *Cal. Close,* 1364–68, 193.
[44] C 136/10/54.
[45] Phillipps, *Wilts. Inst.* i. 66; see p. 64.
[46] C.P. 25(1)/291/63/17.
[47] C 140/10/20.
[48] C.P. 40/916 rot. 329.
[49] *Cal. Inq. Hen. VII,* i, p. 557.
[50] *L. & P. Hen. VIII,* i, p. 282.
[51] Ibid. p. 1329.   [52] C 142/30/44.
[53] C 54/389 no. 12.
[54] C 142/65/33; C 142/67/152; C 142/94/51. Wm. Gorffyn was s. of Marg. Gorffyn, a sister of Sir John de Kingston, Lady Mary's father; Margery Cope was a d. of Katherine Mallory, another sister of Sir John; Katherine Andrews and Marg. Boughton were ds. of Dorothy, another d. of Katherine Mallory; Bridges, *Northants.* i. 604. See also *V.C.H. Berks.* iv. 350.
[55] C 142/94/51.
[56] C.P. 25(2)/65/541/6 Edw. VI Trin.
[57] C.P. 25(2)/65/532/5 Edw. VI East.
[58] C.P. 25(2)/65/532/5 Edw. VI Mich.
[59] C.P. 25(2)/65/541/6 Edw. VI Trin.
[60] C.P. 40/1215 rot. 390.
[61] W.R.O. 132, Deeds of Astley property.
[62] W.A.S. Libr., Devizes, Everett MSS. vol. vi. 25.
[63] See p. 63.
[64] Ibid.
[65] Based on an examination of S.C. 2/208/64, 68, 69.
[66] See p. 63.
[67] Ibid. and *Complete Peerage,* Hungerford, p. 626.
[68] *L. & P. Hen. VIII.* xx (1), p. 527.
[69] C 142/87/101.
[70] See p. 70., and W.A.S. Libr., Devizes, Everett MSS. Large Folder.
[71] C.P. 25(2)/1077/1 Geo. I Trin.
[72] *Cat. Anc. D.* iii, p. 433; *V.C.H. Wilts.* iii. 297.
[73] C.P. 25(1)/251/21/23; *Cal. Feet of F. Wilts.* 1195–1272, ed. Fry, p. 57.
[74] *Valor Eccl.* (Rec. Com.), ii. 98.

building.[75] A lease for the same term to the same persons was renewed in 1543–4.[76] In 1561 the property comprised a capital messuage, with a barn and stable, a number of small closes of meadows, one of which was called Hensford, 40 a. of arable in the fields of Great Sutton, and pasture for 360 sheep.[77] In the same year it was granted by the Crown to Richard Middlecot, clothier, of Bishopstrow.[78] The further descent of the estate has not been traced.

Two other Wiltshire religious houses also had land in Sutton Veny, namely Stanley Abbey in 1227[79] and the Prior of Monkton Farleigh at the beginning of the 15th century.[80] The Stanley land had been given by Andrew Gifford. The descent of these lands has not been traced.

In 1341 the Rector of Sutton Veny had a small estate comprising a carucate of pasture, some meadow and more pasture, and rent and services from tenants valued at 28s. 6d.[81] In 1783 this glebe estate had 53 a. of arable scattered in small lots throughout the common fields, and 6 a. of pasture, meadow, and orchard. There was also grazing for 12 beasts, 1 horse, and 140 sheep, a plantation of elm and chestnut trees, and a farmyard with the usual farm buildings.[82] As shewn below, the glebe estate was greatly enlarged in 1804 by the allotments made in lieu of tithes under the Inclosure Award.[83] In 1880 it comprised about 800 a. and had then been farmed for many years by members of the Parham family.[84] After the death of James Nowlson Parham in 1904 Glebe Farm was rented by David Waddington who was succeeded in 1911 by H. W. Jeans.[85] Jeans bought the farm from the Ecclesiastical Commissioners in c. 1920. From him it was acquired by Mr. G. A. Burt who farmed it in 1963.[86]

ECONOMIC HISTORY. At the time of the Domesday Survey there were three separate estates in Sutton Veny. The largest was William son of Guy's manor of 8 hides.[87] On this the land was divided equally between demesne and tenant farming. Two serfs were attached to the demesne, on which there were 2 ploughs, and on the remainder of the manor there were 6 villeins and 8 bordars with 4 ploughs. This estate had 6 a. of meadow, some pasture, and much woodland. William de Mohun's estate at Little Sutton comprised 5 hides, of which 3 were in demesne.[88] On the demesne there were 3 serfs and 2 ploughs, while 3 villeins and 6 bordars with 2 ploughs farmed the rest of the land. There were 4 a. of meadow, some pasture, and 2 a. of wood. There were at this date on the manor 300 sheep.[89] Niel's 4-hide estate was, like William

son of Guy's, divided equally between demesne and tenant farming.[90] On the demesne there were 3 serfs and 1 plough, and elsewhere there were 5 villeins and 5 bordars with 2 ploughs. There were on this estate 3 a. of meadow, some pasture, and no woodland.

As has been shown above,[91] these three estates continued to share the greater part of the land of the parish until the end of the 17th century. The manors belonging to William son of Guy and Niel in 1086 both eventually became part of the large accumulation of lands belonging to the Lords Hungerford, and were farmed as units in that complex until they were broken up and sold in lots in 1684. The manor belonging to William de Mohun in 1086, except for a part which also became a Hungerford manor, descended to the Thynnes in the mid-16th century, and so became part of the estate of the Marquesses of Bath. Thus, for a considerable time all the manors within the parish were organized as but parts of large estates.[92]

The lands belonging to these manors were dispersed throughout the parish, so that all of them had parts situated in the three tithings of Great and Little Sutton, and Newnham. It is impossible to tell precisely how the common fields were arranged. In the 15th century those of Great Sutton and Newnham lay between what is in 1963 the village of Sutton Veny and the river,[93] and it seems likely that there was another set of fields for Little Sutton. In the 16th century a North and South Field there are mentioned.[94]

A series of 19 account rolls covers the period from 1417 to 1471 on the Hungerford manors in Sutton Veny.[95] At this time the Hungerfords had not yet acquired the manor of Fenny Sutton, but they held the manor of Great Sutton and another in Little Sutton.[96] By the date the accounts begin all the demesne arable was leased out for a rent of £7, and the Hungerfords farmed the land only as a sheep farm. As such, it was organized on an inter-manorial basis with sheep coming and going between Sutton Veny and the other neighbouring Hungerford sheep farms, the interchange being usually with Heytesbury and Farleigh Hungerford (Som.). Between 1417 and 1436 Sutton Veny contributed between 400 and 600 fleeces annually to the Hungerford wool store. The demesne arable continued to be leased out for the entire period covered by the accounts, and for the first 17 years the lessee was the chief stock-keeper of the Hungerford estates in Wiltshire. For one year only (1439–40) the Sutton Veny flock was leased with the demesne land, but thereafter its management was resumed by the lord of the manor.[97]

[75] S.C. 6/Hen. VIII/3969 m. 5.
[76] S.C. 6/Hen. VIII/3982.
[77] E 318/2436.
[78] *Cal. Pat.* 1560–63, 234.
[79] *Cal. Ch. R.* 1226–1257, 39.
[80] *Feudal Aids*, vi. 531.
[81] *Inq. Non.* (Rec. Com.), 170.
[82] Sar. Dioc. R.O. Glebe Terrier, 1783.
[83] See p. 70.
[84] W.A.S. Libr., Devizes, Everett MSS. vol. vi. 140.
[85] W.R.O. 212A, undated notes on Sutton Veny by C.R. Everett.
[86] Ex inf. Mr. G. A. Burt, Glebe Farm.
[87] See p. 64.
[88] See p. 65.

[89] Little Sutton is the only Wilts. manor included in the Exon. Domesday which gives information about livestock: *V.C.H. Wilts.* ii, p. 44.
[90] See p. 63.
[91] See pp. 63–66.
[92] Ibid.
[93] *W.A.M.* xxxvii. 38.
[94] W.R.O. 442/1, Survey of Manor, 1582.
[95] S.C. 6/1059/1–19.   [96] See pp. 63, 66.
[97] For some account of the manorial economy of Sutton based upon the study of these accounts see R. C. Payne, 'Agrarian Conditions on Wilts. Estates of Duchy of Lancaster, the Lords Hungerford, and the Bishopric of Winchester 13th–15th centuries', Ph. D. (Econ.), London, thesis, 1940.

In 1582, by which time the Hungerfords had acquired the manor of Fenny Sutton in addition to that of Great Sutton, but had lost their estate in Little Sutton, there were 6 freeholders, 24 copyholders, 3 tenants at will, and 4 leaseholders on the two manors.[98] The two farms were leased separately. Fenny Sutton farm had 125 a. of arable, 19½ a. of meadow, and 21 a. of pasture. There was pasture for 500 sheep on the downs, possibly inclosed, for there was additionally common pasture upon the East and West Downs, on the heath 'under the wood', and upon the west heath, known as the 'Sands'. The tenant of this farm at this time had to act as bailiff to the Lords Hungerford, and the manor had to provide hospitality when the steward of the Hungerford estate and his officers came to hold the manor courts. Great Sutton farm had c. 180 a. of arable as well as another 40 a. in the North Field of Little Sutton, and 69 a. in the South Field. There were 15 a. of meadow, 4 a. of pasture, and a number of odd acres of meadow lying in various fields. The farm had its own pasture for 12 sheep, and common pasture for another 640 sheep in Great and Little Sutton. There were also some 200 a. of common downland shared between the lord of this manor and the lord of the manor of Little Sutton.

Much of the land of the manor of Little Sutton, acquired by Sir John Thynne in 1563,[99] lay in Newnham and in the extreme west of the parish, although the demesne farm was on the east side. Special arrangements were necessary to provide for grazing rights for the tenants of this manor who were scattered throughout the parish, and those living in Great Sutton, Newnham, or Crockerton had a fixed share in the common pasture of those places.[1] In 1613 the demesne farm of Little Sutton had grazing for 160 sheep in the sheep-sleight of Little Sutton, 240 in that of Fenny Sutton, and 40 upon Tytherington Common. It also had grazing rights for other animals upon the downs and fields of Great Sutton.[2] In 1676 there were upon this manor 4 freeholders, 6 copyholders, and the tenant of the demesne farm.[3]

In the 18th century the land of the parish was still mainly devoted to sheep-farming. Little Sutton Farm, and two farms called Great Sutton Farm, and Sutton Farm, which were possibly the farms of the former manors of Great and Fenny Sutton, had between them grazing for 1,000 sheep on Cow Down, and the rector had grazing for another 140 sheep there. The sheep were pastured on the down from Michaelmas until May, after which month the down was left for about a month and then stocked with cattle until Michaelmas.[4] In the mid-18th century a certain amount of inclosure was said to have taken place within the previous 20 years. Pasture rights on these inclosed lands were,

however, shared in common,[5] and little inclosure seems in fact to have been done before the time of the Inclosure Award in 1808.[6] By the date of this award many of the meadows along the river, north of the village, had been artificially irrigated to make water-meadows, and provision had to be made in the award to ensure the fair control of the numerous channels.

Sutton Veny lies in that region of south-west Wiltshire where in the 15th and 16th centuries the production of wool was closely connected with the manufacture of cloth.[7] Within the parish lay one of the fulling-mills which were strung out along the upper reaches of the Wylye.[8] Mount Mill was a fulling mill at least as early as 1541 and from that date until the 19th century it was owned, or leased, by a succession of local clothiers.[9] Many of the inhabitants, were thus doubtless occupied with both agriculture and industry. A weaver in the parish is mentioned in 1576;[10] Richard Randall a clothier of Sutton Veny occurs in 1717 and 1749.[11] Towards the end of the 18th century a woolsorter and a tailor in the parish were taking apprentices,[12] and in 1798 it was recorded that there were spinning houses in the parish working for the Warminster clothiers.[13]

In the 20th century many of the inhabitants of Sutton Veny found employment in Warminster, although in 1963 there were still five or six farms of over 150 a. in the parish as well as a number of small holdings. Two of these farms, namely the two lying in Little Sutton, belonged to one farmer, who also farmed much land outside the parish.

MILLS. There were two mills at Sutton Veny at the time of the Domesday Survey. One belonged to the Little Sutton estate of William de Mohun, and the other was divided between the holders of the other two estates in Sutton, namely William son of Guy, who held ⅔, and Niel who held ⅓.[14] The mill belonging to the manor of Little Sutton was situated on the Wylye on the west side of the parish, and later became called Wylye Mill. The mill which was divided between William son of Guy and Niel was presumably the one later called Mount Mill, which also stood on the Wylye, north-east of the village. Mount Mill derived its name from the family of Mount which held land in Sutton and the surrounding district in the 14th century.[15] By 1455 this mill was held by members of the atte Bergh family of Robert Hungerford (d. 1459)[16] and in 1476 of his widow Margaret Botreaux, Lady Hungerford.[17] By 1469 it was a fulling mill.[18] It is probably the mill said at the court of the Hungerford manor of Little Sutton to be ruinous in 1510[19] and it seems to have been regarded at least for a time as belonging to this manor and to have passed like that estate from the Hungerfords to William Button, who was overlord in 1550.[20] There is some

98 W.R.O. 442/1, Survey of Manor, 1582.
99 See p. 66.
1 W.A.S. Libr., Devizes, Everett MSS. vol. 1. 161.
2 Ibid. 216.
3 Longleat MSS. Thynne Papers Bk. 83, f. 30.
4 E 112/1309/111.
5 E 134/17 Geo. II Hil. 3.
6 W.R.O. Inclosure Award.
7 V.C.H. Wilts. iv. 122, 129; Ramsay, Wilts. Woollen Industry, 12, 13.
8 V.C.H. Wilts. iv. map facing p. 117.
9 See p. 69.

10 Sess. Mins. 1563, 1574–92 (W.A.S. Rec. Brch.), p. 23.
11 W.R.O. 132, Deed of 1717, and Longleat MS. 9061.
12 W.R.O. 212A, undated notes on Sutton Veny by C.R. Everett.
13 Universal Brit. Dir. (1798), iv. 684.
14 V.C.H. Wilts. ii, pp. 150, 152, 157.
15 B.M. Add. Ch. 17397, 17408; C.P. 25(1)/255/46/22.
16 C 139/161/8.
17 C 140/56/49.
18 Cal. Close, 1468–76, 59.
19 S.C. 2/208/28.   20 C 140/92/125 and see p. 66.

doubt about this, however, for in 1561 and 1591 Sir Walter Hungerford (d. 1596) was granting leases of the same mill.[21]

About the middle of the 14th century Mount Mill was held by Walter atte Bergh, whose widow, Isabel, married Sir Hugh Tirell and died in 1369 holding the mill and other lands.[22] The mill was presumably held of the Hungerfords as it is known to have been in 1455 and 1476 (see above). Isabel's son, John atte Bergh, succeeded and his widow, Christine, died in 1396 holding extensive lands in south and west Wiltshire.[23] Christine was succeeded by another John atte Bergh who conveyed his lands in 1431 to Drew atte Bergh and Anne his wife with reversion in default of issue to John and his heirs.[24] In 1469 the atte Bergh property, including the mill, was settled by Walter atte Bergh upon himself and his wife Eleanor.[25] Eleanor was succeeded in 1476 by her son Maurice,[26] and in 1513 Sir Maurice Barowe (or atte Bergh) settled his estate, which was described then as the manors of Newnham, Sutton, and Bemerton upon himself and his wife Dorothy.[27] In 1541, after the execution of Lord Walter Hungerford, the lease of the mill was granted by the Crown to John Keysbye.[28] In 1561 the mill was leased by Sir Walter Hungerford, Lord Walter's son, to Thomas Ashlock and his son, also called Thomas,[29] and in 1591 a 60-year lease was made to Geoffrey Hawkins, clothier, of Norton Bavant, on the surrender of a previous lease to Thomas Ashlock.[30] In 1765 the mill was advertised for sale as a fulling mill with 2 a. of water-meadow and 1a. of pasture .[31] The purchaser was probably Thomas Benett, of Norton Bavant, who owned it in 1771 and 1780.[32] It was still owned by the Benetts in 1830 when Joseph Everett, clothier of Heytesbury was the occupier.[33] In 1963 the site of the mill could clearly be seen, but no trace of the buildings remained. It had probably ceased to be used about the middle of the 19th century.

Walter, the miller, of the mill at Little Sutton is mentioned in the 13th century.[34] In 1558 John Holgate was the tenant of the mill which was a grist mill and had pasture rights attached at West Heath and Crockerton Heath.[35] No other mention of the mill has been found until after the manor of Little Sutton had passed to Sir John Thynne.[36] In 1702 Lord Bath's tenant at the mill was Samuel Lewis,[37] who two years later was involved with William Adlam, clothier of Bull Mill, Longbridge Deverill, in a dispute over the regulation of the water at

the two mills.[38] Samuel Lewis died in 1725 and was succeeded by his son and his grandson.[39] Both were called Job and henceforth the mill was sometimes called Job's Mill, its name in 1963. In 1782 the mill was described as a newly built grist mill with one pair of French, and one pair of Welsh stones, and with 7 a. of land belonging to it.[40] After the death of Job Lewis, the younger, the lessee in 1786 was John Phipps, of Chilmark.[41] Three years later the mill was leased to John Gale Everett, clothier, of Heytesbury,[42] and at the beginning of the 19th century J. G. Everett was succeeded by his son, Joseph Everett, who also leased Mount Mill from the Benetts.[43] In 1963 the mill-house was the home of Lord Bath.

CHURCHES. The first mention found of the church of Sutton Veny occurs in 1220,[44] but there are traces of Norman work in the old parish church and it is probable that the church of Sutton was among the gifts made by Hamelin de Ballon about the beginning of the 12th century for the endowment of the priory of Abergavenny.[45] The small church, dedicated to St. Leonard, served the parish until towards the end of the 19th century when because of the condition of its fabric it was abandoned for a new church built about 700 yds. to the north-west (see below). There was a free chapel dedicated to St. Nicholas at Little Sutton by 1291.[46] This was the chapel of the manor of Little Sutton in which Sir Thomas de Kingston obtained licence to hear divine service in 1343.[47] The presentation of a fourteen-year old clerk to the chapel was allowed in 1312 because there was no cure attached.[48] The chapel survived until suppressed in the 16th century. Its site is unknown but is said to have been quite close to the parish church.[49]

The living of Sutton Veny is a rectory. Since 1953 it has been held in plurality with that of Norton Bavant.[50] Apparently presuming that the advowson belonged to the manor of Great Sutton, Nicholas de Limesy, Margery his wife, and Margery's sisters, Denise and Florence, claimed in 1220 the right of presentation from the Prior of Abergavenny.[51] The dispute was evidently decided in favour of the prior, for in 1291 Richard, Prior of Abergavenny, conveyed to Robert Burnell, Bishop of Bath and Wells, a rent of 50 s. in Sutton Veny and the advowson of the church.[52] Robert died in 1292 and was succeeded by his nephew Philip Burnell.[53] Philip died seised of the advowson in 1294 and his son Edward, a minor, succeeded,[54]

[21] W.R.O. 442/1, Survey of Manor, 1582; 490, Cover of a Ct. R. 1593.
[22] Wilts. Inq. p.m. 1327–77 (Index Libr.), 356.
[23] C 136/91/3.
[24] C.P. 25(1)/257/62/19.
[25] C 140/56/49.
[26] Ibid.
[27] C.P. 25(2)/51/360/5 Hen. VIII Trin. Sutton here may be Sutton Mandeville.
[28] L. & P Hen. VIII, xvi, p. 428.
[29] W.R.O. 442/1, Survey of Manor, 1582.
[30] Ibid. 490, Cover of a Ct. R. 1593.
[31] Notice of Sale quoted in W.A.S. Libr., Devizes, Everett MSS. Large Folder.
[32] W.A.S. Libr., Devizes, Everett MSS. Large Folder.
[33] C.P. 43/990 rot. 5.
[34] Longleat MS. 9088.
[35] Ibid. Ct. R. 1558.   [36] See p. 66.

[37] W.A.S. Libr., Devizes, Everett MSS. Large Folder.
[38] W.R.O. 130/22.
[39] Longleat MSS. Ct. R. 27 May 1725.
[40] Sar. Jnl. 4 Feb. 1782.
[41] W.A.S. Libr., Devizes, Everett MSS. Large Folder.
[42] Longleat MSS. 8930.
[43] W.A.S. Libr., Devizes, Everett MSS. Large Folder.
[44] Cal. Pat. 1216–25, 262.
[45] See. p 63.
[46] Tax. Eccl. (Rec. Com.), 181 b.
[47] W.A.M. x. 311.
[48] Reg. Ghent (Cant. and York Soc.), ii. 795.
[49] E 301/56/37.
[50] Order in Council, 20 Oct. 1953.
[51] Cal. Pat. 1216–25, 262.
[52] Feet of F. Wilts. 1272–1377 (W.A.S. Rec. Brch.), 36.
[53] Complete Peerage, Burnell, 434, n.b.
[54] Wilts. Inq. p.m. 1242–1326 (Index Libr.), 201–2.

the king presenting to the church in 1304 on account of the minority.[55] In 1309 Henry Lorty, lord of the manor of Fenny Sutton, tried to present an incumbent to the parish church.[56] But he failed to establish his claim to the advowson, and so far as is known, the lords of Fenny Sutton never presented, although the advowson of the church was often said to accompany that manor in the disputes which arose over the lordship in the 14th and 15th centuries.[57] Edward Burnell died in 1316,[58] and the advowson was assigned as dower to his wife Alice.[59] Edward's heir was his sister, Maud, wife of Sir John Haudlo,[60] and in 1339 the advowson was said to be held for life by Joan, widow of Thomas Burnell, eldest son of Sir John Haudlo and Maud.[61] At the same time Sir John settled the reversion of the advowson, after Joan's death, upon himself for life with remainder to his younger son Nicholas and Mary, wife of Nicholas.[62] Sir John Haudlo died in 1346 and was succeeded by Nicholas, who, like his elder brother, assumed the name Burnell.[63] Nicholas died in 1382–3 and was succeeded by his son Hugh, who presented in 1398 and died in 1420.[64] Hugh's son died before his father, leaving three daughters, one of whom, Margery, married Edmund, a younger son of Sir Walter Hungerford (d. 1449).[65] The first presentation after the death of Hugh Burnell was by Sir Walter Hungerford and six other persons.[66] Thenceforth the advowson descended in the Hungerford family like the manor of Great Sutton, until the forfeiture of Walter, Lord Hungerford's possessions in 1540.[67] Then, with the Hungerford manor in Little Sutton, the advowson was granted in 1545 to James Tutt and Nicholas Hame.[68] From them it passed, with the Little Sutton manor, to William Button. Button died in 1547 leaving William his son and heir.[69] Shortly before his death in 1591 this William had settled the manor of Little Sutton, and probably the advowson also, on a younger son William,[70] who eventually became the heir of his eldest brother, Ambrose.[71] William's son and successor, another William, was created a baronet in 1622,[72] and died in 1654 when the advowson passed successively to his sons, Sir William and Sir Robert, who both died without issue.[73] Sir Robert was succeeded in 1679 by his brother Sir John Button who died, also without issue, in 1712.[74] The advowson then passed to Sir John's great-nephew, Heneage Walker, grandson of his sister Mary.[75] Heneage Walker was succeeded in 1731 by his brother John Walker, whose eldest son John succeeded his

father in 1758, and assumed the name Heneage. He died childless in 1806 and the advowson passed to his great-nephew George Heneage Wyld, who assumed the name Walker Heneage in 1818. The advowson then passed in the Walker Heneage family until 1946 when John David William Graham Walker Heneage presented. After that the patronage passed to the Bishop of Salisbury.[76]

In 1291 the church was valued for taxation at £26 13s. 4d.[77] Out of it in 1341–2 a pension of 50s. was paid to the Prior of Abergavenny.[78] This is the only reference found to the pension and it is therefore not known for how long it was paid. In 1535 the rectory with its lands and tithes was said to be worth £21 10s. 1d. and the only charge upon it was 10s. 9d. paid for synodals and procurations.[79] In c. 1580 the value of the rectory was said to be £40.[80] The gross average income of the benefice in 1831 was £850, and the net average income £800.[81] It was thus one of the richer livings in Wiltshire.[82]

In 1341 a ninth of the value of the corn, wool, and lambs, including the corn belonging to the free chapel of St. Nicholas in Little Sutton, but excluding the corn, wool, and lambs belonging to the Prior of Maiden Bradley, was assessed at £12 7s. A ninth of oblations and other tithable commodities was at the same date reckoned at £5.[83] Under the Inclosure Award of 1804 the rector was awarded over 600 a. of land in lieu of almost all tithes, to which he was entitled, and as compensation for the existing glebe which lay in the open fields.[84] In the few cases where no allotment of land could be made, tithes were commuted for money rents which were eventually redeemed in 1924 for £50.[85] From certain land in the parish which had once belonged to the free chapel of Little Sutton the rector was entitled to only ⅓ of tithes. The other ⅔ were impropriated and in 1759 belonged to Thomas Buckler of Sutton, later Church, Farm.[86] Out of these impropriated tithes the Crown had an annual rent of 26s. In 1804 the impropriated tithes were called 'Thirties' and were redeemed by an allotment of 22a. of land to Francis Dugdale Astley, by then the largest land owner in the parish and owner of Church Farm.[87]

At an unknown date Sir Walter Barrow granted 5 a. of land in the North Field of Great Sutton to the church for the maintenance of 5 tapers before the image of Our Lady. In 1549–50 this land was leased to the rector for an annual rent of 4s.[88] In 1554 William Benett of Norton Bavant conveyed

[55] Phillipps, *Wilts. Inst.* i. 5.
[56] *Reg. Ghent* (Cant. and York Soc.), ii. 270.
[57] C.P. 40/499 rot. 346; C.P. 40/898 rot. 537; B.M. Harl. Ch. 53 G. 41.
[58] *Wilts. Inq. p.m.* 1242–1326 (Index Libr.), 408.
[59] *Cal. Pat.* 1313–17, 612.
[60] *Complete Peerage*, Burnell.
[61] *Cal. Pat.* 1338–40, 302; for Thos. Burnell, see *Complete Peerage*, Haudlo, 399, n.o.
[62] *Cal. Pat.* 1338–40, 302.
[63] C 135/129/73.
[64] C 136/24/20; Phillipps, *Wilts. Inst.* i. 84.
[65] *Complete Peerage*, Burnell and Hungerford.
[66] Phillipps, *Wilts. Inst.* i. 111.
[67] See p. 63.
[68] See p. 66.
[69] C 142/87/101.   [70] C 142/239/173.
[71] G.E.C. *Complete Baronetage* (1900), i. 193.

[72] Ibid.
[73] Ibid.
[74] Ibid.
[75] Burke, *Landed Gentry* (1906), Heneage Walker.
[76] Sar. Dioc. R.O. Presentation Deeds.
[77] *Tax. Eccl.* (Rec. Com.), 181.
[78] *Inq. Non.* (Rec. Com.), 170.
[79] *Valor Eccl.* (Rec. Com.), ii. 103.
[80] W.R.O. 442/1, Survey of Manor, 1582.
[81] *Rep. Com. Eccl. Revenues*, H.C. 54 pp. 850–1 (1835), xxii.
[82] *V.C.H. Wilts.* iii. 53.
[83] *Inq. Non.* (Rec. Com.), 170.
[84] W.R.O. Inclosure Award.
[85] Ibid. Cert. Redemption Corn Rents.
[86] B.M. Harl. MS. 6826; see p. 65.
[87] W.R.O. Inclosure Award.
[88] Hoare, *Mod. Wilts.* Warminster, 87–8.

the reversion of the lease to George Cotton and William Manne.[89] This land was exchanged for an allotment of just over 3 a. at North End under the Inclosure Award of 1804.[90] In 1955, by which date the rent was being used for the general maintenance of the church, the land was sold and the proceeds of the sale invested.[91]

There have been a number of distinguished men among the incumbents of Sutton Veny, although some of them had little direct influence upon the parish. Simon Sydenham, rector 1417–21, was elected Bishop of Salisbury in 1426, but his election was quashed the following year.[92] Thomas Benett (d. 1558), rector 1502–7, subsequently rose to high office in the church, and became Precentor of Salisbury in 1542.[93] Cuthbert Tunstall, successively Bishop of London and Durham, was instituted to the livings of Steeple Langford and Sutton Veny in 1509, but almost immediately resigned the latter.[94] Thomas Hyde, Chancellor of Salisbury after 1588, held the living of Sutton Veny by 1613, and until his death in 1618.[95] He presumably seldom, if ever, visited the parish, but employed a curate,[96] as did Thomas Dobbs, who in 1582 was instituted by William Button to the livings of Sutton Veny and Woodborough, some 30 miles apart.[97]

In 1646 the rector, Henry Swaddon, was apparently deprived of his living in favour of Daniel Burgess, one of the Wiltshire signatories to the Presbyterian Testimony of 1648.[98] But by 1662 Swaddon had been restored to the benefice, for that year he was presented by the churchwardens for saying no prayer in the pulpit before preaching his sermon.[99] Between c. 1779 and c. 1783 the Rector of Sutton also served the church of Norton Bavant because of the ill-health of the incumbent there.[1] The living was held from 1780 to 1854 successively by Brounker Thring and his son William Davidson Thring. After 1829 W. D. Thring was also Rector of Fisherton de la Mere and in both parishes he employed a curate.[2] On census day 1851 there were 130 people in church at Sutton for the morning service and 240 were present in the evening. Sunday school that day was attended by 42 children in the morning and 44 in the afternoon.[3] In 1863 the average number of the congregation was said to be 250.[4]

The church of *ST. LEONARD*, with the exception of the chancel, has fallen into ruins since the building of the church of St. John the Evangelist about 700 yds. to the north-west in 1868.[5] The old church was cruciform in plan with nave and chancel, north and south transepts, and central tower.[6] There are traces of a Norman doorway in the ruined north wall of the nave, but the rubble walls of the nave and chancel are of 13th-century date. The arches of the crossing and the lancet windows on the north wall of the chancel also date from the 13th century. On the south wall of the chancel there was once a large 15th- or 16th-century window. In 1868 the chancel was re-roofed and the chancel arch filled in to enclose this part of the church for use as a mortuary chapel. The rest of the church was abandoned. In 1963 there was little trace left of the transepts. The roofless walls of the nave still stood, although much broken down and overgrown with ivy.

The building evidently began at quite an early date to cause concern, and traces remain of the buttresses which had to be built in the 14th and 15th centuries on both sides of the nave and at the north-east corner of the chancel.[7] It was possibly for the work of buttressing that Nicholas of Bonham gave by his will, dated 1386, 8 bushels of wheat and the same quantity of barley for the fabric of the church.[8] In 1698 the room in the parsonage pew had to be taken away because of a buttress built there to support the tower. Another pew was allotted to the parsonage 'under the south window behind the pulpit'.[9] In 1825 the church was much in need of repair and in the following year extensive works of restoration were begun,[10] so that in 1831 it could be said 'the whole of the building has been repaired in good taste'.[11] Among the work undertaken was the addition of an organ and gallery at the west end, and the insertion of a new east window.[12] But within thirty years more repairs were needed, and it was decided to abandon St. Leonard's for a church which certain members of the Everett family offered to build for the parish in memory of Joseph Everett (d. 1865).[13] In 1963 the small ruined church stood in an overgrown and disused church yard, which was lined on two sides by well-grown chestnut trees. At the end of the 18th century the maintenance of the churchyard was shared between the parish, the rector, Sir Walter Long, owner of Polebridge Farm, and William Buckler, owner of Sutton, later Church, Farm.[14]

The foundation stone of the church of *ST. JOHN THE EVANGELIST* was laid in 1866 and the church was dedicated two years later by the Bishop of Sodor and Man.[15] The church was built in memory of Joseph Everett (d. 1865) by his widow,

[89] *Cal. Pat.* 1553–4, 474–5.
[90] W.R.O. Inclosure Award.
[91] Char. Com. Files Correspondence G, and 136718.
[92] Phillipps, *Wilts. Inst.* i. 106, 111.
[93] Ibid. i. 181, 184; Jones, *Fasti Eccl. Sar.* 332.
[94] *D.N.B.*; Phillipps, *Wilts. Inst.* i. 187.
[95] Sar. Dioc. R.O. Metropolitan Vis. 1613; Phillipps, *Wilts. Inst.* ii. 10; Jones, *Fasti Eccl. Sar.* 341.
[96] Sar. Dioc. R.O. Metropolitan Vis. 1613.
[97] Phillipps, *Wilts. Inst.* i. 231; W.A.S. Libr., Devizes, Everett MSS. Memoranda Bk.
[98] Phillipps, *Wilts. Inst.* ii. 18, 31; *Calamy Revised*, ed. Matthews, 88.
[99] Sar. Dioc. R.O. Chwdns' Pres. 1662.
[1] Ibid. Vis. Queries, 1781.
[2] Phillipps, *Wilts. Inst.* ii. 90; Note in church under portrait of W. D. Thring; *Rep. Com. Eccl. Revenues*, H.C. 54 pp. 850–1 (1835), xxii; see p. 45.
[3] H.O. 129/10/260.

[4] Sar. Dioc. R.O. Vis. Queries, 1864.
[5] See below.
[6] There are S.E. and N.W. views of the church in 1804 by John Buckler: W.A.S. Libr., Devizes, vol. ii. 20, and an interior view looking E. in c. 1860 by Ric. Kemm. See pls. facing p. 61.
[7] *W.A.M.* xxvii. 264–5 gives a detailed description of the church in 1893.
[8] B.M. Add. Ch. 15174.
[9] W.R.O. 554, Chwdns'. Acct. Bk. 1692–1718.
[10] W.A.S. Libr., Devizes, Everett MSS. Notebk. i. 134, vi. 137.
[11] Hoare, *Mod. Wilts.* Warminster, 86.
[12] Ibid.; W.A.S. Libr., Devizes, Everett MSS. Notebk. vi. 137.
[13] *W.A.M.* xxxiii. 66–7.
[14] Sar. Dioc. R.O. Glebe Terrier, 1783.
[15] W.A.S. Libr., Devizes, Everett MSS. Notebk. vi. 75.

Frances Alice, and their children.[16] The architect was J. L. Pearson. The church is cruciform in plan with a central tower and a spire. It is built in Early Decorated style of Frome stone with Box ground-stone dressings.[17] The chancel and crossing are rib-vaulted in stone. The altar was presented to the church at the time of its consecration by the then Bishop of Salisbury, and the reredos was given by the parish. The carved oak lectern was displayed at the Exhibition of 1862.[18] A portrait of William Davidson Thring (rector 1819–54) hangs in the south transept, and there are two water-colour pictures of the old church. The belfry and ringing chamber in the tower are reached by an outside staircase. The six bells were brought from the old church and in 1927 were re-hung in a metal frame. Nos. 1, 2, and 3 are of 17th-century date. The others date from the 18th century. No. 5 was cast by Robert and James Wells; no. 6 by William Cockey of Warminster.[19] Edward VI's commissioners took away 4oz. of silver, and left the church a chalice of 9oz.[20] Among the plate in 1963 were a chalice, paten, and flagon inscribed with the names of Samuel and Stephen Long, churchwardens in 1792. The registers begin in 1564 and are complete.[21] In 1918 a corner of the churchyard was set apart as the burial place of the service men, many of them Australians, who had been attached to the military camp and hospital in the parish. Many had died in the influenza epidemic of that year and others were battle casualties. Five Australian nurses are also buried there, and until 1963 there were the graves of 39 German prisoners from the First World War. That year the remains of the German prisoners were transferred to a German prisoner-of-war cemetery in Staffordshire.

The first institution found to the free chapel of St. Nicholas in Little Sutton is in 1312 when John de Kingston, lord of the manor, presented.[22] Until 1333 presentation was by the lords of the manor of Little Sutton. In 1382 Robert Ashton, who may have had a manor in Little Sutton, presented,[23] and in 1423 the patron was William Fyndern who held land formerly belonging to the Kingstons in Corsley.[24] Thenceforth, so far as is known, the lords of the manor presented. The last institution recorded is in 1530.[25]

In 1291 the chapel was worth £1 and was held by John of Berwick.[26] At the time of its suppression the tithes belonging to it were worth 26s. 8d. and were leased to Walter Bullour.[27] In 1563 the tithes of corn in Little Sutton which belonged to the chapel were leased for 21 years.[28] The last reference found to the chapel is in 1705 when it and all its tithes were conveyed by Matthew Davies to Thomas Buckler.[29]

The house called in 1963 the Manor House has for much of its history been the home of the rectors of Sutton, although it has been suggested that it may once have been a manor house.[30] So far as is known, those rectors who were resident in the parish lived here until c. 1913 when the present Rectory was built. In 1783 the parsonage house was said to be built of free stone and roofed with stone tiles. It had two parlours with oak floors, and five chambers, three of which had floors of elm. It also had a study, kitchen, cellar, and pantry, but no garret.[31] In 1831 it was known that the house contained a medieval hall with a number of pointed openings, although this was obscured by the partitions, floors, and ceilings that had been inserted.[32] The Revd. G. F. S. Powell, rector 1854–88, added a kitchen wing at the south end of the house, demolished the farm buildings, and built the retaining wall bordering the lane to North End.[33] In 1921 the 14th-century hall was restored by the then owner, D. E. W. Cowie. The roof was opened up and 4 pointed windows with stone tracery were inserted in existing jambs. One traceried head is original, another has been moved to the coach-house. The end doorways to the screens passage were also restored.[34] In the medieval house, the hall formed, as now, the central range. The service rooms were apparently under the same roof to the south, entered from the screens passage by two pointed doorways which still survive. A solar wing to the north of the hall has been almost entirely rebuilt.

NONCONFORMITY. The Baptist chapel at Crockerton Green, founded at least as early as 1669, has the longest history of the nonconformist places of worship within the parish of Sutton Veny. It played an outstanding part in the early Baptist organization of the district.[35] But although situated until 1934 just within the Sutton Veny parish boundary, the chapel belonged to the hamlet of Crockerton in Longbridge Deverill, and its history is reserved for treatment under the account of that parish. In 1662 there were reported to be 15 sectaries in Sutton, and in 1679 18 nonconformists there were returned, these figures probably representing mainly the Baptists meeting at Crockerton.[36] At the end of the 18th century Thomas Gibbons, minister of the New Meeting in Warminster, preached to a group of Independents in a house in Sutton Veny.[37] In 1793, largely through the exertions and enthusiasm of Gibbons and a family called Imber, a chapel was built for this congregation. The building of this chapel met with some opposition in the village, and one farmer threatened to pull down the walls as they were being erected.[38] A schoolroom and burial ground were added to the chapel in 1818.[39] In c. 1800 average attendance at the chapel on Sunday mornings was 116, in the afternoons 151, and in

[16] Plate in church.
[17] W.A.S. Libr., Devizes, Everett MSS. Notebk. i. 88.
[18] Note in church.
[19] Walters, *Wilts. Bells*, 211–13.
[20] Nightingale, *Wilts. Plate*, 96.
[21] Deposited with other parish records in W.R.O.
[22] Phillipps, *Wilts. Inst.* i. 11.
[23] Ibid. 66, and see p. 66.
[24] Phillipps, *Wilts. Inst.* i. 114.
[25] Ibid. 201.
[26] *Tax. Eccl.* (Rec. Com.), 181.
[27] E 301/58/61.
[28] *Cal. Pat.* 1560–63, 517.
[29] C.P. 25(2)/979/4 Anne Mich.
[30] Hoare, *Mod. Wilts.* Warminster, 86.
[31] Sar. Dioc. R.O. Glebe Terrier, 1783.
[32] Hoare, op. cit.
[33] W.A.S. Libr., Devizes, Everett MSS. Notebk. i. 192.
[34] *W.A.M.* xli. 386.
[35] *V.C.H. Wilts.* iii. 111.
[36] Sar. Dioc. R.O. Chwdns'. Pres. (1662); *W.N. & Q.* iii. 537.
[37] G.R.O. Retns. of Regns.; for the New Meeting, Warminster, see p. 126.
[38] *V.C.H. Wilts.* iii. 140; H.M. Gunn, *Nonconformity in Warminster*, 45.
[39] H. M. Gunn, *Nonconformity in Warminster*, 45.

the evenings 300, and in 1829 the regular congregation was reckoned at *c.* 100.[40] The chapel was rebuilt in Romanesque style in the later 19th century. Its log-book at this period, with its list of meetings, lectures, and tea-parties, illustrates vividly the social and educational importance of the congregation within the parish.[41] In 1962 membership was 8 and the chapel had no resident minister, but was supplied by a visiting minister who also served the chapels at Horningsham and Maiden Bradley.[42]

In 1839 a house in the parish occupied by Thomas White was licensed as a dissenters' meeting place,[43] but nothing more is known of the group that met there. By 1864 there was a Primitive Methodist chapel at Little Sutton,[44] but by 1959 it had long been out of use and that year was pulled down and two cottages built on its site.[45]

PARISH GOVERNMENT. There is a set of court rolls for the Hungerford manors of Great and Little Sutton covering the period 1492–1537.[46] Often a single court was held for the two manors, but occasionally there were separate courts held on the same day. Courts were held annually. There are records of courts held for Lord Bath's manor of Little Sutton from 1605 until the mid-19th century.[47] A court house for this manor existed in 1812 when it was in disrepair.[48] Deposited in the Wiltshire Record Office there are churchwardens' accounts from 1686 until 1828 and from 1829 to 1947, and overseers' accounts from 1686 to 1746.[49] At the time these records begin there were two churchwardens, two overseers, and two waywardens. In the later 18th century, and probably at other times too, one churchwarden was chosen to represent Little Sutton and the other Great Sutton. In 1867 a paid assistant overseer was appointed and by the mid-19th century the number of waywardens had been reduced from two to one.[50]

The later 19th century was a time of considerable activity for the vestry.[51] The closing of the old church, the building of the new, and the provision of a new school required its attention.[52] In 1868 a sub-committee was formed to supervise the building of the school. The vestry was also at this time much concerned with the sanitary state of the parish. An outbreak of scarlet fever had caused several deaths among children in the village and created some alarm. In 1868 the vestry asked the parish officers to report on drainage facilities and to arrange a rate to provide for any improvements found necessary.[53] At the same time the Turnpike Commissioners agreed to pay £25 towards improvements in the village if the same sum were to be

subscribed by the parish. In 1878 scarlet fever was still prevalent and the vestry appointed a sub-committee to carry out another inspection. This body recommended that an investigation should be undertaken by an officer of the Board of Health, and this was done in the following year. The officer's report, although somewhat critical of the water supply and drainage arrangements, found that the outbreaks of sickness were largely due to the lack of proper isolation precautions.[54]

SCHOOLS. In 1732 the poor children of the parish repeated their catechism to the rector regularly on Sundays.[55] At the end of the 18th century there was a boarding school for 'young gentlemen' in the village. Here boys were taught subjects to qualify them for business. In 1794 Mr. Shapcot had succeeded Mrs. Lawes as head teacher.[56] In 1833 there was a small infants' school and 3 other day schools in the parish. About 25 boys and 33 girls, all paying fees, attended these schools.[57]

In 1850 a site was acquired and a school built in which in 1859 about 50 children were taught by a certificated teacher.[58] This school was at the southeast end of the village not far from the church of St. Leonard. It was originally a small stone building with brick dressings. In the later 19th century it was converted into a private house and was still inhabited as such in 1963. In 1873 this school was sold and the money used to build a new one in Gothic style just to the west of the new church.[59] Financial assistance was provided by the National Society and a further grant was made by the society in 1898 for the addition of another schoolroom.[60] In 1903–4 average attendance was 73.[61] By 1938 the school had become a junior mixed and infants' school with about 36 pupils.[62]

A school connected with the Congregational chapel, and later supported by the British Society, was established in the village by 1856.[63] A school adjoining the chapel was built to house it in 1869.[64] In 1893 average attendance was about 34 children.[65] The school was closed in *c.* 1908.[66] In 1859 there was a dame-school for about 40 children in the part of Crockerton which then lay within the parish of Sutton Veny.[67]

CHARITIES. At an unknown date Joseph Dew and Anthony Long bequeathed between them £80 to be invested for the benefit of the poor of the parish. In 1823 most of the money was spent on buying a cottage which formed part of some premises called Old Castle. The rent from the cottage was then spent on clothing for the poor at Christmas. The poor were also remembered in the will of Mary

[40] H.O. 129/10/260; W.R.O. Retns. of Nonconformist Meetings, 1829.
[41] *V.C.H. Wilts.* iii. 145.
[42] *Congregational Year Bk.* 1962, 281.
[43] W.R.O. Certs. of Dissenters' Meeting Houses.
[44] Sar. Dioc. R.O. Vis. Queries, 1864.
[45] Local information.
[46] S.C. 2/208/63–70, 72–3, 75–80.
[47] Longleat MS. 8943 and index to Thynne papers.
[48] W.A.S. Libr., Devizes, Everett MS. 'Court Rolls'.
[49] W.R.O. 554.
[50] Ibid. 554, Vestry Min. Bk. 1864–75.
[51] Ibid.
[52] See p. 71.   [53] See p. 62.
[54] *Rept. to Medical Dept. Local Govt. Bd.* 1–3 Feb. 1872; W.R.O. 554, Vestry Min. Bk. 1864–75.

[55] Lambeth MS. 1732.
[56] *Sar. Jnl.* 8 Apr. 1793, 23 June 1794.
[57] *Educ. Enq. Abstract*, H.C. 62 (1835), xliii.
[58] *Endowed Char. Wilts.* (1908), pp. 668–9; *Acct. of Wilts. Schools*, H.C. 27 (1859 sess. 1), xxi (2).
[59] *Endowed Char. Wilts.* (1908), pp. 668–9.
[60] Nat. Soc. Files.
[61] *List of Schools under Admin. of Bd. 1903–4* (Cd. 2011), H.C. (1904), lxxv.
[62] *Bd. of Educ. List 21*, 1938.
[63] *Rtn. of Non-Provided Schools*, H.C. 178–xxxi (1906), lxxxviii.
[64] *Kelly Dir. Wilts.* (1907).
[65] *Rtn. of Schools, 1893* [C 7529], H.C. (1894), lxv.
[66] *Bd. of Educ. List 21*, 1909; *Kelly Dir. Wilts.* (1907).
[67] *Acct. of Wilts. Schools* (1859), xxi (2).

Long, proved in 1807. In 1825 the £50 she had bequeathed, with a roughly equal amount raised by subscription, were used to build two cottages at Little Sutton. In 1833 the three properties and a small investment produced nearly £11, and in the previous year 8 coats, 8 shirts, and 8 shifts had been distributed. In 1903 the cottages at Little Sutton were derelict, and the older one produced an income of about £4 a year.[68] In 1917 all the property was sold and the money received from the sale invested for the benefit of the poor.[69] In 1957, from the charity so formed, 12 persons received 10s. each.[70]

TEFFONT MAGNA

FOR most of its history Teffont Magna, or Upper Teffont, has been a chapelry of Dinton.[1] Ecclesiastically it remained dependent upon Dinton until 1922,[2] but in the earlier 19th century it seems to have been regarded as a parish for certain administrative purposes.[3] In 1934 it was joined with Teffont Evias to form the civil parish of Teffont.[4] The ancient parish contained 1,734 a.[5] and extended about 2½ miles from north to south, and a mile from east to west. The Grovely Grim's Ditch formed its northern boundary, and the southern boundary ran along the present (1962) main road between Dinton and Teffont Magna as far as the Black Horse Inn. It then left the road and proceeded westward for about ½ a mile skirting Upper Holt Copse before turning north and running up to Grim's Ditch.[6]

Much the greater part of the ancient parish lay on the chalk downs that rise between the valleys of the Wylye and the Nadder. On top of the downs, in the extreme north of the ancient parish, the land reaches nearly 600 ft. It then falls gently southwards to a height of about 300 ft. on the lower chalk, but rises again to 450 ft. on the ridge of upper greensand that borders the chalk. At Springhead, towards the foot of the downs, a stream emerges from the chalk and forms a shallow valley through the greensand ridge as it flows southwards through the village to join the Nadder ½ mile beyond the boundary of the ancient parish.[7] The sandy land is well wooded on the Common, to the east of the stream, and at Upper Holt Copse to the west. Thickthorn Wood on the downs is the most westerly offshoot of Grovely Wood and in 1567 covered about 10 a.[8]

Neolithic and Bronze Age implements have been found on the downs behind the village, and finds indicating Roman occupation have been made at Upper Holt Copse.[9] The land of the ancient parish, being mostly chalk, was devoted mainly to sheep- and corn-farming.[10] The parish boundary stopped short of the River Nadder by about ½ mile, so that Teffont Magna had but a small share of the clay and loam soils of the valley, and consequently could not exploit to the same extent the water-

meadows which contributed so much to the farming of its neighbour, Dinton.[11] Perhaps this dearth of rich pasture land explains in some measure the interdependence which existed between the farming of the two manors of Dinton and Teffont Magna in the Middle Ages. In the 20th century this lack of naturally rich pasture has been overcome with the widespread use of fertilizers and mixed farming on the chalkland has become possible.

It is impossible to estimate the population of Teffont Magna before the 19th century. The chapelry contributed 100s. to the 15th of 1334 when Dinton contributed only 6s. more, and in 1377 there were 75 poll-tax payers in Teffont and 156 in Dinton.[12] In 1543 there was only one inhabitant of sufficient substance to contribute to the benevolence of that year while in Dinton there were 6, and in 1576 there were 12 taxpayers in Teffont and 18 in Dinton.[13] When the Census figures begin in 1801 the population of Teffont Magna was 199. It rose to 292 in 1881 but thereafter dropped until it reached 172 in 1931. In 1951 after Teffont Magna had been joined with Teffont Evias, the population of the parish of Teffont so formed was 297.[14]

The Roman road from the Mendip lead mines to Old Salisbury passes through the extreme north of the parish[15] and the green-way, called the Ox Drove, of possibly greater antiquity, runs in roughly the same direction just south of it. Until about the mid-19th century the main road from Salisbury to Hindon was that running along the top of the sandy ridge, north of Dinton village, and entering Teffont Magna almost opposite the church.[16] This road was turnpiked in c. 1760.[17] From the south, the village was approached either by the road running through the village of Teffont Evias, or by a track which led from Dinton across Teffont Common.[18] At the beginning of the 19th century the present (1962) main road between Dinton and Teffont Magna skirting the Common was made.[19]

The village lies along the main road and along the road which leads north from it towards the downs. Several of the cottages are built on the bank of the swift-flowing stream which borders the road and have stone bridges spanning the stream to

[68] Endowed Char. Wilts. (1908), p. 686.
[69] Char. Com. Correspondence File G. 42.
[70] Ibid. File 201696.
[1] Thanks are due to Mr. R. Lever for his help during the compilation of this article.
[2] See p. 31.
[3] It was so classed by the compilers of the Census Reports and by the Charity Commissioners: Endowed Char. Wilts. (1908).
[4] V.C.H. Wilts. iv. 358.
[5] Census, 1931.
[6] O.S. Map 6″ Wilts. LXV (1st. edn.).
[7] O.S. Map 1/25,000 sheets 31/93, 41/03 and for

some further account of the physical geography of the region see Fry, Land Utilization Wilts. 156, 158, 234.
[8] First Pembroke Survey, ed. Straton, 230.
[9] V.C.H Wilts. i (1), p. 113.
[10] See p. 77.
[11] See p. 30.
[12] V.C.H. Wilts. iv. 302, 311.
[13] Taxation Lists (W.A.S. Rec. Brch.), 35, 145.
[14] V.C.H. Wilts. iv. 358.
[15] Ibid. i(1), 113 and map viii.
[16] Andrews and Dury, Map (W.A.S. Rec. Brch.), pl. 5.
[17] V.C.H. Wilts. iv. 262.
[18] Andrews and Dury, Map (W.A.S. Rec. Brch.), pl. 5.
[19] Salisbury and Winchester Jnl., 27 May, 1816.

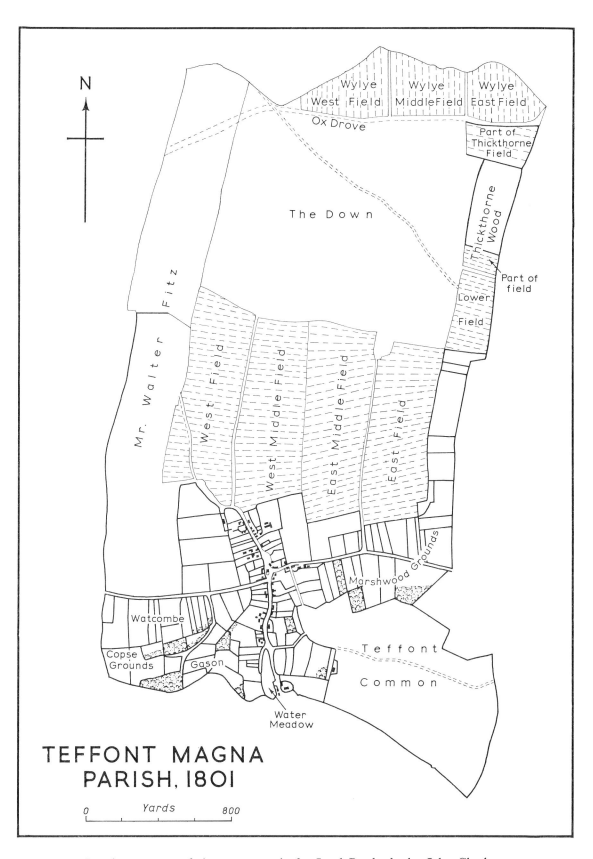

N

Wylye
West Field

Wylye
MiddleField

Wylye
East Field

Ox Drove

Part of
Thickthorne
Field

The Down

Thickthorne
Wood

Part of
field

Mr. Walter Fitz

West Field

West Middle Field

East Middle Field

East Field

Lower
Field

Marshwood Grounds

Watcombe

Copse
Grounds

Gason

Water
Meadow

Teffont

Common

TEFFONT MAGNA
PARISH, 1801

0   Yards   800

Based on a map of the manor made for Lord Pembroke by John Charlton

the road. Many of them date from the 17th and 18th centuries and are built of local stone, and some in 1963 retained their thatched roofs. Few of the houses are larger than cottages. North-west of the church the house called (in 1962) Buck's Close was probably originally a small farm-house. In the late 19th and early 20th century it was an off-licence public house known as 'The Hole in the Wall', and a part of it was used as a malt house.[20] In 1962 it was a private house. Fitz House, the largest house in Teffont Magna, to the west of the village street, was a farm-house until the 1920's. The house, with an adjoining barn on the north, approximately covers three sides of a square. The main house, of squared rubble with dressed quoins and stone mullioned windows, is of late 16th- or early 17th-century date. In 1700 a projecting wing was added at the south end of the main house. This, which bears a tablet inscribed 'R. Fitz 1700', was originally built as a store house, according to local tradition, for wool,[21] and it was not converted for domestic use until the 20th century.[22] The 'Black Horse', an early 18th-century building with stone mullioned windows, at the south end of the village was also once a small farm-house. It became an inn in the 19th century after the present main road between Dinton and Teffont Magna was made.[23] An inn of the same name stood on the south side of the old turnpike road just as it left the village for Dinton. This 17th-century house of stone with thatched roof became a private dwelling when this road ceased to be a main road.[24] Manor Farm, the largest farm in Teffont Magna, lies to the north of the village at the foot of the downs. The farm-house is of early 19th-century date. The cottages beyond the farm at Springhead were built by the Pembroke Estate in the mid-19th century.[25] Apart from a few privately built bungalows, there has been very little building in the village in the 20th century and in 1962 there were no council houses. In c. 1896 water was piped from Springhead and brought to the village by standpipes at intervals all the way down the road.[26] Main water supply came to the village in 1962.[27]

MANOR. Two charters relating to land in 'Teffont' are included in the 15th-century cartulary of Shaftesbury Abbey.[28] The earlier, dated 860, is a grant by King Æthelbald of 14 *cassati* to Osmund, a thegn.[29] The other is a grant by King Edgar of 5 *cassati* to his thegn Sigestan in 964.[30] It is not known to precisely what area of land these two

charters relate, but they presumably represent Shaftesbury's title to the manor of *TEFFONT MAGNA* which it acquired some time before the Conquest. Teffont Magna is not mentioned in the Domesday Survey and is most probably included under Dinton, also a Shaftesbury Abbey manor.[31] It was treated as a part of Dinton throughout the Middle Ages and after the Dissolution passed with Dinton to William Herbert, later Earl of Pembroke (d. 1570).[32] The manor continued to descend as Dinton with the Pembroke title until 1919 when it was sold to Lord Bledisloe (cr. Viscount Bledisloe 1935).[33] In 1950 Lord Bledisloe's son, the Hon. Charles Hiley Bathurst, sold the estate to the Hon. J. J. Astor who sold it the following year in lots.[34]

Until the mid-17th century the demesne lands in Teffont Magna were considered part of the Dinton manorial estate and were farmed with that estate.[35] In 1650 the Teffont lands were leased separately for the first time when the lessee was John Rawlins.[36] In 1679 Richard Maddox was the lessee, and he was followed by his sons, Nathaniel and Samuel.[37] In 1705 the lease was assigned to Joseph Mould who was succeeded in Teffont by his sons, Joseph and John.[38] In 1781 the lease was granted to Oliver Smith and he, or a son of the same name, was still farming the lands in 1836.[39] The farm had a number of lessees in the later 19th century and until it was sold in 1919.[40] It was then bought with the rest of Lord Pembroke's lands in Teffont Magna by Lord Bledisloe, but Lord Bledisloe sold the farm, called Manor Farm, almost immediately to the tenant farmer.[41]

LESSER ESTATES. Among the freeholders on the combined manor of Dinton and Teffont in 1567 two were said specifically to hold their lands in Upper Teffont.[42] They were Leonard Newe, and Thomas South, who also had a freehold estate in Dinton.[43] The South estate in Dinton passed in the late 17th century, as has been shown elsewhere,[44] to William Wyndham and the lands in Teffont were included in the conveyance. In 1567 the Teffont lands comprised 2 virgates called Westbyes and 4 called Sawcers.[45] The descent of Leonard Newe's estate has not been traced. The first mention found of the Fitz family in Teffont Magna is in 1656 when Walter Fitz conveyed land there to John Baverstock, a tailor.[46] In 1736 a descendant, Walter Fitz, was the most substantial freeholder in Upper Teffont.[47] By the beginning of the 19th century the Fitz estate lay in a compact

[20] Teffont W.I. Scrapbk.
[21] Ibid.
[22] Edith Olivier, *Without knowing Mr. Walkley*, 187.
[23] Teffont W. I. Scrapbk.
[24] Ibid.
[25] Ibid.
[26] Ibid.
[27] Ex. inf. Mr. R. Lever, Teffont.
[28] B.M. Harl. MS. 61, ff. 18d., 13, 13d.
[29] Birch, *Cart. Sax.* ii. 105. Consideration of the boundaries given has led to the suggestion that this refers to land in both Teffont Magna and Teffont Evias: Grundy, *Arch. Jnl.* lxxvi. 181 sqq.; *V.C.H. Wilts.* ii, p. 95.
[30] Birch, op. cit. iii. 384–5; *V.C.H. Wilts.* ii. p. 95.
[31] See p. 27.
[32] Ibid.
[33] Ex inf. Col. F. S. Kennedy Shaw, C.B.E., one-time

agent of the Bledisloe estate; Sale Cat. in W.A.S. Libr., Devizes.
[34] Ex inf. Col. F. S. Kennedy Shaw.
[35] See p. 29.
[36] Wilton House MSS. Surveys of Manors, vol. iii. 282.
[37] Ibid. 285.
[38] Ibid.
[39] Ibid. 286; Survey of Teffont, 1836.
[40] Ibid. Rent Roll and Audit Bk.
[41] Ex inf. Col. F. S. Kennedy Shaw.
[42] *First Pembroke Survey*, ed. Straton, 216–17.
[43] Ibid.; C 142/291/144 (inq. p.m. Thos. South).
[44] See p. 28.
[45] *First Pembroke Survey*, ed. Straton, 217.
[46] Conveyance dated 30 Dec. 1656 *penes* Mr. Ronald Lever, Teffont.
[47] *Q. Sess. and Ass.* (W.A.S. Rec. Brch.), 147. Wm. Wyndham was assessed under Dinton.

Dinton House

Village Street, Teffont Magna

block along the west side of the ancient parish,[48] and in 1837 comprised 286 a.[49] Towards the middle of the 19th century the estate was sold to William Wyndham [50] and remained part of the Wyndham estate in Teffont and Dinton until it was sold in *c.* 1920 to Lord Bledisloe.[51] It was sold with the rest of Lord Bledisloe's property in Teffont Magna in 1950.[52]

ECONOMIC HISTORY. Teffont Magna is not mentioned in the Domesday Survey but was almost certainly included under the survey of Dinton.[53] It was indeed farmed by Shaftesbury Abbey as part of Dinton throughout the Middle Ages. No separate medieval surveys for Teffont Magna exist and its tenants are included in the mid-12th-century survey for Dinton contained in the early-15th-century Shaftesbury Abbey cartulary.[54] This shows some tenants with lands on both manors. The interdependence of the two estates is further emphasized by the fact that there was no mill at Teffont Magna and corn from there had to be ground by one of the Dinton mills.[55] Teffont Magna is not named among the lands of Shaftesbury Abbey in the *Valor Ecclesiasticus* and was again, no doubt, included under Dinton.[56]

It was surveyed with Dinton in 1567, shortly after both estates had passed to Lord Pembroke, and from this survey some information may be had about the agricultural organization of Teffont Magna as a separate unit.[57] At this date there was no separate demesne farm there. Teffont Magna had, however, its own three open arable fields and in these lay some 80 a. of Dinton's demesne arable. The Dinton demesne farm also had a small amount of meadow in Teffont and grazing for 300 sheep on Teffont Down. Of the seven freeholders, whose holdings are precisely located in this survey, two appear to have had lands in Teffont Magna and two in both Dinton and Teffont. The survey rarely locates the holdings of the customary tenants on the two estates, but, in the few cases where these are stated to be in Teffont Magna, they comprised a few small closes of meadow, an allotment of strips in the three common arable fields, and certain grazing rights for sheep and other beasts on the downs.

A survey of 1631 provides more information since the tenants of Upper Teffont are separately listed.[58] There was still no demesne farm, and the demesne farm of Dinton had 66 a. in Teffont's common fields, about 9 a. of meadow in the chapelry, and certain rights to fuel from Teffont Common. As in 1567, Dinton's demesne arable at Teffont was distributed among the open fields and was not, as it was by then in Dinton, consolidated into a single field. Inclosure was, however, proceeding,

and was specifically given as the reason for the decline in the number of sheep that could be grazed upon the downs. Fifteen customary tenants are named at Upper Teffont, all holding by copy of court roll. Most, by this date, had small closes of arable, as well as their closes of meadow and their uninclosed strips in the common fields. Nearly all had, besides their grazing rights on the downs, an acre or so in Thickthorn Wood.

In 1650, for the first time, the demesne lands in Teffont Magna were leased as a separate estate.[59] They comprised a small close of arable in which stood a barn, a coppice, another small close, and 66 a. of arable in the common fields, namely 22 a. in West Field, 28 a. in Middle Field, and 16 a. in East Field. There was also grazing on the downs for 270 sheep and an allotment out of Teffont Common for fuel. There was a dwelling house attached to the estate.[60] Henceforward the Teffont demesne lands formed a separate estate which later was enlarged and became known as Manor Farm.

A map of 1801 shows the open fields still in being, although the three-field system had been slightly modified by a certain amount of sub-division.[61] The manor farm at about this time had 47 a. of inclosed arable and just over 100 a. of arable distributed between the three fields. Walter Fitz, the largest freeholder, had 32 a. of inclosed arable and 124 a. said to be in the common fields, but they had been largely consolidated in one field along the western boundary of the parish.[62] Consolidation of the rest of the lands was achieved by the joint Inclosure Award for Dinton and Teffont Magna in 1837. At this time Lord Pembroke's manor estate comprised 823 a. and his leasehold estate 282 a. William Wyndham had a freehold estate in Teffont Magna of 228 a., and other freehold estates there, including that of Walter Fitz, amounted to 309 a.[63]

In the 20th century the productivity of the chalk lands of Teffont Magna has been at least doubled by the use of artificial fertilizers.[64] The lack of much of the more inherently fertile lands along the river has thus been largely overcome. In 1956 there were two farms within the area of the ancient parish. Manor Farm, with over 1,000 a., had dairy and beef cattle, pigs, sheep, and a large number of chickens, and turkeys. Fitz Farm was also a mixed farm.[65] Agriculture has always been virtually the only employment available within Teffont Magna.

CHURCH. The church of Teffont Magna was a chapel-of-ease of Dinton until 1922 and its history until then has been recorded with that of the church of Dinton.[66] No endowments were specifically allotted to Teffont Magna and the chapel was always served either by the Vicar of Dinton or by his curate.

---

[48] B.M. map 5710 (27).
[49] W.R.O. Inclosure Award.
[50] Ex inf. Mr. R. Lever, Teffont.
[51] Ex inf. Col. F. S. Kennedy Shaw, C.B.E., one-time agent of the Bledisloe estate.
[52] See above.
[53] See. p. 29.
[54] B.M. Harl. MS. 61.
[55] Ibid.
[56] See p. 29.
[57] *First Pembroke Survey*, ed. Straton, 216–31.
[58] *Pembroke Manors* (W.A.S. Rec. Brch.), 35.

[59] Wilton House MSS. Surveys of Manors, vol. iii. 282; see p. 30.
[60] Wilton House MSS. Surveys of Manors, vol. iii. 382.
[61] W.A.S. Libr., Devizes, map of Teffont Magna, 1801; see p. 75.
[62] Wilton House MSS. Survey Bk. of Teffont (n.d. but apparently early 19th cent. with later additions); W.A.S. Libr., Devizes, map of Teffont Magna, 1801.
[63] Wilton House MSS. Survey of Teffont, 1836.
[64] Teffont W. I. Scrapbk.
[65] Ibid.   [66] See p. 31.

In c. 1870 a house was built in Teffont Magna so that the curate could live there.[67] In 1922 the chapel of Teffont Magna was detached from the church of Dinton and annexed as a chapelry to the church of Teffont Evias.[68] The chapel was then served by the Rector of Teffont Evias and the advowson of the church of Teffont Evias was shared by M.W. and G.F. Keatinge and the patrons of the church of Dinton.[69] In 1957 the advowson of Teffont Evias was transferred to the Bishop of Salisbury, already by then patron of the church of Dinton.[70] Since 1952 the church of Teffont Evias with the chapelry of Teffont Magna and the church of Dinton have been held in plurality.[71]

The church of Teffont Magna has no known dedication. It is a small rectangular building of local stone. It is mainly late 13th century in date, but fragments of a Saxon cross-shaft found re-used in the walls suggest the possibility of an earlier church on or near the same site. The south porch was added in the 14th century and the jambs of the south doorway have representations of medieval ships scratched upon them, an unusual subject for an inland church.[72] The nave and chancel are structurally undivided but between them is a screen, probably of early 16th-century date. There is a 13th-century circular font bowl and on the south side of the chancel there was, in 1963, a 17th-century communion table. The church was restored in 1955. There is an Elizabethan cup with hall marks for 1571 belonging to the chapelry and a paten of pre-Reformation date.[73] One of the two bells was removed from the bell-cote in the west wall in 1930 and placed within the church. This is a narrow-waisted bell with no mark but thought to date from the late 13th century.[74] The present No. 1 bell was given to the church in 1947 and No. 2 bell, dated 1764, was recast at the same time.[75] Record of births, deaths, and marriages was kept in the registers of Dinton until 1852 when separate registers for the chapelry were begun. No ground was consecrated for burials until 1925.[76]

At the time of Dinton and Teffont Inclosure Award two small pieces of land lying ¾ mile north of the church were allotted to the chapel-wardens.[77] These were called Bell Halves and Bar Acre and the rent from them, which was 30s. in 1925,[78] was used for the general expenses of the church. In 1959 authority was given for the land to be sold.[79]

NONCONFORMITY. In 1783 there were said to be no dissenters in the chapelry.[80] About 30 years later two houses in the village were licensed as nonconformist meeting places[81] and in c. 1820 a Primitive Methodist chapel was built.[82] In the later 19th century the Vicar of Dinton attributed the decline in the congregation from Teffont Magna to the successful activities of the nonconformists in the chapelry.[83] In 1905, however, the Primitive Methodist chapel ceased to be used and was closed.[84] It was subsequently converted into a private dwelling house.

SCHOOL. In the early 19th century children from Teffont Magna attended the school in Dinton.[85] By 1859 there was a school in the village conducted by a dame in a roadside cottage and attended by about 40 children.[86] The National Society was giving support to a village school by 1871.[87] Some time before 1881 this school received a building grant from the Treasury.[88] In 1893 average attendance was 52.[89] The school was closed in 1936 and the children have since attended schools in Dinton or Wilton.[90] In 1962 the former school building was used for village meetings and social activities.

CHARITIES. By his will proved in 1836 John Lush gave £50 to provide blankets every year for the two oldest poor in the chapelry. In 1906 the income from the investment was 25s. and 6 blankets were distributed.[91] In the 1950s the income of this charity was the same and was allowed to accumulate until a reasonably large sum was in hand.[92]

Edward Harris by his will proved in 1876 left £100 to provide coal at Christmas time for the poor of Teffont Magna. Subsequently the income on this was used as a donation to the parish coal club.[93] In 1952 it was spent on coal for 10 persons.[94] A scheme was drawn up in 1928 for the administration of this charity with that of John Lush (see above). By this the incumbent and two representatives of the parish council became trustees.[95]

UPTON SCUDAMORE

THE parish of Upton Scudamore divides the urban districts of Westbury and Warminster. The paro-chial status of the districts of Norridge and Thoulstone, which lie to the west of the village of Upton,

[67] Teffont W. I. Scrapbk.
[68] *London Gaz.* 31 Nov. 1922.
[69] *Kelly's Dir. Wilts.* (1931) and see p. 32.
[70] Order in Council, 26 Jan. 1958.
[71] Ibid. 18 July 1952.
[72] There is a S.E. view of the church in 1804 by John Buckler: W.A.S. Libr., Devizes, vol. ii. 15.
[73] Nightingale, *Wilts. Plate*, 50.
[74] Notice beside bell in church.
[75] Ibid.
[76] *Kelly's Dir. Wilts.* (1931).
[77] W.R.O. Inclosure Award; *Endowed Char. Wilts.* (1908).
[78] Char. Com. Correspondence File G. 43.
[79] Ibid.
[80] Sar. Dioc. R.O. Vis. Queries, 1783.
[81] W.R.O. Certs. of Dissenters' Meeting Houses.
[82] Teffont W. I. Scrapbk.
[83] Sar. Dioc. R.O. Vis. Queries, 1864.
[84] Teffont W. I. Scrapbk.
[85] See p. 34.
[86] *Acct. of Wilts. Schools*, H.C. 27 (1859 sess. 1), xxi (2).
[87] *Rtn. relating to Elem. Educ.* H.C. 201 (1871), iv.
[88] *School Building Grants* [Cd. 1336], H.C. (1902), lxxviii.
[89] *Rtn. of Schools, 1893* [C. 7529], H.C. (1894), lxv.
[90] *Bd. of Educ. List* 21, 1938; ex. inf. the Head Teacher, Dinton School.
[91] *Endowed Char. Wilts.* (1908), p. 698.
[92] Char. Com. Accts. File G. 43.
[93] Endowed Char. Wilts. (1908), p. 698.
[94] Char. Com. Accts. File G. 43.
[95] Ibid. File 66374.

was doubtful. Each contained a free chapel to which tithes belonged in the Middle Ages. Thoulstone chapel apparently belonged to Warminster in 1341,[1] and the permission of Warminster was needed to annex it to Upton c. 1437.[2] Norridge was apparently claimed as part of Warminster in the 16th and early 17th centuries.[3] The agriculture of the manor of Norridge was closely connected both with Warminster and Corsley,[4] and the tithes of about 170 a. in it belonged to the impropriate rectories of those places.[5] When both Norridge and Thoulstone were reckoned part of Upton, the parish was almost 5 miles long and in most places not more than a mile wide; its area was 2,461 a.[6] In 1884 Hisomley Farm, a small detached part of Upton, was transferred to Westbury, and Upton Cottage and Smallbrook Mill, also detached pieces, to Warminster. At the same time small pieces of Warminster and Corsley, locally in Upton, were added to the parish.[7] In 1934 the western end of the parish was transferred to the newly formed parish of Chapmanslade. This reduced the area of Upton to 2,359 a.[8]

In the east of the parish the chalk downs of Salisbury Plain rise to a height of 650 ft., but here a broad valley of greensand runs into them east of the road from Westbury to Warminster, which roughly bisects the parish from north to south. The part west of the road occupies the flat top of a greensand ridge some 400 ft. above sea-level which forms the watershed between the valleys of the Bristol Avon to the north and the Wylye to the south. At the northern boundary of the parish is a deep combe in which are the springs of the Biss, a tributary of the Avon. The village of Upton stands about ¼ mile west of the main road; its position is distinctive, for it is on a low mound rising from the greensand ridge, so that it commands extensive views of the surrounding countryside in all directions save the east. The site was attractive to prehistoric man, for early Iron Age material has been found south of the church, while the church itself appears to be on or near the site of a Roman building.[9] In the 14th century the village was of a good average size and prosperity, assessed at 108s. in 1334 and with 85 poll tax-payers in 1377.[10] There were apparently 191 adults in the parish in 1676.[11] In 1801 the population of the whole parish was 409; ten years later it was only 314, and if the figures are accurate this considerable decline can only be accounted for by the inclosure of the parish. It had grown again to 392 by 1831, and did not begin to decline significantly until the decade 1871-81. By 1901 it was 236, and has not since then been much above 200.[12] The inhabitants have always been chiefly concerned with agriculture, although there was probably some domestic cloth-working done

until the decline of the industry in the early 19th century.

In the early 18th century the village of Upton was almost on the main road from Bath and Frome to Salisbury. This road entered the parish at Dead Maids as at present, but continued directly east from Thoulstone to near Upton by a route now marked only by a green lane. At its eastern end a turnpike gate stood in 1773, and still in 1838.[13] Just before it reached the village, the road turned south to join the present road from Upton to Warminster at the parish boundary.[14] The northern part of this stretch also remains as a green lane, but the southern part is lost.

At the inclosure of the parish in 1807 the village of Upton consisted chiefly of about ten farmhouses, the Angel Inn, the rectory, and a few cottages. The ancient site of the manor house is near the church in a field called Court Furlong; in the early 18th century 'plain marks of a considerable fabric' could be seen there.[15] It has usually been assumed that the site was marked by a rectangular enclosure in the north-west corner of the field, but recent excavation has failed to confirm this, and it now seems more likely that the house stood on the site of the cow yard west of the church.[16] In 1471 a tenement called 'le Garyet' stood on the site.[17] The later site of the manor farm is marked by the house now called Temple Farm after the Temple family of Bishopstrow, which leased and later owned the demesnes from the mid-17th century. The brick house probably dates from that time. It is of two stories and attics, the symmetrical front having 3 gables with stone copings and finials, and a central porch of two stories with round-arched doorway. At the attic story stone-mullioned windows remain, but below they have been replaced by sash windows. This was probably done in the early 19th century, when the front of the house was hung with shaped tiles and a kitchen wing was added at the back, perhaps replacing part of the earlier house. Inside is an original fireplace with four-centred arch and some contemporary oak panelling. Behind the house the large thatched barn, and granary on staddle-stones, are probably of the same date as the house.

Manor Farm, although it is so called, represents the homestead site of the considerable freehold which in the Middle Ages was held of the lords of Upton by the Park family.[18] In 1482 a new tenant was ordered to rebuild a kitchen and repair the rest of the house.[19] The stone house incorporates a single-storied open hall of two bays probably of the 15th century. The timbers of its roof, some smoke-blackened, are largely original, and include an arch-braced collar-beam truss and curved

[1] *Inq. Non.* (Rec. Com.), 170.
[2] See p. 89.
[3] E 301/58 no. 76; *Early Stuart Tradesmen* (W.A.S. Rec. Brch.), 18; Daniell, *Warminster*, 181; Longleat MS. 8845; W.A.S. Libr., Devizes, Everett MSS. Pedigrees i. 88.
[4] See p. 86.
[5] W.R.O. Tithe Award.
[6] Ibid. The following maps were used: O.S. Maps 1/2,500 Wilts. XLIV. 15, 16, XLV. 9, 13, LI. 3, 4 (all edns.); 1/25,000, ST 84.
[7] *Census*, 1891.
[8] *Census*, 1951.
[9] From an interim report on excavations carried out

by Mr. J. W. G. Musty, in 1962, kindly supplied by him.
[10] *V.C.H. Wilts.* iv. 302, 311.
[11] *W.N. & Q.* iii. 537.
[12] *V.C.H. Wilts.* iv. 359.
[13] *Andrews and Dury, Map* (W.A.S. Rec. Brch.), pl. 7; W.R.O. Tithe Award.
[14] Halliday, Information, f. 99; *Q. Sess. and Ass.* 1736 (W.A.S. Rec. Brch.), 62.
[15] M. Gibson, *View of the Ancient and Present States of the Churches of Door, Home Lacy, and Hempstead* (1727), 57.
[16] Report as in n. 9 above.
[17] S.C. 2/209/63.
[18] See p. 82.
[19] S.C. 2/209/64.

wind-braces supporting the purlins. It was probably when the Seaman family became tenants of the farm in the early 17th century that the house was extended by the addition of gabled side wings and a stone entrance arch and porch at the west end of the hall. It was perhaps at this time also that the hall was divided into two floors and a chimney inserted near its centre; one of the upper rooms has a plaster barrel ceiling of the period. East of the entrance doorway a two-light window with cusped lights and a carved head in late 15th-century style has been reset.

The houses now called Millard's Farm and Keyford were both farmhouses in 1807; both are timber-framed buildings and Keyford has a thatched roof. Several other farmhouses date from the 18th century, after the manorial lands had been sold as several freehold farms. A good example is the house just south of the Angel Inn, which formerly belonged to the Heytesbury Hospital farm. It is of brick with stone quoins and stone mullioned windows and is dated 1723. In 1807 the Angel Inn stood opposite its present site, where a row of cottages now stands. Nearby is the former Baptist chapel, built in 1850 and used since 1920 as a dwelling-house. The large 19th-century rectory stands at the southern entrance to the village, and on the opposite corner is the former school, used as a dwelling-house since it was closed in 1925.

In 1807 there were few cottages in the village, and this is still true to some extent, although several council houses have been built since the Second World War. At inclosure, however, the outer parts of the parish were more populous than they are now. At Fulmoor Common just north of Norridge Wood stood five cottages, which have all since disappeared. In the north-west part of the parish at least seven houses formerly at Row and near Chapmanslade have gone, and six or seven more were in Biss Bottom, north of the village. Most of these must have been built on waste land, probably from the 16th century onward. At Norridge, however, still lay a hamlet which existed in the Middle Ages. In 1377 there were 16 poll-tax payers there,[20] and 7 or 8 cottages still remained in 1807. Some of these were burnt in the late 19th century, and others remained, derelict, until a few years ago. The hamlet was reduced to the farmhouse and two cottages until a few more houses were built after the Second World War. In 1333 the manor house of Norridge consisted of a hall with various chambers, a chapel, a kitchen, and a dovehouse.[21] It may have stood on what appears to have been a moated site just west of the present farmhouse. In 1572 the house consisted of nine rooms: hall, parlour, buttery, two kitchens,

and four rooms over. The hall had then just been lofted over.[22] The present farmhouse is partly of stone rubble and partly timber-framed; it appears externally to be of the 17th century, but has been much altered. Nearby the owner of the farm, Mr. J. Meinl, has built a house with a colonnaded portico, designed by R. Vallis of Frome *c.* 1960.[23]

Thoulstone had 22 poll-tax payers in 1377. In 1428 it had fewer than ten households,[24] and in the later 16th century there were about seven houses there.[25] By 1807 there were only three farms; one, the Breach Farm, which lay south of the sharp bend in the road, has since disappeared. Of the other two, that south of the road is a large brick building of the late 18th century, while the one on the other side displays the Gothic taste of a few years later.

The works of the Trowbridge Water Company were established at Biss Bottom in 1873, despite some objection from the parish.[26] They are invisible from the village, but the water tower raised near the main road in 1906 is a prominent landmark. It was given in memory of John Baron, a former rector, to provide a supply for the village.[27]

MANORS. In 1086 the largest of the three holdings mentioned in Upton was held of Alfred of Marlborough's fief.[28] By 1100 Alfred's castle of Ewyas in Herefordshire had passed, with other of his lands, to Harold, son of Ralph, first Earl of Hereford.[29] Upton formed part of these lands, and was held of the honor of Ewyas until the 14th century.[30] The lordship of the honor descended to Harold's grandson Robert (II) de Ewyas, whose daughter and heir Sibyl married Robert de Tregoze. Her grandson John left two daughters and coheirs, and the barony was divided. The fee at Upton fell to Sibyl who married William de Grandison.[31] Their son John de Grandison, Bishop of Exeter, conveyed the overlordship of certain fees in Wiltshire, including Upton, to his nephew Sir John de Montagu, whose son John succeeded to the earldom of Salisbury in 1397.[32] From that time the overlordship descended with the earldom to Margaret, Countess of Salisbury;[33] on her attainder and execution in 1541 it passed to the Crown, and when the manor was regranted to Walter Hungerford in 1552, it was to be held directly of the king.[34]

A certain Ralph was tenant of this holding under Alfred of Marlborough in 1086,[35] but nothing is known of him. He may, however, have been ancestor of the Scudamore family. It has been said that a Walter Scudamore was lord of Upton in the reign of Stephen,[36] and in the mid-12th century Robert de Ewyas, lord of the honor, granted the whole vill of Upton Scudamore to Godfrey Scudamore;

[20] *V.C.H. Wilts.* iv. 311.
[21] *Wilts. Inq. p.m.* 1327–77 (Index Libr.), 95.
[22] Longleat MS. 8860.
[23] Local inf.
[24] *V.C.H. Wilts.* iv. 311, 314.
[25] W.R.O. 442/1; Longleat MS. 8860.
[26] Printed *Mins. of Evidence* on proceedings on 36 and 37 Vic. c. 134 (copy *penes* West Wilts. Water Bd.); *V.C.H. Wilts.* vii. 150.
[27] *Wilts. Times*, 31 Aug. 1962.
[28] *V.C.H. Wilts.* ii, p. 142.
[29] *Herefordshire Domesday*, ed. Galbraith (P.R.S. N.S.

xxv), 111.
[30] e.g. *Bk. of Fees*, 725; *Rot. Hund.* (Rec. Com.), ii. 276.
[31] I. J. Sanders, *English Baronies*, 43; *Wilts. Inq. p.m.* 1327–77 (Index Libr.), 110.
[32] E 329/207; *Cal. Pat.* 1364–7, 312; *Complete Peerage*, s.v. Grandison and Salisbury.
[33] E 326/8993.
[34] See below.
[35] *V.C.H. Wilts.* ii, p. 142.
[36] M. Gibson, *View of the Ancient and Present State* of *the Churches of Door, Home Lacy, and Hempstead* (1727), 55, which refers to deeds then extant.

the use of the suffix in the grant implies that the family had some previous interest there.[37] By it Godfrey was bound to do the service of one knight at the castle guard of Ewyas Harold. In 1166 he held five fees of the honor of Ewyas in Wiltshire.[38] He was probably dead by 1190,[39] and was succeeded by a Peter Scudamore who held the five fees in the early 13th century.[40] He forfeited all his possessions in 1216, but regained them in the following year.[41] By 1222 he had been succeeded by Godfrey Scudamore,[42] who held the property until at least 1262.[43] By 1267 his son Peter Scudamore had succeeded him.[44] He died c. 1293,[45] leaving a daughter Alice, wife of Adam Bavant.[46] Shortly before his death, however, he had granted Upton to his nephew Walter,[47] who died in 1318 and was succeeded by his son, another Peter.[48] In 1338 Roger Bavant, grandson of Alice, brought an action against Peter Scudamore to recover the manor.[49] The suit seems to have lasted for many years, and was not finally ended until 1358, when John, son of Roger Bavant, released his claim to Sir Walter Scudamore, son of Peter.[50]

Peter was still living in 1339, but his son Walter had succeeded by 1347, and was alive in 1360.[51] He had a son Peter, who settled the manor on himself and his wife in 1368,[52] and died c. 1382.[53] His widow, Joan, remarried Sir Robert Corbet, who still held Upton in 1412.[54] Peter's heir was his only daughter Katharine, who married Sir John Reynes and had a son Thomas.[55] Thomas died in 1417, holding Upton by permission of his father,[56] and leaving a son John who died without issue in 1421. Sir John's other son Ralph was apparently childless, and the heir to the property was William Street of Meldreth (Cambs.), son of Sir John's daughter Cecily.[57] After the younger John's death, Sir John obtained a grant of Ralph's right,[58] and re-settled the property on himself and his second wife Alice.[59] In 1426 they conveyed the manor to feoffees,[60] to whom William Street released his right in 1428.[61] Sir John was then dead.[62] His feoffees were perhaps charged with the payment of his debts, for in 1435 the manor of Upton was taken in execution and delivered to two of his creditors.[63] By then the feoffees had already sold the reversion of it

after Alice's death to Sir Walter Hungerford.[64]

Sir Walter, later styled Lord Hungerford, died in 1449. Upton passed to his son Robert and thence to his grandson, another Robert, who was attainted in 1461 for his part on the Lancastrian side, and executed in 1464.[65] The manor remained in the king's hands until 1474, when it was granted to Richard, Duke of Gloucester.[66] When Richard obtained the throne in 1483 he granted it to John, Duke of Norfolk, who was killed at Bosworth.[67] By this time the heir to the Hungerford property was Mary, Lady Botreaux, grand-daughter of Robert, Lord Hungerford and Moleyns, being the only daughter of his elder son Sir Thomas Hungerford. Upton was among the properties which Margaret, Lady Botreaux, widow of Robert, 2nd Lord Hungerford (d. 1459), had directed by her will to remain in the male line of the family. On the restoration of the house of Lancaster, therefore, it came to Sir Walter Hungerford, younger brother of Sir Thomas.[68] He died in 1516 and was succeeded successively by his son Edward and grandson Walter, later Lord Hungerford of Heytesbury; the latter was attainted and executed in 1540, and his property was again forfeited to the king.[69]

In 1544 Upton was among many manors granted to Queen Catherine Parr.[70] In 1552, however, it was restored to Sir Walter Hungerford,[71] who died in 1596 leaving as his heir male his half-brother Edward.[72] He too died without issue, but had adopted as heir his great-nephew Edward Hungerford, heir to the Down Ampney Hungerfords, and son of one of the female coheirs of Sir Walter (d. 1596).[73] Sir Edward died in 1648 and his estates passed to his half-brother Anthony Hungerford of Blackboughton (Oxon.). On his death in 1657 he was succeeded by his son Sir Edward Hungerford, 'the spendthrift',[74] who sold Upton in 1684 to Sir Stephen Fox.[75]

Sir Stephen Fox sold the manor in lots in 1689,[76] and the manorial rights seem to have lapsed. The demesne farm had been let to the Temple family of Bishopstrow since 1662 and was sold to Peter Temple in 1689.[77] It descended in the same way as the manor of Bishopstrow until the present century.[78]

[37] Gibson (op. cit. 56) had seen an original of the grant; a copy is in W.R.O. 490, Hungerford Cart. f. 111.
[38] *Red Bk. Exch.* (Rolls Ser.), 245.
[39] *Pipe R. 1190* (P.R.S. N.S. i), 122.
[40] *Red Bk. Exch.* (Rolls Ser.), 153.
[41] *Rot. Litt. Claus.* (Rec. Com.), i. 285, 300.
[42] Ibid. 513.
[43] *Bk. of Fees*, 712, 725; C.P. 25(1)/251/20/23.
[44] *Cal. Chart. R. 1257–1300*, 73; for the relationship, see *Visitation of Hunts.* (Camd. Soc. 1st ser. xliii), 82.
[45] *Wilts. Inq. p.m. 1242–1327* (Index Libr.), 194.
[46] Hoare, *Mod. Wilts.* Warminster, 77.
[47] *Visitation of Hunts.* (Camd. Soc. 1st ser. xliii), 82, a deed of after Oct. 1289 because Ric. de Combe was sheriff.
[48] *Cat. Anct. D.* v. A 13410.
[49] G. Wrottesley, *Pedigrees from the Plea Rolls*, 37; *Rot. Parl.* i. 408; the dispute had probably begun by 1320: see below p. 89.
[50] W.R.O. 490, Hungerford Cart. ff. 117–8.
[51] Hist. MSS. Com. *Hastings*, i. 220–2.
[52] W.R.O. 490, Hungerford Cart. f. 116 v.
[53] C 136/28/2.
[54] *Cal. Close, 1392–6*, 181; *1405–9*, 443; *Feud. Aids*, vi. 532.
[55] *Visitation of Hunts.* (Camd. Soc. 1st ser. xliii), 83; W.R.O. 490. Hungerford Cart. f. 125 v.

[56] C 139/20/34.
[57] C 139/33/36; cf. *Visitation of Hunts.* (Camd. Soc. 1st ser. xliii), 88 where he is called Henry Street.
[58] *Cal. Close, 1419–22*, 255.
[59] C.P. 25(1)/256/60/40; *Cal. Close, 1419–22*, 211.
[60] C.P. 25(1)/257/61/19; C.P. 25(1)/257/61/31.
[61] *Cal. Close, 1422–9*, 412.
[62] W.R.O. 490, Hungerford Cart. f. 124 v.; *Feud. Aids*, v. 273.
[63] W.R.O. 490, Hungerford Cart. ff. 120–1.
[64] *Cal. Close, 1429–35*, 56 (1430).
[65] *Complete Peerage.*
[66] *Cal. Pat. 1467–77*, 466.
[67] Ibid. 1476–85, 359.
[68] Hoare, *Mod. Wilts.* Heytesbury, 109; Sir John Maclean, *Deanery of Trigg Minor*, i. 357–60; *Complete Peerage*; C 1/80/45.
[69] Maclean, op. cit. 360–1; *Complete Peerage.*
[70] *L. & P. Hen. VIII*, xix (1), p. 83.
[71] *Cal. Pat. 1550–53*, 438–9.
[72] C 142/306/159.   [73] C 142/306/160.
[74] Collinson, *Somerset*, iii. 356.
[75] C.P. 25(2)/747/Trin. 36 Chas. II.
[76] For other parts of the manor, see pp. 83–84.
[77] W.R.O. 132, Deeds of the Upton property.
[78] See p. 6; the manor house is mentioned above, p. 79.

Before the Conquest Tous held 2½ hides in Upton, which by 1086 had passed to Ernulf of Hesdin.[79] The overlordship of this land passed in the same way as Ernulf's estate at Great Chalfield to the Earls of Salisbury,[80] and it was held of the earl in 1242-3, when it was described as a knight's fee in *NORRIDGE*.[81] A moiety of the manor of Norridge was said to be held of the Earl of Salisbury in 1333, the remainder being held of the lords of Upton.[82] The land held under the earls descended with the title,[83] but the tenure has not been found mentioned later than the early 15th century.[84] The tenure under the lords of Upton was still marked by the payment of a chief rent in the 17th century.[85]

Rainbold was tenant under Ernulf of Hesdin in 1086.[86] In the early 13th century the 2½ hides of his holding were in dispute between Ralph Fitz-William and Thomas de Cormeilles; Ralph asserted that Roger, his grandfather, held the land in 1189, while Thomas claimed to hold in right of his wife Alice, according to a division made between her and her sisters.[87] Ralph seems to have lost, for in 1229 he relinquished his right to Godfrey Scudamore and William Bastard and Alice his wife.[88] Nothing more is known of a direct Scudamore interest in the estate. William Bastard held it in 1242-3;[89] his wife Alice was probably the same who had been wife of Thomas de Cormeilles. It was perhaps from the issue of her two marriages that the two families, who in the early 14th century contested the ownership of the manor, descended. It was said in 1289 that John de Cormeilles held a knight's fee in the hundred of Warminster,[90] and in the same year he held land in Norridge of the Prioress of Studley (Oxon.).[91] In 1313, when this or another John presented to the chapel of Norridge, which was appurtenant to the manor, the presentation was disputed by Walter Gascelyn and Annice his wife.[92] In 1315 John le Warrener and Joan his wife and John de Bassingbourne and Christine his wife released their right in the manor to Walter Gascelyn. It is not clear who they were, for John de Cormeilles put in his claim then,[93] and was still maintaining it in 1318.[94]

Walter Gascelyn seems, however, to have made

his claim good, and died holding Norridge in 1333.[95] His son William died in 1346 leaving as heir his sister Julia, wife of Geoffrey de Stawell.[96] After Geoffrey's death in 1362, his son Matthew succeeded to Norridge,[97] and sold it in 1368 to John Lye, subject to a life interest which Sir Peter Scudamore held, apparently by lease.[98] Nicholas Lye died possessed of the manor *c.* 1420, leaving a life estate to his widow Elizabeth.[99] She still held it in 1440, when Nicholas's son John settled the reversion on his marriage with Joan Newburgh.[1] This or another John held the manor under Edward IV,[2] and was dead by 1482 leaving a son John,[3] probably Sir John Lye, who died *c.* 1523, leaving several daughters and coheirs.[4] Norridge was evidently assigned to Anne, wife of Sir James Worsley of Appuldurcombe in Godshill (I.o.W.).[5] Norridge remained in the Worsley family for several generations, descending in the same way as Appuldurcombe[6] to Sir Robert Worsley, who in 1690 married the daughter of Thomas, 1st Viscount Weymouth.[7] Two years later Sir Robert sold the manor to his father-in-law, and it descended from that time with the Longleat estate.[8] The manor house is mentioned above.[9]

LESSER ESTATES. Among the freehold estates held of the lords of Upton Scudamore in the Middle Ages the chief was held by a family called Park (*de Parco*). Simon Park held ⅓ knight's fee of Godfrey Scudamore in 1242-3.[10] Walter Park was active by about 1270,[11] and was engaged in lawsuits in Upton later in the century.[12] He was still alive in 1307.[13] The next probable holder was Walter, son of William Park, who occurs in 1332 and 1334.[14] He was dead by 1347, when his son John was at variance with his overlord, Walter Scudamore, over the payment of a relief. It was found that John held his lands of Scudamore by a rent of 40*s.*[15] He was soon succeeded by a Nicholas Park, to whose brother and heir Walter the estate had passed by 1352.[16] From that time it was held by a succession of men called Walter Park.[17] One died in the early 15th century, leaving a widow Alice, who remarried John Osebarn, and a son

[79] *V.C.H. Wilts.* ii, p. 140.
[80] Ibid. vii. 59.
[81] *Bk. of Fees,* 710.
[82] *Wilts. Inq. p.m.* 1327–77 (Index Libr.), 95.
[83] i.e. unlike the manors of Trowbridge and Aldbourne: *V.C.H. Wilts.* vii. 129.
[84] *Feud. Aids,* v. 274; *Cal. Close,* 1405–9, 458.
[85] W.R.O. 442/2.
[86] *V.C.H. Wilts.* ii, p. 140.
[87] *Cur. Reg. R.* 1201–3, 243, 305; 1203–5, 83; 1220, 5–6, 285; 1221–2, 13; *Bracton's Note Bk.* ed. Maitland, iii. 411.
[88] C.P. 25(1)/250/8/12.
[89] *Bk. of Fees,* 710, 719; for Bastards holding land in Upton a century later, see Hist. MSS. Com. *Hastings,* i. 221.
[90] J.I. 1/1006 m. 55d.
[91] *Feet of F.* 1272–1327 (W.A.S. Rec. Brch.), 31.
[92] Phillipps, *Wilts. Inst.* i. 13.
[93] *Feet of F.* 1272–1327 (W.A.S. Rec. Brch.), 92.
[94] *Cal. Close,* 1313–8, 547.
[95] *Feud. Aids,* v. 212; *Wilts. Inq. p.m.* 1327–77 (Index Libr.), 95.
[96] *Glos. Inq. p.m.* 1302–58 (Index Libr.), 312.
[97] *Wilts. Inq. p.m.* 1327–77 (Index Libr.), 317, 326.
[98] W.R.O. 492, Deed Stawell to Lye; C.P. 25(1)/255/51/33.

[99] C 138/48/60; *Cal. Close,* 1419–22, 95. In 1428 it was said that the land was late of Rich. de Penlegh, but it is not known why: *Feud. Aids,* v. 274.
[1] B.M. Harl. Ch. 53. C. 11; Longleat MSS. 8836, 8838–9.
[2] S.C. 2/209/63.   [3] Longleat MS. 8839.
[4] S.C. 2/208/68; C 142/42/153; Hoare, *Mod. Wilts.* Downton, 4; Hutchins, *Hist. Dors.* iv. 144; P.C.C. 18 Bodfelde.
[5] Longleat MSS. 8840–3; Berry, *Hants Genealogies,* 134.
[6] *V.C.H. Hants,* v. 171.
[7] G.E.C. *Complete Baronetage,* i. 66–7.
[8] Longleat MSS. Parcel XXVII, Title Deeds of Manor
[9] See p. 80.
[10] *Bk. of Fees,* 712; see also C.P. 25(1)/250/9/11, C.P. 25(1)/251/13/46, and B.M. Add. Ch. 26695, 26698.
[11] B.M. Add. Ch. 26702.
[12] *Plac. Abbrev.* (Rec. Com.), 189; *Cal. Close,* 1288–96, 404.
[13] B.M. Add. Ch. 26706.
[14] Hist. MSS. Com. *Hastings,* i. 220, 222.
[15] W.R.O. 490, Hungerford Cart. f. 118 v.
[16] Hist. MSS. Com. *Hastings,* i. 222–3.
[17] C.P. 25(1)/255/50/18 (1362); B.M. Add. Ch. 40046 (1388); *Rot. Parl.* iii. 258 (1389); B.M. Add. Ch. 26718 (1417), 26719–20 (1440–2).

Walter.[18] The younger Walter was dead by 1447, and Alice Park, a free tenant in 1450, was probably his widow.[19]

By 1471 the property had fallen into the hands of the lords of Upton, perhaps by escheat;[20] the demesne lands with the house called 'Parkescourte' were held as a customary holding of the manor of Upton in the late 15th century.[21] They remained a separate farm, which in 1542 had been let to Christopher Eyre, local bailiff of the Hungerford family.[22] Three virgates were apparently added to the farm then; in 1582, when it was in hand, it consisted in all of over 200 a.[23] In 1606, when it was let to William Seaman, it was called Acres Farm.[24] It must have been the same property as that which was bought by the Seaman family when the manor was broken up in 1689.[25] It descended to Lionel Seaman, Archdeacon of Wells, who died in 1760.[26] By his wife Jane, daughter of Edward Willes, Bishop of Bath and Wells, he had an only son Lionel, who died unmarried in 1783,[27] and two daughters, who held the land jointly for many years. Mary Seaman never married; her sister Jane married the Revd. William Somerville of Dinder (Som.) and survived her sister, dying in 1830.[28] The farm then passed to Francis Willes, their cousin, son of the elder Jane Seaman's brother William.[29] His daughter Margaret Sophia married W. A. Mackinnon of Acryse Park, Kent, who still held the farm at his death in 1903.[30]

In 1205 the king confirmed to the Abbot of Waverley (Surr.) a virgate of land in Norridge, and certain land in Corsley given by Walter Giffard.[31] Seven years later Thomas de Cormeilles, who claimed the manor of Norridge, acknowledged that he owed rent to the abbot for these lands.[32] No more is known of them, but in 1536 the rent was still paid, for it was granted with other Waverley property to Sir William FitzWilliam.[33]

In 1496 William Champion of Croscombe (Som.) was licensed to grant a small estate in Norridge and Thoulstone to the Guild of St. Anne in Croscombe church.[34] It consisted of three closes and a few acres of field land, and was held by the guild until the dissolution of chantries.[35] In 1548 it was granted to Sir John Thynne,[36] and descended with the Longleat estate.[37]

The property which formed the endowment of the Scudamore and Park chantries in Upton church was appropriated in the 15th century to the use of the Hungerford chantry, later hospital, at Heytesbury.[38] It consisted in 1833 of a farm of 96 a., and was retained by the hospital until the present century.[39]

Giles Powell was a free tenant of the manor in 1525.[40] In 1582 Roger, son of Christopher Powell, held a virgate of land called Palmer's freely of the lord of the manor by a rent of 7s.[41] He still held it in 1609;[42] in 1638 Christopher Hill died seised of it, and was succeeded by his son Stephen.[43] In the late 18th century this land was held by William Bayly, who paid the rent to Lord Bath.[44] It descended in the same way as Middleton in Norton Bavant to J. B. O. Bayly,[45] who in 1838 held a farm of some 77 a., the house of which lay south of the road from the village to the Warminster road.[46]

Several farms which probably became freeholds only at the break-up of the manor in the late 17th century may be briefly mentioned. In 1582 Robert Green held three virgates in right of his wife Alice, daughter of Richard Escott.[47] In 1737 Philip Ballard of Bratton devised lands called Green's, which probably once formed part of the property, in trust for his son Jonathan, who died c. 1741.[48] By 1773 they were held by William Tree, whose name survives in Tree's Farm; after his death c. 1801 the farm passed to John Pearce.[49] His family held it until 1849, when it was sold to the trustees of the Stockton Almshouse, as Green's Farm of 67 a.[50] Early in the 20th century it was held by W. H. Laverton.[51] Another holding formerly Green's was held in 1773 by Lord William Seymour, third son of Edward, 8th Duke of Somerset (d. 1757), At Lord William's death in 1800 it passed to his widow Hester, and after her death in 1812 to Edward Seymour, their son. By 1821 it was held by Peter Awdry of Seend, whose first wife had been their daughter.[52] Awdry's son Ambrose held the farm in 1838.[53] This holding was farmed from the house adjoining Tree's Farm to the east. Another farm was apparently originally two virgates held in 1582 and 1609 by Christopher Carpenter.[54] In the early 18th century it consisted of about 60 a. and was held by the Keyford family,[55] which had probably bought it at the sale of the manorial lands. In 1773 it was still held by that family, but by

[18] *Feud. Aids*, v. 274; Hist. MSS. Com. *Hastings*, i. 222.
[19] S.C. 2/209/62; S.C. 6/1061/14; Hist. MSS. Com. *Hastings*, i. 225.
[20] S.C. 2/209/63.
[21] S.C. 2/209/64.
[22] *L. & P. Hen. VIII*, xvii, p. 60.
[23] W.R.O. 442/1.
[24] Ibid. 442/2.
[25] See p. 81.
[26] Foster, *Alumn. Oxon.* 2nd ser. iv. 1270.
[27] Hoare, *Mod. Wilts.* Warminster, 52; Burke, *Landed Gent.* (1846), ii. 1263.
[28] W.R.O. Land Tax Assessments and Inclosure Award; Burke, op. cit. ii. 1262–3.
[29] W.R.O. Land Tax Assessments and Tithe Award; Burke, op. cit. ii. 1592.
[30] Burke, *Landed Gent.* (1906), ii. 1094; *Kelly's Dir. Wilts.* (1903).
[31] *Rot. Chart.* (Rec. Com.), 161.
[32] C.P. 25(1)/250/3/40.
[33] *L & P. Hen. VIII*, xi, p. 88.
[34] *Cal. Pat.* 1494–1509, 78.
[35] Longleat MS. 8850; *Somerset Chantries* (Som. Rec. Soc.), 311.

[36] *Cal Pat.* 1548–9, 52.
[37] Longleat MS. 7031.
[38] See p. 87.
[39] *W.A.M.* xliv. 258; *Endowed Char. Wilts.* (1908), pp. 202, 224. [40] S.C. 2/208/70.
[41] W.R.O. 442/1.
[42] Ibid. 442/2.
[43] Ibid. 490, Court Bk. 1628–41.
[44] Longleat MSS. Rental 1775.
[45] See p. 50.
[46] W.R.O. Land Tax Assessments and Tithe Award.
[47] Ibid. 442/1.
[48] *W.N. & Q.* iii. 527, 529.
[49] W.R.O. Land Tax Assessments.
[50] Ibid. Tithe Award; *Endowed Char. Wilts.* (1908), p. 669; J. Baron, *Reasons against Alienation of Property of Stockton Almshouse in Upton Scudamore*, 1877 (copy in Wilts. Tracts cviii).
[51] W.R.O. Tithe Award, Altered Apportionment.
[52] W.R.O. Land Tax Assessments; Burke, *Land. Gent.* (1846), i. 39; Hoare *Mod. Wilts.* Mere, 132.
[53] W.R.O. Tithe Award.
[54] Ibid. 442/1–2.
[55] Ibid. 78, Settlements of 1713 and 1719.

1780 it had passed to the Seamans,[56] and subsequently descended in the same way as Manor Farm.[57]

In 1582 William Escott held a virgate in Upton which included closes called Pilton's and Lokyer's. He still held it in 1609, but it subsequently passed to a family called Daniell,[58] which probably bought the freehold in 1689. In the early 18th century Elizabeth, daughter of Christopher Daniell, married William Barton,[59] and took the estate to him. The same lands were settled on their son William in 1731.[60] Daniel Barton held them in 1773, and was succeeded by William Clerk Barton (d. c. 1794) and then by William Kington Barton (d. 1801). For some years they were held by his widow's second husband, William Waldron, but in 1819 they were settled on Barton's only daughter, Louisa Margaret, when she married Stephen Flower Knight of Semington. In 1844 Knight sold the farm to James Chapman, and parts of it were later added to the Longleat and Temple estates.[61] In 1807 the farmhouse of this holding stood just south of Millard's Farm,[62] but has now disappeared.

In 1437–8 John Ewyn and John Colston paid a rent of 2 lb. of wax to the lords of Upton.[63] In 1472 Richard Ewyn of Bower Chalke, son of John, sold lands in Thoulstone, Upton, and Chalcot, once of William his grandfather, to Thomas South.[64] In 1487–8 the lord of the manor released a rent of 12s. 6d. charged on these lands, then described as in Thoulstone, to Robert South.[65] They probably later passed to the lords, for in 1582 Agnes Sainsbury held a copyhold of some 75 a. in Thoulstone which included lands called 'Ewens'.[66] In 1609 William May held this farm and also another virgate in Thoulstone called Taylors.[67] In 1630 Laurence Kington was admitted as tenant of these lands.[68] It was probably a descendant of his who bought the freehold at the sale of the manorial lands. The farm, on the north side of the road at Thoulstone, evidently descended in the Kington family, who acquired the rectory of Norridge in 1736. From that time it passed in the same way as the rectory.[69]

In 1572 the manor of Norridge included several small holdings at Thoulstone.[70] These too must have later been held by the Kington family as lease- or copyholders; in the mid-18th century, after the manor had passed to the Thynne family, John Barter held lands late Kington's at a rack rent. Other lands, some formerly part of Norridge Farm, were later added to them, and the holding was called Thoulstone Farm;[71] the house was that which stands on the south side of the road there.

Clear Wood belonged to Peter Scudamore c. 1290.[72] It was not sold with the part of Norridge Wood belonging to the manor, for in 1569 Sir Walter Hungerford obtained a declaration from some old inhabitants that Clear Wood, which contained four coppices, was distinct from Norridge Wood.[73] By 1682, however, it had been added to the Thynne estate; it then contained 63 a.[74]

ECONOMIC HISTORY. There was land for 6 ploughs on the main holding at Upton in 1086; land for two of these was in the demesne, and 9 villeins and 22 bordars held the remainder.[75] Apart from this little is known of agriculture in the village before the 15th century. In 1351 the lord of the capital manor let pasture for 240 sheep on Odyngdon, later called Upton Cow Down; they were to be folded on his arable land.[76] In 1377 an agreement for the maintenance of five ploughs shows that the demesne arable was still farmed.[77] By 1438 Odyngdon, for which a rent of 106s. 8d. had formerly been paid, was in hand again and used for the pasture of the lord's sheep.[78] Between then and 1454, and probably for some years before and after that period, Upton was one of the group of Hungerford manors in Wiltshire and Somerset which were carefully organized for the production of wool.[79] The number of sheep sheared on this manor was generally over 500, and in 1451 reached 721. All the pastures and downs of the manor were used for their feed; the rest of the demesne was let in small parcels except for a few acres of meadow which were mown to provide hay for the sheep in winter. The sheep were folded on parts of the arable land, which could then be let at a higher rate than the rest. The costs of this kind of farming must have been small; the only payments recorded were the wage of the shepherd and of men at shearing time, the cost of necessaries such as hurdles and tar, and the wages of men to mow the meadows and carry the hay to the downs. Leases of parcels of demesne arable and meadow land could bring in as much as £18 a year. Rents of assize brought in rather more than this, and sales of timber and underwood often brought £6 or £8.[80]

This intensive sheep farming was not resumed when the Hungerford family recovered the manor in 1485,[81] for the demesne was immediately let as a whole to John Hill at a rent of £12. He also held the demesne of the estate which had formerly belonged to the Park family, which he had occupied for some years.[82] The Hill family still held the demesne farm, then called Odyngdon Farm, c. 1530,[83] and half of it in 1582. The other half was

[56] W.R.O. Land Tax Assessments.
[57] See p. 83.
[58] W.R.O. 442/1–2.
[59] Genealogists' Mag. ix. 360.
[60] W.R.O. 194, Settlement, 1731.
[61] Ibid. 132, Deeds of the Farm; ibid. Land Tax Assessments and Tithe Award, Altered Apportionment.
[62] Ibid. Inclosure Award.
[63] S.C. 6/1061/10.
[64] Antrobus D. before 1625 (W.A.S. Rec. Brch.), 27.
[65] S.C. 6/Hen. VII/919.
[66] W.R.O. 442/1.
[67] Ibid. 442/2.
[68] Ibid. 490, Hungerford Court Bk. 1628–41.
[69] Ibid. Land Tax Assessments and Tithe Award; see p. 89.
[70] Longleat MS. 8855.   [71] Ibid. Rentals.

[72] Visitation of Hunts. (Camd. Soc. 1st ser. xliii), 82.
[73] B.M. Add. Ch. 40080.
[74] Longleat MS. 10652.
[75] V.C.H. Wilts. ii, p. 142. The agricultural history of Norridge and Thoulstone is mentioned separately later in this section.
[76] Hist. MSS. Com. Hastings, i. 221. See also Visitation of Hunts. (Camd. Soc. 1st ser xliii), 83. For the identity of the downs see Hoare, Mod. Wilts. Westbury, 55.
[77] Hist. MSS. Com. Hastings, i. 221.
[78] S.C. 6/1061/10.
[79] See V.C.H. Wilts. iv. 19–25.
[80] S.C. 2/209/62–4; S.C. 6/1061/10–18.
[81] See p. 81.
[82] S.C. 6/Hen. VII/918; S.C. 2/209/63; see above, p. 83.
[83] C 1/642/15.

then held by Christopher Cabell, and the whole was called Kinton's Farm. It included a pasture called Perry's Breach and 192½ a. of arable land. Park's Farm held by Christopher Eyre included 24 a. of inclosed meadow and pasture and 124 a. of arable land, but was held with three virgates which added another 91 a. to its area. In 1582 the customary holdings of the manor in Upton amounted, apart from cottages and small closes, to 16½ virgates; these were divided between 11 copyholders in holdings varying between 4 virgates and ⅓ virgate.[84] By 1609 the two halves of the demesne farm had been re-united, and the number of larger copyholders had been reduced to 10 by the anexation of a single virgate to a larger holding.[85] Such concentration of holdings must have given rise to the several farms into which the manorial lands were divided when they were broken up in 1689.[86] Thus the farm held by the Keyford family in the 18th century was identical with the two virgates held by Christopher Carpenter in 1582,[87] and the three virgates held by Robert Green then were still distinguished as Green's Farm in the 19th century.[88] The demesne farm of the manor was sold to the Temples of Bishopstrow in 1689,[89] and let by them at rack rents from at least 1717. After inclosure it amounted to over 450 a., and was let at £340 in 1824.[90]

Little is known about the layout of the fields of Upton before the 16th century. A number of furlong names are recorded, and there was an East Field in 1341.[91] In 1582 the arable lands of holdings in Upton lay in East, South, and West Fields, and in the Garston, which lay north of the village between the Warminster road and the lane to Biss Bottom.[92] The total extent of the arable at that time was probably not greatly different from that at the inclosure of the parish in 1805,[93] when it covered the open hollow between Upton Cow Down and the Warminster boundary and extended westward to surround the crofts of the village and join the lands of the holdings in Norridge and Thoulstone. In 1582 the South and East Fields of Upton followed a two-year course,[94] and the division of the rectory glebe into two parts in 1608 probably indicates that this was still the course for the whole of the arable land. A century later the same glebe was classified into East Field, West Field, and 'other fields',[95] and at the inclosure more than half a dozen fields and furlongs were named on the award. This no doubt reflects a more elaborate course, but nothing is known of it.

The demesne arable land lay in many pieces in the 15th century,[96] but improvement by the exchange and consolidation of strips had begun in 1582, when at least 30 a. in the Garston, and perhaps all the farm lands, had already been divided off.

Much had also been done on Park's Farm, for the 124 a. belonging to it was divided into only 20 pieces, some as large as 20 a. This was a strong contrast to the three virgates held with Park's, where 84 a. were divided into over 90 pieces,[97] or the rectory glebe, where in 1608 22½ a. lay in 33 pieces. The glebe still lay in many pieces in 1705.[98] In 1582 the inclosure of common field land in Upton had not begun, for the only closes mentioned were crofts adjoining the village houses and inclosures of land, probably formerly waste, at Chalcot.[99] It had indeed made little progress by the time of the inclosure of the parish in 1805. Inclosed land not subject to common rights lay mainly round the village and west of it toward Norridge Farm, and few inclosures had been made in other parts of the fields. Those which were still subject to common were included in the allotments made by the award.[1]

The dearth of streams in Upton must have always made meadow land scarce and no commonable meadows seem to have existed; what little meadow there was lay in small inclosures about the village or near the Biss.[2] The commons on the other hand were in 1582 extensive and important. Beside the unsown field, which was used for cattle from the breach and sheep from Martinmas, the downs provided much pasture. Odyngdon, or Upton Cow Down, provided 200 a. of summer pasture for cattle and was several to the farmer of the demesne for his sheep for the rest of the year. The tenants had 60 a. of sheep pasture in Tenantry Down for the whole year, and another 100 a. in Ridgeway Down for the winter, partly shared with the farm flock. The farmer of Park's could keep 273 sheep in Whiteway Down and Durtley Hanging all the year, and had winter common for them in High Hook in Warminster; in addition he had spring pasture in Warminster Hill Field every second year. The stints of the Upton customary tenants amounted to 970 sheep. For cattle and horses, the tenants of Upton had common at the rate of 5 beasts to a virgate in all the extensive commons belonging to Norridge, including Norridge Wood, Clear Wood, Norridge Down, and Fulmoor Common.[3]

For a century before inclosure Upton had been divided into several freehold farms of considerable size. The extent to which this had modified the course of the fields, their division into strips or the common rights over them is not known, although we have seen that there had not been extensive inclosure. In 1805 all the commonable land of the parish was allotted; in Upton village there were about eights farms, varying from about 50 to 450 a. in size. Although inclosure must have resulted in an increase in permanent grass, the parish remained

[84] W.R.O. 442/1.
[85] Ibid. 442/2.
[86] See p. 81.
[87] See p. 83.
[88] Ibid.
[89] See p. 81.
[90] W.R.O. 132, Leases of the Farm, and Valuation, 1824.
[91] Ibid. 490, Hungerford Cart. ff. 111, 114 v., 115 v., 116 v.
[92] Ibid. 442/1 and Inclosure Award.
[93] Ibid. Inclosure Award, hereafter in this section used without specific reference.

[94] Ibid. 442/1.
[95] Sar. Dioc. R.O. Glebe Terriers, 1608, 1705; W.R.O. 109, Deed Sturges and Pearce to Matravers, 1750 gives W., S.W., S.E., and N.E. Fields and other furlongs.
[96] S.C. 2/209/62.
[97] W.R.O. 442/1; the wording of the survey is ambiguous.
[98] Sar. Dioc. R. O. Glebe Terriers, 1608, 1705.
[99] W.R.O. 442/1.
[1] c.g. Ponton's and Upthorn's Tynings in the allotment in Hay Furlong Field made to Green's Farm: Endowed Char. Wilts. (1908), p. 669.
[2] W.R.O. 442/1.   [3] Ibid.

predominantly arable. In 1838 there were 1,368 a. under the plough compared with 1,024 a. of pasture which included 530 a. of downland.[4] In 1905 out of a rather smaller area there were 1,050 a. of arable land and 1,148 a. of pasture.[5]

In 1333 the demesnes of the manor of Norridge consisted of 103 a. of arable land and small quantities of meadow, pasture and wood, and free and customary tenants paid just over £4 in rents.[6] The demesnes were still farmed in 1389, when 57 qr. of wheat, 63 qr. of barley and 5 qr. of oats were winnowed.[7] By 1468 the house and demesnes were let at farm.[8] In 1572 William Cabell, the lessee, held a farm which comprised some 27 a. of meadow, 50 a. of pasture, 15 a. of wood, and 140 a. of arable land. Most of the arable lay in the North and South Fields of Norridge, but some lay in Thoulstone Field. The farmer had common on Norridge Down for 260 sheep all the year, and in Norridge Wood and Clear Wood for his oxen and horses, besides certain rights in the fields of Upton and Warminster. Besides this large farm, Cabell held two smaller ones, a house near Norridge Farm called the Crosshold, and over 50 a. and a rowless tenement in Upton called Barn Close and about 40 a. The rest of the manor consisted of two holdings at Norridge, of 60 a. and 25 a., and four small holdings at Thoulstone.[9] Norridge Down, which lay south of Clear Wood, ceased to be used as a common pasture in 1698, another indication of the dominance of the farm in the economy of Norridge. William Seaman, the lessee, broke it up and sowed it with oats, and in 1739 it was producing good corn crops.[10] By 1750 part of the farm which lay in Thoulstone had been subtracted from Norridge Farm, which was then held at a rack rent of £130. Later in the century part of Clear Wood had been grubbed up and added to it.[11]

At inclosure much of the western part of the parish, stretching from Norridge Farm to Chapmanslade, consisted of old inclosures, many of which had existed in the 16th century. Commonable arable land lay north of the Bath road surrounding Hedge Croft Wood. It was divided into Thoulstone Field, Cold Castle Field, and Norridge Hill. On the parish boundary north of Norridge Wood lay Norridge Common. By that time the Longleat estate in the parish consisted of only two farms, at Norridge and Thoulstone.[12]

In 1267 Peter Scudamore obtained a grant of a weekly market and a yearly fair at Upton,[13] but nothing is known of either being held.

Mills belonged to two of the holdings at Upton

in 1086.[14] That of the capital manor may have been Smallbrook Mill which, although it lay beyond Warminster, was in Upton Scudamore parish until the 19th century.[15] It paid a chief rent to the manor of Upton in the 14th century, and was no doubt once Scudamore property. Its history is dealt with below.[16] A mill at 'Biss sub Clyve', no doubt Biss Bottom, existed in the late 13th century,[17] but no more is known of it.

CHURCH. Norman work still remaining shows that there was a church at Upton Scudamore in the 12th century. The advowson of the rectory was annexed to the manor until the mid-14th century.[18] In 1352 Walter Scudamore granted it to a canon and two vicars of Wells Cathedral, in return for a payment of 40 marks and the inclusion of his family in the prayers offered there. In 1357 Sir Peter de Grandison, Scudamore's overlord, licensed the grantees to assign the advowson to the Dean and Chapter of Wells.[19] William de Cudeworth, a vicar choral of Wells, was instituted as rector in 1361,[20] and the church seems to have been destined for the support of the college of vicars choral then recently organized there.[21] Canons of Wells were still presenting to the church in 1395,[22] but between then and 1428 the advowson was evidently regained in some way by the lords of the manor, for Walter, Lord Hungerford, presented at the later date.[23] Successive lords continued to present until the break-up of the manor in 1689. In 1701 Sir Stephen Fox gave the advowson to his nephew, Richard Barry, who had been rector since 1691.[24] After the death of his son Richard, rector from 1749 until his death in 1766, it was sold, subject to the life interest of his son Richard, who succeeded him as rector and died in 1779, to the John Michel Foundation in Queen's College, Oxford.[25] The college still retained the living in 1962.

There was a vicar at Upton Scudamore in the mid-13th century[26] and until the sale of the advowson to the Dean and Chapter of Wells many of the rectors seem to have presented vicars to serve for them.[27] When it was held by the chapter the church may have been appropriated. Early in Elizabeth I's reign the Hungerfords were treating the rectory as though it were impropriate and making leases of it to laymen.[28] In 1582, however, Thomas Hickman, the rector, evidently took his patron to law and must have been successful in regaining all the profits of the rectory.[29] The church was valued at £8 in 1291,[30] and at £16 6s. 11d. clear in 1535.[31] In 1582 it was reckoned to be worth

[4] W.R.O. Tithe Award.
[5] Information supplied by Bd. of Agric. 1905.
[6] *Wilts. Inq. p.m.* 1327–77 (Index Libr.), 95.
[7] Longleat MS. 8852.
[8] Ibid. 8855.
[9] Ibid. 8860.
[10] E 134/13 Geo. II/Mich. 5.
[11] Longleat MSS. Rentals.
[12] W.R.O. Inclosure Award.
[13] *Cal. Chart. R.* 1257–1300, 73.
[14] *V.C.H. Wilts.* ii, pp. 142, 150.
[15] See p. 79.   [16] See p. 115.
[17] Hist. MSS. Com. *Hastings*, i. 219.
[18] Phillipps, *Wilts. Inst.* i. 3, 17, 23, 38.
[19] W.R.O. 490, Hungerford Cart. ff. 121v.–122v.; *Wilts. Inq. p.m.* 1327–77 (Index Libr.), 245–6.
[20] W.R.O. 490, Hungerford Cart. f. 123.
[21] *Reg. Ralph of Shrewsbury* (Som. Rec. Soc.), ii. 765;

V.C.H. Som. ii. 167.
[22] Phillipps, *Wilts. Inst.* i. 81.
[23] Ibid. i. 118.
[24] Queen's Coll. Oxon. MSS. 5F. 16a; Hoare, *Mod. Wilts.* Warminster, 50; Foster, *Alumn. Oxon.* 1st ser. i. 79.
[25] Queen's Coll. Oxon. MSS. 5F. 22; Hoare, op. cit. 52. For the foundation see J. R. Magrath, *The Queen's College*, ii. 104–8.
[26] *Sar. Chart. and Doc.* (Rolls. Ser.), 319.
[27] Phillipps, *Wilts. Inst.* i. 2, 26, 44, 54; Hist. MSS. Com. *Hastings*, i. 219. Wm. Burgoyne, instituted in 1330, was described as perpetual vicar: *Tropenell Cart.* ed. Davies, i. 301.
[28] W.R.O. 490, List of Deeds, 1651.
[29] *Acts of P.C.* 1581–2, 344.
[30] *Tax. Eccl.* (Rec. Com.), 181.
[31] *Valor Eccl.* (Rec. Com.), ii. 103.

£40 a year,[32] and in 1634 £100.[33] About 1770 the glebe and tithes were let at £200 a year.[34] In 1835 the average income was £456,[35] which by 1864 had increased to £520.[36] When the tithes were commuted in 1838, the rector owned those of all but about 419 a. of the parish. Of the remainder 23 a. had been exempted from tithes under the Warminster Inclosure Award; the tithes of 77 a. belonged to the Dean and Chapter of Salisbury as part of Warminster rectory, of 92 a. to the Prebendary of Luxfield in Wells Cathedral, and of 227 a. to the former free chapel of Norridge. For his tithes the rector was allotted a rent-charge of £490, of which £10 represented the tithes of the glebe when it was let. The Chapter of Salisbury received £50 and the Prebendary of Luxfield £35.[37] When the advowson was conveyed to the Dean and Chapter of Wells 2 a. of land were included;[38] this probably represents an augmentation of the glebe belonging to the living. In 1608 the glebe was reckoned at 23½ a. and in 1705 at 28 a.[39] After the inclosure of the parish it amounted to 23¾.[40]

In 1311 John, parson of Upton Scudamore, was pardoned for breaking out of prison in Dorset because he had done good service in Scotland.[41] Adam of Usk, chronicler and canon lawyer, held the living from 1387 to 1393, but probably never resided, for he was at Oxford at that time.[42] Thomas Hickman, rector from 1579, was soon at variance with his parishioners. Several of them were brought before the Privy Council for bringing a malicious action against him at Quarter Sessions; they had evidently complained of his Puritanism, but the Council approved of 'his finding fault with sundry Papistical abuses by them used in the said parish, worthy of reformation'.[43] In spite of this the parishioners continued to complain to the bishop of Hickman's practices, such as making them receive the sacrament standing and wear their hats in church, and not himself wearing the square cap and surplice. It was rumoured, too, that he had the benefice by simony, and by 1585 he had been excommunicated.[44]

The 17th and 18th centuries were notable for long incumbencies; between 1628 and 1850 only seven rectors held the living. William Seaman, 1628–80, was head of a family which held a farm in the parish on lease[45] and there is little doubt that he resided. The Barrys, of whom father, son, and grandson served the cure successively between 1691 and 1779, also seem to have lived in the village, although the second of them held benefices

in Dorset and Gloucestershire in plurality.[46] Thomas Owen, 1779–1812, was a man of some learning who translated classical works on agriculture into English.[47] Upton was his only benefice and he resided on it. In 1783 he held morning and afternoon services on Sundays with a sermon at the former, and administered the sacrament four times a year to about 40 people.[48] Henry Barry, 1812–50, is the only known absentee rector, for he himself served the living of Draycot Cerne and employed a curate at Upton.[49] John Baron, 1850–85, published works on theological and antiquarian subjects, but is chiefly remembered for his part in the production of Scudamore organs, which is described below.[50] He held morning and afternoon services on Sundays, both with sermons; communion services were held at the major festivals and monthly, and about 25 people attended. One assistant curate was employed.[51] A Sunday School had about 18 pupils in 1851.[52]

In 1331 Peter Scudamore was licensed to give lands in mortmain to found a chantry in Upton church.[53] When he granted his Warminster property to his son three years later, he reserved an estate of over 40 a. there to endow it. The gift was not, however, made until 1349, when Walter, Peter's son, conveyed the land in Warminster to a priest to celebrate daily in Upton church for the souls of the Scudamore family.[54] When the manor passed to the Hungerford family, licence was obtained in 1442 to use the endowment of this chantry for the Hungerford chantry at Heytesbury.[55] The later history of the property is described above.[56]

An inquisition in 1359 found that it would be no damage to anyone to allow Walter Park to grant 60 a. in Upton to found a chantry in the church there.[57] Nothing more is known of this chantry; it is probable that the lands given for its support were, like those of the Scudamore chantry, appropriated for the Heytesbury chantry in the 15th century.[58]

In the mid-16th century there were 2 a. of land in the fields of Upton which had been given by an unknown donor for the maintenance of a lamp in the church.[59] It was probably the same 2 a. the profits of which it was said in 1582 had been employed on the repair of the church time out of mind.[60] In 1783 it was said that there were 4 a. which had been left before the Reformation for that purpose.[61] At the inclosure of the parish an allotment of 2½ a. was made to the churchwardens. In 1903 the rent of the allotments for which it was

[32] W.R.O. 442/1.
[33] W.R.O. 490, Rental 1633–4.
[34] Ibid. Sale Particular.
[35] Rep. Com. Eccl. Rev. H.C. 54, pp. 852–3 (1835), xxii.
[36] Sar. Dioc. R.O. Vis. Queries, 1864.
[37] W.R.O. Tithe Award.
[38] Ibid. 490, Hungerford Cart. ff. 121 v.–122 v.
[39] Sar. Dioc. R.O. Glebe Terriers.
[40] W.R.O. Inclosure Award.
[41] Cal. Pat. 1307–13, 394.
[42] Emden, Biog. Reg. Oxon. iii. 1937; Chronicon Adae de Usk, ed. Thompson; D.N.B.
[43] Acts of P.C. 1581–2, 269, 292, 324, 328, 334, 337, 344.
[44] Sar. Dioc. R.O. Ep. Vis. 1583 and 1585; V.C.H. Wilts. iii. 35; see also Sess. Mins. (W.A.S. Rec. Brch.), 123.
[45] See p. 83.
[46] R.F. Scott, Admissions to St. John's, Cantab. iii. 13,

[con't] iii, 540.
[47] D.N.B.
[48] Sar. Dioc. R.O. Vis. Queries, 1783.
[49] Rep. Com. Eccl. Rev. (1835), pp. 852–3.
[50] W.A.M. xxii. 349–51.
[51] H.O. 129/10/260; Sar. Dioc. R.O. Vis. Queries, 1864; Warminster Miscellany, April 1859.
[52] H.O. 129/10/260.
[53] Wilts. Inq. p.m. 1327–77 (Index Libr.), 74; Cal. Pat. 1330–34, 185.
[54] W.R.O. 490, Hungerford Cart. ff. 115v., 118v. For the earlier history of this estate, see p. 105.
[55] W.A.M. xxvii. 242.
[56] See p. 83.
[57] Wilts. Inq. p.m. 1327–77 (Index Libr.), 258.
[58] See p. 83.
[59] E 301/58 no. 95.
[60] W.R.O. 442/1.
[61] Sar. Dioc. R.O. Vis. Queries, 1783.

A HISTORY OF WILTSHIRE

used amounted to about £7 a year and was used for church expenses.[62] In 1885 Sophia Mary Baron gave two cottages at Biss Bottom to the churchwardens. They were sold for £100 in 1890 and the income from that sum has since then been used for church expenses.[63]

The church of *ST MARY THE VIRGIN* stands south of the village, and consists of nave, chancel, north aisle, and porch, and a square western tower. The dedication is mentioned in 1331.[64] The oldest remaining work is the Norman surround of the north doorway,[65] which is of the late 12th century; a 15th-century arch has been inserted in it. In the north wall of the nave is a small pointed lancet of which the head is not original; this may once have been Norman, while at the west end of the same wall 'long and short' quoins have been preserved. The circular Norman font is decorated with bands of saw-tooth and lozenge ornament.[66] These are the surviving remains of a church which probably consisted only of a nave and chancel. In the late 13th or early 14th century a small aisle or chapel of two bays was added north of the nave; in its east wall is an original window of three graded and cusped lancets. The chancel was probably rebuilt in the 15th century. The chancel arch of this time remains, and a square-headed east window of the period existed until 1855. The tower was rebuilt in 1750, and retains a round-headed window of that date at the belfry stage. According to Hoare, the remainder of the church was also rebuilt at this time.[67]

By the mid-19th century the church had become 'an offensive charnel house', with 'all sorts of deformities and material obstructions to worship'. Under the direction of G. E. Street it was extensively remodelled in the 13th-century style. The chancel was entirely rebuilt, and so was the south wall of the nave, which incorporates a built-in arcade to allow for the future addition of a south aisle. A gallery at the west end of the nave was removed, plaster ceilings in the nave and aisle were replaced by the present roofs, and a north porch was added. The west door and lower window of the tower were renewed, the pinnacles taken off, and an external frame was built on the tower to hold the bell, which had previously been almost inaudible at the rectory. The churchyard was extended on three sides, and a stone wall replaced the dead hedge and rotten palings which had surrounded it.[68]

In the north aisle are two effigies of knights, probably members of the Scudamore family;[69] one is probably of the late 13th century and the other about 100 years later.[70] The church also

contains several monuments dating from the late 17th century onwards. There were three bells in 1553 and the same number in 1750, when two were sold to pay for the work then done on the church. The remaining one, dated 1614, was recast in 1882, and two new bells were then added.[71] In 1553 a chalice of 11½ oz. was left for the parish, and 15 oz. of silver taken for the king. The plate consisted in 1963 of chalices of 1652 and 1878, a paten of 1733, and a flagon of 1883.[72]

Upton Scudamore church was the scene of an experiment in organ building which had some influence on mid-Victorian builders. At the restoration of the church in 1855–9 John Baron found himself unable to afford an organ, and so devised a design for a small organ with only one manual and no pedals, based on medieval models. He employed Nelson Hall, an organ-builder living in the village, to make the instrument, and G. E. Street, the architect for the restoration, designed the case. The idea was taken up by other churches both on account of its cheapness and the small space needed. Hall soon moved to Warminster, and supplied churches in several parts of the country before his early death in 1862. Many more Scudamore organs, as Baron called them, were built by Henry Willis, the celebrated London builder.[73]

There was a chapel at Norridge in the reign of Edward I.[74] Peter Bolymer was Rector of Norridge in 1306,[75] and in 1311 was described as parson of the chapel.[76] Institutions to this chapel are recorded between 1313 and 1521, the patrons being the lords of the manor of Norridge.[77] It was perhaps the chapel in the manor house there, mentioned in 1333.[78] In 1428 it was not taxed because of the small number of inhabitants.[79] In 1531 it was let to Richard Hill, apparently a layman, although the incumbent, William Hill, was a clerk described as well-learned, and holding only one other small benefice. The income of 52s. 6d. clear came from 25½ a. of land and the tithes of certain furlongs in the manor of Norridge. The chapel was covered with tiles and contained one bell.[80] It was dissolved as a free chapel, and the property was let to John Stockman for 21 years in 1555.[81] The reversion of the lease was granted to Richard Middlecott of Bishopstrow, clothier, in 1562.[82] The property was sold by John Middlecott to John Sainsbury in 1572.[83] From that time the descent is obscure until in 1655 William Whitaker bought ¼ share of the parsonage from a number of interested parties,[84] and left it at his death ten years later to his daughter Anne, wife of Anthony Kington.[85] In 1662 Elnathan Holwey acquired a half share from John Holwey and Richard Clase,[86] and in 1697 Edward Buckler

[62] *Endowed Char. Wilts.* (1908), p. 731.
[63] Ibid. p. 733; Char. Com. Accts. File G. 45.
[64] *Cal. Pat.* 1330–4, 185.
[65] There is a drawing of the church before restoration by Buckler in W.A.S. Libr. Devizes.
[66] *W.A.M.* liii. 469.
[67] Hoare, *Mod. Wilts.* Warminster, 51.
[68] J. Baron, *Report on the Partial Restoration of Upton Scudamore Church*, 1858 (Copy in Wilts. Tracts cv); *Warminster Miscellany*, Dec. 1859.
[69] J. Baron, *Scudamore Organs* (1862), 112.
[70] Pevsner, *Wilts.* (Buildings of England), 484.
[71] Walters, *Wilts. Bells*, 223–5; Hoare, *Mod. Wilts.* Warminster, 51.
[72] Nightingale, *Wilts. Plate*, 97.
[73] J. Baron, *Scudamore Organs* (edns. of 1858 and 1862);

Warminster Miscellany, Oct. 1858, April 1862; inf. kindly supplied by Mr. Peter Madeley of Devizes.
[74] Hist. MSS. Com. *Hastings*, i. 219.
[75] *Cal. Pat.* 1354–8, 167.
[76] *Feet of F. Wilts.* 1272–1327 (W.A.S. Rec. Brch.), 80.
[77] Phillipps, *Wilts. Inst. passim*; Hoare, *Mod. Wilts.* Warminster, 107; see above, p. 82.
[78] *Wilts. Inq. p.m.* 1327–77 (Index Libr.), 95.
[79] *Feud. Aids*, v. 297; *V.C.H. Wilts.* iv. 314.
[80] *Valor Eccl.* ii. 104; *W.A.M.* x. 298; E 301/56 no. 36, 58 no. 76.
[81] *Cal. Pat.* 1554–5, 166.   [82] Ibid. 1560–3, 234.
[83] C.P. 25(2)/239/14 & 15 Eliz. I Mich.
[84] C.P. 25(2)/609/1655 Mich.
[85] *W.N. & Q.* iv. 114.
[86] C.P. 25(2)/744/14 Chas. II Trin.

bought the other quarter, again from several parties.[87]

In the early 18th century Norridge parsonage was held in 3 parts; half belonged to the Holwey family, a quarter to Edward Buckler of Bristol, and a quarter to Lawrence Kington. In 1734 Buckler bought the Holwey share, and two years later sold all his interest to Anthony Kington, son of Lawrence, who thus obtained the whole.[88] Anthony Kington's daughter, Elizabeth, married John Gallimore Hulbert who held the parsonage until c. 1799. It then passed to another Anthony Kington, perhaps brother of Elizabeth, who died c. 1805.[89] His death again left several parties interested, whose shares passed c. 1820, probably by sale, to S. F. Phelps, a Warminster attorney.[90] In 1838 the impropriator was John Norris Clark of Trowbridge. He owned the great and small tithes of 227 a.; he also owned the freehold of 97 a. of these lands, and the tithes on them were extinguished by the award. Most of the rest of the land titheable to Norridge formed part of Norridge Farm. The parsonage glebe amounted to $23\frac{1}{2}$ a., which was apparently free of tithe.[91]

Although the chapel must have been near Norridge Farm, its exact site is unknown. It was completely gone by 1783,[92] and probably long before then. The only vestige remaining is a stone panel with a carving of the crucifixion which is built into the wall of a cottage; it is thought to be of the 13th or 14th century.

There was a chapel at Thoulstone in the reign of Edward I.[93] In 1320 there was a dispute between Roger Bavant and Peter Scudamore over the advowson,[94] which was annexed to the manor of Upton Scudamore.[95] In 1341 it was described as a free chantry worth 5 marks.[96] In 1428 it was not taxed because there were fewer than 10 inhabitants.[97] It was apparently annexed to the church of Upton about 1440 at the instance of Walter, Lord Hungerford.[98] The chapel may have stood in Chapel Close, which adjoins Thoulstone Farm on the south. This close was later part of the glebe of Upton church.[99]

NONCONFORMITY. There were two sectaries in Upton Scudamore in 1662,[1] but in 1669 and 1676 there were said to be none.[2] A man who objected to infant baptism lived in the village in 1683,[3] and a century later there was one Presbyterian family.[4] A building was licensed for Baptist worship in 1798,[5] but no permanent congregation grew up.[6] In 1841 another building was licensed[7]; this was probably also for Baptists, for in 1850 there were enough in the village for the Warminster congregation to build a chapel there. It provided 100 sittings, and a congregation of 60 attended in 1851, when afternoon and evening services were held on Sundays and the minister from Warminster preached on Thursday evenings.[8] The chapel fell out of use in 1907 and was sold in 1920, the proceeds going toward paying off the debt on the Warminster chapel.[9] It still stood in 1963, and was used as a dwelling house.

SCHOOLS. There was a school in Upton Scudamore in 1818, but it was said to be of little use.[10] Six fee-paying children attended a school in 1833[11] and five years later between 20 and 30 children were being taught by a mistress in her own cottage.[12] Grants towards building a new school were made by the state and the National Society in 1839.[13] By c. 1858 some 40 or 50 children were being taught by a mistress, trained at Salisbury Diocesan Training College. The older boys at this date went to school in Warminster.[14] In 1864 there was besides the day school an evening school two nights a week in winter; it was successful in teaching boys to read, write, and cipher, 'but not much in Christianizing or civilizing them'.[15] In 1871 there were the National School for about 28 children and a private school for 18 children.[16] The National School had an average attendance of 43 in 1903-4.[17] In 1917 it had dropped to 34, and in 1925 the school was closed.[18] It still stood in 1963, and was used as a dwelling house.

CHARITIES. John Neat, by his will proved in 1844 left £150, the income from which was to be paid on Christmas Eve to 5 old men and 5 old women, regular attenders at Upton church.[19] Mary Ann Wheeler gave £200 in 1878 and a further £50 in 1908 to provide small sums of money, or food and clothing, for 6 poor men or women, who also had to be regular churchgoers.[20] The income from both these charities amounted in 1962 to just over £12 and was given away to between 6 and 10 people.[21]

---

[87] C.P. 25(2)/889/9 Wm. III Mich.
[88] E 134/13 Geo. II/Mich. 5; C.P. 43/607 rot. 184. Lawrence Kington was of Pond Close in Corsham: W.R.O. 194, Barton Settlement, 1731.
[89] Misc. Gen. et Her. 2nd ser. iv. 306; W.N. & Q. iv. 510; W.R.O. Land Tax Assessments.
[90] W.R.O. Land Tax Assessments.
[91] Ibid. Tithe Award.
[92] Sar. Dioc. R.O. Vis. Queries, 1783.
[93] Hist. MSS. Com. Hastings, i. 219.
[94] Reg. Martival (Cant. and York Soc.), i. 147.
[95] Cal. Close, 1419-22, 255; see above, p. 81.
[96] Inq. Non. (Rec. Com.), 170.
[97] Feud. Aids, v. 297; V.C.H. Wilts. iv. 314.
[98] Hoare, Mod. Wilts. Warminster, 15.
[99] Sar. Dioc. R.O. Glebe Terriers, 1608, 1705.
[1] Sar. Dioc. R.O. Chwdns.' Pres. 1662.
[2] G. L. Turner, Orig. Records of Early Nonconformity, 121; W.N.&.Q. iii. 537.
[3] Sar. Dioc. R.O. Chwdns.' Pres. 1683.
[4] Ibid. Vis. Queries, 1783.

[5] G.R.O. Retns. of Regns.
[6] W.R.O. Retn. of Nonconformist Meetings, 1829.
[7] Ibid. Certs. of Dissenters' Meeting Houses.
[8] Ibid.; Gunn, Nonconformity in Warminster, 61; H.O. 129/10/260.
[9] Char. Com. Files 89246 and G. 45.
[10] Digest of Returns to Cttee. on Educ. of Poor, H.C. 224 (1819), ix (2).
[11] Educ. Enq. Abstract, H.C. 62 (1836), xliii.
[12] Nat. Soc. files.
[13] Ibid.
[14] Acct. of Wilts. Schools, H.C. 27 (1859 Sess. 1), xxi (2).
[15] Sar. Dioc. R.O. Vis. Queries, 1864.
[16] Return relating to Elem. Educ. H.C. 201 (1871), lv.
[17] List of Schools under Admin. of Bd. 1903-4 [Cd. 2011], H.C. (1904), lxxv.
[18] Bd. of Educ. List 21, 1919; Char. Com. File 79294.
[19] Endowed Char. Wilts. (1908), p. 731.
[20] Ibid. p. 732; Char. Com. File 30565.
[21] Char. Com. Accts. File G. 45.

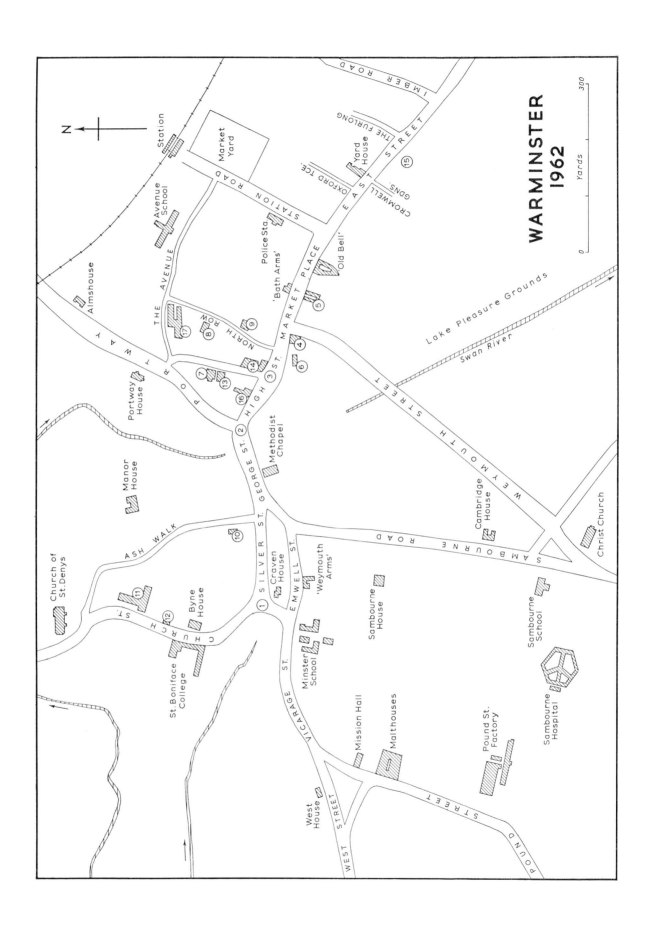

WARMINSTER 1962

Station

Market Yard

IMBER ROAD

THE FURLONG

EAST STREET

Yard House (15)

CROMWELL GDNS.

OXFORD TCE.

Avenue School

STATION ROAD

THE AVENUE

Almshouse

Police Sta.

'Bath Arms'

MARKET PLACE

'Old Bell' (5)

(9)

(17)

NORTH ROW

(8)

(4)

PORTWAY

(14)

(6)

(7)

(3)

HIGH ST.

(13)

(16)

Portway House

(2)

GEORGE ST.

Manor House

Methodist Chapel

Lake Pleasure Grounds

Swan River

WEYMOUTH STREET

ASH WALK

(10)

SILVER ST.

Craven House

EMWELL ST.

'Weymouth Arms'

Cambridge House

SAMBOURNE ROAD

Christ Church

(11)

CHURCH ST.

(12)

Byne House

Minster School

Sambourne House

Sambourne School

Church of St. Denys

St. Boniface College

VICARAGE ST.

Mission Hall

Malthouses

Pound St. Factory

Sambourne Hospital

West House

WEST STREET

POUND STREET

N

0   300
Yards

WARMINSTER

WARMINSTER[1] lies at the foot of the downs, near the north-west corner of Salisbury Plain, which ends here in the conspicuous Arn Hill (694 ft.).[2] From Arn Hill a ridge of land about 400 ft. high joins the Plain to the isolated height of Cley Hill to the west, and forms the watershed between the valley of the Biss and Frome to the north and that of the Wylye to the south. Warminster grew up at the confluence of two small streams which rise in the southern slope of the ridge; after their junction they form the Were which gave the town its name.[3] The stream, called the Swan River since at least the mid-19th century,[4] is still only small as it flows on to join the Wylye, which skirts the parish on the south. To the west of the town begins rather higher and more broken country, formerly heathland but now largely wooded, which forms the eastern verge of the Longleat estate.

The ancient parish of Warminster differed considerably in its boundaries from the present urban district.[5] From the 1962 boundary between Tascroft Farm and Botany Farm a narrow strip extended westward to the Somerset border near Stalls Farm, so that the parish was over seven miles long. South-east of Bishopstrow the former common meadow of Pit Mead was manorially part of Warminster, but was parochially divided between the parishes of Warminster, Bishopstrow, and Norton Bavant. Adjoining it the former farm at Moot Hill belonged to Warminster; smaller detached pieces included Eastleigh Farm and some land near Norridge. Inside the Warminster boundary lay small detached pieces of Corsley, Upton Scudamore, and Boyton. By the Divided Parishes Act of 1882[6] and an order of 1883,[7] Pit Mead and Moot Hill Farm were assigned to Sutton Veny and Eastleigh Farm to Bishopstrow, and the smaller detached pieces were included in the parishes which surrounded them. In addition, detached parts of Bishopstrow and Norton Bavant, which adjoined Warminster on the south, were included within it; together they stretched from Botany Farm to Henford's Marsh. These changes made the area of the parish 6,564 a.[8] In 1934 the western part of the parish, from Tascroft Farm to the Somerset border, was added to Corsley, leaving the urban district with an area of 5,658 a.[9]

Within its boundaries Warminster parish included a diversified stretch of country. The high chalk downland of Salisbury Plain, which provided good sheep pasture, is penetrated by deep combes at Mancombe and Oxendean. On either side of them ridges of high land reach to the south, culminating in Arn Hill to the west and Battlesbury to the east. They enclose a lower area of greensand, separated from the Wylye valley to the south by the chalk outliers of Cop Heap and Chalk Hill. This greensand, and a similar area west of Arn Hill to the north of the town, provided most of Warminster's open field arable land before the parish was inclosed in the late 18th century. The town itself lies roughly in the centre of the parish, on well-watered land protected from the north by the downs, providing good meadow and garden land. More meadow and pasture lay along the Wylye and to the west of the town. Most of the south-western extremity of the parish was open common until the inclosure; it has since been planted with woods and forms the outlying part of Longleat Park. Of the hamlets outside Warminster, Smallbrook was mentioned separately in 1086 and still in the 14th century,[10] but has long been reduced to a single farm. Bugley and Boreham remain semi-rural, connected to the town only by sporadic ribbon-development. The origin of the large hamlet of Warminster Common is discussed below.[11]

Apart from prehistoric occupation, of which considerable evidence has been found in the hill-fort of Battlesbury, the earliest known inhabited site in Warminster is that of two Roman villas found in the late 18th century at Pit Mead, while deposits of Roman coins have been found at the Common, and Romano-British remains at Arn Hill and Mancombe Down.[12] No Roman road ran this way, but the site of the town lay on a viable route from Salisbury to Bath; there the traveller could descend from the downs and perhaps spend a night before going on to meet the road south from Bath near Beckington.[13] Warminster seems to have owed its comparative inportance in Saxon times rather to its being a royal manor than to its position on a north-south route. Its status as a borough may be inferred from the late 10th century, when moneyers,

---

[1] Grateful thanks are due to Mr. H. N. Dewey of Warminster for much advice in the preparation of this article, and for the loan of material from his collection.
[2] The following maps were used: O. S. Maps Wilts. 1/500, LI, and 1/2,500, LI and LII (all edns.); 1/25,000, ST 84 and ST 94.   [3] *P. N. Wilts.* (E.P.N.S.), 157.
[4] *Warminster Miscellany, passim.*
[5] W.R.O. Inclosure and Tithe Awards; J. J. Daniell, *History of Warminster,* 10–12.
[6] 45 and 46 Vic. *c.* 58.

[7] *Bounds of Wilts.* 15–16.
[8] *Census,* 1901–31.
[9] *V.C.H. Wilts.* iv. 359; *Census,* 1951.
[10] *V.C.H. Wilts.* iv. 302, 311.
[11] See p. 96.
[12] *V.C.H. Wilts.* i (1), 110, 118.
[13] For this road, see I. D. Margary, *Roman Roads in Britain,* i. 99, 116–7; its course between Donhead St. Mary and Frome has not been found, and it may have run fairly close to the site of Warminster.

KEY TO THE MAP ON THE OPPOSITE PAGE

1. Site of High, or Emwell Cross.
2. Site of Almshouse Bridge.
3. Site of former Town Hall.
4. Town Hall.
5. Former Corn Market.
6. Chapel of St. Laurence.
7. Congregational Church.
8. Baptist Church.
9. Former Unitarian Church.

10. Christian Scientist Church.
11. Lord Weymouth's Grammar School.
12. Former National School.
13. Former British School.
14. Former Athenaeum and Secondary School.
15. Site of East End House.
16. Chantry House.
17. Cottage Hospital.

who were limited to boroughs by law, worked there,[14] while the minster which gave the town its name must have supplied the spiritual needs of a considerable district around it in even earlier times.[15] It was a royal residence in the early 10th century,[16] and at the Conquest its obligation to provide the farm of one night was probably of ancient standing. There is no evidence, however, that its importance arose from its urban character. There were, it is true, 30 burgesses in 1086, but they lived on the royal demesne, and were probably only the traders and craftsmen who served the needs of the large estate which surrounded them. There is no indication of heterogeneous tenure or the payment of the third penny, two of the hall-marks of the urban Domesday borough.[17] No moneyers are known to have worked in Warminster after the reign of Harold I,[18] and the town never developed any organ of self-government or achieved parliamentary representation.[19]

The development of Warminster into a relatively prosperous town, which with its 304 poll-tax payers in 1377 stood tenth in the county,[20] was based on its market, first mentioned in the 13th century.[21] In the 12th century the capital manor was granted away from the royal estate,[22] and there are slight indications of growth in the town which may have taken place under the new lords, and may even have been artifically fostered by them. They are to be deduced from the plan of the town. The parish church stands at the very end of the town, and nearby is the site of the manor house. They stand on a slight rise, almost surrounded by two small streams, which no doubt marks the area of the earliest settlement. From the church a curved street leads southwards to an open space at the junction of other roads leading east and west; here until the 18th century stood the remains of a cross called the High Cross or Emwell Cross.[23] In the early 19th century the tradition still remained in Warminster that this place had once been the centre of the town, which had extended no further east than Almshouse Bridge (now the junction of George Street and High Street).[24] The present centre of the town, the wide and straight High Street and Market Place, extends on the opposite side of the bridge. This was called the market of Warminster in the earlier 13th century, when a shop covered with stone stood there adjoining the Chapel of St. Laurence.[25] Other permanent buildings there were mentioned later in the century.[26] Such a street or market-place, distinct though not

necessarily separate from an older settlement, is a feature of the artificially-fostered new towns of the 13th century.[27] It may be that in Warminster development was less formal than the founding of a new town attached to the rural manor, but the occurrence of the place-name Newport applied to at least part of this end of the town in the 14th century[28] must add some weight to the supposition that the town grew eastwards in the 13th century.

Little else is known of Warminster's development in the Middle Ages. Houses in Byne Street, the modern Church Street, are regularly mentioned from the 13th century.[29] West Street was so-named by 1325,[30] and houses lay in Newport Street, now Portway, by 1366.[31] The whereabouts of 'Curtstrate' of the 13th century,[32] and 'Pidemannes-lane' of 1384[33] is not known. Nor are there visible remains of building to fill in the picture of the medieval town. It seems reasonable to assume, however, that at the end of the Middle Ages Warminster stretched from the church to the east end of the Market Place; the part west of Almshouse Bridge was probably not very closely built, for even in the 18th century some lessening of density and greater informality in the layout of the houses and plots could be detected there.[34]

By the 16th century the fame of Warminster market was well-established, and the clothing and malting trades, which with the market were to be the economic mainstays of the town until the 19th century, had begun.[35] Some expansion may have resulted from the growth of these industries. A house with a timber-framed upper story (now no. 34 Vicarage Street) standing in the former West Street, past its junction with Pound Street, shows its extent to the west, and the mention of a house adjoining the Common Close in 1572[36] probably indicates growth to the north too. Other timber-framed houses perhaps of this period survive in Silver Street (nos. 39, 44-50) and High Street (nos. 36-37), though all have been variously refronted. The central block of the house in Emwell Street, now the 'Weymouth Arms', contains a 16th century-fireplace. All but the most important houses in the town were probably of timber at this time; in 1638 13 out of 14 houses in the town belonging to the manor of Furnax were of timber, thatched with straw or reed.[37] The most substantial buildings in the town were perhaps the inns, with which the town was well supplied for the convenience of visitors to the market. In 1686 Warminster stood fourth for accommodation

[14] V.C.H. Wilts, ii, pp. 16–18; R. H. M. Dolley (ed.) Anglo-Saxon Coins, 146.
[15] V.C.H. Wilts. ii, p. 32.
[16] Ibid.
[17] Ibid. pp. 20, 116.
[18] H. de S. Shortt, 'Mints of Wilts.', Arch. Jnl. civ. 117.
[19] See p. 128.
[20] V.C.H. Wilts. iv. 311–12.
[21] See p. 115.
[22] See p. 96.
[23] Longleat MS. 9531 (1667); Longleat Estate Office, Survey 1743, p. 42; W.R.O. 194, Ferris to Webb, 1763.
[24] J. E. Halliday, Information about Warminster, f. 12; this MS. was compiled c. 1820–40, and is in 1963 penes Mr. H. N. Dewey.
[25] Longleat MS. 8966, a deed of Thos. Mauduit, fl. c. 1204–44.
[26] Ibid. 9096, 9101; B.M. Add. Ch. 26702.
[27] M. W. Beresford, 'Six New Towns of the Bishops of Winchester', Medieval Archaeology, iii. 187–215, and

Time and Place (Leeds, 1961), 11–18. But cf. Stenton, Anglo-Saxon England, 526, where it is suggested that the growth might be pre-Conquest.
[28] Longleat MS. 9147 (1339); the name Newport was that of an estate whose chief house later lay in Portway, formerly Newport St., but may perhaps have once been nearer the Market Place.
[29] Longleat MSS. 8982 (Edw. I), 9014 (1354); C.C.C. deeds K. 1. 20 (1344).
[30] Longleat MS. 9000; until the 19th century the name West St. or West End applied to all the town west of Emwell Cross.
[31] Ibid. 9169.
[32] B.M. Add. Ch. 26700–1.
[33] Longleat MS. 9181.
[34] W.R.O. Inclosure Award.
[35] See pp. 110, 113.
[36] Longleat MS. 9419.
[37] C.C.C. MSS. Survey 1638.

among Wiltshire towns, with 116 beds and stabling for 328 horses,[38] and it was said that there were 51 inns and alehouses in the town in 1710.[39] The value of the principal ones may be judged from the price of £1,000 paid for the 'Red Lion' in 1636.[40] The best example of the old inns of the town is the 'Old Bell'; its exterior of coursed rubble stone probably dates from the late 18th century, but the interior has earlier timber work which may connect it with the 'Bell' of 1483.[41] The open arcade across the pavement, said to have been for the protection of buyers and sellers at the market, was formerly a feature of other Warminster inns, including the 'Anchor'[42] and the 'Red Lion'.[43]

Warminster was the scene of some activity in the Civil War. Henry Wansey, a Warminster man, was a major in the Parliamentary forces; in 1644 when he was besieged at Woodhouse in Horningsham, another force under Edmund Ludlow was prevented from relieving him after a skirmish on Warminster Common.[44] The town also contained other parliamentary sympathizers;[45] in 1646 it was said that it had suffered to the extent of £500 by being a parliamentary garrison.[46]

It is in the 17th century that we first know anything of the external road connexions of Warminster. The only road through the town mentioned in Ogilby was a now lost way over the Plain from Amesbury through Shrewton, which descended into the Wylye valley near Norton Bavant and, passing through Warminster, went on to Maiden Bradley. This was the main road from London to Barnstaple in 1675,[47] and in 1754 it was still as a place on the road from London to the west that Warminster was noted.[48] There were routes from Salisbury to Bath which avoided Warminster altogether, and even if the traveller kept roughly to the line of the present main road between the two places, he did not actually pass through the town. From Thoulstone the road skirted Upton Scudamore village, joined the road from Westbury, and passed east of Warminster by Cop Heap Lane and Woodcock to join the road down to the Wylye valley beyond the present Bishopstrow House.[49] The present main road from Thoulstone to Warminster church, which brought the route through the centre of the town, was turnpiked in 1752.[50]

The 18th century was a prosperous time in Warminster; the malting and woollen trades and the market all flourished, and in 1751 it was described as a 'Populous place with good inns'.[51] The population grew somewhat. In 1665 there were 354

householders in the town,[52] which indicates a total of perhaps 1,800 people. In 1781 the town within the turnpike gates contained 539 houses and 2,605 inhabitants.[53] In extent it probably grew most towards the west. By 1783 houses stretched along West Street on both sides for ½ mile beyond the High Cross and along Pound Street further than the end of Princecroft Lane.[54] Houses in Pound Street are mentioned by 1748,[55] and some at Topps, near Princecroft Lane, rather earlier.[56] In 1783 cottages, some evidently built on waste at the side of the road, extended sporadically along Portway as far as the bottom of Elm Hill.[57] East of the town houses extended as far as the Imber road, and some of the cottages of the Furlong were built. The row of houses built on the grounds of the prebendal mansion house (from the 'Masons' Arms' to East End Garage) was at least partly built by 1751, when the Packhorse Inn stood in it.[58] East of the Imber road a number of houses stood in the Boreham road on plots probably made available by the inclosure of open-field land. Houses bearing the dates 1712, 1718, and 1739 still stood there in 1962.[59] In the older area of the town courts began to develop on what had been the gardens of houses. Meeting House Lane, now North Row, probably dates from the establishment of the Old Meeting there in the late 17th century.[60] Other surviving courts are Three Horseshoes Yard, off the Market Place, and Oxford Terrace and Cromwell Gardens (formerly Ludlow's Court), off East Street.

The period has left ample evidence of its prosperity in buildings, and the amount which remains will allow only general observations to be made. The most common building material was a roughly-squared rubble stone, apparently quarried locally,[61] and laid in courses of about the depth of brickwork. It was used in buildings ranging in size from cottages to all but the largest houses, and in 1796 Arthur Young described Warminster as a stone town.[62] Many groups of cottages built of this rubble can be seen in West Street and Pound Street; good examples of its use in larger buildings are West House (no. 12 West Street) and Lord Weymouth's Grammar School of 1707 in Church Street. The latter is of two stories and attics, with mullioned and transomed windows, and has an elaborate central doorcase which came from Longleat, and was designed by Wren.[63] In larger rubble houses ashlar was used for quoins and window surrounds; it was used with great effect to embellish no. 32 Vicarage Street. Only the most pretentious houses

[38] *Early Stuart Tradesmen* (W.A.S. Rec. Brch.), p. xv.
[39] Halliday, Information, f. 85.
[40] Longleat MSS. 9461–6.
[41] C.C.C. Deeds K.1. 63.
[42] *Warminster Miscellany*, Feb. 1854; C. V. Manley, Regional Survey of Warminster, iv. 206–7 (MS. *penes* Warminster U.D.C.).
[43] Longleat Estate Office, Survey 1743, p. 73.
[44] Ludlow, *Memoirs*, ed. Firth, i. 91, 460–1.
[45] Hist. MSS. Com. *Var. Coll.* i. 119; *W.A.M.* xxxvii. 483.
[46] Hist. MSS. Com. *Var. Coll.* i. 110.
[47] Ogilby, *Britannia* (1675), pl. 32.
[48] *Travels of Richard Pococke*, vol. ii (Camden Soc. 2nd ser. xliii), 38.
[49] Halliday, Information, f. 99; the eastern part of this road is lost, but can be seen on *Andrews and Dury, Map* (W.A.S. Rec. Brch.), pl. 7.

[50] 25 Geo. II, c. 12.
[51] [S. Whatley], *England's Gazetteer*, vol. ii.
[52] Daniell, *Warminster*, 115–9.
[53] Halliday, Information, f. 72.
[54] W.R.O. Inclosure Award, which is used in this section without further reference.
[55] Longleat MS. 10252.
[56] W.R.O. 212 B Wa. 10–15.
[57] The name Scotland applied to houses at the N. end of Portway probably derives from their remoteness rather than any connexion with the estate of Edw. Scutt, as supposed by Daniell (*Warminster*, 48).
[58] *W.N. & Q.* i. 129.
[59] Nos. 21, 27, and 36 Boreham Road.
[60] See p. 125.
[61] Daniell, *Warminster*, 256; O.S. Map 1/2,500 Wilts. LI (1st edn.); U.D.C. Local Bd. Min. Bks.
[62] Young, *Annals of Agriculture*, xxviii. 460.
[63] Hoare, *Mod. Wilts.* Heytesbury, 72.

such as Portway House and the Manor House, both described below,[64] were entirely faced with ashlar. Brick does not appear to have been in general use, but was evidently highly thought of from the mid-18th century. The earliest surviving example is probably in the wings of the house in Emwell Street, used since 1928 as the 'Weymouth Arms',[65] where its use may date from 1749; Craven House in Silver Street, dated 1774, where it is used for the front only, and nos. 3–4 Church Street are prosperous brick houses of the second half of the century. In cottages it was used extensively for quoins and window surrounds. Tiles were the most common roofing material, although much thatch survived on smaller buildings until the 19th century.[66] Large and prosperous houses are to be found in all parts of the town, but there is a striking group in Church Street. Byne House, built by John Wansey in 1755,[67] has three-light windows with the central light taller than the outer ones, similar to those in the Chantry, High Street, and the house, dated 1767, now converted into the Regency Arcade in East Street. These houses are also notable for their Venetian windows, of which there is another good example at no. 25A High Street. They were probably by a local architect, unlike the house in Church Street, which William Wansey had built by Joseph Glascodine, a Bristol man, in 1796;[68] this must be the house now incorporated in St. Boniface's College, which bears that date. Elaborate doorways can be seen at nos. 3 and 4 Church Street. The buildings of three of the chief 18th-century inns of the town survive. The 'Angel', now no. 4 High Street, and the 'Lamb', no. 51 Market Place, are both three-storied houses of rubble, used as shops. The building which still houses the 'Bath Arms' must date, externally at least, from 1732 when the 'Three Goats' Heads', which stood on the site, was let on condition that it was rebuilt. The new house was first called the 'King's Arms', but the name 'Lord's Arms' or 'Weymouth Arms' was used by 1769.[69]

The deliberate improvement of Warminster streets probably began soon after the first Turnpike Act affecting the town was passed in 1727. It affected seven roads radiating from Warminster; none was over three miles long and some did not leave the parish, so that the purpose of the Act was clearly local improvement rather than the care of a long stretch of a nationally important route. The roads in the town were described in the Act as 'ruinous' and 'impassible in winter',[70] and although the phrases were conventional, it is clear that they were also accurate. Water ran over the road through the town at four places, Coldharbour, High Cross, Chain Street, and Almshouse Bridge. Chain Street

itself was closed to all except foot passengers by chains at either end, and the horse road ran behind the houses along 'shallow water, or the backside of Chain Street', which was often flooded in winter.[71] The way in East Street was so deep that it was possible to jump from the footpath on to the top of a loaded hay-waggon.[72] The earliest improvements of which we know were carried out in 1759, when Portway, which had previously been only a bridle track, was made into a road by the demolition of a number of cottages.[73] In 1765 Thomas Marsh, a timber-merchant, took a lease of all the ground on the west side of Portway from Almshouse Bridge to Portway House, and built several houses on it.[74] The hollow way in Pound Street was filled up in 1759, and a new road, probably the present Sambourne Road, was made to the Common, replacing a deep and winding lane.[75] In 1763 a road bridge was made at Almshouse Bridge to replace the narrow wooden footbridge, and the stream at Coldharbour was bridged in 1770.[76] In 1769 the base of the High Cross, and a barn which stood in the street near it, were removed to improve the junction of Church Street and West Street; the obelisk, which commemorates the inclosure of the parish, was placed on the site of the cross in 1783.[77] In 1792 the turnpike commissioners obtained additional powers to make and maintain pavements in the town.[78] Such improvements no doubt encouraged improvement in buildings, and several substantial houses in the Market Place date from about the end of the century. The terrace which extends east from the 'Old Bell' was built after 1783 to replace several scattered houses, parts of which may still be seen at the rear. On the same side of the road no. 14 is of about 1800, built on the site of the Bush Inn.

In the first half of the 19th century Warminster's clothing trade collapsed, and malting declined somewhat, though it still remained important. The market suffered for a time from the competition of other towns with better communications. In spite of this the town seems to have suffered no permanent depression. Increase in retail trade, and new occupations such as brewing and iron-founding had, it was considered in 1860, made up for the loss of the clothing trade, while the silk mill at Crockerton provided employment for many women and girls.[79] This is borne out by population figures. From 4,932 in 1801 the number declined slightly by 1811, when the slump in the cloth trade was severe, but rose to 6,115 by 1831, and slightly more, to 6,285 by 1851.[80] Cobbett approved of Warminster as a 'solid and good town', with 'no villainous gingerbread houses running up',[81] and in 1830 it was said that a spirit of improvement was

[64] See pp. 98, 99.
[65] Manley, Regional Survey, vii. 568.
[66] *Warminster Miscellany* and *Herald*, reports of fires *passim*.
[67] Transcripts of Wansey papers made by Mr. H. N. Dewey.
[68] Ibid.
[69] Longleat MSS. 10216, 10284; Longleat Estate Office, Survey 1743, p. 79 and Survey 1837, p. 84; The 'Three Goats' Heads' existed in the late 17th century: Longleat MSS. Survey 1682.
[70] *V.C.H. Wilts.* iv. 258; Daniell, *Warminster*, 111.
[71] Halliday, Information, ff. 2, 13; Longleat MS.

10253.
[72] Halliday, Information, f. 13.
[73] Daniell, *Warminster*, 115.
[74] Longleat Estate Office, Survey 1743, p. 46.
[75] Daniell, *Warminster*, 115; the old lane probably ran east of Sambourne Road; traces of it can be seen on the inclosure map.
[76] Halliday, Information, f. 12.
[77] Ibid.; Longleat Estate office, Survey 1743, p. 42.
[78] 32 Geo. III, c. 141.
[79] *Warminster Miscellany*, Oct. and Nov. 1860.
[80] *V.C.H. Wilts.* iv. 359.
[81] *Rural Rides*, ed. G. D. H. Cole, 397.

Village Street, Bishopstrow

Byne House, Warminster, built 1755

The Ship Inn, demolished *c.* 1900

Town Hall, demolished 1830

WARMINSTER

very apparent.[82] This spirit has left a permanent mark on the town. The first movement of the century was initiated by the bequest of George Wansey, who in 1807 left £1,000 to be laid out in improvements provided that another £1,000 was raised for the same purpose. A committee was formed which bought all the houses on the south side of Chain Street and demolished them, so making the wide road called George Street, presumably after the donor.[83] On the north side land which had previously been gardens was let for building, and a row of three-storied brick houses of uniform design was built on it c. 1815.[84] Further east a fire which destroyed a number of houses at the corner of Portway and High Street gave an opportunity for rebuilding, and the plain three-storied houses which stand there are of c. 1825.[85] On the opposite corner the two-storied houses nos. 36–40 George Street are of c. 1831,[86] and the widening of the road here, completely covering the stream so that all semblance of a bridge disappeared, was carried out in 1832.[87]

There were also notable changes in the Market Place. In 1830 Weymouth Street was made from it to provide a new road to Sambourne. Its cutting provided an opportunity to build a new Town Hall and demolish the old one which stood inconveniently in the middle of the Market Place.[88] Edward Blore, the architect of the new building, also designed the group built in the Tudor style, an early example of its use, at the opposite corner of the new road,[89] on the site of an inn called the 'King's Arms'.[90] The corner building, which housed the newly formed Literary and Scientific Institute, was opened in 1838.[91] Other buildings were improved by their occupiers. No. 3 High Street, which had been built c. 1730, was improved in 1841 at a cost of over £700, and its plain front of ashlar must date from then.[92] Some new buildings were also put up, such as those at the east corner of North Row and the Market Place, built in 1831,[93] and the terrace of early-19th-century houses, now nos. 52 and 53 Market Place.

While the centre of the town was being transformed, the movement of the wealthier inhabitants to the outskirts which was typical of the period went only slowly. The earliest suburban house in Warminster was probably Sambourne House, built by Henry Wansey c. 1800.[94] Cambridge House, also in Sambourne Road (nos. 54–55), must be of about the same time. Several smaller houses dating from

the earlier part of the century may be seen along the Boreham road, such as no. 89 East Street, a stone-built villa, and nos. 35–37 Boreham Road, a pair of brick houses. Boreham Terrace is of six brick houses of three stories (nos. 24–34 Boreham Road); all these were probably among the 'elegant and lofty houses' which had been very recently built in 1822.[95] By 1840 a group of cottages and four larger houses (nos. 81–87) had been built further along the road near what was to be the site of St. John's Church, and at Boreham itself two large villas, Heronslade and Boreham Villa.[96] Other parts of the town were less favoured. Even after Christ Church was built at Sambourne in 1830, New Road and Sambourne Road did not prove attractive to builders; perhaps they were too near the Common and the Union Workhouse, built in 1836, or perhaps freehold land was not available. The west end of the town, West Street and Pound Street, was a predominantly working-class area which did not expand at this time.

The railway from Westbury to Warminster was opened in 1851, and extended down the Wylye to Salisbury in 1856.[97] Its coming marked the beginning, and was largely the cause, of a period of comparative depression. The great market declined almost to nothing, the retail trade suffered in consequence, and hardly any industry was carried on. Even in 1860, before the full effects had been felt, Warminster was 'a clean-swept, semi-aristocratic, decidedly poor place', in a 'lukewarm, stagnant, bankrupt state'.[98] By 1871 many inns had been closed, and carriers and others connected with the market had left the town.[99] In the 1890's shopkeepers did not get one busy day a month, and a traveller was told that the town had 'gone to sleep and never wakes up' so that 'men rust out rather than wear out'.[1] The population declined slightly at each census until it was 5,547 in 1901, a decrease of over 700 since 1851.[2] Building in the town was discouraged by its declining state and by the policy of not renewing long leases pursued by the Longleat estate.[3] Several public buildings were, however, built in the 1850's. The Savings Bank at the east end of the Market Place is of 1852. The name of its site, Hatchet Corner, is derived from an inn which stood there from the 16th century until c. 1789.[4] The Corn Market, opened in 1855, was built on the site of the 'Red Lion' which had been burnt down four years earlier,[5] and the Athenaeum, designed by the local architect, W. J. Stent, in an early

[82] Pigot, *Nat. Com. Dir.* (1830).
[83] Halliday, Information, f. 13; Longleat Estate Office Survey 1743, pp. 71, 110, 119.
[84] Longleat Estate Office, Survey 1743, p. 65, and Survey 1837, pp. 67, 115, 116, 130, 132; the 3 western houses have recently (1962) been demolished, leaving 12 (nos. 25–36).
[85] Longleat Estate Office, Survey 1837, pp. 49–51, 65.
[86] Ibid. pp. 54–55.   [87] Halliday, Information, f. 12.
[88] Daniell, *Warminster*, 122–3.
[89] Longleat Estate Office, Survey 1837, p. 34.
[90] Ibid. Survey 1743, p. 72; it was formerly the 'Plume of Feathers', and in the 17th cent. the 'Prince's' or 'States' Arms'; Longleat MS. 9380.
[91] W.R.O. 132, papers relating to Warminster Lit. & Sc. Inst.; W.A.S. Libr. Devizes, Everett MSS. ix.
[92] Longleat Estate Office, Survey 1743, p. 34, and Survey 1837 p. 31; before 1731 the 'Rose and Crown' stood there.

[93] Halliday, Information, f. 20; *Endowed Char. Wilts.* (1908), p. 737; the site of a 'King's Arms' which existed before the one mentioned above.
[94] Longleat Estate Office, Survey 1837, p. 92.
[95] Pigot, *New Com. Dir.* (1822–3).
[96] W.R.O. Tithe Award; the first lease of Boreham Villa was in 1834: Bishopstrow Parish Records, Eastleigh Estate Sale Catalogue.
[97] *V.C.H. Wilts.* iv. 284.
[98] *Warminster Miscellany*, Oct. 1860.
[99] *V.C.H. Wilts.* iv. 325.
[1] J. J. Hissey, *Through Ten English Counties*, 132.
[2] *V.C.H. Wilts.* iv. 359.
[3] *Warminster Miscellany*, Oct. 1860.
[4] Daniell, *Warminster*, 132; Longleat MSS. 9299, 9301; Longleat Estate Office, Survey 1743, p. 43.
[5] Ibid. June and Sept. 1854, Dec. 1855; Longleat Estate Office, Survey 1837, p. 78; since the 1920's it has been used as a garage and 2 small shops.

Renaissance style, replaced the London Inn in 1858.[6] The improvement made in 1856 by exposing St. Laurence's Chapel to the street has been mentioned below.[7] There are few buildings of the later part of the century in the centre of the town; among them are those occupied in 1962 by Lloyds and Barclays Banks and nos. 36 and 40 Market Place and 11 High Street. An important improvement carried out *c.* 1900 was the opening of Common Close into the High Street by the removal of the 'Ship'.[8]

New building was desultory in the suburbs of the town. The Boreham road continued to be the most favoured site for villas; its attraction was increased by the building of St. John's Church in 1865. Boreham Villas, three pairs of stone houses, now nos. 52–62, date from before 1860,[9] and another pair, nos. 35–37, were built by 1874.[10] St. John's Lodge, built in 1883,[11] and Highbury, of about the same time, are large detached houses. North of the town nos. 67–68 Portway are perhaps the new pair of villas built there in 1863,[12] and Downside and Portway Villa are of much the same time.[13] A few houses were also built near Christ Church by 1886, including Christ Church Terrace and Hampton House.[14] In the 1890's a future direction of suburban expansion was indicated by the building of a number of houses on the Imber road north of the railway.[15]

The early years of the 20th century saw little change in Warminster. Combination in the brewing industry led to the closing of the small breweries which had grown out of the older malting businesses, and what little manufacturing industry there was in the town employed few hands. There was a tendency to regard the town's future chiefly as residential. It had a pleasant position and many well-built large houses. During the incumbency (1859–97) of Sir James Philipps it had become a centre of Anglican activity.[16] Sporting facilities included good fishing and hunting country and a golf course opened in 1891.[17] In 1907 a Town Advertisement Committee was formed. It authorized the production of a town guide, and inserted advertisements in the G.W.R. publication *Holiday Haunts*. An ambitious project to build a hotel and villas in Elm Hill and Cop Heap Lane only broke down because the committee insisted on refusing the plots offered by Lord Bath, and asked for others more favourably placed.[18] The population of the town declined slightly in each decade between 1851 and 1931,[19] so that it was little bigger in 1931 than in 1801. It was the approach of the Second Word War which finally halted the eco-

nomic decline. Camps and permanent barracks in the town were begun in 1937,[20] and a large workshop for vehicle repairs was opened in 1940.[21] After the war Warminster remained a permanent garrison town, housing the School of Infantry and a R.E.M.E. workshop. Large estates of married quarters were built. Several light industries were also begun, and the population of the town in 1961 was estimated at 9,900.

The growth of a settlement of houses built on the waste at the edge of Warminster Common can be traced from the late 17th century. A cottage which adjoined other cottages there belonged to the Longleat estate in 1668,[22] and by 1727 a parish workhouse was built there.[23] In 1739 it was complained that one cottage, built 20 years before, had since been enlarged to hold four families, and an attempt was made to prosecute the inhabitants for not having the statutory four acres adjoining their dwellings.[24] About 1770 an attempt to establish the lord of the manor's ownership of the cottages ended in failure.[25] By 1781 there were 200 houses in which lived 1,015 people.[26] The squalor of the place in the late 18th century was vividly described by William Daniell. Hovels of one room up and one down, unceiled, unplastered, and with earth floors housed families which were without the commonest necessities of life. Outside piles of filth corrupted the stream which was the only water supply, so that typhus was rarely absent and smallpox not uncommon. The rudeness of the Commoners matched that of their houses; respectable people would not go there, and Sundays were occupied in brutal sports, fighting, and drunkenness. The ill-fame of the place for crime was known as far away as Devon.[27] The labours of Daniell himself, and of the Anglican clergy, to reform the inhabitants are mentioned below.[28] They were accompanied by a gradual physical improvement, and by 1833 the hamlet was neat, clean, and respectable.[29] The seal was set on its respectability in the following year, when the streets were named by a committee of the vestry.[30] By 1862 even the name of the Common had begun to be abandoned in favour of New Town.[31] Many of the rubble cottages which still stand there in 1962 date from the early 19th century. A survivor of an earlier time is the thatched house at the corner of Broadway Road.

MANORS. *WARMINSTER* belonged to the kings of England before the Conquest, and was still in the hands of William I in 1086.[32] By 1156 it had been granted to William FitzHamon,[33] a tenant in

[6] *Warminster Miscellany*, Oct. 1855, April 1857, Nov. 1858; an inn called the 'Search Hoop' stood on the site until 1818; *W.A.M.* xx. 140–4; Hist. MSS. Com. *Var. Coll.* i. 118. The building has been a cinema since before the First World War.
[7] See p. 123.
[8] See pl. facing p. 95.
[9] *Warminster Miscellany*, May 1860.
[10] *Warminster Herald*, 3 Jan. 1874.
[11] 'Highways and Byways', vi. (A series of numbered articles by W. Middlebrook which appeared in the *Wilts. Times* between Dec. 1959 and June 1961.)
[12] *Warminster Miscellany*, Aug. 1863.
[13] Downside was built by 1865 for W. J. Stent: *Harrod's Dir.* (1865).
[14] O.S. Map. 1/2,500 Wilts. LI, 1st edn.
[15] Ibid. 2nd edn.; U.D.C. Local Bd. Min. Bks.

[16] See p. 120.
[17] Manley, Regional Survey, vii. 579.
[18] U.D.C. Min. Bk. of Cttee. 1907–9.
[19] *V.C.H. Wilts.* iv. 359.
[20] *W.A.M.* xlviii. 468; *Wilts. Times*, 20 Feb. 1937.
[21] *V.C.H. Wilts.* iv. 206–7.
[22] Longleat Estate Office, Survey 1743, p. 118.
[23] See p. 129.
[24] Longleat MSS. Parcel XXI.
[25] W. Daniell, *Warminster Common*, 3–4.
[26] Ibid. 7.   [27] Ibid. 9–15 and *passim*.
[28] See p. 128.
[29] W. Daniell, *Warminster Common*, 202.
[30] Ibid. 217.
[31] *Warminster Miscellany*, July 1862.
[32] *V.C.H. Wilts.* ii, p. 116.
[33] *Pipe R.* 1156–8 (Rec. Com.), 57.

several counties and constable of Salisbury Castle in the earlier part of the reign of Henry II.[34] William held it until 1175,[35] when it reverted to the Crown, probably by his death. It was immediately regranted in fee to Robert Mauduit,[36] a royal chamberlain and younger son of a family whose chief estates were in Buckinghamshire.[37] He had succeeded FitzHamon in his constableship of Salisbury, and it is possible that the estate was regarded as appurtenant to that office.[38] Robert obtained a renewal of the grant when Richard I succeeded to the throne,[39] but was dead by 1191.[40] His son and heir Thomas was a minor, and was in the successive wardships of Robert de Tregoze[41] and Hugh de Bosco[42] until he came of age by Michaelmas 1204.[43] Thomas held Warminster, except for a forfeiture when he joined John's enemies,[44] until his death c. 1244, when he was succeeded by his son William.[45] William was dead by 1264, leaving a son Thomas, a minor, whose wardship was granted to Warin de Bassingburn, his uncle.[46] In 1270 Thomas was given licence to let the manor of Warminster while he went to the Holy Land with Prince Edward.[47] He probably died abroad, for in 1271 the wardship of his heir Warin was granted to Richard, King of the Romans.[48] In 1275 Thomas's widow Joan held Warminster in dower.[49] Warin came of age c. 1290 and in 1294 was licensed to let Warminster to Bogo de Knoville, the last holder of his wardship, for six years.[50] At Warin's death in 1300 he was succeeded by his son Thomas,[51] who came of age in 1308[52] and was executed after the battle of Boroughbridge in 1322.[53] Warminster was immediately granted to Hugh le Despenser the elder,[54] but on the accession of Edward III Thomas's widow Eleanor was assigned her dower in it,[55] and the custody of the remainder granted to John de Kingston during the minority of John, the heir.[56] John came of age in 1332, and settled Warminster on himself and Juliane his wife in the same year.[57] He died in 1364 leaving as heir, after the termination of his widow's estate, his granddaughter Maud, daughter of his son Thomas who was already dead.[58]

Maud took the Mauduit inheritance to a Northamptonshire family, for she married Sir Henry Greene of Drayton near Kettering.[59] He was executed in 1399 and succeeded in turn by his sons Ralph, who died without issue in 1417,[60] and John, who died in 1433.[61] John's son Henry died in 1467 leaving an only daughter and heir Constance, who married John Stafford, third son of Humphrey, Duke of Buckingham.[62] Stafford was created Earl of Wiltshire in 1470 and died three years later. His only son Edward died without issue in 1499, and after a long dispute his property passed to the heirs of his maternal grandfather Henry Greene, who were the descendants of Greene's sisters Isabel and Margaret.[63] Of these, Margaret left by her husband Sir William Huddleston a daughter Elizabeth, who married Sir Thomas Cheney and died without issue in 1502.[64] The whole inheritance thus passed to the issue of Isabel Greene, who had married Sir Richard Vere. Their son Sir Henry Vere left four daughters; of these one died without issue, so that Warminster was divided into thirds amongst the others.[65]

Of these three coheirs, Anne married Sir Humphrey Brown of Abbess Roding (Essex), a Justice of the Common Pleas who died in 1562. Their only son George died without surviving issue soon after his father, and this share of Warminster descended to his three half-sisters by his father's second marriage.[66] The second coheir Audrey married into the same family of Browns, and by her husband John left a son George and a grandson Wistan.[67] The third coheir Elizabeth married John Mordaunt created Baron Mordaunt in 1532, and her share of Warminster descended to her grandson Lewis, the 3rd baron.[68] In the reign of Mary Sir John Thynne of Longleat attempted to buy the share of Warminster which belonged to Audrey's issue. Conveyances were made[69] but for some reason never implemented, which gave rise to extended litigation.[70] In 1577, however, the manor passed by sale for the first time since the original grant to the Mauduit family when all the interested parties

34 *Red Bk. Exch.* (Rolls Ser.), 664 and *passim*; *V.C.H. Wilts.* vi. 54–5.
35 *Pipe R.* 1175 (P.R.S. xxii), 99, and preceeding volumes in the same series.
36 Ibid. 1176 (P.R.S. xxv), 171; *Cartae Antiquae Rolls* (P.R.S. N.S. xxxiii), 184.
37 The elaborate account of this family in Robert Halstead (pseud.), *Succint Genealogies of the . . . Houses of . . . Mauduit of Warminster . . .* (1685), was followed by Hoare, *Mod. Wilts.*, Warminster, 2–8, but its earlier part is corrected in R. W. Eyton, 'Pedigree of the Baronial Houses of Mauduit', *Herald and Genealogist*, vii. 385–94. For a criticism of Halstead's work see *Beds. Hist. Rec. Soc.* xi. 84–87.
38 *V.C.H. Wilts.* v. 8.
39 Halstead, *Succint Genealogies*, 128; *Pipe R.* 1190 (P.R.S. N.S. i), 121.
40 *Pipe R.* 1191 & 1192 (P.R.S. N.S. ii), 121.
41 Ibid. 281.
42 Ibid. 1195 (P.R.S. N.S. vi), 136.
43 Ibid. 1204 (P.R.S. N.S. xviii), 247. Halstead printed a deed settling Warminster on Robert's younger son Robert; if genuine it cannot have taken effect, but deeds settling a smaller estate on him are in W.R.O. 490 Hungerford Cart. ff. 112v.–113.
44 *Rot. Litt. Claus.* (Rec. Com.), i. 285, 315.
45 *Ex. e Rot. Fin.* (Rec. Com.), i. 418; Eyton, *Antiquities of Shropshire*, iv. 65.
46 *Close R.* 1261–4, 339–40; *Cal. Pat.* 1258–66, 532; Longleat MS. 8971.
47 *Cal. Pat.* 1266–72, 440.
48 Ibid. 533.
49 *Rot. Hund.* (Rec. Com.), ii. 276.
50 *Cal. Pat.* 1292–1301, 177; Longleat MS. 8978. For previous holders of the wardship see *Cal. Pat.* 1272–81, 253 and J.I. 1/1006 m. 55d.
51 *Wilts. Inq. p.m.* 1242–1326 (Index Libr.), 249–53.
52 Ibid. 372.
53 T. Walsingham, *Hist. Anglicana* (Rolls Ser.), i. 165.
54 *Cal. Chart. R.* 1300–26, 444.
55 *Cal. Close,* 1327–30, 16.
56 *Cal. Fine R.* 1327–37, 28.
57 *Wilts. Inq. p.m.* 1327–77 (Index Libr.), 85–87; *Abbrev. Rot. Orig.* (Rec. Com.), ii. 74.
58 *Wilts. Inq. p.m.* 1327–77 (Index Libr.), 371.
59 *Cal. Fine R.* 1377–83, 136. The pedigree of the Greene family is in Halstead, *Succint Genealogies*, 153 f., and Bridges, *Hist. Northants.* ii. 251–2.
60 C 137/20/1; C 138/27/41.
61 C 139/58/32.
62 C 140/23/1; Longleat MS. 9039.
63 *Complete Peerage,* s.v. Wiltshire.
64 *Cal. Inq. p.m. Hen. VII,* iii. pp. 408–9.
65 Ibid.; Halstead, *Succint Genealogies,* 223–4.
66 C 142/135/4; *Visitations of Essex,* pt. i (Harl. Soc. xiii), 166; George had a son Thomas living in 1557: C 54/528 m. 23d.
67 *Visitations of Essex,* i. 166–7; Audrey's husband was the nephew of her sister Anne's husband.
68 *Complete Peerage.*
69 Longleat MSS. 9248, 9257.
70 Ibid. Parcel XXI; C2/Eliz. I/W 1/2 and W 17/13.

conveyed their shares to George Tuchet, Lord Audley (d. 1617).[71] In 1611 he sold Warminster to Sir Thomas Thynne,[72] and the manor has since descended in that family, created Viscounts Weymouth in 1682, and Marquesses of Bath in 1789.[73] Most of the property in the town was sold in lots in 1919, but several farms west of the town still belong to the Longleat estate in 1962.[74]

A capital messuage is mentioned in the earliest known extent of the manor,[75] and was clearly the regular dwelling-place of the Mauduit family. Henry Greene made agreements for its repair in 1386 and 1389, and a new kitchen and chamber were built in 1390.[76] It is not known to have been used by any later lords of the manor, and was regularly let with the demesne farm.[77] When the farm was divided in the 17th century parts described as the old and the new buildings were let with the two portions.[78] About 1790 the lessee under Lord Bath sold the lease of the house to Thomas Marsh, a timber merchant, who rebuilt it in 1791.[79] The plain house, of 3 storeys and attics, has since been altered by the addition of bay windows to one side of the front. In 1851 it was held with 30 a. of land under Lord Bath, and was described as a gentleman's residence.[80] In the 20th century it has been used both as a guest house and as flats, and in 1961 the park round it had been covered with an estate of small private houses.

Among the properties held freely of the lords of Warminster were several which were styled manors, and for which courts are known to have been held. The manor of *BOREHAM* or *BURTON DELA-MERE* or *BISHOPSTROW*[81] took its suffix from a family which was seated at Nunney Castle (Som.). The de la Meres may have acquired the land *c.* 1200 by the marriage of Nicholas de la Mere with Grace de Meysey, who was heir to considerable estates in Wiltshire and Somerset[82] which apparently included Nunney.[83] In 1217 Nicholas was given seisin of his land of Bishopstrow on returning to the king's service.[84] He was succeeded by his son by Grace, Ellis de la Mere; he held the manor by 1227,[85] and was still living, as was his mother, in 1263.[86] He was dead by 1271[87] and succeeded by his son Nicholas;[88] he or another Nicholas still held it in 1300, when the property was described as

2 carucates of land held at a rent of 3s.[89] In 1303 it was said to be ⅕ knight's fee.[90] By 1330 the manor had passed to Thomas de la Mere, who then settled it on himself and his wife Margery.[91] They were the parents of Sir John de la Mere[92] from whom the manor descended in the same way as the manor of Fisherton de la Mere to the Paulet family.[93] In 1574 John Paulet, Marquess of Winchester, sold Boreham to Thomas Webb of Beckington (Som.), clothier. In 1590 Thomas's son Robert sold the manor to Alexander Staples of Yate (Glos.).[94] His son Richard, who succeeded him in the same year,[95] sold parts of the property,[96] and by 1656 apparently only retained the demesne farm.[97] He left no issue, and Boreham Farm passed to his nephew Oliver, who in 1663 sold it to Benjamin Gifford of Boreham.[98] Its subsequent history is dealt with below.[99]

The manor house of Boreham stood on the south side of the road from Warminster to Salisbury just east of the turning to Bishopstrow.[1] Between the house and the Wylye lay fishponds[2] which survived in Daniell's time.[3] In 1821, however, the site was occupied by three cottages.[4] Later in the century the large Victorian house called Boreham Manor was built on it.

The estate later known as the manor of *NEW-PORT* or *PORTWAY* seems to have originated in property held in Warminster by junior members of the Mauduit family. In the earlier 13th century William Mauduit granted an estate to his younger son Warin with remainder to another son William.[5] Warin apparently left no issue, for *c.* 1293 William Mauduit held estates in Warminster which his brothers Warin and John had formerly held.[6] Thomas, son of William Mauduit, held land there in 1322;[7] it was perhaps his son, another William, described as of Newport, who granted all the corn growing on his lands in Warminster to the lord of Warminster in 1339.[8] This William was succeeded by his son John, who in 1356 granted his lands to Thomas Mauduit, lord of Warminster, for Thomas's life;[9] they included at least one house in Newport.[10] It is fairly certain that this was the same property which in the early 15th century had descended to Alice, daughter and heir of another William Mauduit.[11] She married John Laffull and

[71] Longleat MSS. Parcel XXVIII.
[72] Ibid. 9355.
[73] Hoare, *Mod. Wilts.* Heytesbury, 60–61; *Complete Peerage.*
[74] Longleat Estate Office, Rental, 1919.
[75] *Wilts. Inq. p.m.* 1242–1326 (Index Libr.), 249–53.
[76] Longleat MSS. 9178, 9184 and Parcel XXVII, Acct. Roll, 1389–90.
[77] See p. 108.
[78] Longleat MS. 10652.
[79] Halliday, Information, f. 3; *Univ. Brit. Dir.* (1798), iv. 682.
[80] W.A.S. Libr. Devizes, Sale Cat.
[81] It must have extended into Bishopstrow, but the manor house was in Warminster and the property was held of the lords of Warminster.
[82] *Feodary of Glastonbury Abbey* (Som. Rec. Soc. xxvi), 11, 13, 66, 96, 108; *Glastonbury Cart..* ii (Som Rec. Soc. lxiii), 413–5 530–1. Nicholas was of Wilts. in 1199: *Rot. Cur. Reg.* (Rec. Com.), ii. 9.
[83] *Somerset Fines, Rich. I to Edw. I* (Som. Rec. Soc. vi), 38.
[84] *Rot. Litt. Claus.* (Rec. Com.), i. 301.
[85] *Cal. Pat.* 1225–32, 299; *Bracton's Note Bk.* ed. Maitland, iii. 193.
[86] *Glastonbury Cart.* ii (Som. Rec. Soc. lxiii), 413–5.

[87] *Ex. e Rot. Fin.* (Rec. Com.), ii. 536.
[88] *Feodary of Glastonbury Abbey* (Som. Rec. Soc. xxvi), 66; *Rot. Hund.* (Rec. Com.), ii. 276.
[89] *Wilts. Inq. p.m.* 1272–1326 (Index Libr.), 249–53.
[90] Ibid. 305.
[91] C.P. 25(1)/254/41/18.
[92] E. Green, 'On the Parish and Castle of Nunney', *Som. Jnl.* xxii. 71–105.
[93] See p. 38.
[94] W.R.O. 132, Title Deeds of the Manor.
[95] C 142/227/217.
[96] W.R.O. 132, Staples to Wm. Gifford 1626 and to Bailey 1641.
[97] Ibid. Settlement 1656.
[98] Ibid. Title Deeds of Manor.
[99] See p. 103.
[1] *Andrews and Dury, Map* (W.A.S. Rec. Brch.), pl. 7.
[2] W.R.O. Inclosure Award.
[3] Daniell, *Warminster,* 45.
[4] W.R.O. 132, Astley to Temple, 1821.
[5] B.M. Add. Ch. 26695.
[6] Longleat MS. 8984.
[7] S.C. 6/1145/12 m. 13.
[8] Longleat MS. 9147.
[9] Ibid. 9164.
[10] Ibid. 9169.
[11] Ibid. 9292.

left an only daughter and heir Maud, who married William Mohun. They left three daughters and coheirs,[12] and the manor was divided in thirds for over a century.

One daughter Alice married William Barrell; their son William[13] had a son Robert, who was dealing with the Warminster property in 1474,[14] but is said to have sold his share of it *c.* 1480 to the Poole family[15] of Sapperton (Glos.).[16] It descended in this family to Sir Giles Poole who in 1565 sold it to John Poole of Stanton St. Bernard. Three years later John Poole sold his third share of the manor to Richard Middlecott of Bishopstrow, clothier.[17]

Another coheir of Alice Mauduit, Eleanor, married John Wolley. She apparently left two coheirs, Maud Jakes and Agnes Nowers, who in 1499 sold their share of the manor to John Gilbert of Steeple Ashton.[18] In 1515 Gilbert sold it to William Bird, Vicar of Bradford, and Thomas Horton.[19] This was no doubt to endow Bird's chantry in Bradford church, but in 1540 he was attainted of high treason and his property forfeited to the Crown.[20] In 1546 it was granted to Sir Thomas Moyle,[21] who two years later sold the lands in Warminster to John Wysse, the purchaser in 1550 of the manor of Smallbrook.[22] Wysse died in 1554,[23] and in 1559 his son Thomas sold his share of the manor to Richard Middlecott.[24]

The third of Alice Mauduit's coheirs, Agnes, married Thomas Blanchard of Cutteridge in North Bradley, and her share descended in the same way as Cutteridge manor to Richard Kirton, who held it by 1481 and still in 1497.[25] Another Richard Kirton died seised of it in 1558,[26] and in 1565 Christopher Kirton of Cheddar (Som.) sold it to Richard Middlecott.[27] The whole manor of Newport was thus reunited in his hands, and remained in his family for 250 years. In 1820 Edward Middlecott sold all his lands in Warminster, amounting to about 500 a., to Lord Bath.[28]

Portway House was built by Edward Middlecott in the early 18th century; a panel bearing his initials is dated 1722. It is of three stories and basement and built of ashlar Bath stone. The front is of seven bays, the centre one slightly projecting and with its windows enriched with fluted pilasters at the two upper stories. In the 19th century the main entrance was moved to a newly-erected two-

story wing on the south side, and a large bay window replaced it in the centre of the east front A similar two-story wing on the north side was added in the present century. The house has a fine staircase, and several panelled rooms. In front of it the low garden wall carries elaborate wrought iron railings with central gateway, contemporary with the house. In 1963 they were under repair following much discussion about whether it was possible to preserve them because of their bad state.

The manor of *WARMINSTER SCUDAMORE* probably originated in a conveyance of over 100 a. of land from Nicholas Malemayns to Walter Scudamore, lord of Upton Scudamore in 1312.[29] In succeeding years several conveyances of small estates in Warminster were made to Walter's two successors,[30] and the estate was referred to as a manor in 1372.[31] It descended in the same way as Upton Scudamore[32] to Walter, Lord Hungerford, who added to it a considerable estate bought of Peter Morgan in 1537 and 1538.[33] Still in the same way as Upton this manor passed from the Hungerfords to Sir Stephen Fox, who in 1687 sold it to Thomas, Viscount Weymouth.[34] Lord Weymouth sold the demesne farm of the manor in the same year to Edward Halliday, a dyer, who had held it on lease from the Hungerfords since 1664.[35] From Halliday a considerable property descended for several generations to John Edmund Halliday who died in 1913.

If the Hallidays lived on the site of the manor in the 19th century, the manor house lay on the north side of East Street. The house called Yard House is a plain building of stone, partly of the late 18th century with a large addition of the mid-19th. There was however a strong tradition that the manor house of the Hungerfords lay near the junction of Common Close and High Street. Daniell had heard that it was on the site of Bartlett's brewery in the High Street.[36]

In 1298 John le Squire conveyed to Gilbert Francis a half-virgate of land[37] held under the lords of Warminster by a rent of 8*d*.[38] Francis conveyed this property to John de Kingston in 1317,[39] and it probably formed part of the estate later known as the manor of *KINGSTON'S*. By 1329 Kingston held a considerably larger property, described as two carucates of land in Warminster,

[12] Hoare, *Mod. Wilts.*, Warminster, 9–10; the husbands of the coheirs are named in B.M. Add. Ch. 26718 (1417).
[13] S.C. 2/209/62.
[14] *Cal. Close*, 1468–76, 323; see also B.M. Harl. Ch. 76. A. 41 (1471).
[15] Daniell, *Warminster*, 39.
[16] *Visitation Glos.* 1623 (Harl. Soc. xxi), 125–6; the buyer was probably John Poole, said to have been in the service of the Abbess of Wilton. It was certainly held by his son by 1497: *Cal. Inq. p.m. Hen. VII*, ii, pp. 212–13.
[17] Hoare, *Mod. Wilts.* Warminster, 42.
[18] *Cal. Close*, 1485–1500, 356; C.P. 25(1)/257/66/25, 27.
[19] *W.N. & Q.* ii. 420; C1/411/26.
[20] *V.C.H. Wilts.* vii. 25–26.
[21] *L. & P. Hen. VIII*, xxi(1), p. 74.
[22] C.P. 40/1141 m. 1; see below, p. 103.
[23] C 142/101/118; Daniell, *Warminster*, 42–43.
[24] Hoare, *Mod. Wilts.* Warminster, 41; C.P. 25(2)/239/1 Eliz. I East.
[25] S.C. 2/209/63; *Cal. Inq. p.m. Hen. VII*, ii, pp. 212–13; see below, p. 223.
[26] Longleat MSS. Parcel XXI, Papers in Thynne v. Middlecott.

[27] Hoare, *Mod. Wilts.* Warminster, 42; C.P. 25(2)/239/7 Eliz. I Trin.
[28] Daniell, *Warminster*, 40. No authentic pedigree of the family has been found, although a conjectural one is in Halliday, Information, f. 81 **; for early members see C142/152/70, C 142/258/141.
[29] W.R.O. 490, Hungerford Cart. ff. 111v., 113.
[30] e.g. ibid. ff. 112v., 114, 114v., 116.
[31] Ibid. f. 117.
[32] See p. 81.
[33] C 1/827/54–55; C.P. 25(2)/46/321 and C.P. 25(2)/46/322; S.C. 6/*Hen. VIII*/3918; some of this property was derived by the Morgans from the Page family: see below, p. 104.
[34] C.P. 25(2)/803/3 Jas. II Trin.; Halliday, Information, f. 79.
[35] Lease Hungerford to Halliday, 1664, *penes* Mr. H. N. Dewey; Longleat Estate Office, Survey 1743, p. 125; Longleat MS. 10652.
[36] Daniell, *Warminster*, 111.
[37] *Feet of F. Wilts.* 1272–1327 (W.A.S. Rec. Brch.), 44.
[38] *Wilts. Inq. p.m. 1242–1326* (Index Libr.), 249–53.
[39] *Feet of F. Wilts.* 1272–1327 (W.A.S. Rec. Brch.), 96.

which was then settled on him and his son Thomas.[40] This descended in the same way as the manor of Little Sutton to Chidiock Paulet,[41] who apparently sold it to William Clevelode of Warminster, clothier. At his death in 1558 Clevelode left his freehold property to William, son of William Bird, citizen and mercer of London,[42] who in 1577 mortgaged it under the name Kingston's.[43] Soon afterwards he sold the estate to Edward Horton of Westwood.[44] Horton died in 1603, and Kingston's was sold by his trustees to Edward Scutt of Warminster in 1609.[45] Its descent from this time is probably the same as the manor of Cheyneys.[46]

In 1268 the Prior of the Hospital of St. John at Wilton recovered arrears of a rent of a qr. of wheat and a qr. of rye which was payable to him out of lands at Warminster held by Humphrey of Bradley.[47] These lands were probably the same as the five virgates held by William of Bradley early in the 13th century.[48] They can more certainly be identified with the property known in the 15th century as the manor of CHEYNEYS, for in 1465 the same rent was payable out of it to St. John's Hospital.[49] They had probably passed from the Bradleys to the Cheyneys by 1300, for then Walter de Cheyney held a carucate of land of the lords of Warminster by the rent of 10s.[50] John Cheyney, mentioned in 1356,[51] but dead by c. 1363,[52] must also have held this property. By 1364 some property which had belonged to him was held by Thomas Hungerford.[53] Thomas was a free tenant under the lord of Warminster c. 1360–70[54] and at his death in 1397 he held property at Henford's Marsh.[55] The manor of Cheyneys Court was certainly held by Thomas's son Walter, who settled it on his son Robert in 1421.[56] It cannot, therefore, have formed part of the property which Robert's son Robert derived from his marriage to the heir of William, Lord Moleyns; yet on the partition of the Hungerford estates after the death of Margaret, Lady Hungerford and Botreaux, in 1479, Cheyneys was separated from the other Hungerford property in the district, and instead went to Mary, daughter and heir of Sir Thomas Hungerford (d. 1469) with a group of

properties which had formed part of the Moleyns inheritance.[57] Mary Hungerford married Edward, Lord Hastings (d. 1506). In 1538 their son George, Earl of Huntingdon,[58] conveyed Cheyneys to William Dauntsey, alderman of London, who was apparently acting on behalf of Stephen Agard,[59] of a family seated at Broughton (Northants.).[60] Stephen's son Ambrose Agard sold Cheyneys to Robert Manley in 1609,[61] who in the following year sold it to Edward Scutt of Warminster.[62] Scutt's daughter Joan married Ralph Hastings;[63] in 1647 they sold the manor to William Gifford[64] of Boreham and thereafter it descended in the same way as the remainder of the Gifford property.[65]

The manor of FURNAX or AVENEL'S FEE was not held of the lords of Warminster and so must have been granted away from the Crown before the capital manor was. In 1130 the sheriff accounted for the issues of land in Warminster which had belonged to Robert Malet.[66] It evidently descended in the same way as his barony of Curry Mallet (Som.) to William Malet (d. c. 1216) and then with a moiety of the barony to William's daughter Mabel, who married as her first husband Nicholas Avenel.[67] In 1242–3 her second husband, Hugh de Vivon, was overlord of this manor, which was held of him by the service of enclosing one perch of his park at Curry Mallet.[68] The overlordship evidently descended with the ⅛ of the barony which passed to the Beauchamps of Hatch Beauchamp (Som.), for in 1343 Avenel's Fee was held of John, Lord Beauchamp.[69] No further mention of their overlordship has been noted, and in 1401–2 Furnax was held of the Duchy of Lancaster.[70] This tenure still continued in the 17th century.[71]

The earliest known tenant under the Malets was perhaps Robert de Pirou, who, it was said late in the 12th century, had received land in Warminster and the church there by gift of Henry I.[72] Robert was steward to the Earl Ferrers early in the reign of Henry II,[73] and a tenant under him in Derbyshire.[74] He was still living in 1172,[75] but probably died soon after, leaving a son William.[76] William was probably father of Ralph FitzWilliam,

[40] C.P. 25(1)/254/40/42.
[41] See p. 66.
[42] Longleat MSS. Parcel XXI, Papers in Thynne v. Middlecott; P.C.C. F. 39 Noodes.
[43] C 54/1007.
[44] In 1586 Horton paid the chief rent of 8s. to the manor of Furnax which Bird had paid: C.C.C. MSS. K 2(1) 14, 21.
[45] Longleat MS. 9327.
[46] See below.
[47] C.P. 25(1)/251/21/22; V.C.H. Wilts. iii. 365.
[48] C.P. 25(1)/250/4/1; see also C.P. 25(1)/250/3/21 and Cur. Reg. R. iv. 166, 192 and vii. 290,321.
[49] S.C. 6/1061/24.
[50] Wilts. Inq. p.m. 1242–1326 (Index Libr.), 249–53.
[51] B.M. Add. Ch. 26712.
[52] Hoare, Mod. Wilts. Warminster, 45.
[53] W.A.S. Libr. Devizes, Jackson Hungerford MSS., Places, iv. 233.
[54] Longleat MSS., Parcel XXVII, Custumal of Free Tenants; the property he held is not specified, but this is before the Hungerfords had the manor of Warminster Scudamore, or Butler's Coombe.
[55] C 136/100/31.
[56] W.R.O. 490, Fragment of Hungerford Cart.; S.C. 6/1061/23.
[57] Hoare, Mod. Wilts. Heytesbury, 90–103; Aubrey Topog. Coll. ed. Jackson, 285.
[58] Complete Peerage.
[59] C.P. 40/1099 rot. 803.

[60] Bridges, Hist. Northants. ii. 85.
[61] C.P. 25(2)/369/7 Jas I Mich.
[62] C.P. 25(2)/369/8 Jas. I Mich.
[63] Wilts. Visitation Pedigrees (Harl. Soc. cv–vi), 175.
[64] C.P. 25(2)/512/23 Chas. I East.
[65] See p. 103.
[66] Pipe R. 1130 (H.M.S.O. facsimile), 5.
[67] I. J. Sanders, English Baronies, 38–39, on which the remainder of this paragraph is based.
[68] Bk. of Fees, 717, 737.
[69] Cal. Inq. p.m. viii, p. 325; Complete Peerage, s.v. Beauchamp of Somerset; see also Two Beauchamp Registers (Som. Rec. Soc. xxxv), 66. In 1253 it was said that the estate was held of Nicholas, son of Martin, by rent of a sore goshawk or 10s., but this cannot be explained: Cal. Inq. p.m. i, p. 278.
[70] Feud. Aids. vi. 628; cf. E 329/75, an acknowledgment by Alice Stury that she held the manor of the Abbot of Our Lady of Grace by the Tower of London, 1402.
[71] Early Stuart Tradesmen (W.A.S. Rec. Brch.), 8–9.
[72] Hist. MSS. Com. Wells, i. 58; since the grant was made by Hen. I, what was later the Malet barony was probably in royal hands at the time; the Malets are not known to be connected with any part of the barony before 1130: Sanders, op. cit. 38.
[73] Sir Chr. Hatton's Bk. of Seals, ed. Lloyd and Stenton, p. 104.
[74] Red Bk. Exch. (Rolls Ser.), 339.
[75] Cal. Doc. France, ed. Round, 440.
[76] Darley Cart. ed. Darlington, pp. iii, 412.

who gave the church of Warminster to Wells Cathedral,[77] and also of Robert FitzWilliam, mentioned as a former tenant in a lawsuit of 1243.[78] Robert left three daughters and coheirs. His Warminster property passed to the husband of one of these, Nicholas Avenel,[79] who held it in 1242–3.[80] His relationship to the Nicholas Avenel, who married Mabel Malet and was dead by November 1223, is not clear.[81] The second Nicholas Avenel died *c.* 1246,[82] and was succeeded by his son William who died without issue in 1253. His heir was Matthew de Furneaux,[83] who was descended from another coheir of Robert FitzWilliam, who had married Henry de Furneaux.[84] This Matthew was dead by 1284–5,[85] and was succeeded by another Matthew. By 1297 the second Matthew had conveyed his Warminster property to his son Simon,[86] and in 1308 this conveyance was confirmed with remainders to three of Simon's brothers.[87] Simon died in 1358 leaving as heir his daughter Elizabeth, the wife of John Blount.[88] She in turn left an only daughter and heir Alice, wife of Sir Richard Stury, who held this manor in 1412,[89] but died childless in 1414. Alice's property was divided up between the descendants of her four great-aunts, the daughters of the last Sir Matthew de Furneaux, Simon's younger brothers having left no issue.

The Warminster property was allotted to the descendants of the youngest of these daughters, Margaret, who had married Sir John Beaupré. Their daughter Isabel married John Longland[90] and left three daughters and coheirs. Of these the eldest, Margaret, married Sir Leonard Hackluyt, and left a daughter who married into the Stapleton family of Shropshire and had a son Leonard. The third, Anne, married John Farwaye and left two daughters, one of whom married Thomas Berkeley. At the division of the Furneaux property in 1421, Warminster was divided between Leonard Stapleton, who received $\frac{2}{3}$, and Thomas Berkeley, who received $\frac{1}{3}$.[91]

Leonard Stapleton died without issue, and his widow Joyce sued his feoffees for a life estate in the lands in Warminster which had been promised her.[92] Stapleton's estates, however, went to the heirs of a certain John Stapleton, perhaps his brother,

whose lands in Shropshire were the subject of a lawsuit in 1470.[93] The Warminster property was evidently divided between two of the coheirs of John Stapleton, for in 1483 William Ruynon quitclaimed all the lands in Warminster which he had by feoffment of Leonard Stapleton to George Booth and Katharine his wife, John Leighton, and Robert Cressett and Christine his wife.[94] Of these, Leighton was the son of Elizabeth, one of John Stapleton's coheirs. Elizabeth's sister Margaret had married a Cressett of Upton Cressett (Salop.), and left two daughters, one of whom married Robert Cressett and the other Robert Mountfort.[95] Mountfort's daughter and heir married George Booth of Dunham Massey, (Cheshire).[96] Thus of Stapleton's $\frac{2}{3}$ of Furnax, $\frac{1}{3}$ had passed to John Leighton and $\frac{1}{6}$ each to Robert Cressett and George Booth.

The remaining descent of all these shares derived from Stapleton can be quickly dealt with. In 1511 George Booth's son, Sir William Booth, sold his $\frac{1}{6}$ to John FitzJames, later Lord Chief Justice, who used it to endow the grammar school which he helped to found in the Abbey of Bruton (Som.) in 1519.[97] Although it passed to the Crown at the Dissolution, this part of Furnax was regranted to the school at Bruton refounded by Edward VI in 1550. In 1516 Thomas Cressett, son of Robert, and Sir Thomas Leighton both sold their shares to Richard Fox, Bishop of Winchester, who used them for the endowment of Corpus Christi College, Oxford, which he founded.[98].

The $\frac{1}{3}$ of Furnax which passed to Thomas Berkeley descended to John Berkeley, who left it at his death in 1479 to endow a chantry in the church of Tickenham (Som.), and specifically ordered the exclusion of his sister and heir, Cecily Ashe.[99] In spite of this Cecily brought a successful action against his feoffees and obtained the whole of the estate.[1] Furnax descended in the Ashe family to her great-great-grandson, John Ashe of Tickenham,[2] who apparently left three daughters and coheirs. One of these, Jane, married William Bassett of Uley (Glos.), and her $\frac{1}{9}$ of the manor passed to her son Edward.[3] Edward's widow Isabel joined with her second husband in conveying it to

[77] See p. 117.
[78] K.B. 26/128 rot. 11.
[79] *Misc. Gen. et Her.* 3rd ser. iii. 272–3; all 3 coheirs and their husbands held Robert's Devonshire property in 1212 (*Bk. of Fees*, 96). See below, pp. 117–18.
[80] *Bk. of Fees*, 717, 737.
[81] Sanders, *English Baronies*, 39.
[82] *Ex. e Rot. Fin.* (Rec. Com.), ii. 2.
[83] *Cal. Inq. p.m.* i, p. 71; *Close R.* 1253–4, 8.
[84] The pedigree of this family in Cussans, *Hist. Herts.* Edwinstree Hundred, 138, is apparently incorrect. If Hen. de Furneaux died in 1214 his son Matthew must have been of age by 1235, when he was engaged in a lawsuit: Sir H. C. Maxwell Lyte, *Some Somerset Manors* (Som. Rec. Soc. extra series), 316. Yet a second Matthew, who was under age in 1243, was said to be the son of Hen. de Furneaux: ibid. It seems more likely that Nicholas had the wardship of two successive Matthews, and the document quoted by Maxwell Lyte refers to the first. The succession would then be 1. Henry d. 1214, 2. Matthew d. 1235–43, 3. Matthew, aged 28–29 in 1253, and so under age in 1243.
[85] *Feud. Aids*, iv. 275; this supports the correction made to the pedigree given by Cussans, for if the Matthew who succeeded Wm. Avenel in 1257 had lived to 1317 he would have been almost 90.
[86] C.C.C. Deeds K.1.3.

[87] *Feet of F. Wilts.* 1272–1327 (W.A.S. Rec. Brch.), 72.
[88] *Coll. Top. et Gen.* i. 243–7, from which the genealogical information used here is taken; see also *Some Somerset Manors*, 316–321.
[89] *Feud. Aids*, vi. 536.
[90] Margaret's stepson by her second marriage to Sir Hugh Longland.
[91] These were not the only descendants of Margaret de Furneaux who received a share of the whole Furneaux estate: the deed of partition is printed in *Coll. Top. et Gen.* i. 245–6.
[92] C 1/17/64.
[93] *Shropshire Arch. Soc.* 4th ser. v. 221–2.
[94] C.C.C. Deeds K.1.62; there were other coheirs, so the Warminster settlement was probably the result of a partition. Ruynon was a kinsman of the Stapletons, being also a descendant of Margaret Furneaux.
[95] *Shropshire Arch. Soc.* 4th ser. v. 222.
[96] Ormerod, *Hist. Ches.* i. 524.
[97] King's School Bruton MSS. B IV. 1; for the foundation, see *V.C.H. Som.* ii. 448.
[98] C.C.C. Deeds I. 2(1).25, 31, 35–6; I.2 (2).1.
[99] Ibid. I.2(3).1.
[1] Ibid. I.2(3).2.
[2] J. Byrchmore, *Parochial History of Tickenham* (1895), 9–11.
[3] *Visit. of Glos.* (Harl. Soc. xxi), 206.

Simon Sloper of Warminster.[4] The names or marriages of the other coheirs of John Ashe are not certainly known.[5] One may have married or been mother of William Rosseter, grocer of London, who in 1572 sold a share of Furnax to William Fry *alias* Gysse of Combe St. Nicholas (Som.). In the following year Fry sold it to Thomas Fry of North Petherton (Som.) who in 1589 sold it to Corpus Christi College.[6] The third of the Ashe coheirs may have married or been mother of Michael Godwin of Longbridge Deverill who in 1595 sold a share of Furnax to Edmund Ludlow of Hill Deverill.[7]

By 1638 then, Furnax was divided among four lords in various proportions; in that year the school and the college brought proceedings against Simon Sloper and Henry Ludlow, because, as was alleged, they were using their nearness to the property to deprive the larger but more distant owners of their profits. A decree in chancery ordered the division of the manor, and Sloper and Ludlow were allotted land in proportion to their shares but no part of the manorial rights.[8] The rest of the manor remained in the undivided lordship of the college and the school in the proportion $5\frac{1}{2}$ to $1\frac{1}{2}$ until 1883, when a partition was authorized by the Charity Commissioners;[9] the college retained some property in Warminster until the 1920's, when the last lots were sold.[10]

There was a capital messuage belonging to the manor in the 14th century,[11] but in the 16th century the demesnes were let without a house.[12] In 1638 the tenant of the demesne farm held under the lords two houses at the east end of the Market place on the south side,[13] and this site is still remembered traditionally as the site of the manor house.[14]

The manor of *SMALLBROOK* was held by Mainard before the Conquest, and in 1086 by Aubrey the chamberlain.[15] In the 12th century this manor was held of the honor of Gloucester,[16] and the overlordship descended with the honor to Richard de Clare. At his death in 1314 the honor was divided between two sisters and coheirs,[17] and Smallbrook passed to Eleanor, whose husband, Hugh de Audley, died in 1347.[18] His daughter Margaret married Ralph, Earl of Stafford,[19] and the overlordship descended with that title to

Humphrey, Earl of Stafford, who was created Duke of Buckingham and died in 1460, and thence to Edward, Duke of Buckingham, who was executed in 1521.[20] It remained in the Crown until 1585, when it was granted to Anthony Collins and others,[21] but no further mention of it has been found. From the 14th century it was regularly described as the profits of a court leet at Smallbrook.[22]

Smallbrook was probably among the five fees held of the honor of Gloucester by Roger Waspail in 1166,[23] and by another Roger Waspail in the early 13th century.[24] In 1233 this Roger was succeeded by another Roger[25] who held in 1242–3.[26] By this time it had, however, been long subinfeudated by these Waspails to another branch of the same family. The first known tenant of Smallbrook was Osbert Waspail[27] who was succeeded, probably by 1194,[28] by his son also called Osbert. This second Osbert left a daughter Cecily, who died under age, leaving Smallbrook disputed between Robert Waspail and Henry Waspail, which Henry apparently held Hill Deverill under Roger Waspail.[29] The outcome of the suit was in Henry's favour, but in 1232 he acknowledged that Robert held the manor of Smallbrook of him by the service of two knights and suit at his court of Deverill.[30] Smallbrook was thus held by Robert of Henry of Roger of the honor of Gloucester, but these intermediate overlordships are not mentioned after 1242–3,[31] and the Waspails who held it held directly of the honor.

Robert Waspail's heir was his brother Godfrey,[32] who had succeeded him by 1242–3.[33] He in turn was succeeded by William Waspail, who was dead by 1268, when his widow claimed dower in Smallbrook.[34] His son and heir was no doubt the William Waspail who held the manor at the end of the 13th century,[35] and whose son John had apparently succeeded him by c. 1318.[36] This John was apparently succeeded by another John,[37] who died in 1361 leaving a son and heir William.[38] By this time the family was principally seated at Hartley Wespall (Hants),[39] and Smallbrook descended in the same way as that manor to William's grandson John Waspail who died in 1448 having settled his property on Hugh Pakenham, son of his wife by her first husband John Pakenham.[40] In 1460 Pakenham sold Smallbrook to Thomas Rogers of Bradford, serjeant-at-law,[41] who died in possession in 1478.[42]

[4] C.P. 25 (2)/371/13 Jas. I East; Hoare, *Mod. Wilts.* Warminster, 106.
[5] But see Crisp, *Somerset Wills*, 1st ser. 19.
[6] C.C.C. Deeds K.2(1). 1–11, 17.
[7] Hoare, *Mod. Wilts.* Warminster, 107.
[8] King's School, Bruton MSS. B IV. 8–10.
[9] Longleat MSS. Deeds, schedule IV, bundle 24; King's School, Bruton MSS. Sale Cat.
[10] Ex inf. the Bursar.
[11] C.C.C. Deeds K.1.3, K.1.5, K.1.48.
[12] C.C.C. MSS. K.b.1, K.b.3.
[13] C.C.C. MSS. K.b.3.; W.R.O. Inclosure Award.
[14] Daniell, *Warminster*, 46; *Wilts. Times*, 21 Oct., 30 Dec. 1960
[15] *V.C.H. Wilts.* ii. p. 167.
[16] See below, n. 31.
[17] Sanders, *English Baronies*, 6.
[18] Ibid.; *Cal. Close*, 1337–9, 201.
[19] *Wilts. Inq. p.m.* 1327–77 (Index Libr.), 373.
[20] *Feud. Aids*, v. 264; *Complete Peerage*.
[21] C 66/1254 no. 4.
[22] e.g. *Cal. Close*, 1313–18, 131; S.C. 6/1148/1; B.M. Add. Ch. 28005–8 and 26769–80.
[23] *Red Bk. Exch.* (Rolls Ser.), 289.
[24] Ibid. 608.

[25] *Ex. e Rot. Fin.* (Rec. Com.), i. 236.
[26] *Bk. of Fees*, 718.
[27] *Bracton*'s *Note Bk.* ed. Maitland, ii. 414, on which the following descent to 1231 is based.
[28] *Cur. Reg. R.* 1193–5 (P.R.S. xiv), 103.
[29] Bracton has Robert as the name of the overlord, but the suit is only intelligible in the light of other known facts if Roger is substituted.
[30] C.P. 25(1)/250/8/23.
[31] *Bk. of Fees*, where it is mentioned on p. 718 and disregarded on p. 723.
[32] C.P. 25(1)/251/15/10.
[33] *Bk. of Fees*, 718, 723.
[34] J.I. 1/998 m. 7.
[35] *Feud. Aids*, v. 217; B.M. Add. Ch. 26696–7; C.C.C. Deeds K.1.32.
[36] Hoare, *Mod. Wilts.* Warminster, 45.
[37] Ibid.
[38] *Cal. Inq. p.m.* xi, p. 183.
[39] Jn. Waspail did not live at Smallbrook in 1343: *Cal. Close*, 1343–6, 31.
[40] *V.C.H. Hants*, iv. 42.
[41] Hoare, *Mod. Wilts.* Warminster, 46; B.M. Add. Ch. 26721.
[42] C 140/66/7.

It descended in the same way as Rogers's manor of Bradford to his great grandson Anthony Rogers,[43] who in 1550 sold it to John Wysse, citizen and founder of London,[44] and owner of a share of the manor of Portway.[45] After Wysse's death his son Thomas sold the manor in 1559 in two parts; the manor house and demesne lands to John Bennett and the remainder to Richard Middlecott of Bishopstrow, clothier.[46] The manor descended in the same way as Portway in the Middlecott family, and was probably sold with their estate to the Thynnes in 1820.[47]

John Bennett, the purchaser of the demesne farm, died in 1584, leaving a son and heir, John, aged 13.[48] This younger John was probably the father of Francis, who held the estate and died in 1667, leaving a son John.[49] It was probably a grandson of this John, also called John, who married Susan Halliday in 1696 and died in 1744.[50] Their son John married Ann Temple in 1723, and died in 1734 leaving a son John.[51] By 1769 the estate was heavily encumbered by mortgages and about 250 a. had to be conveyed to trustees to sell for paying off the debts. Most of this was sold and at the inclosure in 1784 the estate was reduced to a few fields near the manor house.[52] It was then held by yet another John, on whom it had been settled in 1767.[53] His only son Edward died unmarried in 1826 and the estate was divided between his three sisters.[54]

The manor house of Smallbrook stood in front of the present Smallbrook Farm, where an elaborate pair of gate pillars may still be seen in 1962. It was demolished in the 19th century.[55]

LESSER ESTATES. From the 15th century a considerable estate which lay mainly on the Boreham side of Warminster was built up by the Gifford family. It derived first from John Osborne, reeve of the capital manor of Warminster in the early 15th century[56] and a freeholder in 1434.[57] His son John Osborne[58] had a son Richard, whose widow died possessed of lands in Boreham in 1527. Richard's heir was Thomas Gifford, grandson of Elizabeth, sister of the younger John Osborne, who had married Edward, son of Walter Gifford of 'Rodhurst'.[59] Later in the 16th century the

Gifford family acquired a freehold estate in the parish which had belonged to a family named Cutting, which had held land in the 14th century.[60] Thomas Cutting held 100 a. in 1402,[61] and about 40 years later John Cutting died seised of it and John Newburgh claimed to be his heir.[62] It descended to John's grandson, Roger Newburgh, who held it in 1493.[63] In 1504 Henry Daccombe and Christian his wife, who was probably the daughter of Newburgh, conveyed it to Richard Elyot, sergeant-at-law.[64] Elyot died in 1522;[65] by 1536 Cutting's Farm was held by Robert Coker of Mappowder (Dors.).[66] In 1567 Henry Coker sold it to Sir John Thynne,[67] who in 1571 conveyed it with other lands to Thomas Gifford in exchange for land in Longbridge Deverill.[68] It then consisted of a holding of about 60 a. called Cutting's Farm, and a smaller holding of 13 a.[69]

Thomas Gifford was succeeded in turn by his son John and grandson and great-grandson, both called William;[70] the younger William added to the estate two small holdings, parts of the manor of Boreham, which he bought from Richard Staples in 1626,[71] and the manor of Cheyneys, bought of Ralph Hastings in 1647.[72] William's son, Benjamin, bought the large manor farm of Boreham in 1663.[73] The family estate descended to Benjamin's grandson, John Hoskins Gifford of Cucklington (Som.), who died without issue in 1744. Of his three sisters and coheirs only one had issue, and so the whole estate eventually passed to her son, William Buckler.[74] At his death in 1790 he left the estate to be divided between his two daughters, and in 1801 a partition was agreed upon by which the Wiltshire estates were allotted to Mary, the younger daughter, wife of Francis Dugdale Astley of Everleigh.[75] In 1810 Astley exchanged with Lord Bath outlying parts of the estate in Corsley and the western part of Warminster parish for about 300 a. in Boreham which had once been copyholds of the capital manor of Warminster.[76] In 1821, however, Astley's trustees sold all of his estate in Boreham which lay north of the Wylye, to William Temple of Bishopstrow, who thus became owner of almost the whole of Boreham tithing on that side of the river.[77] In succeeding years, he bought most of the small

43 V.C.H. Wilts. vii. 16; W. H. Jones, Bradford on Avon, ed. J. Beddoe (1907), 196.
44 Hoare, Mod. Wilts. Warminster, 46.
45 See p. 99.
46 C 54/553 nos. 13–14; Bristol Univ. Hodge (Baker) MSS. D.M. 76/34.
47 See p. 99.
48 C 142/207/48.
49 Bristol Univ. Hodge (Baker) MSS. D.M. 76/105; Hoare, Mod. Wilts. Warminster, 24–25.
50 Hoare, op. cit. 24–25.
51 Bristol Univ. Hodge (Baker) MSS. D.M. 76/44–46; W.A.S. Libr. Devizes, Everett MSS. Pedigrees, i. 73 f.
52 Bristol Univ. Hodge (Baker) MSS. D.M. 76/68–90; W.R.O. Inclosure Award.
53 Bristol Univ. Hodge (Baker) MSS. D.M. 76/65–6.
54 W.A.S. Libr. Devizes, Everett MSS. Pedigrees, i. 73 f.
55 It appears on W.R.O. Tithe Award but not on O.S. Map 1/2,500 Wilts. LI. 8 (1st edn.).
56 Longleat MSS. 9062, 9421.
57 Ibid. 9063.
58 Tropenell Cart. ed. Davies, i. 59.
59 C 142/46/109; Wilts. Visitation Pedigrees (Harl. Soc. cv–vi), 64, where Elizabeth is given as the immediate heir of John Osborne.

60 Longleat MSS. Parcel XXVII, Custumal of free tenants c. 1360.
61 C.P. 25(1)/256/58/3.
62 C 1/14/31.
63 W.N. & Q. vi. 282; for this family, see Hutchins, Hist. Dors. i. 366.
64 C.P. 25(2)/257/66/41; Roger Newburgh left an only dau. and heir Christian, whose only recorded marriage was to John, Lord Marney.
65 D.N.B.
66 Longleat MSS. Thynne Papers, Bk. 63, p. 41, and Parcel XXI, Rental c. 1540.
67 W.N. & Q. v. 357.
68 Longleat MS. 8283; C.P. 25(2)/239/14 Eliz. I Hil.
69 Longleat MS. 11260.
70 Wilts. Visitation Pedigrees (Harl. Soc. cv–vi), 64–65; the pedigree printed by Hoare, Mod. Wilts. Warminster, 76 is wrong in omitting one of the Williams entirely.
71 W.R.O. 132, Staples to Gifford, 1626.
72 See p. 100.
73 W.R.O. 132, Staples to Gifford, 1663.
74 Ibid. Wills of J. H. Gifford, 1744, and of Dorothy Newman, 1752.
75 Ibid. Partition, Astley and Lethbridge, 1801.
76 Ibid. Exchange, Bath and Astley, 1810.
77 Ibid. Exchange, Astley to Temple, 1821.

properties of other owners there. Chief of these was a farm called Chamberlayne's, which had been a copyhold of the manor of Boreham. It was sold by Richard Staples to William Bailey in 1641 and passed with his daughter to the Slade family of Warminster, in which it descended until the Revd. William Slade sold it to William Temple in 1823.[78] The Temple family retained the Boreham estates until 1921, when they were sold.[79]

Several small estates which were eventually added to the Longleat estate must also be mentioned. In the 14th century John de la Mere, probably a younger son of the family which held the manor of Boreham, held a small estate in Warminster. He died c. 1349 leaving three coheirs; two were his daughters, Cecily, wife of Henry Montfort, and Joan, wife of Richard Scammell,[80] and the third was Thomas de Sindlesham, infant son of a third daughter.[81] The whole estate apparently passed to the Montforts of Nunney, for in 1412 John Montfort held lands in Bishopstrow and Warminster worth 40s.[82] By the late 15th century the Montfort property here and at Nunney and other places in Somerset was held by Simon Wiseman. He sold much of it, including Warminster, to Richard Mawdley,[83] in whose family it remained until the 17th century.[84] A survey of 1603 shows that the estate consisted of a virgate of land without a house on it;[85] Roger Mawdley, who owned it then, left three daughters.[86] After his death they joined with their husbands in conveying it to Sir Thomas Thynne.[87]

A family called Laffull held land in Warminster in the 14th century.[88] In 1459 Thomas Laffull sold property there to Richard Page,[89] who in 1464 held a number of properties, including over 100 a. called 'Laffellisland alias Felthamps'.[90] Page's son was probably Edmund Page of Warminster, whose grand-daughter Ann Page married Richard Brayfield and left a daughter Elizabeth, wife of James Heath of London, mercer.[91] It was from Heath that Sir John Thynne bought part of the Page property, amounting to about 35 a., in 1568.[92] The remainder passed in an unexplained way to the descendants of Gregory Morgan, who was the second husband of Edmund Page's wife Ann,[93] and must have formed part of the estate sold by Peter Morgan to Walter, Lord Hungerford.[94]

Another estate which eventually passed to the

Thynne family once belonged to Roger Twynyho, and passed at his death in 1497 to his brother George.[95] He died in 1525 leaving a son Edward,[96] who in 1550 sold the property to William Stump of Malmesbury.[97] Stump's son William sold it in 1580 to William Yerbury, a Trowbridge clothier,[98] whose son Edward sold it in 1615 to Edward Scutt of Warminster.[99] Scutt mortgaged the property to Sir Thomas Thynne in 1626 and released his right in the following year. It then consisted of six houses and a small amount of land, mainly near Portway.[1]

The chief ecclesiastical estate in Warminster was that belonging to the Prebend of Warminster in Salisbury Cathedral. In about 1115 Henry I gave, or more probably confirmed, to the church of Salisbury two hides of land at Warminster which Walter, son of Edward of Salisbury, had held.[2] By the early 13th century this land formed the endowment of the prebend; it was then valued at £5,[3] but in 1226 was only worth 41s.[4] In 1222 the prebend was declared exempt from archidiaconal jurisdiction.[5] It was valued at £5 in 1291,[6] and at £7 net in 1535.[7] In 1550 the whole estate was let to Robert Whatley for 60 years at a rent of £7 6s. 8d.[8] In 1635 it was let to Thomas Ludlow,[9] a member of a younger branch of the Ludlows of Hill Deverill, and ancestor of a family that held the prebend for almost 200 years.[10] In 1829 William Heald Ludlow sold his leasehold interest in parts of the estate to several persons, to whom new leases were made.[11] In 1847 the freehold of the property was vested in the Ecclesiastical Commissioners in return for an annuity of £150 to the prebendary.[12] Two years later they were authorized to sell parts of the estate.[13] The prebendal manor house, called East End House, stood south of East Street on the site of Ridgeway.

Part of the estate of the Prebend of Warminster alias Luxfield in Wells Cathedral lay in Warminster, but its history is described in the account of the parish of Corsley.[14]

Several religious houses held estates in Warminster. That of the Priory of Longleat was probably the land granted to it by Robert le Bore in 1324.[15] It was included in the grant of the site of Longleat to Edward, Earl of Hertford, in 1541, and was sold by him to Sir John Thynne in the same year.[16]

The house of Maiden Bradley also held property

[78] W.R.O. Deeds of property bought from Slade; see also W.R.O. 212B, Wa. 5, 8–9.

[79] W.R.O. 132, Sale Temple to Bazley, 1921; W.A.S. Libr. Devizes, Sale Cat. For the Temples, see p. 7.

[80] Halstead, *Succint Genealogies*, 144; the authenticity of the doc. printed by Halstead is borne out by *Cal. Fine R.* 1347–56, 184.

[81] Longleat MS. 9009.   [82] *Feud. Aids*, vi. 511.

[83] *Cal. Close*, 1476–85, 274 and 1485–1500, 222.

[84] Longleat MSS. 16th cent. Rentals, *passim*. For the Mawdley family see *Visitation of Somerset*, 1623 (Harl. Soc. xi), 73.

[85] Longleat MS. 7344.

[86] C 142/762/155; Hist. MSS. Com. *Egmont*, i. 85n.

[87] C 142/765/47.

[88] B.M. Add. Ch. 40046.

[89] C.P. 25(1)/257/64/48.

[90] *Tropenell Cart.* ed. Davies, ii. 66–7.

[91] Longleat MSS. 9413–4.

[92] Ibid. 9428.

[93] Ibid. 9413–4.

[94] See p. 99.

[95] *Cal. Inq. p.m. Hen. VII*, ii. pp. 212–3.

[96] C 142/44/13; C 1/1304/7.

[97] Longleat MS. 9350; *W.N. & Q.* viii. 392–5, 483.

[98] Longleat MS. 9319.

[99] Ibid. 9323.

[1] Ibid. 9334, 9342.

[2] *Reg. St. Osmund* (Rolls Ser.), i. 202; *Complete Peerage*, xi. 374, note f.

[3] *Interdict Documents* (P.R.S. N.S. xxxiv), 20.

[4] *Reg. St. Osmund* (Rolls Ser.), ii. 73.

[5] Ibid. i. 338.

[6] *Tax. Eccl.* (Rec. Com.), 182.

[7] *Valor Eccl.* (Rec. Com.), ii. 77.

[8] Ch. Com. 136777, f. 202; C 3/79/29.

[9] C 54/3494 no. 39.

[10] See pedigree, *W.A.M.* xxvi, opp. p. 172.

[11] Ch. Com. 3608–13; W.R.O. 442, Abstr. of Title to Prebend, c. 1849.

[12] *Lond. Gaz.* 1847, p. 45.

[13] Ibid. 1849, p. 2223.

[14] See p. 21.

[15] Hoare, *Mod. Wilts.* Heytesbury, 56, and Addenda, 22; S.C. 6/Hen. VIII/3144 m. 48.

[16] *L. & P. Hen. VIII*, xvi, pp. 381, 463.

in Warminster, but its history is described above with that of the larger estate at Whitbourne in Corsley.[17]

The manor of Cheyneys, which was held of the Prior of St. John of Wilton, has been mentioned above.[18] Other property held of the hospital included seven houses which formed part of the estate of Philip Morgan at his death in 1473 for a chief rent of 2s. 6d.[19] Land re-granted to the restored order of St. John of Jerusalem in 1558 included property of very small value in Warminster which had belonged to Ansty Preceptory.[20]

Robert Mauduit, the first of the family to hold the capital manor, endowed his younger son Robert with a tenement which Gilbert the knight of Warminster had held, to hold by the service of $\frac{1}{8}$ knight's fee.[21] Thomas Mauduit added certain pasture rights to the gift.[22] It was perhaps this same tenement which was held by another Robert Mauduit by the rent of 1d. in 1300[23] and granted to him by Peter Scudamore, lord of Upton, in 1328.[24] In 1331 Scudamore obtained licence to use the land, still held at the same rent, to endow a chantry in Upton Scudamore church.[25] In 1334 and 1349 it was described as a place called the Dryehey, $39\frac{1}{2}$ a. of arable land, $2\frac{1}{2}$ a. meadow, pasture for certain stock and rents of £1.[26] In 1442 the property of the chantry of Upton was used to endow the Hungerford chantry and hospital at Heytesbury.[27] When the hospital let its Warminster property in 1586 it included the $39\frac{1}{2}$ a. of arable land and some 12 a. of meadow and pasture;[28] in addition a chief rent of 4s. was received from William Middlecott.[29] The estate continued to be let as a whole until the late 18th century.[30] By the early 19th century it was much reduced in size, amounting only to some 12a., and half of this had been sold by 1903.[31]

At the Dissolution of chantries the property given for the support of St. Laurence's chapel consisted of a house and about 30 a. of land, let at a rent of 40s.[32] It was let to William Deacon in 1590.[33] In 1606 it was granted in fee farm at the same rent to Thomas Emerson and William Benett.[34] It probably soon passed to the Thynne family, by whom it was certainly held in the later 17th century.[35] The Crown rent was redeemed c. 1788.[36]

AGRICULTURE. The earliest references to open-field land in Warminster are in deeds of the

13th century, when North[37] and West[38] Fields are mentioned. East and South Fields are so -named in 1334[39] and 1349[40] respectively. All these names were still in use in the 17th century,[41] but the more detailed surveys of that period commonly defined arable land by the furlong in which it lay rather than the field. Furlongs were often themselves referred to as fields; thus in 1682 arable lay in Sand Field, Gillidge Bridge Field, Hill Field, Copripp Field, and Wetridge Field, beside the four fields mentioned in the Middle Ages. Wetridge Field was probably the same as the Wetridges in Mancombe Field which appears in the same survey.[42] But although it is difficult to be certain about the exact division and nomenclature of the town fields continuously between the 13th and the 18th centuries, the regular references to arable land at such known places as Chedlanger, Fernicombe, Mancombe, and Morley, which all occur in the 14th century or before,[43] show that much of what was still open arable in the 18th century had been so in the 13th.[44] It is also possible tentatively to identify three of the medieval fields with those which still existed in the 18th century. The West Field, in which land at Chedlanger lay in 1284,[45] is no doubt the Chedlanger Field which before inclosure stretched south and east of Norridge Woods from near Bugley across the Bath road to the Westbury road below Arn Hill.[46] In 1349 the North Field included land below Cop Heap, at Mancombe, and at Oxenpit.[47] Mancombe and Oxendean both lay in Warminster Field in 1780 and Cop Heap adjoining it; it then included all the arable land on the downs between the Upton Scudamore boundary and the Westbury and Imber roads as far eastward as the edge of the sheep down above Mancombe and Oxendean. If West and North Fields do indeed correspond with Chedlanger and Warminster Fields, then the medieval East Field must be the Morley Field of the inclosure award, which extended south of the Imber road between Cop Heap and Battlesbury. Land 'over Morligh' lay in the South Field in 1349,[48] however, so that the position is not very clear. No open arable land to the south of Warminster remained at the time of inclosure. Some lay at Sambourne in the early 14th century,[49] and at Ryehill, between East Street and the Were, as late as 1687;[50] both may well have formed part of the medieval South Field.

Of the outlying hamlets of Warminster, Boreham had its own fields and its agriculture is dealt

[17] See p. 16.
[18] See p. 100.
[19] C 140/525/48.
[20] Cal. Pat. 1557-8, 317.
[21] W.R.O. 490 Hungerford Cart. f. 113.
[22] Ibid. f. 112v.
[23] Wilts. Inq. p.m. 1242-1326 (Index Libr.), 249-53.
[24] W.R.O. 490 Hungerford Cart. f. 115.
[25] Wilts. Inq. p.m. 1327-77 (Index Libr.), 74; Cal. Pat. 1330-34, 185; see above, p. 87.
[26] W.R.O. 490 Hungerford Cart. ff. 115v., 118v.
[27] See p. 87.
[28] W.R.O. 251, Lease Hosp. to Alford.
[29] W.A.M. xliv. 258.
[30] W.R.O. 251 various leases; ibid. 212A (Everett section), Lease to Clavey, 1765.
[31] W.R.O. 251, Surveys of the Estate; Endowed Char. Wilts. (1908), p. 202.
[32] E 301/58 no. 131.
[33] Longleat MS. 9386.
[34] E 308/4/35 no. 12.

[35] Longleat MS. 10652.
[36] Ibid. Estate Office, Survey 1743, p. 56.
[37] Longleat MSS. 9071, 9091.
[38] Ibid. 9092.
[39] Ibid. 9141.
[40] W.R.O. 490, Hungerford Cart., f. 118v.
[41] Longleat MS. 10652.
[42] Ibid.
[43] Ibid. 9070, 9092; 8988, 9081; 8975; W.R.O. 490, Hungerford Cart., f. 118v.; Hist. MSS. Com. Hastings, i. 218-9.
[44] This ignores variations of extent depending on the demand for land, which cannot be determined.
[45] Longleat MS. 9092.
[46] W.R.O. Inclosure Award, which is referred to hereafter without footnotes.
[47] Ibid 490 Hungerford Cart. f. 118v.
[48] Ibid.
[49] Ibid. ff. 114, 115.
[50] Longleat MS. 10652.

with separately below.[51] About Bugley the position is rather less certain. Arable land lay in Bugley Field in 1320,[52] and is occasionally referred to in or near Bugley until the 17th century. In 1652, for instance, arable land lay 'near Haygrove on the Lyes', and in 1671 in Princecroft, south of the road to Warminster.[53] But the district was one of early inclosure, and only three or four pieces of land there still lay open at the inclosure. Arable land which belonged to holdings at Bugley lay regularly, from the 16th century at least, in Chedlanger Field and Cley Field.[54] The former was shared by the tenants of Warminster and Corsley, and the latter, although it was one of the fields of Corsley, included much land which belonged to holdings in Warminster.[55]

In 1086 there were 80 a. of meadow in Warminster.[56] Some of this must have lain at Pit Mead, a large meadow which lies along the Wylye between Norton Bavant and Sutton Veny, but was partly in Warminster until the 19th century.[57] The lord of Warminster had meadow there in the early 13th century.[58] Possibly at that time, and certainly by the 15th century, he shared it not only with some of his freehold tenants of Warminster,[59] but also with the lords of Bishopstrow and Norton Bavant.[60] The other principal common meadow of Warminster was Woodman Mead, which extended from near Bugley to Warminster church along the stream north of the road, and is first mentioned in 1323.[61] In it the copyholders of the capital manor and the lords and tenants of the manors of Furnax, Warminster Scudamore, and Portway had their meadow.[62] Smaller meadows which were common lay at Bristol Mead and Laurence Mead. Bristol Mead lay on the stream between the Bath and Westbury roads, north of Gas House Farm; meadow land lay there in 1328,[63] and is occasionally referred to from that time, mainly attached to holdings of the capital manor.[64] It survived partly open until the inclosure. Laurence Mead, south of St. Laurence's chapel, was apparently common in 1618, when an illegal inclosure was made there[65] but inclosed before the parliamentary award.

The common pasture of the manor lay in Warminster Common or Heath to the west of the town, extending in a long strip to the Somerset border; in the common fields and meadows after harvest or while they lay fallow; and in the common downs beyond the arable land in the east of the parish.

It is fairly clear that a two-field course was practised until the 17th century. In 1218 a half-virgate of land had for its arable 7 a. in the field between Warminster and Bishopstrow and 7 a. in the field between Upton and Warminster.[66] West and North Fields, then, apparently lay fallow when East and South Fields were sown; this probably explains the conventional division of 39½ a. arable into North and South Fields in 1349, when, as noted above, the South Field included land which might have been expected to be in the East Field.[67] In 1238 a tenant was to receive half his leasehold estate sown with winter corn 'at champarty',[68] and in 1327 half the demesne arable was sown each year, when it was worth three times as much as that which lay fallow and common.[69] Of the meadows Woodman Mead was subject to this course, and lay in with Chedlanger Field when it was fallow every other year in the late 15th and early 16th centuries.[70] The course of Pit Mead is not known. The two-field rotation persisted until at least the early 17th century. In 1603 a freehold yardland had common after harvest either in Mancombe Bottom or Cop Heap Field,[71] so that the North and East Fields were still sown in alternate years, and in 1616 land at Topps (near Sambourne), which should have lain common every other year, was being sown every year contrary to the custom.[72] Chedlanger Field was in a two-year course with Cley Field in Corsley in the early 18th century.[73]

Linked with the field course were the regulations which governed the stocking of the commons and the fallows. Warminster Common provided pasture for a common herd of horses and other beasts in 1574, but its use for sheep was confined to 'lying-in weather', which meant only in time of snow. Pigs also ran there.[74] In the early 17th century it was said that every inhabitant could have one horse and one cow there, and those who held land could have them there without stint. All could cut fern and furze as much as they wished,[75] paying a hen at Christmas and five eggs at Easter.[76] The common milking place of the town lay at the north end of the hamlet at the Common.[77] More important was the feeding for sheep and oxen provided by the common fields and downs. The course of the lord's and freeholders' feeding was apparently as follows.[78] In the winter, which was reckoned from 29 September to the Sunday after 23 April, the sheep were kept on the downs, those of the lord of Warminster (or

[51] See p. 110.
[52] Longleat MS. 9131.
[53] W.R.O. 130a, Lease by Wm. Bailey; ibid. 194, Adlam to Adlam, 1671.
[54] e.g. Longleat MS. 11260 mentions a holding with 31 a. in Cley Field and 24 a. in Chedlanger Field, c. 1570.
[55] See e.g. Longleat MS. 10649.
[56] V.C.H. Wilts. ii, p. 116.
[57] See p. 90.
[58] Longleat MS. 9066.
[59] Ibid. Parcel XXI, plan of Pit Mead, 1711; W.R.O. 132, Survey of Boreham 1582; Ch. Com. 66630.
[60] Longleat MSS. 9063 (Rental 1434) and later rentals passim.
[61] Ibid. 9005.
[62] Ibid. Surveys and Leases passim; C.C.C. MSS. K.b. 3; W.R.O. 194, Middlecott to Hotkins, 1648.
[63] W.R.O. 490 Hungerford Cart. f. 115.
[64] Longleat MS. 10652.
[65] Ibid. 9340.
[66] C.P. 25(1)/250/4/1; H. L. Gray, English Field Systems (1959), 501.

[67] W.R.O. 490, Hungerford Cart. f. 118v.; see also C.C.C. Deeds K.1.1. [68] Longleat MS. 8969.
[69] Halstead, Succint Genealogies, 141.
[70] S.C. 6/Hen. VII/957–9; S.C. 6/Hen. VIII/3902.
[71] Longleat MS. 7344.
[72] Ibid. Parcel XXI, Presentment 1616; the two-field system also probably accounts for the variation of freehold rents in alternate years which is a feature of Warminster rentals.
[73] Longleat MS. 6981.
[74] Soc. Antiq. Jackson MSS. s.v. Warminster.
[75] C.C.C. MSS. K.b.3 Survey c. 1605.
[76] W.R.O. 442/1.
[77] Longleat Estate Office, Survey 1743, p. 42 and W.R.O. Inclosure Award.
[78] Based on statements of custom in Longleat MSS. 7344 (1603); ibid. Parcel XXI, survey of Warminster c. 1577; ibid. Parcel XXVIII, Papers in Bennett v. Sloper, and Freeholders v. Sloper, early 17th cent.; C.C.C. MSS. K.b. 3, Surveys 1577 and c. 1605. Variations, apart from points at variance, between these sources are only minor ones of date.

later his farmer) on his own down and those of the freeholders on their down. During this time oxen were kept in the field which had last been cut and was to lie fallow. On 2 February Woodman Mead, and presumably the other common meadows, were hained from the fields for the grass to grow. At the end of winter, or the Sunday after 23 April all the downs were hained, and the sheep moved down into the fallow field to follow the oxen. The lord of Warminster's down was broken at Whitsun for his and the freeholders' oxen. The freeholders' down remained hained until 23 June, when all the oxen were moved into it and the farmer's down was kept for lambs. Finally on 1 August the lambs followed the oxen into the freeholders' down, and the oxen were moved into the meadows which were then broken after haymaking. Whether the stock of the copyholders followed this course is not clear. They are not known to have had their own down, and in 1603 it was said that their sheep could go in with the freeholders' sheep on 21 December.[79] Perhaps before that day they had to keep their sheep in part of the field destined for spring sowing. In addition to the general course, at least one freeholder had winter common for a stint of sheep on limited parts of the fallow fields. This was Roger Mawdley, who in 1603 had in alternate years pasture for 100 sheep from 11 November to the middle of March in Mancombe Bottom or Cop Heap Field, whichever lay in wheat stubble.[80] The common rights over 60 a. of arable land near the Sands Cross and Morley, which belonged to the lords of Furnax in the 16th and 17th centuries,[81] and William Chandler's winter field in Chedlanger, which in 1698 had bounds long fixed by custom,[82] were probably similar. An early instance of this practice is perhaps the winter pasture in the fields below 'Orebury' in the mid-13th century.[83] The practice may have arisen from obligations on certain tenant flocks to fold on the demesne arable in the winter, for such obligations existed in the 14th century.[84]

In addition to the commons which followed this course, the lord of Warminster and some freeholders had their own several pastures. That of the lord was a coppice called the Frith, which lay near the Common;[85] it provided pasture for his oxen in 1292–3,[86] and was evidently part of the demesne as long as it was farmed.[87] The 'more' of the lord of Smallbrook, in which pasture for one beast was sold in 1327,[88] was also probably a several pasture, and perhaps the same as the Waspail's Marsh of 1585.[89] To the manor of Furnax belonged a coppice near Norridge Woods, first mentioned in 1483.[90]

Apart from this tentative reconstruction of the course of the fields and commons, little is known of the agriculture practised in Warminster in the Middle Ages except on the demesne of the capital

manor. In 1300 the demesne was said to consist of 240 a. of arable and 30 a. of meadow,[91] but in 1327 the arable was reckoned at 400 a., of which half was sown yearly.[92] The most extensive work on this land was done by 8 virgaters, who in 1348–9 worked 5 days a week from Lammas to Michaelmas, and 3 days a week for the remainder of the year. In addition they ploughed 2½ a. and weeded 8 a. each year.[93] In 1364–5 31 half-virgaters did a day's ploughing at the spring sowing, a day's weeding in summer and a day's reaping at harvest, and 17 cottagers did the last two of these, but not the first. Since only 5 half-virgaters and 6 cottagers were mentioned as belonging to the capital manor in 1300 and 1327, it is possible that many of these were small freeholders. Some of the larger freeholds also owed works, mainly of carrying crops from the fields and ploughing, in the mid-14th century. The crops threshed from the demesne are known for three years in the 14th century. In each wheat and barley were the largest crops; wheat was rather larger than barley in 1348–9 and 1385–6, but in 1390–1 barley was the larger. In 1410 78 a. of the demesne were sown with barley and 42 a. with wheat.[94] The only other considerable crop in the 14th century was oats; the quantity threshed was $\frac{1}{3}$ to $\frac{1}{2}$ that of the wheat crop. In 1410 52 a. of oats were sown on the downs.[95] Crops grown in small quantities were bere, or inferior barley, in 1322[96] and 1348–9; rye in 1348–9; dredge-corn in all the recorded years; and peas and beans in 1410.[97] The only other crop known to have been grown in Warminster in the Middle Ages is flax. In 1315 a tenant of Cheyney's manor was obliged to dig sufficient land to take a bushel of flax seed, and afterwards to treat and prepare the crop 'as far as the water'.[98]

In 1296 the stock on the demesne of the capital manor consisted principally of 32 plough-oxen, 16 cattle, 48 pigs, and 250 sheep and lambs.[99] In 1327 the demesne was said to have common of pasture for 300 sheep,[1] and it is clear that sheep were kept in considerable numbers as long as it was farmed. In 1379–80, for instance, 350 sheep and 90 lambs were sheared, and in 1390–1 the whole flock amounted to over 700. The larger freeholders too kept considerable numbers of sheep. In the later 14th century the stints allowed to 10 chief freeholders amounted to 1,956 sheep, and in 1379–80 they paid for the agistment of 1,080 lambs on the lord's down. The fold of at least one free tenant's flock was reserved for the lord's land during the winter.[2]

To complete the account of medieval agriculture it only remains to consider how the lands, which were under the system here described, were divided between the various holders. Much of this is de-

[79] Longleat MS. 7344.
[80] Ibid.; Longleat Estate Office, Survey 1743, p. 30.
[81] C.C.C. MSS. K.b. 1, K.b. 3.
[82] Longleat MS. 6681.   [83] Ibid. 9077.
[84] Ibid. Parcel XXVII, Custumal of Free Tens.
[85] Its position is mentioned in 16th-cent. leases: ibid. Parcel XXVIII.
[86] Ibid. 8984.
[87] Ibid. 9062; S.C. 6/1145/12 m. 3.
[88] B.M. Add. Ch. 26711.
[89] W.R.O. 132, Middlecott to Audley, 1585.
[90] C.C.C. Deeds K. 1.3; see also surveys in ibid. K.b.3.

[91] *Wilts. Inq. p.m.* 1242–1326 (Index Libr.), 249–53.
[92] Halstead, *Succint Genealogies*, 141.
[93] Longleat MSS. Parcel XXVII. The remainder of this paragraph is based, unless otherwise stated, on account and other rolls in this parcel.
[94] Ibid. 9200.
[95] Ibid.
[96] S.C. 6/1145/12 m. 12.
[97] Longleat MS. 9200.
[98] Ibid. 9120.
[99] Ibid. 8977.
[1] Halstead, *Succint Genealogies*, 141.
[2] Longleat MSS. Parcel XXVII, Acct. and other rolls.

duced from surveys of the 16th and 17th centuries, but the conclusions seem to be borne out by what earlier evidence is available. The most noteworthy feature of land-holding in Warminster was the preponderance of freeholders over copyholders. In 1300 there were 35 freeholders of the capital manor, of whom 17 held land reckoned at 7 carucates and 10½ virgates;[3] this is exclusive of the manors of Furnax and Smallbrook, which were not held of the capital manor.[4] Against this there were only 8 bond tenants who held a full virgate and a few smaller tenants; there is, moreover, little doubt that most, if not all, these virgaters held their land in Boreham, being the predecessors of the group of large copyholders there which belonged to the manor until the 18th century.[5] Thus in 1300 Warminster manor was already apparently what it certainly was later: a manor in which the demesne outstripped in size the total of the copyholds, which were generally small.[6] Demesnes were also important on other holdings of which details are known. Thus in the late 16th century Warminster Scudamore comprised a demesne of some 60 a. and about 100 a. divided between 21 copy- and leaseholders.[7] Somewhat earlier Furnax demesne was 80 a. and 19 tenants held about 190 a.[8] In the early 17th century Cheyneys manor had a demesne of 200 a. and about 50 a. divided between 13 tenants.[9] Smaller freeholds consisted of single units farmed or let by their owners, such as Roger Mawdley's virgate or Cutting's Farm.[10] Thus as far back as information is available, Warminster never had the hierarchy of copyholders of various degrees typical of some manors. The multiplicity of freeholds and the smallness of copyholds made the farm consisting of a freehold, or the demesne of a freehold, the typical unit; an important factor in considering the effect of the changes in agriculture which began in the later Middle Ages.

The process by which the works of the customary tenants were commuted and the demesnes leased out can again only be traced on the capital manor.[11] In 1348-9 the 8 full-virgaters on it were obliged to perform 1,396 days work and actually performed 1,086. By 1379-80, however, two of them had had their whole obligation commuted; of the 1,050 owed by the remainder, 727 were still performed. The proportion was much the same in 1390-1, but in 1401-2 only three virgaters still owed 497 works, of which they performed 290. In that year little arable farming was done on the demesne, and most of the works were haymaking; a flock of 163 sheep

was kept. The first known lease of the whole demesne was made for eight years in 1410 when the land sown amounted to 185 a.[12] Leasing evidently continued until 1437-8, when 102 a. of land sown with corn and 5 oxen were bought from the farmer, evidently for a partial resumption of farming. In 1441-4 a small part of the arable was used and the remainder let in small parcels, but a large flock of sheep was kept. This partial revival was over by 1462-3, when the demesnes were already let at farm again. Of the other manors of Warminster, the demesnes of Cheyneys were let at farm by 1421,[13] and those of Furnax as early as 1352;[14] information for the others is lacking.

From the 16th century, then, the agriculture of Warminster was based largely on a number of considerable farms. The farm of the capital manor, consisting of over 400 a., was let as a whole from the 15th century until the late 17th century,[15] but after the long tenure of the Sloper family, from 1598 until c. 1670, it was divided into two parts of roughly equal size, and remained so until the inclosure.[16] Cheyneys Farm was of c. 200 a. in the early 17th century,[17] and continued to be let as a whole until the 18th century.[18] In the 16th century Warminster Scudamore had, in addition to a demesne farm of about 65 a., another farm of 83 a.,[19] which had been added to it in 1537 and 1538 by Walter, Lord Hungerford's purchase from Peter Morgan.[20] The demesne farm of Furnax consisted of some 85 a. let as a whole until the inclosure.[21] The demesnes of Portway were let as a whole by 1509,[22] but after the whole of the manor was the property of the Middlecott family,[23] they may have been kept in hand as a home farm. This was certainly so at the time of the inclosure, when Edward Middlecott held a farm of several hundred acres.[24] The demesne farm of Smallbrook, which amounted to over 160 a. in 1723, was kept in hand by its owners, the Bennett family, in the 17th and 18th centuries.[25] Among other farms which may be mentioned are the estate belonging to the Prebend of Warminster;[26] the holding of Heytesbury Hospital, leased as a whole from the 16th to the 18th centuries;[27] and the slightly larger farm in Bugley, formerly of Maiden Bradley, which was let as a whole until the inclosure.[28]

Compared with these the typical copyhold in Warminster was small, often a house and an acre or two in the fields. Thus in the late 17th century the estate of Lord Weymouth, which by then included the former Hungerford property, only had

[3] *Wilts. Inq. p.m.* 1242–1326 (Index Libr.), 250–1.
[4] See pp. 100–03.
[5] See p. 103.
[6] For the smallness of most of the holdings apart from the demesne, see Longleat MSS. Parcel XXVIII, rental 1578; later rentals also show this if the accretions to the manor under the Thynnes are disregarded.
[7] W.R.O. 442/1; this is neglecting the farm of some 80 a. bought of Morgan earlier in the century; see above, p. 99.
[8] C.C.C. MSS. K.2(1), 23.
[9] Longleat MS. 9341.
[10] See pp. 103, 104.
[11] This paragraph is based, unless otherwise stated, on acct. rolls in Longleat MSS. Parcel XXVII.
[12] Ibid. 9199.
[13] S.C. 6/1061/23.
[14] C.C.C. Deeds K.1.48.
[15] Longleat MSS. Leases and Rentals, *passim*; B.M.

Add. MS. 34566, f. 2.
[16] Longleat MS. 10652 and later rentals *passim*.
[17] Ibid. 9341.
[18] C.P. 25(2)/508/5 Chas. I Hil.; W.R.O. 132, Will of J. H. Gifford, 1744.
[19] W.R.O. 442/1.
[20] See p. 99.
[21] C.C.C. MSS. K.b.3, Surveys of various dates; King's School, Bruton MSS. B. iv.4.
[22] C.C.C. MSS. K.1.64.
[23] See p. 99.
[24] W.R.O. Inclosure Award.
[25] Ibid. 212 B, Wa. 6; Bristol Univ. Hodge (Baker) MSS. 76/39.
[26] See p. 104.
[27] W.R.O. 251, bundle of Leases; ibid. 212A, pt. 12, bundle of Leases.
[28] S.C. 6/Hen. VIII/3969 m. 4d.; Longleat MS. 11260; Bristol Univ. Hodge (Baker) MSS. 76/56.

6 copyholds of over 20 a. (apart from the Boreham ones mentioned below) out of a total of over 90.[29] Some engrossment of these small estates was inevitable. In the mid-16th century John Stanlake held the manor of Furnax at farm,[30] and took advantage of his position to amass 16 copyholds, amounting in all to over 70 a. [31] In addition Stanlake held land of the manor of Warminster Scudamore,[32] and of the Prior of Longleat.[33]

The changes in agriculture on these holdings from the 16th century onwards by inclosure and consolidation of open field land can only be intermittently traced. Closes near Warminster town are mentioned in the 13th century,[34] but were probably no more than crofts attached to houses. The earliest reference to the inclosure of land which had once formed part of the common fields is in a deed, probably of the mid-14th century, of a croft in Sambourne and 1 a. of arable land lying outside it in Nicholas Nobount's inclosure.[35] Closes are occasionally referred to from that time onwards. Some, like the pasture called Pathcroft, with parcels of arable adjoining, of 1465[36] were probably the result of the inclosure of low-lying arable land near Warminster and Bugley for conversion to meadow or pasture.[37] Sixteenth-century surveys show that most closes lay there. Thus in 1582 Warminster Scudamore manor included closes at Fernhill and Ryehill, both near Smallbrook, and at Sambourne,[38] and about the same time five closes near the church belonged to Furnax manor.[39] In Bugley the farm formerly of Maiden Bradley had 8 closes amounting in all to some 20 a.[40] Inclosures of land further from the town were made by encroachment on the waste. 'Tercecroft', now Tascroft, south-west of Bugley, where pasture was let in 1322,[41] may be an early example of this. In 1585 50 a. of coppice newly inclosed lying on both sides of Redford Water were let for the first time; in 1606 the land was described as pasture,[42] and probably formed the nucleus of Stalls Farm, north of Longleat.

Inclosure of both kinds probably continued spasmodically until the award of 1783. Thus in 1618 two tenants of Cheyneys manor had inclosed land in Woodman Mead and Laurence Mead.[43] Parts of Bristol Mead were inclosed by 1609,[44] and in 1638 a close at the east end of Warminster had recently had 2 a. of arable which had been let down to pasture added to it.[45] The inclosure of the arable land called the Sands, between Woodcock and the Boreham road, which already contained some inclosed land by 1577,[46] may have been completed in the early 18th century, for some inclosure had recently taken place there in 1723.

Inclosure had at the same time been taking place at Battlesbury.[47] An inclosure at Brickhill was made by 1768.[48] In Pit Mead, Lord Weymouth's holding of 30 a. had been made several by 1711.[49] The sheep sleights on the downs were not inclosed but by the 16th century had been divided so that they were several to their owners during the winter, when each flock kept to its own down. Thus 100 a. at High Hook (now Mancombe Down) were claimed as parcel of the farm of Smallbrook in 1607; it had formerly been a rabbit warren but this had been destroyed 50 or 60 years before to protect the tenants' corn.[50]

On some holdings consolidation of the strips of open-field arable land was well advanced by the 16th century. Thus in 1577 83½ a. belonging to the demesne farm of Furnax lay in 19 pieces, including pieces of 9 a. and 8 a. and four of 6 a.[51] Mawdley's freehold virgate, on the other hand, had 28 a. in 17 pieces in 1603,[52] and the Warminster Scudamore demesne farm in 1687 had its 65½ a. of field land in 56 pieces, of which 25 were ½ a. or less. At that time one moiety of Warminster Farm had 144 a. in 19 pieces, of which 10 were 8 a. or over, and the other moiety had 143 a. in 16 pieces, one as large as 20 a.[53] At the time of inclosure many small pieces of arable land remained in the fields, and only the larger holdings had their land much consolidated. Chedlanger Field and Woodman Mead had been considerably affected by piecemeal inclosure, and so had much land near Woodcock and Heronslade. Warminster Field and Morley Field remained largely open, and some of the inclosures that did exist in them were probably still commonable, for they were ignored by the award.[54]

Little is known of the practice of agriculture in Warminster between the 16th century and inclosure, although there is little doubt that it was generally very similar to that of the chalk country of south Wiltshire.[55] It is clear that all the arable land did not follow the two-field course; the 'hockefelde' in which corn was grown in 1574 was probably a part of the fallow field put aside for a second crop, but the significance of fields called the Heath Common on which corn was also grown at that time is not known.[56] After the parliamentary inclosure of the common fields and downs, much of the Longleat estate property was consolidated into several large farms. Thus in the mid-19th century Parsonage Farm consisted of 939 a. to which 288 a. of Portway Farm were added in 1858, when the rent was increased to £1,065. At the same time Bugley Farm consisted of the old farm of 168 a., another group of old copyholds of 75 a., and 60 a. belonging to the Luxfield Prebend.[57] On

[29] Longleat MS. 10652.
[30] C.C.C. MSS. K.a.1; King's School, Bruton MSS. B.IV.3.
[31] C.C.C. MSS. K.b.3.
[32] S.C. 6/Hen. VIII/3918.
[33] Longleat MS. 9488.
[34] B.M. Add. Ch. 26696, 26699.
[35] W.R.O. 490 Hungerford Cart. f. 119v.
[36] S.C. 6/1061/24.
[37] See p. 105–06.
[38] W.R.O. 442/1.
[39] C.C.C. MSS. K.b.3.
[40] Longleat MSS. 11260.
[41] S.C. 6/1145/12 m. 3.
[42] Longleat MSS. 9228 and Parcel XXVII, Audley to Thynne, 1606.

[43] Ibid. 9340.
[44] W.R.O. 130, Lease by Edw. Scutt 24 June 1609.
[45] C.C.C. MSS. K.b.3.
[46] Ibid.
[47] Bristol Univ. Hodge (Baker) MSS. 76/44–46.
[48] W.R.O. 130, Weymouth to Larkham, 1768.
[49] Longleat MSS. Parcel XXI, plan of Pit Mead, 1711.
[50] Ibid. Parcels XXVII–XXVIII, Papers in lawsuits about the downs.
[51] C.C.C. MSS. K.b.3.
[52] Longleat MS. 7344.
[53] Ibid. 10652
[54] Draft Inclosure Map penes Mr. H. N. Dewey.
[55] See V.C.H. Wilts. iv. 43–64.
[56] Soc. Antiq. Jackson MSS. s.v. Warminster.
[57] Longleat Estate Office, Rack Rental 1853–60.

these farms the conventional sheep and corn husbandry of south Wiltshire gave way as the century progressed before the advance of dairy farming. Thirteen cows imported from the Channel Islands were sold in the market in 1855.[58] By 1905 there were almost 4,000 a. of permanent pasture in the parish compared with about 1,600 a. of arable land.[59]

Market gardening had probably begun in Warminster by 1671, when the vicar complained that he was deprived of the tithes of 'great parcels of ground' occupied by gardeners.[60] In the 18th century many gardeners occupied small holdings which belonged to the Longleat estate.[61] Most of them lay west of Warminster near the Common. Arthur Young remarked on the extent of the business in 1796,[62] and it continued during the 19th century. There was a public house called the 'Gardeners' Arms' at the Common, and in the 1850's Warminster onions were well known at Bath.[63] In 1867 there were 18 market gardeners, almost all at Warminster Common.[64] The firm of T. H. Harraway and Son, nurserymen in Sambourne Road, was founded in 1876; in 1963 it occupied some 20 a. of land for the production of rose and fruit trees, hedging plants, and cut flowers, and had a shop in the Market Place.[65]

The agriculture of the manor of Boreham was separately organized from that of Warminster, and it had its own common fields. These must have been on the greensand levels between Boreham and Battlesbury as far as the high downs. In the late 16th century the manor of Boreham consisted of a demesne farm containing 20 a. of meadow, 11 a. of several pasture, and 164 a. of field-land, and four small copy- and leaseholds amounting in all to about 50 a. more.[66] There was, however, a group of considerable copyholders who held their lands in Boreham directly of the lords of the capital manor.[67] Little is known about the practice of agriculture there, but it was no doubt the typical sheep and corn farming of south Wiltshire. Little inclosure had taken place before the general inclosure of the parish.[68] By that time the tithing consisted of four farms: the manor farm, the holding of the Slade family, which apparently consisted of the old tenantry land of the manor, and two farms made up of the former copyholds of the capital manor.[69] In the early 19th century

the whole came into the possession of the Temple family of Bishopstrow, and most of it was let as Boreham Farm.[70]

INDUSTRY AND TRADE. Dyers lived in Warminster in 1334[71] and 1452,[72] but little else is known of the existence of the woollen industry in the town before the 16th century.[73] John Eyre, a Warminster clothier, bought wool worth £67 from John Thynne in 1548,[74] but the taxation list of 1545 shows that he was only moderately prosperous.[75] Thomas Clevelode, described as a Warminster clothier at his death in 1558,[76] amassed a sufficient fortune to buy the estate called Kingston's.[77] In 1545 he was assessed at Longbridge Deverill,[78] where he probably occupied a mill, perhaps at Crockerton. Clothiers whom the 1576 subsidy[79] show to have been fairly prosperous included Thomas Cockell,[80] William Rawlings,[81] and Robert House.[82] The richest clothier, and indeed the richest man, in the town at that time was William Middlecott,[83] but much of his wealth must have derived from the freehold property which he had inherited from his father[84] and his leasehold estate under the manor of Furnax.[85] His family carried on business for many years from Smallbrook Mill.[86]

Our knowledge of most 17th-century Warminster clothiers is limited to their names, such as Joel Girdler (died c. 1657),[87] William Wilton (fl. 1668),[88] and William Slade (fl. 1695)[89]. In 1610 William Bailey of Boreham was able to pay £205 for the lease of some property there,[90] and in 1664 Edward Halliday, a dyer, paid £400 for a lease.[91] The one Warminster business of this period about which more than the barest facts are known was probably typical of many others. This is that of George Wansey, accounts of whose affairs from 1683 to his death in 1707 have survived.[92] Wansey made little cloth of the finest variety, so that he was able to buy much of his wool locally, occasionally mixing Spanish wool with it for his better pieces. In addition to medium-grade cloths he also made druggets in the 1690's and occasionally linsey-woolsey and serge. Most of the processes were, as usual, put out, but Wansey possessed his own dressing shop and dyehouse. The maximum capacity of his business was ten cloths a week, and he was able to spend as much as £1,400 in a single

---

[58] *Warminster Miscellany*, Aug. 1855.
[59] Statistics supplied to *V.C.H.* by Bd. of Agriculture, 1905.
[60] Sar. Dioc. R.O. Glebe Terrier, 1671.
[61] Longleat Estate Office, Survey 1743, pp. 5, 27; W.R.O. Inclosure Award.
[62] *Annals of Agriculture*, xxviii. 460.
[63] *Warminster Miscellany*, Feb., July, 1854.
[64] *P.O. Dir. Wilts.* (1867).
[65] Ex inf. T. H. Harraway and Son.
[66] W.R.O. 132, Survey of Boreham.
[67] Longleat MSS. Rental *c.* 1550 and later rentals *passim*.
[68] W.R.O. Inclosure Award
[69] Longleat Estate Office, Survey 1743, pp. 7, 9, 10, 18, 20, 55; Wilts. Cuttings, xvii. 141.
[70] W.R.O. 132, Deed Astley to Temple, 1821; see p. 103.
[71] Longleat MS. 9139.
[72] *Cal. Pat.* 1452-61, 45.
[73] See, however, *V.C.H. Wilts.* iv. 128-9, 138.
[74] Longleat MS. 323.
[75] *Taxation Lists* (W.A.S. Rec. Brch.), 35.

[76] *W.N. & Q.* iv. 231.
[77] See p. 100.
[78] *Taxation Lists* (W.A.S. Rec. Brch.), 42.
[79] Ibid. 148-9.
[80] Longleat MS. 6947; he was also described as a fuller: ibid. 6346.
[81] *Sess. Mins.* (W.A.S. Rec. Brch.), 53.
[82] Ibid. 125; 3 other members of this family, 2 fullers and a clothier, are mentioned in 1588-9: ibid. 125, 126, 128.
[83] *Taxation Lists.* (W.A.S. Rec. Brch.), 149; he was regularly described as a clothier, e.g. Hoare, *Mod. Wilts.*, Warminster, 31.
[84] See p. 99.
[85] C.C.C. MSS. K.b.3.   [86] See p. 115.
[87] P.C.C. 285 Ruthen.
[88] B.M. Add. Ch. 40122.
[89] C.10/504/210.
[90] W.R.O. 132, Staples to Bailey, 15 July 1610.
[91] Deed *penes* Mr. H. N. Dewey.
[92] J. de L. Mann, 'A Wiltshire Family of Clothiers', *Econ. Hist. R.* ix. 241-53.

year on wool. He left his widow and son a modest fortune and estate and a business which would afford them a comfortable livelihood.

George Wansey was probably typical, not only of his own generation of clothiers, but of Warminster clothiers until the final extinction of the trade there. There is no indication of large fortunes such as were made at Trowbridge and Bradford, but more of modestly prosperous family businesses which might be kept up for two or three generations. Little is known in detail of the trade, and the 18th-century clothiers of the town must be judged largely by extraneous details of their lives. Pitman Warren, for instance, lived in the elaborate house, now no. 32 Vicarage Street, which he held with a small estate in land under Lord Weymouth.[93] He also owned freehold houses in West Street,[94] and land in Morley Field.[95] He was active as a clothier from at least 1753, when £100 was paid him as a premium for an apprentice,[96] until his death in 1788.[97] His son Peter Warren succeeded him in the business for some years,[98] but when he went bankrupt in 1822 he was described as a mealman.[99] The Wansey family provided a succession of clothiers after George described above. In 1724 his son Henry Wansey received £100 with an apprentice.[1] At least two members of the family were active in 1755.[2] In 1783 George and William Wansey both lived in Church Street, George apparently in Byne House and William opposite in either No. 3. or No. 4.[3] Both these and another Henry were in business at the turn of the century.[4] When George died in 1807 he left £1,000 to endow a charity[5] and £1,000 to be laid out in improving the town.[6] Many of the family were generous in supporting the Old Meeting in the town, and seem to have been genuinely pious and cultured, and intelligent observers of local and national affairs.[7] Henry Wansey (d. 1827) retired from his clothing business to follow mainly antiquarian pursuits; he was partly responsible for the account of Warminster[8] hundred in Hoare's *Modern Wiltshire*, and also wrote on economics and travel.[8]

In considering the rapid decline of this seemingly well-established industry in the early 19th century, there are two factors which must be stressed. The first is that there are indications that Warminster clothiers did not regularly make cloth of quite the same quality as, say, those at Trowbridge and Bradford. We have seen that this was true of George Wansey in the late 17th century, and the setback in the superfine trade from 1730 to 1750, which

caused Henry Wansey embarrassment,[9] may have led to a permanent change to rather poorer quality material. At any rate, almost all the clothiers in the town in 1784 were described as 'superfine and seconds' clothiers,[10] and in the early 19th century the common opinion was that 'a bad trade reputation was the cause of its decay'.[11] A second factor was the town's poor position to take advantage of the mechanization of the industry from the late 18th century. No stream which ran through it was powerful enough to drive water-wheels, and there was no canal to bring coal. The only steam engine known to have been erected belonged to George Warren in 1806,[12] and Warminster never developed factories as the towns further north did. At most, it seems to have had only one worthy of the name, which was suspended because of the harvest when Cobbett passed through in 1826.[13] It was probably the same one which was later said to have employed 100 hands when it was working; in 1860 it was a malthouse.[14]

The course of the decline can be traced fairly accurately. In 1784 there were 13 clothiers in the town,[15] and the same number in 1798, when it was said that the trade had recently much increased, and that 100,000 yards were produced annually.[16] A list of 1801 gives the names of 17 clothiers.[17] In that year, however, riots began in the town against the introduction of machinery, particularly 'the wooden shearman'. They continued intermittently until 1803, and seem to have succeeded in their object. Because of this the Warminster cloth could not compete with that with the improved finish given by machinery; one clothier had a large quantity returned, and by 1809 several had gone out of business.[18] It was probably at this time that Edward Butler, of a family that had been in the trade for almost a century,[19] left Warminster for Stroud.[20] By 1812 there were only 9 firms in business, but some of these were very small, and none in full employment. George Wansey started in 1814,[21] but further riots occurred in 1817, following attempts to introduce the spring loom.[22] By 1822 the trade was 'hardly worthy of observation', and only three clothiers remained.[23] George Wansey closed down in 1829 'thus settling the fate of the town'.[24] In 1830, when one firm remained, producing only four yards a week, John Raxworthy, who had apparently been forced out of business, petitioned the Commons to amend the laws relating to truck payments, and blamed the decline of the trade on the improvements made in machin-

[93] W.R.O. Inclosure Award.
[94] Longleat MSS. Title Deeds, Schedule I.
[95] W.R.O. 132, Bennett's Trustees to Warren, 1769.
[96] *Wilts. Apprentices* (W.A.S. Rec. Brch.), 125.
[97] Bailey, *Brit. Dir.* (1784); Halliday, Information, f. 33.
[98] *Univ. Brit. Dir.* (1798), iv. 683; Halliday, Information, f. 15 (1801).
[99] *Lond. Gaz.* 1822, 684.
[1] *Wilts. Apprentices* (W.A.S. Rec. Brch.), 89.
[2] W.R.O. 212A, Wansey to Wansey.
[3] Ibid. Inclosure Award; Bailey, *Brit. Dir.* (1784).
[4] *Univ. Brit. Dir.* (1798), iv. 683; Halliday, Information, f. 33.
[5] See p. 135.
[6] Halliday, Information, f. 13.
[7] Wansey Papers *penes* Mr. H. N. Dewey.
[8] *D.N.B.*
[9] *V.C.H. Wilts.* iv. 162.

[10] Bailey, *Brit. Dir.* (1784); cf. the Trowbridge entry.
[11] *Warminster Miscellany*, Dec. 1860.
[12] Longleat Estate Office, Survey 1743, f. 123; the engine is mentioned because a man who was a life on a lease was killed by it.
[13] *Rural Rides*, ed. G. D. H. Cole, 396.
[14] *Warminster Miscellany*, Nov. 1860.
[15] Bailey, *Brit. Dir.* (1784).
[16] *Univ. Brit. Dir.* (1798), iv. 681–3.
[17] Halliday, Information, f. 15.
[18] *Warminster Miscellany*, Dec. 1860.
[19] *Wilts. Apprentices* (W.A.S. Rec. Brch.), 125; Longleat Estate Office, Survey 1743, p. 12.
[20] Gunn, *Nonconformity in Warminster*, 37.
[21] *Warminster Miscellany*, Dec. 1860.
[22] Ibid. Nov. 1860; Middlebrook, 'Highways and Byways', no xxvi.
[23] Pigot, *New Com. Dir.* (1822–3).
[24] *Warminster Miscellany*, Dec. 1860.

ery.[25] George Wansey must have re-started his business, for he was the only manufacturer in the town in 1842; six years later none remained.[26]

Other textile industries which have existed in Warminster can be briefly mentioned. The names of three feltmakers who were working between 1721 and 1753 are known.[27] A silk-weaver lived in the town in 1637.[28] References to the silk industry in the mid-19th century probably refer to the mill at Crockerton,[29] but in 1874 the firm which owned that mill, Charles Jupe and Sons, opened a factory at Pound Street, bringing 70 hands from Crockerton. By 1883 over 150 hands were employed,[30] but the factory no doubt closed at the same time as the other mills belonging to the firm in 1891.[31] After being empty for some years, the Pound Street factory was taken over c. 1903 by Moore and Marshall and used for the manufacture of shirts and other goods with linen brought from Ireland. This business was later acquired by Berry & Co., a London firm, and employed as many as 130 people, but it was closed at the beginning of the First World War. In 1925 the Macclesfield firm of J. & T. Brocklehurst & Sons (later Brocklehurst-Whiston Amalgamated) began silk, rayon, and woollen weaving there. The factory was enlarged in 1932, but closed at the end of 1958.[32]

Connected both with Warminster's textile industry and with its position near large tracts of downland was the trade of wool-stapling. The names of Robert and John le Wolmangere[33] indicate its existence in the 13th century. Scales and weights were provided to weigh wool at the market in 1425–6,[34] and much wool was sold in the market in the late 17th century.[35] A number of prosperous wool-staplers lived in the town from the 17th to the 19th centuries. Among them may be mentioned several members of the Wilton family, freeholders and leaseholders under the Thynnes and Corpus Christi College, who were active from the mid-18th century until the 1820's.[36]

While the cloth industry declined, the manufacture of horsehair articles enjoyed a brief prosperity in the town. J. T. Morgan was a hair-sieve manufacturer in Silver Street in 1822–3; by 1830 his business was carried on by Godfrey Morgan, and T. P. Ubsdell was in the same trade in Back Street.[37] In 1842 Morgan was described as a 'hair and silk and sieve bottom and stock manufacturer',[38] and in 1848 the making of hair-seating, sieves, and

stock-foundations was carried on in the town, the stocks giving employment to many hundred children.[39] The trade of sieve-making was also carried on by several basket-makers, among whom may be mentioned several members of the Ball family between 1822–3 and 1903.[40] There was a ropemaker in the town in the early 18th century.[41] Isaac Watts, in business in 1822–3 and 1830, and Edward Price, 1842 and 1851, were no doubt forerunners of the firm of Watts and Price, rope and sacking manufacturers, which was active in the fifties and sixties.[42]

Several small engineering businesses flourished in the 19th century. The earliest was probably that carried on in the Boreham road by Benjamin Dutch at the end of the 18th century, which survived until the 1860's, later carried on by Mary Dutch. It was then taken over by E. Collins, and finally by Hole and Roberts, iron and brass founders, wind engine manufacturers, waterworks engineers, agricultural implement makers, and cycle and motor manufacturers, who were active there in 1903.[43] The main foundry stood at the junction of Boreham Road and Smallbrook Lane; it was replaced by houses in 1886.[44] Another was founded by Hugh Carson, a Scot, in 1816, and run in the 1820's as Carson and Miller.[45] At first it was described as an iron foundry, but the making of agricultural implements had begun by 1842.[46] In 1860 the business was handed over to W. H. Carson and J. V. Toone, son and son-in-law of the founder, and was carried on until c. 1906, when W. C. Toone left the town. Gray and Turner continued it for a few years. The main premises were behind the buildings south of East Street.[47] Another firm of long standing was that of Thomas Petherbridge, who was active as a millwright and agricultural implement maker in Boreham Road between 1848 and 1890.[48] His works lay behind the Rose and Crown Inn.[49]

The only survivor of these and other firms is that of John Wallis Titt. Titt came to Warminster in 1870 as agent for Brown and May, steam engine makers of Devizes; he first set up at Portway, but by 1875 had built his own factory for agricultural implements at Woodcock. By c. 1900 the main business of the firm was in the manufacture of an advanced type of elevator invented by Titt, and in the installation of water supply fittings, especially artesian wells and wind-pumps, which were supplied to many parts of the world. Agricultural

[25] Halliday, Information, f. 15; C. J. lxxxv. 272; the firm still working was John and Joseph Gaisford, Pound St.: Pigot, Nat. Com. Dir. (1830).
[26] Pigot, Nat. Com. Dir. (1842); Hunt, Dir. (1848).
[27] Wilts. Apprentices (W.A.S. Rec. Brch.), 113, 117, 118, 121.
[28] V.C.H. Wilts. iv. 176.
[29] Hunt, Dir. (1848); Slater, Nat. & Com. Dir. (1851).
[30] U.D.C. Local Board Min. Bks.; Middlebrook, 'Highways and Byways', no. xxvi.
[31] V.C.H. Wilts. iv. 177, where n. 78 is wrong in suggesting that the Warminster and Crockerton mills were identical.
[32] Middlebrook, 'Highways and Byways', no. xxvi; V.C.H. Wilts. iv. 177; Wilts. Cuttings, xxi. 60.
[33] B.M. Add. Ch. 26702; Longleat MS. 9090.
[34] Longleat MS. 9454.
[35] Econ. Hist. R. ix. 242.
[36] Longleat MS. 10250; Bailey, Brit. Dir. (1783); Univ. Brit. Dir. (1798), iv. 683; Pigot, New Com. Dir. (1822–3); W.R.O. Inclosure Award; Wilts. Poll. Books, 1705, 1772.

[37] Pigot, New Com. Dir. (1822–3) and Nat. Com. Dir. (1830).
[38] Pigot, Nat. Com. Dir. (1842).
[39] Hunt, Dir. (1848); the stocks must be the article of clothing worn round the neck, which could be of horsehair: O.E.D.
[40] Univ. Brit. Dir. (1798), iv. 681–3, and later Dirs. passim.
[41] Wilts. Apprentices (W.A.S. Rec. Brch.), 21.
[42] Pigot, New Com. Dir. (1822–3) and later Dirs. passim.
[43] Univ. Brit. Dir. (1798), iv. 682, and later Dirs.; ex inf. Mr. H. N. Dewey.
[44] U.D.C. Local Bd. Min. Bks.
[45] Inscription on gates of Nonconformist Cemetery, Boreham Road, dated 1828.
[46] V.C.H. Wilts. iv. 194; Pigot, Nat. Com. Dir. (1842).
[47] V.C.H. Wilts. iv. 194–5, where more detail about the firm is given.
[48] Hunt, Dir. (1848) and later Dirs.
[49] O.S. Map 1/2,500 Wilts LI (1st edn.); U.D.C. Local, Board Min. Bks. s.a. 1873.

implements and water supply were still the main concerns of the firm in 1962.[50]

The firm of Hall and Churchill, wholesale ironmongers and nail manufacturers, was in business in the Market Place in 1859.[51] It is said to have succeeded an ironmonger named Reynolds who was in business c. 1830. By 1867 only the name Hall was used,[52] and the manufacture of paints was begun then or soon afterwards. New buildings were erected in Weymouth Street in 1876,[53] and the site was still used in 1962 by the firm of John Hall and Co. for the manufacture of paints, distempers, and varnishes.[54]

There were lime burners in Warminster in 1798 and 1830.[55] A limekiln existed under Arn Hill north of the Westbury road by 1840,[56] and was apparently in use for most of the remainder of the century.[57] It was out of use by 1924[58] and was afterwards replaced by the house called Southdown. Brick Hill on the Bath road was so called in the early 17th century,[59] and a brickmaker lived in the town in 1687.[60] Kirk and Daniell in 1822–3, and Harry Joy in the mid-19th century worked at the trade at Brick Hill.[61]

The gloving industry and bell-founding in Warminster are mentioned elsewhere in this history.[62]

The earliest maltster known to have worked in Warminster is Henry Garratt (fl. 1554).[63] Twenty years later it was ordered that furze was not to be cut on the common for making malt,[64] and in 1648 the malting activities of four people in the town were stopped because they had other means of support.[65] It is clear that in the later 17th century Warminster contained a number of prosperous maltsters, among them members of the families of Buckler[66] and Adlam.[67] In 1720 there were 36 malthouses in the town,[68] and in the middle of the century the malt trade there was said to be bigger than at any town in the west of England, so that Bristol and much of Somerset were largely supplied by it.[69] The sign 'Warminster Malt' could be seen on many inns in Somerset.[70] Members of some of the principal families, such as the Bucklers, Wanseys, Aldridges, and Slades were maltsters.[71] By the early 19th century the trade had somewhat declined, but was still considerable. In 1818 there were 25 malthouses,[72] and throughout the first half

of the century there were over a dozen maltsters at work in the town.[73] By 1860 there were complaints that the trade had fallen off and many malthouses had been demolished; in answer to them it was said that although the trade was in fewer hands, the malting capacity of the town had actually increased.[74]

In the second half of the century the number of firms engaged in malting declined to about half a dozen in the sixties and to two twenty years later.[75] The chief of these belonged to the Morgan family, maltsters in Silver Street as early as 1822–3.[76] W. F. Morgan succeeded his father in the business and carried it on until shortly before his death in 1907.[77] It was carried on by Dr. E. S. Beaven until his death in 1941; the firm of E. S. Beaven (Maltings) Ltd. is now a subsidiary of Messrs. Guinness. Its chief malthouses are in Pound Street and were built in 1879.[78] In addition it owns a small 'one man' malthouse in the Market Place. Dr. Beaven began a 'barley nursery' to breed and test new varieties of malting barley in 1895. Here, single-handed and at his own expense, he produced his Plumage Archer barley, which, it has been estimated, made the barley-growing land of this country produce from 15 to 20 per cent. more to the acre. After his death his work was taken over by Messrs. Guinness; their Barley Research Station in Boreham Road is on the site where Beaven's work was carried out.[79]

In the later 19th century several breweries developed from malting concerns. One of these also belonged to the Morgan family and was begun c. 1830. In the 1890's it was known as Morgan and Bladworth's Warminster Brewery, and stood north of the 'Ship and Punchbowl' in Silver Street, on the site of Obelisk Terrace.[80] The High Street Brewery of James Bartlett and Co. flourished from c. 1830 until after the First World War, when it was taken over by Usher's of Trowbridge and closed. The large brick building of 1885 was, after various uses, reconstructed as a shop and showrooms in 1956.[81] The West Street Brewery belonged to Charles Price, a member of a family which occupied the Cock Inn there from the late 18th century, while the East Street Brewery was connected with the 'Masons' Arms'; both were active in the 1880's and 1890's.[82]

---

[50] *V.C.H. Wilts.* iv. 195, where more detail about the firm is given.
[51] *P.O. Dir. Wilts.* (1859).   [52] Ibid. (1867).
[53] Local Bd. Min. Bks. s.a. 1876.
[54] Ex inf. John Hall and Co.
[55] *Univ. Brit. Dir.* (1798), iv. 682; Pigot, *Nat. Com. Dir.* (1830).
[56] W.R.O. Tithe Award.
[57] Longleat Estate Office, Rack Rental 1853–6, Occupation Book 1892.
[58] O.S. Map 1/2,500 Wilts. LI (1st edn.).
[59] *P.N. Wilts.* (E.P.N.S.), 159.
[60] Salisbury Marr. Licenses (TS. in Inst. of Hist. Research Libr.), 43.
[61] Pigot, *New Com. Dir.* (1822–3) and *Nat. Com. Dir.* (1842); Slater, *Com. Dir.* (1851).
[62] *V.C.H. Wilts.* iv. 237, 239, 253.
[63] Longleat MS. 9252.
[64] Soc. Antiq. Jackson MSS. *s.v.* Warminster.
[65] *Wilts. Q. Sess. Rec.* ed. Cunnington, 183.
[66] Longleat MSS. Parcel XX.
[67] W.R.O. 194, Hotkins to Adlam, 1671 and Adlam to Adlam, 1671 and 1681, by which Wm. Adlam obtained a freehold of over 30 a.
[68] Halliday, Information, f. 15.

[69] [S. Whatley], *England's Gazetteer*, 1751, ii.
[70] Halliday, Information, f. 15; Daniell, *Warminster*, 256.
[71] *Wilts. Apprentices* (W.A.S. Rec. Brch.), 25; Gunn, *Nonconformity in Warminster*, 18; Halliday, Information, f. 15; W.R.O. 194, Ferris to Slade, 1763; *Univ. Brit. Dir.* (1798), iv. 681–2.
[72] Halliday, Information, f. 15.
[73] Pigot, *New Com. Dir.* (1822–3) and *Nat. Com. Dir.* (1830); Hunt, *Dir.* (1848); Slater, *Nat. & Com. Dir.* (1851).
[74] *Warminster Miscellany*, Oct. 1860.
[75] *P.O.* and *Kelly's Dirs. Wilts.*
[76] Pigot, *New Com. Dir.* (1822–3).
[77] *W.A.M.* xxxv. 151.
[78] U.D.C. Local Bd. Min. Bk. See pl. facing p. 174.
[79] *The Times*, 20 Nov. 1941; ex. inf. Mr. T. Davies of the Research Station; A. D. Hall, *Pilgrimage of British Farming* (1913), 8–11.
[80] Manley, Regional Survey, iv. 195a; Pigot, Slater, *P.O.* and *Kelly's Dirs. passim*; Middlebrook, 'Highways and Byways', xxiv.
[81] *Directories, passim*; Middlebrook, 'Highways and and Byways', xix
[82] *Directories, passim.*

The importance of Warminster market must have ensured that it was a place of retail trades and services for the supply of a considerable area around it. At the end of the 18th century the town contained, beside shopkeepers like grocers, bakers, shoemakers, and drapers, specialized tradesmen such as a printer, a gunsmith, a watchmaker, and a bookbinder.[83] The quality of the work of one Warminster craftsman of the 18th century can still be seen; a monthly astronomical and equation clock made by Edward Cockey is in the British Museum, and another similar one at Longleat.[84] In 1822–3 it was said that the shops in the town were 'in general very select and attractive',[85] while the variety of services which could be obtained in the town in 1860 may be judged from the occupants of a yard near Portway, comprising a stonemason, a timber merchant, a builder, an ironfounder, a cooper, a sieve- and basket-maker, and a blacksmith.[86] The town has also been a centre for professional services. The earliest known surgeon was Robert Olden who flourished in 1620,[87] while among later ones may be mentioned several members of the Seagram family in the 18th and 19th centuries.[88] Apothecaries included Thomas Squire, whose son Samuel, born at Warminster, became Bishop of St. David's in 1761.[89] There was a veterinary surgeon in Warminster as early as 1822–3,[90] and many firms of lawyers have flourished in the town.[91] Banking had begun by 1783 when there were two houses, Horlock, Everett, Mortimer and Everett, and Kington, Bayly and Lye.[92] The former was known as the Warminster and Wilts. Bank or the Old Bank; several families held interests in it at different times, but the connexion with the Everetts was constant, and it was as Everett, Ravenhill and Co. that the firm merged with the North Wilts. Bank in 1860.[93] The second bank was called the Warminster Bank. By 1798 it belonged to George Lye,[94] who went bankrupt c. 1810; the bank was taken over by the firm of Phipps, Biggs and Bannister.[95] On the dissolution of that partnership in 1834,[96] John Bannister remained in the business alone until the 1850's.[97] Larger banking houses had come to the town by 1838 when both the North Wilts. and the Wilts. and Dorset had branches there.[98]

There was a printer in Warminster in 1798.[99]

J. L. Vardy was in the business there by 1822–3;[1] a successor, R. E. Vardy, began the first local newspaper in 1854. This was the monthly *Warminster Miscellany*, which was published until 1863. The *Warminster Herald*, begun by W. H. Tayler in 1857, ran until 1893, when it ceased because of the competition of the *Warminster and Westbury Journal*. This was founded by B. W. Coates, successor to the Vardy family in the Market Place, and was still published weekly by the firm of Coates and Parker in 1962.[2]

MILLS. Seven mills belonged to the manor of Warminster in 1086[3] but in 1300 the lord of Warminster held only one water mill in demesne, while another was held under him by a free tenant.[4] There is little doubt that the demesne mill was that at Boreham, which was held by Thomas Mauduit, lord of the manor, in the early 13th century.[5] Boreham Mill was in hand in 1385 and 1391, and still, or again, in 1409, when it was repaired, and in 1412.[6] By 1442 it was let for 66s. 8d. a year, which was reduced to 53s. 4d. in 1454–5 when the new tenant was John Bowerman.[7] It continued to be let on lives at this rent until the 18th century. Among long tenancies may be mentioned those of the Bowerman family, who still held it in 1508,[8] the Goodridge or Goodrose family between 1626 and 1682,[9] and the Marsh family, 1700–65.[10] In 1810 the mill was included in the Longleat property exchanged with F. D. Astley,[11] and remained the property of his family until 1884, when it was sold.[12] The new owners evidently rebuilt it, for the large brick mill is dated 1886. It contained a 20 h. p. turbine in 1893.[13] In 1962 it was used by Wiltshire Farmers Ltd. for grinding animal food; water power was still used.

The mill which was held as a freehold of the capital manor in 1300 may have reverted to the lord very soon afterwards, for in 1309 Thomas Mauduit let the water mill of Fishwear to Robert the Miller.[14] It was still let at farm in the late 14th century,[15] and in 1496.[16] A tenant held it at a rent of 28s. in 1578,[17] and in 1659 the same rent was paid for Henry Allen's mills.[18] By 1690, however, a close 'on which formerly stood a mill called Fisher's Mill' was let with other lands;[19] it lay on the Cannimore stream near the western end of

[83] *Univ. Brit. Dir.* (1798), iv. 681–3.
[84] A third clock of the type is believed to be in private hands in 1962: ex. inf. B. M. See also *W.N. & Q.* vi. 310, 320. Clocks by Cockey are in Old Dilton Church and Corsham Court.
[85] Pigot, *New Com. Dir.* (1822–3).
[86] *Warminster Miscellany*, Oct. 1860.
[87] *Early Stuart Tradesmen* (W.A.S. Rec. Brch.), 19.
[88] Longleat Estate Office, Survey 1743, p. 60; *Wilts. Apprentices* (W.A.S. Rec. Brch.), 9; *Directories, passim.*
[89] *Wilts. Apprentices* (W.A.S. Rec. Brch.), 86; *W.N. & Q.* ii. 397.
[90] Pigot, *New Com. Dir.* (1822–3).
[91] *Directories, passim.*
[92] Bailey, *Brit. Dir.* (1783).
[93] *Univ. Brit. Dir.* (1798), iv. 680 and later *Dirs.*; *Warminster Miscellany*, Nov. 1856, May 1860.
[94] *Univ. Brit. Dir.* (1798), iv. 680.
[95] Printed Sale Particular in Longleat Estate Office.
[96] *Lond. Gaz.* 21 Oct. 1834, p. 1897.
[97] *P.O. Dir. Wilts.* (1855).
[98] *List of Country Banks* (1838).
[99] *Univ. Brit. Dir.* (1798), iv. 683.

[1] Pigot, *New Com. Dir.* (1822–3).
[2] H. Richardson, 'Wilts. Newspapers Past and Present', *W.A.M.* xliii. 34–7.
[3] *V.C.H. Wilts.* ii, p. 116.
[4] *Wilts. Inq. p.m.* 1242–1326 (Index Libr.), 249–53.
[5] Longleat MS. 8987.
[6] Ibid. 9062, 9421, and Parcel XXVII, Acct. Rolls 1385–6 and 1390–1.
[7] Ibid. Parcel XXVII, Acct. Rolls 1441–2 and 1454–5.
[8] Ibid. Rental 1508.
[9] Ibid. Rental 1626 and MS. 10652.
[10] Ibid. MSS. 10211, 10274, 11254.
[11] W.R.O. 132, Bath to Astley, 1810, and see above, p. 103.
[12] Bishopstrow Parish Records, Eastleigh Estate Sale Catalogue.
[13] U.D.C. Mins. of Sewage Cttee. 1893–8.
[14] Longleat MSS. Parcel XXVIII, Lease.
[15] Ibid. Parcel XXVII, Acct. Rolls 1379–80, 1385–6, 1390–1.
[16] Ibid. MS. 9040.
[17] Ibid. Rental 1578.
[18] Ibid. Parcel XXVII, Rental 1659.
[19] Longleat Estate Office, Survey 1743, p. 42.

Warminster Common, between the roads leading to Folly Farm and Cannimore Farm,[20] where a weir still remains in 1962.

No mill belonging to the manor of Smallbrook was mentioned in 1086,[21] but there was one in 1268.[22] In 1366 John Mauger paid a rent for Smallbrook Mill to the manor of Upton Scudamore,[23] and the mill and land immediately around it may already have lain in Upton parish, as it did in the 18th and 19th centuries.[24] It was probably the mill which belonged to the manor of Warminster Scudamore in 1444–5,[25] but nothing more is certainly known of it until the end of the 15th century, when it was appurtenant to the manor of Portway.[26] It passed in the same way as that manor[27] to the Middlecott family, for in 1582 William Middlecott paid the chief rent of 1s. 6d. for it to the manor of Warminster Scudamore.[28] After his death his son Edward sold the mill in 1602 to William Adlam,[29] although it was held on lease by members of the Middlecott family for many years afterwards.[30] In 1650 this or another William Adlam sold it to John Bennett, lord of the manor of Smallbrook, and it descended in his family as the manor did.[31] By 1837, however, the chief rent was paid by John Webb.[32] Before 1849 it had passed to the Astley family, and was sold with the rest of their estate in 1884.[33] Smallbrook Mill seems always to have been a corn mill.[34] It was still so used in the late 19th century, but in c. 1900 it was converted to pump sewage to the Warminster sewage works nearby.[35] After the abandonment of the sewage works the mill was partly demolished, but part of the 19th-century brick building remained in 1962.

The mill at Henford's Marsh lay in a detached part of Norton Bavant, and is dealt with in the account of that parish.[36]

MARKET AND FAIRS. There was a market in Warminster in the time of Thomas Mauduit, lord of the manor c. 1204–44.[37] In the middle of the 13th century the toll of it belonged to his son William Mauduit,[38] and stalls and shops in it were the subject of conveyances before 1300.[39] The toll of the market and fair of St. Laurence was said to be worth only 15s. a year in 1300,[40] but was valued at 100s. in 1327.[41] In 1322 the toll of the market for about six weeks was 32s.[42] In 1348–9, perhaps a bad year, the markets and fairs together produced almost £8. In 1379–80 the market alone

produced over £18 and fines paid for stalls another £4, and in 1385–6 the profits of the market were almost £20. In the 15th century profits were accounted for in 'home' and 'foreign' boxes; perhaps traders from the town paid at a different rate from those from outside. Together they amounted to between £8 and £10 in 1443–4, 1454–5 and 1455–6, but were under £6 in 1462–3.[43]

From the 16th century the tolls of the market and the profits of the stalls and shambles in the Market Place were let with the bailiwick of the town.[44] In 1711, however, the tolls alone were let at rack for £100 a year, reduced to £82 in 1737. The other profits of the bailiwick were added to this lease in 1758,[45] and let at rack until 1802. When the market rights were in hand between 1802 and 1805 the profits amounted to over £100 a year, of which the largest part was toll on corn, and the remainder profits of stalls and pig pens.[46] The whole was re-let at rack rent in 1806, and remained so until 1856 when the toll of corn was taken into hand on the building of the new corn market.[47] This toll was still in hand and collected in kind in the late 19th century, and the rest of the market profits were let at £25 a year.[48] In 1904 the Urban District Council became lessee of the whole of the tolls and in 1920 purchased them of the Marquess of Bath for £1,600.[49]

Tolls of corn and other produce sold in front of a certain house in the Market Place had in 1801 been taken from time immemorial by the lessee of the house, which was held on a 1,000-year lease. In that year they were given up to the Marquess of Bath in return for the reversion of another house.[50] It is possible that the right of taking them originated in a mid-13th century grant of a house in Warminster quit of tolls at markets and fairs.[51]

The market was held on Saturday in the 17th century,[52] and that continued to be the day of the corn market as long as it was held. Although cattle were sold at the Saturday market in 1887, a separate monthly cattle market was held by 1903, and Monday has been the cattle market day since then; sales have been sometimes weekly and sometimes less often.[53]

In the 16th century Leland mentioned Warminster as a great corn market.[54] Its fame was probably well-established by his time, for there can be little doubt that the large tolls collected in the 14th and 15th centuries came from the sale of

[20] W.R.O. Inclosure Award.
[21] V.C.H. Wilts. ii, p. 167.
[22] J.I. 1/998 m. 7.
[23] S.C. 6/1061/9.
[24] See p. 79.
[25] S.C. 6/1119/11.
[26] C.P. 25(1)/257/66/25, 27; C 1/411/26.
[27] See p. 99.
[28] W.R.O. 442/1.
[29] C.P. (25)2/242/44 Eliz. I East.
[30] C 6/154/113.
[31] Bristol Univ. Hodge (Baker) MSS. 76/105; see above, p. 103.
[32] Longleat Estate Office, Rental 1837.
[33] W.R.O. 160 a, Astley Settlement, 1849; Bishopstrow Parish Records, Eastleigh Estate Sale Catalogue.
[34] C 6/154/113; W.R.O. 442/1, Newspaper cutting stuck to f. 56 v.
[35] U.D.C. Min. Bks.
[36] See p. 55.
[37] Longleat MS. 8966.   [38] B.M. Add. Ch. 26695.

[39] Longleat MSS. 8976, 9101.
[40] Wilts. Inq. p.m. 1242–1326 (Index Libr.), 252.
[41] Halstead, Succint Genealogies, 141.
[42] S.C. 6/1145/12 m. 3.
[43] Longleat MSS. 9455–6 and Acct. Rolls in Parcel XXVII.
[44] Ibid. Parcel XXVIII, Lease Brown to Stote, 1573, and later leases of the bailiwick passim; see below, p. 129.
[45] Longleat Estate Office, Survey 1743, pp. 123–4.
[46] Longleat MSS. Manor Bk. 1801–8.
[47] Longleat Estate Office, Rack Rental 1853–60.
[48] Royal Com. on Market Rights, vol. xiii, pt. 2 [C. 6268–vi A], pp. 544–51, H.C. (1890–1), xl.
[49] Wilts. Cuttings, xvi. 141.
[50] W.R.O. 144, Morgan to Bath, 1801.
[51] B.M. Add. Ch. 26695.
[52] Daniell, Warminster, 128.
[53] Kelly's Dir. Wilts. (1903 and later edns.); Royal Com. on Market Rights, vol. xiii, pt. 2, pp. 544–51; Manley, Regional Survey, iv. 230, 562.
[54] Leland, Itin. ed. Toulmin Smith, v. 83.

corn.[55] In the late 16th century the quantity brought to the market was 'scarce credible',[56] and in Aubrey's time it was held to be much the greatest corn market in the west of England. He was told that 12 or 14 score loads were brought there on market days, but that it had declined somewhat, owing, it was said, to the growth of the market at Bristol, where farmers from Gloucestershire took samples in bags.[57] In contrast, Warminster remained a 'pitched' market, in which one sack from every load was pitched in the street, a practice which still prevailed in the 19th century.[58] In spite of the loss of the Bristol trade, however, the market still flourished, and was noted by Celia Fiennes in the late 17th century,[59] and by Richard Pococke in 1754.[60] About 60 maltsters attended to buy barley in 1757,[61] and in 1798 the corn market was said to be the largest at an inland town in England.[62] In 1805 the toll amounted to 478 bushels, mainly wheat and barley; if, as seems likely, the rate was the same as in Daniell's day, 2 quarts out of each sack pitched, over 7,500 sacks were pitched in a year, which gives an average of over 150 loads brought to market each week throughout the year.[63] Warminster was the only market in the county from which weekly returns of sales of corn had to be made under the Importation of Corn Act of 1828.[64] Between that year and 1835 the quantities sold varied between 58,000 and 76,500 quarters a year; the largest turnover in money was £184,000 in 1831.[65] In the 1830's Warminster was second only to Bristol among corn markets in the west of England, and was particularly notable for the quantities of barley sold.[66] From 1829 to 1841 between 25,000 and 30,000 quarters of wheat were generally sold yearly, and the figures for barley would certainly be rather higher.[67] Even in 1831, however, trade was beginning to decline because of the lack of a canal to the town, and it was thought that Devizes market promised to rival Warminster within a few years.[68] Sales of corn at the two towns bear out the accuracy of this forecast,[69] but in the next decade Warminster market increased again and 'far exceeded' other markets in the county; this was said to be due to the coming of the railway.[70]

In spite of this the inhabitants of the town and those frequenting the market complained in 1854 to the Marquess of Bath that railways made or projected would put Warminster into competition with Devizes, Melksham, Chippenham, and Salisbury, and that they all had excellent market houses.[71] The building of the Market House in 1855[72] helped the market in its recovery, and in the early 1860's the quantities sold at Warminster were no smaller than they had been 30 years before,[73] and the average turnover was still £10,000 a week.[74] About this time Scott and Smith, the largest corn-factors in the town, built new corn stores near the station.[75] In 1871, however, the railway was blamed for diverting traffic from the market, and many sack carriers and others had left the town.[76] Weekly sales often fell to only a few quarters,[77] and in 1894 the corn market was almost dead.[78] It finally ceased to be held after the council had taken over the tolls.[79]

Besides corn, the market was used for the supply of the town with butcher's meat and vegetables. In Cobbett's time the town was well-known for fine meat.[80] Pigs were sold in the early 19th century[81] but in the 1850's, although cattle were sold occasionally, attempts to hold regular cheese, wool, cattle, and poultry markets failed.[82] By 1887 regular livestock markets were held on Saturdays.[83] By the turn of the century they were replaced or supplemented by monthly sales of cattle held on Mondays, and Monday has been Warminster's regular market day, either weekly or fortnightly, since the Saturday corn market ended. After a busy period between the World Wars the sales of cattle declined again, and in 1962 the frequency of the market had again to be reduced to once a fortnight.[84]

Until the 19th century Warminster market was held in the open Market Place; the arcades which several of the inns had for the protection of dealers have been mentioned above.[85] The only other facilities were the stalls which since the late Middle Ages had clustered around and under the Town Hall.[86] There, too, were butchers' shambles,[87] while pigs were sold in front of the site later occupied by the London Inn, now the way into Common Close.[88] When the Town Hall was demolished in 1832, new shambles and a pig market were provided behind it; the shambles still stood, derelict, in 1962. The provision of a building for the corn market was undertaken by Lord Bath in 1855. It was designed by T. H. Wyatt[89] in the form of a four-sided piazza supported by cast-iron arcades and opening upon a central court-yard. After it ceased to be used it was roofed over and was in

[55] See above, and compare Trowbridge market: *V.C.H. Wilts.* vii. 143.
[56] Camden, *Britannia* (1695), 90.
[57] Daniell, *Warminster*, 128–9.
[58] *App. Rep. Sel. Cttee. on Sale of Corn*, H.C. 517, p. 23 (1834), vii; *Warminster Miscellany*, Oct. 1856.
[59] *Journeys of Celia Fiennes*, ed. Morris, 8.
[60] *Travels of Richard Pococke vol. ii* (Camden Soc. 2nd ser. xliii), 38.
[61] *W.N. & Q.* ii. 20.
[62] *Univ. Brit. Dir.* (1798), iv. 679.
[63] Longleat MSS. Manor Bk. 1801–8.
[64] 9 Geo. IV, c. 60, s. 8, which listed 150 principal markets in England and Wales.
[65] Halliday, Information, f. 11.
[66] *Lond. Gaz. passim.*
[67] *Rep. Sel. Cttee. on Agric.* H.C. 79, p. 216 (1836), viii, pt. i; *Weekly Ave. Price of Wheat*, H.C. 78, p. 10f. (1842), xl.
[68] Lewis, *Topog. Dict. Eng.* (1831), iv. 391; Halliday, Information, f. 10.   [69] *Lond. Gaz. passim.*
[70] *Warminster Miscellany*, Feb. 1854, Nov. 1856.

[71] Ibid. June 1854.
[72] Ibid. Dec. 1855.
[73] *Lond. Gaz. passim.*
[74] Wilts. Cuttings xvi. 137.
[75] Longleat Estate Office, Survey 1837, p. 150.
[76] *V.C.H. Wilts.* iv. 325.
[77] *Warminster Herald, passim.*
[78] J.J. Hissey, *Through Ten English Counties* (1894), 132.
[79] Manley, Regional Survey, iv. 230.
[80] *Rural Rides*, ed. Cole, 399.
[81] Longleat MSS. Manor Bk. 1801–8.
[82] *Warminster Miscellany*, Sept. 1854, Aug., Nov. 1855, Dec. 1859, Oct. 1860.
[83] *Royal Com. on Market Rights*, vol. xiii, p. 544.
[84] *Kelly's Dir. Wilts.* (1903 and later edns.); *Wilts. Times*, 8 July 1960, 23 Febr., 9 March 1962.
[85] See p. 93.
[86] e.g. Longleat MSS. 9455 (1454–5), 10238 (1737), and see p. 129.
[87] Longleat Estate Office, Survey 1743, pp. 4, 54.
[88] Halliday, Information, f. 107.
[89] *Warminster Miscellany*, Sept. 1854, Dec. 1855.

1962 used as a garage and two lock-up shops.

A yearly fair on the vigil, day, and morrow of the feast of St. Laurence (9–11 August) was granted to William Mauduit, lord of Warminster, in 1253,[90] and a second fair, lasting from 22 to 29 October to Henry Greene in 1447.[91] Thomas Thynne obtained a grant of a third fair, from 10 to 12 April, in 1679.[92] All three fairs were still held in 1770, when the dates were given as 11 April, 10 August, and 28 October.[93] By the end of the 18th century the date of the first fair was 22 April.[94] All three fairs survived into the 20th century,[95] and the April and October fairs were still held in 1961.[96] The August fair was called Hang Fair in the 19th century because of some executions which took place on Sutton Common on that day in 1783.[97]

The tolls of the fairs belonged to the lords of the capital manor. In the 14th and 15th centuries they generally yielded between 30s. and 50s. a year.[98] They were subsequently let with the bailiwick in the same way as the market. When the office was in hand in the early 19th century only the October fair was of much value, yielding as much as £22 in 1805.[99]

In 1770 the fairs were for cattle, sheep, pigs, and cheese.[1] Of these, sheep were apparantly sold only at the October fair,[2] which from at least the early 19th century was the principal one of the three.[3] In the 1820's as many as 20,000 sheep had changed hands at it,[4] and large quantities of cattle were sold.[5] This fair continued to be important throughout the century, between 10,000 and 20,000 sheep being regularly sold.[6] The April fair also remained a business fair, but by c. 1880 the August one was given over entirely to amusements.[7] It fell out of use soon after that time, but in 1963 the April and October fairs were still held in the Market Place, mainly for pleasure.[8]

The April and August fairs were regularly held in the street, but in the 18th century the sheep fair in October had long been held in a paddock called Carrion Close, lying immediately north of Portway House.[9] After the inclosure of the parish in the 1780's a more convenient place was found in a field belonging to Warminster Farm just north of Chain Street (now George Street), and Carrion Close and the old hurdle house in the Common Close were let.[10] By 1839 this field had been abandoned in favour of one in Beastleaze opposite the end of North Row.[11] Finally in 1856 a field near

the station was chosen;[12] after the Urban District Council had acquired the tolls of the market it was asphalted and made into the present market yard.[13]

CHURCHES. The name Warminster first occurs in the early 10th century, when the church on the Were from which it is derived must already have existed.[14] It was no doubt one of those minster churches, often found on royal manors in Saxon times, which had the rule of a large area of surrounding country before many villages had churches of their own.[15] The only medieval church known to have been dependent on it is that of Corsley, which was regarded as a chapel to Warminster until the 15th century.[16] The former chantry chapel of St. Laurence in the centre of the town has been used as a chapel-of-ease to the parish church by permission of its feoffees since the 16th century.[17] In the 19th century a new church and parish of Christ Church were founded on the south of the town, and St. John's, Boreham Road, was built as a chapel-of-ease to the parish church. St. John's was separated from it in 1957 and is now held with Bishopstrow.[18]

The early history of the advowson of Warminster is one of dispute between the lords of the capital manor of Warminster and those of the manor of Furnax about which manor the church belonged to. The lords of Furnax claimed that it had been given by Henry I to Robert de Pirou, the original grantee of the manor.[19] His descendant Ralph Fitz William gave it *in prebendam* to Reynold Fitz Jocelin, Bishop of Bath and Wells, whose episcopate began in 1174, and Richard I confirmed the gift in 1189.[20] The church was reckoned part of the possessions of Wells in 1190,[21] and Richard I's charter was again confirmed between then and 1197. A dispute between the bishop and the incumbent of the church was settled by a quitclaim of the latter's right to the church of Wells.[22] The earliest evidence of opposition to the lords of Furnax disposing of the church is a plea between William Revell and the guardians of Thomas Mauduit, begun in 1194 and still undecided in 1199.[23] By 1199 Henry de Furneaux was associated with Revell in the case, and since they both claimed in right of their wives, it is clear that they were the husbands of two of the coheirs of Robert FitzWilliam, lord of Furnax.[24] The cause was left

[90] *Cal. Pat.* 1247–58, 252.
[91] *Cal. Chart. R.* 1427–1516, 85.
[92] *Cal. S. P. Dom.* 1678, 116; C 66/3205 no. 15.
[93] *Ogilby and Morgan's Book of the Roads* (1770), 294.
[94] *Univ. Brit. Dir.* (1798), iv. 679.
[95] *Kelly's Dir. Wilts.* (1939).
[96] *Wilts. Times,* 10 Jan. 1961.
[97] Halliday, Information, f. 9.
[98] Longleat MSS. 9455–7 and Parcel XXVII, Acct. Rolls.
[99] Ibid. Manor Bk. 1801–8.
[1] *Ogilby and Morgan's Book of the Roads,* 294.
[2] Longleat MSS. Manor Bk. 1801–8.
[3] Pigot, *New Com. Dir.* (1822–3); Halliday, Information, f. 9;
[4] Hoare, *Mod. Wilts.* Warminster, 13.
[5] Halliday, Information, f. 9
[6] *Warminster Miscellany* and *Warminster Herald, passim.*
[7] Ibid.
[8] *Wilts. Times,* 3 Aug. 1962.
[9] Longleat MS. 10238; Longleat Estate Office, Survey

1743, p. 103; W.R.O. Inclosure Award. Woodmead Home for old people was built on the Close, 1961–2.
[10] Longleat Estate Office, Survey 1743, p. 103.
[11] Ibid. Survey 1837, pp. 67, 129; ibid. Rack Rental 1838–44.
[12] Ibid. Rack Rental 1853–60.
[13] Manley, Regional Survey, iv. 562.
[14] *P.N. Wilts.* (E.P.N.S.), 157.
[15] Stenton, *Anglo-Saxon England,* 148.
[16] See p. 21.
[17] See p. 123.
[18] See pp 10–11.
[19] Hist. MSS. Com. *Wells,* i. 58; see above, p. 100.
[20] *Archaeologia,* l. 356–9; but cf. Hist. MSS. Com. *Wells,* i. 59, where a William Fitz Reynold is mentioned as patron.
[21] Hist. MSS. Com. *Wells,* i. 435–6.
[22] Ibid. 58.
[23] *Abbrev. Plac.* (Rec. Com.), 6; *Rot. Cur. Reg.* (Rec. Com.), i. 63, ii. 54.
[24] See p. 101.

undecided at this time, apparently because of the minority of Thomas Mauduit,[25] but the right of presentation was again in dispute between the lords of the two manors in 1217. Then, however, Nicholas Avenel, lord of Furnax, disputed the Bishop of Bath and Wells's right to present, whereas Thomas Mauduit supported it.[26] An agreement which partially settled the dispute was made in 1235, when Richard Poore, Bishop of Durham, acted as arbitrator. The Bishop of Bath and Wells abandoned any claim to the church in return for the endowment of a prebend in his cathedral worth 30 marks issuing from land and tithes in Warminster and Corsley.[27] The question of the ownership of the advowson was left vague by this agreement. It was again the subject of litigation in 1243, when a jury said that the church had been included in the capital manor when it was given by Henry II to Robert Mauduit;[28] after that time the claim of the Mauduits was not disputed.

About twelve or fifteen years after this William Mauduit gave the advowson of Warminster to the Dean and Chapter of Salisbury.[29] This grant included the rectory, for in 1259 the chapter granted the patronage of the church to the Bishop of Salisbury, who in return appropriated the rectory to the chapter.[30] The rectory was charged with yearly obits for the then bishop, Giles of Bridport, and his predecessor, William of York; the charge still remained in the 16th century.[31] From 1259 until the present time (1962) the patronage of the vicarage of Warminster has been regularly exercised by the bishops of Salisbury.[32]

The rectory of Warminster was valued at £23 6s. 8d. in 1291.[33] In 1341 it was apparently let at farm[34] and in 1580 it was said that the lessees of the rectory had been making certain underleases for at least a century.[35] The first surviving lease of the whole rectory, however, is of 1523 to Thomas Benett, Vicar of Warminster, at a rent of £33 6s. 8d.[36] The clear value of this rent to the chapter was £28 15s., the rest going in alms and the maintenance of the obits charged on the rectory.[37] Benett's lease evidently passed to his brother William Benett of Norton Bavant, who left it to his younger son John.[38] He sold his interest in the rectory to William Perry and others before his death in c. 1566; they sub- let the tithes of Boreham and Smallbrook separately for the proportionate rent of £13 13s. 4d. to the chapter.[39] The next

lessee was William Blacker of Salisbury, whose lease in reversion of the previous one was granted in 1565 at the same rent.[40] It was probably after the termination of this estate that, in 1641, the first of a long series of leases to the Young family of Little Durnford was made. In 1655 parcels of the rectory were sold to Henry Wansey of Salisbury.[41] After the Restoration the leases to the Youngs were renewed, at the same rent of £33 6s. 8d., until 1783. Four years later the trustees of T. W. Young, the last of the line, sold the lease of the rectory to Lord Weymouth for £6,664.[42] In 1808 the rectory was reckoned worth about £670 a year.[43] Leases were renewed to the Marquesses of Bath until 1868, when the reversion of most of the land, and all the tithes, belonging to the rectory was conveyed (with the prebend of Luxfield) to the 4th Marquess. In return Lord Bath surrendered his interest in the remainder of the land and conveyed his freehold estate in the rectory of Imber to the Ecclesiastical Commissioners.[44]

The tithes of corn, hay, and mills were kept in hand by the Rector of Warminster when he instituted a vicar to the church c. 1250.[45] In 1341 the tithes of hay were worth £9 5s. and of mills 30s. 4d.[46] In 1649 the whole of the rectorial tithe was worth about £250 a year.[47] When Warminster was inclosed in 1784 most of the tithes were commuted either for allotments of land or for a fixed rent charge. Beside allotments, the lessee under the chapter received at the inclosure a rent charge of £36 3s. 4½d. and the still-uncommuted great tithes of 200 a., which in 1808 were let at £27 a year.[48] These remaining tithes were commuted in 1840 for £28.[49] The lessee also had the tithes of 76 a. of land in Upton Scudamore, which were commuted for £20.[50] All three rent-charges were conveyed to the Marquess of Bath with the chapter estate in 1868. The tithes of certain lands in Warminster belonged to the Prebendary of Luxfield and their history is dealt with above.[51]

William Mauduit's original gift to the chapter included 4 a. of his demesne land.[52] This was probably an addition to land already belonging to the church, for in 1341 the rectory estate included 40 a. of land, and meadow and pasture worth 30s., in demesne, beside other property producing 33s. 4d. in rent.[53] A small piece of land in Boreham was added to the chapter estate in 1392.[54] In 1649, however, the rectorial glebe only amounted to 25½ a.[55] At the inclosure in 1784 the chapter was

[25] Cur. Reg. R. i. 42.
[26] Bracton's Note Bk. ed. Maitland, iii. 330.
[27] Hist. MSS. Com. Wells, i. 365–6. For the prebend, see above, p. 21.
[28] K.B. 26/128 rot. 11.
[29] Sar. Chart. and Doc. (Rolls Ser.), 329–30.
[30] Ibid. 330–1.
[31] Valor Eccl. (Rec. Com.), ii. 78.
[32] Phillipps, Wilts. Inst. passim.
[33] Tax. Eccl. (Rec. Com.), 194.
[34] Inq. Non. (Rec. Com.), 170; at least part of the estate was at farm in 1313: Longleat MS. 8989.
[35] C 2/Eliz. I M. 5/23.
[36] Ch. Com. 136777, f. 138.
[37] Valor Eccl. (Rec. Com.), ii. 78.
[38] W.N. & Q. vi. 135; W.R.O. 413, Will of Wm. Benett.
[39] C 2/Eliz. I M. 5/23; C 3/21/10; C 3/137/17; C 3/179/57; Req. 2/62/10.
[40] Ch. Com. 67388.

[41] C 54/3886 no. 14.
[42] Ch. Com. 67390–5; Longleat MSS. Abstract of title of T. W. Young; for the family, see Hoare, Mod. Wilts. Amesbury, 125.
[43] Ch. Com. 66630.   [44] Ibid. 125663–5.
[45] Sar. Chart. & Doc. (Rolls Ser.), 319.
[46] Inq. Non. (Rec. Com.), 170.
[47] W.A.M. xli. 116–8.
[48] Ch. Com. 66630.
[49] W.R.O. Tithe Award.
[50] Ibid. Upton Scudamore Tithe Award.
[51] See p. 21.
[52] Sar. Chart. & Doc. (Rolls Ser.), 329. A previous gift to Warminster church of land at Bapton is recorded (see above, p. 40), but nothing is known of this.
[53] Inq. Non. (Rec. Com.), 170.
[54] Cal. Pat. 1391–6, 97.
[55] W.A.M. xli. 116–8; a largely illegible terrier of the 17th cent. in Sar. Dioc. R.O. mentions 18a. of arable land, and so must refer to the rectory.

allotted 19 a. in lieu of the open-field glebe in addition to 6½ a. of old inclosures. In lieu of tithes commuted by allotments of land it received over 600 a. more,[56] making a farm estimated to be worth £606 a year in 1808.[57] All but 71 a. of this land was sold to Lord Bath in 1868; the remainder has been sold in the present century.[58]

No formal ordination of a vicarage in Warminster has survived, although c. 1250 the rector endowed an individual vicar with the small tithes,[59] and in 1259 the endowment of a competent vicarage was specified when the rectory was granted to the chapter.[60] The vicarage was valued at £5 a year in 1291,[61] at £18 clear in 1535,[62] and at £50 in 1649.[63] An augmentation of £50, later reduced to £20, was allowed by the Commonwealth authorities, and a further £22, payable out of the rectory, in 1656.[64] These must have ceased at the Restoration. In 1665 the incumbent derived £89 from the living,[65] and in 1745 it was said to be worth £80 a year.[66] The vicarial tithes were largely commuted for land at the inclosure, and it may have been this that raised the value of the benefice to a net figure of £324 in 1831, of which half was paid to a curate.[67] An endowment of glebe in 1850 (see below) helped to bring the value up to £450 a year in 1864,[68] and in 1865 a further £120 a year was allotted from the common fund.[69]

Little is known about the small tithes with which the vicarage was endowed until 1671. They then consisted of the usual small tithes with the tithes of 16 coppices in Norridge Wood and of 100 sheep from Seaman's Farm in Upton Scudamore, because part of its sheep pasture lay in Warminster. The impropriator took, unjustly as the vicar believed, the tithes of 'great parcels' of ground occupied by gardeners and of grounds summerfed with unprofitable cattle.[70] At about this time the tithes were taken largely by composition.[71] In 1784 the vicar's tithes were commuted in the same way as the impropriator's, leaving him, beside allotments of land, the small tithes of 200 a. and a rent-charge of £22 6s. 4d.[72] In 1840 the remaining tithes were commuted for a rent charge of £40.[73]

In the mid-13th century the vicar's glebe only consisted of the house and small meadows adjoining it.[74] It was probably the same as the 1 a. of glebe about the house mentioned in 17th and 18th century-terriers.[75] At the inclosure in 1784, however, the vicar was allotted some 20 a. of old in-

closed land and 99 a. of commonable land in lieu of the small tithes. A piece of about 10 a. was sold, so that he retained 109 a.[76] An endowment of about 14 a. was made by the Ecclesiastical Commissioners in 1850,[77] and another small addition was made in 1869.[78] In 1887 the glebe was worth £403 a year.[79] In 1919 117 a. of the vicarial glebe was offered for sale; the 102 a. sold realized £4,760.[80]

An annual payment of a *pondus* of cheese or 10s. was reserved by the rector when he gave the vicarage to Stephen the chaplain c. 1250.[81] The vicars still paid 10s. to the dean and chapter in the 19th century, when the memory of its origin remained.[82] The history of the 26s. 8d. paid yearly by the rectors of Corsley to the vicars of Warminster is dealt with above.[83]

There is no record of the endowment of any permanent chantry in the church. In 1388 Thomas Laffull's feoffees regranted his lands in Warminster to him charged with 5s. a year to provide two torches on Good Friday,[84] and in 1493 John Hewett, parson of Winterbourne Monkton (Dors.), charged a cottage in 'Newport Street' and 8 a. of land with the provision of a 2 lb. taper on festival days before the altar of Our Lady and a yearly distribution of 2s. to poor men.[85] In the same year John Chaffyn of Salisbury charged property in Warminster with the provision of paschal and font tapers as his ancestors had provided them, and to found an obit for himself. The poor were to receive 20d. yearly and the residue of the profit was to go to the church funds.[86] Other lights were endowed at unknown dates by Richard Fytor, John Shepherd, and Ellen Hildewe.[87] The property supporting these lights seems to have become part of the property of St. Laurence's Chapel.[88]

William Benett, Vicar of Warminster, was deprived in 1554, no doubt for his Protestant sympathies.[89] In 1556 two parishioners were alleged to have sold the church goods and kept the money.[90] Benett was restored at the beginning of Elizabeth I's reign,[91] no doubt on the deprivation of Peter Weaver who had replaced him. He held the Prebend of Warminster, and may not have served the vicarage himself, for the burial of a parish curate is recorded in 1564.[92] His successor, Lewis Evans, may have been the man of that name who, having been formerly a staunch Romanist, and written a book against heretics, later became a violent partisan and prolific controversialist in favour of the

[56] W.R.O. Inclosure Award.
[57] Ch. Com. 66630.
[58] W.A.S. Libr. Devizes, Sale Cat.
[59] *Sar. Chart. & Doc.* (Rolls Ser.), 319.
[60] Ibid. 332.
[61] *Tax. Eccl.* (Rec. Com.), 194.
[62] *Valor Eccl.* (Rec. Com.), ii. 103.
[63] *W.A.M.* xli. 116–8.
[64] *Cal. S.P. Dom.* 1656–7, 198.
[65] Halliday, Information, ff. 86–7.
[66] *Clergyman's Intelligencer* (1745), 181.
[67] *Rep. Com. Eccl. Revenues*, H.C. 54, pp. 852–3 (1835), xxii.
[68] Sar. Dioc. R.O. Vis. Queries, 1864.
[69] *Lond. Gaz.* 1865, pp. 570, 3883.
[70] Sar. Dioc. R.O. Glebe Terrier, 1671.
[71] Daniell, *Warminster*, 172–3.
[72] W.R.O. Inclosure Award.
[73] Ibid. Tithe Award.
[74] *Sar. Chart. & Doc.* (Rolls Ser.), 319.
[75] Sar. Dioc. R.O. Glebe Terriers, 1609, 1671, 1705, 1783.

[76] W.R.O. Inclosure Award; U.D.C. Map of Vicarial Glebe, 1835.
[77] *Lond. Gaz.* 1850, p. 865.
[78] *Lond. Gaz.* 1869, p. 2014.
[79] *Retn. of Glebe*, H.C. 307, p. 167 (1887), lxiv, where the area is wrongly given as 228 a.
[80] W.A.S. Libr. Devizes, Sale Particular.
[81] *Sar. Chart. & Doc.* (Rolls Ser.), 319.
[82] Ch. Com. 66630; Daniell, *Warminster*, 151–2.
[83] See p. 21.
[84] B.M. Add. Ch. 40046.
[85] W.R.O. 61, Hewett to Gylwhyte; it is not clear whether this foundation is distinct from that mentioned by Hoare, *Mod. Wilts.* Warminster, 35 (erroneously dated 5 Hen. VI) and Daniell, *Warminster*, 155.
[86] *W.A.M.* xlix. 452
[87] E 301/58 no. 131; Daniell, *Warminster*, 154–5.
[88] See p. 122.   [89] Phillipps, *Wilts. Inst.* i. 216.
[90] Sar. Dioc. R.O. Ep. Vis. 1556.
[91] *V.C.H. Wilts.* iii. 33.
[92] *Fasti Eccl. Sar.* ed. Jones, ii. 428; Daniell, *Warminster*, 170.

Anglican church.[93] In 1585 it was alleged that he had churched harlots and let them go unpunished, and did not say service in the appointed place.[94] Nothing more is known of the views of the vicars or their conduct of their cure until 1642, when William Maxwell, the then vicar, was among 17 men appointed by the Commons to preach at Warminster.[95] This official approval may have been given because he agreed with the Presbyterianism of some of the others then named,[96] but by 1646 he had been sequestered by the County Committee. One Webb then obtained the support of a company of factious men and women in the town, who hoped to have him admitted in spite of his not being a minister because he had the spirit and the word was revealed to him.[97] He failed in this and William Woodward was appointed by the Committee of Plundered Ministers in 1647.[98] Woodward's presence evidently caused violent controversy among his parishioners; some objected to his doctrine and his being a pluralist, but others, led by Francis Bennett of Smallbrook, wished for his continuance.[99] He was still at Warminster in 1649, but at least two others held the living between then and 1660.[1]

Paul Latham, who was admitted in 1660, was presented in the following year for not reading Common Prayer according to law.[2] He was author of a theological work and a preacher of considerable note.[3] Both he and his successor Edward Chubb, were canons of Salisbury,[4] and Chubb held the living of Brixton Deverill in plurality from 1710,[5] but both appear to have resided regularly at Warminster. Chubb was succeeded in both livings by James Legertwood, who is said to have been the first master of Lord Weymouth's school.[6] The next vicar, John Rogers, employed a number of curates; among them was Richard Hart, curate 1753–8, described as an earnest preacher of evangelical truth, whose sympathy with Methodism earned him some persecution. His preaching converted John Pearce of Meeting House Lane, who held Sunday evening service in his house, supported by a few members of the established church, for nearly 50 years; they were for much of that time the only services held in the town at that hour.[7]

Millington Massey (later Massey-Jackson) held the living of Kingston Deverill in plurality,[8] and although he lived in the vicarage at Warminster, seems to have performed few of his duties personally. The preaching of Dacre Youngson, curate under him, attracted such overflowing congregations

that a public meeting was called to propose the enlargement of the church.[9] After Youngson's early death in 1783, William Elliott became curate. In his time services were held in the parish church twice on Sundays, each with a sermon, and on Wednesdays and Fridays and holidays in St. Laurence's Chapel. The sacrament was administered at the three major festivals and once a month besides, and between 40 and 50 people usually received it.[10] A third curate under Massey was Robert Herbert, who for over 40 years did nearly all the duties of the parish for £80 a year, and spent a 'handsome' fortune on relieving the poor.[11] William Dalby, vicar 1825–41, was an active preacher who began to hold services at the workhouse on Sunday evenings for the people of Warminster Common, and a weekday evening service with sermon at St. Laurence's Chapel.[12] He was instrumental in building Christ Church in the face of considerable opposition from the vestry.[13] His successor, Arthur Fane, was talented and zealous, and made great efforts to reduce dissent.[14] Among his activities were the foundation of the Reformatory School,[15] and preaching to the navvies employed on the railway works.[16]

Outstanding among 19th-century vicars was Sir James Erasmus Philipps, Bt., who held the living from 1859 to 1897. Apart from founding St. Boniface's College and St. Denys's Home,[17] he was instrumental in the rebuilding of the parish church and the foundation of St. John's Church and schools, the cottage hospital, the orphanages of pity, and a school for girls. The cost of these projects was well over £30,000, most of which he raised himself. In doctrine he was a high-churchman[18] and met with some opposition, especially for his practices at St. John's.[19] Early in his incumbency services had been increased to three each Sunday at the parish church and one at St. Laurence's, each with sermon, and one daily at one of these churches in the week. An average of 1,400 people attended the Sunday evening service. Holy Communion was administered each Sunday, and about 400 parishioners received it. Four curates assisted Philipps in 1864,[20] and three in 1896.[21] By 1903 communion was celebrated at St. Laurence's Chapel each Thursday and on saints' days.[22]

Late in Philipps's incumbency began a series of lawsuits which attained some national celebrity as the Warminster Pew Case. From the 17th century it had been the custom for the churchwardens to grant space in the church on which pews could be

[93] Daniell, *Warminster*, 170; the identification is not certain: Wood, *Athenae Oxon*. ed. Bliss, i. 411.
[94] Sar. Dioc. R.O. Ep. Vis. 1585.
[95] *C.J.* ii. 559.
[96] *W.A.M.* xxxiv. 175f.
[97] *Walker Revised*, ed. Matthews, 377; Hist. MSS. Com. *Var. Coll.* i. 111.
[98] *Walker Revised*, ed. Matthews, 300, 377.
[99] *Humble Petition of Well-Affected Inhabitants of Warminster* (1648) (Wilts. Tracts lii).
[1] W. A. Shaw, *Hist. Eng. Ch.* 1640–60, ii. 597; Hist. MSS. Com. *Var. Coll.* i. 137.
[2] Hist. MSS. Com. *Var. Coll.* i. 138.
[3] Daniell, *Warminster*, 171.
[4] *Fasti Eccl. Sar.* ed. Jones, ii. 358, 428.
[5] Phillipps, *Wilts. Inst.* ii. 50.
[6] Daniell, *Warminster*, 171.
[7] Halliday, Information, ff. 38, 69 and inserted memoir of J. Draper; W. Daniell, *Warminster Common*, 18.
[8] Phillipps, *Wilts. Inst.* ii. 85, 106.

[9] Halliday, Information, inserted memoir of J. Draper; Daniell, *Warminster*, 171–2, 191; Venn. *Alumni Cantab.* 2nd. ser. vi. 626; at the meeting the vicar was advised to preach more often to do away with the necessity of enlargement.
[10] Sar. Dioc. R.O. Vis. Queries, 1783.
[11] W. Daniell, *Warminster Common*, 20.
[12] Ibid. 120–2; *Endowed Char. Wilts.* (1908), p. 748.
[13] W. Daniell, *Warminster Common*, 132–3, 157–9.
[14] Ibid. 256–7, 282.
[15] H. R. Whytehead, *Minster and Ch. Life in Warminster*, 17.
[16] *Warminster Miscellany*, Aug. 1854.
[17] See p. 133.
[18] *W.A.M.* xxxvii. 463–4; *The Times*, 22 Feb. 1912; *V.C.H. Wilts.* iii. 67–8.
[19] e.g. *Warminster Herald*, 18 Jan. 1868.
[20] Sar. Dioc. R.O. Vis. Queries, 1864.
[21] *Crockford*, 1896.
[22] *Endowed Char. Wilts.* (1908), p. 765.

erected, which could then be the subject of lease, conveyance, or bequest by the families which occupied them. This kind of traffic, not unique to Warminster, seems to have reached here an uncommon intensity, perhaps because of the limited church accommodation.[23] In the late 18th century the vestry tried to limit the tenure of pews to leasehold for 3 lives, but in the 1830's 4 pews were regarded as freehold, belonging to the manor houses of Portway, Smallbrook, and Boreham, and to the house in East Street formerly belonging to the manor of Warminster Scudamore, but held since the 17th century by the Halliday family.[24] It was the Halliday pew which caused the trouble. At the restoration of the church Philipps had it removed; J. E. Halliday, who was a dissenter, began an action against the vicar for the pew to be replaced, which he won in the House of Lords in 1891. The pew was not put back in the church until 1897, when some friends of Halliday wished to attend a service. Halliday was very unpopular in the town, and the pew was soon removed from the church by night, smashed and partially burnt. It was, however, roughly repaired and put back under police escort, fixed to the floor by a blacksmith, and it remained on its site in the south chancel aisle until after its owner's death in 1913, when it was finally surrendered.[25]

The church of *ST. DENYS* stands at the north-western extremity of the town, about ½ mile from the Market Place. The dedication is mentioned in the 12th century.[26] The present church was almost entirely rebuilt in 1887–9. The oldest work which survived in the old building was a small window, thought to be of the 11th century, which was found blocked in the east wall of the south transept.[27] The church was apparently largely remodelled or rebuilt in the 14th century, as a cruciform building with central tower and nave of four bays.[28] Provision was made for an octagonal spire, but there is no evidence that it was ever built. Aisles which extended the whole length of both sides of the nave and were as wide as the length of the transepts were also either included in the original plan, or added before the end of the Middle Ages. In the late 15th or earlier 16th century an aisle was added to the south of the chancel, to which it was connected by two arches, while another panelled arch was made into the south transept. Square-headed transomed windows in the transepts and similar smaller ones in the nave aisles probably dated from about the same time. A south porch was also added. Another addition was probably the turret rising from the rood-loft openings in the east wall of the north transept nearly to the top of the tower; the stairway in it then joins one in the diagonal turret at the north-east corner of the tower, but

the reason for this awkward arrangement is not clear.

In 1583 the chancel was out of repair,[29] and by 1626 the whole building was in decay; the church 'weeps many a fresh tear for her decayed house, especially when the wind is in the west', wrote the vicar. Extensive repairs were made in 1626–9, and in 1638 the tower was repaired. In 1650 the building was again 'mightily in decay', so that the people dared not assemble there.[30] A gallery was built under the tower in 1660 and, probably at this time, a plaster ceiling in the form of vaulting was made under it. In 1723–4 the arcade of the nave and the clerestory were demolished and rebuilt. The clerestory was given four round-headed Georgian windows on each side, and the walls of the aisles were raised and small circular windows inserted above the old ones to light the galleries. In 1745 the galleries were extended to the whole length of the aisles of the nave, and a gallery was made in the south aisle of the chancel in 1813. In 1745 a Grecian altar piece was erected by subscription; its 'beautification' in 1760 involved the blocking-up of the east window.[31]

The building which was the result of these, and many other, minor alterations was sufficiently in accord with contemporary taste to receive at least conventional approval. In 1798 it was described as handsome, and the 'praise-worthy exertions' of the inhabitants in enriching its interior were commended,[32] and in 1831 it was 'handsome and spacious'.[33] Six years later, however, a visitor complained of the disparity of the styles of architecture in the church, and of the interior being crowded with pews.[34] Some improvements in the interior were made. In 1846 the reading-desk was re-sited and the pulpit altered, and two years later new stalls were fitted in the chancel; in 1852 the whole church was re-seated. The east window was reopened in 1842,[35] but little could be done to make the exterior of the building conform with newer ideas of ecclesiastical architecture, and Daniell, who had been curate there, considered that it was probably the ugliest church in the diocese. It was largely rebuilt by Sir Arthur Blomfield in 1887–9; the central tower, the south aisle of the chancel, inner parts of the transepts, the south aisle wall, and the south porch were kept from the old church, and the nave was extended to the west and a porch added there.[36] Blomfield's work is in his favourite Perpendicular style. Many monuments dating from the 17th to the 19th centuries were retained from the old church.[37]

There was an organ in the church in 1630; in 1639 the angel on top of it was newly gilded, but in 1643 the pipes had to be hidden to escape destruction by soldiers.[38] The organ loft was repaired in 1676,

[23] Daniell, *Warminster*, 187–8.
[24] Halliday, Information, ff. 37, 40A.
[25] Wilts. Cuttings xvi. 136, 140–1; Report on the trial *penes* Mr. H. N. Dewey; Char. Com. File 92130.
[26] Hist. MSS. Com. *Wells*, 1. 59.
[27] *W.A.M.* xxvii. 197.
[28] The following account of the church before 1889 is based largely on Daniell, *Warminster*, 152f.; also consulted were *W.A.M.* xvii. 347–8; ibid. xlii. 302; Hoare, *Mod. Wilts.* Warminster, 15–16; prints in W.A.S. Libr. Devizes, and in the church.
[29] Sar. Dioc. R.O. Ep. Vis. 1585.
[30] Hist. MSS. Com. *Var. Coll.* i. 122.

[31] Dates given in Halliday, Information, f. 40.
[32] *Univ. Brit. Dir.* (1798), iv. 680.
[33] Lewis, *Topog. Dict. Eng.* (1831), iv. 390.
[34] Notes by Sir S. Glynne, *W.A.M.* xlii. 302.
[35] The altarpiece of 1745 was given in 1845 for the chapel of Salisbury Infirmary, where it still remains in 1962: Daniell, *Warminster*, 189.
[36] *W.A.M.* xxxiii. 350; Wilts. Cuttings. xvi. 136.
[37] M.I.'s printed in Daniell, *Warminster*, 190–203; many churchyard M.I.'s are in *Rambles in and Round Warminster* (1883) (copy in Wilts. Tracts xc).
[38] Daniell, *Warminster*, 158–9, 165–6, on which this account is based.

but the organ was out of repair in 1683,[39] and it may have been at this time that it was replaced by 'an orchestra of wind and other musical mechanisms'. An organ gallery was built in 1770, perhaps to house a new instrument. In 1792, however, the parish raised 400 guineas to buy an organ which had been built for Salisbury Cathedral by G.P. England, a celebrated organ builder of London, but had proved of insufficient power.[40] This organ was repaired and modernized *c.* 1903,[41] and in 1962 was still in use. There was a choir in the church in 1770.[42] In 1820 Elizabeth Townsend left £3 a year to be distributed to the vicar, organist, clerk, and a choir of ten voices, on condition that they should sing on the Sunday before Midsummer Day an anthem on the 150th psalm which had been composed by Roger Townsend of Warminster (d. 1730), her husband's grandfather. The choir had 'fallen to decay' by 1832 and been replaced by the charity children, who were not competent to sing the anthem, so it was discontinued and the endowment added to the other charity founded by Mrs. Townsend.[43] The anthem was sung in 1871 with the music altered.[44]

There were five bells and a sanctus bell in the church in 1553. Two of these bells survived until the 19th century, the old 3rd and 5th of the peal of six, which remained until 1881; one had an inscription naming it Giles, and the other, cast in London *c.* 1410, was called Gabriel. The remainder were variously recast in the 17th and 18th centuries by the Lotts of Warminster and other founders.[45] In 1879 the peal had not been used for many years; it contained two medieval bells, both cracked, three 18th-century bells, one of them broken, and one bell of 1805. All except the last were recast in 1881, and two new bells, given by G. J. Vicary, added to the peal.

In 1553 Warminster parish had the second largest quantity of plate in the county; 60 oz. were taken and a cup of 12½ oz. left. This chalice or its Elizabethan successor was probably replaced by the one of 1682, still remaining in 1962. Another was obtained in 1750, which also survives. The two patens are of 1706, the gift of Edward Chubb, Vicar of Warminster, and 1761. Two alms-plates, dated 1766 and 1789, were remade into alms bowls in 1844. A silver flagon is hall-marked 1710.[46] The parish registers begin in 1558 and are complete.

There was a chapel of St. Laurence in the Market Place of Warminster in the first half of the 13th century.[47] It was traditionally said to have been endowed by two maiden sisters called Hewett, and members of a family of that name may have been benefactors in the 14th century.[48] John Langton, parochial chaplain of Warminster in the mid-14th century, was apparently connected with the chapel,[49] and there was certainly a chaplain of St. Laurence in 1500.[50] By the middle of the 16th century two houses and about 30 a. of land had been given for the support of the priest of St. Laurence. In addition several other small properties and rents, which had been given for the maintenance of lights and obits in the parish church,[51] had been converted to the support of the chapel. Because of its convenient position in the heart of the town, the inhabitants met the remaining charges out of their own purses. At the dissolution of chantries they endeavoured to have the chapel continued because of this,[52] and also petitioned for the continuance of a school which the priest had been teaching.[53] In spite of this the foundation was dissolved, and in 1550 the chapel and priest's chamber were granted to Richard Roberts of London, the Crown reserving the bells and lead.[54] Roberts immediately sold them to John Hartgill of Kilmington, and they passed from him to John Eyre of Warminster and thence to John Warder of Warminster in 1562.[55]

The inhabitants of the town had apparently intended to re-establish some foundation such as the chapel as early as 1570, for then Thomas Hewett of Erlestoke conveyed to four feoffees the freehold of a cottage and 8 a. in Warminster, which had been charged with a payment to a light in the parish church before the Dissolution. In 1574 they bought the chapel from Thomas Warder of Trowbridge, son of the last purchaser, and by 1592 had acquired a small meadow, a curtilage, and a cottage in Boreham.[56] The purpose of the foundation was said to be for the repair of the chapel and the parish church, the relief of the poor and the maintenance of a school,[57] but there is no evidence that any of these objects except the maintenance of the chapel has ever been provided for. This was indeed said to be the principal object of the foundation, and in the early 17th century prayers were said there three times a week and there was a sermon on most Saturdays.[58] In the reign of James I a chancery suit alleging misappropriation of the property was brought against the feoffees by some of the other inhabitants, who claimed that no payments to the poor or the parish church were made.[59] The next appointment of new feoffees, in 1651, limited their obligation to keeping the chapel,

[39] Sar. Dioc. R.O. Chwdns.' Pres. 1683.
[40] *D.N.B.*
[41] Wilts. Cuttings, xvi. 29.
[42] Daniell, *Warminster*, 187.
[43] *Endowed Char. Wilts.* (1908), p. 739; Hoare, *Mod. Wilts.* Warminster, 16–17; see below, p. 135.
[44] *Rambles in and round Warminster* (Wilts. Tracts xc), 12.
[45] Full details of the various recastings are given in Daniell, *Warminster*, 159–61 and Walters, *Wilts. Bells*, 226–7, on which this paragraph is based; see also Soc. Antiq. Jackson MSS.
[46] Daniell, *Warminster*, 156–7; Nightingale, *Wilts. Plate*, 97–8.
[47] Longleat MS. 8966, a deed of Thos. Mauduit fl. *c.* 1204–*c.* 1244.
[48] Hoare, *Mod. Wilts.* Warminster, 29, 34–6; Daniell, *Warminster*, 206–7; it is not possible to detect any particular benefaction from surviving deeds, and the

tradition that they were benefactors may only have arisen because the later feoffees had from 1570 an estate which had belonged to them, and acquired some earlier deeds with it.
[49] B.M. Add. Ch. 26712; Hoare, op. cit. 34.
[50] S.C. 6/Hen. VII/958.
[51] For these, see p. 119.
[52] E 301/58 no. 131.
[53] *W.A.M.* x. 314.
[54] *Cal. Pat.* 1549–51, 5; Hoare, *Mod. Wilts.* Warminster, 30.
[55] C 54/616 no. 41; Hoare, op. cit. 30.
[56] Hoare, op. cit. 31–33; the acquisition of Hewett's property may have been a coincidence or a further benefaction by the family. The feoffees did not regain any of the chantry property.
[57] C 2/Jas. I/W. 24/22.
[58] Daniell, *Warminster*, 216.
[59] Ibid. 216–20; C 2/Jas. I/W.24/22.

bell, and clock in repair and causing the bell to be rung at 8 p.m. each day for a curfew and at 9 a.m. on Sundays to call the people to the parish church.[60] A further bell at 4 a.m. each day was ordered in 1694, and continued to be rung until c. 1800;[61] the evening bell is still rung. Successive groups of feoffees have allowed the chapel to be used by the vicars of Warminster, without stipend but at no cost, both for various services[62] and for baptisms. The estate was little altered except for changes brought about by the inclosure, until the early part of the present century, when it was sold and the proceeds invested.[63] In the 19th century three bequests of money were made to the feoffees, by W. F. Seagram (£100 in 1865), Susannah Seagram (£500 in 1872), and Charles Bleeck (£100 in 1878). In 1903 the income from these sums was about £15, and from the property £37.[64] In 1950 the income of the feoffees from stock was about £80 a year.[65]

The chapel of *ST. LAURENCE* consists of a nave and an eastern tower with a spirelet at one corner. Although a chapel on the site existed in the 13th century, the present one contains little medieval work owing to successive rebuildings and repairs. Some building is thought to have been done in the reign of Henry VII, and the lower stage of the tower appears to be of that time.[66] The upper stage of the tower was rebuilt in 1642, and in 1725 the nave also, in 'a miserable bastard Grecian . . . with four round-headed windows, and lofty and unsightly pews'. The architect was William Leigh.[67] Further piecemeal repairs and alterations followed; in 1829 the spirelet was rebuilt and the interior redecorated and reseated,[68] but by the middle of the century the chapel was again in a bad state. It was restored in 1855–6 by the efforts of Arthur Fane, the then vicar. A new roof with parapet was added to the nave and battlements to the tower, and the windows were remade in the Decorated style. At the same time six houses, which had been built on the old graveyard between the chapel and the High Street as early as 1651,[69] were demolished. In 1897 the spirelet was damaged by lightning and rebuilt.[70]

There was one bell in the chapel in the 16th century, called the town bell, which, having been retained by the Crown when the chapel was sold, was discovered under a patent for concealed lands and sold by the patentee to Thomas Warder in 1574.[71] From him it passed with the chapel to the feoffees. It was recast by John Lott, the Warminster founder, in 1657; many people threw silver coins

into the metal, which was said to account for its silvery tone.[72] There was a clock in the tower in 1651; a later one bore the inscription 'God made Cockey and Cockey made me 1723'.[73] A new one made by Thomas Rudd was placed there in 1765,[74] and was restored in 1949.[75] The quarter bells were cast by Thomas Rudhall of Gloucester.[76] A set of altar plate bought in 1856, proved to be of base metal and unsatisfactory, and in 1879 a set which belonged to the vicar personally was in use at the chapel.[77]

Informal services, sanctioned by the church authorities but apparently conducted by laymen, were begun in houses at Warminster Common in the late 18th century. In 1826 the vicar, William Dalby, began to hold services for the people of the Common at the workhouse there, preaching to crowded congregations in spite of miserable accommodation. He conceived the idea of building a church there after the erection of the Methodist chapel in 1827, and displayed much energy in advancing the scheme. A public meeting held to sponsor it decided, in opposition to his wishes, that it should be at Sambourne.[78] Over £2,800 was raised by subscription,[79] and most of the rest of the cost was met by a grant of £1,676 by the Church Building Commissioners.[80] The church was called Christ Church and consecrated in 1831. It remained at first a chapel-of-ease to the parish church, although a perpetual curate was appointed from the beginning. In 1838 a district including the Common, Boreham, and part of the town was assigned to the church.[81] By subsequent Acts of Parliament it has become an ecclesiastical parish and the incumbent is styled a vicar. The advowson has remained with the Vicar of Warminster.[82] The benefice had an income of £100 at its foundation,[83] probably derived from pew-rents, offerings, and an allotment from the vicarial tithe. It was endowed with several sums through Queen Anne's Bounty between 1832 and 1840, owing much to the generosity of H. Walsh, the first curate,[84] and in 1841 with £21 a year from the common fund of the Ecclesiastical Commissioners.[85] In 1864 the income was £150,[86] to which £120 was added in the same year.[87] By 1879 it had risen to £300 a year gross. In 1920 William Hickman, a former vicar, left over £4,000 in further augmentation.[88]

CHRIST CHURCH occupies a dominant position at the top of the hill at Sambourne at the junction of Weymouth Street and Sambourne Road. The building of 1830–1, to the design of

[60] *Endowed Char. Wilts.* (1908), p. 745.
[61] Daniell, *Warminster*, 221.
[62] See p. 117.
[63] Char. Com. Corr. File and Accts. File G 36.
[64] *Endowed Char. Wilts.* (1908), pp. 764–5.
[65] *Wilts. Times*, 7 Jan. 1950.
[66] Daniell, *Warminster*, 225–8, on which this paragraph is chiefly based.
[67] H. M. Colvin, *Biog. Dict. Eng. Architects*, 361.
[68] *Endowed Char. Wilts.* (1908), p. 748.
[69] Daniell, *Warminster*, 221.
[70] *Endowed Char. Wilts.* (1908), p. 765.
[71] Hoare *Mod. Wilts.* Warminster 31–33.
[72] Daniell, *Warminster* 226; Walters (*Wilts. Bells*, 229) contradicts Daniell's assertion that it was again recast in 1783.
[73] Halliday, Information, f. 62.

[74] Daniell, op. cit. 220, 226.
[75] *Wilts. Times*, 7 Jan. 1950.
[76] Walters, *Wilts. Bells*, 229.
[77] Daniell, *Warminster*, 228.
[78] W. Daniell, *Warminster Common*, 120, 132–3, 157–9.
[79] Daniell, *Warminster* 229–34, on which the account of Christ Church is based unless otherwise stated.
[80] M. H. Port, *Six Hundred New Churches*, 164–5.
[81] *Lond. Gaz.* 1838, p. 2956.
[82] *Crockford* (1955–6).
[83] *Rep. Com. Eccl. Revenues*, H.C. 54, pp. 852–3 (1835), xxii.
[84] Hodgson, *Queen Anne's Bounty* (1845), pp. ccxxii, ccxxvii, cccxxxv. [85] *Lond. Gaz.* 1841, p. 2590.
[86] Sar. Dioc. R.O. Vis. Queries, 1864.
[87] *Lond. Gaz.* 1864, p. 4213.
[88] Char. Com. File 100110.

John Leachman,[89] consisted only of a nave and western tower with prominent pinnacles, in a simple 'Early English' style. The accommodation, augmented by a western gallery, was for over 800. Later in the century great efforts were made to transform the building from 'a huge, naked, oblong hall to the uses and character of an English church'. In 1871 a chancel was added by T. H. Wyatt, and stained glass was inserted both in the chancel windows and in those in the nave, where stone tracery was added. Carved oak doors and a pavement of encaustic tiles also helped to improve the building.[90] Ten years later slender arcades were built to divide the body of the church into nave and aisles, an open timbered roof replaced the old plaster ceiling, and the gallery was removed. It was probably at the same time that the western entrance was remodelled by building small porches flanking the tower to replace the former entrance under it. Rose windows at the west end also probably date from this second renovation, for which the architect was Mr. Vialls of London.[91]

An organ was provided in 1843, and replaced by the present one when the chancel was built in 1871. The peal of eight tubular bells dates from 1888.[92] The communion plate was partly given by the first curate.

By the 1860's there was great need to relieve again the strain on the accommodation provided by the parish church and to get rid of some of the galleries which crowded it. The foundation of a chapel-of-ease on the Boreham road owed much to the generosity of William Temple of Bishopstrow, who gave the land for it and started the building fund with £500. More than one set of plans were produced for his approval by G. E. Street, who was 'so much in fashion all over the country, with low as well as high, that it would be easier to get £2,000 for a church designed by him than £1,000 for a church designed by an inferior or less known architect'.[93] In the end designs for both a round tower with steeple and a square tower were rejected, and the present building, dedicated to *ST. JOHN*, erected. It consists of a nave with north aisle, chancel also with north aisle to contain the organ and a vestry, south porch, and bell-cote with one bell at the east end. The apsidal western baptistry was added after the First World War at the cost of Mrs. F. M. Rule, formerly Miss Temple. The whole church is in the Early English style. The interior is remarkable for a series of illustrations of scriptural scenes on the walls, designed by C. E. Ponting, and carried out in *opus sectile* by J. Powell of Whitefriars in the years before the First World War.[94]

Stock worth £100 to begin a repair fund was bought by subscription at the foundation of the church. Since then St. John's has received various bequests, some considerable, to provide for repairs and the payment of a curate and to keep the churchyard in repair.[95] In 1930 Mrs. F. M. Rule gave a house in Boreham Road to house the curate; it was sold when St. John's Church was united to the parish church of Bishopstrow in 1957.[96]

There was a chapel of St. Nicholas in the manor house of Warminster in the earlier 13th century. Thomas Mauduit (fl. c. 1204–44) endowed the chaplain serving it with a virgate of land which had formerly belonged to Roger his clerk, certain rents and pasture rights, and 6 cartloads of wood yearly.[97] At another time when granting the chapel to a priest he gave certain other lands, and granted him maintenance at his table.[98] One of the rents which supported the chaplain was later exchanged for another.[99] In 1269 a chaplain was appointed.[1] In the early 14th century the incumbent was called rector,[2] and the chapel the free chapel of St. Mary and St. Nicholas.[3] In 1400 Ralph Greene, the lord of the manor, let 'the chantry of Warminster', with the lands which had lately been held by chaplain, to a layman.[4] This probably marked the end of the use of the chapel for worship.

ROMAN CATHOLICISM.

ROMAN CATHOLICISM. One papist, an apothecary, lived in Warminster in 1783.[5] No permanent mass centre was founded in the town until 1922 when the church of St. George was built on Boreham Road.[6] This was then served from Frome for some years.[7] In 1938 a presbytery was added to the church.[8]

PROTESTANT NONCONFORMITY.

PROTESTANT NONCONFORMITY. In 1642 a woman was presented for disturbing the minister of Warminster in church and holding conventicles at the house of Elizabeth Cripps.[9] The group of people who were opposed to the preaching of the vicar in 1648[10] probably included many of the early supporters of nonconformity in the town. William Gough, a puritan who was afterwards ejected from a living in Berkshire, was preaching and keeping a school in Warminster before 1653.[11] In 1659 the vicar complained that over 300 parishioners refused to pay him his dues.[12] There is thus considerable evidence for sectarian activity in the town before the Restoration. In 1662 64 people were presented for not coming to church but going elsewhere to hear other preachers; they included members of the families of Wansey, Wilton, and Buckler, all of considerable wealth.[13] In 1669 a congregation of 200–300 men and women, rich and poor, was meeting at St. Laurence's Chapel and at William Buckler's house. They were described as Presby-

[89] Port, *Six Hundred New Churches*, 164–5.
[90] Daniell, *Warminster*, 232.
[91] *Rambles in and round Warminster* (Wilts. Tracts xc), 99.
[92] *Wilts. Times*, 23 May 1888.
[93] W.R.O. 132, papers connected with the building; the opinion of Street is in a letter from the Vicar of Upton Scudamore.
[94] H. R. Whytehead, *Minster and Ch. Life in Warminster*, 35.
[95] *Endowed Char. Wilts.* (1908), pp. 772–3; Char. Com Files 50660, 104273, 112918, 132042, and Accts. File G 36.
[96] Char. Com. File 112918.

[97] Longleat MS. 8972.
[98] Ibid. 8968.
[99] Ibid. 8974.
[1] Ibid. 8971.   [2] Ibid. 8992, 9000, 9135.
[3] Soc. Antiq. Jackson MSS.
[4] Longleat MS. 9024.
[5] Sar. Dioc. R.O. Vis. Queries, 1783.
[6] *Kelly's Dir. Wilts.* (1939).
[7] *V.C.H. Wilts.* iii. 97.
[8] *Kelly's Dir. Wilts.* (1939).
[9] Hist. MSS. Com. *Var. Coll.* i. 108.
[10] See p. 120.
[11] *Calamy Revised*, ed. A. G. Matthews, 230.
[12] Hist. MSS. Com. *Var. Coll.* i. 137.

terians, Anabaptists, and Independents 'promiscuously'. Their teachers were six ejected ministers, all of whom lived at a distance, one as far away as London.[14] In 1672 another ejected minister, Robert Bartlet, who was a Presbyterian, was licensed to preach at Buckler's house.[15] Two years later the churchwardens presented two Anabaptists and two Quakers by name, and 'great multitudes' more, for frequenting conventicles.[16] In 1675 there were 56 nonconformists in the town compared with 544 churchgoers.[17] Of these nonconformists of the earlier part of Charles II's reign, the largest group appears to have been the Independents and Presbyterians, who were clearly the forerunners of the Old Meeting. No early congregation of Baptists formed in Warminster, and Baptists from the town went to Crockerton to worship.[18]

For some years after the first period of indulgence in the 1670's the history of the group which had met at William Buckler's house is obscure. John Buckler was probably preaching in the town before 1687, and was imprisoned for being unlicensed in 1690.[19] Nonconformists were clearly numerous and influential in and around the town in 1683,[20] but during the period of persecution it seems most likely that Horningsham was to Warminster what Southwick was to Trowbridge[21]—a meeting place near enough to reach but distant enough to discourage interference. In 1719 there had been until lately several Warminster families who 'always belonged to Dr. Cotton's church at Horningsham, and used to be ranked with the disaffected here'.[22] At the second Declaration of Indulgence in 1687, a congregation began to meet openly in the town, and from then the continuous history of what was generally called the Old Meeting can be traced.[23]

In 1687 the group fitted up temporary accommodation in a barn in Beastleys Meadow belonging to Edward Middlecott of Portway. Compton South, who had been living at Donhead St. Mary since his ejection from Berwick St. John in 1662, was invited to take half the services, and did so, although still living at Donhead, until his death in 1705. On other Sundays the pulpit was taken by a variety of preachers who included John Buckler and Rowland Cotton, minister of the Independent church at Horningsham, and William Dangerfield, minister of the Presbyterian congregation at Bradford-on-Avon.[24] In 1691 a plain meeting house was built not far from the barn, in what was later known as Meeting House Lane, now North Row. In 1704 some adjoining land was bought and the meeting house demolished and rebuilt so that it could seat 500 people.[25] The names of those who subscribed to the cost and bought pews in the new

building are eloquent of the social standing and wealth of the congregation. They included Edward Middlecott, lord of the manor of Portway and probably the richest man in the town; William Temple, lord of the manor of Bishopstrow; the heads of the land-owning families of Halliday, Buckler, Bayly, and Langley, and the clothing families of Slade, Warren, and Wansey; and a number of prosperous tradesmen. The new building was opened by Cotton Mather, an eminent divine from Boston, New England, who was apparently a relative of Rowland Cotton.[26] After Compton South's death in 1705, Samuel Bates was appointed as resident and full-time minister. His doctrine soon caused a schism in the meeting; a minority of his hearers suspected him of Arianism, and seceded to form the New Meeting whose history is traced below. In 1719 a defence of Bates's position which exonerated him from the charge was subscribed by 44 members of his congregation; it shows that it was little impaired in wealth or influence, for most of the principal families remained, including the Middlecotts and the Temples. Four years previously the congregation was reckoned at 800, including 4 members whose estates totalled together £90,000, and 20 voters for the county.[27]

After the secession the Old Meeting was usually described as Presbyterian.[28] Bates's long pastorate, from 1706 to 1761, was afterwards peaceful, and most of the important families remained faithful. Bates lived for many years with the Middlecott family at Portway House,[29] and received £40 a year from the congregation. The cause declined greatly in the time of his successor, William Lush, whose sermons were critical dissertations on the accurate meaning of a sentence of scripture which the poor could not understand, and which were made duller by the extreme slowness of their delivery. Nathaniel Andrews, 1782–94, was a more lively preacher, who began a Sunday School in 1785. Some difficulty was experienced in finding 'a minister of free sentiments' to replace Andrews.[30] Thomas Tremlett, who was eventually appointed, began to preach the Unitarian doctrine which had forced him to leave Oxford. Theophilus Browne who succeeded him was an Anglican clergyman who had become 'fatigued with the Trinitarian Forms of worship'. While he was at Warminster he published a statement of the principles of Unitarianism and a new translation of selected passages of scripture. The introduction of the latter into the services was one of the numerous subjects on which he quarrelled with the congregation before he left in 1807.[31]

The change in doctrine under these two men was

[13] Sar. Dioc. R.O. Chwdns.' Pres. 1662.
[14] G. L. Turner, *Original Records of Early Nonconformity*, i. 121.
[15] Ibid. 403, 515.
[16] Sar. Dioc. R.O. Chwdns.' Pres. 1674.
[17] *W.N. & Q.* iii. 537.   [18] *V.C.H. Wilts.* iii. 111.
[19] H. M. Gunn, *History of Nonconformity in Warminster* (1853), 16–17; Gunn's statement that Rowland Cotton was preaching in the town from 1672 has been disproved —he did not come to Warminster until after 1700: correspondence to the *Warminster Jnl.* 1932, *penes* Mr. H. N. Dewey.
[20] *V.C.H. Wilts.* iii. 121.
[21] Ibid. 109–10; vii. 157.
[22] Gunn, *Nonconformity in Warminster*, 36.

[23] The history of this meeting is based, except where otherwise stated, on Gunn, *Nonconformity in Warminster*.
[24] *V.C.H. Wilts.* vii. 33.
[25] It was not certified until 1710: W.R.O. Certs. of Dissenters' Meeting Houses.
[26] Not a grandson, as Gunn supposed; see *Dict. Amer. Biog.*
[27] Dr. Williams's Libr. Evans MS. f. 123; this estimate may have been before the schism was complete: see below.
[28] e.g. Sar. Dioc. R.O. Vis. Queries, 1783.
[29] Dr. Williams's Libr. Wilson MS. F3, f. 408.
[30] Wansey papers *penes* Mr. H. N. Dewey.
[31] Ibid.; T. W. Marshall, *Notes on the Episcopal Polity of the Holy Catholic Church* (1844), 456; for Browne, see *D.N.B.*

permanent, although the meeting was still called Presbyterian until its end. Tremlett's teaching is known to have alienated two members of the Butler family who left for the New Meeting,[32] but the trustees appointed in 1805 comprised 4 Bucklers, 3 Wanseys, a Warren, and a Hinton, [33] all of families which had supported the meeting a century before. They were typical of the prosperous clothiers, maltsters, and tradesmen who formed the backbone of the congregation. So too was John Langley who at his death in 1799 left £400 to provide yearly payments of £6 to the pastor, 10s. to the clerk, and 5s. each to 38 poor members of the congregation.[34]

In the 19th century the Old Meeting suffered a steady decline. Many of its poorer supporters were attracted to newer meetings,[35] while economic changes reduced the prosperity of the richer ones. Apart from Langley's gift, there was no endowment to pay the pastor which probably accounted for the succession of short pastorates, seven between 1825 and 1850. In 1829 there were 250 attenders,[36] but in 1851 on a Sunday in March there were not many over 50, and many of the pews were out of repair.[37] In 1845 the Vicar of Warminster claimed that most of the poor that attended did so from motives of gain. He had refused to bury a Unitarian in the churchyard,[38] and the vigour of his attack on this, as on other sects, may have furthered its decline. The last settled pastor left in 1866,[39] and the chapel was closed in 1868. The last communicants were members of the family of Buckler and Wansey.[40] The meeting house was sold in 1870, and in 1881 the proceeds were assigned to augment the trust fund of the Conigre Unitarian Church at Trowbridge.[41] The endowment of Langley's charity passed, as the donor had provided, to augment that of the other charity he had founded.[42] The set of five pieces of plate, also given by Langley in 1790, was eventually deposited with the British and Foreign Unitarian Association, and later lent to congregations in London.[43]

The meeting house was later used as the Girls' British School,[44] and was in 1962 used by the Avenue School as an annexe. The building of 1704 has been little altered. It is very plain, of brick with stone dressings and stone mullioned windows; the double roof is supported in the centre by massive square columns of timber.

The origin of the congregation of Independents called the New Meeting is to be found in the dis-

satisfaction of some members of the Old Meeting with the teaching of Samuel Bates, whom they suspected of Arianism. Within a few months of his coming to Warminster Bates had offended the Butler family,[45] and in 1709 John Butler, who had been a trustee of the Old Meeting, certified a barn or shop at the back of Richard Lott's house as a place of worship.[46] Lott was no doubt the bell-founder of that name who worked in Common Close,[47] so that the building was probably near the site of the later meeting house. It seems that a further secession from the Old Meeting to the New took place in 1719, apparently occasioned both by doctrinal difference and by a dispute over the co-pastorate of Joseph Pike. In 1715 Pike was associated with Bates at the Old Meeting,[48] but was not approved by most of the congregation. A group, led apparently by Nathaniel Butler, left and no doubt joined those already worshipping in Common Close.[49] At the same time the doctrinal dispute was renewed, the Old Meeting asserting its orthodoxy in an entry in the church book and the New publishing a vindication of the secession written by Pike.[50] The seceders were joined by some families from the town who had been worshipping at the Independent chapel at Horningsham, and the congregation built a meeting house in Common Close which was licensed early in 1720.[51] Although at first clearly inferior to the Old Meeting in wealth and numbers, it included several prosperous families such as the Baylys, Butlers, Slades, Adlams, and Aldridges. In 1734 four members united to buy the freehold of the chapel, and in 1754 it was vested in trustees who included a maltster, a tanner, a clothier, and two woolstaplers.

Little is known about the size of the congregation in the first half of the 18th century. Daniel Fisher, minister from 1752 to 1771, was said to have added many members, and also kept a boarding school. Thomas Gibbons, 1786–93, was evidently a zealous pastor who began to hold services on Monday evenings in a house at the Common.[52] He also began a Sunday School at a house in Portway, and during his ministry village evangelization began with the building of a chapel at Sutton Veny.[53] Gibbons's successor, Edward Dudley Jackson, was a powerful preacher, whose influence made the chapel too small for the crowds that wished to hear him. In 1798 it was pulled down except for the front wall and rebuilt with new galleries and pews. He continued the work at the Common, expounding the *Pilgrim's Progress* on winter evenings, until

[32] Gunn, *Nonconformity in Warminster*, 18.
[33] *Endowed Char. Wilts.* (1908), p. 742.
[34] Ibid. pp. 741–2.
[35] J. Murch, *Hist. of Presbyterian and General Baptist Chs. of West of England*, 89–90.
[36] W.R.O. Retns. of Nonconformist Meetings, 1829.
[37] H.O. 129/10/260.
[38] John Owen, *Letter to the Inhabitants of Warminster*, 1845 (copy in Wilts. Tracts clvii); Wm. Morgan, *Letter to Revd. A. Fane*, 1847 (copy *penes* Warminster U.D.C.).
[39] G. E. Evans, *Vestiges of Protestant Dissent*, 249.
[40] Wansey papers *penes* Mr. H. N. Dewey.
[41] *Endowed Char. Wilts.* (1908), pp. 779, 996; *V.C.H. Wilts.* vii. 158.
[42] See p. 135.
[43] Wansey papers *penes* Mr. H. N. Dewey; Evans, *Vestiges of Protestant Dissent*, 249.
[44] See p. 133.
[45] *V.C.H. Wilts.* iii. 125.

[46] W.R.O. Certs. of Dissenters' Meeting Houses; the secession of 1709 was apparently known to one of the Wansey family (papers *penes* Mr. H. N. Dewey) but not to Gunn.
[47] Walters, *Wilts. Bells*, 304.
[48] Dr. Williams's Libr. Evans MS. f. 123.
[49] Murch, *Hist. of Presb. & Gen. Bapt. Chs.*, 89–90; Letter from Butler in Wansey papers *penes* Mr. H. N. Dewey; Gunn, *Nonconformity in Warminster*, 30. The account of the New Meeting which follows is largely based on Gunn, 35–38, where much detailed information is given.
[50] *An Impartial View of the Principal Difficulties that Affect the Trinitarian, or Clog the Arian Scheme* (copy in B.M.).
[51] W.R.O. Certs. of Dissenters' Meeting Houses.
[52] W. Daniell, *Warminster Common*, 21; G.R.O. Retns. of Regns. (12 June 1790).
[53] See p. 72.

in 1802 a chapel was built there in Bread Street so that evening services could be held on weekdays.[54] A girls' school held on Saturday afternoons at the Bread Street chapel was also begun during his pastorate. After Jackson's early death in 1803, Joseph Berry carried on the work of his predecessors with vigour. The Sunday School flourished, and many members were added to the congregation. During his time chapels were built at Hindon, Heytesbury, and Codford St. Mary. It was probably due to these vigorous pastorates that the Common Close society was by far the largest in the town in 1829, when its congregation numbered 900, and 150 attended at the Bread Street chapel.[55] In 1836 school rooms for the Sunday School were built at a cost of over £1,000, and three years later a further £2,000 was spent on the entire rebuilding of the chapel. In 1846 side galleries were added, so that the accommodation was 700, and an organ was installed. In March 1851 the morning congregation numbered 292, afternoon 232, and evening 470, and there were 140 pupils at the Sunday School.[56] Classrooms and a vestry, designed by W. J. Stent, were added to the north of the chapel in 1862,[57] and in the same year open stalls replaced the old pews.[58]

In the 19th century bequests for the benefit of poor members of the congregation were made by Thomas Morgan (£200 in 1809), John Barnes (£200 in 1837), John Everitt (£100 in 1838), Jane Rebbeck (£100 in 1847), and Anne Butt (£100 in 1865). These sums produced in the 1950's about £20 a year, which was distributed to needy members in sums of £1 and under. Morgan also left £100 for the benefit of the Sunday School, and in 1894 Albert Lucas left £100 to provide a choir picnic fund. Caroline Carpenter's gift of £50 in 1901–2 was to provide a yearly distribution of coal, and is still so used.[59] A house and malthouse in Common Close were bought in 1886, and the income, which amounted to £18 a year in 1903, was applied to general chapel expenses.[60] In 1907 W. F. Morgan left the reversion of £5,000 to the congregation for general expenses and to buy a manse. No. 22 Boreham Road was bought in 1930. In that year Frank Moody left £100 to provide an income which was to be spent on giving parcels of groceries to poor members at Christmas.[61]

The two Quakers who were presented in 1674[62] were the forerunners of a small group which appeared openly after the Toleration Act. One of them was joint author of a pamphlet containing an apology for Quakers directed to the people of Warminster in 1693.[63] The house of James Hedges was certified for Quaker worship in 1701;[64] it may have been the building in Common Close which was remembered as a Quaker meeting house in the 19th century although it had long been converted into a malthouse.[65] There were still a few Quakers in the town in 1783,[66] but the last one died in 1794.[67] Their burial ground was in a field near Cley Hill, where it could still be seen in Daniell's time.[68]

Methodist preachers first visited Warminster in 1753, and held services in cottages at the Common for about three years.[69] John Wesley preached in the town in 1758,[70] but no group formed until 1770, when Warminster was termed a new place with 14 members.[71] It met in Back Lane, where a house was licensed in 1773,[72] but soon encountered cruel persecution. On one occasion the pulpit and stools were taken from the meeting house and broken into fragments which were hung on the direction post at Emwell Cross, and on another the fire engine played water over the preacher. Two of the ringleaders were prosecuted and bound over at the Assizes in 1773,[73] but the society was reduced to 6 members, and dissolved in 1776.[74]

From 1780 a group of poor people met privately in the town; in 1789 they obtained a room at the junction of Pound Street and West Street,[75] but it was used only for prayer meetings and scripture meetings. Until 1804 all Methodists in the town attended the parish church and took the sacrament there. In that year the group built a chapel in Chain Street (now George Street).[76] About 1818 the congregation was torn by internal dissension; some of the oldest members were expelled, many others left, and numbers were reduced by nearly half.[77] In 1829, however, there were 200 attenders,[78] and in 1835 92 members.[79] Further strife followed, and in 1850, according to William Daniell, perhaps a jaundiced witness, the cause was languishing and saddled with an oppressive debt.[80] In 1851 the average attendances at morning and evening services were 50 and 90 respectively, and there was a Sunday School with 25 pupils.[81] In 1861, however, the society had recovered sufficiently to rebuild the chapel, to a design by W. J. Stent.[82] An organ by Nelson Hall was installed in 1862.[83]

From the earliest visits of Methodists to Warminster Common in the 1750's, there is a fairly continuous record of prayer meetings, scripture readings and preaching in cottages there by groups more or less influenced by Methodist teaching.[84] Typical of them was probably that held for many years in the house of Jeremiah Payne, a blind man,

54 W. Daniell, *Warminster Common*, 22.
55 W.R.O. Retns. of Nonconformist Meetings, 1829.
56 H.O. 129/10/260.
57 *Warminster Miscellany*, May 1862, June 1863.
58 Ibid. Dec. 1862.
59 *Endowed Char. Wilts.* (1908), pp. 742–3, 777–8; Char. Com. Accts. File G. 36.
60 *Endowed Char. Wilts.* (1908), p. 777.
61 Char. Com. File 9889.
62 Sar. Dioc. R.O. Chwdns.' Pres. 1674.
63 *V.C.H. Wilts.* iii. 119.
64 W.R.O. Certs. of Dissenters' Meeting Houses.
65 Gunn, *Nonconformity in Warminster*, 41; Halliday, Information, f. 69.
66 Sar. Dioc. R.O. Vis. Queries, 1783.
67 Halliday, Information, f. 69.
68 Daniell, *Warminster*, 240.
69 W. Daniell, *Warminster Common*, 17.

70 *Journal*, ii. 459.
71 Halliday, Information, f. 69
72 G.R.O. Retns. of Regns.
73 W. Daniell, *Warminster Common*, 14–15.
74 Halliday, Information, f. 69.
75 Gunn, *Nonconformity in Warminster*, 62; probably G.R.O. Retns. of Regns. 24 Feb. 1790.
76 W. Daniell, *Warminster Common*, 23; G.R.O. Retns. of Regns.   77 W. Daniell, op. cit. 55–56, 58–59.
78 W.R.O. Retns. of Nonconformist Meetings, 1829.
79 Halliday, Information, f. 69.
80 W. Daniell, op. cit. 55–56.
81 H.O. 129/10/260.
82 *Warminster Miscellany*, Aug. 1860.
83 Ibid. April 1862.
84 The account of Methodism at the Common is based except where otherwise stated on W. Daniell, *Warminster Common*.

where ten or a dozen people regularly met for reading and prayer on Sunday evenings. In 1803 the Methodists from the town borrowed the Independent Chapel in Bread Street and held services for a short time. In 1807 a fresh start was made at a cottage in King Lane where services were held on Sunday afternoons and Friday evenings. It was enlarged in 1809, but still proving insufficient, the Independent Chapel was again borrowed for Sunday evenings, and used until 1818. In that year the town Methodists left the Common; their leaving was either a cause or a consequence of the quarrels which took place among them at that time. The work was taken up by a group of those whom they had expelled, and especially by William Daniell.

Daniell, who was styled in his later days the Bishop of Warminster Common, has left a vivid description of his work there. Even before 1818 he had been active in forming a Bible Association and holding 'Christian Experience' meetings. When he began services at the Bread Street chapel, only four or five members took an active part, while a gang of men and youths interrupted them with curses and stones, breaking the lanterns and damaging the clothes of the worshippers. 'I have been sometimes obliged', wrote Daniell, 'to stop the service, and go and lay hold of the offender, and by physical force, single-handed, drag him out from among the congregation and throw him out of the door.' In spite of such annoyances, which only abated very slowly, the cause prospered, and the cottage used on Sunday afternoons was often crowded to suffocation. In 1827 the congregation was able to build its own chapel, in what was afterwards called Chapel Street, with accommodation for 300. Sunday afternoon attendances soon rose from 50 to 250, and a new gallery was made in 1838. In 1841 the congregation suffered from the zeal of the new vicar, Arthur Fane, whose opposition lasted until 1846. In spite of this a new vestry was built in 1844, containing a boiler which could provide tea for 500 people in 40 minutes. In 1851 average attendances at the afternoon and evening services were 170 and 150 respectively, and there was a Sunday School 160 strong.[85] Daniell had always concentrated on the instruction of children since the earliest days of his work at the Common, holding tea meetings, catechizing, and distributing tracts among them. In 1846 a schoolroom was built for the school.

Daniell's work continued until his death in 1860.[86] The cause had never been affiliated to the Wesleyan Conference; the chapel and two houses in Bread Street, bought in 1844, were vested in trustees who were to allow Daniell to use it for life. After his death the meeting seems to have languished. The chapel was let to the Salvation Army later in the century,[87] and is still occupied by them in 1963.

An Independent Methodist Chapel in Pound Street was licensed for worship in 1842.[88] It provided accommodation for 150, and in 1851 the average attendance at three Sunday services was between 40 and 60, while 25 children attended the Sunday School.[89] The congregation still survives in 1963.

No early Baptist congregation formed in Warminster, and any Baptists from the town attended the ancient chapel at Crockerton.[90] In 1810, however, Ebenezer Chapel was built in Meeting House Lane (now North Row). The congregation, small at first, gradually increased,[91] and in 1829 numbered 250.[92] On a Sunday in 1851 the attendance at morning and evening services was 160 and 175 respectively.[93] A schoolroom was built in 1858;[94] in 1861 the organ was moved from the gallery to a platform behind the pulpit, and the old square pews were replaced by stalls.[95] The meeting received an important bequest in 1913, when J. E. Halliday left the reversion of his estate, amounting to some £17,000.[96]

A Christian Scientist Meeting began in the town in the 1930's, and in 1963 was still meeting in the former police station in Ash Walk.

In 1822 a small burial ground for the use of the nonconformists of the town was laid out on the Boreham road.[97] Its contemporary railings and gates and a small free-standing entrance arch of stone, inscribed *Mors Janua Vitae*, still remain. The ground was levelled and turfed and the stones arranged round the walls in 1950.[98] In 1907 W. F. Morgan left £100 to the trustees to provide wages for a caretaker.[99]

TOWN GOVERNMENT AND PUBLIC SERVICES.

Warminster had the status of a borough in late Saxon times, and still contained burgesses in 1086.[1] In the 14th and 15th centuries a court called a portmote was held in the town every three weeks; in 1348–9 it was kept by a portreeve.[2] It was distinct from the manorial courts, and no doubt only had jurisdiction over the urban area, perhaps even only over the area east of Almshouse Bridge which, it is suggested above, formed the 'new port'.[3] Nothing is known of any other burghal institutions, and the town was never represented in Parliament.

In the mid-13th century William Mauduit was holding a court in which he claimed the liberty of trying and hanging thieves.[4] Later in the century the lord of Warminster had a gallows called Alkemere, which it was said interfered with the jurisdiction of the Abbot of Glastonbury in Longbridge Deverill.[5] A three-weekly manorial court and a twice-yearly court-leet were being held in the late Middle Ages.[6] No records remain to illustrate their work before the 17th century. They were then described as the courts of Warminster town and

[85] H.O. 129/10/260.
[86] *Warminster Miscellany*, Sept. 1860.
[87] *Endowed Char. Wilts.* (1908), p. 779.
[88] W.R.O. Certs. of Dissenters' Meeting Houses.
[89] H.O. 129/10/260.
[90] *V.C.H. Wilts.* iii. 111, 112, 138.
[91] Gunn, *Nonconformity in Warminster*, 61
[92] W.R.O. Retns. of Nonconformist Meetings, 1829.
[93] H.O. 129/10/260.
[94] *Warminster Miscellany*, May, 1858.
[95] Ibid. Dec. 1861.
[96] Char. Com. File 92130.

[97] Daniell, *Warminster*, 240.
[98] Middlebrook, Highways and Byways. no. vi.
[99] Char. Com. File 86635.   [1] See p. 90.
[2] Longleat MSS. 9062, 9455, and Parcel XXVII, Acct. Rolls *passim*; S.C. 6/1145/12 m. 3.
[3] See p. 92.
[4] *Crown Pleas Wilts. Eyre*, 1249 (W.A.S. Rec. Brch.), 213–4.
[5] *Rot. Hund.* (Rec. Com.), ii. 276, 277; *Cal. Pat.* 1272–81, 348.
[6] Longleat MSS. 9062, 9455, and Parcel XXVII, Acct. Rolls *passim*.

liberty, or of the in-hundred, and were attended by the tithingmen of Warminster, Avenel's Fee, and Boreham. In the 17th and 18th centuries they appointed haywards, bread weighers, shamble wardens, leather sealers, ale tasters, viewers of commons, viewers of firehearths, and constables. The chief business was presentment of breaches of the agricultural custom, of strays, and of nuisances.[7] It is not known how long the three-weekly courts continued to be kept, but the court-leet was still held in the mid-19th century.[8] Its meeting was only annual, and was largely occupied with food and drink.[9]

Sir John Thynne was high steward of Warminster in 1553,[10] and Giles Estcourt in 1574.[11] No more is known of this office, and the chief manorial officer in later times was the bailiff. From the 16th century it was customary to lease the bailiwick of the town on lives, generally though not always with the hundred bailiwick.[12] The lessee occupied, or could underlet, the office, and enjoyed the profits of the courts leet and baron, of the fairs and markets, of the guildhall and the stalls and shambles in the Market Place, and of certain houses near Almshouse Bridge.[13] The lease was clearly profitable and was held by men of substance; lessees for a large part of the 17th century were the Sloper family, tenants of the manor farm.[14] In the early 18th century the tolls of the markets and fairs were deducted from the lease, although the profits of the stalls and shambles remained. The last lease of the bailiwick on lives fell in hand in 1758, and the profits were afterwards let at rack with the tolls added again.[15] They were still held like this in the mid-19th century,[16] and the office of bailiff was held by the manager of the corn market in 1903,[17] long after it had ceased to have any significance in local government. Of the other manorial officers, the high constable was still performing some minor functions in the 1860's,[18] and a hayward was still exercising his office in 1868, when he was involved in a lawsuit about impounding cattle.[19]

A 'tolseld' stood in Warminster in the late 14th century.[20] In the middle of the next century rents were received both for a *novam aulam placitorum*, with shops beneath it, and a *vetus aulam placitorum*.[21] The latter was probably the same as the old tolseld repaired in 1563–4.[22] It may have stood near the eastern corner of the Market Place and Weymouth Street, for the 'Plume of Feathers', later the 'King's Arms', which stood there until the 1830's, was

traditionally said to be a former town hall.[22] The new hall was no doubt that called in 1516–17 the 'yelde hall' and council house,[24] and later generally the Guildhall.[25] It stood in the centre of the road where High Street and the Market Place join, opposite the entrance into Common Close. The medieval building was subsequently added to. A 'little shed house' which stood at the west end in 1575[26] had been replaced a century later by a 'new-erected' hall, with an open place underneath it.[27] The date 1711 which appeared on the west wall when it was demolished may have referred to a further extension or to repairs.[28] The building was used for public meetings ranging from the holding of the summer Quarter Sessions to balls and assemblies; part of the lower stage was used as a blind house or town prison, and the poor were customarily paid there.[29] Market stalls stood beneath it, and part was used as a wool hall.[30] It was a serious obstruction to the highway through the town, and was demolished in 1832; the present building at the junction of the Market Place and Weymouth Street was provided by the Marquess of Bath and opened in the same year.[31] It was designed by Edward Blore. The stone front is in a Tudor style reminiscent of Longleat. The building was given to the town by the fifth marquess in 1903.

The vestry, which shared the government of the town with the decaying court leet, was active from at least the early 17th century.[32] It was always 'open', and in the 19th century was evidently attended by considerable numbers of ratepayers, sometimes as many as 200.[33] There were overseers of the poor in 1616, when the manor court ordered that certain poor cutters of wood should be taken before them to decide their fitness for that liberty.[34] The overseers were no doubt the same as the collectors for the poor, who were appointed in the vestry in 1620.[35] There was a poor man's box, in which a few shillings a year were collected, in the later 1620's.[36] Little is known about poor relief, however, until near the end of the century, when a volume of overseers' accounts begins in 1687. From that date expenditure rose gradually and intermittently, from under £200 in the 1680's to a figure generally over £400 between 1710 and 1720.[37] About 1727 a poor house was built at Warminster Common by Lord Weymouth, apparently in exchange for consent to his inclosing some waste lands. An offer by him to undertake the perpetual relief of all the chargeable poor of the parish in

7 Ibid. Parcel XXI, Court papers.
8 Slater, *New Com. Dir.* (1851).
9 W. Daniell, *Warminster Common*, 227–9.
10 Daniell, *Warminster*, 60.
11 Soc. Antiq. Jackson MSS.
12 Longleat MSS. 9042, 9356, 9450, and Parcel XXVIII; earlier leases of the bedelry are recorded, but it is not clear to what they relate.
13 Ibid. Parcel XXVIII, Leases Brown to Stote, 1573, and Francis and Foster to Hawkins, 1671.
14 Ibid. MSS. 9356, 10652; Hist. MSS. Com. *Var. Coll.* i. 78, 102; W.R.O. Q. Sess. Great Roll, Trin. 1686.
15 Longleat Estate Office, Survey 1743, pp. 123–4.
16 Ibid. Rack Rental, 1853–60.
17 *Kelly's Dir. Wilts.* (1903).
18 U.D.C. Inspectors' Min. Bk. 1860–7; see also Daniell, *Warminster*, 131.   19 *Warminster Herald*, 25 Jan. 1868.
20 Longleat MSS. Parcel XXVII, Acct. Roll 1385–6.
21 Ibid. MSS. 9455–6.
22 Ibid. Parcel XXVII, Acct. Roll 1463–4.
23 Daniell, *Warminster*, 122.

24 Longleat MSS. Parcel XXVIII, List of repairs 8 Hen. VIII.
25 e.g. ibid. MSS. 9264 (1575), 10254 (1749).
26 Ibid. MS. 9264.
27 Ibid. 10652 and Parcel XXVIII, lease Francis and Foster to Hawkins, 1671.
28 Daniell (*Warminster*, 122) assumed that this was the date of the whole, but drawings of it indicate a much older building (see pl. opp. p. 95) and W. Daniell, (*Warminster Common*, 192) believed it to be very old.
29 Daniell, *Warminster*, 122; W. Daniell, *Warminster Common*, 192; *Salisbury and Winchester Jnl.* 25 Feb. 1788.
30 Longleat MSS. Rental 1775.
31 Halliday, Information, f. 14.
32 Daniell, *Warminster*, 178–89; Halliday, Information, ff. 39–44.
33 W. Daniell, *Warminster Common*, 72, 121–2; Halliday, Information, f. 41.
34 Longleat MSS. Parcel XXI, Presentment 1616.
35 Daniell, *Warminster*, 180.
36 Halliday, Information, f. 38A.   37 Ibid. f. 45.

return for permission to inclose all the waste lands was rejected. The workhouse was a failure in the end,[38] although it was perhaps responsible for a fall in expenditure between 1732 and 1736, when the highest figure was only £318. For the next two decades it was generally over £500, and more than twice that sum in the worst years.[39] In 1757 Lord Weymouth paid the parish £300 for the right to inclose some more common lands, and the money was used towards building a workhouse at Warminster Common and inclosing some land near it for a garden.[40] Salaried masters were appointed for the remainder of the century, and there is no evidence of farming out the poor there.[41] Expenditure on the poor rose slightly in the 1770's and 1780's. The average from 1774 to 1782 was £1,138; the appointment of a salaried assistant overseer from 1783 resulted in a slight improvement for a few years, and a committee of the vestry found that further improvement might be made by reducing the number of inmates in the workhouse, whose upkeep cost over 2s. a week each, while those on outdoor relief cost less than 1s.[42]

In 1790 distress in the town was so great that £140 was subscribed and distributed in money, bread, and fuel to 466 families.[43] From that time expenditure on the poor increased rapidly, reaching over £5,500 in 1801 and being generally between £3,000 and £5,000 between then and 1835.[44] In 1821 the workhouse, 'a most grievous concentration of every species of vice', usually contained from 90 to 100 paupers, but by 1824 rigid scrutiny had reduced the number to about 30.[45] An account of the administration of the poor law in Warminster in 1832 is probably typical of most of the period of large expenditure since 1790. The vestry appointed four overseers, chiefly tradesmen, who with the churchwardens assessed and levied the rates and spent the money. They were assisted by a salaried assistant overseer, and subject to the scrutiny of the vestry at its monthly meetings. Only 18 poor were in the workhouse, mainly aged and impotent; their upkeep cost the parish about £12 each a year. Some 70 or 80 labourers were wholly on the parish during the summer and 120 or 140 in the winter. They were employed upon the roads when possible. A much larger number, 900 in September 1832,[46] received out-relief because their earnings were not sufficient to support their families. The parish objected to employers paying under 9s. a week; with that sum, a man was given 1s. 6d. a week if he had four children, and 2s. 6d. for five, but nothing for less than four.[47]

The vestry appointed surveyors of the highways

by 1620,[48] but they were probably able to do no more than deal with the worst places, for the roads of the town were generally in a miserable state.[49] The appointment of scavengers in 1736 with power to raise a 6d. rate[50] was probably ineffective, and the earliest real improvements in the town probably date from the establishment of a turnpike trust in 1727. The trust's activities were largely confined to roads within the parish; some of its road improvements have been described above.[51] In 1792 the trustees were given additional powers to provide and repair pavements in some streets and to order the removal of nuisances.[52] The surveyors appointed by the vestry still remained responsible for most of the parish. Together they seem to have achieved a certain amount. In 1809 a barrel-drain was made in the Market Place.[53] William Daniell, the Methodist overseer, was appointed surveyor in 1822, and after great exertions was able to remove the heaps of filth which stood before most of the doorways at the Common and to prevent them from being replaced.[54] In the early 1830's the parish improved many roads, the money coming from the poor rates and labour from the unemployed poor.[55]

In 1835 the parish was able to set up a more effective authority for the repair of the roads. This was a Highway Board, a committee of the vestry appointed under the Act of that year.[56] The board was active in its early years; William Daniell was appointed as salaried assistant surveyor, and between 1836 and 1840 the board laid several drains in various parts of the town and widened the road in East Street. In 1840 it successfully opposed the renewal of the turnpike commissioners' powers relating to pavements and the removal of nuisances.[57] In 1856 it proceeded against tradesmen who obstructed the pavement with their goods.[58] In 1859–60 it spent £386,[59] presumably on the maintenance of minor roads, pavements, and drains, and these were probably its chief concern until it was replaced in 1867. The vestry also delegated some of its local government powers to a body of Inspectors of Lighting and Watching appointed under the Lighting and Watching of Parishes Act of 1833.[60] In the early 1860's its chief functions were the supervision of the lighting of the main streets of the town by gas and of the town's fire engines. Between £300 and £400 were spent each year, most of which was paid to the Gas Company.[61] Beside these two permanent bodies it was customary to appoint boards of health to deal with outbreaks of disease in the town. Such a board was appointed in the cholera outbreak of 1832;[62] in 1858 a board of

---

[38] W. Daniell, *Warminster Common*, 2–3.
[39] Halliday, Information, f. 45.
[40] Daniell, *Warminster*, 187.
[41] Halliday, Information, f. 43; W. Daniell, *Warminster Common*, 22.   [42] W. Daniell, *Warminster Common*, 6–7.
[43] Halliday, Information, f. 47, inserted newspaper cutting.
[44] Ibid. f. 46 and inserted printed sheet; *App. Sel. Cttee. on Poor Rate*, H.C. 556, p. 190 (1822), v; ibid. H.C. 334, p. 230 (1825), iv.
[45] W. Daniell, *Warminster Common*, 82.
[46] Daniell had 1,000 poor constantly to provide for in 1828: ibid. 139.
[47] *App. Rep. Poor Law Com.* H.L. 8 h–m, pp. 247 f–k and 850 a–e (1834), v–xi.
[48] Daniell, *Warminster*, 180.
[49] *Wilts. Q. Sess. Rec.* ed. Cunnington, 108–9; see

above p. 94.
[50] *Q. Sess. and Ass.* 1736 (W.A.S. Rec. Brch.), 75.
[51] See p. 94.   [52] 32 Geo. III, c. 141.
[53] Daniell, *Warminster*, 110.
[54] W. Daniell, *Warminster Common*, 94–96.
[55] Ibid. 161; Halliday, Information, inserted printed sheet, 'Comparative View of Parish Expenditure, 1822–41'
[56] 5 & 6 Wm. IV, c. 50; such boards were limited to parishes of over 5,000 inhabitants, and only a few were ever elected: S. and B. Webb, *The King's Highway*, 205.
[57] Posters and extracts from minutes *penes* Mr. H. N. Dewey; *C.J.* xcv. 120; 3 & 4 Vic., c. 21 (local and personal Act).
[58] *Warminster Miscellany*, Nov. 1856.
[59] Ibid. April 1860.   [60] 3 & 4 Wm. IV, c. 90.
[61] U.D.C. Inspectors' Min. Bk. 1860–7.
[62] *V.C.H. Wilts.* v. 324.

health was compelled to undertake the abatement of the nuisance created by the sewage in the Swan River, and the vestry appointed a committee to co-operate with it.[63]

Thus before the formation of the Local Board of Health, the government of Warminster was shared between the vestry and its committees, the turnpike trusts, and the *ad hoc* boards of health. Little money was available, and some of the greatest permanent improvements, such as the reconstruction of George Street from 1807[64] and the supply of water to the Common in 1849,[65] were the result of private efforts. In 1860 the road from Portway to the station, now the Avenue, was repaired by subscription.[66] Even normal services were given grudgingly; in 1859 the Highway Board decided not to water the streets at the expense of the parish, but to make the carts available to private people who wished to do so.[67]

A Local Board of Health was set up in 1867.[68] It consisted of 15 members, a third of whom retired each year. It immediately appointed a clerk, a treasurer, a surveyor, and a rate-collector, none of them apparently full-time officials. The practice of appointing permanent committees was begun in 1869, when finance and general purpose committees were formed; other committees followed as the work of the board increased.

The board at first simply assumed the functions of the Highway Board and the Inspectors of Lighting and Watching. An inspector of nuisances was appointed, and some show of ordering their abatement was made, particularly the cleaning of water-courses, the fixing of gutters on houses, and the cleansing of slaughterhouses. The three town fire engines were found to be in as good order as their age would allow, and a proposal to buy a new one was dropped. The largest items in the first year's estimate of £743 were £324 for street lighting and £210 for highways and cleaning the streets. Only £30 were allowed for drains and pavements. An outbreak of smallpox was dealt with by the old expedient of a temporary board of health. The town board had little inclination to seek new responsibilities. In 1869 it resolved that it had no present intention of altering the system of drainage, and it would only proceed with the reconstruction of the Common water-supply if half the cost could be raised by subscription.[69] In 1873, however, the board appointed a medical officer of health. Three years later the Local Government Board asked what the board intended to do about the unsatisfactory privies mentioned in the medical officer's reports. Between 1876 and 1878 there were outbreaks of scarlet fever and typhoid, and the government began to complain repeatedly about the lack of sewerage and the pollution of the Swan River. It was the threat of action under the Rivers Pollution Prevention Act of 1876[70] that eventually forced the board into tardy action in 1880.

The sewerage committee appointed by the board produced a scheme amended from one which had been prepared for the former Highway Board in 1867. It involved collecting most of the town's sewage in a sewer, running down the Swan River from Almshouse Bridge, and taking it to meadows near the Wylye on the Bishopstrow boundary, where it would be filtered by being spread over several acres of land. Smaller schemes were to take sewage from Boreham to the same area and from the Common to another site at Henford's Marsh. After much discussion the lease of a piece of land was secured from Lord Bath, and the scheme came into use in 1883. The board experienced much difficulty in making property owners connect their houses to the scheme; in 1884 few cesspits had been done away with, and in 1886 the river was still very foul from sewage which ran into it from the Manor House. In spite of the imperfections of the system, Warminster was the first of the smaller towns in the county to have one at all.[71]

The other main problem which faced the local board was that of water supply, and on this it was also slow to act. We have seen that the Common supply was left to private initiative and only received partial support from the board. In 1872 its extension to the Marsh side of the Common was carried out in the same way, and even in the late 1880's, after the inauguration of the town supply, the Common scheme was still run by a private committee. The first move to supply the town itself came from a London civil engineer in 1882. This provoked a public meeting in the town the following year at which a motion in favour of having a supply was defeated. A majority of the members of the board at this time wanted a supply, and an engineer was called in, and negotiations begun with Lord Bath for the use of a spring at Aucombe near Shearwater. At the 1884 election four of the five members returned were opposed to having a supply, but this still left a narrow majority in favour. A public enquiry was held, and much evidence given about the pollution of the wells from which the town was supplied; in the courts off East Street the water was the colour of porter. Nevertheless a majority of ratepayers, led by Sir James Philipps, the vicar, were violently opposed to being supplied by the board. The plans were approved by the government, and pushed on with as fast as possible; by the next election in 1885 they were well advanced, but again four opponents of the scheme were returned, including Philipps himself. A resolution was immediately passed that the works should be transferred to a private company, and Philipps began to negotiate privately with Lord Bath for him to take it over. This action, taken without the knowledge of the board, evidently caused much offence to the other members, and was probably the reason why several of the opponents changed sides and enabled the board to carry out the original scheme after all.

The minor activities of the board can be quickly dealt with. The houses of the town were numbered in 1876. Three years later the board bought a house in South Street at the Common for an infectious diseases hospital to replace the old practice of using any empty house available. Medical opinion in the

[63] *Warminster Miscellany*, Sept., Oct. 1858.
[64] See p. 95.   [65] Daniell, *Warminster*, 103.
[66] *Warminster Miscellany*, Jan. 1860.
[67] Ibid. April 1859.
[68] The following account of the board's activities is

taken from the Minute Bks. in the U.D.C. offices. Thanks are due to Mr. W. H. Edwards, clerk to the council, for making these records available.
[69] Daniell, *Warminster*, 103.
[70] 39 & 40 Vic., c. 75.   [71] *V.C.H. Wilts.* v. 327.

town was against the site, and the Local Government Board refused a loan. The collection of house refuse was begun in 1880, and in the same year a Fire Brigade committee was formed. In 1886 a Volunteer Fire Brigade was established, to which the board agreed to contribute. An anonymous donor gave a second-hand manual engine which required 22 men to work it,[72] and the three old engines were sold.

Warminster Urban District Council was formed under the Local Government Act of 1894. It consists of 15 members of whom a third retire annually. As with its predecessor, the first problem which faced the council was one of sewage disposal. There were still parts of the town not served by the system, including The Furlong and new houses on the Imber road, beside more outlying parts such as Woodcock and Hillwood Lane. At the Common some sewage still ran into the stream. There were also frequent complaints about smells from the sewage farm, and the government urged

URBAN DISTRICT OF WARMINSTER. *Gold, a man in armour mounted on a horse and riding towards the sinister, brandishing in his right hand a sword, its blade bendwise-sinister, all proper the surcoat and shield azure lined gules, the horse sable with bardings gules lined azure.*
[granted 1948]

that the whole system should be reviewed. When this was done it was found that the farm was ill-arranged and too small. After much consideration it was decided to pump the sewage to a more suitable area. Smallbrook Mill was bought for the purpose, and a piece of sloping land north-east of Butler's Coombe Farm was adopted as the new farm. The work of laying new sewers in areas not previously served was still going on in 1901. Since the turn of the century the council has taken many new responsibilities which can only be briefly summarized here. In 1904 it took a lease of the markets and fairs from Lord Bath, and bought them from him in 1920.[73] A housing committee was established in 1911 and the first housing scheme was begun in 1919.

The Volunteer Fire Brigade was taken over in 1913, and the Lake Pleasure Grounds were laid out in 1924.[74] In 1955 the council bought Portway House for use as offices, and in 1960 the sewage works were reconstructed.

In 1895 the council adopted for use on its seal the device of the Mauduit family as depicted by Hoare, an armed knight on horseback. A grant of this device as arms was obtained in 1948.[75]

A cottage hospital was built in 1866 on the site of Portway Farm;[76] it was enlarged in 1892 and 1899,[77] and replaced by the present building in 1932. The Isolation Hospital on Bradley Road was built by a joint committee of the urban and rural councils in 1915, and transferred to the Trowbridge committee in 1934.[78]

In 1840 the inspector in charge of the newly-formed county police at Warminster lived at the London Inn.[79] Two years later the police office was in Weymouth Street;[80] it was subsequently moved to the yard ajoining no. 6 Market Place.[81] In 1857 a police station was built in Ash Walk;[82] it remained in use until 1932, when the present one in Station Road replaced it.[83] The building in Ash Walk was in 1963 used partly as a Christian Science church.

In 1723 the deputy-postmaster of Hungerford (Berks.) had the supervision of the postal service at Warminster.[84] In the early 19th century the post office was in George Street; it moved to the building now no. 6 Market Place *c.* 1862, and thence to part of the Savings Bank building opposite in 1903.[85]

The Warminster Gas and Coke Company was founded in 1834,[86] and a gasworks built at Brick Hill. Lighting of the streets was begun in the same year.[87] The company obtained fresh powers in 1889.[88]

SCHOOLS. The chantry priest of St. Laurence was teaching a school in Warminster before the Dissolution.[89] Simon Forman, the astrologer, was a schoolmaster in the town in 1577,[90] and William Lockier[91] and Giles Daniell[92] taught there in the earlier 17th century. William Gough kept a school in the town during the Interregnum.[93] In 1662 three men were presented by the church-wardens for teaching unlicensed, and one of them was recommended as fit to keep a school.[94] Lord Weymouth's Grammar School was founded in 1707 to teach the youth of Warminster, Longbridge Deverill, and Monkton Deverill, but, owing to a lack of definition in the master's obligation to take free scholars, few seem to have been educated there;[95] in 1783 the curate wrote that there was no public or charity school in the town.[96] It was about that time, however, that the beginnings of public elementary education in Warminster are to be found in the Sunday Schools. That begun at the Old Meeting in 1785 was directly under the influence of Robert Raikes. The children were instructed in reading for three hours on Sunday mornings, and returned in the afternoon for another reading lesson before going to the meeting; after it they went back to the school for instruction in the catechism. They had to be recommended for admission by subscribers, and three years instruc-

[72] *Wilts. Times,* 3 Sept. 1887.   [73] See p. 115.
[74] *West Wilts. Dir.* (1932).
[75] *W.A.M.* liii. 265; an example of the seal is on E 326/11087, a deed of the first half of the 13th cent.
[76] *P.O. Dir. Wilts.* (1867); Char. Com. File 91800.
[77] Wilts. Cuttings, v. 272, vii. 38.
[78] *V.C.H. Wilts.* v. 345.   [79] Halliday, Information, f. 116.
[80] Pigot, *Nat. Com. Dir.* (1842).
[81] Manley, Regional Survey, vii. 564.
[82] *Warminster Miscellany,* March 1857.
[83] Manley, Regional Survey, vii. 564.
[84] *Cal. Treas. Papers,* 1720–8, 219.

[85] Manley, Regional Survey, vii. 603.
[86] Printed copy of deed of settlement *penes* U.D.C.
[87] Halliday, Information, f. 9.
[88] 52–3 Vic., c. 64 (local and personal Act.).
[89] *W.A.M.* x. 314.   [90] Ibid. xlvi. 656.
[91] *Genealogist* N.S. xxiv. 52.
[92] Halliday, Information, f. 107.
[93] *Calamy Revised,* ed. Matthews, 230.
[94] Sar. Dioc. R.O. Chwdns.' Pres. 1662.
[95] *Endowed Char. Wilts.* (1908), pp. 743–4, 760–3; for an account of the school, see *V.C.H. Wilts.* v. 361.
[96] Sar. Dioc. R.O. Vis. Queries, 1783.

tion was considered long enough for each child.[97] A Sunday School was begun at the New Meeting six years later,[98] and it was the establishment of another at the Methodist chapel in the early 19th century which first encouraged the establishment of a public day school in the town. The Methodists had over 200 children, and failed because numbers were too big for the teachers to control, but their effort provoked the New Meeting not only to double the size of their Sunday School, but to begin a day school as well. This failed, but roused the Anglicans to establish a National School in 1815.[99] From that time the histories of the individual schools are dealt with below.

Other educational provision in the town can only be briefly mentioned. Sunday Schools continued to supply the lack of day schools in the early 19th century; in 1833 eight schools of all the chief denominations instructed 800 children.[1] In 1798 there were five private schools, two of them boarding schools for ladies;[2] in 1822 five private schools out of eight took boarders.[3] The Christ Church Establishment for Young Ladies was conducted for many years from 1842 by Miss Haskew and Miss Cruse at Cambridge House, Sambourne,[4] and another successful ladies' boarding school of the same period was Mrs. Hardick's at East End House.[5] Sir J. E. Philipps founded St. Boniface Missionary College in a house in Church Street in 1860, and subsequently raised £17,000 for a new range of buildings adjoining which was opened in 1910.[6] The design was by J. A. Reeve;[7] a chapel designed by Sir Charles Nicholson was added in 1927. Since 1948 the college has been associated with King's College, London, as a postgraduate training centre for mission work.[8] Philipps also founded the Community of St. Denys; in addition to training women for work abroad, it has run St. Monica's School for Girls, founded in 1890, and, until 1959, the Orphanage of Pity.[9] A Reformatory School for Wiltshire was begun by another vicar, Arthur Fane, in 1856. In the buildings now known as Tascroft Farm boys committed by the magistrates worked 20a. of land, the produce of which partly supported them.[10] In 1868 they spent 10 or 15 hours a week at lessons, and worked for the rest of the time in the fields.[11] The school was closed c. 1925.[12] There was a Mechanics' Institute in East Street in 1842.[13] Its place in popular education was probably taken by the Athenaeum, which from its foundation in 1858 was used for many years for programmes of winter

lectures on an enormous variety of subjects, generally to packed audiences.[14] It also housed a reading-room, library, and class-rooms, in one of which a government school of art was begun in 1861.[15] The Literary Institution, opened in 1838, provided a reading-room and library for more exalted inhabitants of the town and district.[16]

The day school which the New Meeting established early in the 19th century[17] was educating about 100 children in 1808,[18] but only lasted for a short time. A new school for girls on the Lancastrian principle was begun in 1827 in a large room in Ash Walk.[19] In 1833 80 girls attended, paying 2d. a week.[20] Three years later the committee was granted the use of the newly-built schoolrooms at the Common Close chapel, and moved the school there in 1837. In 1842 a British School for boys was started in the same building.[21] In 1859 there were altogether 85 children under a certificated master and two pupil teachers; the school 'bore the stamp of managerial indifference', and the top class were unusually ignorant.[22] The girls' section was moved to the disused Unitarian meeting house in North Row in 1872.[23] By 1890 there were separate boys' and infants' sections in the Common Close, the boys south of the chapel and the infants north of it. The girls were still at North Row, and total average attendance was about 220.[24] After the 1902 Act the schools were taken over by the county. In 1923 the girls were moved to the Close and united with the boys, and the infants sent to North Row. The senior children were moved to the Avenue School in 1931, which then took over the North Row building as a manual training room. The buildings adjoining the Common Close chapel became a junior mixed school. In 1959 the New Close Junior School was built at Woodcock by the county, but the old buildings in the Close were in 1963 still in use as part of the new school.[25]

A British School was begun at Warminster Common in 1845[26] in a building adjoining the Methodist chapel there; it began to receive a grant c. 1868–70.[27] In 1893 average attendance was 96 boys and girls.[28] The building was enlarged in 1898, and taken over by the county in 1902. In 1903–4 the average had risen to 88 mixed senior children and 44 infants.[29] Senior children were removed to the Avenue School in 1931, and the Common School, later called New Town, remained in use as a junior mixed and infants' school until 1959.[30]

A National School was begun in 1815 in a building in Church Street which bears that date, and was

[97] Acct. Bk. and other papers in Wansey MSS. *penes* Mr. H. N. Dewey.
[98] Gunn, *Nonconformity in Warminster*, 44.
[99] W. Daniell, *Warminster Common*, 84.
[1] *Educ. Enq. Abstract*, H.C. 62 (1835), xliii.
[2] *Univ. Brit. Dir.* (1798), iv. 679.
[3] Pigot, *New Com. Dir.* (1822–3).
[4] Pigot, *Nat. Com. Dir.* (1842); Longleat Estate Office, Rack Rental, 1853–60; *Warminster Herald*, 4 Jan. 1879.
[5] Pigot, *Nat. Com. Dir.* (1842); Manley, *Regional Survey*, xi. 2013.
[6] *W.A.M.* xxxvii. 463–4.   [7] Wilts. Cuttings, vii. 38.
[8] *Crockford* (1956).
[9] *W.A.M.* xxxvii. 463–4; *Official Yr. Bk. of Ch. of Eng.* (1951), 466; Nat. Soc. Files; Wilts. Cuttings, xxi. 258.
[10] *Acct. of Wilts. Schools*, H.C. 27 (1859 Sess. 1), xxi (2).
[11] *Rep. Com. Empl. of Children in Agric.* [4202–i], p. 283, H.C. (1868–9), xiii.
[12] *Sar. Dioc. Kalendars*, 1923, 1925.

[13] Pigot, *Nat. Com. Dir.* (1842).
[14] *Warminster Miscellany* and *Herald*, *passim*.
[15] Daniell, *Warminster*, 132–3; *Warminster Miscellany*, Sept. 1861.
[16] W.R.O. 132, Papers about the Institution.
[17] See above.   [18] Lambeth Palace Libr. MS. 1732.
[19] Copies of Wansey MSS. made by Mr. H. N. Dewey; Gunn, *Nonconformity in Warminster*, 51.
[20] *Educ. Enq. Abstract* (1835).
[21] Gunn, *Nonconformity in Warminster*, 51.
[22] *Acct. of Wilts. Schools*, H.C. 27 (1859 Sess. 1), xxi (2).
[23] Char. Com. File 79294.
[24] *Kelly's Dir.* (1890).
[25] Ex inf. Mr. H. N. Dewey.
[26] *Kelly's Dir. Wilts.* (1890).
[27] *Rep. of Educ. Cttee. of Council*, 1870–1 [C 406], pp. 270–1 (1871), xxii.   [28] *Rtn. of Schools*, 1893 (1894).
[29] *List of Public Elem. Schools*, 1 Jan. 1906 [Cd. 3182], H.C. (1906), lxxxvi.   [30] Ex inf. L.E.A.

evidently converted then from a small private house. It was supported by subscription and provided for about 200 boys and girls of the poorest families.[31] In 1835 another National School was built at Sambourne near Christ Church; it apparently housed girls and infants, and the Church Street school remained in use, presumably for boys.[32] In 1842 207 boys and 128 girls attended on weekdays and Sundays, and another 369 children attended on Sundays only. In summer 145 infants attended, but in winter only 85, and there was a winter evening class in Church Street for 60 working youths, run by the vicar and his friends.[33] In 1846 a new building at the junction of Back Street and West End, now Emwell Street and Vicarage Street, was opened,[34] and the Church Street school given up.[35] In 1848 the National day and Sunday schools were providing for 800 children.[36] In 1859 the National Schools in Warminster were divided into boys', girls', and infants' departments, but it is not clear how they were divided between the two buildings. About 300 children attended, and the schools were regarded as very good both for accommodation and instruction.[37] The Vicarage Street school was extended in the 1880's, and by 1890 was divided into girls' and infants' schools;[38] the girls' school was called the Hall School, but was united with the infants' school in 1904.[39] At Sambourne there were separate boys' and girls' schools. In 1890 combined attendance at the Vicarage Street and Sambourne Schools was 350.[40] In 1923 the Sambourne school was re-organized as a senior mixed school, and the Vicarage Street, or Minster School, for junior mixed children and infants.[41] No change was made until 1955, when the senior children from Sambourne were sent to the Avenue School;[42] since then the Sambourne and Vicarage Street schools have been junior mixed and infants' schools. Both have controlled status under the 1947 Act.

In 1868 it was announced that a small school in connexion with Christ Church was to be built in Kettle Alley at Warminster Common, where children of parents who were too poor to send them elsewhere could be educated.[43] Grants were made by the government and the National Society, and a small building was put up at the corner of Cannimore Road and South Street.[44] It was extended in 1878.[45] In that year Matthew Davies left £1,000 for the benefit of the school, then known as the Ragged School, and the income was subsequently used toward its maintenance.[46] In 1893 average attendance was 68.[47] It remained in use as an infants' school until 1922, when it was closed.[48]

The establishment of a school on the Boreham road followed naturally on the building of St. John's

Church there. The National Society made a grant, and the building was finished in 1872 and called St. John's School.[49] The stone building, designed by G. E. Street, was added to by the Temple family in memory of Vere Temple (d. 1892).[50] In 1903–4 it contained mixed and infants' departments, and was attended by some 95 children.[51] Since the removal of the older children in 1931 it has remained a junior mixed and infants' school. It received controlled status under the 1947 Act.

When the County took over the administration of education under the 1902 Act, a Secondary School for boys and girls was built in the Common Close adjoining the Athenaeum.[52] In 1931 a new county Secondary School was built at the Avenue; some children from the old school went to grammar schools in Trowbridge, and the rest to the Avenue School, which became a Secondary Modern School under the 1947 Act.

CHARITIES. In the 17th century a number of people gave or left small sums of money to the parish; they were to be lent out at interest and the proceeds applied to the relief of the poor. Some of the money had been lost by 1683, and by 1724 only £15 remained out of about £100. This money was borrowed by the parish towards the repair of the church, and it was agreed that 15s. a year interest should be paid. This, however, was only done intermittently, and in 1869 the charity was allowed to lapse with the consent of the parish and the Charity Commission.[53]

There was an almshouse in Warminster in the mid-16th century; it stood at the lower end of the High Street, and gave its name to the bridge which crossed the stream there. In 1607 Clement Abath gave £5 to the inmates, and the building was still in use in the early 18th century. It later fell into decay and was removed about 1750.[54]

In 1627 Henry Smith, silversmith of London, founded a charity for the benefit of the poor of a number of places including Warminster. The sum allotted to Warminster was at first £10 out of an estate at Stoughton (Leics.) worth £220 a year. In the late 17th and early 18th centuries the sum received was only £6 or £8 a year, but in the 19th century £24 or £25 a year was the usual amount. In 1833 this was usually laid out in calico and dowlas shirting, which was given away in lengths worth 4s. each. In 1868 the Stoughton estate was exchanged for one at Thurlaston (Leics.); by 1903 the annual receipt had fallen to £18, which was distributed in 4s. tickets for buying food.[55]

In 1670 Stephen Pilchard of London left £120 to the parish of Warminster where he was born, to

[31] Pigot, *New Com. Dir.* (1822–3); *Educ. Enq. Abstract* (1835).
[32] Pigot, *Nat. Com. Dir.* (1842); *Retn. of Non-Provided Schools*, H.C. 178 (1906), lxxxviii.
[33] W.A.S. Libr. Devizes, Everett MSS. Pedigrees xi, Report for 1842.
[34] Extracts from Wansey MSS. made by Mr. H. N. Dewey.
[35] Longleat Estate Office, Survey 1837, p. 107.
[36] *Hunt's Dir.* (1848).
[37] *Acct. of Wilts. Schools* (1859 Sess. 1).
[38] *Kelly's Dir. Wilts.* (1890).
[39] *List of Public Elem. Schools*, 1 Jan. 1906 [Cd. 3182], H.C. (1906), lxxxvi.
[40] *Kelly's Dir. Wilts.* (1890).
[41] *Bd. of Educ. List* 21, 1927.

[42] Ex inf. L.E.A.
[43] *Warminster Herald*, 6 June 1868.   [44] Nat. Soc. File.
[45] U.D.C. Local Board Min. Bk.
[46] *Endowed Char. Wilts.* (1908), p. 775.
[47] *Retn. of Schools*, 1893.
[48] *Bd. of Educ. List.* 21, 1927.   [49] Nat. Soc. File.
[50] H. R. Whytehead, *The Minster and Ch. Life in Warminster*, 35.
[51] *List of Public Elem. Schools*, 1 Jan. 1906.
[52] *Kelly's Dir. Wilts.* (1903).
[53] *Endowed Char. Wilts.* (1908), pp. 739, 780; Longleat MSS. Parcel XXI, List of gifts, 1683; Daniell, *Warminster* 186, 241–2.
[54] Daniell, *Warminster*, 120–1, 162.
[55] *Endowed Char. Wilts.* (1908), pp. 733, 752; Halliday, Information, f. 20.

buy lands; of the revenue 10s. was to be paid to the officiating minister for a sermon on St. Stephen's Day, and the residue was to be distributed to 20 old and needy natives of the town. In 1682 the sum of £7 4s., to allow for the gifts to be of 6s. 8d. each, was secured as a rent-charge on some houses near Almshouse Bridge, which later included the Organ Inn.[56]

At his death in 1688 John Wadman of Imber left a rent-charge of 50s. a year out of Flint-ford Farm in Frome to be given away to 20 poor inhabitants.[57] In 1723 William Slade left a rent charge of 50s. a year out of the former 'King's Arms' in the Market Place to be distributed in the same way.[58] William King of London by his will dated 1769 left a small piece of land, the rent to be given away yearly at the rate of 10s. a year to each recipient. The income has varied from £2 to £6. In 1949 the land was sold and the proceeds invested.[59] At his death in 1799 John Langley left £1,000 stock to provide annual payments of 5s. each to 120 poor people. In 1869 the capital was increased by £400 transferred, as Langley had provided, from the charity he founded in connexion with the Old Meeting.[60] From that time the number of recipients was increased.[61]

In 1807 George Wansey left £1,000, which was subsequently allowed to accumulate to £1,250, to provide yearly payments of £1 each to aged widows; they had to be nominated to go on the list, and once on it remained recipients for life.[62] By his will proved in 1818 Ralph Hotchkin left £100 stock so that the interest could be distributed to deserving poor, especially widows and people with large families.[63] At her death in 1820 Elizabeth Townsend left £200 to provide a number of great coats and cloaks for poor old men and women. In 1833 £3 a year from another charity she founded for singing an anthem in the parish church was allotted to this one.[64] About 1830 Sarah Lawes gave just over £100 for the benefit of the industrious poor. Similar bequests or gifts were made later in the 19th century by Jane Benett, £100, Mary Anne Wyche, £100, J. S. Halliday, £100, Mary Aldridge, £100, Susan T. Taylor, £98, F. H. Langley, £1,000, and G. T. Vicary, £50.[65] Other bequests were made by Letitia Leat, £100 to provide fuel, Charles Bleeck, £400 to give away beef at Christmas, and John Doel, £200 to provide boots and shoes.[66]

Since at least the early 19th century it has been customary to distribute the income from most of these charities at Christmas. In the 1820's and 30's some £120 was generally given to nearly 400 recipients.[67] The same method was still in use in 1962; in 1957 about £140 was given away, mainly in small sums as directed by the donors.[68]

In 1873 Louisa Warren built four almshouses in Portway in memory of her late husband. They were to provide homes for 4 Protestant widows or spinsters over 60; an endowment of £2,500 was made to allow for the upkeep of the houses and for small weekly payments to the inmates. In 1893 Jane Fish, an almswoman, left £122 to the endowment. The charity still functioned in its original form in 1963.[69]

Several charities have been endowed for the poor of the district or parish of Christ Church. In 1878 Matthew Davies left £2,000 to provide weekly supplies of coal for old people during the winter. In 1903 the income was sufficient to provide over 100 people with 1 cwt. a week and an extra 1½ or 2 cwt. at Christmas. In 1959 it was given away in 8s. vouchers.[70] In 1867 Margaret Elling gave a house and 6a. of land at Rehobath near Warminster Common for the general relief of the poor of the district. The estate was sold c. 1922 and the proceeds invested; in the 1950's some £26 a year was given away in money and vouchers.[71] By his will proved in 1901 S. P. Collier left £100 to provide meat for poor people; this too has been given away in vouchers.[72]

The formally-endowed charities were supplemented by several subscribing bodies for the relief of the poor. Warminster Infants' Friend Society was founded in 1800 to lend clothes and linen to lying-in women, and to give the infants that lived an adequate set of clothes. The Society for the Relief of the Aged Poor, established in 1814, collected subscriptions of 1d. a week from its members and allowed a number of aged paupers 1s. a week in winter and 6d. in summer to provide comforts in addition to the parish pay, which was not cut. Warminster Ladies' Benevolent Society was founded in 1818 to give small sums of money or clothes and comforts to the sick poor, and the Blanket Lending Society dated from 1827.[73] There were clothing clubs attached to the church Sunday Schools at the parish church and the Common in 1828,[74] and in 1835 a Penny Clothing Society was instituted. Members could pay from 1d. to 4d. a week, and at the end of the year were supplied with tickets to buy clothing worth a small amount over what they had paid, the increase coming from subscriptions.[75] The Society for the Aged Poor and the Blanket Lending Society still carried on their work in 1962. Each had accumulated endowment by gift and bequest, and still received subscriptions from its members.[76]

[56] Endowed Char. Wilts. (1908), pp. 735, 754; Daniell, Warminster, 243–4.
[57] Endowed Char. Wilts. (1908), pp. 737, 754; Hoare, Mod. Wilts, Heytesbury, 164.
[58] Endowed Char. Wilts. (1908), pp. 737, 754; Daniell, Warminster, 244.
[59] Endowed Char. Wilts. (1908), pp. 738, 754; Char. Com. File 29888.
[60] See p. 126.
[61] Endowed Char. Wilts. (1908), pp. 738, 754; Daniell, Warminster, 245–6.
[62] Endowed Char. Wilts. (1908), pp. 738, 757.
[63] Ibid. p. 755.
[64] Ibid. pp. 739, 758.   [65] Ibid. pp. 740, 755–9.
[66] Ibid. pp. 759, 771; Char. Com. File 90316.
[67] Halliday, Information, f. 116.

[68] Endowed Char. Wilts. (1908), p. 751; Char. Com. Files 29888, 74430.
[69] Endowed Char. Wilts. (1908), pp. 768–71; Char. Com. Corr. File G. 36.
[70] Endowed Char. Wilts. (1908), p. 774; Char. Com. Accts. File G. 36.
[71] Endowed Char. Wilts. (1908), p. 773; Char. Com. Accts. and Corr. Files G. 36.
[72] Endowed Char. Wilts. (1908), p. 775; Char. Com. Accts. File G. 36.
[73] Printed Accounts, Rules etc. penes Mr. H.N. Dewey.
[74] Select Psalms and Scripture Hymns, Warminster, 1828 (copy in W.A.S. Libr. Devizes).
[75] Printed Accounts, Rules etc. penes Mr. H. N. Dewey.
[76] Endowed Char. Wilts. (1908), p. 766; Char. Com. Accts. File G. 36; Warminster and District Dir. 1960–1.

THE HUNDRED OF WESTBURY

THE hundred, which was coterminous with the ancient parish, may have been included in the grant of the manor of Westbury by Henry II to Reynold Pavely.[1] In 1274 the jurors in the hundred court did not know by what authority Reynold, grandson of the above Reynold, held it, but they agreed that it was in his hands, as it had been in those of Walter, his father, after the baronial wars of John's reign.[2] Edward I disputed the right of Reynold's son, Walter, to it in 1281 and maintained that his ancestors, Richard I and John, had been possessed of it. The jurors on this occasion declared that the hundred had been held by the Crown only during a minority and that Walter was lawfully seised of it.[3]

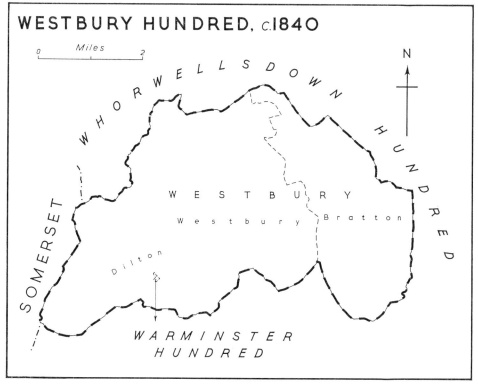

WESTBURY HUNDRED, c.1840

The course of boundary between the tithings of Westbury and Dilton is uncertain

The hundred descended with the manor of Westbury until the death of Sir John Pavely in 1361,[4] when it was divided between his two daughters Joan, later wife of Ralph Cheyney, and Alice, wife of John St. Lo.[5] Alice survived her father by half a day only,[6] and when John St. Lo died in 1375 the moiety inherited by his wife was divided between her two surviving daughters, Joan, wife of John Chidiock, and Eleanor, wife of Thomas of Bradeston.[7] The quarter inherited by Joan Chidiock

[1] *Rot. Hund.* (Rec. Com.), ii. 278.   [2] Ibid. 279.
[3] *Plac. de Quo Warr.* (Rec. Com.), 798.
[4] See p. 149.
[5] *Wilts. Inq. p.m.* 1327–77 (Index Libr.), 209–1. This

division was not revoked by the second partition of Sir John's lands, see below p. 149.
[6] *Wilts. Inq. p.m.* 1327–77 (Index Libr.), 291.
[7] Ibid. 291, 391.

passed to her grandson, John, who died seised of it in 1450 and left two daughters as co-heirs.[8] Their rights in the hundred, however, appear to have lapsed, for none is found among the possessions of John's descendants who held the manors of Westbury Stourton and Westbury Arundell.[9] The quarter inherited by Eleanor of Bradeston descended in the same way as the estate later called Westbury Seymour and passed in 1621 to Sir James Ley.[10]

The half of the hundred assigned in 1361 to Joan, later wife of Ralph Cheyney, passed with the manor of Brook, which she also inherited, until 1599 when with a part of that manor it was conveyed by Charles Blount, Lord Mountjoy (d. 1606), to Sir James Ley.[11] The whole hundred with all profits, the court house, and the house called the 'guildhall' were confirmed to Sir James by letters patent in 1610,[12] and from that date the hundred descended with the manor of Westbury.[13] It is mentioned in connexion with the sale of the manor in 1920 when the lordship of manor and hundred was sold for £42 10s. to Mr. Frank Parsons of Westbury.[14]

The lords of the hundred claimed in it rights of *extractas brevium*, gallows, assize of bread and ale, and view of frankpledge.[15] They did not have return of writs, however, and the sheriff held half-yearly tourns in the hundred. The earliest reference found to a sheriff's tourn in Westbury hundred is in 1393.[16] At the sheriff's tourn of 1501–2 two millers were presented for exacting excessive tolls, and a complaint was made that the tithing of Edington, which was in the hundred of Whorwellsdown, had neglected to repair the highway at 'Sweetappleshill'.[17]

In 1249 the Precentor of Salisbury, with the cooperation of five men of the town, attempted unsuccessfully to withdraw the suit due from his tithing of Chantry from the hundred court.[18] In 1274 the Priors of Steventon and Monkton Farleigh had successfully withdrawn the suits due from their manors in Westbury.[19] At an unknown date Walter Pavely, lord of the hundred, granted exemption to the Abbot of Stanley and his men of Chapmanslade.[20] The Abbot of Westminster was granted exemption for his manor of Westbury Priory by royal charter in 1399.[21]

In 1651 with a number of other Wiltshire hundreds in private hands Westbury was surveyed by the Parliamentary Commissioners as a late possession of Charles I.[22] The three-weekly courts for the hundred were, like the courts leet, held by appointment of Sir John Danvers, lord of the manor of Westbury. It was stated, however, that at this date much of the business of the hundred court was undertaken in the lord's other courts. Presentments and fines were said to be rare except for fines from the tithing men for the nonpayment of tithing silver. The hundred court at this date was held at Westbury, presumably in the court house mentioned in 1599 and 1610.[23] The sheriff's tourns were held about Lady Day and Michaelmas at Bratton Marsh.[24]

When the second partition of Sir John Pavely's lands and possessions was made in 1368, the appointment of the steward and bailiff of the hundred and of the port-motes was granted to John St. Lo for life and after his death was to go to his daughters, granddaughters of Sir John Pavely.[25] From this it seems that the steward and bailiff of the hundred were also the officers of the borough court, and of the manor court as

[8] C 139/139/26.
[9] See pp. 149, 150.
[10] See p. 150.
[11] See p. 151.
[12] C 66/1847 no. 14.
[13] See p. 150.
[14] W.A.S. Libr. Devizes, Sale Cat. xvi.
[15] J.I. 1/1000 m. 54 d.; B.M. Lansd. MS. 442, f. 145-6; *Rot. Hund.* (Rec. Com.), ii. 279.
[16] J.I. 3/179 m. 19, 18.

[17] S.C. 2/208/29.
[18] *Crown Pleas Wilts. Eyre*, 1249 (W.A.S. Rec. Brch.), pp. 209-10.
[19] *Rot. Hund.* (Rec. Com.), ii. 279.
[20] *W.A.M.* xv. 255.
[21] *Cal. Chart. R.* 1341–1417, 378–80.
[22] E 317/Wilts./17.
[23] C 54/1521/Mountjoy and Ley; C 66/1847 no. 14.
[24] Bratton Marsh is an area on the northern outskirts of the village of Bratton.

well. What their duties were in their various capacities is not clear. But it was as bailiff of the hundred that Henry Barker attempted to impound animals from off the common arable in 1736.[26] There were also two constables for the hundred who were that year assaulted as they attempted to execute their office.[27]

At the sheriff's tourn of 1501–2 only the tithings of Leigh, Bratton, and Dilton appear to have been represented,[28] and in 1651 the same three alone were liable for tithing silver at the hundred court.[29] In 1736, however, nine tithings were listed as responsible for producing jurors, namely Westbury Chantry, Westbury Priory, Short Street, Chapmanslade, Westbury Town, Borough of Westbury, Leigh, Leigh Bailiffe, and Bratton.[30] In 1575 a perambulation was made of the bounds of the hundred and parish showing these to be marked at frequent intervals by 'balls', or occasionally by boundary oaks.[31] Further examination into the various tithings into which the hundred and ancient parish were divided is reserved for treatment below.[32]

[25] *Cal. Close*, 1364–68, 457–8.
[26] *Q. Sess. and Ass.* 1736 (W.A.S. Rec. Brch.), p. 64.
[27] Ibid. p. 57.
[28] S.C. 2/208/29.
[29] E 317/Wilts./17.
[30] *Q. Sess. and Ass.* 1736 (W.A.S. Rec. Brch.), p. 69.
[31] Hoare, *Mod. Wilts.* Westbury, 54–57.
[32] See p. 139.

WESTBURY

THE ancient parish of Westbury[1] was co-extensive with the hundred.[2] It was roughly crescent-shaped, stretching some seven miles from east to west, and approximately four miles from north to south, and included within its bounds were the later civil parishes of Bratton, Dilton Marsh, Heywood, and part of Chapmanslade. It remained a single parish, with the town of Westbury roughly in the centre, until the late 19th century, but a number of other centres of settlement are early discernible, some of which were as large as many rural parishes. In 1334 there were besides the town of Westbury eleven vills or tithings liable for taxation. These were Bratton, Melbourne, and Stoke in the east, Hawkeridge and Heywood in the north, Brook, Penleigh, Bremeridge, Dilton Marsh, and Westbury Leigh in the west and south, and Chapmanslade in the extreme southwest corner.[3] Of these Melbourne and Stoke became merged in Bratton;[4] Bremeridge was coupled with Dilton Marsh in 1377 and has not been found to occur again as a separate tithing; Brook continued to constitute a separate area for the purposes of taxation until the 17th century. Westbury Leigh was probably a suburb of Westbury town from early times, but it retained its separate identity as a fiscal and administrative unit until the 19th century; Penleigh remained a distinct hamlet or tithing until the end of the 17th century when it was divided into Upper and Lower Penleigh. By the 19th century, however, it probably comprised little more than Penleigh House and Farm and a few farm cottages. Bratton, Heywood, Hawkeridge, and Chapmanslade survived as distinct centres of population. In the 14th century both Dilton, which had a church and was a chapelry of Westbury,[5] and Dilton Marsh were centres of population for taxation purposes, but for some centuries afterwards Dilton seems to have been more important than Dilton Marsh. By the beginning of the 19th century, however, Dilton was a mere hamlet and Dilton Marsh the more populous district with a thriving weaving industry.[6]

In the 16th century the town of Westbury was divided for purposes of taxation into the tithing of the precentor, or 'chantry', which lay around and to the south of the church, and the town and the borough of Westbury, which were not co-extensive.[7]

The borough of Westbury, it seems from later evidence, was the part of the urban area in which the burgage tenements lay.[8] The first evidence found for the location of the burgages occurs in 1777 when there were 61 distributed among 10 manors or lesser estates, all part of the capital manor of Westbury. These estates were Westbury Arundell, Seymour, and Stourton, Heywood, Hawkeridge, Brook with Mauduits, Westbury Leversage, Leigh Priors, Leigh Marsh (Westbury Leigh), and Bremeridge.[9] As is shown below,[10] these estates were made up of lands scattered throughout the ancient parish, and the burgages must have been in those parts which were situated in, or converged upon, the town. In 1835 it was reported that the burgages lay in three separate areas of the urban area, namely around the Market Place, in the vicinity of Eden Vale, and at a place called the Knoll, which lay between the southern end of Church Street and the Warminster road.[11]

Outside the urban area a tithing of Bayly is mentioned in the 16th century. This does not, so far as is known, occur in the 17th century, but in 1645 Hawkeridge is divided into two parts: 'Bailief Hawkeridge' and 'Priorie Hawkeridge', and Westbury Leigh is divided into 'the Bailief of Leigh' and 'the Tithing of Leigh' which suggests that the former tithing of Bayly may have been formed out of parts of Hawkeridge and Westbury Leigh.[12] In 1542 the tithing of Short Street, lying between Dilton Marsh and Chapmanslade, was coupled with Chapmanslade, and later, on one or two occasions, appeared as a tithing on its own.[13] The freehold book of 1736 possibly affords a very rough indication of the importance of the various areas of settlement at that date. The names of the more substantial free-, lease- and copyholders were collected for 12 places within the ancient parish. Brook, Dilton, and Hawkeridge returned no names. Heywood and Short Street returned one each; Westbury Leigh and Penleigh 3; Chapmanslade and the tithing of Chantry 5; the borough of Westbury 8, the 'Bailief of Leigh' 10, and Bratton 17.[14]

In 1882 the area of the ancient parish was very slightly increased when Hisomley Farm, previously a detached part of Upton Scudamore, was trans-

[1] This article was written between 1951 and 1953 and was revised in 1960. Any reference to later years is dated. Grateful thanks are due to Mr. W. G. Bush, Mr. H. Ross, and Mr. R. Tuffin for much help. [2] See p. 136.
[3] V.C.H. Wilts. iv. 302.
[4] These deductions about the various tithings within the parish of Westbury are based upon a study of 'Fifteenths and Tenths, Quotas of 1334', and 'Poll-Tax Payers 1377', V.C.H. Wilts. iv. 302 and 311; 'Commission to take Musters', L. & P. Hen. VIII, xiv (1), p. 300; Taxation Lists (W.A.S. Rec. Brch.), 34, 70–72; 'Assessment to Parliamentary 25th', W.A.M. xxxix. 445; Parish Records, Rate Bks. 1687–1705, 1729–60, Vestry Bk. 1801–26 (in parish ch.); E 179/197/53; E 179/197/207.
[5] See p. 180.
[6] See n. 4 above, and below, p. 170.

[7] Rep. Munic. Corps., H. C. 116, pp. 1377–9 (1835), xxiv. The town and the borough were distinguished in the taxation return of 1576: Taxation Lists (W.A.S. Rec. Brch.), 70–71.
[8] See p. 186.
[9] W.R.O. 490, Notice of sale of Lord Abingdon's lands.
[10] See p. 167.
[11] Rep. Com. Munic. Corps. (1835), xxiv, p. 1377.
[12] E 179/197/53; E 179/197/207; Taxation Lists (W.A.S. Rec. Brch.), 34; W.A.M. xxxix. 447–8. The 'Bailief of Leigh' as distinct from the tithing of Leigh also occurs in the 18th century: Q. Sess and Ass. 1736 (W.A.S. Rec. Brch.), 148.
[13] W.A.M. xxxix. 445; Parish Bk. 1729–60.
[14] Q. Sess and Ass. 1736 (W.A.S. Rec. Brch.), 148.

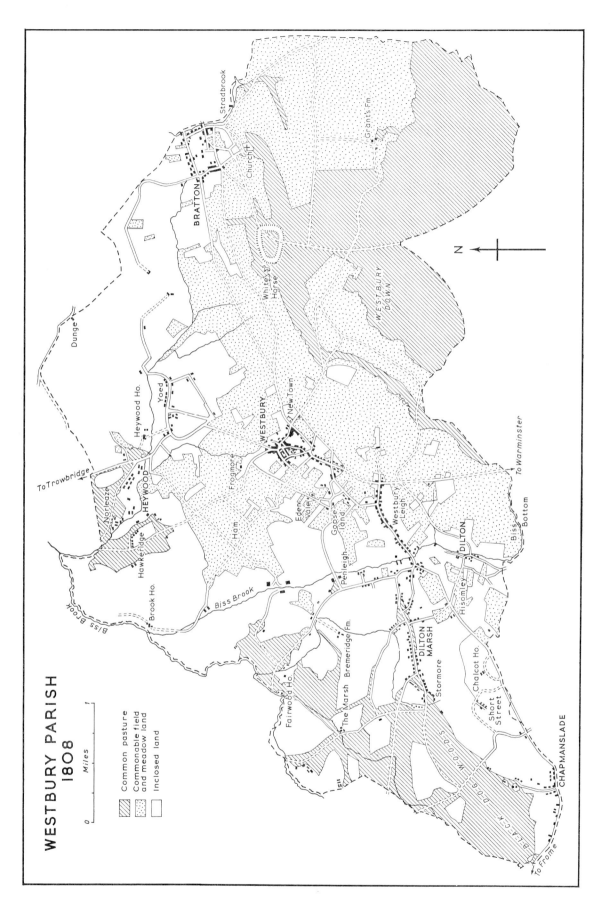

WESTBURY PARISH
1808

Miles
0   1

Common pasture

Commonable field
and meadow land

Inclosed land

This map is based on the inclosure award map

ferred to Westbury.[15] In 1894, however, the ancient parish was split up with the formation of the three separate civil parishes of Westbury, Bratton, and Dilton Marsh.[16] Two years later the civil parish of Heywood was created out of the northern part of the civil parish of Westbury.[17] The civil parish of Chapmanslade was created in 1934 when parts of Dilton Marsh, Corsley, and Upton Scudamore were taken to form it.[18] In 1899 the civil parish of Westbury was constituted an urban district retaining the same boundaries.[19] These were slightly enlarged in 1909 by the addition of a part of the parish of Heywood.[20] In 1951 the area of the urban district, which is roughly square in shape, was 3,686 a.[21]

The town of Westbury lies in the centre of the urban district on the strip of upper greensand, which runs beneath the north-western escarpment of Salisbury Plain, and divides the chalk uplands in the south-east of the urban district from the gault and Kimmeridge clay in the north-west.[22] On the chalk uplands in the south-east a height of over 700 ft. is reached, but beneath the escarpment in the rest of the urban district the land nowhere rises much above 250 ft. From its position beneath Salisbury Plain the town has sometimes been called Westbury-under-the-Plain.[23]

Biss Brook, which later becomes the River Biss, forms the western boundary of the urban district. To the east and south of the town, along the foot of the steep chalk downs, there are numerous springs and wells. A spring rising at Wellhead to the south of the town runs westwards to join the Biss Brook. Bitham Brook also rising from a spring in the town runs northwards.[24] In the north-west corner of the urban district, in the district called the Ham, there is a chain of lakes and ponds formed by the waterfilled iron-ore workings abandoned after the First World War.[25] The only woodland in the urban district lies at the foot of the chalk downs to the south-east of the town.

The main road from Trowbridge to Warminster runs from north to south through the centre of the urban district. This forms the town's main street passing through the Market Place, continuing as Maristow Street, and Edward Street, and leaving as the Warminster Road. A secondary road running from West Lavington under the escarpment of Salisbury Plain passes through Bratton and joins the main Trowbridge-Warminster road in the town. Another secondary road leaves the main road in a westerly direction at the southern end of the town. The roads to Westbury from Trowbridge and from Market Lavington were turnpiked in 1758, as was a road now (1960) a mere track, which led over Westbury Hill via Bowls Barrow to Chitterne.[26] The road leaving the town for Warminster was

turnpiked in 1769.[27] A toll-house at Chalford on this road survived in 1960.

The railway station lies at the Ham in the north-west of the urban district, nearly a mile from the centre of the town. It was opened in 1848 when the line was brought to Westbury through Trowbridge from Thingley on the main line from London to Bristol.[28] The line running westwards from the the station towards Frome was opened in 1850 as the first stretch of the line from Westbury to Weymouth.[29] The first part of the line running south from the station through Warminster to Salisbury was opened the following year.[30] In 1900 the line running eastwards to join the main line from London to Bristol at Patney and Chirton was opened and later became part of the main route from London to Taunton and the west of England.[31] There are also two loop-lines by-passing the station: the first made in 1933 for trains on the route from London to the west of England;[32] the second made in 1942 for trains travelling between Trowbridge and Reading.[33]

The town of Westbury is nearly a mile to the south-east of the site of a Romano-British settlement at the Ham.[34] The oldest part of the present town lies in and around the roughly triangularshaped area formed by West End (formerly Cheap Street), Edward Street, Bratton Road, and Alfred (formerly Duck) Street. Within this area lies the Market Place, the church, Angel and Bitham Mills, and, until the late 19th century, a considerable part of the southern end of it was occupied by Church or Parsonage Farm.[35] Most of the houses in this area appear to be of 18th- or early 19th-century date, but in many cases re-fronting done in those centuries must obscure earlier buildings of stone or timber-framing. Interspersed with these, and sometimes lining such streets as West End, Edward, and Fore Streets, are many rows of workers' cottages dating from the 18th and early 19th centuries. Many of the 19th-century houses are roofed with pantiles, probably made locally.

The Market Place, in which no markets have been held since the middle of the 19th century,[36] lies in the north-west corner of the area. Many of the houses flanking it were converted into shops in the 19th century. The 'Lopes Arms' on the east side is an apparently 18th-century building. Between c. 1754 and 1809 it was the 'Lord Abingdon Arms', and it may stand on the site of an inn called 'St. George and the Dragon' in the 16th century.[37] The 'Crown' and the 'White Hart' on the west side of the Market Place are 18th-century buildings, but probably have not such long histories as inns. The Market Hall on the east side was presented to the town by Sir Manesseh Massey

[15] V.C.H. Wilts. iv. 360.
[16] Ibid. 342, 347.
[17] Ibid. 349.
[18] Ibid. 343.
[19] FitzMaurice and Bown, Administrative Bounds Wilts. 24.
[20] Census, 1911 and V.C.H. Wilts. iv. 349, where the date is incorrectly given as 1904.
[21] Census, 1951.
[22] For a more detailed account of the geology of the area see Fry, Land Utilization Wilts. 200, 219–22.
[23] It was so called in 1574: C 142/211/186.
[24] Among the maps used are: O.S. Maps 6″ Wilts. XLIV; 1/2,500 Wilts. XLIV. 8 (1st and later edns.).

[25] See p. 171.
[26] 31 Geo. II c. 68; Andrews and Dury, Map (W.A.S. Rec. Brch.), pl. 7; V.C.H. Wilts. iv. 270.
[27] 9 Geo. III c. 73.
[28] V.C.H. Wilts. iv. 283.
[29] Ibid. 283–4.
[30] Ibid. 284.
[31] Ibid. 289.
[32] Ibid. 292.
[33] Ibid. 293.
[34] Ibid. 1(1), 119.
[35] See p. 153 and pl. facing p. 142.
[36] See p. 175.
[37] Notice on building.

Lopes in 1815.[38] It is built of Bath stone and has a colonnaded ground floor of 3 bays. The upper floor also has 3 bays and in the central one is an arched panel with a clock face. Above this is a pediment with the Lopes arms carved in stone in the tympanum. It was used for a time as a Town Hall, and as long as county courts were held in Westbury, they sat here,[39] but in 1960 the upper part was used only for a branch of the County Library. At the southwest corner, where Maristow Street leaves the Market Place, stands the Manor House, occupied occasionally by Sir Manesseh Lopes after he acquired the manor in 1810.[40] It is a late Georgian house with two stories and attics. Over the front-door is a semi-circular stone porch supported by two Tuscan columns. To the left of this a shop-window has been inserted. Between the Manor House and the church there is a terrace of double-fronted houses of about the same date set behind front gardens.

There are two other medium-sized residential houses in the neighbourhood of the Market Place which are comparatively unaltered. Bank House, called for a time in the 1940's Marlborough House, in West End, facing into the Market Place, is an early-18th-century brick building of 5 bays with stone dressings, a moulded eaves-cornice, and a steeply pitched hipped roof. Above the central doorway is a shell hood on foliated brackets and internally there is a contemporary staircase. In 1960 it was the bank house of a branch of Barclays Bank. The other house of some size lies in Alfred Street as it leads eastwards out of the Market Place. At the end of the 19th century it was called Ferndale, and is thought locally to have been once the rectory house.[41] It is a stone house, perhaps of 17th-century date. Its two-storied brick front, however, is of the mid-18th century with stone Venetian windows and Gothic glazing-bars. It stands in fairly extensive grounds for a town house.

The church of All Saints lies south of the Market Place. The churchyard is inclosed by brick walls and by some cottages of 18th- and early 19th-century date, which face the church, and by contrast give it height. The tithing of Chantry lay to the south and east of the church. Through it, running south from the church, winds Church Street, a narrow street, with three even narrower ways or footpaths leading off its east side. At the north end of the street there is a tall early-19th-century brick house, with an older rear wing facing the churchyard. This has a stone gable-end containing a two-light medieval window, and the first-floor room has an arch-braced collar-beam roof, probably also of late medieval date. This may possibly represent part of a house once used by the Precentors of Salisbury who held the rectory and exercised peculiar jurisdiction in the parish.[42] In the southern part of the tithing of Chantry, within the area inclosed by Church and Edward Streets, Bratton Road, and the footpath called Chantry Lane, was Church or Parsonage Farm. The farm-

house and buildings are shown on a map of 1899.[43] Fields, called Chantry Lease, belonging to the farm lay some two miles away, north of the lower road to Bratton, a mere track in 1960.[44] Shortly after 1870 the farm ceased to be worked as such, and much of the site was used for allotments.[45] In 1960 some of the land was being built over, but some of it was still open and was used for a builder's yard and as allotments. Two houses with modernized frontages on the east side of Church Street, called Little Chantry, were formerly part of the farm buildings. On the same side of the street and at its southern end are two medium-sized 18th-century houses, both with some features of distinction.

Opposite the site of the former Chantry Farm, and in the angle formed by the junction of Church and Edward Streets, lies the Angel Cloth Mill. Bitham Cloth Mill lies to the north-east and abuts on to Bitham Lane and Alfred Street.[46]

There are a number of 18th-century houses along Maristow and Edward Streets, and the beginning of the Warminster road. Some are medium-sized town residences, and have been little altered, but many of the smaller houses have been converted into shops. Westbury House, in Edward Street, is a red-brick house built in the early 19th century with later additions. In the 19th century it was the home of the Laverton family until 1888 when William Henry Laverton bought Leighton House.[47] In 1960 an extension on the north side of the house was used by C. Rickards, Ltd., Umbrella Manufacturers.[48] Fontainville House, once the home of the Jefferies family, stood in a large garden nearly opposite Westbury House and was of approximately the same date. It was built of Bath stone, and had some distinguished architectural features, including a Doric porch and a balcony above with wrought-iron rails of lattice pattern. In 1959, however, the house was a ruin, and in 1961 it was pulled down to make way for a new shopping precinct. Number 24 Warminster Road is an early-19th-century stone house now partly converted into a shop. It has a three-storied ashlar front and its 5 bays are divided by pilasters with incised line ornament. The Greek revival influence is evident in the honey-suckle ornament and the acroteria of its top story.

In Bratton Road, near the junction with Warminster Road, there is a two-storied building with timber-framed upper part of different dates. This was formerly called Bere's Well, and a spring rising beneath it is carried under Bratton Road and by underground conduit down Church Street.[49]

Besides the small group of 18th-century houses at the beginning of Warminster Road there are a few further south, but a map of 1773 shows that at that time the town extended no further south than the junction with Leigh Road, formerly Lower Road.[50] This point was, indeed, called 'Townend'.[51] Between this point and the hamlet of Chalford there is a medium-sized late-18th-century house built of brick surrounded by a large garden. This was formerly called Hill Tyning[52] and since the

38 *Kelly's Dir. Wilts.* (1931).
39 See p. 188.
40 See p. 150.
41 Ex inf. Mr. R. Tuffin.
42 See p. 176.
43 O.S. Map 1/2,500 Wilts. XLIV. 8 (1st edn.).
44 Ibid.; W.R.O. Inclosure Map.

45 Ex inf. Mr. R. Tuffin.
46 See pl. facing p. 180.
47 See p. 156.   48 See p. 171.
49 See p. 187.
50 *Andrews and Dury, Map* (W.A.S. Rec. Brch.), pl. 7.
51 Ex inf. Mr. R. Tuffin.
52 W.R.O. Inclosure Map.

WESTBURY

Air view of the town from the south, showing Westbury Mills in the foreground, the church in the centre and the market place beyond.

The Court House

Scott's Farm

BRATTON

Second World War has been the Cedars Country Club Hotel. Beyond this, standing in its park, is Leighton House built in 1800.[53] In the 18th century the park was divided into two parts by the road which turns west off the main Westbury-Warminster Road, called in 1960 Laverton Road. In the part lying south of Laverton Road was Leigh House which was abandoned after Leighton House was built in the northern part of the park. At the junction of the two roads is the hamlet of Chalford.

Parallel with Warminster Road, and about $\frac{1}{4}$ mile to the west, is the district known as Eden Vale. There are a few 18th-century houses here, and the Westbury Union Workhouse was established here in the early 19th century. An earlier workhouse, built at the end of the 18th century, is probably represented by the front range of the present building which has alterations and additions of c. 1835.[54] In 1960 the workhouse was used as the offices and yard of T. Holdoway & Sons, Builders. The Indigo Factory, or Dye House, was built in this district in the early 19th century, and throughout that century there were considerable brick works here, which are now abandoned. The map of 1773 also shows some building at the beginning of the road leading off the Bratton road and over the downs towards Chitterne.[55] Even at that date the district was called New Town, and may have been designed as a new housing scheme to meet the needs of the prosperous 18th-century town. A few 18th-century cottages remain on the south side of the road, but there is nothing to show that the site was ever further developed.

Several of the town's public buildings bear witness to the revival of the cloth industry and the position of the Laverton family in Westbury in the later 19th century. The Laverton Institute, built by Abraham Laverton, is a red-brick building in Gothic revival style in Bratton Road opened in 1873. It was originally used for recreational and cultural activities, and for a time housed a British School for boys, but since 1899 it has been the offices of the Urban District Council.[56] Abraham Laverton also laid out Prospect Square on the south side of Bratton Road. This comprises 39 houses, of which seven are almshouses, built of brick and stone round three sides of an open space used as allotment gardens.[57] William Henry Laverton built the public baths in Church Street in 1887, and the Technical School of Science and Art in the same street in 1897.[58]

In the 20th century there has been a certain amount of building on the east side of the town where the upper greensand gives way to the chalk. Small detached houses and bungalows have been built along the Butts and Bratton Road, and around New Town. Much of the town's expansion, however, has been westwards towards the station and along Eden Vale and Leigh Road to the west of the Warminster road. In addition to the railway work-

shops, several of Westbury's industries are situated in the region of the station.[59] The Avenue, and the Crescent, the council's housing estates built between the two World Wars, and the Old Field Park council housing estate, built after the Second World War, all lie on the west of the town.[60]

Westbury Leigh lies within the urban district of Westbury about a mile from the centre of the town. Like Westbury, it is situated on the upper greensand strip at the foot of Salisbury Plain.[61] The houses are built close to the road and extend along it for about $\frac{1}{2}$ mile. They include several dating from the 18th century. At the north-east end of the street no. 18 has a red-brick front with stone dressings which apparently dates from the earlier 18th century, but has Victorian alterations. It is of 2 stories and 5 bays and has round-headed windows to the first floor. Above the central doorway is a scrolled pediment. The gloving factory of Messrs. Boulton Bros. is at the same end of the village, standing back from the road, and occupying as part of its premises the mill called Balls Mill in the later 19th century.[62] Westwards along the street, on its south side, the malthouse of Messrs. Samuel Thompson & Sons is an early-19th-century building, probably on the site of a considerably older malthouse.[63] The church was built on the north side of the street in the late 19th century. Three blocks of council houses have been built on the same side of the street since the Second World War. The nearby 'Phipps Arms' dates from the early 19th century. Just north of the road, and not far from the track leading across the fields from Westbury to Penleigh House,[64] is a moated site, traditionally called Palace Garden.

Dilton, locally called Old Dilton, lies about $\frac{3}{4}$ mile south-west of Westbury Leigh on the boundary between Westbury Urban District and the parish of Dilton Marsh. It is a mere hamlet consisting of the church of St. Mary, Dilton Farm, and a few cottages situated in, and on the sides of, the valley of the Biss Brook, which is here quite steep. A minor road running between the secondary road from Westbury to Chapmanslade and the main road from Westbury to Warminster winds through the hamlet.

The civil parish of *BRATTON* was created in 1894 out of the eastern part of the ancient parish of Westbury.[65] It comprises 3,695 a.[66] and is the long, narrow shape, typical of the 'springline parish'.[67] About $\frac{2}{3}$ of the parish lies on the chalk downs of Salisbury Plain, which rise steeply south of the village to over 750 ft. near the Iron Age camp at Bratton Castle. Until the end of the 19th century there were three or four substantial farms on the slopes of the Plain, but in 1960 much of this area belonged to the War Department. The northern end of the parish is clay-land and low-lying. The village of Bratton is situated in the extreme east

[53] See p. 156.
[54] See p. 187.
[55] *Andrews and Dury, Map* (W.A.S. Rec. Brch.), pl. 7.
[56] *Endowed Char. Wilts.* (1904), p. 26, and see below pp. 187, 189.
[57] See p. 191.
[58] See p. 188.
[59] See p. 171.

[60] See p. 188.
[61] Fry, *Land Utilization Wilts.* 200, 219–22.
[62] See p. 174.
[63] See p. 171.
[64] See p. 160.
[65] *V.C.H. Wilts.* iv. 342.
[66] *Census*, 1951.
[67] Fry, *Land Utilization Wilts.* 200, 203.

of the parish at a height of about 300 ft. on the strip of upper greensand dividing chalk and clay.[68] A small stream, called the Milbourne in the Middle Ages, and locally sometimes called the Bratt,[69] forms part of the eastern boundary of the parish and on this were a number of mills.[70] Church Spring, rising just south of the church, flows round it on the west side and down to join the larger stream. The only woodlands in the parish are the clumps of beech trees scattered here and there on the downs, but the thick hedges on high banks, and the numerous small ochards in and around the village create a well-wooded effect.[71]

The secondary road from West Lavington to Westbury runs through the parish at the foot of the downs. For its course through the village it is called Melbourne Street. This is joined at the western end of the village by a secondary road from Steeple Ashton in the north, and a former toll-house stands at the junction of the two roads. A minor road turns west off this road from Steeple Ashton and runs across the parish to Heywood. A road from the village of Bratton running south-westwards over the top of the downs to join a road from Westbury to Chitterne was turnpiked between 1751 and 1775.[72] In 1960 this was a mere track, as was the road running from Bratton to Westbury just north of the present secondary road, and known as Westbury Lower Road. The railway line from Westbury to Patney and Chirton passes through the northern part of the parish. The station of Edington and Bratton lies in the parish of Edington, but was closed to passengers in 1952.[73]

The village lies roughly round an incomplete circle of roads and along Melbourne Street, which runs through the middle. On either side of this street there was originally space for orchards and allotments, but in the 20th century this has been encroached upon by private building and a council estate built c. 1922. More recent building has extended the village westwards, and here there is another council estate built in 1948-9. The church lies ¼ mile to the south of the centre of the village on the steep slopes of the downs.[74]

In the early 19th century Bratton was still said to be made up of the three tithings of Stoke, Melbourne, and Bratton,[75] which existed in the 14th century and probably much earlier.[76] There was also another tithing, or estate, called Headinghill.[77] The first mention found of this is in 1166 and in the 13th and 14th centuries it emerges as an important member of the manor of Westbury.[78] It is mentioned with other lands in Bratton in a 16th-century suit,[79] and was assessed under Bratton for land tax in the 18th century,[80] and for church rates in the 17th and 18th centuries.[81] It has not, however, been precisely located. In 1960 the three separate settle-ments of Stoke, Melbourne, and Bratton were still distinguishable. Stoke, or Little Stoke, lay around the church,[82] so that the church probably once lay in the centre of a village, or hamlet, not, as now, on the fringe. Melbourne lay along the stream as it flows from the point called Stradbrook, and along Melbourne Street. Bratton is thought to have been the district around the Court House[83] which stands at the junction of Lower Road and Court Lane. This ho e was probably once the court house of the manor of Bratton which descended to the Marquesses of Bath. It formed part of Lord Bath's estate in 1840.[84] Just north of the Court House there are traces in a field of a moated site, probably of medieval date, thought locally to have been the site of the manor house of the same manor.[85] Traces of a moat are also to be seen at Dunge Farm, an 18th-century farm house about a mile to the north-west of the Court House.

The Court House is a timber-framed building with a thatched roof, standing on a stone base. Infilling between the timbers is of wattle and daub, partly replaced by brick. The structure is of several periods and its evolution is difficult to trace. It consists of a principal range parallel to the road with a cross wing at its north end; there are comparatively modern additions at the rear and at one time the building was divided into several cottages. A single cruck blade in a cross wall, near the centre of the principal range indicates that this part of the house was originally a single-storied structure of medieval date. The cross wing, which has close studding and a jettied first floor at the gable end, may be an early 16th-century addition. The principal or 'hall' block was later remodelled and raised to two stories, probably in 1626, a date which is carved on a bracket supporting the ceiling in the present central room. Moulded and carved fireplaces here and in the room above appear to be of the same period. The present front door, immediately south of the central room, has a lintel dated 1656. It is approached by a contemporary timber porch with turned balusters and the whole south end of the range may have been built, or rebuilt, at this time.

Bratton contains a high proportion of old houses of many periods, showing the use of a wide variety of building materials. In addition to the Court House, timber-framed examples include Ivy Cottage, Yew Tree Farm, and a derelict cottage (all in Lower Road), Court Lane Farm, and several houses at the south-east corner of the village. Most of these appear to date from the 16th and early 17th centuries; in some cases their thatched roofs have been replaced by slate. On the south side of Melbourne Street one of the few stone houses in the village has a thatched roof and a door lintel dated 1621; the adjoining cottage was formerly

[68] For a general survey of the geology of the region, see Fry, op. cit. 219-22.
[69] Ex inf. Miss J. S. Whitaker, Bratton. Thanks are due to Miss Whitaker for much help with this section.
[70] See p. 174.
[71] The maps used for this description are O.S. Maps 1/25,000 sheets 31/85, 94, 95; 1/2,500 Wilts. XLV. 2 (1st and later edns.).
[72] V.C.H. Wilts. iv. 257.
[73] Ibid. 293.
[74] See p. 179.
[75] Hoare, Mod. Wilts. Westbury, 57 n.
[76] See p. 139.

[77] P. N. Wilts. (E.P.N.S.), p. 152 has included some spellings of Headinghill under the entry for Huntenhall in Corsley. It has no entry for Headinghill in Bratton. In the 17th century the following spellings occur: Heddingshill, Higingshill, Higonshill, Higginghill, Hidgons Hill: Parish Records, Rate Bks.
[78] See p. 163.
[79] W.N. & Q. iii. 203-6.   [80] See p. 163.
[81] Parish Records, Rate Bks. 1687-1705, 1729-59.
[82] See p. 179.
[83] Bratton W.I. Scrapbk.
[84] W.R.O. Tithe Award, and see pl. facing p. 143.
[85] Ex inf. Miss J. S. Whitaker, Bratton.

timber-framed. The village also contains a notable number of small farm houses and medium-sized dwelling houses of the later 17th and 18th centuries. These are built of brick with stone dressings and several have considerable architectural character. The Manor House, partly of the 17th century, is an example.[86] Rosenhime Farm has a symmetrical front, a central gabled porch, and stone mullioned windows with drip moulds; its thatched roof was raised and tiled in 1962. The Poplars in Court Lane and Fir Tree Cottage in Lower Road date from the early 18th century and have two-light stone mullioned windows without drip moulds.[87] Ivydene in Lower Road is a much altered house of the same period. The older part of Grange Farm is dated 1739 and Scotts Farm is a somewhat similar house with a stone-slated roof.[88] A tall thatched house to the north of the Court House with a symmetrical brick front was formerly timber-framed; the brick alterations and additions date from the 18th century. Ballards, next to Scotts Farm, is a later 18th-century example with 19th-century additions.

There are also some larger 18th-century houses of which the most important is Bratton House in Melbourne Street, home of the Ballard family until the 19th century.[89] Melbourne House in Melbourne Street, built of red brick with stone dressings, has a two-storied front and a hipped roof of stone slates with dormer windows. The central doorway is surmounted by a stone hood on moulded brackets and above it is a pedimented window. Flanking these are three-light windows with raised central lights. The initials 'WW' and date '1768' are inscribed on a chimney stack and the same date appears on the wall enclosing the forecourt. Yew Trees in Lower Road consists of two distinct parts, each with a symmetrical 18th-century brick front. Between 1718 and c. 1789 members of the Whitaker family conducted a boarding school for boys in the house, and it was here, under the leadership of the Whitakers, that the early meetings of the Baptists were held before their chapel was built.[90] The school continued for many years after the retirement of the Whitakers. It is probable that the western part of the house, which contains a single large room on the ground floor, was built as an extension to the school in the middle of the 18th century. Unusual angle buttresses at the west end may have been added for structural reasons. The eastern part of the house, with an extension to the rear, is probably the original building and may date from the 17th century. A fire is said to have destroyed much of it in 1790[91] and the present brick front, which has a fluted stone frieze to the parapet and a decorative fanlight above the doorway, appears to have been rebuilt at this period. The sash windows are set within the frames of wider windows, and these may have belonged to the

original house. Behind the building is an avenue of ancient yews.

The presence of the foundry of Messrs. J. and R. Reeves[92] on the west side of the village caused Bratton to receive certain services earlier than many other rural villages. A telegraph service was introduced in 1892, gas in 1904, and the telephone in 1907. A street lighting scheme by oil lamps was first put into operation in 1902. This was adapted to gas in 1904 and to electricity in 1945.[93]

On the steep western slope of Bratton Down, just within the parish and at a height of about 600 ft., the so-called Westbury White Horse is cut out of the chalk (length 166 ft. height 163 ft.). A tradition, which apparently goes no farther back than the 18th century, has it that a horse was carved here to commemorate Alfred's victory over the Danes at Ethandun in 878. There is, however, no evidence for the existence of a horse here before the early 18th century. An engraving of the horse as it was in 1772 exists in Gough's edition of Camden's *Britannia* showing it to be quite different from the present horse, and certainly suggestive of a Saxon, or more primitive, origin.[94] In 1778 the horse depicted by Gough was destroyed and re-modelled by a Mr. Gee, steward to Lord Abingdon, this time facing left instead of right.[95] In 1873 a local committee appointed to supervise its restoration directed that an edging of upright stones should be made to prevent the horse from losing its shape. This work cost between £60 and £70. The outline of the present horse thus dates from 1873. Minor improvements were made in 1903 and 1936, and a number of scourings have taken place during the past 50 years. In 1936 the scouring was done under the auspices of the Office of Works. In 1953 the chalk was excavated from the tail and that area was covered with a mixture of cement.[96] In 1957 the whole surface of the horse was excavated to a depth of about 1 ft. and then recovered with a special mixture of cement with a chalk base. This work took about three months to complete and cost some £4,000.[97]

The civil parish of *DILTON MARSH* was created in 1894 out of the western part of the ancient parish of Westbury.[98] It lies, therefore, in the extreme west of the county, and its western boundary is the county boundary between Wiltshire and Somerset.[99] Until 1934 the parish extended southwestwards to include the houses on the north side of the village street at Chapmanslade, but in that year Chapmanslade became a civil parish and the south-west corner of Dilton Marsh was transferred to it[1].

The parish of Dilton Marsh comprises 2,507 a.[2] and is roughly square in shape with a projecting tongue of land in the north-east corner. It is low-

[86] See p. 161.
[87] A cottage with similar windows has a date stone of 1722.
[88] See pl. facing p. 143.   [89] See p. 165.
[90] Bratton W.I. Scrapbk. and see p. 183.
[91] B. H. Cunnington, *Annals of Devizes*, ii. 267; Bratton W.I. Scrapbk.
[92] See p. 171.
[93] Bratton W.I. Scrapbk.
[94] *Camden's Britannia*, ed. R. Gough (1806), p. 146,

pl. xiii, fig. 2.
[95] See *frontispiece*. Unless otherwise stated, information about the whitehorse is from M. Marples, *White Horses and other Hill Figures*, 67–76.
[96] *The Times*, 22 Aug. 1953.
[97] Ibid. 15 July, 1957.
[98] *V.C.H. Wilts.* iv. 347.
[99] For maps used see p. 141, n. 24.
[1] See p. 147.
[2] *Census*, 1951.

lying and nowhere reaches a height of over 250 ft. The soil of the north and west is clay, but the south-eastern part of the parish lies mostly on the upper greensand, and the extreme south-east corner touches upon the chalk of Salisbury Plain.[3] The southern part of the parish is well wooded. Much of it is occupied by the park of Chalcot House.[4] Black Dog Woods, once part of the forest of Selwood, which begin in Berkeley (Som.) and run through Chapmanslade, extend for over ½ mile into the south-western corner of the parish. There is also some woodland on the western boundary near Standerwick (Som.). The Biss Brook forms the eastern boundary of the parish, and a stream named the 'Alleburne' enters the parish in the north and runs through the Fairwood estate.

The main railway line from London to the west of England runs across the parish from east to west, and the line between Westbury and Warminster, opened in 1851,[5] runs southwards for about two miles just within the eastern boundary of the parish. There is a halt for Dilton Marsh on this line at the extreme east end of the village.

No main roads run through the parish, but the main road between Bath and Warminster forms its south-western boundary for about a mile. The secondary road from Westbury enters the parish at a point called Penknap. Here it forks and the northern branch crosses the parish and leads to the main Bath-Warminster road, while the southern branch leads to Chapmanslade and Frome (Som.). Just beyond Penknap a road leads north towards Penleigh and leaves the parish near Fairwood House.

The village of Dilton Marsh lies along the northern branch of the secondary road from Westbury, which forms the village street, and along two smaller roads leading off either side of it. The church, built in the 19th century, stands on the south side of the street, approximately in the middle of the village. There is little evidence of any building before the late 18th century. The houses on both sides of the street are spread out, and many stand in fair-sized gardens well back from the road. These houses are mostly cottages, often in blocks of two or more, and many of them were clearly built for the hand-loom weavers who, in the early 19th century, worked in their homes for the clothiers of Westbury and Warminster.[6] At the time of the Inclosure Award some of these craftsmen were allotted small parcels of land in front of their houses forming the verge of the road. Many of the houses are of brick, but others are of stone rubble with red-brick dressings, and in some instances the front walls only are of brick. One unit on the north side of the road, opposite the church, consists of a terrace of 4 two-storied weavers' cottages with a three-storied, double-fronted master's house at one end.[7] Behind the master's house is a two-storied workshop with wide windows to each floor. These buildings, which probably date from c. 1830, have front walls of red brick and are

of rubble behind. Along the narrow road branching south from the village street the cottages are close-packed and at all angles to the road.

There is a brick and tile works on the east side of the parish just north of the Dilton Marsh halt, and north of this a line of disused iron quarries stretches for about a mile.[8] On this side of the parish there are several rows of red-brick houses of late-19th-, and early-20th-century date, very probably built for workers at the nearby Leigh Works, the leather works of Charles Case & Son. These works occupy the former cloth mill called Boyer's Mill[9] standing beside the Biss Brook, which forms the boundary between Dilton Marsh and Westbury Leigh. Boyer's House, a large, early-19th-century building, stands in fairly extensive grounds on the Westbury Leigh side of the stream. On the west side of the same stream, and thus in Dilton Marsh, although in fact situated at the west end of the village street of Westbury Leigh, is Bridge Farm, formerly the Apple Tree Inn. This is an L-shaped building, originally timber-framed, and of 16th- or early-17th-century date. The front facing the street dates from the late 18th century. It is of stone ashlar with pediments to the first-floor windows, a central carved panel below the parapet, and a doorway with an enriched frieze.

At the west end of Dilton Marsh village there is a small council housing estate built since the Second World War. In the 19th century this end of the village was called Dilton's Lower Marsh.[10] From a point in this neighbourhood called Redpit a smaller road branches off the secondary road and forms a loop joining the larger road again about ½ mile west of Dilton Marsh village. The houses along this loop-road form the hamlet of Stormore, called Stormore Common, or St. Maur Common or Green in the 19th century,[11] and thus presumably part of the former manor of Westbury Seymour, or St. Maur.[12] Many weavers lived at Stormore in the early 19th century[13] and here, as at Dilton Marsh, some of the cottages still bear traces, often on the back elevations, of the wide windows beneath which the hand-looms stood.

Chalcot Park is the largest estate in the parish. In its finely landscaped park there is the site of a Romano-British settlement from which much pottery has been excavated. There are also several other large farms and houses in the parish. On the Biss Brook, about two miles north of Penknap, are Penleigh House and Farm, standing on either side of a private road leading through fields to Westbury.[14] North of Penleigh House, also on the Biss, are Brook Farm and Mill.[15] The farm can be approached either from the east by a road from the Ham in Westbury, or from the west by a private road called Brook Drove. On the western boundary of the parish is Fairwood House, a mainly 19th-century house, standing in a large park. Two farms, both called Fairwood, lie to the south-east and south-west of the park. At the western end of the Fairwood estate is an area

[3] For an account of the geology of the region, see Fry, *Land Utilization Wilts.* 155, 219–22.
[4] For Chalcot House see p. 155.
[5] *V.C.H. Wilts.* iv. 284.
[6] See pl. facing p. 249.
[7] See pl. facing p. 174.
[8] See p. 171.
[9] See p. 174.
[10] W.R.O. Inclosure Award.
[11] Ex inf. Mr. R. Tuffin.
[12] See p. 150.
[13] W.R.O. Inclosure Award.
[14] See p. 160.
[15] See p. 172.

known as Stourton Bushes, presumably named after the Lords Stourton who had a manor in Westbury in the 15th and 16th centuries.[16] South from Stourton Bushes is Five Lords' Farm. According to Hoare, the boundaries of the five manors of Westbury Stourton, Arundell, and Seymour, Leigh Priors, and Bremeridge met at this point.[17] Several of their boundary stones are said to have stood until the time of inclosure in 1808.[18] Bremeridge Farm, which gave its name to one of the Westbury manors, lies in an isolated position about two miles north of the village of Dilton Marsh.[19]

HEYWOOD lay in the north of the ancient parish of Westbury and when in 1894 the ancient parish was split up into the three civil parishes of Westbury, Bratton, and Dilton Marsh, Heywood was included in the new parish of Westbury. In 1896, however, Heywood, with an area of 1,701 a., was created a separate civil parish. In 1909 87 a. in the south-west corner of the parish were returned to Westbury,[20] so that in 1951 the area of Heywood was 1,614 a.[21]

The parish is roughly oblong in shape.[22] It is situated in the clay region of mid-west Wiltshire[23] and is consequently low-lying. Only in the extreme north-east corner does the land rise to 300 ft., and for the most part it does not lie above 175 ft. The Biss Brook forms the western boundary of the parish. A stream rising at Brittle Springs at the foot of Salisbury Plain enters the parish on the east, near Fulling Bridge Farm, a late-18th- or early-19th-century farmhouse, and runs past Heywood House where it is dammed to form a lake. The bridge carrying the main road over this stream was repairable by the county between 1852 and 1855.[24] The stream is joined just beyond the lake by the Bitham Brook, which rises in Westbury and enters the parish in the south. The combined stream, called the 'Bere Burne', runs northwards out of the parish to join the Biss Brook. The only woodland in the parish in 1960, besides the landscaped park of Heywood House, was the large wood in the north-east corner called Clanger Wood.

The railway line between Trowbridge and Westbury runs through the middle of the parish, and the main line from London to the west of England just enters the parish for about $\frac{1}{4}$ mile in the south. The main road from Trowbridge to Westbury also runs through the middle of the parish. A minor road, called Yoad Lane, branches east off this and leads to the road between Steeple Ashton and Bratton. About $\frac{1}{2}$ mile further north along the main road, another minor road forks north-west and runs out of the parish near Dursley to join a minor road coming in from Yarnbrook (North Bradley) and running through Heywood to Westbury.

There is no one compact area of settlement in the parish. The mid-19th-century church stands in the angle formed by the junction of the minor

road from Dursley with the main Westbury-Trowbridge road. Some houses, mostly of late-19th- or early-20th-century date, are strung out along this minor road, for the most part on its southern side. The school lies along this road, and on its northern side there is a small council housing estate built since the Second World War. A lane turning south of the minor road leads to a small group of houses called Norleaze. A more obvious and older area of settlement is the hamlet of Hawkeridge which is approached by a lane turning east off the road between Yarnbrook and Westbury. The congregational chapel was built here in 1844 and an inn and a number of cottages are of early-19th-century and later dates.

Until the end of the 19th century there was another area of settlement in the south-east corner of the parish. In the 18th century this was called Yoed and lay to the south of Heywood House along the narrow road called, in 1960, Yoad Lane, and along the lane leading to Apsley Farm. A small group of houses here is shown on maps of 1773 and 1817, but by the end of the 19th century the hamlet had apparently disappeared.[25] In 1960 there were only a few 20th-century houses along the lane.

In the mid-20th century a fairly extensive housing estate has been built in the south-west of the parish where Heywood adjoins Westbury at the Ham.

The largest house in the parish is Heywood House built in the mid-19th century.[26] Brook House, on the site of the manor house of the manor of Brook, lies to the east of the Biss Brook just within the parish.[27] To the north-east and south-east respectively of Brook House are Hawkeridge and Lodge Wood farms.[28] Hawkeridge Farm is a brick house of early-18th-century date with later alterations. Lodge Wood Farm was acquired by the War Department during the Second World War and was used for a time as part of an Ordnance Supply Depot. Just to the south-west of Lodge Wood Farm there is a moated site.

The civil parish of *CHAPMANSLADE* was created in 1934 out of parts of Dilton Marsh, Corsley, and Upton Scudamore.[29] Until 1894 Chapmanslade was a tithing within the ancient parish of Westbury, but after the civil parish of Dilton Marsh was made out of Westbury that year,[30] most of Chapmanslade came within the southern boundary of the new parish. This boundary ran down the middle of the road from Westbury to Frome (Som.), which for about $\frac{3}{4}$ of a mile forms the village street of Chapmanslade, so that the houses on the south side of the village street were in Corsley, while those on the north side were in Dilton Marsh.[31] All the land lying south of this road was, therefore, until 1934 either in the parish of Corsley or in that of Upton Scudamore.[32] Thus the tithing of Huntenhull Green lay in Corsley

[16] See p. 149.
[17] Hoare, *Mod. Wilts.* Westbury, 43.
[18] Ibid.   [19] See p. 158.
[20] For all above information see p. 141.
[21] *Census*, 1951.
[22] O.S. Map 1/25,000 sheet 31/85.
[23] For some account of this region see Fry, *Land Utilization Wilts.* 209–13.
[24] W.R.O. Q. Sess. Order Bk. 1852–55.

[25] *Andrews and Dury, Map* (W.A.S. Rec. Brch.) pl. 7; O.S. Map 1″ sheet 14 (1st edn.).
[26] See p. 163.
[27] See p. 152.
[28] See p. 156.
[29] *V.C.H. Wilts.* iv. 343.
[30] See p. 145.
[31] O.S. Map 6″ Wilts. XLIV. SW (2nd edn.).
[32] Ibid.

and is treated with the history of that place,[33] and the tithing of Thoulstone lay in Upton Scudamore and is dealt with under the history of that place.[34]

The civil parish of Chapmanslade is small, comprising some 1,136 a., and extending about 1½ mile from north to south and the same distance from east to west.[35] The Rodden Brook, about ½ a mile south of the village street, makes the southern boundary of the parish for most of its course, and the main road between Warminster and Bath forms part of the northern boundary. The western boundary of the parish is the county boundary between Wiltshire and Somerset. The soil of the parish is divided approximately equally between the light, highly fertile, greensand on the east side and the heavier gaults and clays on the west side.[36] In the north-west corner the land is fairly low-lying, but it rises to about 500 ft. near the centre of the parish, and from there falls rather steeply to the south and west. Black Dog Woods, once a part of Selwood Forest, occupy the entire north-west corner of the parish, and in 1959 were being extensively replanted. The secondary road from Westbury to Frome crosses the main Warminster-Bath road at Dead Maids Corner and runs from east to west through the middle of the parish. The only other metalled road is a minor road branching off the secondary road near the village and leading south through Huntenhall Green to Corsley.

The village of Chapmanslade lies approximately in the centre of the parish along the road from Westbury to Frome. The houses are spread out along this for about ¾ of a mile. They include a number of small houses and cottages, arranged singly or in pairs, of 18th- and early-19th-century date. These are either of stone, or brick with stone dressings, and many have stone door hoods on moulded brackets. The church and the Congregational and Baptist chapels all lie on the north side of the street, the church standing roughly in the middle of the village.[37] The narrow lane leading to the Baptist chapel continues northwards for about ¼ of a mile to Godswell Grove Farm which in the Middle Ages gave its name to the manor later known as Chapmanslade.[38] A number of buildings along the village street bear witness to Chapmanslade's former weaving industry.[39] Almost opposite the church is a much altered early-19th-century weavers' workshop. It is a two-storied building of rubble with brick dressings. On the west side of the upper floor there is an eight- or nine-light window, which has been blocked up. On the east side both ground and upper floors had seven-light windows, now reduced to six-lights. In 1960 this building was almost derelict, and was used as a workman's shed. Further east, nearly opposite the 'Wheelwrights' Arms', is another building which in the early 19th century may have been a weavers' workshop. It is built of similar materials,

but the wide window openings have been altered and the building converted into two cottages.

Huntley House, at the east end of the village, may originally have been timber-framed. But it was given brick walls, a third story, and a symmetrical front in the 18th century. Adjoining it to the south is a 3-storied structure of the early 19th century which was originally a weavers' workshop and more recently a small retail shop. At the back of the house a long range of brick and stone, possibly of 17th-century date, was at one time a bakehouse. The 'Wheelwrights' Arms', on the north side of the village street, was built as a residential house of some size and importance in the later 18th century. Close by is an early-19th-century ashlar pair of houses with some notable features. One of these has been converted into the village shop and Post Office. At the extreme east end of the village is a group of council houses built c. 1948, and there has been some more recent building at the west end of the village.

In the north-east corner of the parish, just inside the boundary with Dilton Marsh, are the few houses which form the hamlet of Short Street. This is approached by a minor road turning north off the secondary road between Westbury and Chapmanslade.

MANORS. In 1086 the king, as successor to Queen Edith, held *WESTBURY*.[40] It could thus later claim to be ancient demesne of the Crown.[41] The royal manor was assessed at 40 hides, and was co-extensive with the hundred.[42] The process of fragmentation of this large manor by royal grant had begun before 1086, for by then William Scudet, the king's cook, held an estate of 4½ hides which was to form later the manor of Dilton.[43] Several further grants of land in the manor were made in the 12th century. Henry I gave 4 bovates to Salisbury Cathedral which later formed the Rectory manor.[44] The Empress Maud granted land to Humphrey FitzOdo,[45] and also made a large grant to William Defuble. A gift by Defuble to the priory of Le Pré (dép. Seine-Inférieur) later formed the manor of Westbury Priory.[46] The rest of Defuble's land was regranted by Henry II to Joce de Dinan, and by division between his heirs and subinfeudation formed the manors later known as Westbury Mauduits, Leigh Priors, Westbury Leversage, and Bremeridge.[47] Other unrecorded grants by Henry II or his predecessors gave rise to the manors of Leigh, Penleigh, and Bratton.[48] What was left after all these gifts was granted away in 1173, and by successive division between coheirs formed the estates later known as Westbury Stourton, Westbury Seymour, Westbury Arundell, and Brook.[49] Other estates, acquired by religious houses from various gifts, were known as the manors of Godswell and Heywood.[50]

[33] See p. 16.
[34] See p. 78.
[35] Among maps used were O.S. Map 6″ Wilts. XLIV. SW; 1/2,500 Wilts. XLIV. 8 (1st and later edns.).
[36] For some account of the geology of the region see Fry, *Land Utilization Wilts.* 219–22.
[37] See pp. 181, 184.
[38] See p. 161.
[39] See p. 168.
[40] *V.C.H. Wilts.* ii, p. 118.
[41] J.I. 1/996, m. 17d.

[42] *V.C.H. Wilts.* ii, p. 213.
[43] Ibid.; see below, p. 152.
[44] See p. 153.
[45] J.I. 1/996, m. 11; in 1248–9 it was held by Augusta, a descendant of Humphrey's brother and wife of John de Aure: ibid. Its further descent has not been found.
[46] See p. 154.
[47] See pp. 155–7.
[48] See pp. 158–61.
[49] See below.
[50] See pp. 149–52.

The capital manor of Westbury, after its reduction by the grants mentioned above, was held at farm by four men from 1170 to 1173,[51] when it was granted by the king to Reynold Pavely.[52] He was holding the manor in 1194,[53] and must have died c. 1200, when the wardship of his heir was given to Ralph de Beauchamp.[54] In 1209 the Pope threatened to place Westbury under an interdict if it were not restored to Queen Berengaria of whose dower it was then claimed it formed a part.[55] The outcome of this threat is unknown. On his death in 1256 Walter Pavely was holding Westbury by the service of one knight's fee.[56] The manor at that time comprised the four estates or hamlets of Brook, Headinghill, Stoke, and Dilton.[57] It passed from Walter Pavely to his son, Reynold (d. 1280);[58] from Reynold to his son Walter, who was sheriff of Wiltshire in 1289 and 1296,[59] and died in 1323;[60] from Walter it passed to his son Reynold (d. 1347), [61] and from Reynold to his son John.[62] Sir John Pavely died in 1361. His heirs were Joan, Elizabeth, and Eleanor, daughters of his daughter Alice by his first marriage, who had married John St. Lo and survived her father by half a day only, and Joan, his daughter by his second marriage. All the girls were under age.[63]

The wardship of Joan Pavely was granted to the Bishop of Winchester. By the partition of her father's lands Joan received the manor of Westbury, the hamlet of Headinghill,[64] and half the profits and perquisites of the view of frankpledge, the hundred, fairs, market, and portmote of Westbury. The rest of Sir John's property went to John St. Lo for his daughters.[65] After Joan's marriage, her husband, Ralph Cheyney, objected that his wife's share was inferior in value to that allotted to the daughters of John St. Lo, and a second partition was made in 1368.[66] By this Ralph and Joan Cheyney were to hold the manor of Brook, the hamlets of Ditteridge,[67] and Hawkeridge, and half the profits of the view of frankpledge, the hundred, fair, market, and portmote of Westbury; the manor of Westbury with the hamlets of Headinghill, Stoke, Milborne, and Leigh, the other half of the profits mentioned above, and the whole of the rent of the 'shamelhouse' in Westbury were assigned to John St. Lo for his daughters.[68] John St. Lo died in 1375 and the manor of Westbury with the hamlet of Headinghill was divided between his

two surviving daughters, Joan, wife of Sir John Chidiock, and Eleanor, wife of Thomas of Bradeston.[69]

Sir John Chidiock died in 1390 and his heir was his son John (II) aged twelve.[70] Joan, his widow, survived her husband and married secondly John Bache upon whom she settled the manor in 1392.[71] John Bache died in 1409 and the manor reverted to John Chidiock (II).[72] John Chidiock (II) died in 1415 and was succeeded by his son John Chidiock (III), also a minor.[73] On the death of John Chidiock (III) in 1450 his share in the manor of Westbury was divided between his daughters, Katharine, wife of William Stafford, and Margaret, wife of William Stourton (d. 1477).[74]

William Stourton succeeded to the title of Lord Stourton in 1462 and his share in the manor of Westbury descended with the title until the execution of Charles, Lord Stourton, in 1557 for the murder of Thomas Hartgill,[75] when it was fortfeited to the Crown. In 1570 this estate, by now known as *WESTBURY STOURTON*, was granted to Edward Dyer.[76] Dyer conveyed it in the same year to Stephen Whitaker[77] on whose death in 1576 it passed to his son Henry.[78] Henry was succeeded by his second son, William,[79] who sold it in 1619–20, with the exception of Bitham House, a fulling mill called Bitham Mill,[80] and a close called Gaston, to Sir James Ley (cr. Earl of Marlborough 1626).[81] Among the property which comprised the manor at this time was land near Dogget's Lane, a close called Apsleys, presumably near the present Apsley Farm, Stourton's Wood, no doubt to be identified with Stourton Bushes, in Dilton Marsh,[82] and land scattered throughout the fields of Westbury, Dilton, Leigh, Heywood, Hawkeridge, and Bratton.[83]

William Stafford, husband of Katharine Chidiock, died in 1450, and his share in Westbury passed to his son Humphrey, who was created Earl of Devon in 1469 and executed the same year.[84] He left no issue,[85] and the fee of the manor remained with his mother, who survived him. She married as her second husband Sir John Arundell. The manor, with certain other estates, was mortgaged to raise money for the fine imposed upon Arundell for his part at the battle of Tewkesbury.[86] He died deeply in debt, and his wife, who married thirdly Roger Lewkenore, died in 1479 leaving as her heir Thomas

[51] *Pipe R. 1171* (P.R.S. xvi), 23; ibid. *1172* (P.R.S. xviii), 128; ibid. *1173* (P.R.S. xix), 105.
[52] *Rot. Hund.* (Rec. Com.), ii. 278.
[53] *Pipe R. 1194* (P.R.S. N.S.v), 18.
[54] *Rot. Oblat. et Fin.* (Rec. Com.), 49.
[55] *Cal. Pap. Let.* i. 33.
[56] *Wilts. Inq. p.m.* 1242–1326 (Index Libr.), 18–19.
[57] See pp. 151, 163, 144, 143.
[58] *Wilts. Inq. p.m.* 1242–1326 (Index Libr.), 130.
[59] P.R.O. *List of Sheriffs* s.v. Wilts.
[60] *Wilts. Inq. p.m.* 1242–1326 (Index Libr.), 434–6.
[61] Ibid. 1327–77 (Index Libr.), 176–7.
[62] Ibid.   [63] Ibid. 290–1.
[64] For the location of Headinghill see p. 144.
[65] *Cal. Pat.* 1361–64, 162–3; *Wilts. Inq. p.m.* 1327–77 (Index Libr.), 290–1.
[66] B.M. Lansd. MS. 442 f. 145; *Cal. Close*, 1364–8, 456–8.
[67] This is Ditteridge in Box in which place Sir John Pavely held a messuage and a carucate at the time of his death in 1361: *Wilts. Inq. p.m.* 1327–77 (Index Libr.), 291.

[68] *Cal. Close*, 1364–8, 456–8.
[69] *Wilts. Inq. p.m.* 1327–77 (Index Libr.), 387–9, 391.
[70] C 136/66/3.
[71] C.P. 25(1)/289/56/235.
[72] C 137/76/15.
[73] C 138/17/58.
[74] C 139/139/26.
[75] *Complete Peerage*; J. E. Jackson, 'Lord Stourton and the Murder of the Hartgills', *W.A.M.* viii. 242–336.
[76] C 66/1071 m. 28.
[77] C.P. 25(2)/239/13 Eliz. Trin.
[78] C 142/179/105.
[79] Hoare, *Mod. Wilts.* Westbury, 43.
[80] See p. 172.
[81] C.P. 43/147 m. 45d; for James Ley see *D.N.B.*
[82] O.S. Map 1/25,000 Wilts. 31/84; see p. 147.
[83] C.P. 43/147 m. 45d.
[84] *Complete Peerage*, Devon.
[85] For the contingent interest of his heir-at-law, Sir Robert Willoughly, and his issue, see e.g. C.P. 40/1113 mm. 5 d., 6.
[86] *Cal. Inq. p.m. Hen. VII*, i, p. 13.

Arundell her son by her second husband.[87] Thomas died in 1485 before he had been able to pay off his father's debts, and the manor passed to his son John, who was said to hold it of Sir Robert Willoughby, who was a cousin of Humphrey Stafford.[88] Thomas's son, Sir John Arundell, sold, in 1549–50, to Thomas Long, clothier of Trowbridge, a mill and various tenements in Westbury, which probably comprised the whole of this part of the manor.[89] Thomas Long died childless seised of the manor in 1562,[90] and the manor passed under his will to his nephew Edward Long. Edward and his son Gifford sold the manor in 1613 under the name of Westbury and *WESTBURY ARUNDELL* to Sir James Ley.[91] The estate at this date included a mill, and was said to lie in Westbury, Bratton, Imber, and Edington.[92]

Eleanor of Bradeston, the second daughter of Sir John St. Lo, married secondly Sir Richard Seymour, who died seised of his wife's share of the manor in 1401.[93] His heir was his son Richard, but Eleanor survived her husband, and in 1408 conveyed the manor to John Seymour, presumably a younger son, and his wife Margaret, a daughter of John Erlegh, and their issue.[94] After the death of John Seymour, Margaret married Sir Walter Sondes, who held the manor in her right at the time of his death in 1428.[95] Margaret married thirdly Sir William Cheyney and died in 1443 when the property passed to her grandson, Thomas, son of John Seymour.[96] Thomas settled the manor upon his son John Seymour and Elizabeth his wife and their heirs. Elizabeth outlived John and married secondly John Biconill and on her death in 1505 was succeeded by her granddaughter Joan, daughter of her son William Seymour who died in 1503.[97] Joan married William Drewry and died childless in 1517, and her heirs were her cousins John Stawell and Edward Bamfield, sons of her aunts Anne and Margaret, sisters of William Seymour.[98] Edward Bamfield died in 1528 and was succeeded by his son John.[99] John Stawell sold his share in 1566 to Thomas Webbe and Margaret his wife,[1] who also acquired from Richard Bamfield that part of the manor which had belonged to John Bamfield.[2] In 1574 they settled the two parts upon themselves with remainder in tail to their daughters, Joan, wife of Alexander Chocke, and Elizabeth, wife of Robert Webbe.[3] Thomas Webbe died in 1585,[4] and in 1602 Robert and Elizabeth Webbe conveyed their interest, which was the remainder in default of heirs of Joan and Alexander

Chocke, to trustees for the queen and her successors.[5] This interest was granted in 1616 by James I to Sir Francis Popham and Richard Organ.[6] Between 1605 and 1607 Alexander and Joan Chocke settled the manor on themselves and their heirs, with remainder to their nephew Alexander, son of Alexander the elder's younger brother Francis.[7] This apparently superseded the settlement of 1574, for on Alexander the elder's death without issue in 1607, the manor, then known as *WESTBURY SEYMOUR*, passed to his nephew Alexander.[8] In 1621 this Alexander, his wife, his father, and representatives of Elizabeth and Robert Webbe conveyed the manor to Sir James Ley, who thus became possessed of the whole manor of Westbury.[9]

Sir James's son Henry, Earl of Marlborough, died in 1638 and his widow married Thomas Wanklin, who compounded for his life interest in the manor in 1651.[10] Henry's son James, Earl of Marlborough (d. 1665) sold the manor in 1639–40 to Henry, Earl of Danby (d. 1644).[11] On the death of Danby, Westbury apparently passed to his brother Sir John Danvers, the regicide, who in 1651 was receiving the profits of the hundred.[12] Danvers died in 1655 and his heirs were his two daughters, Elizabeth, wife of Robert Villiers, who assumed the name Danvers, and Anne, wife of Sir Henry Lee. Anne and Henry Lee had two daughters, Eleanor, wife of James, Lord Norris, and Anne, wife of Thomas Wharton (cr. Marquess of Wharton and Malmesbury 1714–15).[13] In 1670 a moiety of the manor was settled on Robert and Elizabeth Danvers.[14] Robert died *c.* 1675, and his widow, who assumed the title Viscountess Purbeck, married John Duvale. In 1681 they conveyed their share in the manor to James, Lord Norris,[15] who had married Eleanor, a daughter of Anne and Henry Lee. By a conveyance of the same date the share belonging to Anne and Thomas Wharton was apparently sold to James and Eleanor Norris,[16] and in 1689 the whole manor was settled on them.[17] James was created Earl of Abingdon in 1682,[18] and Westbury descended with the title until 1777 when a large part of it was advertised for sale.[19] The Abingdon lands were then sold in parts at sales held in 1788, 1790, 1797, 1799, and 1808.[20] In 1810 the manorial rights were sold to Sir Manasseh Massey Lopes, bt.[21] The manor then passed with this title until *c.* 1904 when Sir Massey Lopes conveyed it to his nephew Henry Ludlow Lopes, Baron Ludlow of Heywood (d. 1922).[22] In 1920 the lordship of the hundred and manor of Westbury were

[87] C 140/71/47.
[88] *Cal. Inq. p.m. Hen. VII*, i, pp. 13, 83–84.
[89] C.P. 25(2)/65/531/3 Edw. VI Mich.
[90] C 142/132/22.
[91] C.P. 25(2)/370/11 Jas. I Hil.; C.P. 25(2)/371/12 Jas. I East.
[92] Ibid.
[93] C 137/26/55.
[94] C.P. 25(1)/256/59/10; *Cal. Pat.* 1405–8, 396.
[95] E 179/196/87.
[96] C 139/110/37.
[97] *Cal. Inq. p.m. Hen. VII*, iii, p. 425.
[98] C 142/32/107.
[99] C 142/48/77.
[1] C.P. 25(2)/259/8 Eliz. Trin.; see also C 66/999 m. 7.
[2] C 3/188/27.
[3] C 142/211/186.
[4] Ibid.
[5] C.P. 43/76 m. 10d.

[6] C 66/2071.
[7] C.P. 25(2)/369/3 Jas. I Trin.; C.P. 25(2)/369/4 Jas. I East.; C.P. 43/93 m. 53.
[8] C 142/296/132.
[9] C.P. 25(2)/372/19 Jas. I Mich.
[10] *Cal. Cttee. for Compounding*, 1643–60 pt. 4, p. 2732.
[11] C 54/3202 no. 5; *Complete Peerage*, Danby.
[12] E 317/Wilts./17.
[13] Macnamara, *Memorials of the Danvers Family*, 102; *Complete Peerage*, Norreys and Wharton.
[14] C.P. 25(2)/761/22 and 23 Chas. II Hil.
[15] C.P. 25(2)/747/35 Chas. II Trin.; C 54/4548 no. 8.
[16] C.P. 25(2)/747/33 Chas. II Trin.; C.P. 43/395 rot. 182.
[17] C.P. 25(2)/897/1 Wm. & Mary East.
[18] *Complete Peerage*.
[19] W.R.O. 490, Notice of Sale.
[20] Hoare, *Mod. Wilts.* Westbury, 44.
[21] Ibid. 6, 44.
[22] Burke, *Peerage and Baronetage*, and see p. 163.

sold to Mr. Frank Parsons, of Westbury. It was said to be worth £3 a year.[23]

Until 1361 the estate which became the manor of *BROOK* formed part of the capital manor of Westbury. In 1216 when Ralph de Beauchamp had the wardship of Walter Pavely this property was described as Westbury and Brook,[24] and in 1256 Brook was named as one of the five estates, or townships, which composed Walter Pavely's manor of Westbury.[25] Brook was possibly the principal residence of the Pavely family in the 14th century, for Reynold Pavely is styled 'of Brook'.[26]

Brook was assigned to John St. Lo for his three daughters on the death of Sir John Pavely in 1361,[27] but on the second partition of Sir John's estates in 1368 the manor was allotted to his daughter Joan, wife of Ralph Cheyney.[28] Sir Ralph Cheyney died in 1400 holding the manor in right of his wife, and in 1402[29] his son, Sir William Cheyney, settled it upon himself and his wife Cecily.[30] Cecily outlived her husband and their eldest son, Edmund, who had married Alice, daughter and coheir of Sir Humphrey Stafford of Southwick (d. 1442),[31] and on Cecily's death in 1430–1 her heirs were the three daughters of Edmund, Elizabeth, Cecily, and Anne.[32] The younger Cecily died shortly after her grandmother,[33] and the manor was eventually assigned to Anne, who married Sir John Willoughby.[34] In 1461 a general pardon was granted to Sir John, who was presumably a Lancastrian, for all offences and all forfeitures of lands.[35] His son Robert also forfeited his lands for his adherence to the Lancastrian cause, and in 1485 Brook was granted to Edward Ratcliffe for his services against the rebels.[36] Robert Willoughby's estates were restored to him by Henry VII, under whom he held high office, including those of lord steward and admiral of the fleet, and by whom he was created in 1491 Baron Willoughby de Broke.[37] Brook was presumably the chief residence of Lord Willoughby de Broke and, according to Leland, he rebuilt the house there. On his death in 1502 the manor passed to his son, Robert.[38] Robert died in 1521 leaving no son, and Brook was settled upon his daughters by his second wife, Dorothy Grey. They were Anne, later wife of Charles Blount, Lord Mountjoy (d. 1544), and Elizabeth, later wife of John Paulet, Marquess of Winchester (d. 1576).[39] A claim to the manor by Sir Anthony Willoughby of Goreley (Hants) was unsuccessful and in 1542 Anthony released his claim to Charles Blount and

John Paulet.[40] Charles Blount, Lord Mountjoy, died in 1544.[41] His wife, Anne, then married Richard Broke,[42] and after his death she apparently married Sir John Bonham,[43] for in 1574 as Anne Bonham, widow, she alienated her life interest in her moiety of the manor to John Pavy and John Goldwell.[44] In 1596–7 Lord Mountjoy (d. 1606), grandson of Anne, and William, Marquess of Winchester (d. 1598), son and heir of Elizabeth Paulet, obtained permission by Act of Parliament to divide the property which had come to them from Robert Willoughby, and Brook was allotted to Lord Mountjoy.[45] On the death of Anne Bonham in 1582[46] the park at Brook had been disparked and made into several grounds and portions.[47] Closes called Rush Lanes, Oxen Leaze, and Bushy Leaze, comprising 45 a., were conveyed in 1599 by Lord Mountjoy to Sir James Ley and thereafter descended as the capital manor.[48] Another part of the manor was conveyed in 1599 by Lord Mountjoy to Sir Edward Hungerford,[49] and at Sir Edward's death in 1607 this estate was called the manor of Brook.[50] The exact extent of the estate is not known, but it seems to have excluded Brook House and included Brook Farm, 'Storadge and Dowesfield', three fulling mills, a grain mill, and Brook Marsh, as well as land and common of pasture in the surrounding hamlets and townships.[51] It passed in the Hungerford family until 1684 when Sir Edward Hungerford sold it, apparently with the exception of Storridge Pastures, to Sir Stephen Fox. Between 1692 and 1698 Sir Stephen's son, Charles, conveyed it to Robert, Lord Lexinton. From Lord Lexinton it passed in c. 1718 to Sir Edward Desbouverie and descended in the Bouverie family of Longford Castle. In 1785 Jacob Pleydell-Bouverie, Earl of Radnor, sold much of the property to Gaisford Gibbs and John Gawen.[52] The same year Brook Farm was conveyed to Thomas Phipps of Chalford (d. 1792), who was already lessee of Brook Mill, a grist and fulling mill.[53] In 1794 Phipps's executors sold the Brook Farm estate, comprising some 150 a., to William Aldridge Ballard of Bratton.[54] After Ballard's death Brook Farm was sold in 1803 by his executors to Thomas Henry Hele Phipps of Leighton House (d. 1841).[55]

Storridge Pastures (see above), comprising 160 a., passed in 1688 from Sir Edward Hungerford to John Hall of Bradford,[56] and descended with Hall's other Wiltshire estates to the Duke of Kingston.[57] In about 1745 Evelyn, Duke of Kingston, sold the

[23] W.A.S. Libr., Devizes, newspaper cutting in Sale Cat. xvi; see above p. 137.
[24] *Rot. Litt. Claus.* (Rec. Com.), i. 285.
[25] *Wilts. Inq. p.m.* 1242–1326 (Index Libr.), 18–19.
[26] *Cal. Close,* 1327–30, 528, 538.
[27] See p. 149.
[28] Ibid.
[29] C 139/13/52.
[30] *Cal. Pat.* 1401–5, 91.
[31] C 138/46/46.
[32] C 139/49/42.
[33] C 139/51/53.
[34] Hoare, *Mod. Wilts.* Westbury, 26.
[35] *Cal. Pat.* 1461–6, 126.
[36] Ibid. 1476–85, 424.
[37] *D.N.B.* Willoughby.
[38] C 142/18/1.
[39] C 142/40/12; *Complete Peerage,* Willoughby de Broke and Winchester; *Burke's Peerage,* Willoughby de Broke.
[40] C.P. 40/1113 mm. 5d., 6.
[41] *Complete Peerage.*
[42] Ibid.

[43] C 2 Eliz. I/43/52.
[44] C 66/1113 m. 17.
[45] C 2 Eliz. I/Hh. 15/47.
[46] C 142/202/194.
[47] C 2 Eliz. I/H. 3/52.
[48] C 54/1621 Chas. Blount, Lord Mountjoy and Jas. Ley.
[49] C 54/1621 Chas. Blount, Lord Mountjoy and Edw. Hungerford.
[50] C 142/306/160.
[51] C 54/1621 Chas. Blount, Lord Mountjoy and Edw. Hungerford; Hoare, *Mod. Wilts.* Westbury, 30. Unless otherwise stated, facts about the descent of this estate come from Hoare, op. cit.
[52] MS. Cal. Deeds at Chalcot House, 127.
[53] Ibid. 121–3.
[54] Ibid. 127.
[55] Ibid. 133, and see p. 156.
[56] Unless otherwise stated, facts about the descent of this estate come from Hoare, *Mod. Wilts.* Westbury, 30–33, and MS. Cal. Deeds at Chalcot House.
[57] *V.C.H. Wilts.* vii. 14–15.

estate to Thomas Phipps (d. 1792), who on the marriage of his son, Thomas Hele Phipps (d. 1790), with Penelope Clutterbuck in 1788 made over the property as part of her marriage settlement. On Penelope's death in 1830 Storridge Pastures passed to her son Thomas Henry Hele Phipps of Leighton House (d. 1841).[58]

In 1599 Brook House with some land adjoining was sold by Lord Mountjoy to William Jones of Edington.[59] The estate comprised some 280 a. at this time, of which 58 a. were leased to Peter Polden, and 63 a. to Sir James Ley.[60] William was succeeded by his son Sefton Jones,[61] whose granddaughters Anne, wife of Peter Whatley of London, and Elizabeth, wife of Henry Long, styled of Brook, sold the estate in 1651 to Nicholas Greene of Brook, who already had a life interest in the estate by his marriage with the widow of Sefton Jones.[62] Part of the estate was settled in 1662 by Nicholas Greene upon his son, another Nicholas. Nicholas the younger died c. 1688 and his son, Richard Greene, sold the house and estate in 1689 to Edward Lisle of the Middle Temple, London. From Lisle it was purchased in 1693 by Stephen Blatch of Westbury. Blatch died childless and left Brook House by his will dated 1718 to his brother John Blatch. From John Blatch it passed to Richard Tuck of Rowdford whose mother was an aunt of the brothers Stephen and John Blatch. In 1758, after the death of Richard Tuck, the house, together with the adjoining Lodgewood Farm, was sold to Henry Hele, of Salisbury. Hele's daughter and heir, Jane, brought the house into the Phipps family on her marriage to Thomas Phipps of Chalford and after his death in 1792 it passed to her grandson Thomas Henry Hele Phipps (d. 1841), who also acquired the Brook Farm estate in 1803 and Storridge Pastures in 1830.[63]

When Leland visited Brook House in c. 1541 part of a much older manor house was still to be seen, but the main building was that newly erected, according to him, by the 1st Lord Willoughby de Broke (d. 1502). The windows, Leland remarked, were full of rudders, which he suggested were Lord Willoughby de Broke's badge as admiral of the fleet.[64] The park he described as fair, although not large, and with a great number of fine-grained oaks.[65] Aubrey, writing just over a hundred years later, described the house as very large and stately. The hall, which was large and open at that time, contained, according to him, very old windows with the coat of arms of the Pavelys. Other shields of arms were then to be seen in windows in the 'canopie chamber', the dining room, the parlour, and the chapel. Aubrey also records a tradition that Edward III was at Brook, and that a bridge

there, called Kingbridge, was built at the time.[66] In 1872 it was said that only one wing survived of the 'newly erected' house which Leland saw.[67]

In 1960 this wing, which may well have been built in the late 15th century by Lord Willoughby de Broke (d. 1502), as suggested by Leland, was used as a farm building and formed one side of a farmyard. It is a two-storied structure of 7 bays with stone-rubble walls with freestone dressings. The west gable-end and south side have stepped buttresses. On the south side there are 3 moulded stone doorways with arched heads and several two-light windows with uncusped arched lights. The range was always two-storied and the upper floor consisted of at least 3 rooms, each of which had an external door in the north wall. The central room has a blocked stone fireplace. The open roof of the wing is of the arch-braced collarbeam type with 3 tiers of wind braces. At right angles to this wing, at its east end, a farmhouse was built in the 17th century, probably soon after Aubrey's visit (see above). It is built of stone-rubble with mullioned and transomed windows, and has a steeply pitched roof covered with stone slates. Early-19th-century Gothic windows have been inserted in its east front. The medieval hall, part of which Leland saw, was probably demolished at the time of the building of the farmhouse, but at the junction of the house with the late-15th-century wing, a short length of steeply pitched roof may have formed part of this earlier hall. A fire at this point in 1958 has destroyed the old roof timbers.[68]

The $4\frac{1}{2}$ hides held by William Scudet in Westbury in 1086 possibly lay partly in Dilton and partly in Bratton.[69] It was probably this estate, then comprising 4 carucates, which in 1210–12 William Dauntsey held in chief, in Bratton and Dilton by the serjeanty of keeping the king's larder.[70] William died c. 1221 and was succeeded by his son Richard,[71] who held $4\frac{1}{2}$ hides in Bratton and Dilton in 1236 and 1242 in chief by service in the king's army.[72] By 1250 Richard Dauntsey had alienated a number of holdings in Bratton and Dilton to various persons,[73] but on his death that year 4 carucates in those places passed to his heir, Richard, aged twelve.[74] Richard (II) died c. 1266 and the wardship of his heir, Giles, was granted to William de Aete.[75] In 1288–9 the manor of *DILTON* was in the possession of Richard Dauntsey (III),[76] possibly a brother of Giles, and identical with the Richard, son of Richard Dauntsey, who died in 1315 holding the manor of Dilton.[77] This he held by the service of $\frac{1}{2}$ knight's fee, and the payment of 10 marks annually to the castle guard of Old Salisbury. Richard (III)'s son, Richard (IV), died holding the manors of Bratton and Dilton in 1348 and was

[58] For sale of Storridge Farm, see p. 156.
[59] C 54/1621 Chas. Blount, Lord Mountjoy and Wm. Jones.
[60] MS. Cal. Deeds at Chalcot House.
[61] C 142/423/61.
[62] Subsequent facts about descent of Brook House from Hoare, *Mod. Wilts*. Westbury, 28–9, and MS. Cal. Deeds at Chalcot House.   [63] See above.
[64] Canon Jackson thought it more likely that the rudder was a device of the Pavelys: *W.A.M.* i. 183, n; see p. 248.
[65] Leland, *Itin*. ed. Toulmin Smith, v. 83.
[66] Aubrey, *Topog. Coll*. ed. Jackson, 399–402.
[67] *W.A.M.* xiv. 36–38.

[68] *Wilts. Times*, 5 Aug. 1958.
[69] *V.C.H. Wilts* ii. pp. 73, 118 n., 167 n.; see above, p. 148.
[70] *Red Bk. of Exch*. (Rolls Ser.), ii. 486.
[71] *Excerpta e. Rot. Fin*. (Rec. Com.), i. 76.
[72] *Bk. of Fees*, i. 586, ii. 740. The service had been changed with royal consent temp. Hen. III: ibid. ii. p. 1178.
[73] *Bk. of Fees*, ii. pp. 1178, 1225, and see p. 164.
[74] *Wilts. Inq. p.m.* 1242–1326 (Index Libr.), 11.
[75] *Wilts. N. & Q.* ii. 359; J.I. 1/998 m. 32.
[76] J.I. 1/1006 m. 50d.
[77] *Wilts. Inq. p.m.* 1242–1326 (Index Libr.), 394–5.

succeeded by his grandson, John Dauntsey.[78] On John's death in 1355 the manor, at this time called of Dilton only, together with one carucate in Bratton, passed to his brother William,[79] and William appears to have been succeeded before 1362 by another brother Walter.[80] Walter died seised of the manor of Dilton in 1369, leaving as his heirs his sister, Margaret, wife of Sir Ralph Norton, and his nephew John St. Manifee, son of his sister Joan.[81] St. Manifee conveyed his share in the manor to trustees for Sir Ralph and Margaret.[82] Maud, wife of Thomas de Cantesangre, and presumably widow of Walter Dauntsey, held a life interest in a third of each share.[83] In 1380 the entire manor was conveyed to the Rector and Bonhommes of Edington.[84] In the following year the rector re-granted to Sir Ralph Norton and Margaret and their issue their share in the manor with reversion to Edington.[85] Margaret died childless in 1388 and the manor thus reverted to the Bonhommes, and formed part of the property of that community until the Dissolution.[86]

In 1540 the manor was granted to John Bush, probably brother of Paul Bush, the last Rector of Edington.[87] John's son, another John, mortgaged it in 1566 for £500 to Jerome Hawley, who ten years later entered into possession.[88] Hawley then sold the manor in 1587 to Sir Walter Hungerford.[89] It descended in the Hungerford family until 1684 when Sir Edward Hungerford sold it to Sir Stephen Fox.[90] In 1689 Fox conveyed it to two persons,[91] presumably trustees for Thomas Phipps and Bridget his wife, who were in possession of the manor in 1693.[92] Thomas Phipps died c. 1715 and in 1721–2 his son, also called Thomas (d. 1724), conveyed the manor to Paul Phipps of Chalford (d. 1722), and to Paul's sons John (d. 1739), and Thomas (d. 1747).[93] It passed from Paul's son Thomas (d. 1747) to his son, another Thomas, who devised it in 1792 to his younger grandson, Charles Lewis Phipps.[94] Charles Lewis Phipps styled himself of Dilton Court after the house which he built on the estate.[95] From Charles Lewis, who died without issue in 1862, the estate passed to his nephew Paul Phipps.[96] Paul Phipps sold it to a cousin, Charles Paul Phipps, who also acquired Chalcot House and died in 1880.[97] From then on the Dilton Court estate followed the same descent as Chalcot House which became the

residence of this branch of the Phipps family. Dilton Court later came to be called Chalcot Home Farm.[98]

The manor of the *RECTORY* of Westbury, sometimes called the Parsonage or Chantry manor, comprised in 1086 $1\frac{1}{2}$ hide of land held by the church of Westbury.[99] Henry I gave the church to Salisbury Cathedral and it came to be appropriated to the office of precentor.[1] A virgate of land which had belonged to Richard Dauntsey was added to the manor in the 13th century.[2] Apart from a sale by the Parliamentary trustees in 1652,[3] the manor was held by the precentors until 1842 when, on the death of the then precentor, it passed under the Cathedrals and Ecclesiastical Commissioners Act (1840–1) to the Ecclesiastical Commissioners.[4] Authority for the sale of the property was given in 1863,[5] and the bulk of it was sold in 1899 to Lord Ludlow of Heywood (d. 1922).[6]

In 1574 William Benett, nephew of Thomas Benett, Precentor of Salisbury (d. 1558), bequeathed the lease of the rectory manor, which he had presumably obtained from his uncle, to his son, Thomas Benett.[7] Thomas died without issue in 1605, and the lease probably passed to his brother, William Benett of Norton Bavant. It was renewed to William's son, Thomas, in 1641,[8] and descended in the same way as Norton Bavant to William Benett who died without issue in 1781.[9] The Benetts' connexion with the manor then ceased and it was leased until the end of the 18th century by William Parry.[10] In 1800 the lessees were Richard White, of London, and John Gale, of Stert.[11] White also leased the manor of Westbury Priory.[12] In 1851 Richard White was replaced by William White and from this date until 1874 the Rectory Manor was leased by William White in partnership with two or three other lessees, who sub-let the property to 'persons resident in the tithing of chantry'.[13]

The farmhouse and buildings of the rectory manor lay just south of Westbury Church within the tithing of Chantry. Much of the land of the manor lay in Bratton.[14] In 1614 besides the 'mansion house' there were three pastures called Chantry Lease (26 a.), a pasture called Parson's Croft (6 a.), and 45 a. in the common fields. There were also numerous other parcels of land all let out, including 28 a. in the arable fields of Bratton.[15] In 1642 the estate was described as the 'manor of Westbury be-

[78] Ibid. 1327–77 (Index Libr.), 174.
[79] *Cal. Inq. p.m.* x, p. 200–1.
[80] *Wilts. Inq. p.m.* 1327–77 (Index Libr.), 311.
[81] Ibid. 351–2. For the descent of the carucate in Bratton, see p. 164.
[82] B.M. Lansd. MS. 442, f. 127d.
[83] *Cal. Pat.* 1377–81, 491.
[84] Ibid. 486, 491; C.P. 25(1)/256/54/25, 26.
[85] *Cal. Pat.* 1381–5, 7.
[86] C 136/57/18.
[87] *L. & P. Hen. VIII.* xv. p. 299; *V.C.H. Wilts.* iii. 323.
[88] C 54/995 Jerome Hawley and John Bush; C.P. 25 (2)/239 8 Eliz. Trin.
[89] C 66/1291 m. 51.
[90] C.P. 25 (2)/747 36 Chas. II Trin.
[91] C.P. 25 (2)/887/1 Wm. and Mary Trin.
[92] C.P. 25 (2)/888/5 Wm. and Mary Trin.
[93] C.P. 25 (2)/1078/8 Geo. I Hil; and see H.R. Phipps, 'Phipps Notes', v, pp. 13, 15, TS in B.M. For Paul Phipps of Chalford and his son John, see p. 155.
[94] MS. Cal. Deeds at Chalcot House, 41; Hoare, *Mod. Wilts.* Westbury, 50.
[95] Burke, *Landed Gentry* (1906), Phipps of Chalcot, and

ex inf. Lady Sybil Phipps, Chalcot House.
[96] Ex inf. Lady Sybil Phipps.
[97] Ibid. and see p. 155.
[98] Ex inf. Lady Sybil Phipps.
[99] *V.C.H. Wilts.* ii, p. 118.
[1] See p. 176.
[2] *Bk. of Fees*, ii. 1226; see p. 164.
[3] C 54/3648 no. 8.
[4] 3 & 4 Vic., c. 113.
[5] *Lond. Gaz.* 20 Nov. 1863, 5562–3.
[6] Ex inf. Ch. Com.
[7] *W.N. & Q.* vi. 184. For Thos. Benett, precentor, see Jones, *Fasti Eccl. Sar.* ii. 332.
[8] C 54/3648 no. 8.
[9] Court papers relating to manor courts held by the Benetts c. 1551–c. 1729 are in W.R.O. 413, and 1736–1778 in Ch. Com. 176055.
[10] Ch. Com. 176054.
[11] Ibid.; Hoare, *Mod. Wilts.* Westbury, 10.
[12] See p. 154.
[13] Ch. Com. 176055; Hoare, *Mod. Wilts.* Westbury, 10
[14] See p. 142.
[15] Sar. Dioc. R.O. Glebe Terrier, 1614.

longing to the Rector', and included the Parsonage House with Bittumes Close, the Chantry Leases, Parsonage Croft, and a cottage adjoining the church house.[16]

William Defuble gave 10 out of the 30 librates of land in Westbury which he received from the Empress Maud to the priory of Notre-Dame du Pré (dép. Seine-Inférieur).[17] The grant was confirmed by Henry II.[18] When Defuble's property was regranted by Henry to Joce de Dinan it must have included the overlordship of the priory's property, for in 1242–3 Walter Plucknet and Fulk FitzWarin, to whom Defuble's property had descended,[19] were the chief lords under the king.[20] Nothing more of their overlordship is known.

The estate was known as the manor of *WEST-BURY PRIORY*. Notre-Dame du Pré was one of the French priories dependent in certain respects upon the abbey of Bec (dép. Eure),[21] so that the ½ hide said to be held in Westbury by Bec in 1193–4 refers to the same holding.[22] In 1238 Thomas of Clopton conveyed 5 a. in Westbury to the Prior of Pré.[23] In 1242–3 the priory of Steventon (Berks.), an English cell of Bec, assigned to the maintenance of the monks of Pré,[24] held the land in Westbury.[25]

A final grant of land in Westbury to Bec was made in 1248 when Henry III granted ½ a. of assart in Selwood Forest. This had been assarted at the instigation of William de Guineville, the Prior of Ogbourne, the representative of the Abbot of Bec in England.[26]

In 1389 the prior and convent of Le Pré conveyed to Hugh de Calvyley the holding in Westbury, then called 'a manor' and described as 'parcel of the possessions of their priory of Steventon'.[27] The grant was confirmed by the Abbot of Bec and royal licence for the transaction was subsequently obtained.[28] Hugh de Calvyley conveyed the manor to Thomas Chalumley and others, who after Hugh's death, granted it in 1394 to John Waltham, Bishop of Salisbury, and Roger Walden.[29] Roger Walden, consecrated Archbishop of Canterbury in 1398, survived Waltham and sold the manor in 1399 to the king.[30] In the same year it was granted by the king to Westminster Abbey with the same liberties, including the return of royal writs, which the abbey enjoyed on its other estates.[31] In 1400 John de Calvyley, as guardian of David de Calvyley, heir of Hugh de Calvyley, claimed the estate then described as a member of the manor of Steventon.[32] The claim was unsuccessful and the Abbot of

Westminster obtained an exemplification of the grant from Archbishop Walden to the king, and the abbey remained in possession.[33]

After the Dissolution the manor was granted in 1542 with the former abbey's other possessions to the newly created Dean and Chapter of Westminster.[34] During the Interregnum the manor was sold by trustees in 1649 to John Sibley and John West,[35] but it was returned to the chapter at the Restoration and remained part of its property until 1869 when it was transferred to the Ecclesiastical Commissioners.[36] The estate was then disposed of bit by bit by the commissioners, the bulk of it being sold in 1899 to Lord Ludlow of Heywood (d. 1922).[37]

In 1522–3 the manor was leased to William Lovell, and later to John Whitaker, but in 1551 the chapter made another lease to Jerome Reynolds, causing considerable friction between the lessees.[38] In 1640 the manor was leased to William Wheler of Westbury Leigh[39] and it continued to be leased by members of the Wheler family until *c.* 1776.[40] In 1778 Edward Moore held the manor court as lord of the manor, and from 1792–1810 the courts were held by Peter and Stephen Moore.[41] Between 1810 and *c.* 1848 the manor was leased to Richard White, of London, and from *c.* 1848 until 1862 it was leased to William White.[42]

The lands of this manor lay scattered all over the area of the ancient parish.[43] In 1840 the demesne lands, which lay north of Leigh Road near its junction with Warminster Road,[44] comprised some 29 a. The rest of the manor, totalling just under 200 a., was made up of copyhold lands.[45] On the demesne land there was a barn built of stone in which the manorial courts were held. In 1840 this had recently replaced an old building which had fallen into decay.[46]

The 30 librates of land granted by the Empress Maud to William Defuble[47] must have passed into the hands of Henry II, who granted land, still reckoned at 30 librates in 1274, to Joce de Dinan.[48] Joce died *c.* 1166 leaving two daughters. One, Sybil, married Hugh Plucknet, and received a half share of the inheritance.[49] Of this, five librates already formed half of the manor of Westbury Priory.[50] The remainder had been subinfeudated to the Pavely family, lords of the capital manor, by 1210–12, when it was held by Ralph de Beauchamp, who had the wardship of the heir.[51] In 1242–3 it was held as ½ fee by Walter Pavely of

[16] C 54/3648 no. 8.
[17] *Rot. Hund.* (Rec. Com.), ii. 278.
[18] Dugdale, *Mon.* vi. 1100.
[19] See below.
[20] *Bk. of Fees*, ii. 740; it was probably a misapprehension that there were two mesne lords between Fitzwarin and the monks.
[21] Poirée, *Histoire de L'Abbaye du Bec*, i. 395.
[22] *Plac. Abbrev.* (Rec. Com.), 96.
[23] *Cal. Feet of F. Wilts.* 1195–1272, ed. Fry, 29.
[24] M. Morgan, *English Lands of the Abbey of Bec*, 21.
[25] *Bk. of Fees*, ii. 740.
[26] *Cal. Chart. R.* 1226–57, 331; Morgan, op. cit. 39.
[27] *Cal. Pat.* 1388–92, 6; D. & C. Westm. no. 7401. Steventon was alienated to Hugh de Calvyley at the same time.
[28] D & C. Westm. nos. 7401 and 7402; *Cal. Pat.* 1391–6, 417.
[29] Ibid.
[30] *Cal. Anct. D.* iv. A 6975.
[31] *Cal. Chart. R.* 1341–1417, 376–8.

[32] *Cal. Pat.* 1399–1401, 260.
[33] Ibid. 320.
[34] *L. & P. Hen. VIII*, xvii, p. 392.
[35] C 54/3463 no. 1.
[36] *Lond. Gaz.* 13 Aug. 1869, 4524.
[37] Ex inf. Ch. Com.
[38] C 3/149/22.
[39] D. & C. Westm. Register Bks., and see p. 158.
[40] D. & C. Westm. Register Bks.; Ch. Com. 145934.
[41] Ch. Com. 145934.
[42] Ibid. 142297–142305. Between 1810 and 1866 the manor courts were held by the dean and chapter: ibid. 145934.
[43] Ch. Com. 146117.
[44] Ibid. and Map 12494/3.
[45] Ibid. 146117.   [46] Ibid.
[47] *Rot. Hund.* (Rec. Com.), ii. 278.
[48] B.M. Lansd. MS. 442, f. 141.
[49] *V.C.H. Berks.* iv. 253; *Rot. Oblat. et Fin.* (Rec. Com.), 38.
[50] See above.
[51] *Red. Bk. Exch.* (Rolls Ser.), ii. 488–9.

William Plucknet.[52] In 1280 Reynold Pavely held the land of Jocelin Plucknet and it was said to be worth £10.[53] No more is heard of the Plucknet overlordship, and the land was probably merged into the Pavely inheritance.[54]

Hawise, Joce de Dinan's other daughter, married Fulk FitzWarin (d. c. 1198). Her share of the inheritance also included the overlordship of half the manor of Westbury Priory. She was still living in 1226;[55] before her death she is said to have given the part of Westbury which she held herself to her son Fulk. By c. 1219 he had given the land which his mother gave him to his brother Eudo, who soon after gave it to their sister Eugenia. She married William Mauduit, lord of Warminster c. 1244–64,[56] and took her Westbury property into that family, from which it was called the manor of *WESTBURY MAUDUITS*. A grant of free warren in his demesne lands made in 1317 to Thomas Mauduit described these as lying in Westbury, Westbury Leigh, and Chalcot.[57] In 1562 Chalcot alone was described as a manor.[58] But no evidence of any independent manorial organization has been found and Chalcot was probably only a part of the Mauduit lands in Westbury.

These lands followed the same descent as Warminster[59] until 1585 when George Tuchet, Lord Audley (d. 1617), sold them to the brothers Henry and Nicholas Phipps.[60] Henry and Nicholas apparently conveyed some part of the property to Sir James Ley (cr. Earl of Marlborough 1626), and this became annexed to the earl's manor of Brook under the name of Westbury Brook cum Mauduits.[61] Henry and Nicholas also added to their estate by the purchase in 1599 of a fulling mill at Westbury Leigh from Charles, Lord Mountjoy (d. 1606),[62] and by lands bought at an unknown date from Thomas Saunders.[63] Henry Phipps died in 1600 leaving his house at Westbury, his mill at Chalford, and his new house at the 'sheep-washing' at Chalford to his nephew Henry, son of Nicholas, with remainder to Nicholas in default of male issue of Henry.[64] Nicholas Phipps died in 1615 seised of the manor of Westbury Mauduits,[65] which presumably represented the bulk of the property he and his brother had acquired from Lord Tuchet (see above). Livery of this manor was made to Nicholas's son Henry in 1618.[66]

Henry Phipps, the younger, died in 1620 leaving an infant daughter Christine who later married William Bishop of Mere.[67] In 1639–40 livery of the manor of Westbury Mauduits was made to Christine and her husband and to Margaret Phipps, Christine's sister.[68] In the same year these three with Christine, widow of Henry Phipps, sold the manor to John and Edward Ash.[69] It seems to have remained in the Ash family[70] until sold by them to Zachary Bayly, a West India merchant, who owned it in 1689 and 1713.[71] It passed from Zachary to his son, another Zachary, who sold it to his nephew Bryan Edwards, author of the *History of the British Colonies in the West Indies*, who married Maria, daughter of Thomas Phipps of Leighton House (d. 1792).[72] Before his death in 1800 Edwards sold the estate to his younger brother, Zachary Bayly Edwards, who also died in 1800, and was succeeded by his son another Bryan Edwards.[73] The estate was bought from Edwards some time after 1842[74] by Charles Paul Phipps (d. 1880), who was the first member of the Phipps family to be styled of Chalcot and Dilton Court.[75] From Charles Paul the Chalcot estate passed to his son Charles Nicholas Paul Phipps (d. 1913), and from him to his son Charles Bathurst Hele Phipps (d. 1960).[76]

Chalcot House is a mid-18th-century building of 3 stories on the site of an earlier one, which Hoare suggests may have been the manor house of the manor of Westbury Mauduits.[77] Extensive alterations were made in 1870, leaving only the south-east front unaltered. This front has 5 bays with pilasters flanking the windows. The first, central, and fifth bays have panels with swag ornaments. A central niche on the first floor contains a large urn.

The property at Chalford and Westbury, which Henry Phipps (d. 1600) devised to his nephew Henry (see above) passed on the death of the younger Henry in 1620 without male issue to a younger brother.[78] Paul Phipps (d. 1722), a descendant of this brother, added largely to the property which lay mostly in Chalford and Westbury Leigh.[79] He probably did not, however, occupy Leigh House, which at this date was leased from the Earl of Abingdon, lord of the manor of Westbury, by Thomas Phipps of Heywood.[80] Thomas Phipps of Heywood died in 1724 without issue and the lease was assigned to John Phipps (d. 1739)

[52] *Bk. of Fees*, 736.
[53] *Wilts. Inq. p.m.* 1242–1326 (Index Libr.), 130.
[54] But cf. *Feet of F. Wilts.* 1272–1327, 102, which is a settlement of land in Westbury on Robert Plucknet. He was not, however, the representative of the main line of the family: *Complete Peerage* s.v. Plugenet.
[55] Eyton, *Antiquities of Shropshire*, vii. 68–71.
[56] R. Halstead, *Succint Genealogies* (1685), 131–2. For the unreliability of this work, see p. 97 n. 37, but the deeds quoted here seem to be genuine.
[57] *Cal. Chart. R.* 1300–26, 374.
[58] C 142/135/4.
[59] See p. 97.
[60] C 66/1262 m. 30.
[61] *Wilts. Inq. p.m.* 1625–49 (Index Libr.), 232–4.
[62] C 54/1623 Mountjoy and Phipps.
[63] P.C.C. 32 Wallopp.
[64] Ibid.
[65] C 152/355/33.
[66] C 60/480/no. 45.
[67] C 142/380/116.
[68] C 60/544 no. 48; and see pedigree in H. R. Phipps, 'Phipps Notes', v, TS. in B.M.

[69] C.P. 25 (2)/511 15 Chas. I Mich.
[70] Hoare, *Mod. Wilts.* Westbury, 40–1.
[71] C.P. 25(2)/887 1 Wm. & Mary Trin.; C.P. 43/522 rot. 148.
[72] Hoare, op. cit.; Burke, *Landed Gentry* (1952); *D.N.B.* Bryan Edwards.
[73] Hoare, op. cit.
[74] W.R.O. Tithe Award. This shows Bryan Edwards at Chalcot House.
[75] Burke, *Landed Gentry* (1952). Chas. Paul Phipps acquired Dilton Court from a cousin in c. 1862: see p. 153.
[76] Burke, *Landed Gentry* (1952); *The Times*, 16 Jan. 1960.
[77] Hoare, *Mod. Wilts.* Westbury, 40.
[78] P.C.C. 32 Wallopp, and for descent of the property in the Phipps family see H. R. Phipps, 'Phipp Notes', v, TS. in B.M. and Burke, *Landed Gentry* (1952).
[79] He also acquired the manor of Dilton in 1721–2 from Thos. Phipps of Heywood: see p. 153.
[80] MS. Cal. Deeds at Chalcot House, facing f. 3. although this summary of the various transactions does not seem to be entirely accurate, and ff. 43–5. For Thos. Phipps of Heywood see p. 162.

eldest son of the above Paul of Chalford and West-bury Leigh.[81] The house continued to be leased by members of this branch of the family until 1791 when it was bought by Thomas Phipps (d. 1792), grandson of Paul, from the Earl of Abingdon.[82] By 1773 there was, besides Leigh House, another house in Leighton Park to the north of the road which cut the park in two and apparently some-what to the west of the present Leighton House. That year Leigh House was apparently occupied by Thomas Phipps, and the one to the north by his brother Paul.[83] Paul died in 1785 and Thomas in 1792, and the Leighton estate, to which Thomas had added much property,[84] descended to Thomas's grandson. This was Thomas Henry Hele Phipps, who abandoned Leigh House for a new one which he built in 1800 in the northern part of the park.[85] Thomas Henry Hele Phipps died in 1841 and was succeeded by his son of the same name. This Thomas Henry Hele Phipps died in 1847 leaving a son Thomas Henry Leckonby Phipps who died without issue. His uncle, John Lewis Phipps, suc-ceeded to the estate and died in 1870. Richard Leckonby Hothersall Phipps, son and heir of John Lewis, sold the house and estate in 1888 to William Henry Laverton (d. 1925).[86] In 1911 some 1,700 a. of the estate including Storridge, Brook House, Hawkeridge, and Lodge Wood farms were sold in lots,[87] and in 1921 Laverton sold the rest of the estate, including Leighton House, Madbrook, Beresmere, and Skye or Hill farms.[88] Leighton House was sold to the proprietors of a school for boys called Victoria College.[89] The school closed in 1936[90] and about three years later the property was taken over by the War Department. Since then it has been the headquarters of the Permanent Com-missions Board.

Leighton House as built in 1800 by Thomas Henry Hele Phipps comprised 3 stories and 5 bays. It was built of stone ashlar and had a central Roman Doric porch. In 1888 the house was bought by William Henry Laverton and was altered and ex-tended in the taste of that time. A wing was added to the east, a conservatory to the west, and a billiard room to the north. The interior was remodelled and completely redecorated. The architect for these alterations was Frank Willis of Bristol.[91] A three-sided stable block approached by a bridge over the Warminster road dates from c. 1800. A coat of arms and a bell cupola, which form the central features, were added in the late 19th century. Nearby is an avenue of araucaria trees. William Henry Laverton also built a private theatre in the park and made a cricket pitch there.

In 1274 it was said that the land given by the Em-press Maud to William Defuble amounted to 30 librates.[92] The descent of these has been described above; 10 formed the holding of the Prior of Le Pré and 10 that of the Mauduit family, and the remaining 10 seem to have been merged into the capital manor.[93] It appears, however, that Defuble's holding was larger than the 30 librates assigned to it in 1274, and in 1210–12 it was definitely said to amount to 50 librates. Of this, part was clearly the land held by the heirs of Joce de Dinan, to whom Defuble's land had been regranted by Henry II. The remainder, presumably 20 librates, was held by Ralph de Lanvaley and William de Lanvaley.[94] This family was associated with a holding of Joce de Dinan at Lambourn (Berks.)[95] and he may have given land at Westbury to it before his death. The first member of the family certainly holding land here was Thomas de Lanvaley, whose estate at Leigh was in the hands of the sheriff in 1190.[96] His relationship to the later members of the family is not known, but he evidently was related to the family that held land at Lambourn, and the honor of Walkern (Herts.). William de Lanvaley of that family died c. 1215, leaving a daughter and heir Hawise, who married John de Burgh (d. 1275).[97] He was overlord of land at Westbury in 1274,[98] the last time the overlordship of the Lanvaley estates is mentioned.

The fragmentation of those estates by subinfeu-dation began in 1204 with the gift of land at Leigh from Ralph de Lanvaley to the priory of Monkton Farleigh, in return for a life pension of 2 marks.[99] This formed the largest part of the manor of *LEIGH PRIORS*. In 1242–3 it was said to be held in chief,[1] and in 1274 it was reckoned at ½ fee.[2]

Subsequent acquisitions show the priory follow-ing a policy of augmenting and consolidating its property in Westbury Leigh. In 1226 Henry III confirmed among the other possessions of the house in Westbury, half the vill of Westbury Leigh and a tenement (*mansura*) there.[3] In 1249 the prior ex-changed with William and Eve Mauduit the wood of Holt for 15 a. in Westbury Leigh next to the wood which Walter of Brookway held.[4] Another exchange was made by the prior in 1285 with Stephen the tanner of land in 'Buricrofta' and 'Cumputte' in Westbury Leigh for other land in the same place.[5] More land was acquired in Leigh and Westbury in 1320–1 by an exchange with Walter Pavely.[6] In 1294 the Westbury Leigh estate along with the priory's other possessions was temporarily taken into the king's hands.[7] In 1331 the manor was leased to John Bradford, parson of the church at Bishopstrow, and Thomas de Croume for their lives. In 1368 licence was granted for John Mareys and Thomas Jordan to grant some 50 a., which they held of the Prior of Farleigh in Westbury

[81] MS. Cal. Deeds at Chalcot House, 44.
[82] Ibid.
[83] *Andrews and Dury, Map* 1773 (W.A.S. Rec. Brch.), pl. 7.
[84] See pp. 151–2.
[85] MS. Cal. Deeds at Chalcot House, ii. 55.
[86] *W.A.M.* xlvii. 134.
[87] W.A.S. Libr., Devizes, Sale Cat. xxi.
[88] Wilts. Cuttings, xvi.
[89] *W.A.M.* xlvii. 134.
[90] *Wilts. Gaz.* 12 Mar. 1936.
[91] *Wilts. Times* 14 July 1888.
[92] *Rot. Hund.* (Rec. Com.), ii. 278.
[93] See p. 154.

[94] *Red Bk. Exch.* (Rolls Ser.), ii. 488–9.
[95] *V.C.H. Berks.* iv. 256, 259.
[96] *Pipe R.* 1190 (P.R.S. N.S. i), 123.
[97] Farrer, *Honors and Knights Fees*, iii. 287–91; Sanders, *English Baronies*, 92.
[98] *Rot. Hund.* (Rec. Com.), ii. 278.
[99] C.P. 25(1)/250/3/12.
[1] *Bk. of Fees*, ii. 740.
[2] *Rot. Hund.* (Rec. Com.), ii. 278.
[3] Dugdale, *Mon.* v. 27.
[4] *V.C.H. Wilts.* iii. 263, and see p. 164.
[5] *Cat. Antct. D.* ii. p. 284, B 2273.
[6] *Rot. Orig. Abbrev.* (Rec. Com.), i. 257.
[7] *V.C.H. Wilts.* iii. 264.

Leigh, to the Bonhommes of Edington.[8] The manor, then leased out, was among the property of Monkton Farleigh when the priory was dissolved in 1536.[9]

In 1545 the manor, with its capital messuage, and the lands leased with it to John Whatley, Leigh Common, and all appurtenances were conveyed to John Adlam, clothier, of Westbury, who also received other rents due to the priory from lands in Westbury.[10] John died seised of the manor in the same year leaving as his heirs his daughters Edith, wife of John Lambe, and Alice, wife of Robert Cogswell.[11] Edith married secondly John Westwell, who, after Edith's death in 1577, held the manor for life.[12] It then passed to John Lambe, Edith's son by her first marriage.[13] John Lambe died in 1615 holding half the manor and was succeeded by his son, John.[14] This John sold his half of the manor to Sir James Ley (cr. Earl of Marlborough 1626) in 1615.[15] The other half, which passed on the death of Alice Cogswell in 1606 to her grandson, Roger,[16] had been sold by him to Sir James Ley in 1611.[17] Ley thus acquired the entire manor of Leigh Priors, which thenceforth followed the same descent as the capital manor.

The half of the township of Leigh which remained after the grant to the priory of Monkton Farleigh in 1204 was by 1242–3 divided into two parts, each reckoned at $\frac{1}{16}$ fee.[18] Robert de Maners held one directly of the heirs of William de Lanvaley, but the other had been three times subinfeudated, and was held by Eve de Bassingburn of Eve de Tracy of Fulk FitzWarin of the heirs of de Lanvaley.[19] Eve de Bassingburn had acquired her part of Eve de Tracy in 1241.[20] By 1274 the two parts had been united, for John de Maners held $\frac{1}{4}$ fee directly of the tenant-in-chief.[21] John probably subinfeudated it before the Statute of 1290. By 1316 it was held by John Rous;[22] at his death in 1330 Rous was said to hold it jointly with his wife Ela of Robert de Maners by the gift of John of Lavington.[23] It descended in the Rous family in the same way as the manor of Baynton in Edington[24] to John Rous, who was holding it in 1412.[25]

The descent of this estate during the next 50 years cannot be traced. By 1464 it had passed to Robert and Agnes Leversage, for that year they were sued by the Chaplain of Baynton for a rent of 40s.,[26] which Richard Rous had granted him from his land in Leigh.[27] Agnes was the daughter of William of Westbury (d. 1482) and among the estates which went to make up the manor of WEST-

BURY LEVERSAGE were lands which she inherited from her father in Heywood, Hawkeridge, and Westbury Leigh.[28] Agnes's lands passed by a settlement of 1475 to her heirs Edmund and John Leversage.[29] Edmund died seised of the property in 1469 and was succeeded by his nephew, Edmund, son of William Leversage.[30] At this date the Leversage estate in Westbury was called the manor of Heywood and it is not known whether the land in Westbury Leigh still formed part of it. The younger Edmund died in 1508 and was succeeded by his son Robert.[31] Robert died in 1549[32] and was followed by his son William who died in 1582, at which date the estate was sometimes called the manor of Westbury Leversage.[33] Grace, widow of William Leversage, married secondly Anthony Williams,[34] and in 1612–13 they conveyed the manor, then called Westbury Heywood, to Sir James Ley (cr. Earl of Marlborough in 1626).[35] From this time the Leversage manor followed the same descent as the capital manor of Westbury, with which it became merged.[36]

The manor of BREMERIDGE is represented in modern times by Bremeridge Farm lying some three miles to the south-west of Westbury. The estate probably originated in the grant to Philip Marmium by Joce de Dinan (d. c. 1166) of 3 hides out of the land which the king had granted Joce in Westbury.[37] The grant was confirmed to Marmium's son, Roger, by Walter Pavely, by then lord of the manor of Westbury.[38] In c. 1276 Philip Marmium, possibly Roger's son, died seised of a virgate held of Richard Dauntsey in Bratton and Dilton, 12 virgates in the manor of Westbury, of which 6 were held of Reynold Pavely, lord of the capital manor, and 6 of Thomas Mauduit, lord of the manor of Westbury Mauduits, 11 librates in Bremeridge, as well as other smaller holdings in Westbury, Brook, and Bremeridge. For all these lands he seems to have held a single court.[39] Philip Marmium was succeeded by a grandson, Roger, whose legitimacy was questioned by his aunt Eve, elder daughter of Philip Marmium.[40] This was apparently of no avail, and Roger added to his holding a wood called Huddesgrove acquired from John of Leigh,[41] and a rent from a tenement in Leigh together with the advowson of the chantry of Heywood, which were granted him by Reynold Pavely.[42] In 1335–6 he settled his entire estate upon himself and his wife Maud. Roger was succeeded by his grandson, William,[43] who in 1350–1 conveyed a messuage and two carucates of land in Bremeridge to his grand-

[8] Wilts. Inq. p.m. 1327–77 (Index Libr.), 347–8.
[9] V.C.H. Wilts. iii. 267; Valor Eccl. (Rec. Com.), ii. 143.
[10] L. & P. Hen. VIII, xx (1), p. 420.
[11] Cal. Pat. 1553. App. 1547–53, 312.
[12] C 142/260/124.
[13] Ibid.
[14] C 142/355/93.
[15] C.P 25(2)/371/13 Jas. I Trin.
[16] C 142/295/44.
[17] C.P 25(2)/369/8 Jas. I Hil.
[18] See p. 156.
[19] Bk. of Fees, ii. 736.
[20] C.P. 25(1)/251/12/35.
[21] Rot. Hund. (Rec. Com.), ii. 278.
[22] Feud. Aids, v. 210.
[23] Wilts. Inq. p.m. 1327–77 (Index Libr.), 56; Lavington may have been the previous tenant, but was more likely a feoffee of Rous.
[24] See p. 242.

[25] Feud. Aids, vi. 531.
[26] B.M. Lansd. MS. 442, f. 232.
[27] Ibid. f. 231; Cal. Pat. 1361–4, 183.
[28] C 140/84/36; C 1/24/199.
[29] Cal. Inq. Hen. VII, i. pp. 513–14.
[30] Ibid.
[31] C 142/24/51
[32] C 142/89/150.
[33] C 142/198/19.
[34] Cal. Proc. Chanc. Eliz. (Rec. Com.), ii. p. 162.
[35] C.P. 25(2)/370/10 Jas. I East.
[36] See p. 150.
[37] B.M. Lansd. MS. 442, f. 141, and see p. 148.
[38] Ibid. for Walter Pavely see p. 149.
[39] Wilts. Inq. p.m. 1242–1326 (Index Libr.), 103–4.
[40] Ibid. 104; Cal. Close, 1272–9, 382; G. Wrottesley, Pedigrees from Plea Rolls, 530.
[41] B.M. Lansd. MS. 442, f. 141d.
[42] Ibid. f. 146.
[43] Ibid. f. 142.

mother, Maud, and her second husband William FitzWarin.[44] This seems to have been a settlement of the manor upon the heirs of Maud and FitzWarin, for it passed to Sir Philip FitzWarin of Great Chalfield,[45] who in 1366, with his wife Constance, exchanged Bremeridge with the Bonhommes of Edington for the manor of Highway.[46] The manor of Bremeridge was at this date held of Gillian Mauduit as of her manor of Westbury by the service of a knight's fee.[47] The manor remained among the possessions of Edington until the dissolution of that house in 1539.[48]

In 1541 the manor was leased by the Crown to Thomas Charde, and in 1543 the reversion after the expiry of this lease was granted to Charles Blount, Lord Mountjoy (d. 1544).[49] James Blount, Lord Mountjoy (d. 1581), son of Charles Blount, conveyed it in 1574 to the queen.[50] In 1609–10 James I sold the manor to John Eldred, James Collymore, and others,[51] but the sale was apparently ineffective, for the following year the king sold it to George and Thomas Whitmore of London.[52] George and Thomas Whitmore sold Bremeridge in 1612 to Sir James Ley (cr. Earl of Marlborough 1626),[53] and it thus became part of the large estate in Westbury, which Ley was acquiring during the first quarter of the 17th century.[54]

In 1631 Henry Ley, Earl of Marlborough (d. 1638), son of Sir James Ley, and lord of the manor of Westbury, sold the capital messuage and farm of Bremeridge with 'Rookesgrove' and 'Knawbone' to Edward Windover, but not, apparently, the manorial rights which remained with the lords of the manor of Westbury.[55] The earl retained certain hunting rights on the estate, and Windover was bound to do suit at the court of the manor of Bremeridge.[56] No more is known of this estate until 1655 when it was sold by John Stedman to William Lant.[57] Lant, a London merchant, died in 1671, and his widow Anne remarried Sir Edward Bromfield, and held Bremeridge until her death in 1696. She was succeeded by her son Thomas Lant,[58] who held the farm in 1709, but by 1727 it was the freehold property and residence of John Watts.[59] After the death of Watts and his wife it passed to a son also called John. The Revd. John Watts, son of the second named John, died unmarried, and the farm passed to the children of his sister, the Thrings of Sutton Veny.[60] They sold the estate in 1825 to Frederick Seagram of Warminster. In 1830 it was

bound to pay 'lord's rent' to Sir Manasseh Massey Lopes, lord of the capital manor of Westbury.[61] Subsequently the farm passed into the possession of Charles Paul Phipps of Chalcot House and Dilton Court (d. 1880).[62]

The farmhouse dates largely from the 19th century, but there are indications, such as a 17th-century doorway, that there may have been an earlier house on the site. A hoard of gold coins of the time of Edward III and Richard II was found buried outside the backdoor in 1877.[63]

In the 12th century two members of a family calling themselves of Leigh (de Lya), and thus presumably holding land there,[64] were wardens of Selwood Forest, within which Leigh then lay: Walter in 1189, and his son, Philip, in 1193–4.[65] In 1210–12 Philip of Leigh held land in Westbury valued at 10s. by the serjeanty of supplying one archer for the royal service.[66] Philip died c. 1226 when his son and heir, James, paid homage for his holding, which he held in chief of the king.[67] John of Leigh, possibly son of James, was holding a virgate in Westbury in 1274–5,[68] and in 1349–50 John Mauduit conveyed a mill, tenement, and garden in Leigh to Joan Huggin to hold during the minority of Thomas, son of John of Leigh.[69]

The estate in *WESTBURY LEIGH* descended in the family of Leigh until the death of Robert Leigh in 1525–6 when it was divided between his daughters.[70] One of these, Margaret Harvey, died in 1527[71] and her son and heir, Nicholas, sold his share in the manor of Westbury Leigh to Thomas Webb.[72] Robert Webb, son of Thomas, sold his share in the manor to Alexander Staples of Yate (Glos.),[73] who died seised of it the same year having devised it to his younger son Thomas.[74] In 1631–2 Thomas Staples sold the manor to Humphrey Lee,[75] and six years later Lee sold it to William Wheler.[76]

From Henry Hussey and Cecily, another daughter of Robert Leigh, part of the manor of Westbury Leigh passed to John Hussey and from him in 1581 to his son, Thomas Hussey.[77] In the following year Thomas Hussey sold his half of the manor to James Powton,[78] of whom it was purchased in 1591–2 by Edward and Jeremy Horton.[79] The capital messuage of the estate was Ludborne House.[80] In 1639–40 the estate was sold by Sir John Horton, son of Jeremy Horton to William Wheler, who thus acquired both parts of the manor.[81] By

[44] Ibid.; C.P. 25 (1)/255/48/10.
[45] V.C.H. Wilts. vii. 60.
[46] *Wilts. Inq. p.m.* 1327–77 (Index Libr.), 339–40; V.C.H. Wilts. vii. 198.
[47] *Wilts. Inq. p.m.* 1327–77 (Index Libr.), 339–40.
[48] V.C.H. Wilts. iii. 323; *Valor Eccl.* (Rec. Com.), ii. 141.
[49] *L. & P. Hen. VIII*, xviii (2), p. 237.
[50] C.P. 25(2)/260/16 Eliz. Hil.
[51] C 66/1812 no. 10.
[52] C 66/1845 no. 2.
[53] C 54/2091 no. 33.
[54] See p. 185.
[55] C.P. 43/196 m. 1.
[56] Ibid.
[57] Hoare, *Mod. Wilts.* Westbury, 36–37.
[58] *London Visitation Pedigrees*, 1664 (Harl. Soc. xcii), 88–9.
[59] Hoare, *Mod. Wilts.* Westbury, 36–7.
[60] See p. 71.
[61] Ibid.
[62] Burke, *Landed Gentry* (1952).

[63] *W.A.M.* xxi. 121–40.
[64] The holding of this family is sometimes said to be in Leigh and sometimes in Westbury, but it is assumed that by Westbury is meant more precisely Leigh in Westbury.
[65] V.C.H. Wilts. iv. 437.
[66] *Red Bk. of Exch.* (Rolls. Ser.), ii. 488.
[67] *Excerpt. e Rot. Fin.* (Rec. Com.), i. 143.
[68] *Rot. Hund.* (Rec. Com.), ii. 278.
[69] Halstead, *Succint Genealogies*, 144.
[70] C 142/43/22.
[71] C 142/51/98.
[72] C.P. 43/29/14.
[73] C.P. 43/29/14; for other property sold by Webb to Staples, see p. 98.
[74] C 142/227/217.
[75] C.P. 25(2)/509/7 Chas. I Mich.
[76] C.P. 25(2)/510/13 Chas. I Mich.
[77] C.P. 25(2)/240/230 24 Eliz. Mich.
[78] C.P. 25(2)/240/24 Eliz. Hil.
[79] C 54/1408 Powton and Horton.
[80] Ibid.
[81] C 54/3206 no. 4.

his will proved in 1667 Sir William Wheler devised the manor to his wife Elizabeth with remainder to George, son of Charles Wheler of Charing (Kent). George Wheler died in 1723, one year before his eldest son, and the estate passed first to his second son Granville Wheler, and on Granville's death in 1770 to Granville's son of the same name.[82] In 1772 some land within the manor was sold to Thomas Phipps,[83] and the rest was sold to Thomas, Viscount Weymouth.[84] This descended to the Marquesses of Bath, and was sold by Lord Bath sometime between the two world wars.[85]

Another share in Robert Leigh's manor (see above) passed to his daughter Anne, wife of William Beckett, and this estate became known as Leigh Becketts. It belonged in 1558 to Henry Beckett,[86] and appears to have descended in the family until 1612–13 when William Beckett and his wife Elizabeth sold it to Sir James Ley (cr. Earl of Marlborough 1626), lord of the capital manor of Westbury.[87]

Land in Westbury held by William Burnel had escheated to the Crown in 1168.[88] It was probably another William Burnel who in 1194 paid 2 marks to have seisin of $1\frac{1}{2}$ hide of land there.[89] From that time until at least 1214 he paid a yearly farm for it to the king.[90] At first the farm was 30s. but from 1200 he began to pay only 10s. out of the 30s. charged on him, and from 1207 his farm was reduced to 10s. at the Exchequer.[91] This was a belated recognition of the fact that the Prior of Monkton Farleigh was overlord of $\frac{2}{3}$ of Burnel's fee. He put forward his claim in 1194,[92] when the land was first said to lie in *PENLEIGH*, and by 1199 it had been established that $\frac{2}{3}$ of Burnel's rent should be paid to the prior.[93] The overlordship of Farleigh is regularly mentioned thereafter,[94] and the 20s. rent was still paid at the Dissolution.[95] In 1236 William Haket held the land *de elemosina domini regis*, paying the rents to the prior and the king,[96] but by 1242–3 Eudo Burnel held it by the same rents.[97] Eudo was succeeded by his brother William in *c.* 1243.[98] William's heir was William the chaplain,[99] and it seems likely that he relinquished his right in Penleigh, for no more is heard of the Burnel overlordship.

William Burnel had subinfeudated his land before his death. In 1256 Walter Pavely was holding land in Penleigh of him by a rent of 10s.[1] Walter's son, Reynold, held it in 1274, when it was said to

be $\frac{1}{3}$ of the Burnel fee,[2] but by 1288–9 it was described as $\frac{1}{3}$ of Penleigh held directly of the king.[3] This land probably became merged into the larger Pavely estate, and is not heard of again. The other part of the Burnel fee, held of the monks of Farleigh, was perhaps subinfeudated by 1243, when Alan FitzWarin seems to have exerted some claim to part of it.[4] In 1260 Eudo FitzAlan, presumably his son, granted the land which Alan had held to Thomas de Tetteburn and Joan his wife for their lives.[5] They still held it in 1274,[6] but by 1288–9 it had reverted to Peter FitzWarin.[7] It was held by William FitzWarin who forfeited it as a rebel in 1322;[8] it was soon restored to his widow Joan and their son William, who were in possession in 1327.[9]

By 1340 Penleigh had passed to Sir Adam de Shareshull and Alice his wife, for that year these two settled it upon themselves and their heirs.[10] How it came to them is not clear; Alice may have been the heir of the FitzWarins. Ten years later they conveyed it for life to Sir Thomas, son of Maurice Berkeley, and his wife Katharine, with remainder to John de Veel and his sister Joan, children of Katharine by her first husband Sir Peter de Veel.[11] John de Veel died without issue and Katharine's heir was Sir John Moigne, son of Joan de Veel.[12] From Sir John Moigne the manor passed to his daughter, Elizabeth, who married William Stourton. Their son, John (cr. Baron Stourton 1448),[13] died seised of the manor in 1462.[14] William Stourton (d. 1477) succeeded his father and married Margaret, daughter of Sir John Chidiock, and in her right became possessed of part of the capital manor of Westbury. Penleigh thenceforth followed the same descent as the part of the capital manor called Westbury Stourton until it was forfeited in 1557 by Charles, Lord Stourton.[15] In 1580 Penleigh was granted by Elizabeth I to Lord Burleigh and others.[16] This grant was apparently made with the purpose of restoring it to John, Lord Stourton, son of Charles, for that year he conveyed it to the same grantees for a settlement upon himself and his wife, Frances, and their issue, with remainder to the heirs of his grandfather, William, Lord Stourton.[17] The manor descended with the title until *c.* 1704 when Lord Stourton sold it to George Turner, on whose death it passed under his will to his widow Martha Turner.[18] Martha Turner left it to her nephew, Gilbert

[82] W.R.O. 212 A, Abstract of title of Granville Wheler, the younger, to the manor of Leigh and Ludborne.
[83] W.R.O. 212 A, Deed Granville Wheler to Thos. Phipps, 1772.
[84] Hoare, *Mod. Wilts.* Westbury, 42.
[85] Ex inf. Longleat Estate Office.
[86] C 3/83/22.
[87] C.P. 25(2)/370/10 Jas. I Mich., and see p. 150.
[88] *Pipe R.* 1167–8 (P.R.S. xii), 158; ibid. 1168–9 (P.R.S. xiii), 18.
[89] Ibid. 1194 (P.R.S. N.S. v), 201.
[90] Ibid. 1195 (P.R.S. N.S. vi), 140 and succeeding volumes to 1214.
[91] Ibid. 1200 (P.R.S. N.S. xii), 156; ibid. 1207 (P.R.S. N.S. xxii), 201.
[92] *Rolls of the King's Ct.* 1194–5 (P.R.S. xiv), 71.
[93] *Memoranda Roll 1199–1200* (P.R.S. N.S. xxi), 13.
[94] e.g. J.I. 1/1006, m. 50d; *Wilts. Inq. p.m. 1327–77* (Index Libr.), 348.
[95] *L. & P. Hen. VIII*, xx(1), p. 420.
[96] *Bk. of Fees*, 586.
[97] Ibid. 740.

[98] *Excerpt. e Rot. Fin.* i. 396.
[99] *Rot. Hund.* (Rec. Com.), ii. 278–9.
[1] *Wilts. Inq. p.m. 1242–1326* (Index Libr.), 19.
[2] *Rot. Hund.* (Rec. Com.), ii. 278–9.
[3] J.I. 1/1006, m. 50d.
[4] *Crown Pleas Wilts. Eyre, 1249* (W.A.S. Rec. Brch.), 207.
[5] C.P. 25(1)/283/15.
[6] *Rot. Hund.* (Rec. Com.), ii. 278.
[7] J.I. 1/1006, m. 50d.
[8] S.C. 6/1145/1.
[9] *Cal. Pat.* 1327–30, 75.
[10] C.P. 25(1)/254/44/35.
[11] C.P. 25(1)/255/48/1.
[12] C 136/38/8.
[13] *Complete Peerage.*
[14] C 140/8/18.
[15] See p. 149.
[16] C 66/1189 m. 6.
[17] C 66/1186 John, Lord Stourton and others to Wm. Burghley and others.
[18] Hoare, *Mod. Wilts.* Westbury, 92.

Trowe Beckett, who was in possession in 1791.[19] He afterwards assumed the name Turner, and it passed from him to his brother, the Revd. Thomas à Beckett Turner, incumbent of Wootton Underwood (Bucks.).[20] The estate remained in the à Beckett Turner family until the last decade of the 19th century.[21] Since the beginning of the 20th century Penleigh House has had various occupiers.

Penleigh House faces east and consists of two ranges of different heights. That on the south has stone mullioned and transomed windows and may be the older of the two. The other, and higher range has a two-storied front of 7 bays. This front has a deep parapet surmounted by four vases and the roof has a central bell-turret with a weather cock. In the gable-end is a stone inscribed '1710 G.T.'. The sash windows in this portion of the house are not the original ones and other alterations, such as the addition of a central porch, seem to have been made. The central stone doorway, surmounted by a broken pediment and a shield of arms, possibly those of the Turner family, may be original, or alternatively the stone doorway which now forms the gateway in the garden wall may have been transferred from the house. The walls of the house are cement-rendered giving the appearance of ashlar, but they were originally wholly or in part of brick. The house contains two staircases of c. 1710. The principal one is lit by a Venetian window. A red-brick stable block to the west is of much the same date as the house, and the farmhouse to the north is of red brick with stone mullioned and transomed windows and has the inscription '1716 G.T.'.

Ernulf de Mandeville, the disinherited eldest son of Geoffrey de Mandeville, Earl of Essex, had received land in Wiltshire by royal grant as early as 1156, and it is quite possible that he had been given it by the Empress Maud.[22] He was apparently dead by 1178, when the sheriff accounted for £3 9s. 9d. for the farm of his lands for half a year.[23] Ernulf was succeeded by his eldest son Geoffrey.[24] In 1201 and in 1210–12 a Geoffrey de Mandeville, probably this son, was holding land in BRATTON.[25] Either this Geoffrey, or his son of the same name,[26] borrowed money from Jews, and the property of the de Mandevilles in Highworth and Bratton was seized for payment of the debt. In 1232 the justices dealing with matters relating to the Jews were ordered to make reasonable terms for Geoffrey de Mandeville for debts owed by him to three Jews. Part of the profits from the two manors was to be assigned every year for payment of the debts, and the rest was to provide for the maintenance of

Geoffrey, his wife and children.[27] In 1236 Geoffrey de Mandeville held one fee in Bratton and Highworth.[28] In 1242–3 he held ⅓ knight's fee in Bratton by castle-guard service to Devizes Castle.[29] Geoffrey de Mandeville, grandson of Ernulf, died in 1246 and was succeeded by his son Ralph.[30] Ralph died in 1280 holding 20 librates of land in Bratton and Highworth of the king in chief. For this he paid £1 a year to Devizes Castle in time of peace, and in time of war owed 40 days service there for himself and a horseman.[31] Thomas, son and heir of Ralph, apparently died soon after his father, for in 1288–9 Amice, widow of Ralph de Mandeville, and wife of Robert de Saucey, was holding part of the estate in dower, of the heritage of Robert de Mandeville.[32] Robert may have been a younger brother of Thomas. He appears to have been succeeded by another Ralph de Mandeville, for in 1299 William de Mandeville was holding the inheritance of Ralph his father in Bratton.[33] William died in 1333, when the estate passed to his brother John.[34] John died c. 1336, and Bratton was settled on his widow Benedicta.[35] In 1361 she conveyed her interest in it to the house of Bonhommes at Edington.[36] This grant was confirmed in 1362 by Nicholas atte Hoke and Joan his wife, kinswoman and heir of John de Mandeville,[37] and in 1372 by Walter Maryner de Langecote and Isabel his wife,[38] possibly another heir of John de Mandeville.

A number of lesser estates in Bratton were also acquired by the Bonhommes soon after the foundation of the house in 1358.[39] In 1401 the property belonging to the community in Bratton and Dilton was described as ½ knight's fee in Bratton late belonging to Walter Dauntsey.[40] Bratton continued to form part of the Edington lands until the Dissolution.

In 1543 Bratton was granted to Sir Thomas Seymour of Sudeley Castle (Glos.), brother of the Protector, who had already acquired the bulk of the Edington property.[41] After Seymour's execution in 1548–9,[42] Bratton appears to have remained with the Crown until 1591 when it was granted by the queen to Richard Knollis and Richard Swale.[43] In the same year these grantees sold it to Sir Christopher Hatton, the Lord Chancellor.[44] Sir Christopher died seised of it in 1591, leaving as his heir Sir William Newport, son of his sister Dorothy, who had married Sir John Newport.[45] Sir William assumed the name Hatton and in 1595 he and his wife Elizabeth conveyed the manor with four watermills to Richard Beconsawe and Francis Shrimpton.[46] Four years later in 1599 it passed from Gerard Fleetwood and Jane his wife to Wil-

[19] C.P. 43/832/387.
[20] Hoare, op. cit. 33.
[21] Wilts. Cuttings, xvi. 223.
[22] J. H. Round, *Geoffrey de Mandeville*, 229–30.
[23] *Pipe R.* 1177–8 (P.R.S. N.S. xxvii), 31.
[24] Round, *Geoffrey de Mandeville*, 232–3; *W.A.M.* xxxiii. 311.
[25] *Plac. Abbrev.* (Rec. Com.), 33; *Red Bk. of Exch.* (Rolls Ser.), ii. 489.
[26] Round, *Geoffrey de Mandeville*, 232; *W.A.M.* xxxiii. 303.
[27] *Cal. Close*, 1231–4, 168.
[28] *Bk. of Fees*, i. 585.
[29] Ibid. ii. 719, 736.
[30] *Excerp. e Rot. Fin.* (Rec. Com.), ii. 3.
[31] *Wilts. Inq. p.m. 1242–1326* (Index Libr.), 129.
[32] J.I. 1/1006 m. 50d.

[33] *W.A.M.* xxxiii. 304.
[34] *Wilts. Inq. p.m. 1327–1377* (Index Libr.), 94.
[35] *Cal. Inq. Misc.* ii, p. 350; *Wilts. Inq. p.m. 1327–1377* (Index Libr.), 113; *Cal. Pat. 1334–8*, 232.
[36] *V.C.H. Wilts.* iii. 321.
[37] C.P. 25(1)/255/50/16; B.M. Lansd. MS. 442, f. 90.
[38] C.P. 25 (1)/255/52/25; B.M. Lansd. MS. 442, f. 90d. and 90.
[39] See p. 164.
[40] E 164/3/316 d.
[41] *L. & P. Hen. VIII*, xviii (1), p. 549; *V.C.H. Wilts.* iii. 324.
[42] *Complete Peerage*, Seymour of Sudeley.
[43] C 66/1372 m. 10.
[44] C 54/1396 Ric. Swale and Ric. Knollis to Sir Christopher Hatton.   [45] C 142/232/82.
[46] C.P. 25(2)/242/37 Eliz. Trin.; Longleat MS. 6614.

liam Lambert.[47] Shortly after this it passed to William Paulet, Marquess of Winchester (d. 1628/9), who already held the Bratton Grange or Farm estate,[48] and in 1620 Paulet sold it to Sir James Ley (cr. Earl of Marlborough 1626),[49] in whose possession it was at the time of his death in 1629.[50] The manor then presumably descended for a time with the capital manor of Westbury but shortly after the death of James Ley, 3rd Earl of Marlborough, in 1665, it apparently passed to William Bromwich, owner of the grange and farm, for he was admitting tenants on the manor in 1667.[51] In 1669 Arthur Bromwich sold the manor to Sir James Thynne,[52] from whom it eventually descended to the Marquesses of Bath. Shortly before the Second World War Lord Bath sold his estate in Bratton.[53]

Members of the Whitaker family, who leased most of the Bratton Grange estate,[54] were also leasing lands in the 17th, 18th, and 19th centuries on this manor.[55]

The 'mansion' house of Bratton is described in a 17th-century survey as a good, tiled house consisting of kitchen, hall, 2 parlours, a pantry, a cellar, brew-house, and other offices. There was also a tiled barn, stables, outhouses, gardens, orchards, and a home-close comprising in all about 4 a.[56] It is not possible to identify this house with any in Bratton now. Grange Farm, in Lower Road, the farmhouse of Lord Bath's former estate in Bratton, dates from 1739 and later.[57].

After the execution of Sir Thomas Seymour, lord of the manor of Bratton, an estate known as *BRATTON GRANGE*, or *FARM*, was conveyed in 1550 to Sir William Paulet (cr. Marquess of Winchester 1551, d. 1571). This estate comprised some 346 a. of arable and 62 a. of meadow or pasture with lands called Little Broadmead, Broadmead, Opencrofts, and Great Opencrofts, and lay in the south of the parish.[58] It passed with the Winchester title[59] until 1600 when William Paulet, Marquess of Winchester (d. 1628/9), mortgaged the estate for 1,000 years to mortgagees, who sold the lease to Thomas Hutchins and William Bower. After the death of Hutchins in 1607 the reversion was granted by the marquess to Sefton Bromwich, who probably redeemed the mortgage.[60] Sefton Bromwich died a few months later and was succeeded by his son William, a minor, to whom livery was made in 1629.[61] William Bromwich, Rachel, his wife, and Arthur Bromwich sold the Grange to Sir Walter Ernley of Etchilhampton.[62] In 1695 it was settled upon Anne, widow of Edward Ernley, son of Sir Walter Ernley, with remainder to her second son

Sir Edward Ernley.[63] Elizabeth, the only daughter and heir of Sir Edward Ernley, married Henry Drax in 1720 and died in 1759. She was succeeded by her eldest son Thomas Erle Drax, on whose death in 1789 the property passed to his brother Edward. Sarah Frances Drax, daughter and heir of Edward, married Richard Grosvenor, who assumed the name of Erle Drax.[64] Richard Erle Drax Grosvenor died in 1819 and his widow in 1822. In 1829 the whole estate was sold in lots.[65] The manor house and a part of the estate were bought by George Watson-Taylor of Erlestoke Park.[66] This still belonged to Watson-Taylor in 1842,[67] but before the end of the 19th century it had passed to Charles Nicholas Paul Phipps.[68]

In 1815 part of the estate, comprising nearly 1,000 a., and including Lower and Upper Garston, and Garston Orchard was leased by Richard Erle Drax Grosvenor to Philip Whitaker.[69] In 1842 the same Philip Whitaker occupied the manor house and another part of the estate was leased to his son, Joshua Whitaker.[70] Members of the Whitaker family continued to farm the estate until well on into the 20th century. When John Saffery Whitaker retired in 1913 Grant's Farm, lying on Salisbury Plain, and the largest farm on the estate, had been farmed by the Whitaker family for some two hundred years.[71]

The manor house of this estate, and still called the Manor House in 1960, stands at the corner of Court Lane and the high road to Westbury. It is partly of the late 17th century and has stone mullioned windows with drip moulds and a stone slated roof.

In the Middle Ages this manor was usually called *GODSWELL*. Later it became known as *GODSWELL AND CHAPMANSLADE* and eventually as Chapmanslade only. The name Godswell survives in Godswell Grove Farm, a small 19th-century farmhouse, about ¾ mile north-east of Chapmanslade village. During the 12th and early 13th centuries Stanley Abbey received a number of grants of land in Godswell and Chapmanslade: land at Godswell was granted by Hugh Plucknet, one of the abbey's earliest benefactors;[72] Walter of Brookway and Peter of Scudamore also granted lands in the same place;[73] among the gifts of Hugh of Raden was pasture for 400 sheep at Godswell;[74] Philip Marmium granted land there formerly held by Edric, and some land once belonging to Bartholomew his father, lying between 'bellus quercus' and the Brookway;[75] Thomas de Lanvaley granted 2 a. of land in Chapmanslade and some land once held by Alfric Ches;[76] a holding in Chapmanslade be-

[47] C.P. 25(2)/262/41–42 Eliz. Mich.
[48] See below.
[49] C 54/2430 no. 29; C.P. 25(2)/372/18 Jas. I Trin.
[50] *Wilts. Inq. p.m.* 1626–49 (Index Libr.), 232–36.
[51] Hoare, *Mod. Wilts.* Westbury, 45.
[52] C.P. 25(2)/745/21 Chas. II Trin.
[53] Ex inf. Miss J.S. Whitaker, Bratton.
[54] See below.
[55] Longleat MSS. 6592, 6593, 6594, 6951, and W.R.O. Inclosure and Tithe Awards.
[56] Longleat MS. 6644.
[57] See p. 145.
[58] *Cal. Pat.* 1548–9, 376, 1549–51, 196; W.R.O. Inclosure Award.
[59] *Complete Peerage*, Winchester.
[60] C 142/295/65.
[61] Ibid.; C 60/509/1 no. 11.

[62] *W.N. & Q.* iii. 350.
[63] G.E.C. *Complete Baronetage*, iii. 156. The eldest son, Sir Walter Ernley, had died unmarried in 1690.
[64] Burke, *Landed Gentry*, Drax.
[65] W.R.O. 148, Terrier of Estates of R.E.D. Grosvenor.
[66] Ibid.; Hoare, *Mod. Wilts.* Westbury, Preface (un-numbered page).
[67] W.R.O. Tithe Map.
[68] *Kelly's Dir. Wilts.* (1899).
[69] W.R.O. 148, Terrier of Estates of R.E.D. Grosvenor.
[70] W.R.O. Tithe Map; Bratton W.I. Scrapbk. *penes* Miss J. S. Whitaker.
[71] Bratton W.I. Scrapbk. *penes* Miss J. S. Whitaker.
[72] *V.C.H. Wilts.* iii. 269; *W.A.M.* xv. 258.
[73] *W.A.M.* xv. 258–9.
[74] Ibid. 259.
[75] Ibid. 258.
[76] Ibid. 255.

longing to the Prioress of Studley (Oxon.) was at an unknown date conveyed to Stanley.[77]

In 1242–3 the estate belonging to Stanley in Godswell comprised a carucate held in free alms.[78] Licence was granted in 1324 for the manor to be leased for 20 years.[79] It remained among the possessions of Stanley Abbey until that house was dissolved in 1536, by which time the manor of Godswell seems to have been annexed to Heywood, another Stanley Abbey estate.[80]

After the Dissolution the manor, then described as Godswell near Chapmanslade, *alias* Godswell and Chapmanslade, was granted with Heywood and most of the rest of the Stanley Abbey property to Sir Edward Baynton, of Bromham.[81] Sir Edward died in 1545[82] and the following year his son, Andrew, conveyed the manor to his brother, Edward.[83] In 1561 Edward Baynton conveyed it to Thomas Long.[84] Thomas Long died in 1562 and his heirs were his nieces Martha, wife of William Meredith, and Magdalen, wife of Roger Sadler, daughters of his brother Robert Long, and his great-nephew Henry, son of Henry Viner and Mary, a third daughter of Robert Long.[85] William and Martha Meredith sold their ⅓ of the manor in *c.* 1578 to Lionel Duckett,[86] and in 1579 John, son of Roger and Magdalen Sadler, conveyed his ⅓ to Lionel Duckett's nephew Stephen.[87] Henry Viner, however, appears to have acquired these ⅔ from the Ducketts, for on his death in 1626 he was seised of the manor of Chapmanslade and Godswell.[88] Richard Viner, Henry's son and heir, died childless in 1649, and his heirs were the daughters of his sister Mary, Mary, wife of John Minshull, and Anne, wife of the Revd. Oliver Chivers.[89] Mary Minshull died without issue and her share in the manor passed to the daughters of her sister, Anne Chivers, Susan, wife of John Lewis, and Mary, wife of Thomas Bythesea.[90] By a partition of 1667 the manor of Chapmanslade was assigned to Susan,[91] who apparently married secondly George Morgan,[92] while Mary Bythesea received Wyke House, Trowbridge.[93] Susan died childless, and the manor passed to her nephew John, son of Thomas and Mary Bythesea.[94] John Bythesea was succeeded in 1747 by his son, another John.[95] This John died in 1782 and Chapmanslade passed to his third son, William.[96]

In *c.* 1801 the manor was sold either by William Bythesea or his son George, to Thomas Thynne, Viscount Weymouth,[97] and it then descended in the family of the Marquess of Bath until sold by Lord Bath just after the Second World War.[98]

The manor of *HEYWOOD* originated in a grant of 1½ virgate of land by Geoffrey Burnel to Stanley Abbey some time about the beginning of the 13th century.[99] Geoffrey had acquired the land by gift of Hugh Plucknet,[1] and in 1224–5 William Burnel confirmed the grant of his uncle Geoffrey to the abbey.[2] Another virgate in Heywood was granted to the abbey by Hawise Pavely, and confirmed by her son Walter in 1240–1.[3] The estate in Heywood belonging to the abbey was leased *c.* 1327 to Peter of Berwick, and Joan de Bouches, and to John and Simon, Joan's sons, for their lives.[4] In 1451 Heywood Grange, which probably represented the whole estate, was let for 20 years at £3 a year.[5] A rent derived in part from Heywood was granted by the abbey in 1460–1 to the chaplain of the chantry of St. Nicholas in Highworth church.[6] At the Dissolution Heywood, still held by Stanley, seems to have been annexed to Godswell, later called Chapmanslade, another of the abbey's manors.[7] It was acquired by Sir Edward Baynton in 1537 along with much of the rest of the Stanley Abbey property.[8] Sir Edward was succeeded in 1545 by his son Andrew, who conveyed the manor, then called Heywood, *alias* Temmys Leys, to Henry Long.[9] From Henry Long it descended to his son, Thomas, who died seised of it in 1592–3 and was succeeded by his son Edward.[10] Edward sold the manor, which included other land in Heywood to James Ley (cr. Earl of Marlborough 1626), and upon 'Temes Leaze' the earl built a new residence for himself.[11] The manor of Heywood descended to James's son and heir, Henry, Earl of Marlborough (d. 1638),[12] but was sold, as was most of the earl's property in Westbury, in 1639–40 by Henry's son James, Earl of Marlborough (d. 1665) to Henry, Earl of Danby (d. 1644).[13] Henceforward it descended with the capital manor of Westbury.[14]

Some time in the later 17th century Heywood House was acquired by the Ash family, and in *c.* 1700 it passed to Thomas Phipps, mercer (d. *c.* 1715), who acquired the manor of Dilton in *c.*

[77] *W.A.M.* xv. 255.
[78] *Bk. of Fees,* ii. 740.
[79] *Cal. Pat.* 1324–7, 11.
[80] *V.C.H. Wilts.* iii. 274; *Valor Eccl.* (Rec. Com.), ii. 114; see below.
[81] *L. & P. Hen. VIII,* xii (1), p. 143; see below.
[82] C 142/72/109.
[83] C.P. 25(2)/46/324/38 Hen. VIII Trin.
[84] *Cal. Pat.* 1560–63, 136; CP 25(2)/239/3 and 4 Eliz. Mich.
[85] C 142/132/22.
[86] C 66/1179 m. 35.
[87] C.P. 40/1371 carte rot. 13; *Wilts. Visitation Pedigrees, 1623* (Harl. Soc. cv and cvi), p. 51.
[88] *Wilts. Inq. p.m.* 1626–49 (Index Libr.), 60–61.
[89] Burke, *Commoners,* ii. 663. The date of Ric. Viner's death was 1649 not 1647 as in Burke: Admin. Act Bk. 1649 f. 45. The second daughter is called Elizabeth in Burke, but in the will of Sir Henry Viner, d. 1626 she is called Anne: P.C.C. Hele 125.
[90] Burke, *Commoners,* ii. 663.
[91] C.P. 25(2)/745/18–19 Chas. II Hil.
[92] C.P. 25(2)/745/23 Chas. II Mich.
[93] *V.C.H. Wilts.* vii. 131 where Thos. Bythesea's wife is incorrectly said to be Mary Minshull.
[94] Burke, *Commoners,* ii. 663–4.
[95] Ibid; Burke, *Landed Gentry* (1906), i. 246.
[96] Ibid.
[97] Hoare, *Mod. Wilts.* Westbury, 41.
[98] Ex. inf. Longleat Estate Office.
[99] *Cat. Anc. D.* iv. A9286.
[1] *W.A.M.* xv. 259.
[2] *Cat. Anc. D.* iv. A9286.
[3] C.P. 25(1)/251/12/32.
[4] *Cal. Pat.* 1327–30. 484. The lease was made by John of Southbury, Abbot of Stanley 1309–27: *V.C.H. Wilts.* iii. 275.
[5] *V.C.H. Wilts.* iii. 272.
[6] C 143/452/27.
[7] *Valor Eccl.* (Rec. Com.), ii. 114. For Godswell see p. 161.
[8] *L. & P. Hen. VIII,* xii (i), p. 143.
[9] *Cal. Pat.* 1548–49, 432.
[10] C 142/236/40.
[11] *Wilts. Inq. p.m.* 1625–49 (Index Libr.), 232.
[12] Ibid. 268.
[13] C 54/3202 no. 5.
[14] See p. 150.

1693.[15] The son of Thomas Phipps, another Thomas, died in 1724 without issue and left Heywood by his will to his mother, Bridget, for life, and after her death to his brother William.[16] William Phipps, Governor of Bombay, died at Heywood House in 1748 and was succeeded by his son Thomas.[7] Thomas's son, Thomas Peckham Phipps, sold the house in 1789 to the clothier Gaisford Gibbs.[18] Gaisford Gibbs died two years later and his widow, Elizabeth, daughter of William Matravers, another Westbury clothier, married secondly Abraham Ludlow, M.D., of Bristol. Susan, daughter and heir of Gaisford Gibbs, then married the son of Abraham Ludlow, also called Abraham, and brought to him her father's property, including Heywood House.[19] Abraham Ludlow, the younger, died in 1822, and his son Henry Gaisford Gibbs Ludlow succeeded him at Heywood House.[20] Susan, daughter of Abraham and Susan and sister of Henry Gaisford Gibbs Ludlow, married Ralph Franco, nephew of Sir Manasseh Massey Lopes, who bought the manor of Westbury in 1810.[21] On the death of his uncle (Sir Manasseh Massey Lopes) in 1831, Ralph Franco assumed the name of Lopes and succeeded to the baronetcy as Sir Ralph Lopes, and to the lordship of the manor of Westbury.[22] On the death of Henry Gaisford Gibbs Ludlow in 1876, Heywood House passed to the third son of Sir Ralph Lopes.[23] This was Henry Charles Lopes, who was created Baron Ludlow of Heywood in 1897.[24] A life interest in part of the estate was also devised by H. G. G. Ludlow to his sister's son, Endymion Porter.[25] Lord Ludlow died in 1899,[26] and was succeeded by his son Henry Ludlow Lopes, who acquired the manor of Westbury in c. 1904 from his uncle Sir Massey Lopes (d. 1908), eldest son of Sir Ralph Lopes.[27] Henry Ludlow Lopes, Lord Ludlow of Heywood, died in 1922 when the peerage became extinct.[28] Since then Heywood House has had a number of owners.

Heywood House was built in Jacobean style by Henry Gaisford Gibbs Ludlow in the mid-19th century.[29] It possibly stands on or near the site of the house built by Sir James Ley in the early 17th century (see above). The present house stands on the east side of the main Westbury-Trowbridge road and commands a wide view over the park and lake towards the northern escarpment of Salisbury Plain. There are two lodges to the park in Yoad Lane dated 1896. Two more on the main road and

the stable block near the house are probably of early-19th-century date.

LESSER ESTATES. Land at *HEADINGHILL* ('Hevedlingell') with a pasture (*vaccaria*) there was held in 1166–7 by Leon de Lohareng'.[30] Ten years later Leon owed the same rent from the holding but had been disseised of it by Alan de Neville.[31] The estate passed to the Pavelys and may have been one of the two pastures stocked for Reynold Pavely when he acquired the manor of Westbury in 1173.[32] On the death of Walter Pavely in 1256 Headinghill was named as one of the estates making up the manor of Westbury,[33] and in 1323 it was said to be one of the manors making up the demesne of Walter's son, another Walter Pavely.[34] On the second partition of Sir John Pavely's lands in 1368 Headinghill, as part of the manor of Westbury, was allotted to John St. Lo for his daughters Joan, wife of Sir John Chidiock, and Eleanor, wife of Thomas de Bradeston.[35] After the death of St. Lo in 1375 Headinghill and the manor of Westbury were divided between these two daughters and Headinghill presumably descended with the capital manor.[36] In 1740 land-tax for Headinghill in the tithing of Bratton was payable by Mr. Houlton and Jonathan Ballard.[37]

In 1323 there was said to be a capital messuage with garden and a little grove at Headinghill besides the arable, pasture, and meadow lands.[38] At the time of the division of the estate between Joan Chidiock and Eleanor of Bradeston the west of the court of Headinghill, with a chamber over the gate, the 'dayhouse', and sheephouse were allotted to Joan and her husband, while the east part of the same court with the gate at the entrance went to Eleanor and Thomas de Bradeston.[39] A rent of £6 from the manor of Westbury and the hamlets of Headinghill, Stoke, Melborne, and Leigh, i.e. Joan and Eleanor's share of Sir John Pavely's lands, was to be paid to Sir John's daughter, Joan, wife of Ralph Cheyney. Headinghill is mentioned in connexion with this rent in 1420.[40]

An estate called *REDLANDS* is probably the same as the *vaccaria de Redelanda* held in 1166–7 by Alfric the cowherd.[41] Alfric continued to pay rent for this until 1173–4 after when his name disappears from the Pipe Rolls.[42] It thus presumably formed part of the capital manor, which was granted away then, and has not been traced as a separate estate until the 17th century. In 1682

[15] Hoare, *Mod. Wilts.* Westbury, 34; MS. Cal. Deeds at Chalcot House, 38.
[16] MS. Cal. Deeds at Chalcot House, 38. He had conveyed Dilton to Paul Phipps in 1721–22, see p. 153.
[17] Hoare, op. cit. and table in H.R. Phipps, 'Phipps Notes', v, TS. in B.M.
[18] Hoare, op. cit. Hoare states that Thos. Peckham Phipps was the son of Wm. Phipps, but he seems to have been his grandson: H. R. Phipps, 'Phipps Notes', v, TS. in B.M.
[19] Hoare, op. cit.
[20] Ibid.; Burke, *Landed Gentry* (1871).
[21] Burke, *Peerage, Baronetage, and Knightage* (1904), under Lopes, and see p. 150.
[22] Burke, *Peerage, Baronetage and Knightage* (1904), under Lopes.
[23] *W.A.M.* xxxi. 89.
[24] *Complete Peerage*, Ludlow.
[25] *Trowbridge Advertiser*, 2 Sept. 1876; W.A.S. Libr., Devizes, Sale Cat. [26] *Complete Peerage*, Ludlow.

[27] See p. 150.
[28] *Complete Peerage*, Ludlow.
[29] Murray's *Handbk. for Residents and Travellers in Wilts. and Dorset* (1899), 154.
[30] *Pipe R.* 1166–7 (P.R.S. xi), 128.
[31] Ibid. 1176–7 (P.R.S. xxvi), 98.
[32] Ibid. 1172–3 (P.R.S. xix), 106.
[33] *Wilts. Inq. p.m.* 1242–1326 (Index Libr.), 18.
[34] Ibid. 435.
[35] See p. 149.
[36] *Wilts. Inq. p.m.* 1242–1326 (Index Libr.), 387 and see p. 149.
[37] Longleat MS. 6594.
[38] *Wilts. Inq. p.m.* 1242–1326 (Index Libr.), 435. Headinghill seems to have been situated somewhere in the tithing of Bratton: see p. 144.
[39] Ibid. 387.
[40] C 138/46/46.
[41] *Pipe R.* 1167 (P.R.S. xi), 128.
[42] Ibid. 1174 (P.R.S. xxi), 30.

Jeffery Whitaker paid rent to the lord of the manor of Bratton for Redlands,[43] and in 1685 Henry Whitaker devised the lease of Redlands to his son Thomas.[44] In 1740 both Mrs. Susannah Whitaker and John Whitaker Hinton were assessed for land-tax for Redlands,[45] and in 1758 William Whitaker devised his freehold estate of Redlands to his son William.[46] In 1840 the property was owned by Philip Whitaker[47] who was leasing a large part of the Bratton Grange estate.[48] Redlands Farm, which probably represents this estate, lies in the north of the parish of Bratton.[49]

An estate, lying partly in *BRATTON* and partly in *DILTON*, was in the 13th century held by the Dauntseys.[50] In *c.* 1250 parts of this were alienated by Richard Dauntsey to Richard of Dene, the chaplain of Dilton, Roceline of Bratton, Richard and John of Bratton, Geoffrey Scudamore, Alan Fitz-Warin, Walter Pavely, Richard Burnel, Philip Marmium, the Prior of Monkton Farleigh, the church of Westbury, and others.[51]

The descent of some of these small estates can be partially traced over a short period. Richard of Bratton held land in Bratton by 1241[52] and pasture in Stoke by 1249.[53] Part of his property appears to have passed to coheirs, for in 1281 John le Lung, Maud his wife, William Sparkeling, Sarah his wife, and Margery, sister of Sarah, conveyed, a messuage and three virgates of land in Bratton to Geoffrey of Bratton.[54] In 1304 Geoffrey conveyed his holding in Bratton to Walter Pavely, retaining only a life interest in the property for himself.[55] This part of Bratton, together with the land there granted by Richard Dauntsey to Walter's grandfather (see above) presumably became merged in the capital manor of Westbury.[56]

The land conveyed to Alan FitzWarin by Richard Dauntsey passed to Nicholas FitzWarin, who forfeited it as a rebel in 1322.[57] It appears to have been restored to his heirs and in 1349 was granted by Margery, widow of Reynold FitzWarin, to her son Robert.[58] The estate conveyed to Geoffrey Scudamore remained in his family until 1342, when it was sold by Margery, wife of Sir Peter Scudamore, to William son of Nicholas FitzWarin.[59] Land in Bratton, which probably included these two holdings, was held by Sir William FitzWarin in 1361 when the reversion was granted to the Bonhommes of Edington.[60]

The conveyances of Richard Dauntsey to Philip Marmium and the church of Westbury probably

went to enlarge the manors already held by them in Westbury.[61] His grant of land to the priory of Monkton Farleigh was presumably added to two virgates in Bratton which Ernulf de Mandeville had given to the priory.[62] The monks had also acquired an assart of 40 a. at Headinghill by grant of Henry II *c.* 1185–9.[63] It was possibly early in the 13th century that they granted their land in Bratton, amounting to ½ hide, to Roger Cook in fee, reserving a rent.[64] Nothing more is known of the descent of this property except that it must eventually have passed to the house of Bonhommes at Edington, and so was re-united with the manor of Bratton.

The Lungs apparently did not alienate all their property in Bratton in 1281 (see above). In 1325–6 Ralph le Lung of Coulston held land there,[65] and in 1343–4 he and his wife Eleanor conveyed land in Bratton and elsewhere to Nicholas Chamberlain.[66] In the same year Nicholas conveyed the property to John of Edington, Ralph le Lung and his wife retaining a life interest in each transaction.[67] From John of Edington it passed in 1362 to the religious house founded at Edington by his uncle, William of Edington, Bishop of Winchester.[68] At about the same date other parcels of land in Bratton were given to the Bonhommes of Edington, possibly by the descendants of those persons to whom Richard Dauntsey alienated his holding. John Videlu and Joan his wife gave some land there in 1373.[69] John Bonham and John Mareys gave a messuage and land in 1392.[70] Other properties were acquired by the rector in 1427 from John Frank, Thomas Touke and others.[71]

The carucate in Bratton which Richard Dauntsey retained for himself in 1250 (see above) passed with the manor of Dilton until 1364 when Walter Dauntsey conveyed it to Robert Gundevyne and Thomas Jurdan,[72] who the same year obtained licence to convey it to the Rector of Edington.[73]

In 1249 the Prior of Monkton Farleigh conveyed a virgate of land at *BROOKWAY* ('Brocweye') to Walter of Brookway.[74] Walter's father had previously acquired a wood called Holt from Robert de Manners and both pieces of property were henceforth to be held of the prior for a rent of 7s. a year.[75] The estate was probably in the south-west corner of the modern parish of Dilton Marsh, and a farm called Brookway Farm is marked there on the Tithe Map of 1848.[76] In 1290 it was found that a conveyance of the estate, then said to comprise a messuage,

43 Longleat MS. 6592.
44 *W.N. & Q.* iv. 202.
45 Longleat MS. 6594.
46 *W.N. & Q.* iv. 207.
47 W.R.O. Tithe Award.
48 See p. 161.
49 O.S. Map 1/25,000 sheet 31/85.
50 See p. 152.
51 *Bk. of Fees*, ii. 1178, 1225.
52 *Cal. Feet of F. Wilts.* 1193–1272, ed. Fry, p. 34.
53 Ibid. p. 42. For Stoke see p. 144.
54 *Feet of F. Wilts.* 1272–1327 (W.A.S. Rec. Brch.), 15.
55 Ibid. 50.
56 See p. 149.
57 S.C. 6/1145 no. 12.
58 *W.N. & Q.* ii. 561.
59 B.M. Lansd. MS. 442, f. 99.
60 *Wilts. Inq. p.m.* 1327–77 (Index Libr.), 301; *V.C.H. Wilts.* iii. 321.
61 See pp. 153, 157.
62 *Rot. Hund.* (Rec. Com.), ii. 279.

63 *Cartae Antiquae*, ii (P.R.S. N.S. xxxiii), p. 59.
64 *W.N. & Q.* iii. 279. The name of the prior, John, is hitherto unrecorded, but he probably flourished between 1208 and 1227: *V.C.H. Wilts.* iii. 268. This grant must be before 1227: Dugdale. *Mon. Angl.* v. 27.
65 *Feet of F. Wilts.* 1272–1327 (W.A.S. Rec. Brch.), 120.
66 C.P. 25(1)/254/45.
67 C.P. 25(1)/255/46/10.
68 *Wilts. Inq. p.m.* 1327–77 (Index Libr.), 301; B.M. Lansd. MS. 442, f. 61; *V.C.H. Wilts.* iii. 321.
69 C.P. 25(1)/255/52/31.
70 *Cal. Pat.* 1391–6, 156.
71 Ibid. 1422–9, 398.
72 B.M. Lansd. MS. 442, f.91d; and for manor of Dilton see p. 152.
73 *Wilts. Inq. p.m.* 1327–77 (Index Libr.), 331–2; B.M. Lansd. MS. 442, ff. 92 and 92d.
74 C.P. 25(1)/251/16/88.
75 Ibid.
76 W.R.O. Tithe Map, and see *P.N. Wilts.* (E.P.N.S.), 150.

30 a. of arable, and 19 a. of meadow in Brookway and Westbury, would be of no damage to the king, but would deprive Walter Pavely of a suit every three weeks at the hundred court.[77] The overlordship of the estate apparently remained with the priory of Monkton Farleigh until the Dissolution. In 1545 the estate was held by John Brookway and a rent of 12s. from it was granted to John Adlam, who at that date acquired the manor of Leigh Priors which had also formerly belonged to Monkton Farleigh.[78]

This estate called *SEWELLS* or *SHEWELLS* probably originated in the holding of the family of Sewale. In 1280–1 Reynold de Sewale held 4 a. in the hundred of Westbury.[79] In 1341 lands and rent in Westbury, Heywood, Bratton, and Leigh were settled upon Walter Sewale and Emma his wife with remainder in tail to Walter son of Walter, and remainder in default to Hugh FitzWarin and Joan his wife.[80] Later the holding passed to the Westbury family probably through the marriage of Katharine, daughter of William FitzWarin, with William of Westbury.[81] William of Westbury held it at the time of his death in 1449 when it is described as the manor of Sewales and was held of John Seymour,[82] lord of the manor of Westbury Seymour.[83] Sewales passed, possibly in the same way as Westbury Leversage,[84] to Sir James Ley who was seised of it, then apparently called Shewells or Sewells, at the time of his death in 1629.[85] The exact location of this estate is unknown but in 1629 it was described as lying in Heywood, Bratton, and Westbury;[86] it was then worth 40s. a year.

HAWKERIDGE was never described as a manor but its existence as a separate estate can be traced back to the 14th century. When the second partition of Sir John Pavely's lands was made in 1368, Hawkeridge, then described as a hamlet, went to Ralph Cheyney and his wife Joan, a daughter of Sir John.[87] Ralph and Joan also received the manor of Brook by this partition and Hawkeridge seems to have descended with that manor to Charles, Lord Mountjoy (d. 1606), who in 1599 sold tenements in Hawkeridge to Sir James Ley.[88] From then on the estate followed the descent of the capital manor of Westbury.

The family of Phipps of Heywood also had an estate in Hawkeridge. This was sold in 1810 by Thomas Peckham Phipps to George Dyer, who also acquired from Thomas in the same year an estate known as the Stert estate.[89]

An estate called *LAYFIELDS* was described as a manor in the 16th century and was apparently a part of the manor of Brook.[90] This, comprising 50 a., was sold in 1599 by Lord Mountjoy (d. 1606) to Jasper More of Heytesbury.[91] The estate passed to

Jasper's two daughters, Elizabeth, wife of Sir William Guise, and the wife of Shilston Calmady. Both shares were later united in John, son of Sir William Guise, and in 1691 were conveyed by this John's son, also called John, to Thomas Phipps. At this time the property was farmed by Cuthbert Elkins. The same year Thomas Phipps let the estate to Rachel Gawen, widow, of Westbury for lives, reserving suit to the manors of Dilton and Chalford. In 1719 the estate was conveyed to Paul Phipps (d. 1722) and from Paul it passed in the Phipps family to Thomas Henry Hele Phipps of Leighton House (d. 1841). In 1756 the estate comprised two pieces of land called Great and Lower Layfield, which lay in Brook.[92]

In 1682 land on the manor of *BRATTON* was being leased by Sir Thomas Thynne (d. 1714) to Henry Ballard.[93] Sir Thomas Thynne leased lands to William Ballard, yeoman, in 1690,[94] and a Timothy Ballard was one of the chief rent-payers on the manor in the later 17th century.[95] In 1732 John Aldridge Ballard had a freehold estate in Bratton and other members of the Ballard family leased lands there from the Marquess of Bath.[96] Some time before 1830 the property of the Ballards in Bratton appears to have passed by marriage to Edward Seagram M.D.[97] In 1842 Edward Frowd Seagram, of Bratton House, was leasing Grange Farm and approximately 200 a. from Lord Bath and had a freehold estate in Bratton of about the same size.[98] Bratton House continued to be occupied by members of the Ballard and Seagram families until the beginning of the 20th century when it passed, also by marriage, to the Diggle family.[99] In c. 1934 it was bought by Sir Horace Seymour.[1]

Bratton House was built in 1715 by William Ballard and his initials with the date appear on the rainwater heads. The original building is of three stories and basement. It is rectangular in plan with tall symmetrical fronts of 7 and 5 bays. The walls are of brick, later cement rendered, and have stone dressings. Above the central door on the south front is a broken pediment and crest, while the doors on the east and west fronts have stone shell hoods. Internally there is a contemporary staircase. The house has been enlarged at two different periods.

AGRICULTURE. Of the 40 hides attributed in the Domesday Survey to the manor of Westbury 17 were said to be in demesne, leaving, after the deduction of the 4½ hides held by William Scudet, 18½ hides for villein farming.[2] The Geld Roll, however, attributes 35½ hides to the villeins, inferring that the king had no demesne.[3] The Domesday entry records 7 demesne and 40 villein

[77] *Wilts. Inq. p.m.* 1242–1326 (Index Libr.), 183.
[78] *L. & P. Hen. VIII*, xx (1), p. 420, and see p. 157.
[79] J.I. 1/1002 m. 44.
[80] C.P. 25(1)/254/45/2.
[81] C 140/84/36.
[82] C 139/139/23.
[83] See p. 150.
[84] See p. 157.
[85] *Wilts. Inq. p.m.* 1626–47 (Index Libr.), 232–6.
[86] Ibid. 235, see also *P.N. Wilts.* (E.P.N.S.), 479.
[87] B.M. Lansd. MS. 442 f. 145; see p. 149.
[88] C 54/1621/Mountjoy and Ley.
[89] Hoare, *Mod. Wilts.* Westbury, 41.
[90] C.P. 40/1113 rot. 5d., 6.

[91] Unless otherwise stated this and subsequent information about the descent of Layfields from MS. Cal. Deeds at Chalcot House.
[92] W.R.O. 212B/We, Plan of the property.
[93] Longleat MS. 6592.
[94] W.R.O. 212B/We, Deed Thos. Thynne–Wm. Ballard, 1690.
[95] Longleat MS. 6593.
[96] Ibid. 6591.
[97] Hoare, *Mod. Wilts.* Westbury, 160.
[98] W.R.O. Tithe Award.
[99] *Kelly's Dir. Wilts.* (1903).
[1] Ex inf. Sir Horace Seymour, Bratton House.
[2] *V.C.H. Wilts.* ii, p. 118.   [3] Ibid. pp. 212–13.

ploughs. There were 80 a. of meadow, and pasture 3 leagues long by 3 leagues broad. On the demesne there were 28 serfs and 16 coliberts, and there were 38 villeins and 23 bordars. There were an unspecified number of potters, and 9 bee-keepers.[4] This is the only reference in Domesday to bee-keepers in Wiltshire, and their presence at Westbury may indicate an exceptionally highly organized manorial economy.[5] Westbury was also one of the only four Wiltshire manors on which swine-herds are recorded.[6] There were 29 of these, the large number perhaps to be attributed to the excellent feeding for pigs provided in the neighbouring woodlands. In 1086 there was woodland 3 leagues long by ½ league broad attached to the manor,[7] which lay in the heart of Selwood Forest, and remained within the forest until its disafforestation in the 16th century.[8] In the 12th century Selwood in Wiltshire was sometimes known as Westbury Forest.[9]

The size of the demesne on William Scudet's estate of 4½ hides in Bratton and Dilton[10] in 1086 is not known, but attached to it were 4 serfs and 4 ploughs. There were also 20 bordars with 3 ploughs. There were 20 a. of meadow and 4 of woodland.[11]

The manor of Westbury was first extended in 1256.[12] Brook still formed a part of it at this date, but the other lands which were carved out of the royal manor after 1086 had come into existence as separate estates or manors. The manor of Westbury with Brook then comprised a demesne of 11 carucates (660 a.), 7 a. of meadow, and pasture for an unspecified number of oxen, cows, and sheep. There was some park and woodland, as well as the garden and 3 dovecots. Free tenants paid nearly 69s., and customary tenants £4 in assized rents. An extent of 1323 distinguishes the estates of Brook and Headinghill, both of which still formed part of the manor of Westbury.[13] At Westbury itself there were 400 a. of arable, 8 a. of meadow, and some pasture. There were 14 free tenants, and 21 villeins. At Brook there were 200 a. of arable, 40 a. of meadow, some pasture, 20 a. of wood, and a park ('le Park'). There were 11 free tenants, 2 virgaters, and 8 other villeins. Headinghill had the same amount of arable, 20 a. of meadow, a little, 'grove', and some pasture. A fragmentary account, probably of approximately the same date, shows that some at least of the labour services which were owed by all these tenants in villeinage, were commuted, for in one year money paid in lieu of services brought in rather over £2.[14]

Another extent of 24 years later (1347) shows something of the method of farming the 420 a. of arable, and 20 a. of meadow which then made up the manor of Westbury and its members, Brook and Headinghill.[15] Every year 280 a. could be sown at the winter and spring sowings, while 140 a. lay fallow and in common. Half the cultivated arable lay on the chalk uplands ('on the hill'), but this was only worth half as much as the arable lying on the richer land beneath the downs. Half the meadow was farmed in severalty, and was twice as valuable as the other half, which lay in common after mowing. In addition there were 20 a. of several pasture for cattle, and a several pasture for sheep on the downs. There were 100 a. of wood, of which 30 a. were in severalty, and 10 a. of oakwood, all of which lay in common. At this date there were 10 customary tenants on the manor, owing summer works only. Rents of assize amounted to £20.

On the eve of the division of the manor of Westbury between the heirs of Sir John Pavely in 1361, the amount of both meadow and pasture farmed in severalty seems to have increased.[16] On the common pasture 12 cattle, 40 oxen, and 400 sheep could be grazed. Rents of both free and customary tenants amounted to £12. When the manor of Westbury, by this time excluding Brook, was divided in 1375 between the heirs of Sir John St. Lo, the arable lay in 'cultures' called Gavilhucce, Blaklond, Doucefurlong, Smalmedfurlong, Lyamcombe, and Wrowodelonde.[17] On the half, later to become the manor called Westbury Stourton,[18] there was a grange, haybarn, dairyhouse and sheep-house. On the other half, later called Westbury Seymour or St. Maur,[19] there was a grange, an ox-house, and a 'carterstable'. A fishweir is also mentioned. At least 11 bond tenants are named. One tenant paid rent for pasture for 200 sheep.

Such information as has been found for the other manors within the parish suggests, as is to be expected, that much the same economy was followed on them all. On the Mauduit manor in 1300 there were 160 a. of arable, 15 a. of meadow, and a common pasture.[20] There were 8 free, and 5 customary tenants, and 28 cottars. All customary tenants owed labour services for part of, or throughout, the year, but there is evidence that by 1321 many of these services had been commuted for money payments.[21] At the same date it is apparent that some of the pasture land belonging to the manor lay in small inclosed fields.[22] On Richard Dauntsey's manor in Bratton and Dilton in 1348 150 a. could be sown every year, while the same amount lay fallow and in common. Two pastures were farmed in severalty, one comprising 3 a., the other with grazing for 300 sheep. A wood of 12 a. was also cultivated in severalty.[23] At Bratton, as on the manor of Westbury, there was some arable cultivation on the chalk downlands as well as on the more fertile soil beneath.[24] In 1364 75 a. lay on the downs but were sown only every other year because they lay in common. Beneath the downs were 29 a. apparently inclosed and farmed in severalty. There was both common and several pasture on which 300 sheep could be supported.[25]

---

[4] *V.C.H. Wilts.* ii, p. 118.
[5] Ibid. p. 55.
[6] Ibid.
[7] Ibid. p. 118.
[8] *V.C.H. Wilts.* iv. 414–17.
[9] Ibid. 414.
[10] See p. 152.
[11] *V.C.H. Wilts.* ii, p. 118.
[12] *Wilts. Inq. p.m.* 1242–1326 (Index Libr.), 18–19.
[13] Ibid. 434–6.
[14] S.C. 6/1061/26.

[15] *Wilts. Inq. p.m.* 1327–77 (Index Libr.), 176.
[16] Ibid. 290–1, and see p. 149.
[17] Ibid. 387–9. [18] See p. 149.
[19] See p. 150.
[20] *Wilts. Inq. p.m.* 1242–1326 (Index Libr.), 252–3, and see p. 155.
[21] S.C. 6/1145/12.
[22] Ibid.
[23] *Wilts. Inq. p.m.* 1327–77 (Index Libr.), 174.
[24] *W.N. & Q.* ii. 454.
[25] *Wilts. Inq. p.m.* 1327–77 (Index Libr.), 331–2.

As is shown above, the land of the ancient parish was divided between numerous manors and estates, all quite small.[26] Few of these formed compact holdings, but were made up of lands often widely scattered over the whole area of the ancient parish. An early-14th-century terrier,[27] probably for the rectory manor, names six fields, or localities, in which a number of lords had holdings. They were the south field of Leigh, the field called 'the hill', the west field, described as being the west part of the court of the Prior of Steventon,[28] Smallmead, the field called 'the Ham', and the east field of Westbury. Roger Marmium, lord of the manor of Bremeridge,[29] held land in five of these places, Walter Pavely, lord of the manor of Westbury,[30] in four, and the Prior of Monkton Farleigh[31] and the Precentor of Salisbury[32] in three.

The manor of Bratton, perhaps because of its remote position in the south-east corner of the ancient parish, was a more compact estate. It was a corn-growing and sheep-rearing manor. In the 17th century its demesne lands comprised, besides the home close, 151 a. of arable on the downs, 36 a. of arable in the 'lower fields', sheepsleights for 1,000 sheep in summer, and 600 in winter, and a common pasture for 16 beasts.[33] In 1682 the arable lands were being extended, but at the same time improvements were being made to the meadowlands so as to offset the loss of common grazing land to the plough.[34] Most of the best grazing for sheep within the ancient parish lay in or near the tithing of Bratton on the chalk downs south of the village, and grazing rights were strictly regulated by the custom of the manor. Certain flocks, including those from the farms of Westbury Stourton and Westbury Seymour, were excluded from the common fields of Bratton in the daytime, and neither beasts nor sheep were allowed without a keeper on the land newly re-claimed from the marsh.[35] Flocks of between 300 and 600 sheep were probably kept on most of the manors in the 16th and 17th centuries. In the middle of the 16th century Bratton Grange had pasture for 700 sheep,[36] and at about the beginning of the 18th Jeffery Whitaker had well over 100 sheep-leazes at Bratton.[37] The need of the various farmers to cross the land of others when bringing their flocks from the downs to water, led to the creation of clearly defined ways or droves. These sheep-droves, usually called after the respective farmers or landowners entitled to use them, are a feature of the inclosure map of 1808. The amount of time a flock could feed on the richer pasture by the water was also carefully regulated.[38]

The land of the ancient parish was divided roughly equally between the sheep- and corn-farming region of the chalk uplands in the south-east, and the pastoral, dairy-farming region of the

clay vale in the north-west. But less evidence has survived for the agrarian history of the pastoral region. In the mid-18th century Brook Farm and Lodge Wood Farm, both in this part of the former parish, were noted for their cheese, and of their 300–400 acres, much was water-meadow.[39] Storridge Farm, when sold in the mid-20th century, had 324 a. of pasture land and accommodation for over 100 cows.[40] The spread of the town westwards in the late 19th and in the 20th centuries has covered some of this former pasture land with building and one or two of the large farms in this area were in the mid-20th century broken up and no longer working as farms.

The process of inclosure has not been traced in any detail. At Bratton there seems to have been but little inclosure of either pasture or arable by the middle of the 18th century.[41] At Brook in the low-lying, clayland region both arable and pasture inclosures were made early in the 17th century when the park there was disparked,[42] and much of the cultivated land in the north-western part of the parish was already inclosed by the time of the inclosure award of 1808.[43] That year some 220 a. of common-land were inclosed. Besides those gaining considerable consolidated estates as did Abraham Ludlow, of Heywood House, and John Whitaker, of Fairwood, there were a notable number of small men acquiring small parcels of land varying in size from 2 to 33 perches. Among these were a number of weavers, almost all living at Dilton Marsh or Stormore, a woodman, a shoemaker, and a sawyer.

In 1842 some 11,541 a. of land were estimated to be liable for tithe. Of these, 4,448 a. were returned as arable, and 6,118 a. as meadow or pasture, including 1,794 a. of downland. There were 261 a. of orchards and 658 a. of woodland.[44] The greensand strip running through the parish from Chapmanslade to Bratton is particularly suitable for market gardening, and in 1815 fruit and vegetables from the region were sent regularly to Trowbridge,[45] as they still were to a limited extent in 1960. In 1842 there were 40 small orchards in Bratton alone,[46] and some still flourished there in 1960.

While in the earlier 19th century the inhabitants of Chapmanslade, Dilton Marsh, and Westbury Leigh were chiefly occupied with the textile industry,[47] those of Bratton were almost entirely employed in agriculture. In 1831 200 out of 300 families there were occupied in farming.[48] Flocks of 1,000 sheep and more were still maintained on the downs by farmers who also grew corn on a large scale.[49] But in the second half of the century this type of farming was declining everywhere and in Bratton the acquisition of much of the downland by the War Department ensured its virtual disappearance in the 20th century. In this century the dairy

[26] See pp. 148–65.
[27] W.R.O. It is undated, but internal evidence suggests a date in the first half of the 14th century.
[28] See p. 154.
[29] See p. 157.
[30] See p. 149.
[31] See p. 156.
[32] See p. 153.
[33] Longleat MS. 6644, Survey of site and mansion house.
[34] Longleat MS. 6592, Survey Bk. 1682.
[35] Longleat MSS. 6590, 11529.
[36] Cal. Pat. 1548–9, 376.

[37] Longleat MS. 10651, Survey Bk. 1696–1733.
[38] W.N. & Q. iii. 307.
[39] Wilts. Times, 7 Oct. 1960 quoting the Salisbury Jnl.
[40] Wilts. Times, 3 June, 1960.
[41] Longleat MS. 10651, Survey Bk. 1696–1733.
[42] C 2 Eliz. I H. 3/52.
[43] W.R.O. Inclosure Award.
[44] W.R.O. Tithe Award.
[45] Bodman, Hist. of Trowbridge (1815), 21.
[46] W.R.O. Tithe Award.
[47] See p. 170.
[48] Census, 1831.
[49] Bratton W.I. Scrap Bk.

farming of the north-west pastoral region is the principal type of farming within the area of the former ancient parish.

INDUSTRY AND TRADE. Like the other towns in the basin of the Bradford Avon, Westbury emerged as a centre of the cloth industry of that region towards the end of the 15th century.[50] As early as 1433 a Westbury clothier, William Gawen, was transacting considerable business with a merchant in the east-coast port of Lynn (Norf.),[51] and in the second half of the century, as has been shown elsewhere, there were a number of substantial 'clothmen' in Westbury and the surrounding townships.[52] Already in the 16th century such men were acquiring the local fulling mills.[53]

In the course of the 16th century the number and prosperity of the Westbury clothiers increased, so that towards the middle of the century Leland could write 'the towne stondithe moste by clothiers'.[54] In addition to acquiring fulling mills for their business, the clothiers began in the 16th century to accumulate lands and estates in Westbury.[55] In 1545 the clothier John Adlam acquired the manor of Leigh Priors, formerly among the possessions of the Prior of Monkton Farleigh.[56] Possibly the most outstanding among these prosperous clothiers were the families of Whitaker and Phipps. The fortunes of the Whitaker family may have been founded by John, one of the Westbury clothiers of the late 15th century.[57] In c. 1545 Richard Whitaker, likewise a clothier, had some 160 acres of inclosed land in Westbury and a sheep house.[58] In 1570 Stephen Whitaker, already a considerable landowner in Westbury, acquired the manor of Westbury Stourton with the important Bitham fulling mill.[59] His sons and grandson were mill owners in Westbury and Bratton.[60] Thenceforth the family continued to acquire land, mostly in Bratton, and gradually it exchanged its occupation with the clothing industry for that of corn- and sheep-farming. The clothier, Henry Phipps, was acquiring property in Westbury towards the end of the 16th century, and his sons Henry and Nicholas, both clothiers, became lords of the manor of Westbury Mauduits in 1585.[61] This large family continued to accumulate lands and manors until by the end of the 19th century the Phippses were some of the largest landowners, occupying two of the biggest country houses in Westbury, namely Chalcot and Leighton House.[62] In 1722 Paul Phipps, who added extensively to the family estates, was still actively engaged in the clothing industry. On his death he left 281 cloths in

London as well as a number of unfinished cloths in local hands.[63] The connexion with the industry was maintained until about the end of the 18th century, but by then the family had entered the ranks of the landed gentry.

Besides the Whitakers and the Phippses mention must be made of the Benetts, also clothiers, who were leasing the rectory manor in the 16th century,[64] but their main estate lay in Norton Bavant.[65] Other Westbury clothiers include Anthony Garland and Robert Adlam (both fl. 1562),[66] Nicholas Passion (d. 1581),[67] Anthony Wilkins (d. 1599),[68] and Thomas Saunders (d. 1602).[69] The wealth of some of these textile capitalists is illustrated by the subsidy assessments of 1545 and 1576. In 1545 the highest contributions in the hundred were paid by two members of the Adlam family, Sybil and John, both assessed at £3, a greater sum than that paid by John Bush, 'gentleman', lord of the manor of Dilton.[70] In the later year only four persons were assessed at over £7, among them Stephen Whitaker (£10), George Adlam (£8), and Henry Phype (£8),[71] the first two certainly, and the third, probably, clothiers.

The effects of the depression which hit the broad cloth industry during the first quarter of the 17th century[72] were accentuated in Westbury by an outbreak of plague in 1603–4. The justices were obliged to order a relief of 40s. a week for the distressed inhabitants, then said to be mostly weavers and spinners, and special arrangements were made for the collection of corn for the town from the markets of Warminster and 'Lavington'.[73] Six years later the town was still impoverished,[74] and further misfortune overtook it in 1616 when a fire caused damage estimated at over £1,000.[75] Westbury shared in the difficulties caused by the disruption of trade during the Civil War, and in 1648 petitioned Sir Thomas Fairfax against the burden of free quartering of soldiers, protesting that Westbury was the least and the poorest hundred in the county, and had suffered far beyond other places. A troop of 100 dragoons had at the time spent 30 days in the town.[76] After the Civil War Westbury, like the rest of the towns in the region, began to expand its manufacture of medley cloths and abandon its old white-cloth export industry.[77] By the end of the century this had brought a period of relative prosperity to the region, but there was still distress in Westbury immediately after the Restoration. In 1662 250 inhabitants petitioned for relief in consequence of the lack of work and dearness of food, claiming that they depended entirely upon the cloth trade 'which is become as nothing'.[78]

There is no evidence of any guild organization

---

[50] V.C.H. Wilts. iv. 133–4.
[51] Cal. Pat. 1429–36, 236; V.C.H. Wilts. iv. 134.
[52] V.C.H. Wilts. iv. 134.
[53] See p. 172.
[54] Leland, Itin. ed. Toulmin Smith, v. 85.
[55] See pp. 147, 149, 155.
[56] See p. 147.
[57] V.C.H. Wilts. iv. 134.
[58] C 1/1281/36.
[59] See p. 149.
[60] See pp. 172, 174.
[61] See p. 155.
[62] See pp. 155, 156.
[63] W.R.O. Inventory of goods of Paul Phipps.
[64] See p. 153.
[65] See p. 48.

[66] E 159/350/329.
[67] W.N. & Q. vii. 320.
[68] Ibid. 541.
[69] C 142/267/84. Saunders acquired a fulling mill in Westbury Leigh in 1584: see p. 173.
[70] Taxation Lists (W.A.S. Rec. Brch.), 34; see above, p. 48.
[71] Ibid. 70–2.
[72] V.C.H. Wilts. iv. 151–55.
[73] Hist. MSS. Com. Var. Coll. i. 74.
[74] Ibid. 84.
[75] Ibid. 93.
[76] J. Waylen, 'The Falstone Day Book', W.A.M. xxvi 384–5.
[77] V.C.H. Wilts. iv. 155.
[78] Hist. MSS. Com. Var. Coll. i. 144.

among the Westbury cloth-workers, although a guildhall is mentioned in 1599 and in 1610.[79] Communal action, however, could be taken to enforce the custom of apprenticeship in the 17th century. William Axford, a weaver of Bratton, was indicted in 1602 for taking an apprentice when he himself had never been apprenticed,[80] and in 1647 there were protests from 27 'ancient weavers of Westbury' that demobilized soldiers who had never been apprenticed were setting themselves up in the trade.[81] On the other hand, unwarranted interference in the industry was resented. In 1658 the inhabitants, led by their vicar, Philip Hunton, and the mayor[82] petitioned the justices to allow the burlers of broad medley cloths to continue their work undisturbed by the indictment that they had not served as apprentices. Burling, like spinning, they claimed, had never been an apprentice trade, but was undertaken mostly by children to augment the family earnings. To restrict it in any way would bring great hardship to the town. The attempt to do so, it was thought, was to enable a few powerful persons to gain control of the process.[83]

Cloth workers are to be found in most parts of the parish in the 17th century. At Bratton there was Thomas Whitaker, fuller (fl. 1638),[84] William Whitaker, cloth worker (d. 1693),[85] John Bennett (fl. c. 1645)[86] and John Lyde (fl. 1694),[87] both sergeweavers. At Westbury Leigh there were John Paineter, weaver (fl. c. 1633),[88] and Henry Adlam, clothworker (fl. 1695).[89] At Westbury there were Edward Hill, fuller (fl. c. 1620),[90] Steven Appleguard, broadweaver (fl. 1630),[91] and John Crew, dyer (fl. 1640).[92] At Dilton there were William Minty, weaver (fl. 1613),[93] and John Whatly, clothworker (fl. 1660).[94] Sixteenth-century Westbury clothiers named were William Harris (fl. c. 1663),[95] Thomas Weekes (fl. 1681),[96] James Black (fl. 1638),[97] William Tipper (fl. 1670),[98] and John Taunton (fl. 1646).[99]

Westbury was the only one of the Wiltshire clothing towns to take any active part in the attempts made at the beginning of the 18th century to control the manufacture of medley cloth.[1] The town petitioned Parliament in 1711 that cloths should be of a prescribed length to be measured at the fulling mill.[2] But there is no reason to suppose that the industry was not thriving in Westbury at this date as it was in the rest of the region in spite of distress among the mass of weavers and spinners. There may, indeed, have been less discontent at Westbury than elsewhere, for when in 1726 there was serious

rioting in Bradford, Trowbridge, and Melksham, Westbury apparently held aloof.[3] But in 1736 the proceedings of the Trinity Quarter Sessions hint at the existence of an unusual amount of violence and lawlessness.[4] Thomas Phipps, alderman and Justice of the Peace, was abused in the execution of his duty by two victuallers and a yeoman of the town, and on another occasion was assaulted by a labourer.[5] Three years later an anonymous letter to Lord Harrington stated that the trade of the town was in a parlous state, and the poor much oppressed by the rich clothiers. Two brothers of Westbury Leigh, clothiers and justices, were accused in particular of forcing their workers to take truck and for building a private prison.[6] In 1748 it was said that the town was noted for 'rough turbulent people'.[7]

A directory of 1783 lists fifteen clothiers working in Westbury, all except two manufacturing superfine cloth.[8] In 1798 there were about the same number of clothiers and it was said that the town's annual clothing return was over £100,000.[9] Many of these men were no doubt only in a small way of business, but one or two were among the more important Wiltshire clothiers of the time, and the few small, but distinguished, 18th-century houses in Church Street and at Westbury Leigh remain as memorials to their prosperity.[10] As elsewhere, the clothiers lent their support to dissent in the district, providing barns and workshops as meeting places in the early days, and later leading the congregations of the nonconformist chapels.[11] Outstanding among these clothiers were the families of Gaisford, Matravers, and Gibbs, who in the course of the 18th century, consolidated their wealth and position by some notable intermarriages. Their wealth led them eventually into the landowning class, as in the case of Gaisford Gibbs, son of Jane Gaisford and Richard Gibbs, and husband of Elizabeth Matravers, who acquired as his country residence in 1789 Heywood House, sometime seat of the lords of the manor of Westbury.[12]

Early in the 19th century there are signs of unemployment and distress, which resulted from the introduction of mechanized methods of manufacture, and measures had to be taken to alleviate the suffering of the poor.[13] In 1817 a number of weavers, gathered at Dilton Marsh, took cloth belonging to Warminster clothiers from the looms there, and marched with it to Warminster as a protest against low wages.[14] Two years later, the unemployed were set to digging, and a person was

[79] C 54/1621/Mountjoy and Ley; C 66/1847 no. 14.
[80] W.A.M. xx. 341.
[81] Hist. MSS. Com. Var. Coll. i. 114.
[82] See p. 177.
[83] Hist. MSS. Com. Var. Coll. i. 135.
[84] Genealogist (N.S. xxx), 239.
[85] Ibid. (N.S. xxxv), 130.
[86] Ibid. (N.S. xxxiv), 44.
[87] W.N. & Q. iv. 58.
[88] Genealogist (N.S. xxvii), 177.
[89] Wilts. N. & Q. iv. 59.
[90] Hist. MSS. Com. Var. Coll. i. 123.
[91] Genealogist (N.S. xxvii), 177.
[92] Ibid. (N.S. xxxi), 184.
[93] Ibid. (N.S. xxxv), 130.
[94] Ibid.   [95] Ibid. (N.S. xxxii), 63.
[96] Ibid. (N.S. xxxviii), 53.
[97] Ibid. (N.S. xxxi), 61.
[98] Ibid. (N.S. xxxiii), 46.

[99] Ibid. (N.S. xxxi), 61.
[1] V.C.H. Wilts. iv. 158.
[2] C.J. xvii. 125.
[3] V.C.H. Wilts. iv. 164; Wilts. Times, 11 Jan. 1919.
[4] Q. Sess. and Ass. 1736 (W.A.S. Rec. Brch.), 57, 59, 60.
[5] Ibid. 57, 61.
[6] Wilts. Cuttings, xiv, 132. There can be little doubt that the two brothers were John and Thomas Phipps: Q. Sess. and Ass. 1736 (W.A.S. Rec. Brch.), passim.
[7] Wesley, Jnl. ed. N. Curnoch, iii. 381.
[8] Bailey's Western and Midland Dir. (1783).
[9] Universal Brit. Dir. (1798), iv. 735–37.
[10] See pp. 142, 143.
[11] See p. 181.
[12] See p. 163; for pedigrees see Hoare, Mod. Wilts. Westbury, 35.
[13] See p. 187.
[14] H. Graham, Annals of the Yeoman Cavalry, 63.

appointed to teach the children to knit stockings. Men received between 8*d*. and 1*s*. a day, but the income of a married couple was limited to 5*s*. a week, with a small extra allowance for every child.[15] That year several families emigrated to the Cape of Good Hope.[16] Cobbett visiting the town in 1826 described it as a 'nasty, odious, rotten borough, a really rotten place'. Its cloth mills seemed 'ready to tumble down, as well as many of the houses'.[17]

By the beginning of the 19th century it is clear that Dilton Marsh had become the centre of the hand-loom weaving industry. Some of the craftsmen were also apparently smallholders and acquired at the time of Westbury's Inclosure Award small plots of land adjoining or in front of their cottages.[18] In 1840 there were still about 150 hand-loom weavers in Dilton Marsh, while there were no hand-loom weavers at all in Bratton. In some cottages there were two or three looms, and frequently a husband worked by day and a wife by night to augment the family's income. An average of each loom's weekly earnings was said to be about 8*s*.[19] In spite of the rapid advance of mechanization, there were hand-loom weavers in Westbury at least as late as 1859.[20]

A Working Men's Association, founded in 1838 in Westbury, had 200 members by 1839.[21] There were also twelve Trade and Benefit Societies, evidently flourishing as centres of local unrest, for they were said to be proposing that year to apply their funds to the purchase of arms.[22] A number of Chartist meetings were held in Westbury in 1839. One, held in the Market Place, was attended by 300–400 persons. At another at Chalford there were 400–500 present, and on this occasion three of the leaders were arrested.[23]

In 1838 there were said to be eight mills working in Westbury employing 421 hands, and three in Bratton employing 73.[24] It is almost certain that none of these survived the catastrophic decline of the industry in the 1840's.[25] The largest, Matravers & Overbury, failed in 1847,[26] and distress due to unemployment in Westbury was acute.[27]

After 1850 there was a general recovery in the industry, and for a time in the second half of the century there were cloth mills operating at Bratton, Westbury Leigh, and Hawkeridge.[28] All these, however, had ceased to manufacture cloth before the end of the century, and the only mills to survive as cloth mills were the Angel and Bitham Mills acquired successively in the 1850's by Abraham Laverton.[29] Laverton was the son of a master-weaver of Trowbridge.[30] By the time of his death in 1886 the firm which he founded for the manufacture of fine woollen cloth was one of the most

progressive and prosperous in the west of England. Laverton made many benefactions to the town,[31] and rose to an eminent public position, becoming a Justice of the Peace and Member of Parliament for Westbury. His nephew, W. H. Laverton, was likewise a benefactor of the town but did not play such an active part in the firm.[32] In 1921 the business nearly failed, but was re-formed as the private limited company of A. Laverton & Co. Ltd. Since then many improvements and additions to both machinery and buildings have been made, and the manufacture of worsteds has been successfully introduced.[33] In 1960 this firm employed some 213 people mostly living in Westbury.[34]

At about the time that the smaller cloth mills were closing down, tanning and gloving became established in Westbury as factory organized industries, although both had undoubtedly been carried on domestically from a much earlier date. The new concerns of the late 19th century were encouraged by the accommodation afforded in the disused mills, and the plentiful supply of suitable labour. The somewhat complex history of these concerns has been told in another volume of the *History* and it will only be summarized here. William Boulton, 'master glover', and inventor of the Boulton Cut Thumb, founded the firm of Boultons at Westbury Leigh some time before 1871.[35] His sons were trading as Boulton Bros. in 1889. In 1901 the firm, manufacturers of various types of gloves, was incorporated and acquired Ball's Mill at Westbury Leigh.[36] A new factory was built beside the mill, and this the firm still occupied in 1960. The firm experienced considerable difficulties after the First World War and the number of people employed fell severely. It re-established itself during the 1920's and in 1952 was employing an average of 120 men and women in the factory, and about 300 women outworkers. A. L. and W. L. Jefferies, who had both been apprenticed to the cloth trade, set up business as fine quality glovers in Fore Street, Westbury, in 1883.[37] In 1908 a disused mill at Hawkeridge was taken over for the dyeing and leather dressing side of the business.[38] In 1920 the firm became a limited company with A. L. Jefferies as the first chairman and managing director. In 1936 the company was taken over by Dent Allcroft & Co. Ltd. Like Boultons it employs both factory and outworkers. A third glove factory was established in Westbury in 1927. This was the Westbury Glove Co. Ltd. and in 1956 employed about 130 workers.[39] The kid leather tanning firm of Case & Sons came to Boyer's Mill, Westbury Leigh, from Frome (Som.) in 1901 and since then has greatly extended its factory site.[40] The factory had to close for a short

[15] Parish Ch. Vestry Bk. 1801–26.
[16] Ibid.
[17] *Cobbett's Rural Rides*, ed. G.D.H. and M. Cole, ii. 400.
[18] W.R.O. Inclosure Award.
[19] *Rep. Com. Handloom Weavers*, H.C. 43–1 p. 427 (1840), xxiii.
[20] *P.O. Dir.* (1859).
[21] *Chartist Studies*, ed. A. Briggs, 177.
[22] B.M. Add. MS. 34245 B. App. 1.
[23] H.O. 40/48; *Chartist Studies*, ed. A. Briggs, 184, 185.
[24] *Ret. Mills and Factories*, H.C. 41, pp. 158–61 (1839), xlii; see below p. 174.
[25] *V.C.H. Wilts.* iv. 174.
[26] Ibid. and see p. 173.
[27] *V.C.H. Wilts.* iv. 174.

[28] See pp. 173 174.
[29] See p. 173.
[30] This and subsequent information about the firm of A. Laverton & Co. Ltd. comes from an unpublished history by B. Little, TS. *penes* the firm.
[31] See p. 143.
[32] Ibid.
[33] *V.C.H. Wilts.* iv. 175.
[34] Ex inf. Messrs. A. Laverton & Co. Ltd.
[35] For the history of this firm, see *V.C.H. Wilts.* iv. 238.
[36] See p. 174.
[37] For the history of this firm, see *V.C.H. Wilts.* iv. 239.
[38] See p. 173.
[39] *V.C.H. Wilts.* iv. 239.
[40] For a history of this firm, see *V.C.H. Wilts.* iv. 236.

time after the First World War, but reopened in 1922. In 1955–6 it employed just over 100 people.[41]

Malting on a considerable scale was probably a local industry at an early date. In 1647 efforts were made to regulate the trade, particularly where it was practised by those who had other means of livelihood. A number of maltsters was then suppressed and the output of others limited.[42] In 1825 Hoare remarked on Westbury's considerable malting industry.[43] Five years later there were 6 maltsters, including 1 at New Town, and 2 at Westbury Leigh.[44] One of the businesses at Westbury Leigh was that of James Knight, and members of this family conducted their malting business there until c. 1925, when the premises occupied by G. H. Knight & Sons were taken over by Samuel Thompson & Son.[45] Samuel Thompson & Son were in 1960 the only maltsters in Westbury.

A brick and tile works in Eden Vale belonged to the family of Greenland for at least 55 years in the 19th century.[46] Between 1885 and 1889 it appears to have belonged to Robert Butcher, but a few years later the only brick and tile works at Eden Vale was one acquired by Abraham Laverton c. 1875.[47] After Abraham Laverton's death this was carried on by W. H. Laverton until the beginning of the 20th century.[48] W. H. Laverton also had a brick works at Penleigh, Dilton Marsh. This later became the Westbury Brick and Tile Pottery Co. and was still working in 1960.[49]

A new industry opened in Westbury in 1857 when the Westbury Iron Co. was formed to exploit the iron ore beds to the north of the town, discovered over ten years earlier when the cutting for the railway line was being made.[50] The ore was worked by open-cast methods, and furnaces were built to the north of the railway line. At first the enterprise flourished, and in c. 1872 weekly production was about 400 tons and some 200 men were employed. After this its prosperity fluctuated, and then declined until 1901 when the works were shut down. They were re-opened as a result of local effort in 1903, and for a time during the First World War the industry throve. After the war, however, it became apparent that it was not an economic proposition, and by 1925 all work had ceased.

The first bank opened in Westbury was that of the North Wilts. Banking Co., in 1858. The Wilts. & Dorset Banking Co. opened a Westbury branch in 1867. Both these subsequently became merged in Lloyds Bank and in 1960 there were branches of Lloyds and Barclays Banks in Westbury.[51]

In 1858 the first printing business in Westbury was set up by William Michael in a room over his stationery shop in Edward Street. In 1900 the business was bought by the West Wilts. Printing Co. and removed to Church Street for printing *The West Wilts. Post*, forerunner of *The Wiltshire Times*. In 1911 Messrs. A. E. and H. Holloway bought the business and set up their presses in a new building behind the stationers' shop in Edward Street. The newspaper machinery was removed to Bath.[52]

Several concerns have either moved branches to Westbury or opened up business there in the 20th century. In 1915 the G.W.R. opened their locomotive workshops there.[53] In 1926 Messrs. Aplin and Barrett established a factory for making processed cheese in a group of former Air Ministry buildings at the Ham. At the beginning of the Second World War the firm of C. Rickards, umbrella makers, moved to Westbury from London. The firm, now C. Rickards (1950) Ltd., occupies a part of Westbury House including the former kitchen quarters and billiard room.[54] Also at the beginning of the war the International Tobacco (Overseas) Co. Ltd. moved part of its plant to Westbury. A permanent factory was built in 1946 and in 1956 employed about 200 people.[55] Messrs. A.E. Farr Ltd., civil engineering contractors, were evacuated to Marlborough in 1939, and in 1942 established a branch in Westbury. It was at first intended only to acquire a plant depot near the railway, but in 1945 the firm's head office moved to Westbury and new premises were built in Station Road.[56] In 1945 the Concrete Products Manufacturing Co. was formed to make building blocks. Later other precast concrete products were made, but by 1950 the firm was concentrating upon the manufacture of building blocks in its works at the Ham.[57]

In 1947 and 1948 planning permission was given in principle for the building of a cement works to the north-east of Westbury town by the Associated Portland Cement Manufacturers. Chalk was to be excavated from the escarpment of Salisbury Plain, near the White Horse, and carried by underground pipe-line to the valley below, where another large excavation would supply clay.[58]

The oldest engineering firm in Westbury or its neighbourhood is the agricultural engineering business founded at Bratton by Thomas Pepler Reeves at the beginning of the 19th century.[59] By 1848 it had a reputation reaching far beyond Wiltshire. At the height of its production the firm employed some 60 hands. In 1960 the business, still a family concern, employed about 40 men.

In 1801 the population of the ancient parish of Westbury was 5,921.[60] Included in this total were Westbury town (1,837), Bratton with Heywood and Hawkeridge (1,085), Dilton, which must have included Dilton Marsh (1,524), and Westbury Leigh (1,475). The population of the ancient parish rose steadily until 1841 when it was 7,588, although between 1831–41 there was a decided drop in the populations of Bratton, Dilton Marsh, and Westbury Leigh, no doubt reflecting the changes in the

[41] *V.C.H. Wilts.* iv. 250.
[42] Hist. MSS. Com. *Var. Coll.* i. 115.
[43] Hoare, *Mod. Wilts.* Westbury, 6.
[44] Pigot, *Nat. Com. Dir.* (1830).
[45] *Kelly's Dir. Wilts.* (1923, 1927).
[46] *Pigot's Nat. Com. Dir.* 1830 and later Directories.
[47] *Kelly's Dirs. Wilts.* (1875–95).
[48] *Kelly's Dir. Wilts.* (1907).
[49] Ex inf. Mr. Cross, Westbury.
[50] For the history of this industry see, *V.C.H. Wilts.* iv. 250–2.

[51] *Souvenir Handbk.* (Westbury Jubilee Celebrations 1950). [52] Ibid.
[53] Ex inf. Brit. Trans. Hist. Recs.
[54] Ex inf. Mr. R. Tuffin; for Westbury House see p. 142.
[55] For this firm see *V.C.H. Wilts.* iv. 242.
[56] Ex inf. Messrs. A. E. Farr Ltd.
[57] *Westbury Official Guide* (n.d.).
[58] *Wilts. Times*, 21 July 1961.
[59] For this firm, see *V.C.H. Wilts.* iv. 193–4.
[60] All figures from the summary of *Census Reports*, 1801–51 given in *V.C.H. Wilts.* iv. 339–61.

organization of the cloth industry. Bratton in that period fell from 1,237 to 721, Dilton from 2,172 to 1,848, and Westbury Leigh from 1,420 to 1,380. Westbury town, on the other hand, rose to 3,631. In 1851 the population of the ancient parish dropped to 7,029, and this was attributed to emigration caused by lack of employment at home. The population of the town, however, had risen again to 6,308, thus emphasising the depopulation of the villages, formerly the chief sources of labour for the cloth industry. In 1861 the population of the ancient parish fell again to 6,495, attributed this time to the installation of power-looms in place of hand-looms.[61] It continued to fall until 1891 when it was 5,634. After the formation of the civil parishes of Bratton and Dilton Marsh in 1894, and Heywood in 1896, the population of Westbury urban district was 3,305 and after then rose steadily until 1951 when it was 5,260. The population of Bratton in 1901 was 560 and rose until in 1951 it was 677. Dilton Marsh had a population of 1,282 in 1901. Between 1921 and 1931 it declined slightly and in 1951 was 1,319, but had then lost 188 persons to the newly created parish of Chapmanslade. The population of Heywood was 411 in 1901 and rose to 528 in 1951. The population of Chapmanslade was 496 in 1951.

MILLS. At the time of the Domesday Survey there were six mills on the capital manor of Westbury.[62] In 1226–7 the grant of a mill, formerly belonging to Alric at Brook, then part of the capital manor, was confirmed to the priory of Monkton Farleigh.[63] It was probably this mill which Walter Pavely acquired from Monkton Farleigh in 1320,[64] and formed part of his estate at Brook on his death in 1323.[65] A fulling mill at Brook was leased by Henry Long, a Westbury clothier, in c. 1539.[66] When the manor of Brook was divided up into a number of small estates in 1599, three fulling mills and a grain mill were included in the Brook Farm estate conveyed by Lord Mountjoy to Sir Edward Hungerford.[67] One of these mills was presumably Brook Mill, which at this date was leased by Anthony Wilkins, a clothier.[68] In 1624 the occupier was Anthony's son, William,[69] and in 1653 it was Richard Wilkins, fuller of Westbury.[70] On a map of 1773 the mill at Brook is called Roses Mill.[71] In 1785 the lessee was Thomas Phipps of Chalford, who that year bought the mill together with Brook Farm. The mill was then said to be a grist and fulling mill.[72] By 1890 the mill was disused, but its pond beside the Biss Brook, and adjoining Brook Mill Farm, was shown on a map of that date.[73]

In 1323, besides the mill at Brook, there were two water mills on the capital manor of Westbury,[74] and there were still two when the manor was divided between the heirs of Sir John Pavely in 1361.[75] A grain mill and a fulling mill belonging to the manor of Westbury Arundell were sold with the manor in 1549–50 by Sir John Arundell to Thomas Long, and passed with the manor to Sir James Ley in 1613.[76] Two water mills were attached to the manor of Westbury Seymour in 1607, and presumably also passed to Sir James Ley with that manor in 1621.[77]

Bitham Mill attached to the manor of Westbury Stourton belonged in 1573 to William Whitaker, grandson of Stephen Whitaker, who had acquired the manor in 1570.[78] It was then described as a large fulling mill, with loft above, and all things fitted for the dressing of cloth. When William Whitaker sold the manor in 1619–20 to Sir James Ley, he expressly reserved Bitham Mill and the adjoining Bitham House.[79] By 1772 the mill had passed to Granville Wheler,[80] and was sold that year to the clothier Thomas Gaisford, who was already the lessee.[81] Power for the mill was supplied from the adjacent pond, through which the Bitham Brook runs.[82] Thomas Gaisford died in 1774[83] and his son, John, sold the mill to John Deane, clothier of Trowbridge, James Cole of Trowbridge, and two Westbury clothiers, Thomas Matravers and John Crosby. In 1795 Deane relinquished his share in the mill to Cole, Crosby, and John Matravers, probably a son of Thomas Matravers. Six years later the share of Thomas Matravers passed to his daughter Elizabeth, on her marriage to Thomas White, and the firm operating the mill became known as Crosby & White. James Cole relinquished his share in the concern in 1811, and John Matravers made over his share in the following year. In 1820 John Crosby left his share in the mill to his two daughters, his son, Thomas, his brother-in-law, Thomas Finnemore Evans, and to Thomas White, and William Matravers. In 1824 Thomas Crosby, White, and Evans conveyed the mill in trust for Benjamin Overbury. By this date spinning shops had been added to the fulling mill. The next year the mill was mortgaged to secure a loan of £4,000 to Overbury, to William Matravers of Melksham, who was probably the owner of Angel Mill about ¼ mile to the south, and in 1842 also owned mills at Hawkeridge and Chalford.[84]

Angel Mill, or its site at the junction of Church and Maristow Streets, was purchased in 1784 from the Earl of Abingdon by John Matravers, then described as a 'shopkeeper'. A partnership between Matravers and Overbury had been formed by 1818,

[61] A single total for the ancient parish only is given this year, so it is not possible to estimate the effects of mechanization upon the villages.

[62] V.C.H. Wilts. ii, p. 118.

[63] Dugdale, Mon. v. 27.

[64] Cal. Pat. 1317–21, 535.

[65] Wilts. Inq. p.m. 1242–1326 (Index Libr.), 435.

[66] Req. 2/101/39.

[67] See p. 151.

[68] W.N. & Q. viii. 541.

[69] Wilts. Inq. p.m. 1625–49 (Index Libr.), 32.

[70] Hoare, Mod. Wilts. Westbury, 23.

[71] Andrews and Dury, Map (W.A.S. Rec. Brch.), pl. 7.

[72] See p. 151.

[73] O.S. Map 1/2,500, Wilts. XLIV (1st edn.).

[74] Wilts. Inq. p.m. 1242–1326 (Index Libr.), 434.

[75] See p. 149.

[76] See p. 150.

[77] C 142/396/132, and see p. 150.

[78] Hoare, Mod. Wilts. Westbury, 42–3, and see p. 149.

[79] See p. 149.

[80] See p. 159.

[81] Hoare, Mod. Wilts. Westbury, 43; unpublished history of firm of A. Laverton & Co. Ltd. by B. Little, TS. penes the firm.

[82] Unless otherwise stated, information about Bitham and Angel Mills comes from unpublished history, see n. 81, above.

[83] Hoare, Mod. Wilts. Westbury, 34 gives 1744 as date of death of Thomas Gaisford, but this is an error for 1774: Phillipps, Monumental Inscriptions, 83.

[84] W.R.O. Tithe Award.

and probably operated Angel Mill, while the firm at Bitham Mill was still Crosby & White. In 1828 Nathaniel Overbury leased Angel Mill from William Matravers, and by 1833 both mills were operated by the firm of Matravers & Overbury. By this date a 20 H.P. engine at Angel Mill, and a 60 H.P. engine at Bitham Mill, had been installed, and a new block built at Bitham Mill. The 60 H.P. engine at Bitham Mill was the most powerful one in the county in 1838. In the 1840's both mills were mortgaged, and for a time Angel Mill ceased to be used for cloth, and became the flour mill of a firm called Cave & Price. In 1849, however, Angel Mill was leased by Abraham Laverton from the trustees of William Matravers, and reconverted for the production of cloth. In 1852 Laverton bought Angel Mill, and in the same year Bitham Mill was bought by James Wilson, M.P. for Westbury 1847–57, and his brother, William. In 1856 the Wilsons sold Bitham Mill to Abraham Laverton, who thus became owner of both mills, and the firm which he founded, A. Laverton & Co. Ltd., still operated them both in 1960.[85]

The buildings at both mills were extended during the life-time of Abraham Laverton. At Bitham Mill a storehouse was built for Laverton's speculative purchases of wool and yarn. In 1930 Pond Farm which adjoined the mill was bought and the site used for additional factory premises. Conversion from steam-power to electric-drive took place at Angel Mill in the middle of the 1930's and at Bitham Mill in 1939. In 1952 the upper stories of the tall early-19th-century building at Bitham Mill were removed to allow for operations on the spatial and horizontal system employed by modern industry. The oldest part of the Angel Mill buildings appears to be a four-storied red-brick range of 10 bays, the 4 central bays projecting and being surmounted by a pediment. The two-light windows have unmoulded stone frames and segmental heads, typical of early-19th-century mill building in Trowbridge and elsewhere. An 8-bay range at right angles to the north end of the above building has similar windows but appears to be of later brickwork.

A corn mill at Westbury was conveyed in 1428 by Sir John Chidiock, Sir Walter Sandes, and Margery, his wife, to John Curteys, Agnes, his wife, and their son, John, for their lives.[86] This may have been the corn mill on the Bitham Brook, about ½ mile north from Bitham Mill, marked on a map of 1890[87] and disused by 1882.[88] In 1959 the former mill buildings were used by the Gas Company on whose premises they stood.

William of Westbury acquired a mill from John Durnell and Alice, his wife, in 1408–9.[89] It was then occupied by John Dyer and his wife, Joan,

and the conveyance to William was confirmed in 1413 by Richard Pavely.[90] This mill may have been included in the property which passed from William of Westbury to Agnes, wife of Robert Leversage.[91] In 1628 when the Leversage property passed to Sir James Ley there was a mill included called Tomars Mill.[92] This may have been in Hawkeridge where much of the Leversage property lay.[93] Jacob Weeks was leasing Hawkeridge Mill from William Matravers in 1842.[94] In 1859 William Dowding was manufacturing cloth at Hawkeridge,[95] presumably at the mill marked on the map in 1890, but shortly afterwards said to be disused.[96] In 1908 this mill was used by the firm of A. L. Jefferies Ltd., of Westbury, for leather-dyeing and dressing.[97] It is a large building of 4 stories and 7 bays and in 1960 was partly derelict. About ½ mile south-east there is another mill on the Bitham Brook in the parish of Heywood. This is Blenches Mill, a corn mill at the end of the 19th century, but disused early in the 20th.[98]

There was a fulling mill attached to the manor of Leigh Priors when this was acquired by the clothier, John Adlam, in 1545. At this date it was leased to John Whitaker, *alias* Bathe.[99] A fulling mill at Westbury Leigh was conveyed in 1550 by John Stanshall and Anne, his wife, to Christopher Stanshall.[1] This may have been the mill, which Adlam Stanshall sold in 1594 to John Lambe,[2] and John Lambe sold to Sir James Ley in 1616.[3] Another fulling mill in Westbury Leigh was conveyed in 1584 by George, Lord Audley, lord of the manor of Westbury Mauduits,[4] to the clothier Thomas Lawrence, or Saunders,[5] who died seised of it in 1602.[6] His son Thomas sold the mill in 1605–6 to Sir James Ley,[7] and it presumably later became annexed to Sir James's manor of Brook cum Mauduits.[8] Henry and Nicholas Phipps, who acquired the manor of Westbury Mauduits in 1585, purchased a fulling mill in Westbury Leigh from Charles, Lord Mountjoy, in 1599.[9] The fulling mill attached to Westbury Mauduits in 1620 was said to be in a field called Highesfield.[10] Henry and Nicholas Phipps also had a mill at Chalford, presumably on the stream called Wellhead Stream. On his death in 1600 Henry Phipps devised this mill to his nephew Henry.[11] In 1668 two water mills called Chalford Mills were conveyed by Thomas Phipps, clothier, of Westbury, to Samuel Ash, clothier, of Chalcot, then lord of the manor of Westbury Mauduits.[12] A corn and fulling mill called Ludborne Mills, and two similar mills called Leigh Mills, were included in the conveyance of the manor of Westbury Leigh and Ludborne to James Powton in 1592.[13] Leigh fulling mill had been leased in 1551 to Geoffrey Whitaker for 61

85 See p. 170.
86 Hoare, *Mod. Wilts.* Westbury, 84.
87 O.S. Map 1/2,500, Wilts. XLIV (1st edn.).
88 Ex inf. Mr. R. Tuffin.
89 C.P. 25(1)/256/59/17.
90 C.P. 25(1)/256/60/2.
91 See p. 157.
92 E 134/4 Chas. I East./27.
93 See p. 157.
94 W.R.O. Tithe Award.
95 *P.O. Dir.* 1859.
96 O.S. Map 1/2,500, Wilts. XLIV (1st and 2nd edns.).
97 *V.C.H. Wilts.* iv. 239, and see p. 170.
98 See n. 96 above.

99 *L. & P. Hen. VIII*, xx (1), p. 420, and see p. 157.
1 C.P. 25(2)/65/532/4 Edw. VI Hil.
2 C.P. 25(2)/242/37 Eliz. East.
3 C.P. 25(2)/371/14 Jas. I Mich.
4 See p. 155.
5 C.P. 25(2)/241/14 Jas. I; C.P. 25(2)/241/26–7 Eliz. Mich.
6 C 142/267/84.
7 C.P. 25(2)/369/3 Jas. I Hil.
8 See p. 155.   9 See p. 155.
10 C 142/380/116.
11 P.C.C. 32 Wallopp.
12 W.R.O. 212 B/We. 2, and see p. 155.
13 C 54/1408/Powton and Horton, and see p. 158.

years,[14] and in 1599 one of the Leigh mills was leased by John Adlam, and Ludborne Mills were leased by Thomas Raymond.[15]

It is impossible to identify with certainty any of these mills at Westbury Leigh and Chalford with the mills in those places in the 18th and 19th centuries. In 1773 there was a mill called Wellhead Mill on Wellhead Stream, east of the Westbury-Warminster road, which was probably one of the mills at Chalford belonging to the Phippses in the 16th and 17th centuries.[16] In 1839 it belonged to the firm of England & Son, cassimere manufacturers.[17] In 1842 William England was leasing this mill, and Samuel Dowding was leasing a mill called Chalford Mill from William Matravers, who owned Bitham and Angel Mills.[18] In 1960 Wellhead Mill was derelict. There was another mill marked on the map of 1773 further to the west along the same stream and at the end of Westbury Leigh nearest Westbury.[19] This was called Ball's Mill in the 1880's, and was then a corn mill.[20] In 1901 it was bought by Boulton Bros. (Glovers) Ltd. and converted into a gloving factory.[21] In 1773 there was also a mill at the other end of Westbury Leigh on the Biss Brook called Woollers Mill.[22] In about 1800 two new buildings were erected on or near this site for the manufacture of cloth, and the mill became known as Boyer's.[23] In 1830 it was the premises of the clothier James Cockell,[24] but by 1834 it was in the hands of Benjamin Overbury,[25] who, in partnership with William Matravers, was also operating Bitham and Angel Mills. There was water power only at Boyer's Mill at this date, and the supply was irregular according to the amount of water available in the Biss Brook.[26] For a time in the middle of the century Boyer's Mill belonged to Abraham Laverton, but in c. 1855 it was leased from a Doctor Gibbs by the cloth manufacturer, Joseph Harrop.[27] In 1872 this mill had 3 steam engines producing together 90 H.P. It was proposed that year to install a new water wheel of 16 h.p., but lack of sufficient water in the Biss was causing concern.[28] In 1875 the mill was occupied by the firm of Wilkins and Cogswell, woolspinners and carders.[29] In 1900 it was acquired by the tanning and leather-dressing firm of Case & Sons, and in 1960, under the name of Leigh Works, was the factory of that firm. A brick range of 4 stories and 6 bays at the southern end of the site is probably one of the buildings erected c. 1800 (see above).[30] Further north the former manager's house, used in 1960 as laboratories, is of about the same period.

A corn mill at Westbury Leigh, also on the Biss Brook, just south of Boyer's Mill, was called Leigh Mill in 1773.[31] This ceased to be used in c. 1930.[32]

A mill at Penleigh on the Biss was devised by Thomas Knight, tucker, of Westbury Leigh, to his son Edmund in 1497.[33] In 1569 Penleigh Mill was leased to Stephen Whitaker and his sons, Henry and Stephen, for their lives.[34] The lessees of the mill were bound to provide the steward of the manor of Bremeridge and his horses with food and lodging for two days and nights twice yearly, and to collect rents on the manor.[35] This mill was undoubtedly one of the group of grist mills at Penleigh belonging to the manor of Bremeridge, which, with other lands at Penleigh, was granted in 1609–10 to Edward Ferrers and Francis Phillipps.[36] This property, including the mills, was purchased from Ferrers and Phillips by Sir James Ley, and he held it at the time of this death in 1629.[37] At the end of the 19th century Penleigh Mill was a corn mill. By 1922, and probably considerably earlier, it was disused.[38]

There was a mill at Melbourne (Bratton) in 1221.[39] A mill at Bratton was given to the Bonhommes of Edington in 1427 by John Frank and others.[40] A grist mill at the same place was sold by the brothers Christopher and William Whitaker in c. 1585.[41] In 1594–5 four water mills were attached to the manor of Bratton,[42] and it was presumably one of these, which was in the possession of Jeffery Whitaker, of Tinhead, in 1599. From Jeffery it descended to his son Nash, and from Nash Whitaker to his son Geoffrey.[43] Only one mill at Bratton is marked on the map of 1773. This is at Stradbrook and is called Bratton Mill.[44] In 1838, however, there were three cloth, or woollen, mills, all working.[45] Just north of the bridge at the bottom of Melbourne Street was Bridge Mill where wool was prepared for manufacture elsewhere.[46] In 1898 the buildings were being used by the Bratton Dairy Co. Ltd., but this concern had closed by the beginning of the First World War.[47] In 1960 the mill and adjoining wool store were used by a building contractor. The wool store has stone windows with segmental heads and a central stone mullion which are typical of early-19th-century mills in this area. South of the bridge was Stradbrook Mill. In 1858 when this was advertised for sale it was said to have power and equipment to produce about 35 cassimeres a week.[48] It was, however, closed before 1890,[49] and has since been converted into a number of dwellings. Luccombe Mill to the south of Stradbrook Mill was

[14] W.A.M. xxiv. 29.
[15] Ibid. xli. 244.
[16] Andrews and Dury, Map (W.A.S. Rec. Brch.), pl. 7.
[17] Robson's Commercial Dir. (1839).
[18] W.R.O. Tithe Award.
[19] Andrews and Dury, Map (W.A.S. Rec. Brch.), pl. 7.
[20] O.S. Map 1/2,500, Wilts. XLIV (1st edn.)
[21] V.C.H. Wilts. iv. 238, and see p. 170.
[22] Andrews and Dury, Map (W.A.S. Rec. Brch.), pl. 7.
[23] Factory Com. Rep. 1834, H.C. 167 B1, p. 106 (1834), xx.
[24] Pigot's Nat. Com. Dir. (1830).
[25] Factory Com. Rep. 1834, B 1, p. 106.
[26] Ibid.
[27] Unpublished hist. of A. Laverton & Co. Ltd. pp. 12, 14 (see n. 81 above); Rep. Trowbridge and Westbury Water Bill, 58.
[28] Rep. Trowbridge and Westbury Water Bill, 59.
[29] P.O. Dir. (1875).

[30] V.C.H. Wilts. iv. 236, and see pl. facing p. 175.
[31] Andrews and Dury, Map (W.A.S. Rec. Brch.), pl. 7.
[32] Ex inf. Mr. R. Tuffin.
[33] P.C.C. 14 Horne.
[34] L.R. 2/86/97.   [35] Ibid.
[36] C 66/1821 Edw. Ferrers and Francis Phillipps.
[37] Wilts. Inq. p.m. 1625–49 (Index Libr.), 233.
[38] O.S. Maps 1/2,500, Wilts XLIV (1st and 3rd. edns.).
[39] W.N. & Q. ii. 271.
[40] Cal. Pat. 1422–29. 398.
[41] Req. 2/43/5.
[42] C.P. 25(2)/242/37 Eliz. Trin.
[43] W.N. & Q. iv. 108, 112.
[44] Andrews and Dury, Map (W.A.S. Rec. Brch.), pl. 7.
[45] Ret. of Mills and Factories, H.C. 41, p. 157 (1839), xlii.
[46] Bratton, W.I. Scrap Bk.
[47] Kelly's Dir. Wilts. (1898–1915).
[48] Wilts. Times, 17 July 1858.
[49] It does not occur in the late 19th-century Directories.

Malthouses, Pound Street, Warminster

Weavers' Workshop and Master's House, Dilton Marsh

Dilton Mill, *c.* 1875, demolished *c.* 1940

Boyer's Mill, built *c.* 1800, part of Leigh Leather Works

WESTBURY LEIGH

occupied by Isaac Brent in 1823.[50] In 1842 he had been succeeded by Samuel Brent,[51] and in the later 19th century the mill was operated by George Brent, woolspinner and carder. By 1895 it had closed,[52] and has since been converted into a single residence. There was also a grist mill on the same stream to the north of Bridge Mill. This still stood in 1960, although derelict.

In 1086 there were two mills on the estate belonging to William Scudet, which was probably the estate held by the Dauntseys in Bratton and Dilton in the 13th and 14th centuries.[53] In 1315 there was a water mill on the Dauntsey manor of Dilton, and in 1348,[54] when some land in Bratton was included within the manor, there were two water mills, and a fulling mill.[55] The mills, with the rest of the manor of Dilton, passed to the Bonhommes at Edington in 1388.[56] When in 1540 the manor was granted to John Bush there was a corn mill and a fulling mill attached to it.[57] Three years later another fulling mill at Dilton was granted to Nicholas Temple and Richard Andrews.[58] According to Hoare a mill called Dilton Mill was bought by John Waldron of Trowbridge, who built a cloth factory on Tun, or Town, Mead, which formed part of the property belonging to the mill.[59] No trace of this factory survives. At the end of the 19th century there was a corn mill on the Biss Brook, just north of Dilton church, but it ceased to be worked some time during the first quarter of the 20th century.[60]

FAIRS AND MARKETS. A weekly market on Friday and an annual fair on the vigil, feast, and morrow of All Saints (1 Nov.) was granted to Walter Pavely, lord of the manor of Westbury, in 1252.[61] In 1291 a further grant was made to the lord of the manor of a market on Tuesday, and a fair on the vigil, and feast of the Translation of St. Benedict (11 July), and the five following days.[62] Six years later Walter Pavely petitioned that the date of this fair might be altered to the vigil, and feast of St. John before the Latin Gate (6 May), and this change was made.[63]

When the lands of Sir John Pavely were divided after his death in 1361, the profits of fairs and markets were divided between his heirs. One half thus went to the lords of the manor of Brook, and the other was presumably divided between the two daughters of John St. Lo who inherited the manor of Westbury with its appurtenant hamlets.[64] In 1460 a market on Thursdays, and three annual

fairs were granted to Thomas Seymour, Katharine Chidiock, and John Willoughby, lords of the manors of Westbury Seymour, Westbury Arundell, and Brook respectively. One fair was to be on the vigil, day, and morrow of St. George (23 Apr.), the second on Whit Monday and the Tuesday and Wednesday following, and the third on the vigil, day, and morrow of the Exaltation of the Holy Cross (14 Sept.). Disputes and matters arising out of the market and fairs were to be dealt with in a special court set up by the grantees and held by a steward appointed by them.[65] In 1515 a market at Westbury on Fridays was granted to Robert Willoughby, Lord de Broke (d. 1521) presumably in place of the former Thursday market. The Whitsun fair was retained, and other fairs were granted for the Monday before the Nativity of St. John the Baptist (24 June), the day of the Translation of St. Edward the Confessor (13 Oct.), and the Friday before the beginning of Lent. A piepowder court was also confirmed.[66]

Leland in c. 1540 described Westbury market as a small one.[67] In 1673 it was still held on Fridays, and was said to be 'very considerable for corn',[68] and in 1751 it was called a 'good one for corn'.[69] The market was still being held on Fridays in 1792,[70] but some time before 1835 it was changed to Tuesday in the hope of making it more convenient as a corn market.[71] The presentation of a Market Hall in 1815 by Sir Manasseh Massey Lopes, lord of the manor,[72] may also have been made in the hope of stimulating trade. Attempts to maintain the market, however, failed, and in 1835 trade was said to have passed to Warminster, and the Westbury market was described as purely nominal.[73] By 1876 the market had become extinct.[74]

In 1751 the Whitsun fair and the fair held at the beginning of Lent were still being held,[75] and by 1825 an Easter fair had been introduced.[76] The profits of this, like those of the fair at the beginning of Lent, belonged to the lord of the manor, but the profits of the Whitsun fair belonged to the mayor.[77] By 1835 the fair at the beginning of Lent had been discontinued and in 1880 the Whitsun fair was said to consist of no more than one or two gingerbread stalls,[78] and by 1888 it had been discontinued.[79] In 1792 a fair was held at Dilton Marsh annually on Easter Monday and 13 September,[80] and in 1888 a fair at Dilton Marsh on 24 September and a fair at Westbury on the first Tuesday in September were the only fairs being held.[81] The Westbury fair survived for the first few years of the 20th

[50] W.A.S. Libr., Devizes, Allenson's Abstract of Edington Ch. Rate Bk.
[51] W.R.O. Tithe Award.
[52] Kelly's Dirs. Wilts. (1880–95).
[53] V.C.H. Wilts ii, p. 167, and see p. 164.
[54] Wilts. Inq. p.m. 1242–1326 (Index Libr.), 394–5.
[55] Ibid. 174.
[56] See p. 153.
[57] L. & P. Hen. VIII, xv, p. 299.
[58] Ibid. xviii (1), p. 529.
[59] Hoare, Mod. Wilts. Westbury, 50.
[60] O.S. Map 1/2,500, Wilts. XLIV (1st and 3rd edns.). See pl. opposite.
[61] Cal. Ch. R. 1226–57, 394.
[62] Ibid. 1257–1300, 389.
[63] Ibid. 467.   [64] See p. 149.
[65] Cal. Ch. R. 1427–1516, 137.
[66] L. & P. Hen. VIII ii, p. 449.
[67] Leland, Itin. ed. Toulmin Smith, v. 83

[68] R. Blore, Britannia (1673), 242.
[69] England, Gaz. (1751), ii.
[70] Rep. Com. Market Rights and Tolls, [C. 5550], p. 215 H.C. (1888), liii.
[71] Appendix to Rep. Com. Municipal Corps. H.C. 116 p. 1379 (1835), xxiv.
[72] See pp. 141–2.
[73] Appendix to Rep. Com. Municipal Corps. (1835), p. 1379.
[74] Mins. Evidence Rep. Com. Municipal Corps. [C. 2490–1], p. 185 H.C. (1880), xxxi.
[75] England, Gaz. (1751), ii.
[76] Hoare, Mod. Wilts. Westbury, 6.
[77] Appendix to Rep. Com. Municipal Corps. (1835), p. 1379.
[78] Mins. Evidence Rep. Com. Municipal Corps. (1880), p. 185.
[79] Rep. Com. Market Rights and Tolls (1888), p. 215.
[80] Ibid. p. 214.   [81] Ibid. p. 215.

century but by then it was being much criticised for the trouble it caused.[82] At the end of the 19th century there was also a sheep fair on Bratton Down. Some 20,000 sheep were brought to this fair in the early 20th century, but by 1914 the numbers had dwindled and the fair did not survive the First World War.[83]

All profits accruing from the markets and fairs, except from the mayor's fair, continued to belong to the lord of the manor until the market and fairs became extinct.

CHURCHES. The church of Westbury is mentioned in 1086 when it was held by a young clerk (*clericolus*).[84] It is not known whether there were any other churches in the ancient parish at this date. Throughout the Middle Ages the churches of Bratton and Dilton were dependent chapels of Westbury church and remained so, in the case of Bratton, until 1845 when a separate parish was assigned to the church, and in the case of Dilton, until the church was closed at the beginning of the 20th century after the creation of the new parish of Dilton Marsh.[85] These three churches with the chantry chapels provided for the spiritual needs of the ancient parish until the 19th century when new churches were built at Dilton Marsh, Heywood, Chapmanslade, and Westbury Leigh.[86]

Between 1109 and 1120 the church of Westbury was granted to Salisbury Cathedral[87] and the rectory was probably immediately, or shortly afterwards, appropriated to the office of precentor. Some time later the church seems to have been granted to Matthew, chancellor to Queen Eleanor, wife of Henry II, for between 1155 and c. 1165 Matthew restored it to the cathedral, acknowledging that it belonged especially to the precentorship.[88] Thenceforth until the 19th century the precentors of Salisbury held the rectory and advowson, and exercised peculiar jurisdiction within the parish,[89] which in 1222 was exempted from archidiaconal jurisdiction.[90] In 1842 the advowson was transferred to the Bishop of Salisbury,[91] and in 1846 all peculiars within the Diocese of Salisbury were abolished.[92]

The church was worth 50s. in 1086.[93] In 1291 the value was £40.[94] In 1720 the value of the benefice was augmented by a grant of £200 from the governors of Queen Anne's Bounty.[95] At the end of the 18th and beginning of the 19th century it

was again increased by private benefactions, a bequest from the precentor, and another grant from Queen Anne's Bounty.[96]

In 1291 the rector's share in the income of the benefice amounted to £33 6s. 8d.[97] He also derived income from the estate in Westbury later known as Rectory, Parsonage, or Chantry manor.[98] In 1342 the rectory was valued at £36 16s. 8d. which included in addition to the great tithes, lands worth £2 10s., customary services worth £3, and pleas, perquisites, and mortuaries worth £1.[99] The division of tithes between rector and vicar led to a dispute in 1377 in which the Bishop of Salisbury intervened. It was then agreed that the vicar should have some great tithes in addition to the lesser tithes, and all oblations except mortuaries and principals. These were to go as hitherto to the rector, whose share of the tithes was also precisely determined.[1] In 1535 the profits of the rectory were leased out for £69 6s. 8d. which included income from land, rents, and perquisites, as well as tithes.[2] The profits were also leased out in 1649–50 for a rent of £69 10s. which was made up of £16 16s. from lands and £52 14s. from tithes.[3] In 1848 the rectorial tithes were commuted for £2,429.[4]

In 1291 the vicar's share in the income of the benefice was valued at £6 13s. 4d.[5] In 1342 it was £3 3s. 4d., which included oblations as well as the lesser tithes.[6] In 1536 the income of the vicarage was £44 16s. from land, tithes, oblations, and other dues.[7] In 1649–50 the vicarage was said to be worth £80.[8] The vicarial tithes were commuted in 1848 for £235.[9]

Licence for the foundation of a chantry at the altar of the Virgin Mary in the parish church was granted in 1341 to William of Grimstead. To endow this William gave land in Westbury, Bratton, Westbury Leigh, and Heywood for the support of a chaplain to pray daily for him and his wife, Alice, and for Sir John Pavely, and his wife and ancestors.[10] The advowson of this chantry apparently passed to the lords of the capital manor and passed with it in 1375 to the daughters of John St. Lo, for a quarter of it belonged to Sir John Chidiock at the time of his death in 1450, and a half passed with the manor of Westbury Seymour.[11]

Another chantry was founded in 1437 at the altar of St. John the Baptist and St. Thomas the Martyr, in a chapel on the north side of the church, by

[82] Min. Bk. Westbury U.D.C.
[83] Bratton, W.I. Scrap Bk.
[84] *V.C.H. Wilts.* ii, p. 118.
[85] See p. 145.   [86] See below.
[87] *Reg. S. Osmund* (Rolls Ser.), i. 201, 208. The grant was confirmed by Stephen and Hen. II: *Sar. Chart. and Doc.* (Rolls Ser.), 10; *Reg. S. Osmund* (Rolls Ser.), i, 204; Hist. MSS. Com. *Var. Coll.* i. 368.
[88] *Sar. Chart. and Doc.* (Rolls Ser.), 17. Matthew's charter is here dated c. 1145–50. The dean of Salisbury between these dates was Robert Warlewast (Jones, *Fasti Eccl. Sar.* ii. 308), whereas the dean mentioned in the charter is Henry, who is presumably Henry Beaumont, dean 1155–c. 1165.   [89] Jones, *Fasti Eccl. Sar.* ii. 223.
[90] *Reg. S. Osmund* (Rolls Ser.), i. 338.
[91] 3 and 4 Vic. c.113.
[92] Jones, *Fasti Eccl. Sar.* i. 52. Since this article was finally revised in 1960 a number of Precentor's records have been identified and become available in Sar. Dioc. R.O. They include visitation papers and chwrdns.' presentments (17th–19th cents.); ct. papers and act bks. (18th cent.); wills and inventories (17th and 18th cents.)

[93] *V.C.H. Wilts.* ii, p. 118.
[94] *Tax. Eccl.* (Rec. Com.), 182.
[95] *Livings Augmented by Queen Anne's Bounty*, H.C. 115, p. 102 (1814–15), xii.
[96] *Hist. of Westbury Church* (Wilts. Tracts, xxi).
[97] *Tax. Eccl.* (Rec. Com.), 182.
[98] See p. 153.
[99] *Inq. Non.* (Rec. Com.), 160.
[1] Hoare, *Mod. Wilts.* Westbury, 19–22.
[2] *Valor Eccl.* (Rec. Com.), 73.
[3] *W.A.M.* xli. 120–22.
[4] *Rt. of Tithes Commuted*, H.C. 298, p. 207 (1847–8), xlix.
[5] *Tax. Eccl.* (Rec. Com.), 182.
[6] *Inq. Non.* (Rec. Com.), 160.
[7] *Valor Eccl.* (Rec. Com.), ii. 105.
[8] *W.A.M.* xli. 120–22.
[9] *Rt. of Tithes Commuted*, H.C. 298, p. 207 (1847–8), xlix.
[10] *Cal. Pat.* 1340–43, 184.
[11] C 137/26/55; C 139/139/26; *Cal. Pat.* 1405–8, 396; C.P. 25 (1)/256/59/10, and see pp. 149, 150.

William of Westbury, serjant-at-law and a justice of the King's Bench.[12] The chapel was built by William and his father, John,[13] and to endow it William assigned lands and rent in Westbury and Honeybridge (North Bradley) worth £10 a year.[14] Neither the chantry founded by William of Grimstead nor that founded by William of Westbury are mentioned in the *Valor Ecclesiasticus* of 1535. There was, however, at least one chantry in the church in 1545, for that year its chaplain held land called 'Grennyngs and Cockstede' from which a rent of 2*s*. 2*d*. was granted to the clothier, John Adlam.[15] In 1566 lands which had belonged to this or another chantry were leased for 21 years to William Betts,[16] and in 1579 to John Mounslowe for the same period.[17] Another lease for 21 years after the expiration of Mounslowe's lease was made to Thomas Hall.[18]

Edmund Leversage by his will dated 1496 requested that he should be buried in the Chapel of St. John the Baptist on the north side of the church and bequeathed £100 to found a fraternity in honour of Corpus Christi.[19] Nothing further is known about this bequest, but the chapel mentioned in the will was presumably that founded by William of Westbury. Obits were founded by William Antony (Antonius) and the ancestors of Robert Leversage. Richard Blatch assigned a rent of 12*d*. from land at Bratton for the maintenance of a light in the church.[20]

In addition to the chantry chapels within the church there was in 1331 a chapel on the manor of Westbury Mauduits, the advowson of which was in the king's hands by virtue of his wardship of the heir of Thomas Mauduit.[21] The advowson presumably descended with the manor, and the chapel is last heard of in 1407.[22] A chapel at Heywood lying ¼ mile from Westbury church,[23] is first mentioned in 1333 when Reynold Pavely granted Roger Marmium, lord of the manor of Bremeridge, the advowson, which Roger's father had previously granted to Reynold's father.[24] Two years later Roger settled the chapel upon himself and his wife Maud.[25] Thenceforth it passed with the manor of Bremeridge which was conveyed to the Bonhommes of Edington in 1366.[26] In 1547–8 John Blyth, Archdeacon of Coventry, was incumbent. A messuage and land called 'Summerleyes' in Heywood then belonging to the chapel were held by Richard Dekyn under a lease of 1541.[27] In 1548 the chapel had disappeared and the land was granted to Richard Were and Bartholomew Gibbs.[28] A chaplain of Brook is mentioned in the early 14th century, but no further reference to a chapel or chaplain there has been found.[29]

At the time of the foundation of William of Westbury's chantry in 1437 there were said to be 1,000 communicants attending the parish church at Easter, and no chantry priest to assist the vicar with the service.[30] In 1535 there were two assistant priests serving the chapels of Bratton and Dilton to whom no stipends had been paid that year.[31] Between 1641 and 1663 Philip Hunton, [32] scholar and an adherent of Cromwell, was Vicar of Westbury. In 1654 he was an assistant to the commissioners for Wiltshire for the ejection of 'scandalous, ignorant, and insufficient ministers and schoolmasters'. Shortly after his arrival in Westbury differences appear to have arisen with some of his parishioners for in 1647 Hunton issued the terms upon which he would resume his ministry.[33] These were first that the chapelries of Bratton and Dilton should desist from their claim to be created separate parishes until the means could be found to pay for incumbents for them, and then only provided that a sermon was preached in both chapels every Sunday either by Hunton or his assistant. Secondly that neither Hunton nor his assistant should be required to attend at burials for longer than they deemed necessary, and thirdly that Hunton should have absolute discretion to bestow or withhold the sacrament to individuals as he thought fit. These terms were presumably accepted, but in 1662 Hunton was ejected from the living for his presbyterian leanings, and shortly afterwards gathered a congregation of dissenters around him in his house in Westbury.[34] He died at Westbury in 1682 and was buried in the church. His curate John Paradise also held presbyterian views, but he succeeded Hunton for a time as vicar.[35]

In the early 19th century the vicar was assisted by two curates who were assigned to the churches of Bratton and Dilton. The vicar at this time officiated on Sunday afternoons alternately at the two churches.[36] After the creation of the separate ecclesiastical parishes of Bratton, Dilton Marsh, and Heywood in the middle of the century (see below) the vicar was assisted by one curate in what remained of the parish of Westbury, which still included Old Dilton and Westbury Leigh.[37] In 1864 there were morning, afternoon, and evening services on Sunday in the church at Westbury, and an afternoon service in the chapel at Old Dilton. Services were also sometimes held in a schoolroom at Westbury Leigh (see below). There were that year estimated to be about 145 communicants in the parish.[38]

The church of *ALL SAINTS*, Westbury, is cruciform with central tower, clerestoried nave of 4 bays, narrow aisles, north and south chancel chapels, another chapel off the north aisle, and south

[12] *Cal. Pat.* 1436–41, 137, 254; Hoare; *Mod. Wilts.* Westbury, 17.
[13] Hoare, *Mod. Wilts.* Westbury, 17.
[14] Ibid.
[15] *L. & P. Hen. VIII*, xx (1), p. 420.
[16] C 66/1020 m. 15.
[17] C 66/1183 m. 4.
[18] C 66/1301 m. 11.
[19] P.C.C. Horne, 4.
[20] E 301/58 mm. 121, 122.
[21] *Cal. Pat.* 1330–34, 184; see p. 155.
[22] Halstead, *Succint Genealogies*, 182.
[23] E 301/56 m. 30.
[24] B.M. Lansd. MS. 442 f. 146.
[25] Ibid. f. 141 d.
[26] Ibid. f. 142 d.; and see p. 158.
[27] E 301/58 m. 77.
[28] E 315/68.
[29] W.R.O. 413, Terrier of Westbury.
[30] *Cal. Pat.* 1436–41, 137, 254.
[31] *Valor Eccl.* (Rec. Com.), ii. 105.
[32] *D.N.B.*; A.G. Matthews, *Calamy Revised*, 285–6.
[33] W.R.O. 413, Terms upon which Philip Hunton would resume his ministry, 1647.
[34] See p. 181.
[35] A. G. Matthews, *Calamy Revised*, 285; Hoare, *Mod. Wilts.* Westbury, 22–3.
[36] C[aroline] B[rown], *Memoir of Stafford Brown* (priv. printed), 143–4.
[37] Sar. Dioc. R.O. Vis. Queries, 1864.   [38] Ibid.

and west porches. The tower rises in two stages with an octagonal stair turret at the north-east corner and weather-vane dated 1710. Both tower and turret have embattled parapets. The parapets of the nave are likewise embattled, but those of the aisles are plain. The chancel has a steeply pitched roof with stone slates replacing an earlier roof of low pitch. The west porch is unusually small and has seats on either side. The south porch has a groined and panelled roof ornamented with Tudor emblems. There is a small room above this porch and on its south wall, above the entrance, is a sundial dated 1821.

All the surviving features of the church are in the Perpendicular style and suggest that there was an extensive re-building in the 15th century. The transepts and the two chapels flanking the chancel, however, have much exposed rubble walling and it seems probable that they formed part of the church before its reconstruction. Some of the windows are similar to those in the church at Edington which date from the later 14th century. But Edington church (consecrated 1361) is a very early example of the transition between the Decorated and the Perpendicular styles,[39] and it is likely that similar work elsewhere in the district is of somewhat later date. The moulded bases of the piers and arch jambs throughout the church at Westbury are of typical 15th-century character, in which they differ markedly from those at Edington. At the same time the mouldings in the chantry chapel in the north aisle, thought to date from 1437 (see below), are identical with those used elsewhere in the church; this suggests that there is little difference in date between the chapel and the rest of the building.

The north aisle chapel is almost certainly the one built by William of Westbury and his father, John of Westbury, in 1437 (see above). In the 19th century this chapel was granted by faculty to the family of Turner of Penleigh as a burial place and it is sometimes called the Penleigh chapel.[40] Since c. 1900 it has been used as a baptistry and is separated from the aisle by a modern traceried stone screen. The font within the chapel dates from the 15th century.

The south chancel chapel is the Lady Chapel, also known traditionally as the Willoughby de Broke chapel, and sometimes called the Phipps chapel. Part of the arms of the first Lord Willoughby de Broke (d. 1502) appear in a window in the chapel, and other windows commemorate members of the Phipps family of Leighton House.[41]

According to Aubrey the north chancel chapel was traditionally built by 'the two maids of Brook'.[42] A brass to Thomas Benett (d. 1605), lessee of the Rectory Manor,[43] and to Margaret, his wife, has been moved from the floor of the chapel to the east wall of the north transept. The glass in the east window commemorates Stafford Brown, Vicar of Westbury, 1845–7. Since c. 1830 the chapel has been used as a vestry, and since 1847 partly as an organ chamber.[44]

The south transept contains an elaborate marble and stone monument with effigies of Sir James Ley (d. 1629), lord of the capital manor,[45] and of his wife. There is also a marble bust of William Phipps, of Heywood House, Governor of Bombay (d. 1748), by Sir Robert Taylor.[46] The glass in the window in this transept was presented by Lord Ludlow of Heywood (d. 1899). Below and to the left of the window is a trefoil-headed piscina. According to Aubrey, there was once a chapel called the Leversage chapel in the 'aisle north of the tower'.[47] His belief was perhaps based upon the fact that in 1496 Edmund Leversage requested in his will that he should be buried on this side of the church in the chapel of St. John the Baptist (see above). But the chapel was presumably the one already founded by William of Westbury which was so dedicated. There is no trace of there ever having been a chapel in the north transept.

Extensive restoration was undertaken in 1847, largely due to the energy of the Revd. Stafford Brown.[48] The nave roof was renewed and all internal stone-work was re-dressed. A new west window, paid for by the church rate, was inserted, and the east window was partly re-glazed. The east wall of the chancel was buttressed, a gallery removed from the west end, and 285 additional free sittings were made. In 1868 new glass was given for the west window by Abraham Laverton (d. 1886).[49] The oak rood screen and stone reredos were given by John Kaye (curate 1891–8) in memory of his wife.[50] In 1903 the external stone-work of the church was restored. The roof of the south chancel chapel was repaired in 1948.[51]

Until 1921 there were six bells dated 1616, 1620, 1671, 1714, 1738, and 1836. These were recast in 1921, when two new bells were added. The present 7th (1616) bell bears the arms of James I and the Earl of Marlborough, with BE YE MERYAL and the emblems of the Passion.[52] Until 1934 curfew was rung.[53] The sanctus bell is known locally as the Kit Bell.[54]

Edward VI's Commissioners left the church a silver chalice (11½ oz.) and took 23 oz. silver. There is a set of plate hall-marked 1844, presented in 1845 by Caroline Brown for her husband, the Revd. Stafford Brown. There are also 2 chalices and 2 patens with late 19th-century hall-marks,[55] and a ciborium added in 1958.[56] The church at one time possessed a silver-gilt cup known as the Westbury Acorn Cup. This is approximately 10½ in. high, with a cover in the form of an acorn. It is hall-marked 1585 and is inscribed 'Given to the Church of Westbury by Colonell Wancklin and Mary Contes of Marlbrou, 1671'. Wanklin was steward

[39] See p. 248.
[40] See p. 159.
[41] See p. 156.
[42] Aubrey, *Topog. Coll.* ed. Jackson, 403. Jackson suggests that the two maids were Joan and Eleanor, co-heirs of Sir John Pavely (d. 1361).
[43] See p. 153.
[44] R. Tuffin, *Guide to Church.*
[45] See p. 150.
[46] Pevsner, *Wilts.* 498.
[47] Aubrey, *Topog. Coll. ed.* Jackson, 403.
[48] C[aroline] B[rown], *Stafford Brown* (priv printed), *passim.* [49] See p. 170.
[50] Wilts. Cuttings, xvi, p. 225.
[51] Tuffin, *Guide to Church.*
[52] Walters, *Wilts. Bells,* 229–30; *W.A.M.* xlii. 122.
[53] Ex inf. Mr. R. Tuffin.
[54] Walters, *Wilts. Bells,* 229–30.
[55] Nightingale, *Wilts. Plate,* 99.
[56] Ex inf. Mr. R. Tuffin.

to Henry, Earl of Marlborough (d. 1638), and after the earl's death married his widow.[57] In 1846 the cup was sold to raise money to buy plate for the new church at Dilton Marsh (see below). In 1898 it was sold at Christie's for £70. In 1906 the price was £1,500 and in 1918 £966.[58] In 1922 the cup was in the possession of the Goldsmiths and Silversmiths Company, London.[59]

There is a chained black-letter copy of Erasmus's 'Paraphrase of the Gospels' in the church.[60] A 17th-century panelled oak chest with carved rails stands in the nave. The registers date from 1556 and are complete.

At an unknown date in the 17th century 6 a. in the common fields of Westbury and ½ a. in Westbury Mead were conveyed by Henry, Earl of Marlborough (d. 1638), to trustees so that the rent from the land might be used for the maintenance of the bells and clock of the parish church. In 1903 about 5 a. of this lying near Bridewell Springs and 1 a. at Townsend brought in £20 and was spent on the bells and clock and on payment to the bellringers. In 1953 this charity had 5 a. of arable called Clock Piece and a small rent-charge from another piece of property, and in 1955 about £3 were paid to the bellringers.[61] The vicar, organist, parish clerk, and choir of Westbury church also benefited under the will of Elizabeth Townsend, proved 1821, subject to the same conditions as were stipulated for their opposite numbers in Warminster. In 1955 the Westbury choir fund received £2 10s. from this charity.[62] In 1882 Sir Massey Lopes (d. 1908) gave £200 to create a trust fund for the repair of the fabric of the parish church. At the beginning of the 20th century some of the accumulated interest on this was used for making a dry foundation round the church and restoring the basement courses.[63] In 1955 the accumulated interest was about £33.[64]

The vicarage was built in 1880 on the site of an earlier one. A single room of the earlier building still stood in 1959 in the vicarage garden. A church house is mentioned in leases of 1564 and 1581, when it adjoined the back of the house and brewhouse belonging to the 'Lord Abingdon Arms' (later the 'Lopes Arms').[65] In 1857 a new burial ground lying along the road to Bratton was purchased by the parish.[66]

In spite of an attempt to achieve independence in the 17th century,[67] Bratton did not form a separate parish for ecclesiastical purposes until the 19th century. No very early precise mention of the church has been found, but the two chapels said in 1256[68] to belong to the manor of Westbury were probably those of Bratton and Dilton, both of which places were at that time included in the manor. In the

14th and 15th centuries the church seems to have been known not as of Bratton, but of Stoke or Little Stoke, the tithing of Bratton in which it lay. A chaplain of Stoke is mentioned in the late-14th century Edington cartulary, where certain persons responsible for his stipend are listed.[69] In 1349 Margery, widow of Reynold FitzWarin, gave an annual payment of 5s. to the chaplain of Stoke to pray for her,[70] and a chantry in Little Stoke is mentioned in 1368.[71] The church was called 'of Little Stoke' in 1558 when Ralph Aldridge of Bratton directed that he should be buried in the churchyard 'of my parish church of Little Stoke in Bratton'.[72]

The advowson of the church belonged to the precentors of Salisbury, as rectors of Westbury, until 1842 when it passed to the Bishop of Salisbury.[73] In 1845 the eastern part of the parish of Westbury was assigned as a parish to the church of Bratton, and the advowson then passed to the Vicar of Westbury.[74] The living is a perpetual curacy and the incumbents have been styled vicar since the creation of the parish. In 1851 the average number attending church on Sundays over the past year was reckoned at 90 at morning service, and 50 in the afternoons.[75]

At an unknown date, or dates, the church of Bratton acquired three pieces of property, comprising 4 a. of land, the Duke Inn, both in Bratton, and 2 small pieces of land in Westbury. In 1861 the vicar and churchwardens and two others were appointed trustees, and a scheme was made for administering the income from the land and applying it for the repair of the church. In 1887 the Duke Inn was sold for over £1,300 and the money from the sale invested. In 1903 the land in Bratton, known as Church Lands, was let as allotments for about £10 a year. This amount, and the interest on the investment, were used for repairs to the church. In 1921 the land was sold and the money received was invested.[76]

James Hurle, by his will proved in 1902, bequeathed £418 towards paying a salary to the organist, who was always to be appointed by the churchwardens. A scheme for administering this charity was established in 1903.[77] In 1952 the organist received about £9.[78]

In 1614 there was one small house with garden and orchard at Bratton belonging to the vicarage of Westbury.[79] The present vicarage was built in 1863 on ground given by the Marquess of Bath.[80]

The church of *ST. JAMES* lies on the lower slopes of the downs some distance from the village. The churchyard is surrounded by tall trees, some of which were planted in 1829.[81] Until a road was

[57] *W.A.M.* xxxiv. 103–8.
[58] Ibid.; ibid. xl. 356.
[59] Note under photograph of cup in church.
[60] *W.N. & Q.* i. 320.
[61] *Endowed Char. Wilts.* (1908), pp. 783, 794; Char. Com. Correspondence File 46.
[62] *Endowed Char. Wilts.* (1908), p. 795; Char. Com. Accts. File 46, and see p. 122.
[63] *Endowed Char. Wilts.* (1908), p. 803.
[64] Char. Com. Accts. File 46.
[65] *W.A.M.* xlii. 108.
[66] *Ret. of New Churchyards*, H.C. 101, p. 53 (1863), xlvi.
[67] See above.
[68] *Wilts. Inq. p.m.* 1242–1326 (Index Libr.), 18.

[69] B.M. Lansd. MS. 442, f. 109.
[70] *W.N. & Q.* ii. 561.
[71] *Wilts. Inq. p.m.* 1327–77 (Index Libr.), 348.
[72] *W.N. & Q.* iii. 207.
[73] See p. 176.
[74] *Lond. Gaz.* 9 May 1845, p. 1393; *Crockford* (1846).
[75] H.O. 129/10/259.
[76] *Endowed Char. Wilts.* (1908), p. 810; Char. Com. Correspondence G. File.
[77] *Endowed Char. Wilts.* (1908), p. 811.
[78] Char. Com. Accts. File 7.
[79] Sar. Dioc. R.O. Glebe Terrier, 1614.
[80] *Kelly's Dir. Wilts.* (1939).
[81] *Wilts. Times*, 9 Dec. 1960.

made in 1832, the church was approached only by a number of field tracks.[82] Early in the 19th century an approach from the north-west by a flight of 208 steps descending and ascending the valley of a small stream was built at the instigation of the Revd. C. Paillerat. The church is cruciform with north and south aisles, central tower, and a south porch which adjoins the west wall of the south transept. A vestry was added to the north side of the chancel in 1926. Nave and aisles are battlemented. On the south face of the tower there is a large, semi-circular, painted sundial, dated 1801. At the north-east corner of the tower there is an octagonal stair-turret which rises slightly above the tower. The church is built of ashlar with the exception of the east walls of the transepts which are of rubble and probably formed part of an earlier church. The present church seems to have been almost entirely rebuilt in the 15th century following the plan of an earlier one. The nave is of two bays only, but is wide and clerestoried. The piers of the crossing rest on massive polygonal bases, possibly survivals from the earlier church. In the east wall of the north transept there are 4 large empty niches and in the east wall of the south transept there is a trefoil-headed piscina with spur stops. In the stone vault of the tower there is a large circular opening for the bell-ropes. Extensive restoration was carried out in the middle of the 19th century by Paillerat. The chancel was entirely rebuilt, the church reroofed, and the internal ashlar redressed. New choir stalls were installed in 1923 and were removed from the chancel to their present position in 1937. In the same year the organ was restored, enlarged, and moved to its present position. It is a Scudamore type organ built by Henry Willis of London between 1858 and 1862.[83] The font dates from the 12th century but has been restored and is mounted on a modern base. The only early memorial is a tablet to Sefton Bromwich (d. 1607).

There are six bells dated 1587, 1617, 1793, 1858, and 1897. All were recast in 1934.[84] The Commissioners of Edward VI left a silver chalice (11 oz.) for the church and took 2 oz. of silver.[85] In 1960 there were a chalice, paten, and almsdish. The registers date from 1542 and are complete.

As in the case of Bratton there was probably a chapel at Dilton attached to the church at Westbury from an early date, but no very early mention of it has been found. A chaplain of Dilton occurs in c. 1250,[86] and in 1362 there is mention of a chapel dedicated to St. Nicholas.[87] Like Bratton, Dilton appears to have desired independence in the 17th century,[88] but in fact remained throughout its history a chapelry of Westbury. Chaplains of Dilton were presented, as at Bratton, by the precentors of Salisbury, as rectors of Westbury, until 1842 when

the advowson passed to the Bishop of Salisbury.[89] It remained with the bishop until the church was closed in 1900.

In c. 1250 the chaplain held 8 a. of land in Dilton by serjeanty.[90] It is possibly this estate which appears as the 'Vicar of Westbury's acre' in a perambulation of 1575.[91] In 1614 there was a house and garden, three yards of ground on which the chapel stood, and 23½ a. in the arable fields.[92]

In 1900, 55 years after a new church was built at Dilton Marsh, the church at Dilton was closed.[93] It was opened again in 1911 for a short time when an anonymous donor gave £300 for the repair of the building.[94] But it was closed soon after this and has since only been used for Harvest Festivals when the service is conducted by the Vicar of Westbury in whose parish the church lies.[95] In 1921 the churchyard was still in use for burials.

The church of *ST. MARY*, Dilton, is a small building and consists of nave, chancel, north aisle, north vestry, and a south porch.[96] The architectural features of the church date from the 15th century onwards, but doubtless the structure is more ancient. The church is built of rubble, plastered over, and in places patched with ashlar. It is roofed with stone slates, and on the west gable is an octagonal bell-cote with a short spire, partly resting on a central buttress. The vestry which flanks the chancel to the east of the north aisle was probably built in the early 18th century. It has a schoolroom in the form of a gallery above it. Both schoolroom and vestry have fireplaces. The windows, most of which are square headed, have been inserted at various times from the 15th to the 18th centuries. In one window there are some fragments of early-15th-century glass. The wagon roof above the nave was formerly plastered. A gallery at the west end of the nave has a panelled front and in the centre of this there is an octagonal wooden clock-dial in black and gilt by Cooksey of Warminster. All the seating is in high, panelled box-pews of pine or oak, and some medieval benches have been converted into box-pews. A pew at the west end of the aisle has a fireplace. The 'three-decker' pulpit of unvarnished pine stands against the middle of the south wall of the nave. On the wall are the royal arms of George III.

There are 2 bells. One probably dates from the 13th century, the other is dated 1813.[97] Edward VI's commissioners left a silver chalice (8½ oz.) and took 1½ oz. silver.[98] In 1844 the chapelwardens authorized the Vicar of Westbury to sell the church plate in order to buy a new set for the church then being built at Dilton Marsh.[99] The registers date from 1585 and are kept in Westbury parish church.

The building of a church at Dilton Marsh was begun in 1844[1] and the following year the south-west part of the parish of Westbury was assigned

[82] Unless otherwise stated information about the architecture and fittings is from personal observation and 'Historical Notes', unpublished material collected by students of Sar. Dioc. Training Coll. at St. Boniface College, Warminster.
[83] Ex inf. Mr. K. H. Rogers.
[84] Walters, *Wilts. Bells*, 37, and 'Historical Notes'.
[85] Nightingale, *Wilts. Plate*, 81–2.
[86] *Bk. of Fees*, ii. 1178, 1225.
[87] *Wilts. Inq. p.m.* 1327–77 (Index Libr.), 311.
[88] See p. 177.
[89] See p. 176.

[90] *Bk. of Fees*, ii. 1225.
[91] Hoare, *Mod. Wilts.* Westbury, 55.
[92] Sar. Dioc. R.O. Glebe Terrier, 1614.
[93] *Kelly's Dir. Wilts.* (1939).
[94] Wilts. Cuttings, xvi. 227.
[95] *Westbury Official Guide*, 1947.
[96] See pl. opposite.
[97] Walters, *Wilts. Bells*, 75.
[98] Nightingale, *Wilts. Plate*, 87.
[99] Dilton Acct. Bk. 1777–1899 in Westbury Church.
[1] *Kelly's Dir. Wilts.* (1939).

BITHAM MILL, WESTBURY

DILTON CHURCH

Baptist Chapel, Bratton, built 1734

Baptist Chapel, North Bradley, built 1779, demolished 1961

to the new church.[2] The living is a perpetual curacy and the incumbents have been styled vicar since the parish was created. The advowson belongs to the Bishop of Salisbury.[3] On census day 1851 200 people attended church in the morning, and 300 in the evening.[4] The church of *HOLY TRINITY*, Dilton Marsh, was designed by T. H. Wyatt.[5] Much of the expense was met by Thomas Henry Hele Phipps (d. 1847).[6] The church comprises apsidal chancel, nave, north and south transepts, and vestry. It is built of ashlar in late-12th-century style. The tower rises one stage above the tiled roof. There is a set of plate hall-marked 1844[7] and there are 2 bells.[8]

The church at Heywood was built and endowed largely at the expense of Henry Gaisford Gibbs Ludlow in 1849.[9] The same year the northern part of the parish of Westbury was assigned to the new church as a parish.[10] The living is a perpetual curacy and the incumbents have been styled vicar since the parish was formed. The advowson belonged at first to H.G.G. Ludlow,[11] but after his death it passed to the Church Pastoral-Aid Society.[12] In 1960 Heywood had no incumbent of its own and was served by the Vicar of West Ashton.[13] The church of the *HOLY TRINITY*, Heywood, is built mainly in a late-13th-century style but its most striking feature is the large east window with reticulated tracery in a 14th-century style. It comprises chancel, clerestoried nave of 4 bays, north and south aisles, and south porch, and is built of squared and coursed masonry with worked dressings. It has a slate roof and a bell-cote at the west end contains 3 bells. There is a set of plate hall-marked 1848.[14]

The church at Chapmanslade was built in 1867 as a chapel-of-ease to the parish church of Dilton Marsh.[15] In 1924 it was transferred to the church of Corsley.[16] The church of *ST. PHILIP AND ST. JAMES*, Chapmanslade, is built of stone and comprises chancel, nave, south porch, and small western belfry containing 2 bells. The architect was G. E. Street. A set of plate was presented by Mrs. Charles Paul Phipps.[17]

In 1855 a church service was held weekly in a schoolroom in Westbury Leigh,[18] but it was not until 1880 that a church was built there as a chapel-of-ease to the parish church of Westbury.[19] The church of the *HOLY SAVIOUR*, Westbury Leigh, was designed by W. H. White.[20] It is a stone build-

ing in the Gothic style, originally comprising chancel, nave, and south porch. A south aisle was added in 1888 as a memorial to W. H. Duke, Vicar of Westbury, 1850–81, and the tower was added to the west end of the aisle in 1890 at the expense of Mrs. Phipps as a memorial to her husband Richard Leckonby Hothersall Phipps (d. 1889).[21] There is one bell and a silver-gilt chalice and paten hall-marked 1847.[22]

ROMAN CATHOLICISM. Walter Clark of Westbury Hundred was presented as a popish recusant in 1676 and 1680[23] and was convicted of recusancy.[24] In 1683 there were said to be no recusants in the hundred[25] and no other references to recusancy have been found.[26]

The church of St. Bernadette of Lourdes was built in West End in 1938.[27]

PROTESTANT NONCONFORMITY. Westbury lies in that area along the Wiltshire-Somerset border in which, during the later 17th and very early 18th century, dissenting influences were particularly active.[28] Conventicles met during this period in private houses or barns, usually in out-of-the-way places. In 1669 a number of Anabaptists met at the house of Roger Cutter (Cator or Cater), their preacher, and a group calling themselves Quakers met at the house of John Gowen with Philip Hunton as their preacher.[29] Hunton, ejected from the living of Westbury in 1662, was licensed to preach in 1672 as a Congregationalist in his own house in the town.[30] A barn and house belonging to Thomas Edwards of Westbury were also licensed that year as Presbyterian meeting places.[31] At Chapmanslade in 1699 a barn belonging to Robert Hopkins and at Westbury in 1700 a house belonging to John Oatbridge were likewise licensed for use by dissenters.[32] In the following year a barn at Bratton belonging to John Hodges of Warminster was licensed for use by Quakers,[33] and in 1702 a dissenters' meeting place was licensed in the house of William Green at Hawkeridge.[34] Between 1713 and 1734 three houses in Westbury and a barn at Penleigh were all similarly licensed.[35]

The Anabaptists, who met in the house of Roger Cutter in 1669, were a congregation which had been founded in 1662[36] as an offshoot of the Old Baptist chapel at Southwick.[37] Cutter remained as their pastor until his death in 1693, and in 1689 he

[2] *London Gaz.* 9 May 1845, p. 1393.
[3] *Crockford.*
[4] H.O. 129/10/259.
[5] *Kelly's Dir. Wilts.* (1939).
[6] Wilts. Cuttings, xvi. 327.
[7] Nightingale, *Wilts. Plate*, 87.
[8] Walters, *Wilts. Bells*, 75.
[9] *Kelly's Dir. Wilts.* (1939).
[10] *London Gaz.* 6 July 1849, p. 2156.
[11] Sar. Dioc. R.O. Vis. Queries, 1864.
[12] *Crockford.*
[13] Ibid.
[14] Nightingale, *Wilts. Plate*, 91.
[15] *Kelly's Dir. Wilts.* (1939).
[16] See p. 21.
[17] Nightingale, *Wilts. Plate*, 87.
[18] *P.O. Dir.* (1855).
[19] Ibid. 1889.
[20] *Local Guide* published by W. Michaels, 1877.
[21] Wilts. Cuttings, xvi. 225.
[22] Nightingale, *Wilts. Plate*, 100.

[23] W.R.O. Q. Sess. R. Trin. 1676, 1680, Westbury Presentments.
[24] E 377/73.
[25] W.R.O. Q. Sess. R. Trin. 1683, Westbury Presentments.
[26] Thanks are due to Mr. J. A. Williams for supplying the information in this paragraph.
[27] *Kelly's Dir. Wilts.* (1939).
[28] *V.C.H. Wilts.* iii. 109.
[29] G. Lyon Turner, *Original Records of Early Nonconformity*, i. 121. For Cutter, see *V.C.H. Wilts.* iii. 110; for Hunton, see above, p. 177.
[30] Lyon Turner, op. cit. 570.
[31] Ibid. 555, 557.
[32] W.R.O. Certs. of Dissenters' Meeting Houses.
[33] Ibid.
[34] Ibid.
[35] Ibid.
[36] Unless otherwise stated, information about the Baptist church, Westbury Leigh, comes from W. Doel, *Twenty Golden Candlesticks!* 91–99.   [37] See p. 230.

represented his congregation at the first Baptist Assembly in London.[38] By 1694 this congregation belonged to the Western Association. Meetings were held at various places in the neighbourhood of Westbury Leigh, and frequently at Clay Close House, belonging to members of the family of Phipps. After 1693 the congregation moved to a barn belonging to Stephen Self, a clothier, standing on the site of the present Baptist chapel at Westbury Leigh, and in 1714 Self converted his barn into a chapel. In 1724 when William Wilkins was pastor (1724-45), John Watts, an elder of the church, with 29 followers left the Westbury Leigh chapel and formed a new congregation in a barn at Westbury called Mallox. Watts, however, soon left Westbury to devote himself to his work as pastor of a Baptist church at Erlestoke,[39] and the congregation re turned to the Westbury Leigh chapel. In 1796-7, when Robert Marshman (1763-1806) was pastor, a new and larger chapel was built on the same site. The foundation stone was laid in 1796 and almost the whole cost of the building, which was about £1,300, was raised by the congregation, which numbered 116. During his ministry Marshman helped to form a church at Chapmanslade (see below). Marshman was succeeded by George Phillips, who was, however, suspected by some of the congregation of Wesleyan leanings. After some dispute Phillips and his followers left the Westbury Leigh chapel to found a new chapel at Penknap (see below). Westbury Leigh was without a pastor for five years, but during this time a Sunday school was formed. Between 1847 and 1871 the Westbury Leigh congregation raised money for many improvements to their chapel. It is a large red-brick building with stone window-dressings and round-headed windows at ground- and first-floor levels.

The Baptist chapel at Westbury Leigh benefited from several bequests. John Wilkins, a clothier, by his will, dated 1729, directed that £20 a year from his farm of Honeybridge, North Bradley, should be divided equally between the minister and poor of the congregation. The £10 for the poor was to be spent on coats, bearing the testator's cloth-mark upon the sleeve. In 1834 a scheme was made for this charity, providing for the maintenance of the farm and investment of surplus income. In 1833 the farm (about 63 a.) was sold and just over £3,000 invested. By a scheme of 1920 the funds of this charity were divided into three equal parts: one for the benefit of the minister of Westbury Leigh Baptist church; the second for the poor of the congregation of that chapel, and the third for the poor of the Anglican congregations of Holy Trinity, Dilton Marsh, and St. Saviour, Westbury Leigh. In 1950 the payments due to the poor were made mainly in contributions to a clothing club.[40] Another charity for the benefit of both the minister and the poor of the Westbury Leigh Baptist congregation was that established by a bequest in the will of Robert Haynes, dated 1851. Some hundred years

later the minister received about £10 annually from this charity, and about £5 were distributed to deserving cases among the congregation.[41] Charities for the benefit of the minister only were established by bequests in the wills of Sarah Cockel (dated 1746), Richard Haynes (dated 1767), and John Turner (dated 1804), and the minister was still receiving small sums from these bequests in the mid-20th century.[42] James Humphries by his will, dated 1805, bequeathed £100 for the benefit of the poor of the congregation. This money was subsequently used to buy a site for a manse, but house and land were sold in 1949 and the money reinvested for the benefit of the poor.[43] The Westbury Leigh Baptist congregation also benefited under the will of Charlotte Laverton (see below).

After his withdrawal from Westbury Leigh in 1810, George Phillips held his first service in the open air at Upton Lovell.[44] For about six months he continued to preach in a farmyard at Dilton Marsh because no house or barn big enough to hold the congregation could be found. The site for a chapel at Penknap was given by Stephen Applegate, a member of the congregation. The first service was held in the chapel, which was called Providence Chapel, in the autumn of 1810. Phillips was chosen as minister and some 30 followers formed themselves into a church. The differences with the chapel at Westbury Leigh were settled and some financial compensation made to Phillips. At the time of Phillips's death in 1833 the Penknap congregation numbered 175. At about this date a stream near Boyer's Mill was used for baptisms, later a stream at Stormore was used. In 1859 some members of the Penknap congregation complaining that the minister, Joseph Hurlestone, preached Arminianism, left the church. One member then opened his own house for services, and later the upper part of a house in Slob Lane was equipped as a chapel, known as Gideon Chapel, but this congregation failed to establish itself. A Sunday school at Penknap was begun in 1810. The chapel was enlarged in 1835. It is a plain red-brick building with pointed windows with y-tracery at ground- and first-floor levels. The chapel benefited under the will of Charlotte Laverton (see below).

The Baptist chapels of Westbury Leigh and Penknap lie within ½ mile of each other on the south-west fringe of Westbury. Early in the 19th century the need for a chapel nearer the centre of the town was felt, and in 1825 about ten people worshipping at Cook's Stile Meeting House formed themselves into a church.[45] In 1829 the congregation numbered 180 and there were two deacons. Visiting ministers, however, supplied the pulpit until 1839 when the first minister for the new congregation was appointed. A new chapel with seating for 350 was built and opened in West End in 1868. Two bequests have been made for the benefit of the minister. Eliza Deacon, by her will

[38] V.C.H. Wilts. iii. 110.
[39] Ibid. vii. 85.
[40] Endowed Char. Wilts. (1908), pp. 786, 812; Char. Com. Accts. File 46.
[41] Endowed Char. Wilts. (1908), p. 801; Char. Com. File 13160.
[42] Endowed Char. Wilts. (1908), pp. 823, 824; Char. Com. Accts. File 46.

[43] Endowed Char. Wilts. (1908), p. 823; Char. Com. File 13160.
[44] Unless otherwise stated, information about the Baptist church at Penknap comes from Doel, Twenty Golden Candlesticks! 161-171.
[45] Unless otherwise stated, information about the Baptist church at West End comes from Doel, Twenty Golden Candlesticks! 196-9.

dated 1893, and Anna Deacon, by her will proved in 1896, bequeathed £40 and £28 respectively for the minister. In 1903 a sum of £70 represented these bequests and in the mid-20th century the interest was being paid annually to the minister.[46]

The exact date of the formation of a Baptist church at Bratton is not known.[47] William Gough, a Presbyterian, who was responsible for the establishment of a Baptist church at Erlestoke,[48] almost certainly also preached at Bratton in c. 1667, and nonconformity in the two places was always closely linked. Members of the Westbury Leigh congregation also preached at Bratton during the ministry of Roger Cutter. The meetings in John Hodges's barn in 1702, said to be of Quakers, may really have been the nucleus of a Baptist church, for no further reference to a Quaker meeting in Bratton has been found. In 1720 John Watts, who left Westbury Leigh and became minister at Erlestoke, undertook to preach once a month at Bratton in the house of Jeffery and Catherine Whitaker. Soon afterwards services were held once a fortnight, then once a week, and the congregation moved to a schoolroom belonging to Jeffery Whitaker.[49] In 1733 a site was given on which a chapel was built.[50] The building was paid for by voluntary subscription. In the same year the chapel joined the Western Association. Some time between 1734 and 1747 the congregations of Erlestoke and Bratton were amalgamated. In 1828 the congregation numbered 100, and later in the century Bratton became a centre for village evangelisation in the region.

The Baptist chapel at Bratton is a small red-brick building standing in the middle of its burial ground at the end of a narrow lane. A public road running through the chapel-yard was diverted in c. 1800. Two stone pillars at either end of the original building bear the date 1734. The chapel was enlarged in 1786 by extending it about 12 ft. backward. Thorough restoration took place in 1807 and windows on the east and west sides were opened. A schoolroom was added at the west end in 1818. In 1856 the roof of the chapel was raised 4 ft., much interior restoration carried out, and another schoolroom, a vestry, and a lecture room were added. The schoolroom on the west side was enlarged in 1874, and new windows were inserted in the chapel in 1899.

The chapel benefits from a number of bequests. Jeffery Whitaker, by his will, proved 1775, gave £350 and a house 'lately erected for pious and religious uses at Brown's Plot'. The interest on £100 of this bequest was to be given to the Baptist minister if he preached occasionally in the house, but when the time came for a house to be built for the minister, the £100 were to go towards the cost

of this. The interest on £150 of the same bequest was to provide £1 1s. for the minister annually, and the interest on the remaining £100 was to be devoted to the poor and the education of poor children in Bratton.[51] In 1961 the minister was still benefiting from this charity, and £1 1s. was paid for an annual sermon.[52] Several other bequests have been made for the benefit of the minister: Joseph Goodenough Blatch, by his will proved 1840, left £500, Thomas Whitaker, by his will dated 1855, bequeathed £100, John Reeves, by his will proved 1892, bequeathed £200,[53] and Emma Pocock, by her will proved 1932, bequeathed £100.[54] A bequest for the benefit of the choir was contained in the will of John Griffin, proved 1882.[55]

In 1777 Daniel Grey was preaching in a friend's house in Chapmanslade.[56] He was followed by other preachers, calling themselves students of the Countess of Huntingdon's Connexion. Later, preachers came from many neighbouring Baptist chapels, and in 1788 the Revd. Robert Marshman, of Westbury Leigh, baptized 8 people at Chapmanslade. Thenceforth services were held in one of the communal workshops connected with the cloth industry until 1799 when a chapel was built in the village to accommodate about 140 people. The first minister was appointed in 1802. In 1846 some trouble broke out among the congregation and the minister resigned, leaving the chapel in debt. The debt was not cleared until 1864, but five years after this there was enough money among the Chapmanslade Baptists to have the chapel repaired at a cost of over £1,000. At about this time the Baptists were joined by the congregation which withdrew from the Congregational chapel in the village (see below). The Baptist chapel is built of coursed rubble with a tiled hipped roof.

By 1826 Baptists living in and around Stormore (Dilton Marsh), which at that time was the home of many hand-loom weavers, wanted a chapel in their hamlet.[57] Services that year were being held in one of the cottages, and for a time they were conducted in a loft over a carpenter's shop, but in 1829 a small mission chapel was built and became known as Scott's Meeting. It stood by the stream used by both Penknap and Westbury Leigh Baptists for baptisms. In 1884 it was rebuilt as a mission church of the Westbury Leigh chapel and in 1890 a preaching service was held there every Sunday afternoon. In 1958 the chapel was still a mission church of Westbury Leigh.[58]

The Old Congregational Chapel in Warminster Road, Westbury, also called the Old Independent Meeting, or Lower Meeting, claims to date from 1662.[59] It clearly derives from the congregation which gathered round Philip Hunton after he had been ejected from his living in 1662 (see above),

[46] *Endowed Char. Wilts.* (1908), p. 826; Char. Com. Accts. File 46.
[47] Unless otherwise stated, information about the Baptist church at Bratton comes from Hugh Anderson, *Memorial of the Lord's Dealings with the Baptist Church in Bratton* (Frome, undated), and *V.C.H. Wilts.* iii. 110.
[48] *V.C.H. Wilts.* vii. 85.
[49] See p. 145.
[50] *Endowed Char. Wilts.* (1908), p. 820, for a picture of the chapel see pl. facing p. 181.
[51] *Endowed Char. Wilts.* (1908), pp. 785, 821.
[52] Char. Com. Accts. File 7.

[53] Information about all the above benefactions from *Endowed Char. Wilts.* (1908), p. 821.
[54] Char. Com. File 115228.
[55] *Endowed Char. Wilts.* (1908), p. 821.
[56] Unless otherwise stated, information about the Baptist church at Chapmanslade comes from Doel, *Twenty Golden Candlesticks!* 172–77.
[57] Unless otherwise stated, information about the Baptist church at Stormore comes from Doel, *Twenty Golden Candlesticks!* 181–82.
[58] *Baptist Handbk.* 1959.
[59] *Congregational Yr. Bk.* 1959.

although there is no precise record of the formation of a church during Hunton's life time.[60] His followers met at his house in Westbury where he preached privately. On his death in 1682, Hunton left to the 'Protestant Nonconforming Church' of Westbury a piece of land called the Hop Ground. During the pastorate of Hunton's successor a barn in Lower (now Leigh) Road was converted into a chapel, but this was burnt down in 1711. The Hop Ground was then sold to pay for the building of a new chapel. This chapel was probably built on the site of the present Congregational chapel on the east side of Warminster Road. In c. 1725 the congregation numbered 800.[61] Among the congregation were some of Westbury's most influential inhabitants and in 1751 there was a certain amount of disagreement with the minister. He was suspected of holding unitarian views and was accused of preaching sermons condemning slavery. Eventually part of the congregation withdrew and a second church, known as the Upper Meeting, was formed. The earlier congregation survived, however, and in 1821 re-built its chapel at a cost of £2,000. It is a red-brick building with stone dressings and a front embellished later in the 19th century. In 1829 the congregation numbered 500.[62] Between 1763 and 1795 a total of £400 was bequeathed for the support of the minister. The origin of this money is unknown but in 1829 it was invested for the benefit of the minister, together with £200 which were bequeathed that year by Thomas Austin. Austin also left nearly £200 to provide cloaks and clothing for the poor of the congregation, and in the mid-20th century the income from the Austin Charity was distributed as small gifts of money or was spent on buying clothing.[63] The Old Congregational Chapel also benefited by the will of Miss Charlotte Laverton (see below).

The members of the Old Congregational Chapel who withdrew in 1751 met at first in a barn which lay somewhere between Westbury and Westbury Leigh.[64] But in 1763 their chapel, which became called the Upper Meeting Chapel, was opened on the west side of Warminster Road. By 1829 the congregation numbered 300.[65] Throughout the 19th century attempts were made to unite the two congregations. The first invitation to re-unite came from the older congregation in c. 1816, but this like several later attempts came to nothing.[66] Union was only achieved in 1940 when the two congregations came together to form the Congregational Church of Westbury.[67] The Upper Chapel was then closed and all services held in the Old Chapel. In 1960 the Upper Chapel, a plain red-brick building, was used as a builder's store.

In the years following its formation the Upper Congregational Chapel benefited by several bequests, made by members of some of Westbury's leading families. Gaisford Gibbs, by his will proved 1790, bequeathed £400. Elizabeth Ludlow, by her will proved 1794, bequeathed £200, and a bequest of £200 was made at an unknown date by William Gaisford. Thomas Matravers, by his will proved 1794, bequeathed £400 to the chapel, but his estate could not meet the bequest. Matravers's nephew, however, made a gift of £100 which was used for building. A bequest of £100 was made by John Crosby, by his will proved 1821. This bequest proved to be void, but Crosby's children made a gift of £100. Jane Fatt, by her will proved 1835, gave £100 for the benefit of the minister, and the minister also benefited under the will, dated 1851, of Robert Haynes, a benefactor of Westbury Leigh Baptist chapel. A bequest to the Upper Chapel was contained in the will of Abraham Ludlow, proved 1807, and for some years £5 were paid annually from this, but nothing is known of it after 1876.[68] In 1926 a scheme was prepared for the joint administration of the charities of Gaisford Gibbs, Elizabeth Ludlow, William Gaisford, John Crosby, and Jane Fatt.[69]

The congregation of the Upper Meeting with those of the Old Congregational Chapel, and the Baptist chapels of Westbury Leigh, Penknap, and West End benefited by the will of Charlotte Laverton. By a deed, dated 1887, Charlotte Laverton, in exercise of a power given her by the will of her brother, Abraham Laverton, appointed that after her death the interest on £1,500 should be paid annually to the minister and deacons of the five chapels. The proportion in which the interest was to be divided was left to the decision of the trustees, and the money was to be used for the poor of the respective congregations.[70] The income of this charity has subsequently been divided equally between the beneficiaries. In 1954, when there were only four chapels concerned, The Upper Meeting having been closed in 1940, about £50 was shared among them for poor members of their congregations.[71]

A Congregational church was formed at Chapmanslade in 1761.[72] This is the first nonconformist church known to have existed in Chapmanslade, but in c. 1725 there was a Presbyterian congregation there numbering 300. Their minister, however, lived in East Knoyle, so it is possible that services were held there.[73] The Chapmanslade Congregationalists met in a barn until 1771 when a chapel was built.[74] This was enlarged in 1810 and repaired in 1819.[75] In the middle of the 19th century disagreement between minister and congregation resulted in the withdrawal of the entire congregation, who joined the Chapmanslade Baptist chapel.[76] The Congregational minister was obliged

[60] Unless otherwise stated, information about the Old Congregational Chapel comes from *Hist. Old Congregational Chapel Westbury* (printed and published W. Michaels, Westbury, 1875).
[61] Dr. Williams's Libr. Evans MS. f. 122.
[62] W.R.O. Retns. of Nonconformist Meetings, 1829.
[63] *Endowed Char. Wilts.* (1908), p. 818; Char. Com. Accts. File 46.
[64] *Hist. Old Congregational Chapel Westbury*, 13.
[65] W.R.O. Retns. of Nonconformist Meetings, 1829.
[66] *Hist. Old Congregational Chapel Westbury*, 24.
[67] *Souvenir Handbk.* (Westbury Jubilee Celebrations,

1950).
[68] For all the above bequests, see *Endowed Char. Wilts.* (1904), pp. 38–44.
[69] Char. Com. Correspondence File 46.
[70] *Endowed Char. Wilts.* (1908), p. 824.
[71] Char. Com. Accts. File 46.
[72] A. Antrobus, *Hist. Wilts. and E. Som. Congregational Union*, 15.
[73] Dr. Williams's Libr. Evans MS. f. 122.
[74] S. B. Stribling, *Wilts. and E. Som. Congregational Union*, 30.
[75] Ibid.   [76] Doel, *Twenty Golden Candlesticks!* 175

to resign and the chapel, much dilapidated, was pulled down.[77] A new chapel to seat 128 was built and opened in 1867.[78] It is a stone building in Gothic style.

In 1844 a Congregational church was built at Hawkeridge (in the parish of Heywood) as a mission chapel to the Old Congregational Chapel at Westbury.[79] It is a small rough-cast building.

John Wesley preached in the open air at Westbury in 1748 and recorded that the congregation behaved well, in spite of the town's reputation for roughness. He preached again in Westbury in 1749.[80] A Methodist chapel was built in c. 1809 at a cost of £400 raised by voluntary subscriptions.[81] In 1829 the congregation numbered 200.[82] The original chapel in Warminster Road was used in 1958 as a Masonic Hall. A new chapel in Station Road was opened in 1926.[83] Until 1869 the Westbury Methodist congregation belonged to the Warminster circuit. It then joined the newly formed Wilts. and Somerset Mission. Between 1910 and 1915 it transferred to the Trowbridge circuit.[84]

There were 16 Methodists in Bratton in 1829.[85] A chapel at Stradbrook there was built in 1870, largely at the expense of Nathaniel Snelgrove, who made a bequest of £400 for its maintenance in his will, proved 1874. By 1956 the chapel was closed and the congregation transferred to the Westbury Methodist chapel.[86]

In the 18th century the Quakers were represented in Westbury by the Matravers family, and the plot outside the south-west corner of the churchyard where they were buried is called the Quakers' burial ground.[87] A Friends Meeting opened in Westbury in 1943, but moved to Trowbridge in the following year.[88]

In c. 1820 a congregation, calling themselves 'New Lights', met for worship in the house of a Mr. Hayter of Eden Vale.[89] Hayter was reputed to have been a former clergyman of the Church of England.[90] After his departure from Westbury his followers continued to meet in the yard of the Horse and Groom Inn.[91] One of the congregation then presented a site at Cooks Stile, and in 1823 the foundations of a chapel were laid. The congregation, however, failed to perpetuate itself and chapel was sold to the trustees of the West End Baptist chapel.[92]

PARLIAMENTARY REPRESENTATION.
Westbury first sent representatives to Parliament

in 1448, the last but one of the Wiltshire boroughs to do so.[93] Thenceforth two representatives were summoned regularly until 1832 when the number was reduced to one.[94] The borough was finally disfranchised in 1885.[95] The franchise was by burgage tenure.

Before the 17th century the representation of the borough seems to have been determined by no obvious influence and followed no particular pattern. It was thus slightly easier for a stranger to be returned than was the case in most of the other Wiltshire boroughs.[96] At Westbury the first signs of domination by a single influence appear during the first quarter of the 17th century. In this period Sir James Ley (cr. Earl of Marlborough 1626) acquired all 10 estates in which the burgages were situated,[97] and in the seven Parliaments, for which returns survive between 1597 and 1627, Westbury was represented either by Sir James or his brother, Matthew, or his son, Henry.[98] For approximately the next 50 years the borough was represented by members of various local families, and no particular influence is apparent, but after 1681 James, Lord Norris (cr. Earl of Abingdon 1682), who acquired the capital manor that year, began to establish his control.[99]

Burgage tenements in Westbury could be held in fee, for lives, or 99 years, determinable on lives, or by copy of court roll, and the payment of an annual rent of 4d. or 2d.[1] By 1715 the 2nd Earl of Abingdon (d. 1743) had acquired 50 out of the 61 burgages,[2] and although the family's control was challenged throughout the middle years of the century, by 1784 it was complete,[3] and the 4th earl on his death in 1799 held all but two of the burgages.[4] This control passed in 1810 to Sir Manasseh Massey Lopes when he bought the manor from the 5th earl (d. 1854).[5] For this Sir Manasseh had to pay over £75,000, and, according to Oldfield, was obliged to rebuild most of the burgages since residence was a necessary qualification for those who were made freeholders for an hour to enable them to play their part in elections.[6] Before his death in 1831 Sir Manasseh had all the burgages in hand.[7]

Besides establishing control by the systematic acquisition of burgages, the lord of the manor, or his agent, could, at any rate from the 18th century onwards, exercise an influence over the General Council which was the machinery for returning the members to Parliament.[8]

[77] Ibid.
[78] Ibid.
[79] Stribling, *Wilts. and E. Som. Congregational Union*, 57
[80] Wesley, *Jnl.* ed. N. Curnock, iii. 381.
[81] *Hist. Old Congregational Chapel Westbury*, 17.
[82] W.R.O. Retns. of Nonconformist Meetings, 1829.
[83] *Souvenir Handbk.* (Westbury Jubilee Celebrations 1950).
[84] Ibid.
[85] W.R.O. Retns. of Nonconformist Meetings, 1829.
[86] Char. Com. File 138208.
[87] Ex inf. Mr. R. Tuffin. For Matravers family, see p. 169.
[88] Soc. of Friends, List of Members Bristol and Som. Quarterly Meeting, 1944.
[89] Doel, *Twenty Golden Candlesticks!* 198.
[90] Ibid.; *Hist. of Old Congregational Chapel Westbury*, 28.
[91] Doel, op cit. 198.
[92] Ibid.

[93] *V.C.H. Wilts.* v. 73.
[94] Ibid. 301.
[95] Ibid. 312.
[96] *V.C.H. Wilts.* v. 121.
[97] See p. 139.
[98] *Rtn. of Members of Parliament*, 1213–1702.
[99] *V.C.H. Wilts.* v. 215. For a more detailed account of Westbury's 18th-century parliamentary history, see J. A. Canon, 'Wilts. Boroughs 1754–90', D. Phil. Thesis, Bristol Univ. 1958.
[1] T.H.B. Oldfield, *Rep. Hist.* v. 145.
[2] *V.C.H. Wilts.* v. 215.
[3] Ibid.
[4] J. A. Canon, 'Wilts. Boroughs 1754–90', D. Phil. Thesis, Bristol Univ. 1958, 293.
[5] *V.C.H. Wilts.* v. 215, and see p. 150.
[6] Oldfield, *Rep. Hist.* v. 145.
[7] *Rep. Com. Munic. Corps.* H.C. 116, p. 1377 (1835), xxiv.
[8] See p. 186.

PARISH GOVERNMENT AND PUBLIC SER-VICES. Like many other royal manors of the Wessex kingdom, Westbury developed urban or semi-urban institutions at a comparatively early date. There were markets and fairs by the late 13th century,[9] and a portmote by 1361.[10] Burgages are mentioned in the later 14th century and their origin is probably considerably earlier.[11] The burgages naturally did not occupy the whole area of the ancient parish but formed a number of small enclaves within it. Indeed at no time are 'Westbury' and 'the borough of Westbury' to be equated. Sixteenth-century tax lists distinguish between the tithing or township of Westbury on the one hand, and the borough of Westbury on the other.[12] This distinction persisted, and by 1835 the borough was held to include the ancient burgages, arranged in three blocks, but to exclude the adjacent tithings of 'the town', and the 'chantry'.[13] Burgages apart, there are other signs of the growth of a borough. The portmote was being called 'the portmote of the borough' in 1443[14] and in 1448 the borough began to be summoned to Parliament and continued to be summoned thereafter.[15]

By the later 16th century there are some signs that the customary organs of municipal government had begun to grow up, a growth fostered perhaps by the knowledge that Westbury could claim to be 'ancient demesne of the Crown' and therefore ought to enjoy some privileges greater than those accorded to a rural estate. A mayor is mentioned in 1571,[16] a corporate seal was acquired in 1591,[17] and a guildhall and court house existed by 1599.[18] So far as is known, these organs of municipal independence, these trappings of civic pride, did not mature and were not multiplied. No charter was granted, nor was there even a declaration of privileges such as the burgesses of Calne secured in 1569.[19] Indeed from the early 17th century onwards the main function of the corporation—for such in name it was—seems to have been to conduct parliamentary elections.

The corporation is not described until 1835, on the eve of its dissolution.[20] It then consisted of a mayor, recorder, and 13 capital burgesses, who formed a deliberative assembly called the General Council. It also possessed a court. The only activity of the council was said to be that of filling vacancies among its own number and returning representatives to Parliament. The recorder was elected for life. The mayor was elected annually by the assembly, but any number of capital burgesses, however small, was considered competent to form a meeting for this purpose. No attempt was made to maintain the full number of 13 capital burgesses, and in c. 1835 there were 8, of whom but 4 were resident

in Westbury. The borough court was presumably the old portmote, last mentioned under that name in 1599.[21] It had come to meet but once a year and to conduct business that was only formal. A steward of the borough, who until the 1830's was also the steward of the capital manor, presided with the mayor. A grand and petty jury were summoned. The grand jury appointed a borough constable and a number of inferior officers.[22] The constable executed warrants and summonses within the borough and also within the tithing of the town. The other officers were virtually without duties. The petty jury, usually composed of inhabitants of the borough only, presented nuisances and assessed fines, though the fines were not enforced.

It is difficult to make a story out of materials so scanty and disconnected. Certainly it seems as though Westbury was on the way to developing a conventional borough constitution by the reign of Elizabeth I. But at no time is there proof of any true autonomy. It was the lord of the manor who collected the profits of markets and fairs,[23] he who appointed to be steward and bailiff of the portmote the steward and bailiff of his own manor court,[24] he who appointed or acted as recorder in the 18th century. In 1460[25] and 1599[26]the town prison was his, and in the later year the guildhall and court house also. In these circumstances it must be supposed that most of the town's business was conducted, as in any rural manor, in manorial courts, or else by the parish officers.

Apart from the courts of the capital manor, mention should be made here of the courts, called 'an assembly of tenants', that Thomas Phipps held for his tenants in Chalford, Brook, and Westbury Leigh.[27] This met, under the chairmanship of a steward, in a house called Whitehall in Chalford, which in 1899 still bore the inscription:

'Here is a stone stand in the wall
'To testify this is Whitehall
'I.M.H. 1704'

It was reputed at one time to have been used for meetings of the local magistrates, and some cells behind could still be seen.[28] Presumably the magistrates took over the building after the manorial courts had ceased to sit and caused the cells to be put up.

Until the end of the 19th century the government of the ancient parish presented a number of peculiar problems. The parish comprised over 11,000 a. with a small urban community in the centre, two fair-sized tithings, each with a church, and a number of scattered rural hamlets. At the end of the 17th century, when the surviving parish records begin, poor relief for the whole parish was

[9] See p. 175.
[10] It is mentioned among the possessions of Sir John Pavely, lord of the manor of Westbury (d. 1361): Cal. Pat. 1361–4, 162–4.
[11] Wilts. Inq. p.m. 1327–77 (Index Libr.), 388.
[12] See p. 139.
[13] Rep. Com. Munic. Corps. H.C. 116 p. 1377 (1835), xxiv.   [14] C 139/110/37.
[15] See p. 185.
[16] T. H. B. Oldfield, Rep. Hist. v. 141.
[17] W.A.M. xlix. 540–1.
[18] C 54/1621/Mountjoy and Ley.
[19] Calne Guild Stewards' Bk. (W.A.S. Rec. Brch.), p. xii.

[20] Rep. Com. Munic. Corps. (1835), pp. 1377–79. All subsequent information about the corporation as it was in 1835 comes from this report.
[21] C 54/1621/Mountjoy and Ley.
[22] There were 2 serjeants, 2 ale-tasters, 2 surveyors of the fire-hearths, and 2 leather-sealers.
[23] See p. 175.
[24] Cal. Close, 1364–8, 457–8.
[25] Cal. Chart. R. 1427–1516, 137.
[26] C 54/1621/Mountjoy and Ley.
[27] MS. Cal. Deeds at Chalcot House, ff. 195, 201.
[28] W.A.M. xxv. 49; W.N. & Q. i. 321. For protests against the high-handed activities of the local magistrates in the 18th century, see p. 169.

administered by the Westbury vestry.[29] The vestry was 'open', and there were at this date besides the two churchwardens, four overseers of the poor. Each overseer had a number of assistants, and was allotted one of the divisions into which the parish was split for purposes of poor relief. The divisions were Westbury, Westbury Leigh, including Brook, Dilton, including Chapmanslade, and Bratton, including Hawkeridge and Heywood.[30]

Dilton, and, it may be presumed, Bratton also,[31] had vestries of their own. In 1689 Dilton had two chapel-wardens.[32] In matters of poor relief the function of the Dilton vestry was restricted to nominating a number of persons as overseer for the division, one of whom was then elected by the Westbury vestry. Both Dilton and Bratton, however, appear to have elected their own surveyors of the highway.[33]

In 1652 the Vicar of Westbury was excused the payment of rates in return for the use of three houses in the churchyard for the poor.[34] The houses were still in use at the end of the century and in 1687 there was also a poorhouse at Westbury Leigh for the use of the poor of that division.[35] In 1732 the vestry decided to buy a house at Westbury Leigh as a workhouse and to employ a salaried master and mistress.[36] It is not known whether this was done, but in 1769 a site at Gooseland was bought for a workhouse.[37] Architectural evidence suggests that this mid-18th-century workhouse may have been incorporated in the Westbury Union Workhouse built on the same site in c. 1835. In 1687 the vestry ordered that those receiving alms should wear the badge of the parish on their shoulders, and that alms in kind should be distributed monthly from the parish church.[38]

In the late 17th, and throughout the 18th century, the vestry, although 'open', was apparently dominated by a few of the wealthier inhabitants, particularly the clothiers, who frequently held office as churchwardens or overseers, appointing deputies to discharge their duties for them.[39] Partly in the hope of remedying this state of affairs, statutory powers were obtained in 1786 for the appointment of a salaried additional overseer.[40] The churchwardens and overseers were to continue to make and collect rates, but all money was to be passed to the additional overseer, who was to have full authority for the care of the poor. The first appointment was not made until 1801, when a committee was also set up to investigate the state of the poor and the management of the workhouse.[41]

The early 19th century was a time of much unemployment in Westbury and the vestry was obliged to concern itself with attempts to alleviate the hardship and distress which abounded.[42] In 1801 it purchased boilers to make soup for the poor and employed a woman to make it.[43] Two years later the parish was divided into new divisions for poor relief, each under the management of a committee, and various measures were taken to provide employment.[44] The divisions on this occasion were Westbury and Hawkeridge, Bratton, Westbury Leigh with Dilton Marsh, Shortstreet, and Chapmanslade.

Gradually the vestry began to assume wider responsibilities. In 1814 it arranged for four women to receive training as mid-wives.[45] In 1827 it employed a constable to feed the prisoners and to clean and maintain the blindhouse.[46] This was presumably the prison under the Town Hall which in 1835 had recently been pulled down.[47] At that date there were neither police officers nor public watchmen in the town.[48] In 1837 a committee was formed to consider a scheme for lighting the town by gas. This committee appointed five inspectors and estimated that 46 lamps would be required and £150 spent annually on lighting the town.[49] A town fire brigade was first formed with 4 engines in 1861 after a disastrous fire had gutted one of the town's cloth mills.[50]

In 1886, under the Municipal Corporations Act of 1883, the corporation was dissolved, and the corporate property, then much diminished, was vested in the Town Trustees.[51] A parish council was then formed, but no record of its activities has survived. In 1894 Bratton and Dilton, and in 1896 Heywood, were made separate civil parishes, and in 1899 Westbury parish was created an urban district with a council of 12 members.[52] The council's first meeting was held at the Laverton Institute on 4 October 1899 when besides a clerk and a treasurer, a sanitary inspector, and a medical officer were appointed. A finance and a general purposes committee were immediately elected and the decision taken to adopt the former borough seal.[53] Among the first matters to concern the council was the supply of water to the urban district. Some houses along Church Street and in the neighbourhood of the Market Place already had a piped supply, brought by force of gravity from the springs at the foot of the downs to the east of the town. The public baths in Church Street opened in 1887 were supplied in this way from a spring at the Hollow, and continued to be so supplied until well into the

[29] Parish Records (kept in parish ch.), Rate Bk. 1687–1705.
[30] Ibid.
[31] Except for the registers the only record known to survive for the tithing of Bratton is an 18th-century bk. of the surveyors of the highways *penes* Miss J. S. Whitaker, Bratton, in 1960.
[32] There are 2 acct. bks. of the Dilton chapel-wardens 1689–1748 and 1777 to date among the Westbury Parish Records.
[33] Dilton Acct. Bk. 1689–1748 and Bratton Bk. of Surveyors of the Highways, see n. 31.
[34] Parish Records, Rate Bk. 1687–1705.
[35] Ibid.
[36] Ibid. 1729–76.
[37] Ibid.   [38] Ibid. 1687–1705.
[39] Ibid. Rate Bks. 1687–1705, 1729–39.

[40] 26 Geo. III, c. xxiii.
[41] Parish Records, Vestry Min. Bk. 1801–26.
[42] Ibid.
[43] Ibid.
[44] Ibid.
[45] Parish Records, Vestry Min. Bk. 1801–26.
[46] Ibid. 1827–39.
[47] *Rep. Munic. Corps.* (1835), p. 1379.
[48] Ibid.
[49] Parish Records, Vestry Min. Bk. 1827–39.
[50] *Trowbridge Advertiser*, 18 May and 3 Aug. 1861.
[51] 46 and 47 Vic., c. xviii; *Endowed Char. Wilts.* (1904), p. 17.
[52] See p. 141 and *V.C.H. Wilts.* v. 258.
[53] Unless otherwise stated, information about the activities of the Westbury U.D.C. before 1912 comes from the Min. Bks. of the council.

second half of the 20th century.[54] In 1899 the West-bury and Dilton Marsh Joint Water Committee, with representatives from the urban and the rural districts, was formed to administer a water works scheme already prepared. In 1901 a pumping station along the Bratton road was opened with a reservoir at the junction of New Town and Long River. The Westbury and Dilton Marsh Joint Water Committee continued to administer the scheme until *c.* 1960 when its functions were taken over by the West Wilts. Water Board. A second pumping station was opened at Wellhead in 1929.[55]

Main water supply was extended only very gradually to the entire area of the urban district, and until quite late in the 20th century many residents remained dependent upon well-water. Throughout the early years of the century there were frequent reports of water pollution and contamination caused by the lack of any proper sewerage system or arrangements for rubbish disposal. In 1907 much of the town's sewage was discharged in its crude state into ditches on the north side of the town and thence made its way into the River Biss. Sewage from Westbury Leigh reached the Biss from ditches near Penleigh. This state of affairs was severely criticized by the Medical Officer of Health for the County in 1907, who also urged the council to introduce a rubbish disposal service. Between 1907 and 1911 his criticisms and recommendations were repeated several times, and were endorsed by representations from the Local Government Board. In 1909 the council was required to prepare a sewerage scheme and eventually in 1911 this was done. But the cost, £13,000, was considered by the council to be prohibitive. Nothing had been done by the time war broke out in 1914, and it was not until 1922 that a sewage works was built for Westbury at Frogmore to the north-west of the town.[56] In 1959–60 over £10,000 was spent on modernizing these works.[57]

The council formed a special committee in 1900 to report on available sites for working mens' houses, and in the following year plans were approved for the building of a few such houses at Eden Vale. Between the two World Wars 120 houses were built by the council and since the Second World War about 400 have been built.[58]

The town continued to be lit by gas until 1947 when electric street lighting was installed. After 1947 many improvements were made to the lighting of all the streets in the town.[59]

The swimming baths in Church Street, presented by W. H. Laverton in 1887, were taken over by the council in 1900 and have since been administered by it. W. H. Laverton also presented a public garden to the town to mark the Diamond Jubilee of 1897. But this was not used by the townspeople in

the way Laverton had intended, and in 1903 it was closed. In 1938 a plot of ground called 'Grassacre' was laid out by the council as a recreation ground.[60] The Leighton cricket ground in Wellhead Lane, which W. H. Laverton had made, and on which many first-class matches have been played, was leased by the council for 21 years in 1951.[61]

The Westbury and District Hospital, also called the Cottage Hospital, was opened in Westbourne Road in 1897, but moved in 1931 to a building with 20 beds in Butts Road.[62] The Prideaux Hospital, with about 10 beds, was opened in Haynes Road in 1928, but was closed in 1950.[63]

The first record of a postal service in Westbury is in 1783 when Sarah Keevil was appointed postmistress.[64] In 1960 the post office was in Edward Street and there were sub-post offices in Leigh Road and at the Ham.

A court for the recovery of debts to the amount of £5 was set up by statute in 1808[65] to sit alternate fortnights at Westbury and Warminster. It was abolished as such by the County Courts Act of 1846.[66] Westbury was, however, the centre of a county court district until shortly before the Second World War when it was included within the Trowbridge county court district.[67]

SEAL. The seal presented to the borough in 1597 was of silver, oval-shaped, $1\frac{3}{4}$ in. × $1\frac{5}{8}$ in. It bore a shield, said to be of the town arms, quarterly or and azure a cross quartered patonce fleury within a bordure charged with twenty lioncels all counterchanged. The surrounding legend read:

SIGILLUM MAIORIS ET BURGEN*SIUM* DE WESTBURIE

The ivory handle, about $4\frac{1}{2}$ in. long, was inscribed 'Matheus Ley Hoc Dedit Anno Domini 1597'.[68] The seal was destroyed by a fire in the offices of the urban district council in 1935.[69]

SCHOOLS.[70] In 1835 there were said to be 18 schools within the ancient parish. In the town of Westbury there were an infants' school, and 5 daily schools: in Westbury Leigh there were 6 schools, in Bratton 3, in Dilton Marsh 2, and in Heywood 1.[71] Brief accounts of some of these schools, and of others which were established later, are given below.

WESTBURY, LAVERTON INSTITUTE SCHOOL. From a bequest of £1,000, made for educational purposes by John Matravers in 1814, £500 was to provide a school for boys and girls.[72] The first school-room was in the Bratton Road in the building later called the Old Athenaeum.[73] In 1819 24 boys attended the school, which was run on the Lancasterian system.[74] No girls' school was provided, but later the British Girls' School benefited from the bequest. For some time after 1832 the rent of the school-room was paid by William Matravers.[75] In 1833 about 50

[54] Letter from Mr. C. G. Ingram, deputy clerk of U.D.C., in *Wilts. Times and News*, 7 June, 1963.
[55] Ex inf. Mr. C. G. Ingram.
[56] Ex inf. the clerk of the Westbury U.D.C. Thanks are due to the clerk for much help with this chapter.
[57] Ex inf. the clerk.
[58] Ibid.
[59] Ibid.
[60] Ibid.
[61] Ibid.
[62] Char. Com. File 82836 and ex inf. Mr. H. Ross.
[63] *V.C.H. Wilts.* v. 344–5 and ex inf. Mr. H. Ross.
[64] Ex inf. the Postmaster General.
[65] 48 Geo. III, c. lxxxviii.
[66] 9 and 10 Vic., c. 95.
[67] *Kelly's Dir. Wilts.* (1931, 1939).
[68] *W.A.M.* xxviii. 56; Hoare, *Mod. Wilts.* Westbury, 6.
[69] *W.A.M.* xlix. 541.
[70] Thanks are due to Miss D. M. Goschen and Mr. W. T. Watkins for much help with this section.
[71] *Educ. Enquiry Abstract*, H.C. 62, p. 1051 (1835), xliii.
[72] *Endowed Char. Wilts.* (1908), p. 781.
[73] School Log Bk.
[74] *Digest of Returns to Cttee. of Educ. of Poor*, H.C. 224, p. 1040 (1819), ix(2).
[75] *Endowed Char. Wilts.* (1908), p. 782.

boys were taught, besides the more usual subjects, enough geometry to qualify them for mechanical pursuits. Fees were 1d. a week.[76] By 1856 the school was associated with the British Society.[77] In 1874 the school moved to the room provided for it in the newly-built Laverton Institute.[78] In 1885 a proposal to share the income from the Matravers bequest among the other Westbury Schools met with local opposition, but henceforth the girls' school connected with the British Society received £10 a year.[79] Boys were not to be required to attend any particular Sunday school or church, but religious instruction was given at the beginning and end of every school session.[80] In 1899 another room in the Institute was used, and there was said to be accommodation for 180 boys.[81] This room was declared unsuitable in 1909, and in 1910 accommodation was reassessed at 86.[82] In 1907 the school was transferred to the Local Education Authority and its name changed from Westbury British Boys School to Westbury Laverton Institute School.[83] In 1925 the school closed and the boys joined the Senior School in Lower (now Leigh) Road, later called the Westbury County Secondary Modern School.[84]

WESTBURY, CHURCH OF ENGLAND JUNIOR SCHOOL. In 1844, largely through the efforts of the vicar, Stafford Brown, a school of about 70 children was started in a hired room.[85] This became the Church of England Day School for which premises were built with the aid of a state grant three years later at the corner of New Town and Bratton Road.[86] In 1859 a separate building was opened for girls and infants.[87] The schools were in union with the National Society.[88] They received favourable reports in 1859 and were then attended by about 60 boys, 70–80 girls, and 100 infants.[89] Some time after this the girls moved to a school-room in Maristow Street, and the infants to a room in Edward Street.[90] Girls and infants were subsequently moved to a Sunday-school room built in the churchyard in 1873.[91] Between 1893 and 1910 the accommodation of the three departments was estimated at about 454.[92] In 1925 the senior children moved to the Westbury Senior Council School, and the juniors were accommodated in the building in the churchyard.[93] Controlled status was granted in 1949.[94] In 1959 an entirely new building was opened at Oldfield Park with accommodation for 280 children. The churchyard premises were

then handed over for the use of the Laverton County Infants' School.[95]

The school building at the corner of Bratton Road and New Town was acquired by the County Council in 1925. For a time it was used as the domestic science and woodwork centre of the Senior School in Leigh Road. It was later used as extra accommodation for the Laverton County Infants' School.[96]

WESTBURY COUNTY SECONDARY MODERN SCHOOL, LEIGH ROAD. In 1844 a single school-room was built in Lower (now Leigh) Road as a girls' school.[97] In 1859 the school, by then associated with the British Society, had about 70 pupils.[98] Between 1893 and 1910 average attendance was about 60.[99] In 1925 two new classrooms were added, the boys brought from the Laverton Institute School, and the senior children from the Church of England School, and the school became the Westbury Senior Council School with 103 pupils.[1] Senior pupils from Westbury Leigh were admitted in 1929.[2] In 1930 the school was enlarged to accommodate children over 11 from Heywood, Chapmanslade, Corsley, Dilton Marsh, Erlestoke, Bratton, and Edington. Between 1931 and 1950 new classrooms for teaching practical subjects, and a kitchen and dining hall were added. Since 1945 the school has been known as the Westbury County Secondary Modern School and has accommodation for 348 children.[3]

Between 1950 and 1960 numbers increased to 475 and much extra temporary accommodation was needed. In 1960 a major building programme was proposed to bring the buildings up to Ministry of Education standards. Since c. 1953 the school has developed the teaching of rural subjects and provides special courses in these for children from Warminster, Trowbridge, and Bradford-on-Avon, as well as from the Westbury area. Extended courses for pupils up to 16 or 17 years were established in 1960.[4]

LAVERTON COUNTY (INFANTS) SCHOOL. Before 1884 some infants attended the girls' school in Lower Road.[5] That year a school was built by Abraham Laverton in Bratton Road close to the Laverton Institute.[6] The school was associated with the British Society,[7] and opened in 1885 with 73 children.[8] Between 1893 and 1910 accomodation was assessed at 144, but average attendance was 55 in 1908 and 46 in 1910.[9] The school was transferred to the Local Education Authority in 1928.[10]

[76] Ibid.
[77] Ibid. p. 791, 793.
[78] Ibid. p. 805 and School Log. Bk. 1874.
[79] *Endowed Char. Wilts.* (1908), p. 793.
[80] Ibid. pp. 805–6.
[81] *Return of Schools, 1899* [Cd. 315], H.C. (1900), lxv(2).
[82] Bd. of Educ. File 46/298.
[83] Ibid.
[84] School Log Bk. and ex inf. Wilts. Educ. Cttee.
[85] C[aroline] B[rown], *Memorial of Stafford Brown.*
[86] *Acct. of Wilts. Schools*, H.C. 27, p. 47 (1859 Sess. 1), xxi (2); *Kelly's Dir. Wilts.* (1903).
[87] Bd. of Educ. File 11022 46/301/1.
[88] *Return of Non-Provided Schools*, H.C. 178–xxxi, p. 29 (1906), lxxxviii.
[89] *Acct. of Wilts. Schools*, 1859, p. 47.
[90] *Westbury Almanack* (publ. and printed Wm. Michael, Westbury 1867).
[91] *Kelly's Dir. Wilts.* (1903.)
[92] *Return of Schools 1893* [C 7529], H.C. (1894), lxv; *Bd. of Educ. List 21, 1010.*

[93] Senior School Log Bk.
[94] Ex inf. Wilts. Educ. Cttee.
[95] Ex inf. Mr. W. T. Watkins.
[96] Ex inf. Wilts. Educ. Cttee.
[97] *Return of Non-Provided Schools*, H.C. 178–xxxi, p. 29 (1906), lxxxviii; *Kelly's Dir. Wilts.* (1903).
[98] *Acct. of Wilts. Schools*, H.C. 27, p. 47 (1859 Sess. 1), xxi (2).
[99] *Return of Schools, 1893* [C 7529], p. 646, H.C. (1894), lxv; *Bd. of Educ. List 21, 1910.*
[1] School Log Bk. 1925.   [2] Ibid. 1929.
[3] Ex inf. Wilts. Educ. Cttee.
[4] Ex inf. Mr. W. T. Watkins.
[5] *Acct. of Wilts. Schools*, H.C. 27, p. 47 (1859 Sess. 1), xxi (2).
[6] *Return of Non-Provided Schools*, H.C. 178–xxxi, p. 34 (1906), lxxxviii. Date on foundation stone.
[7] *Return of Non-Provided Schools* (1906), p. 34.
[8] School Log Bk.
[9] *Return of Schools*, 1893 [C 7529], p. 646, H.C. (1894), lxv; *Bd. of Educ. List 21, 1908, 1910.*
[10] Bd. of Educ. File 11022 46/300/1.

For a time the building, formerly belonging to the National Schools at the corner of New Town and Bratton Road was used as an extra class-room.[11] In 1958 the premises in the churchyard of the former Church of England Junior school became the main building of the Laverton County Infants' School.

WESTBURY LEIGH, CHURCH OF ENGLAND SCHOOL. About 80 children were said to be attending 6 day-schools in Westbury Leigh in 1833.[12] In 1859 it was proposed to amalgamate the 2 existing schools, which had between 60 and 70 pupils each. One of these schools was supported by Mrs. Phipps.[13] By 1893 a National School with accommodation for 125 children had been opened.[14] In 1910 the accommodation of the mixed department was 126, of the infant department 50, and average attendance figures were 77 and 41 respectively.[15] In 1929 the senior children moved to Leigh Road Senior School, and Westbury Leigh became a junior mixed and infant school.[16] Controlled status was granted in 1950.[17]

BRATTON, BRITISH SCHOOL, AND JUNIOR AND INFANTS' SCHOOL. There were 3 schools in Bratton in 1833.[18] It is not possible to connect any of these with the 2 schools which existed in 1859. One of these was built c. 1846 with the aid of a state grant[19] and was associated with the British Society.[20] In 1859 it had over 150 pupils and was considered a satisfactory school with better conditions than those of the National School in Bratton.[21] But in 1913 the building was considered to be unsatisfactory.[22] In 1928 the school was closed, as was the Bratton National School, and all the children went to the newly-opened council school with accommodation for 120.[23] In 1931 the Bratton Council School became a junior mixed and infant school.[24]

BRATTON, NATIONAL SCHOOL. This school was built in 1846 with the aid of a state building grant and assistance from the National Society.[25] It had accommodation for about 20 children in 1858.[26] Conditions in the school were said to have improved when a vicar became resident in Bratton.[27] The school was enlarged in 1877[28] and between 1893 and 1910 accommodation was 83, although average attendance was only 37 in the last year.[29] The school was closed in 1928 and the children transferred to the new Bratton Council School.[30]

HEYWOOD, CHURCH OF ENGLAND SCHOOL. Some children from Heywood attended a school in Bratton in 1833.[31] A school and school-house were built in Heywood in 1836 by Henry Gaisford Gibbs Ludlow.[32] In 1859 it was called Heywood House School and 50 children were doing 'fairly well' there, although in 1857 it had had an unfavourable report.[33] Elsewhere in the village between 20 and 30 children worked under a dame.[34] In 1885 the trustees of the school became tenants at will of Endymion Porter, of Heywood House, and at the same time it was agreed that religious instruction should be in accordance with the 'principles of the Church of England as understood by Evangelical and Protestant churchmen'. The lessor was to determine any dispute which might arise as to the interpretation of a document or teaching.[35] In 1910 the accommodation of the mixed department was estimated at 81, and of the infant department at 29. Average attendance was 82.[36] In 1930 the senior children were removed to the Leigh Road, Westbury, Senior School, and the school became a junior mixed and infant school.[37] Controlled status was granted in 1948.[38]

DILTON MARSH, CHURCH OF ENGLAND (JUNIOR) SCHOOL. There were 2 schools at Dilton Marsh in 1833.[39] In c. 1847 a school in union with the National Society was built with the aid of a state grant.[40] In 1910 accommodation was 178 and average attendance was 135.[41] In 1937 the senior children were moved to the Senior School in Leigh Road, Westbury, leaving a junior mixed and infant school with accommodation for 150 children.[42] In 1938 the infants were moved to Dilton Marsh Council School, which opened as an infant school that year.[43] The junior school became known as the Dilton Marsh Junior Church of England School.[44]

DILTON MARSH, INFANTS' SCHOOL. A school associated with the British Society was built at Dilton Marsh in 1865.[45] The building was enlarged in 1884,[46] and in 1893 had accommodation for 134 children.[47] In 1906 management was assumed by the Board of Education.[48] In 1910 the senior department had accommodation for 102 and the infant department 54.[49] The senior children were transferred to the Senior School in Leigh Road, Westbury, in 1930.[50] From 1930 until 1938 the school was for mixed juniors and infants but

---

[11] Bd. of Educ. File 11022, 46/300/1.
[12] *Educ. Enquiry Abstract*, H.C. 62, p. 1051 (1835), xliii.
[13] *Acct. of Wilts. Schools*, H.C. 27, p. 47 (1859 Sess. 1), xxi (2).
[14] *Return of Schools, 1893* [C 7529], p. 646, H.C. (1894), lxv.
[15] *Bd. of Educ. List 21, 1910.*
[16] Ex inf. Wilts. Educ. Cttee.
[17] Ibid.
[18] *Educ. Enq. Abstract*, H.C. 62, p. 1051 (1835), xliii.
[19] *Acct. of Wilts. Schools*, H.C. 27, p. 47 (1859 Sess. 1), xxi (2).
[20] *Return of Non-Provided Schools*, H.C. 178–xxxi, p. 19 (1906), lxxxviii.
[21] *Acct. of Wilts. Schools* (1859 Sess. 1), p. 47.
[22] Bd. of Educ. File 10764 46/33.   [23] Ibid.
[24] Ibid. File 10764 46/344.
[25] *Return of Non-Provided Schools*, H.C. 178–xxxi, p. 19 (1906), lxxxviii; Bd. of Educ. File 10764 46/34.
[26] *Acct. of Wilts. Schools*, H.C. 27, p. 47 (1859 Sess. 1), xxi (2).
[27] Ibid.
[28] *Kelly's Dir. Wilts.* (1903).
[29] *Return of Schools, 1893* [C 7529], p. 646, H.C. (1894), lxv; *Bd. of Educ. List 21, 1910.*

[30] Ex inf. Wilts. Educ. Cttee.
[31] *Educ. Enquiry Abstract*, H.C. 62, p. 1051 (1835), xliii.
[32] *Kelly's Dir. Wilts.* (1903).
[33] *Acct. of Wilts. Schools*, H.C. 27, p. 46 (1859 Sess. 1), xxi (2).
[34] Ibid.
[35] *Rtn. of Non-Provided Schools*, H.C. 178, p. 39 (1906), lxxxviii.
[36] *Bd. of Educ. List 21, 1910.*
[37] Ex inf. Wilts. Educ. Cttee.
[38] Ibid.
[39] *Educ. Enquiry Abstract*, H.C. 62, p. 1051 (1835), xliii.
[40] Bd. of Educ. File 10815 46/102/1; *School Buildings Grants*, [Cd. 1336], H.C. (1902), lxxviii.
[41] *Bd. of Educ. List 21, 1910.*
[42] Bd. of Educ. File 10815 46/102/2.
[43] Ibid.
[44] Ex inf. Wilts. Educ. Cttee.
[45] *Kelly's Dir. Wilts.* (1903).
[46] Ibid.
[47] *Return of Schools, 1893* [C 7529], p. 646, H.C. (1894), lxv.
[48] Bd. of Educ. File 10815 46/101/2.
[49] *Bd. of Educ. List 21, 1910.*
[50] Bd. of Educ. File 10815 46/101/2.

in 1938 became a school for infants only with accommodation for 94 children.[51]

CHAPMANSLADE, CHURCH OF ENGLAND SCHOOL. A National School was built in Chapmanslade in 1875.[52] In 1894 it was enlarged.[53] In 1910 accommodation in the mixed department was 59 and in the infant department 50. Average attendance at that date was 42 and 11 respectively.[54] In 1930 the school became a junior and infants' school.[55]

CHARITIES. John Gibbs, of London, by his will dated 1772, left £500 to provide six poor men of Westbury annually with an olive-coloured coat and waistcoat. Gibbs's poor relatives, if any, were to receive first consideration, and after them Westbury burgage-holders. In 1833 it was not always possible to restrict the charity to those who had not received parochial relief. In 1954 the income of this charity was a little over £10 and it was spent on underclothing for deserving cases.[56]

John Matravers, of Westbury, by his will dated 1814, bequeathed £1,000 to provide clothing for 20 poor Westbury women, and £1,000 to establish a school for boys and girls. In 1954 the income of the clothing charity was between £30 and £40, and was spent on 9 sets of underclothing for women.[57]

The origin of Henry Smith's charity is dealt with elsewhere.[58] In 1832 Westbury's share in this was about £20 and was spent on calico for 230 poor people. A scheme for the administration of this charity was established in 1905 when it was decided to spend the income on subscriptions to hospitals, sick clubs, etc., or on the provision of goods to needy persons.[59] In 1955 goods worth about 7s. were distributed to 20 poor people.[60]

Thomas Ray, of Salisbury, by his will proved 1615, devised property in Gigant Street, Salisbury, with £13 a year to his daughter, Martha, for life and thereafter for the benefit of the poor clothiers of Trowbridge, Chippenham, Westbury, and Marlborough yearly in turn. In 1652 it was found that the charity had been much defrauded since the death of Martha Ray, and new trustees for each of the towns were appointed. In 1831 the annual rent of £25 from the property was in arrear, although Westbury seems to have received its share of the charity until 1832. In 1833 £100, representing these arrears, were divided among the four towns. The property in Salisbury was sold in 1877 and £1,000 invested. In 1898 a scheme for the administration of Westbury's share of the investment was made. The income was henceforth to be spent on subscriptions to hospitals or clubs, the purchase of certain goods, and the provision of loans and gifts of money. The beneficiaries were to be poor workers in the clothing industry. In 1903 some of the income was spent in maintaining children of cloth workers at a technical school. In

1955 small sums of money were given to 19 needy clothworkers in Westbury.[61]

In 1845 Richard Gaisford formed a trust and endowed it with £1,200 to provide clothing for poor men over 40 years old and women over 30 in alternate years. In 1857, after the death of Gaisford's wife, the endowment was increased to £2,000. In 1954 the charity was still being administered in accordance with Gaisford's wishes. That year clothing was given to 15 women, and the following year the recipients were 15 men.[62]

By his will, dated 1851, Robert Haynes bequeathed a sum, which when invested would yield £42 a year. Out of this, besides the benefactions to the Baptist chapel at Westbury Leigh, and the Upper Meeting in Warminster Road,[63] £18 was to be spent annually on clothing for six poor old men of Westbury, and £3 was to be paid annually to the Westbury Bible Society. In 1957 in addition to a payment to the minister of the Westbury Leigh chapel, about £5 was paid to the poor of that congregation.[64]

ALMSHOUSES.

Prospect Buildings, Laverton Almshouses. In 1886 William Henry Laverton, acting on the wish of his uncle, Abraham Laverton, conveyed in trust the group of 39 houses called Prospect Buildings, then recently built along three sides of a square in Bratton Road. The 7 houses at the south-east end of the quadrangle were to be almshouses, maintained by the rents from the remaining 32 houses. At the beginning of the 20th century the almspeople, who could be either married couples or single persons, and who often were former employees at the Laverton Mills, received a weekly pension of 5s. Two of the almshouses had five rooms, the remaining five had four rooms. In 1923 pensions and maintenance expenses amounted to more than £150.[65]

Stafford Brown, Ivy Court Almshouses. In 1890 Mary Brown, daughter of Stafford Brown, Vicar of Westbury 1845–7, conveyed in trust 14 cottages adjoining the Warminster road near its junction with Edward Street. Four of the cottages which fronted the Warminster road were to be let and their rents used to maintain the entire property. The remaining ten cottages, known as Stafford Brown Almshouses, Ivy Court, were to be almshouses for poor parishioners who were members of the Church of England. The charity was to be managed by the vicar and churchwardens. In 1903 rents from the four cottages totalled £24 and the almspeople paid 6d. a year for their cottages. These formed a double row of two-roomed dwellings in a small court extending back from the Warminster road frontage. In 1937 the cottages facing the Warminster road had been converted into a house and shop and produced a rent of £25. The almshouses

[51] Ibid.
[52] *Kelly's Dir. Wilts.* (1903); Bd. of Educ. File 10815/48/103/1.
[53] Bd. of Educ. File 10815/46/103/1.
[54] *Bd. of Educ. List 21, 1910.*
[55] Ex inf. Wilts. Educ. Cttee.
[56] *Endowed Char. Wilts.* (1908), pp. 780, 792; Char. Com. Accts. File 46.
[57] *Endowed Char. Wilts.* (1908), p. 781; Char. Com. Accts. File 46. For the school founded by Matravers, see p. 188.

[58] See p. 134. [59] Char. Com. File 82380.
[60] Ibid. Accts. File 46.
[61] *Endowed Char. Wilts.* (1908), pp. 784, 795; Char. Com. Accts. File 46.
[62] *Endowed Char. Wilts.* (1908), p. 799; Char. Com. Accts. File 46.
[63] See pp. 182, 184.
[64] *Endowed Char. Wilts.* (1908), p. 801; Char. Com. File 13160.
[65] *Endowed Char. Wilts.* (1908), p. 803; Char. Com. Accts. File 46.

behind were dilapidated and plans were considered for pulling them down. Nothing was done until 1955 when the site with the disused almshouses on it was sold for £560. A scheme was then drawn up for the administration of the charity to provide pensions to persons who would have been qualified for admission to an almshouse.[66]

CHARITIES FOR THE POOR OF BRATTON.

Among the bequests of Jeffery Whitaker, in his will dated 1775,[67] £50 were assigned for the poor of Bratton and £50 for the education of poor children there. In 1833 the stock had been improperly sold and only £1 15s. was spent on these two objects annually. The trustees, however, agreed to put the matter right. In 1913 a sum was set aside from the bequest to form a fund for educational purposes. In 1961 this brought in just over £2 and in the same year a little over £15 was paid to deserving persons within the parish.[68]

CHARITY FOR THE POOR OF DILTON.

In 1697 12 a. of land in Beckington (Som.), known as the Castley Poor Ground, and a paddock there were bought with £97 representing legacies for the poor of Dilton bequeathed by Anthony Self, Christopher Pearce, John Cable, and William Turner, all of Dilton, and William Gilbert, of Portsmouth. In 1833 the paddock had been lost

to the charity, but an annual rent of £13 from the 12 a. was used to buy bread and clothing for the poor of Dilton. A scheme for the administration of this charity was established in 1888 and arrangements made for the income to be spent in the same was as that of Thomas Ray's charity (see above). In 1903 the annual income was £15 rent and £2 from investment.[69] In 1914 another scheme for the regulation of the charity along the same lines was prepared.[70] All the remaining land was sold in 1918 for £340, and in 1950 grants of money were made from this charity to 77 poor people.[71]

CHARITY FOR THE POOR OF WESTBURY, DILTON MARSH, AND BRATTON.

Charles Nicholas Paul Phipps, by his will dated 1875, bequeathed £650 to his wife Emma Mary Phipps to be applied in a fixed proportion by her for the benefit of the poor of Westbury, Dilton Marsh, and Bratton. Emma Mary Phipps later conveyed the money to trustees to be invested and asked that the income should be used to buy blankets once a year for the poor of these three places. From time to time the interest on this investment was allowed to accumulate and in 1956 15 pairs of blankets could be bought for distribution.[72]

---

[66] *Endowed Char. Wilts.* (1908), p. 808; Char. Com. File 119584.

[67] See p. 183.

[68] *Endowed Char. Wilts.* (1908), pp. 785, 821; Char. Com. Accts. File 7.

[69] *Endowed Char. Wilts.* (1908), pp. 787, 813.

[70] Char. Com. File 201149.

[71] Ibid. Correspondence File G and Accts. File 46.

[72] *Endowed Char. Wilts.* (1908), p. 810; Char. Com. Accts. File 46.

THE HUNDRED
OF WHORWELLSDOWN

THE hundred of Whorwellsdown lies in the western part of the county along the southern fringe of the Avon valley south of Bradford and Melksham. From its centre, the village of Steeple Ashton, it extends west between Trowbridge and Westbury, crossing the valley of the Biss and reaching the River Frome and the Somerset border near Rode. To the south it reaches past Edington village well into the downland of Salisbury Plain, and to the north to Semington Brook, another tributary of the Avon, near Melksham. A detached outlier

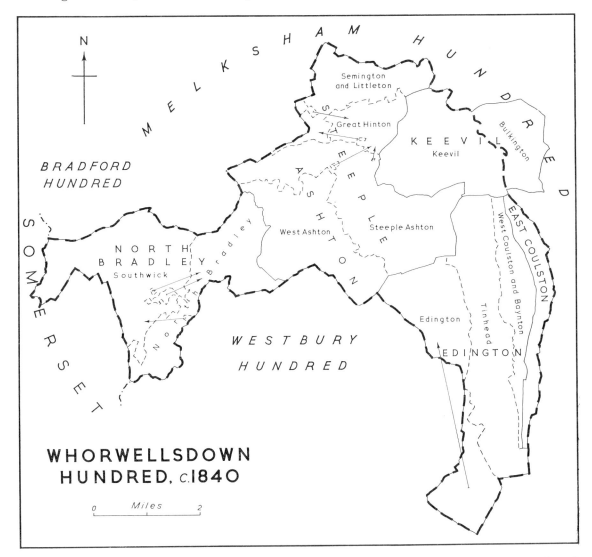

WHORWELLSDOWN
HUNDRED, c.1840

of the hundred, part of Tilshead parish, lies about 5 miles east of the southern tip of the hundred, entirely on the high chalk plateau of the plain. The bulk of the hundred, including all the centres of population, thus lies in the vale. The low flat clay country of the region is varied here, however, by outcrops of Corallian strata around Hinton,

Steeple Ashton, and West Ashton and of cornbrash near Semington, both of which give slightly higher and better-drained land somewhat more suited to arable farming. Most of the vale country is, however, permanent pasture for dairy farming. The downland is given over to arable farming or military training. Although little but agriculture is now carried on in it, the region once had a flourishing cloth industry. It appeared in most of the villages in the hundred in the later Middle Ages, being chiefly centred on the fulling mills driven by the tributaries of the Avon. By 1600 most clothiers had forsaken the villages for Westbury, Trowbridge, and Melksham, but weaving and spinning for the town clothiers were carried on in many of the cottages in the villages until the mechanization of the industry in the 19th century. No place in the hundred has ever grown beyond a village, although Steeple Ashton had a market in the Middle Ages, and North Bradley and Southwick both attained considerable size and prosperity by the 19th century because of their dependence on the trade of nearby Trowbridge.

In 1084 Whorwellsdown hundred included the Abbess of Romsey's manors of Steeple Ashton and Edington, and estates belonging to laymen at Edington, Coulston, and Keevil.[1] North Bradley and Southwick were at this time part of the manor of Steeple Ashton.[2] The tithing of Bulkington in Keevil parish has been part of Melksham hundred since at least the 13th century.[3] It was not mentioned separately from Keevil in 1086, but at least some of the $2\frac{1}{2}$ hides of demesne assigned to Ernulf of Hesdin in 1084 in that hundred may have been there.[4] If this be so, the hundred of 1084 contained Steeple Ashton, North Bradley, East Coulston, and Edington, and the tithing of Keevil, all of which were reckoned to be in it in 1831.[5] To the list at both dates should perhaps be added part of Tilshead, which lay in Whorwellsdown in the 13th century[6] and in 1825, when it was called the tithing of South Tilshead.[7] Its connexion with this hundred must have arisen from the property held there by the Abbess of Romsey by 1206,[8] later reckoned part of Steeple Ashton manor.[9]

The hundred jurisdiction may have been included in the original grant of Steeple Ashton to the abbey of Romsey, for in the 13th century abbesses claimed to hold it by gift of King Edgar.[10] King Stephen, however, granted the hundred to the abbey as Henry I had granted it, to be held at a rent of 40s. paid to the sheriff,[11] and it is quite likely that Henry's was the first grant. The hundred remained with the abbey until the 16th century. Unlike its other property in the district, it was not apparently subject to the arrangement with Sir Thomas Seymour,[12] and must have passed to the Crown at the Dissolution. It was, however, granted to Seymour in 1547,[13] but on his attainder reverted to the Crown and was granted in 1565 to Humphrey Skelton and Nicholas Holbourne.[14] Before the end of the century it had been acquired by the Paulets, lords of Edington Romsey,[15] and thereafter descended in the same way as that manor.[16]

The hundred as granted to Romsey by Henry I was said to include all pleas belonging to it,[17] but in 1233 there was litigation between the abbey and Ela, Countess of

[1] V.C.H. Wilts. ii, p. 188.
[2] See p. 202.
[3] V.C.H. Wilts. vii. 79.
[4] Cf. ibid. ii, pp. 193, 199, and vii. 1, 79. If this were so, it might account for the discrepancy between Ernulf's 7 hides of demesne at Keevil in 1086 and his 6 hides 1 virgate of demesne in Whorwellsdown in 1084.
[5] Ibid. iv. 330.
[6] S.C. 2/208/1; J.I. 1/1004 m. 92d; several small estates in Tilshead in 1086 cannot certainly be assigned to a hundred in 1084.
[7] Hoare, Mod. Wilts. Branch and Dole, 42; its history

is reserved for treatment with the remainder of the parish.
[8] Rot. Chart. (Rec. Com.), 162.
[9] See below.
[10] Rot. Hund. (Rec. Com.), ii. 235, 277; V.C.H. Wilts. v. 45–6.
[11] Cal. Chart. R. 1257–1300, 102.
[12] See p. 241.
[13] Cal. Pat. 1547–8, 26.
[14] C 66/1017 m. 4.
[15] C 142/262/125.
[16] See p. 241.
[17] Cal. Chart. R. 1257–1300, 102.

Salisbury and sheriff of Wiltshire, about the nature of the abbey's liberty. The abbey finally recognized the sheriff's right to two tourns yearly, at which he was to hold the view of frankpledge, enforce the assizes of bread and ale, make attachments of false measures, and hold the pleas of the Crown and pleas about beasts taken and detained against pledge. To the abbey were left pleas of battery and medley where felony was not mentioned, pleas of the wounding of horses and cattle, and actions of debt and other pleas not subject to the king's writ. Permission was, however, given to the abbess to negotiate for the sheriff's rights in return for a payment over and above the 40s. reserved on the original grant, as she had held them before the dispute arose.[18] Some of the rights allotted to him do indeed seem to have passed to the abbey (see below), but sheriffs regularly held two annual tourns in the hundred until at least the 16th century.[19] Yet in 1502 three men were sworn into frankpledge in the abbess's court,[20] so the distinction between her rights and those of the sheriff was perhaps not clear.

The earliest known records of proceedings in the abbess's hundred court are for two courts, one held in December 1261 adjourned from Martinmas, and the other in June 1262 adjourned from Hocktide.[21] Martinmas and Hocktide were the usual seasons for the sheriff's tourn, so that they are no doubt records of the business belonging to the abbess in that court. They show the procedure of presentment of offences by the tithingman of each tithing of the hundred typical of a tourn.[22] Presentments include infractions of the assizes, hue and cry, and bloodshed, so that the abbey had acquired at least some of the pleas allotted to the sheriff in 1233,[23] and in 1274 the abbess did indeed claim the assizes of bread and ale and a gallows.[24] In 1289 the rent paid to the sheriff for the hundred was £4, twice the original sum,[25] which again might indicate an increase of liberties after 1233. In addition to these matters, the courts of 1261-2 heard disputes between party and party; many of them probably related to debt, but one at least concerned a broken contract about the building of houses at Tilshead. A three-weekly hundred court was also held by the abbess in the 13th century.[26] Records exist for both courts for a number of years in the 15th and early 16th centuries.[27] They dealt with pleas of debt and trespass, infractions of the assizes, decay of roads and hedges, bounds of fields, strays, and minor assaults. Between 1412 and 1538 a considerable falling-off of business at all the courts of the hundred is noticeable, both in the presentments of the tithingmen, which became commonly 'all well', and in suits between parties. The profits which accrued to the abbess decreased proportionately, and in the 16th century were often only a few pence at each court.[28] The greatest profit came from the more distant tithings and freeholders who paid fines for respite of suit. Yet the courts were still being held late in the 16th century,[29] and the two views of frankpledge still in the early 18th century. By then no suits were heard in them, and the presentments of the tithings chiefly concerned defects of roads, bridges, bounds, and gates.[30]

In 1261 the tithings of Tilshead, Coulston, Tinhead, Edington, West Ashton, Keevil, Bradley, Southwick, Semington, Littleton, Hinton, and Ashton owed suit

[18] *Bracton's Note Bk.* ed. Maitland, ii, p. 592, iii, p. 128; *Select Pleas in Manorial Courts*, ed. Maitland (Selden Soc. ii), 176-7.
[19] *Rot. Hund.* (Rec. Com.), ii. 278; *V.C.H. Wilts.* v. 20.
[20] S.C. 2/208/7 m. 13.
[21] S.C. 2/208/1; the second was printed by Maitland, *Select Pleas in Manorial Courts* (Selden Soc. ii), 178-83, but he apparently did not know of the first
[22] Pollock and Maitland, *Hist. Eng. Law*, ii. 558-9.
[23] *Select Pleas in Manorial Courts*, 177.
[24] *Rot. Hund.* (Rec. Com.), ii. 278.
[25] J.I. 1/1006 m. 52d.
[26] *Rot. Hund.* (Rec. Com.) ii. 278; *Feet of F. Wilts. 1272-1327* (W.A.S. Rec. Brch.), 32-3.
[27] S.C. 2/208/4 (1-2 Hen. V), /5 (21 Hen. VI), /7 (9, 10, 13, 14, 18, 19 Hen. VII), /8 (2, 3, 6, 7, 9 Hen. VIII), /9 (17-19 Hen. VIII), /10 (25, 26, 30, 31 Hen. VIII), on which what follows is based.
[28] *V.C.H. Wilts.* v. 66.
[29] E 134/26 and 27 Eliz. I/Mich. 4.
[30] Dorset R.O., D. 45.

to the hundred court. Of these Tinhead, Edington, Southwick, and Ashton were each represented at the court by two tithingmen, and the remainder each by one.[31] Two tithingmen from Keevil failed to attend, and it was said in 1268 that the vill had withdrawn its suit for $7\frac{1}{2}$ years.[32] In 1289 Richard de Arundel, lord of Keevil, acknowledged the abbess's right to the suit.[33] All the tithings continued to do suit to the courts in the early 15th century. Those which had been doubly represented were referred to as 'two tithings', and were apparently divided geographically, for one of the Southwick tithings had its suit relaxed, while the other appeared.[34] After the mid-15th century Keevil never appears to have done suit to any of the hundred courts. The distinction between the parts of the other double tithings seems to have been lost by the 18th century, except that Steeple Ashton was divided into upper and lower tithings.[35]

Apart from this change all the tithings of 1261 except Keevil were still doing suit in the 18th century. There had, however, been one addition, a tithing called Battlesfield, which appeared, at views of frankpledge only, fairly regularly from 1413. In that year it appeared by a tithingman and another, 'as accustomed', and presented the default of another suitor.[36] In 1442, however, only a tithingman appeared, but made no presentment, and asserted that he was not bound to do so.[37] Thereafter this right of making no presentment was variously affirmed. Thus in 1493 the tithing 'presented nothing but said "Farewell and have good day"', a phrase which regularly recurred thereafter, and in 1497 the tithingman came with his dog and said the same.[38] Tithingmen were still appearing in the 18th century,[39] and a dim memory of the custom remained at Tinhead in 1897, when an old man said that at a 'manorial' court once held at the 'George' there it was the custom that the hayward should carry a dog in his arms and say 'Here come I and my dog to open this court'.[40] Since Battlesfield was usually the first tithing to appear, there is little doubt that he had heard of this custom. This tithing was almost certainly part or the whole of East Coulston. In all the 15th century courts it is described as the tithing *de Bello Campo*, which is the usual Latin equivalent of the family name Beauchamp, and the Beauchamps were lords of part of East Coulston at that time. It was only in the 16th century that the name was translated as 'Batillisfyld'. The tithing called Coulston in the 15th and 16th centuries apparently included West Coulston in Edington,[41] and may have been only West Coulston. In the 18th century it was distinguished as West, although East Coulston residents owed suit to the hundred.[42]

The hundred was divided into inner and outer parts in the early 18th century,[43] but it is not known in what way or for what purposes.

For purposes other than suit of court the division of the hundred into units has not varied much from that outlined above. In 1334 Baynton in Edington was separately assessed for taxation, but in 1377 it was included with Coulston.[44] In 1576 it was again treated separately for the assessment of a subsidy.[45]

Thomas Tinny was pardoned for acquiring the bedelry of the hundred in 1328,[46]

[31] S.C. 2/208/1; in the part of the roll printed by Maitland (*Select Pleas in Manorial Courts*, 176–83) Ric. Hordy is named by a clerk's error tithingman of Southwick rather than Bradley, which he represented in 1261, and Walt. Nele, made tithingman in court, must have been from Semington.
[32] J.I. 1/998 m. 32.
[33] *Feet of F. Wilts.* 1272–1327 (W.A.S. Rec. Brch.), 32–3.
[34] S.C. 2/208/4.
[35] Dorset R.O., D. 45.
[36] S.C. 2/208/4 m. 2.

[37] S.C. 2/208/5 m. 2d.
[38] S.C. 2/208/7 mm. 2, 7.
[39] Dorset R.O., D. 45.
[40] *W.N. & Q.* ii. 242. For a similar custom at Broughton Gifford, see *W.A.M.* xli. 231–2.
[41] e.g. it presented Baynton Lane in 1502: S.C. 2/208/7 m. 13.
[42] Dorset R.O., D. 45, esp. 1703, 1706.   [43] Ibid.
[44] *V.C.H. Wilts.* iv. 302, 311.
[45] *Taxation Lists* (W.A.S. Rec. Brch.), 141.
[46] *Abbrev. Rot. Orig.* (Rec. Com.), ii. 25.

but it is not clear that it was a grant in fee, and nothing more is known of its being so held. Among those who held the office of steward, Peter of Testwood,[47] Thomas Gore,[48] and Anthony Stileman[49] were all considerable property owners in Steeple Ashton.[50] In the later 16th century two constables for the hundred were chosen in Quarter Sessions.[51] In the 18th century the officers were usually a bailiff and three constables, one each for the outer and inner parts of the hundred and one for Steeple Ashton.[52] In 1770 the bailiwick of the hundred was held at farm for £6 a year.[53]

In the late 13th century,[54] and as long as records of it exist, the three-weekly court of the hundred was held at Steeple Ashton. In the 16th century it was held at the church house there.[55] Almost all the earliest records of the view of frankpledge show that it was held at Whorwellsdown.[56] This is the now lost name of the low rounded hill on which the boundaries of Steeple Ashton, Edington, and Bratton meet near Crosswelldown Farm.[57] In the 16th century it was still held there under an oak or thorn tree, but had also been sometimes held in a field at Steeple Ashton.[58] The hundred court was held at Tinhead in 1708, and this may have been the usual meeting place at that time.[59] The court held at the 'George' there, the tradition of which remained in 1897, was no doubt the hundred court or at least the court for part of it, perhaps the out-hundred of the early 18th century.[60]

Beside the privileges connected with the courts the lords of the hundred also claimed certain rights in woods and commons as appurtenant to it. In 1328 the custody of the abbess's woods in Ashton and Edington was granted with the bedelry.[61] In the late 16th century there was a series of disputes between the Crown and the Marquess of Winchester about the woods in the hundred. Although the Marquess claimed them as appurtenant to the farm of Steeple Ashton,[62] deponents believed that the right of driving them for strays twice a year belonged to him as lord of the hundred, and that he could take trees from them for making pounds.[63] In the early 18th century the hundred court presented the custom of the commons of the hundred and defaults of pounds, and haywards for the various tithings were sworn in it.[64]

The name of Whorwellsdown has retained more meaning than that of many of Wiltshire's hundreds, for it was coupled with Westbury as the name of a rural district from 1872 to 1934,[65] and was in 1960 still the name of a petty-sessional division. No consistent local tradition of the correct way to pronounce the word Whorwellsdown seems to remain.

[47] J.I. 3/130 m. 33 (1343); V.C.H. Wilts. v. 26–8.
[48] J.I. 3/147 (c. 1359).
[49] E 134/25 & 26 Eliz. I/Mich. 4.   [50] See p. 206.
[51] Sess. Mins. (W.A.S. Rec. Brch.), passim.
[52] Dorset R.O., D. 45.
[53] Hants R.O. 11, M 49/121.
[54] Feet of F. Wilts. 1272–1327 (W.A.S. Rec. Brch.), 32–3.
[55] E 134/25 & 26 Eliz. I/Mich. 4.
[56] Feet of F. Wilts. 1272–1327 (W.A.S. Rec. Brch.), 32–3. S.C. 2/208/4–5; W.A.M. xiii. 105–18; but the two

'arrear-hundreds' of 1261–2 were at Ashton: S.C. 2/208/1.
[57] P.N. Wilts. (E.P.N.S.), 135–6.
[58] E 134/25 & 26 Eliz. I/Mich. 4.
[59] Dorset R.O., D. 45.
[60] W.N.& Q. ii. 242.
[61] Abbrev. Rot. Orig. (Rec. Com.), ii. 25.
[62] See p. 208.
[63] ., 134/16 Eliz. I/Trin. 6; E 134/25 & 26 Eliz. I/Mich. 4
[64] Do'set R.O., D. 45.
[65] V.C.H. Wilts. iv. 338.

STEEPLE ASHTON

THE village of Steeple Ashton lies about 3 miles east of Trowbridge.[1] Its name is derived from the church tower.[2] The parish formerly included the tithings of West Ashton, Great Hinton, Semington, and Littleton. The first two of these, and Semington and Littleton together, were assessed for poor rates separately from Steeple Ashton tithing,[3] and so became civil parishes in the late 19th century.

In 1883 small detached parts of Great Hinton and Semington were transferred to Hilperton.[4] In 1894 the whole parish of Whaddon was transferred to Semington civil parish.[5] In 1897 part of Steeple Ashton civil parish, containing a number of houses and a factory which were part of the built-up area of Trowbridge, was transferred to Trowbridge U.D.C.[6] The detaching of West Ashton, Great

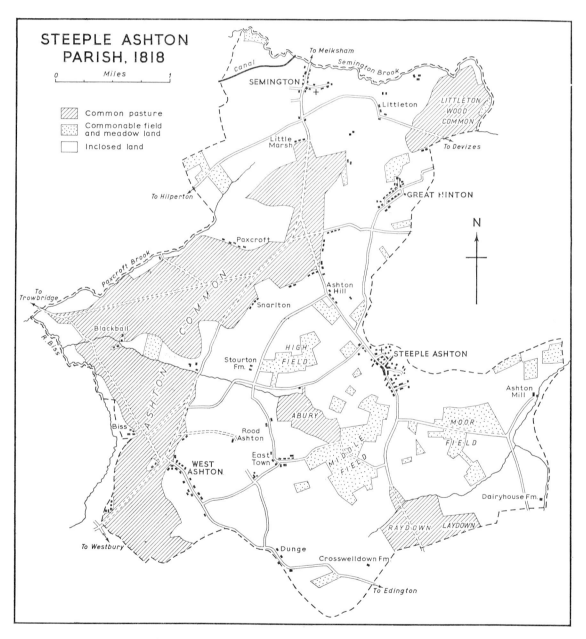

This map is based on the inclosure award map

[1] The following maps were used: O.S. Maps 1/2,500 Wilts. XXXII. 16, XXXIII. 13, 14, XXXVIII. 8, 12, 16, XXXIX. 1, 2, 5, 9, 10, 13, 14 (all edns.); 1/25,000 ST 85, 86, 96, 95.

[2] P.N. Wilts. (E.P.N.S.), 136; see below, p. 213.
[3] Census, 1861.
[4] Bounds of Wilts. (1918), 15.
[5] V.C.H. Wilts. vii. 171.
[6] Ibid. iv. 213.

Hinton, and Semington has left the modern civil parish of Steeple Ashton with a long projection extending westward to the Trowbridge boundary, dividing Semington and Hinton to the north from West Ashton to the south.

Geologically the dominating feature of the ancient parish is the Corallian series, which outcrops here from the clays of the vale of North Wiltshire to form a low plateau with a distinct scarp to the north. This scarp runs north of Great Hinton village, round Hag Hill and south-westward, east of the Semington-Yarnbrook road, to Rood Ashton park and the parish boundary south of West Ashton village. Projections such as Hag Hill and Stourton Hill, show characteristic rounded outlines.[7] South and east of the scarp most of the land is over 250 ft. rising to 265 ft. south of Steeple Ashton and 314 ft. south of West Ashton. The soil of this plateau is lighter than that of the vale, and somewhat more suitable to arable farming.[8] The lower ground in the north-west of the parish is drained by the Biss, which forms its boundary for some distance, and two streams both emptying into the Biss above Trowbridge; one, Paxcroft Brook, rises near Semington and the other near Steeple Ashton. This area is mainly below 150 ft. and contains a large amount of woodland. Woods called Kayred and Slowgrove lay here in 1370,[9] and in 1617 woods, still called by these early names, covered much the same area as those now called Green Lane and Biss Woods. Carter's and Flower's Woods also existed then.[10] Considerable parts of Biss Wood and Flower's Wood have recently (1960) been felled. The north-east of the parish is also in the Oxford Clay region in the valley of the Semington Brook, which forms the parish boundary to the north. Semington village itself, however, stands at the eastern end of a low ridge of Cornbrash which extends westward to Trowbridge and again gives a somewhat lighter soil than the clay of the vale.

Three of the principal ancient settlements, Steeple Ashton, Great Hinton, and West Ashton, stand on the higher ground in the south. The main road from Trowbridge to Devizes crosses the north of the parish, and that from Melksham to Westbury runs through Semington and so south-west, crossing the end of West Ashton village. Both these roads were turnpiked in the 1750's.[11] Great Hinton, Steeple Ashton, and West Ashton all lie on minor roads which connect the main roads with the Westbury-Lavington road at Bratton and Edington. The road from Tinhead to Steeple Ashton and thence by Stony Gutter and Green Lane to Trowbridge was turnpiked in 1752.[12] It formed part of the old route over the downs from Salisbury to Bath, which fell out of use in the later 18th century.[13] In 1768 the road from Horseshoes through Hinton

and Cold Harbour was added to the Trowbridge Trust,[14] and those from Stony Gutter to Hilperton, and Trowbridge to the top of West Ashton Hill were added in 1854.[15] The last part of the old main road to Trowbridge was still not made up in 1961, and the quickest way into the town was through Hilperton.

In the Middle Ages Steeple Ashton was the centre of the great Romsey Abbey estates in the district. The courts of the abbey's hundred of Whorwellsdown were held there,[16] and in 1266 a weekly market and yearly fair were granted to the abbess.[17] In the taxation of 1334 Steeple Ashton paid more than Trowbridge or Westbury, and in 1377 its 260 poll-tax payers placed it 18th in the whole county.[18] In the 16th century Leland described it as 'a praty little market towne', and wrote 'it standithe muche by clothiars'.[19] But Steeple Ashton suffered severely by fire at some time, and Aubrey attributed the decline of the market to this.[20] The fire he referred to may have been in 1503, when at least six houses in the village were destroyed.[21] By 1524 it had fallen well behind the neighbouring towns,[22] and by the end of the 16th century the prosperity of the cloth industry was at an end.[23] From that time Steeple Ashton retained only a certain pre-eminence among surrounding villages, bestowed perhaps by the holding of petty sessions and by being often the home of a medical man or a lawyer.[24] In 1801 the population of the tithing was 618; it increased to 848 by 1831, and then declined intermittently to 603 in 1931. In 1951 it was 1,231,[25] but this number included many Poles temporarily living in a hostel in disused buildings belonging to the airfield at Keevil. The hostel was closed in 1956.

The village still retains something of the aspect of a small town. The principal street, called High Street, opens out into a green on which stand the market cross and a small lock-up or blindhouse, built in 1773.[26] Most of the houses here stand directly by the road, without gardens. To the east of High Street are other streets called Church Street, the Strand, Dark Lane, and Silver Street. Several have stretches of cobbled pavement. The church stands at the north-east corner of the village, adjoining the manor house. The buildings of Steeple Ashton display a pleasing variety of building material. Most of the older buildings are timber-framed with later brick infilling, some colour-washed, and some with bricks set in herringbone. Stone could be fetched from Bradford for more pretentious buildings such as the late-medieval vicarage[27] or the manor house,[28] while brick, often with stone dressings, was in general use from the early 18th century.

The village contains several houses with cruck

[7] Ibid. i. 18.
[8] A. H. Fry, *Land Utilization, Wilts.* 214.
[9] S.C. 2/208/2 m. 1.
[10] B.M. Add. MS. 6027, f. 130.
[11] *V.C.H. Wilts.* iv. 268, 270.
[12] 25 Geo. II, c. 24.
[13] See pp. 239-40.
[14] 8 Geo. III, c. 49.
[15] 17 and 18 Vic., c. 75.
[16] See p. 197.
[17] See p. 210.
[18] *V.C.H. Wilts.* iv. 300–2, 311–2.

[19] Leland, *Itin.* ed. Toulmin Smith, i. 82–3.
[20] *Nat. Hist. Wilts.* ed. Britton, 115.
[21] S.C. 2/208/6 m. 15d.
[22] E 179/197/153.
[23] See p. 209.
[24] Long MSS. Wills of Jn. Long, 1793, and Silas Griffin, 1833; *P.O. Dir. Wilts.* (1855); Soc. Antiq. Jackson MSS. *s.v.* Steeple Ashton. Thanks are due to Viscount Long for permission to use his MSS.
[25] *V.C.H. Wilts.* iv. 340.
[26] *W.A.M.* xxxii. 185. See pl. facing p. 200.
[27] See p. 214.   [28] See p. 202.

trusses. The north wing of the Sanctuary in Dark Lane was formerly a cruck-framed building, probably of the 15th century or earlier. It was apparently of three bays, but only one complete cruck truss remains, with an arch-braced collar-beam. Part of a second truss can also be seen. A jettied cross-wing of two stories was added to the house *c.* 1500. Just south of the Sanctuary is a small cottage with a cruck truss visible at one end, while a similar one with an internal truss remaining stands at the corner of High Street and Silver Street. On the west side of the southern part of the High Street are four timber-framed houses which appear to date from *c.* 1500. They were evidently built for people of means, and in their original form were remarkably uniform in size and design. The northernmost, now called Ashton House, was the home of the Stileman family from about that time until the mid-19th century.[29] It consisted originally of a hall block of three bays parallel to the road and a cross-wing of the same height at its south end projecting eastward. The hall has arch-braced collar-beam trusses with chamfered braces, the chamfers being continued on wall posts down to the windowsills of the ground floor. There are remains of an original wooden window with late medieval tracery at the heads of the lights. The two-storied cross-wing, also with an open roof, has at least three original bays, and evidently contained a 'great chamber' or solar on the upper floor. Alterations were made probably in the mid-16th century; they included the insertion of a large stone chimney and fireplace in the north bay of the hall, and the building of a two-storied addition in the angle between the hall and the cross wing, so that the whole frontage was brought forward to the street. Rooms in this part have heavily moulded beams, and one has the remains of contemporary wall decoration. In 1724 a stone ashlar façade of five bays was added to the house. It had sash windows on two floors; above is a row of 5 blank openings to represent attic windows. On the ground floor the sash windows have been replaced by recent stone-mullioned and transomed windows. In the 1920's the house was carefully restored under the direction of Sir Harold Brakspear. All the original features in the interior were exposed, and if decayed were reproduced, and a new wing was built at the back.[30]

Further south in High Street no. 48 was originally a similar house, also probably of *c.* 1500. It is built on a stone base with small stepped buttresses; the cross-wing has a jettied overhang at first floor level, supported by hollow chamfered brackets continued down as small buttressed shafts. Although the longer wing has been considerably altered and re-roofed at some time, it may well have been an open hall comparable to that at Ashton House. The house contains heavily moulded beams; these can also be seen in the adjoining Black Barn Farmhouse, which may once have been a similar house of which parts have been demolished. To the south again no. 54 has a jettied cross-wing faced with stucco; it retains carved barge boards, and its hall wing may possibly be enclosed in the adjoining house. Nos.

56, 58, and 60 form an L-shaped block of which the south end is a very similar cross-wing, having barge boards with carved quatrefoil ornament. The main block, timber-framed with brick filling and two small gables, may be an early 17th-century reconstruction of a single-storied hall. Similar buildings exist in other parts of the village. The south wing of Church Farm had a jettied overhang until at least the mid-19th century; it has since been built under and the whole house stuccoed.[31] Inside are the heavily moulded beams typical of the other houses, and the main block may include the former hall. The Firs, too, may once have been a similar house, now much restored. The presence of so many houses in the village with the same characteristics suggests considerable building activity at a single period, and this may well have been after the fire of 1503. It may also be significant that most of the houses stand detached and spaced well apart.

The village contains a number of other timber-framed houses, including the 'Rose and Crown', Peartree Cottage, nos. 20, 22, and 24 High Street and nos. 1 and 3 Church Lane. Some of these are probably of later date than those described above, but almost all have the curved braces in the upper panels typical of framing in Steeple Ashton. A particularly fine example is the house facing the green in High Street, used as a shop and the village post office. It is traditionally said to have been a market or merchants' hall,[32] but nothing is known of its history. It stands on a stone base with buttresses; the timber-framing above has later brick infilling in herringbone pattern, and the roof is of stone tiles. If it ever consisted of a single open hall it must have been converted into a house by the late 16th century. There are many features of this period including a small front gable, a newel-staircase, panelling, and doors.

The 'Long's Arms' is a stone building of the 17th century with mullioned and transomed windows. The front has been entirely renewed to include an extension forward on the ground floor. Just north of Ashton House is a small stone house of three bays, no. 32 High Street, which is probably contemporary with the refronting of the larger house in 1724. There are several brick houses with stone-mullioned windows and stone quoins. They include Tyler's Farm in High Street, Moorfields Farm in Church Lane, and the Lodge facing the green south of the 'Rose and Crown'. At the south end of the High Street are three pairs of cottages built for workers on the Long estate, dated 1877, 1879, and 1901. The estate office and yard were opposite. A small council-house scheme at St. Mary's at the north end of the village dates from the 1930's. Beyond it Newleaze is a much larger estate built after the Second World War.

North of the village groups of cottages at Ashton Hill, Ashton Common, and Snarlton, which all existed by 1773,[33] must have begun by encroachment on the great common which covered the northwest of the parish until 1818.[34] Brook Farm and Green Lane Farm were not built until it was inclosed. South of the village only Ashton Mill and

[29] See p. 206.
[30] *Country Life*, 30 Oct. 1942.
[31] Soc. Antiq. Jackson MSS. Drawing by W. W. Wheatley. For drawing by the same of no. 48., see pl. opposite.

[32] e.g. *Country Life*, 23 Oct. 1942.
[33] *Andrews and Dury, Map* (W.A.S. Rec. Brch.), pl. 10.
[34] O.S. Map 1/2,500 Wilts. xxxviii. 12; Steeple Ashton W.I. village history.

The High Street, looking towards the green with lock-up and market cross

A house in the High Street, *c.* 1850

STEEPLE ASHTON

Rood Ashton House, West Ashton

Daubeny Asylum, North Bradley

Dairyhouse Farms date from before inclosure.[35]

West Ashton village lies about 1½ mile south-west of Steeple Ashton, where the minor road from Trowbridge to Bratton climbs on to the Corallian plateau. Most of the older houses of the village are scattered along this road; on the Westbury-Melksham road which crosses it is a group of five pairs of houses, Doreen Cottages, built c. 1850 for workers on the Rood Ashton estate. Another pair, Woodside Cottages, is further down the hill towards Yarnbrook, and two more pairs are in the village street. Another group lies on the far side of Rood Ashton park at Heath Hill. The history of the park is mentioned below.[36] West Ashton Manor Farm at the south end of the village is an early-18th-century brick house with stone-mullioned windows. Opposite Manor Farm is a 17th-century house of stone rubble. A small estate of council houses has been built in East Town Lane, and several bungalows in the village street, since the Second World War. East Town is a hamlet on the way to Steeple Ashton. It was known as Gulden Ashton in the Middle Ages.[37]

Two small groups of houses lay on the lower ground to the north of West Ashton before the inclosure of the parish in 1818. One was at the north end of Biss Wood, upstream from Blackball Bridge. Houses stood there in 1617,[38] and in 1811 the hamlet was called Blackball.[39] It still existed in 1841,[40] but was probably removed very soon afterwards in the reconstruction of Rood Ashton park.[41] It seems likely that this was the place called Lovemead or Lowmead, which is regularly mentioned in medieval records as lying within the manor of Steeple Ashton but near Trowbridge.[42] In 1341 there were 9 houses there,[43] and later in the century its inhabitants appeared at the manor court separately from West Ashton.[44] Another group of houses called Biss stood in the 18th century between the River Biss and the Trowbridge road at the north end of Carter's Wood.[45] This too was probably replaced by Biss Farm on the other side of the road in the 1840's.[46] The population of West Ashton was 344 in 1801, and rose to 374 in 1831; since then it has declined intermittently, and was 243 in 1951.[47] In 1731 a mineral well was discovered at West Ashton, and two years later an attempt was made to attract visitors by advertising in the *London Evening Post*. It was claimed that over 100 people had been cured of such afflictions as leprosy, sore eyes, and the king's evil, and that lodgings were available in the village and in Trowbridge. The well never became established as a place of resort, and its site is uncertain.[48] Thomas King, who was born at West Ashton c. 1694, gave his name to King's Coffee House in Covent Garden, a well-known resort in the 18th century.[49]

Great Hinton lies about a mile north of Steeple Ashton on a road which goes on to join the main road from Trowbridge to Devizes north of the village. It is built along two roads which divide at its south end and re-unite at the north end. Fore Street Farm is a timber-framed building with brick in-filling, probably of the early 17th century. Church Farm is a somewhat later building of stone rubble with a stone-tiled roof, and there are several 18th-century houses of brick with stone dressings. The New Inn is an early-19th-century building of brick, which has been licensed since at least 1842.[50] South-west of the village small groups of houses at Cold Harbour and Bleet both existed in 1773,[51] and were no doubt in origin groups of cottages built on the verges of the common. The population of Great Hinton tithing, later civil parish, rose from 174 in 1801 to 234 in 1831, and then gradually declined to 143 in 1951.[52]

Semington stands at the northern edge of the ancient parish in the valley of the Semington Brook, a tributary of the Avon. Many of its houses are built along the main road from Melksham to Westbury, which is crossed by the Trowbridge-Devizes road just south of the village. The 'Somerset Arms' is an early-18th-century building of brick with stone quoins, which is possibly to be identified with the 'Bell' which existed in 1710.[53] Near it is a two-storied house of stone rubble with stone-tiled roof and mullioned windows, dated 1698. A group of three large late-18th or early-19th-century stone houses stands at the foot of the hill up to the main cross-roads. Semington House is of three stories with rusticated ground floor; it was probably built by a member of the Bruges family.[54] Opposite is Highfield, also of three stories and with a pedimented doorway. Both houses were apparently built by 1811.[55] The Old Parsonage is a two-storied house of rather later date. The church and the adjoining school lie along Church Lane to the east. Here also are the oldest houses in the village. Nos. 26–27 were evidently once a single house on a ½-H plan, probably of the 16th century; the whole is of timber-framed construction, although the framing is only exposed on the wings, and inside are carved and moulded beams and other features. Church Farm is apparently of the same period. It is partly timber-framed, but the exterior has largely been built up in stone. Manor Farm is mentioned below.[56] Also in Church Lane are several council houses built between the World Wars. Another group built after the Second World War is on the other side of the main road in Pound Close.

[35] *Andrews and Dury, Map* (W.A.S. Rec. Brch.), pl. 7.
[36] See p. 204.
[37] *P.N. Wilts.* (E.P.N.S.), 136; see below, p. 206.
[38] B.M. Add. MS. 6027, f. 130.
[39] O.S. Map Wilts. 1″, sheet 14 (1st edn.); on *Andrews and Dury, Map* (W.A.S. Rec. Brch.), pl. 10, the names Blackball and Biss are erroneously transposed.
[40] W.R.O. Tithe Award.
[41] See p. 204.
[42] See the references quoted in *V.C.H. Wilts.* vii. 133.
[43] S.C. 12/699.
[44] S.C. 2/208/2; for later references to these inclosed lands near Trowbridge, see e.g. Soc. Antiq. Jackson MSS. *s.v.* Steeple Ashton, quoting from a survey formerly

at Rood Ashton; Bristol Univ. Libr., Court Bk. of Trowbridge Dauntsey 1593–1600; *W.A.M.* xv. 229. A part of Trowbridge was also called Lovemead.
[45] See n. 39 above.
[46] It still existed in 1842: W.R.O. Tithe Award.
[47] *V.C.H. Wilts.* iv. 340.
[48] *W.A.M.* lv. 16–17, 26.
[49] Aubrey, *Topog. Coll.* ed. Jackson, 354.
[50] W.R.O. Tithe Award.
[51] *Andrews and Dury, Map* (W.A.S. Rec. Brch.), pl. 10
[52] *V.C.H. Wilts.* iv. 340, 350.
[53] *W.N. & Q.* vi. 8.
[54] W.R.O. Land Tax Assessments.
[55] O.S. Map 1″, sheet 14 (1st edn.)   [56] See p. 205.

West of the village St. George's Hospital, the former workhouse of the Trowbridge and Melksham Union, was built in 1836–9 to the design of H. E. Kendall.[57] South of the main cross-roads a group of houses on the edge of the common existed at Little Marsh in 1773.[58] One or two of the cottages which still stand there are probably survivors from that time, and typical of the better type of common cottage; they are of brick, of two stories with thatched roofs. Further south again Hag Hill Farm was not built until after the inclosure of the parish. Paxcroft on the Hilperton boundary is, however, an ancient settlement. Houses stood there in 1254,[59] and in the 18th and 19th centuries there were two or three farms and some other houses there.[60] The only survivor is the present Lower Paxcroft Farm, formerly a detached part of Whaddon and now in Hilperton.[61] Upper Paxcroft Farm, which is just inside the Semington boundary, was built in the 19th century some distance from the old hamlet.

Littleton lies about ½ mile east of Semington on the road to Devizes. It consists only of three farms and Littleton Wood Mill. Littleton Wood Farm is a stone building with stone-tiled roof, probably of the 17th century. Some timber-framing is visible at the back, and there is a moulded plaster ceiling in one of the rooms. In 1801 the combined population of Semington and Littleton tithings was 265. By 1831 it had risen to 398, and ten years later, after the building of the workhouse, to 570. During the later 19th century it fluctuated between 420 and 500, and was 449 in 1931. By 1951 it had risen to 546.[62]

In 1839 William Carrier, the Trowbridge Chartist leader, addressed a small meeting in Steeple Ashton. The next day Thomas Miles, tenant of the Manor Farm, dismissed some of his men for attending. Later he took one back; the others assembled again and threatened to pull down this man's cottage, and Carrier returned and urged them to buy muskets. Later a fire occurred on Miles's property for which the Chartists were blamed.[63]

MANORS. Ashton belonged to King Edgar, who in 964 set forth its bounds and declared that he should enjoy it for life and at his death give it to whom he wished.[64] The estate then included the whole of the ancient parish and also the modern parishes of North Bradley and Southwick.[65] There is no record of Edgar's disposal of the estate, but he must have given or left it to Romsey Abbey (Hants), which he refounded in 967.[66] The nuns held it in 1086,[67] and it remained the property of the abbey until 1539, when it passed in the same way as Edington Romsey to Sir Thomas Seymour, and on his forfeiture in 1549 to the Crown.[68] A year later the manor and demesnes were granted to William Paulet, Earl of Wiltshire;[69] this grant was apparently surrendered, for another of the same year included only the house and demesnes.[70] Later in the century the Paulets, Marquesses of Winchester from 1551, unsuccessfully claimed certain manorial rights, especially those relating to the woods and commons in Steeple Ashton and North Bradley.[71] The capital manor, however, remained in the hands of the Crown. In 1562 it was mortgaged to the City of London, and in 1579 the mortgage was assigned to trustees for Walter Long.[72] In 1610 the manor was assigned for the maintenance of Prince Henry,[73] and in 1617 it was granted to Prince Charles.[74] It was sold to Edward Ditchfield and others in 1629,[75] and they sold it to Walter Long of Whaddon (d. 1672), who held the manor by 1632.[76] Steeple Ashton descended in the Long family in the same way as Whaddon[77] until the present century. Parts of the family estates in Semington and Great Hinton were sold in 1911, and most of the remainder in Steeple Ashton in 1930.[78]

The manor house and farm of Steeple Ashton, granted away separately in 1551, descended to William Paulet, Marquess of Winchester (d. 1629), who in 1601 sold them to John Greenhill,[79] the tenant under him for a number of years before.[80] Greenhill died in 1618;[81] in 1624 his son Henry sold the farm to John Bennett.[82] It descended to his great grandson Thomas Bennett, who died without surviving issue c. 1730 and left it to his sister Mary, wife of Robert Smith of Combe Hay (Som.).[83] At the death of Robert's son John in 1775, an Act was obtained to sell his estates to pay his debts.[84] They were paid without the Steeple Ashton property being sold, but in 1799 John Smith sold the house and farm to Richard Long of Rood Ashton.[85] The house was still in 1963 occupied by his descendant, the third Viscount Long of Wraxall. The manor house, which is dated 1647, is a three-storied building, fronted with ashlar but with the back parts mainly of brick, and roofed with stone tiles. The symmetrical front has three gables, crowned with finials, and a small gabled porch. There are two-light mullioned windows

[57] Pevsner, *Wilts*, 418.
[58] *Andrews and Dury, Map* (W.A.S. Rec Brch.), pl. 10.
[59] *Wilts. Inq. p.m.* 1242–1326 (Index Libr.), 16.
[60] W.R.O. Inclosure and Tithe Awards; Aubrey, *Topog. Coll.* ed. Jackson, 354; O.S. Map 1″, sheet 14 (1st edn.).
[61] W.R.O. Whaddon Tithe Award.
[62] *V.C.H. Wilts.* iv. 340, 357.
[63] *W.A.M* liv. 176; *Chartist Studies*, ed. A. Briggs, 184.
[64] *Cart. Sax.* ed. Birch, iii. 364.
[65] G. B. Grundy, 'Saxon Land Charters of Wilts.', *Arch. Jnl.* lxxvii, 71–5.
[66] *V.C.H. Hants*, ii. 126.
[67] *V.C.H. Wilts.* ii, p. 131; for the tenant William see p. 241.
[68] See p. 241.
[69] *Cal. Pat.* 1548–49, 376.
[70] Ibid. 1549–51, 197; *W.N. & Q.* iii. 212.

[71] *W.N. & Q.* iii. 208f; E 134/16 Eliz. I/Trin. 6; E 134/25 Eliz. I/Trin. 4.
[72] Soc. Antiq. Jackson MSS. s.v. Steeple Ashton, quoting from deeds formerly at Rood Ashton. It is not clear who this Walter was, nor how long his interest lasted. He may have been Walter, son of Sir Robert Long of South Wraxall.
[73] B.M. Harl. MS. 642, f. 239v.
[74] C 66/2109 m. 1.   [75] C 66/2485 m. 13.
[76] *Wilts. Inq. p.m.* 1625–49 (Index Libr.), 328.
[77] *V.C.H. Wilts.* vii. 173.
[78] W.A.S. Libr. Devizes, Sale Cat.
[79] B.M. Eg. Ch. 302; E 134/2 Jas. I/Mich. 12.
[80] E 178/4697.   [81] C 142/375/36.   [82] B.M. Eg. Ch. 304.
[83] Soc. Antiq. Jackson MSS. s.v. Steeple Ashton; Collinson, *History of Somerset*, iii. 336, 350.
[84] 16 Geo. III, c. 118 (priv. act).
[85] Long MSS., Deeds Tracy to Smith, 1782, and Smith to Long, 1799.

with moulded architraves, pulvinated friezes, and cornices. Nearby is a group of contemporary farm buildings of stone rubble, with ashlar quoins and stone-tiled roofs; one, probably formerly a dovecot, has a small open turret of wood. Near the house is an elaborate granary, of brick with ashlar quoins, which stands on circular columns about seven feet high. It is probably of the early-18th century, as is the low brick wall, with rusticated stone gatepiers and enriched ball finials, which bounds the fore-court of the house. Beyond the older farm buildings is a large 19th-century stone barn with a small brick chimney stack, probably for a steam engine to work farm machinery.

Subinfeudation had begun on the Abbess of Romsey's manor in 1086, when tenants named Edward and William held three hides and one hide respectively, and some unnamed Englishmen four hides.[86] Several considerable estates, some called manors, were held freely of the abbey in the Middle Ages. In 1248 Walter de Dunstanville, lord of Castle Combe, obtained permission to hold the park which his father Walter had made by inclosing his wood of Little Ashton.[87] This estate was later subinfeudated again, and was reckoned part of the barony of Castle Combe until the 16th century.[88] In the Romsey Abbey records, however, the intermediate lordship was forgotten, and the actual tenants were spoken of as holding from the abbess. The first of these known to us was probably Thomas of Hurdecote, who perhaps held in the early 13th century.[89] By 1255, and still in 1277, William Bluet held lands in 'Hurdecotes Ashton', reckoned at two carucates.[90] It was no doubt the same two carucates which John Biset died possessed of in 1307,[91] which were then delivered to his widow Katharine.[92] Their only son John died without issue in 1334 leaving as heir his sister Margaret, wife of Robert Martin.[93] In 1339 John de Croucheston complained that Martin and others had wrongfully imprisoned him and seized his goods at Chapel Ashton,[94] and in the following year Martin and his wife released the property to Croucheston.[95] It was then first called the manor of *CHAPEL ASHTON*, but more usually in later times, of *ROOD ASHTON*.

John de Croucheston died *c.* 1374;[96] another John who died *c.* 1390 had during his lifetime settled it on his bastard son Richard. Richard, who was perhaps already dead, left a son Edmund and a daughter Eleanor who possessed it successively but left no issue. The next heir was Joan, daughter of John de Croucheston.[97] In 1390 John Milbourn held it as dower of his wife Margaret, presumably

widow of John or Richard de Croucheston,[98] but on his outlawry for murder it was taken into the king's hands. On this, Joan de Croucheston, who had married Nicholas Temmes, claimed it,[99] and in 1402 John Milbourn and Margaret released their right.[1] Joan married Robert Salmon as her second husband,[2] and in 1433 the manor was settled on the issue of the marriage with remainder to her sons by Temmes.[3] She evidently had no sons by Salmon, for the manor descended in the Temmes family to Robert Temmes, who in 1548 sold Rood Ashton to William Button of Alton Priors.[4] William's son, another William, died holding it in 1591.[5] In the disputes which followed his death it was allotted to his younger son William,[6] who sold it in 1597 to Edward Long of Monkton in Broughton Gifford.[7] Edward's great-grandson, Henry Long, died without issue in 1672, and left Rood Ashton to his nephew Richard, son of his sister Elizabeth by Richard Long of Collingbourne Kingston.[8] From him it descended in the male line to Walter Hume Long, created Viscount Long of Wraxall in 1921.[9] After his death in 1924, the estate was broken up by sale.[10] The mansion house and park were sold to Mrs. Walter Shaw in 1930; after being used by the fighting services in the Second World War, the house was sold in 1950. It has since been stripped of its fittings and the park turned over to agriculture.[11]

Rood Ashton house in 1963 was only a roofless shell. The mansion house of the Long family stood on the site in 1773, but nothing is known of the building at that time. In 1808 Jeffry Wyatt (later Sir Jeffry Wyatville) designed the older part of the present building,[12] and in 1836 his house was altered and extended under the direction of Thomas Hopper.[13] Wyatt's house was of stone ashlar in the 'Tudor' style, with embattled parapets, square-headed stone-mullioned windows, and octagonal pinnacles at the corners. The principal two-storied block was of three bays at the front and sides, the central bay at the front being carried one story higher. The main doorway at the centre of the south-west front had a four-centred arch; its embattled surround was repeated on the large ground floor windows. Behind was a lower block with a single-storied orangery on the south-east. The rest of the house Hopper either rebuilt or completely altered. He adopted Wyatt's window and parapet details, but in the grouping of its various parts his design is much more picturesque and romantic than that of the earlier building. The principal feature is a large *porte-cochère* tower near the centre of the new entrance front, facing north-west. Its elaborate windows, tall angle turrets, and

[86] *V.C.H. Wilts.* ii, p. 131.
[87] *Cal. Pat.* 1247–58, 18.
[88] G. P. Scrope, *History of Castle Combe*, 158, 220, 316.
[89] *W.A.M.* xxxvi. 441.
[90] C.P. 25(1)/251/17/36; *Rot. Hund.* (Rec. Com.), ii. 278.
[91] *Wilts. Inq. p.m.* 1242–1326 (Index Libr.), 334–6; for his assumption of his mother's surname, instead of Wotton, see *Coll. Top. et Gen.* vi. 155.
[92] *Cal. Close*, 1302–7, 517.
[93] *Coll. Top. et Gen.* vi. 155.
[94] *Cal. Pat.* 1338–40, 352.
[95] C.P. 25(1)/254/44/22.
[96] Scrope, *Castle Combe*, 158.
[97] C 136/248/100.
[98] *Cal. Fine R.* 1383–91, 312; *Cal. Pat.* 1388–92, 467.

[99] C 44/17/9.
[1] C.P. 25(1)/256/58/6.
[2] Or perhaps 3rd; the 2nd may have been Nich. Gervase, who held in 1404: Scrope, *Castle Combe*, 158n.
[3] C.P. 25(1)/257/62/26.
[4] C.P. 25(1)/65/531.
[5] C 142/239/123.
[6] B.M. Add. Ch. 40086.
[7] Longleat MS. 10461.
[8] *Misc. Gen. et Her.* N.S. iii. peds. opp. 46 and 70.
[9] Ibid.; *D.N.B.* 1922–30.
[10] W.A.S. Libr., Devizes, Sale Cat.
[11] *Wilts. Times*, 27 Sept. 1930 and 21 Oct. 1960.
[12] Colvin, *Biog. Dict. Eng. Architects*, 738.
[13] Long MSS. Notes by H. E. Medlicott.

enriched frieze are in contrast to the rest of this elevation, which relies for its effect on variations of frontage and roof line. The south-east elevation is again more highly decorated, having carved stone work, a low tower, a two-storied bay, and clustered chimneys. Inside the house remains of elaborate plasterwork can be seen. Some panelling and other material brought from Whaddon House were used in 1836, after being rescued from the fire there the previous year.[14]

In 1773 the house was surrounded by formal gardens, while to the north-west three small lakes lay in the hollow between the house and the main road. Beyond them a lane parallel to the road joined West Ashton village to Mudmead Lane and so to Steeple Ashton.[15] By 1811 this lane had been diverted so that it only ran from the site of the later Castle Lodge to Mudmead Lane.[16] The park was remodelled in the 1840's. The three lakes were replaced by the larger lake called Stourton Water north of the house, and to make this possible the old lane was closed altogether. Beyond the lake Stourton Farm was demolished, and the small inclosures which covered Stourton Hill were levelled; the top was planted with trees to form a background to the water. The old main entrance to the house had been a drive from the main road, with a lodge half way between the cross-roads and the site of Castle Lodge. This was replaced by a drive further east, which extended across the main road and so through the woods to Trowbridge; it was lined with Scotch firs, the whole being laid out by Sir John Nasmyth. Lodges built at the Trowbridge end and on the Westbury to Melksham road still survive; the latter is called Castle Lodge, consisting of a large square and a small round tower. Another drive to the cross roads at West Ashton probably dates from the building of the church in 1847. The lodge at that entrance was designed by T. H. Wyatt.[17] Rood Ashton Home Farm was probably built about the same time. The previous home farm was apparently north of the road between East Town and West Ashton at the point where it is joined by the lane from Dunge.[18]

What was later called the manor of *WEST ASHTON* consisted in 1340 of two properties. Thomas Langford held of the abbess a house and 2 carucates which later passed to William Don.[19] They were settled on Don and Katharine his wife in 1388,[20] but a few years later Don's brother John complained of the breach of an agreement that he should have the reversion of the estate, for William and Katharine had sold it to William Stourton.[21] Stourton was summoned to do fealty for the lands in 1411.[22] The other part of the later manor was held in 1340 by John Oysel, and consisted of a house and 2 virgates.[23] They passed to John Westbury the elder, who held lands in West Ashton in 1412.[24] In 1449 William Westbury, grandson of John, died holding them.[25] Soon after this the property must have passed to John, Lord Stourton, son of the William Stourton who had bought the Don property. John died in 1462 holding lands in West Ashton;[26] his grandson John, Lord Stourton, held at his death lands there which were said to include the properties formerly of Don and of Westbury.[27] These descended with the title to William, Lord Stourton (d. 1548), who in 1544 conveyed them, then referred to as a manor for the first time, to Thomas Long of Trowbridge, clothier.[28] He died without surviving issue in 1554, leaving most of his property to Edward, third son of his younger brother Henry. Edward subsequently bought the manor of Rood Ashton,[29] and from that time the descent of the two manors was the same. The capital house of West Ashton was probably Stourton Farm, which stood on Stourton Hill until the alterations to Rood Ashton park in the 1840's.

In the early 12th century Hawise, Abbess of Romsey, enfeoffed a knight named Herlewin with a hide of land in Ashton, Edington, and Bradley, and also land which a certain Alric had formerly held at a rent of 10s.[30] Alric was probably one of the abbey's English tenants in 1086.[31] About 1170 Abbess Juliana confirmed these and other lands to Richard, son of Michael, son of Herlewin; they included $\frac{1}{2}$ hide in Semington held freely, $\frac{1}{2}$ hide there held by 10s. a year, $\frac{1}{2}$ hide in Ashton freely, $1\frac{1}{2}$ virgate in Edington freely, and land at Feltham there by a rent of sheep and honey.[32] In the mid-13th century at least some of these lands were held by Peter FitzMichael of Semington, and then by his widow Alice;[33] they granted away some estates in Edington, reserving rents which in 1293 were payable to William of Semington.[34] It seems likely that the Semington lands of this family passed, probably by the marriage of an heiress, to the Tinhead family. John of Tinhead held a yardland in Semington in 1281,[35] but in 1329 a larger estate there, described as a carucate of land, was settled on another John of Tinhead and his wife Margaret. They had a daughter Maud,[36] who may have married as her first husband a Percy of Great Chalfield.[37] In 1340 she was the wife of Robert Selyman, who held the carucate by the old rent of 10s.[38] They had a son Robert who was dead by 1374; in that year John Gore, who had married Robert's widow Emma, claimed to hold the lands for her life.[39] What happened to them after her death is not clear, but

[14] Long MSS. and sketches of the house; W.A.S. Libr., Devizes, Sketch by John Britton; Soc. Antiq. Jackson MSS. Sketch, and see pl. facing p. 201.
[15] *Andrews and Dury, Map* (W.A.S. Rec. Brch.), pl. 7.
[16] O.S. Map 1″, sheet 14 (1st edn.).
[17] Long MSS. Notes by H. E. Medlicott and Map 1843.
[18] W.R.O. Inclosure and Tithe Awards.
[19] S.C. 12/699.
[20] C.P. 25(1)/256/55/43.
[21] C 1/68/84.
[22] S.C. 2/208/3 m. 4; *Cal. Close*, 1413–9, 139.
[23] S.C. 12/699.
[24] *Feud. Aids*, vi. 540.
[25] Hoare, *Mod. Wilts.* Westbury, 17.

[26] *Cal. Close*, 1461–8, 125.
[27] S.C. 2/208/6 m. 13; *Complete Peerage*.
[28] C 54/435 no. 59.
[29] *Cal. Pat.* 1560–63, 599.
[30] B.M. Lansd. MS. 442, f. 61v.
[31] *V.C.H. Wilts.* ii, p. 131.
[32] B.M. Lansd. MS. 442, f. 61 v.
[33] Ibid. f. 62–62v.
[34] Ibid. f. 63.
[35] *Feet of F.* 1272–1327 (W.A.S. Rec. Brch.), 16.
[36] C.P. 25(1)/254/40/27.
[37] B.M. Lansd. MS. 442, f. 74.
[38] S.C. 12/699; see below, p. 241.
[39] S.C. 2/208/2 mm. 4, 7.

in the middle of the 15th century lands formerly occupied by Robert Selyman and later by Emmot Percy were held by Robert Long.[40] This Robert Long, the first known member of the family who possessed Wraxall,[41] held at that time another estate in Semington, which had belonged to John of Lilleshulle in 1340,[42] and afterwards to John Gore.[43] These two properties, first called the manor of *SEMINGTON* in 1522,[44] descended in the Long family as did Wraxall to Sir Robert Long, who succeeded his father Sir Henry in 1556.[45] In the following year he renewed a lease of the manor to Thomas Long, farmer of Semington, who already held it for life.[46] At an unknown date, before 1591,[47] the freehold was sold to the Brouncker family, lords of the manor of Melksham. In 1598 Henry Brouncker sold the manor house of Semington and a considerable amount of land there to John Lowe of Orcheston St. Mary.[48] At Lowe's death in 1632 this property was described as the mansion house and farm of Semington; he had since bought two other properties there which had belonged to Thomas Long and Robert Flower.[49] The whole estate, usually still referred to as the manor of Semington, descended to Lawrence Lowe, on whom it was settled when he married Lucy, daughter of Thomas Pile of Baverstock, in 1679. He apparently left no issue, for in 1689 his widow joined with Thomas Chaffin, Edward Lowe, and Robert Hyde in releasing his estates to Thomas Freke and Thomas Pile. Freke died without issue in 1698, leaving his estates to Pile and to Elizabeth, wife of Thomas Freke of Hannington, for their lives, with remainder to George Pitt of Stratfield Saye (Hants), who had married Lucy, Lawrence Lowe's widow. The life interests terminated in 1714,[50] and the manor descended from George Pitt to his grandson George, Baron Rivers (d. 1803), who held it in 1780. By 1800 it had been sold to the Duke of Somerset.[51] In 1838 the Somerset estate consisted chiefly of Manor Farm, Church Farm, and Littleton Wood Mill Farm, in all about 350 a.[52] It has remained the property of the dukes of Somerset until the present century.[53]

Manor Farm, which may have been the capital house of the manor, is probably basically of the 16th century. It has been considerably altered, but has one 16th-century window on the south side.

LESSER ESTATES. In 1086 William Scudet, one of the king's cooks, held a hide of land in Steeple Ashton of the Abbess of Romsey.[54] It seems likely

that his descendants took their surname from his occupation. Edwin *cocus* lived *c.* 1130, and Crispin *cocus* late in the 12th century.[55] The name also appears as le Keu. In the late 13th century Richard le Keu granted to his brother William lands in West Ashton which had formerly belonged to Richard their father and subsequently to Roger, their brother.[56] It was perhaps the same estate which in 1285 Richard le Keu and Sybil his wife conveyed in reversion after their deaths to Margaret, daughter of Roger le Porter of Shaftesbury. It was then described as 2 virgates in 'Rodeschawe'. Margaret's heir was her brother Roger,[57] who in 1306 conveyed 1½ virgate in West Ashton to Robert of Wilmington, clerk.[58]

Robert of Wilmington acquired several other estates in the district. One of them lay at 'Hurdecote's Ashton', and had previously been held by the Sauser family. In the early 13th century Thomas of Hurdecote granted a half-virgate of his fee of Ashton to Henry le Sauser.[59] Henry was apparently the father of another Henry, who granted the half-virgate to his brother Roger, and on another occasion, gave him land at 'Middle Ashton', which had also been held of the Abbess of Romsey by Henry the father.[60] This or another Roger le Sauser was a free-tenant of John Biset, successor of Thomas of Hurdecote in the manor of Rood Ashton, in 1307.[61] Two years later he conveyed 2½ virgates in 'Gyldene Ashton' and 'Hurdecote's Ashton' to Robert of Wilmington.[62] Robert acquired by 1314 1½ virgates in West Ashton and 'La Stone' which had once been held by the Bythewood family.[63] At an unknown date he also obtained a small property in West Ashton from Walter of Wyke.[64]

Robert of Wilmington, who was Rector of Donhead St. Andrew from 1304 to 1321,[65] seems to have had some connexion with Bradford, and settled his property on two of the children of a certain Beatrice Sulleve of that place. They were no doubt his own children, for one of them, called John of Wilmington, obtained a dispensation on account of his illegitimacy and became a priest.[66] Most, if not all, of the lands passed to John's sister Agnes, who married William of Whitecliff in Brixton Deverill.[67] In 1340 William was said to hold two properties, each of two virgates in West Ashton.[68] He was dead by 1358, leaving two or more daughters and coheirs. In 1386 one of these, Margaret, conveyed her share of the lands in West Ashton to William Lyveden and his wife Agnes, who was probably a daughter of one of Margaret's

[40] S.C. 12/16/65; Emmot Percy was daughter of Sir Roger Percy of Great Chalfield: *Tropenell Cart.* ed. Davies, i, pedigree opp. 272; she held the land in 1413: S.C. 2/208/4 m. 1.
[41] Burke, *Commoners* (1833–8), iii. 212.
[42] S.C. 12/699.
[43] S.C. 12/4/3; S.C. 12/16/65.
[44] *W.N. & Q.* ii. 421.
[45] C 142/110/167.
[46] W.R.O. 8, Cartulary; this was evidently Thomas (d. 1593), eldest son of Henry Long of Whaddon (d. 1558).
[47] Longleat MS. 10461.
[48] W.R.O. 8, Cartulary.
[49] Ibid.; *Wilts. Inq. p.m.* 1625–49 (Index Libr.), 326–9.
[50] *V.C.H. Hants*, iii. 414, iv. 22; Hutchins, *Hist. Dors.* iv. 89; Berry, *Hants Genealogies*, 101. It is possible that Freke's interest was as a trustee for Lucy Lowe.
[51] W.R.O. Land Tax Assessments.

[52] Ibid. Tithe Award.
[53] *Kelly's Dir. Wilts.* (1939).
[54] *V.C.H. Wilts.* ii, pp. 73, 131.
[55] B.M. Lansd. MS. 442, ff. 55, 61v.
[56] *W.A.M.* xxxvi. 444.
[57] Ibid. 443–4.
[58] *Feet of F. Wilts.* 1272–1327 (W.A.S. Rec. Brch.), 55.
[59] *W.A.M.* xxxvi. 441.
[60] Ibid. 442.
[61] *Wilts. Inq. p.m.* 1242–1326 (Index Libr.), 335; see above, p. 203.
[62] *Feet of F. Wilts.* 1272–1327 (W.A.S. Rec. Brch.), 75.
[63] Ibid. 89; S.C. 12/699.
[64] *W.A.M.* xxxvii. 4.
[65] Phillipps, *Wilts. Inst.* i. 6, 18.
[66] Emden, *Biog. Reg. Oxon.* 2051.
[67] *W.A.M.* xxxvi. 441, xxxvii. 6, 11.
[68] S.C. 12/699.

sisters.[69] Another coheir, Lettice, married Thomas Ward, and in 1390 granted a life estate in her share of lands in West Ashton to her son John.[70] In some unexplained way this share of the Ward family evidently passed to the Lyveden family. In 1445 John Lyveden conveyed his lands in West Ashton and 'Rodshaw' to feoffees.[71] In 1476 he settled lands there on his daughter and heir Margaret when she married Nicholas, second son of Sir Nicholas St. Lo.[72] John Lyveden died c. 1502, and Nicholas St. Lo succeeded him.[73] His estate was only for life, however, for Margaret was long since dead,[74] presumably without issue, and on his death the estate reverted to John Westley, who had succeeded to John Lyveden's estates in Whitecliff and elsewhere. He held the West Ashton property in 1511,[75] and it descended to his grandson, Leonard Westley, who died in 1562. At his death the West Ashton property was held by Anne Tichebourn, widow, for her life but the reason for this is not clear.[76] Leonard's son Thomas held a house and 160 a. of land in West Ashton at his death in 1621.[77] By 1642 Samuel Martyn held lands in East Town and West Ashton which he had bought of another Thomas Westley.[78]

Although the names of 'Sauser's', 'Gyldene' and 'Hurdecote's Ashton', 'Rodshaw', and 'La Stone' are all lost, there can be little doubt that the estate which Robert of Wilmington built up in the early 14th century represents the present East Town Farm. This is indeed indicated by the use of the form Sauser's Ashton *alias* East Town in 1614.[79] The Martyn family held the property well into the 18th century.[80] By 1780 it had passed, probably by sale to Gaisford Gibbs, and it descended in the same way as Heywood House to the Ludlow family.[81] About 1844 it was conveyed to the Longs of Rood Ashton in exchange for Fulling Bridge Farm in Heywood.[82] The house at East Town is a 17th-century building of stone rubble.

Robert Stileman was a leaseholder under the Abbess of Romsey in 1478,[83] and he and his son Anthony were bailiffs of the manor.[84] In 1500 the abbess granted two houses, about 80 a. of land, and various meadows and pastures to Anthony Stileman in fee.[85] Parts of this property remained in the family for almost 350 years. Anthony's son Richard was dead by 1561; Richard's son Anthony had a son John on whom the estate was settled in 1582. John died in 1601 leaving a son Anthony,[86] who was perhaps father of the John who died in 1649.

His son John died in 1691, and was succeeded by another John.[87] By 1699 some of the family lands had been sold, for John Stileman paid only part of the original chief rent charged on the premises in 1500.[88] He died in 1713, his widow Christian surviving him until 1765.[89] From there the descent is not clear, but some lands remained in the family until the death of Dr. William Stillman in 1843. His sons sold them to Walter Long and emigrated to Australia.[90] The home of the family was the house now called Ashton House, which is described above.[91]

In 1524 John Loveday of Melksham bought a virgate of land in West Ashton from Walter Ballard of Hilperton.[92] Loveday sold it in 1545 to Henry Brouncker.[93] Brouncker also bought lands in West Ashton which had been customary holdings of the manor, and had been granted in 1553 to Sir William Sharington and Richard Roberts.[94] His grandson Henry Brouncker sold them to Tristram Flower, who died in 1604 holding 3 virgates in West Ashton.[95] Later in the 17th century these lands passed to the Beach family by the marriage of Robert Beach and Grace Flower. Their son Thomas died in 1729, and was succeeded in turn by his son and grandson, both of the same name.[96] In 1763 the latter held a house and about 100 a. of land.[97] After his death in 1774 the estate appears to have been broken up; most of it probably passed to the Longs. The house stood at the top of West Ashton Hill.[98]

ECONOMIC HISTORY. When the bounds of the manor of Ashton were set forth by King Edgar in 964,[99] the estate included the whole of the ancient parish of Steeple Ashton and also North Bradley and Southwick. The furthest points to the west were thus about 6 miles from the village of Steeple Ashton, near the Somerset border north of Rode, where Romsey Oak Farm still recalls the connexion. In 1086 the manor was assessed at 40 hides, of which tenants of the abbess held eight.[1] By 1340 the number of freeholders under the abbess was 28, who paid rents totalling about £15. Their properties lay chiefly in Southwick and West Ashton, although some land nearer Steeple Ashton itself had also been granted out.[2] By c. 1540 the free rents had increased to almost £20, largely owing to a rent of £4 6s. 8d. from the lands granted to the Stileman family.[3] In 1553 the free rents from holdings in Semington were included in the property

[69] *W.A.M.* xxxvii. 9.
[70] Ibid. 10.
[71] Ibid. 13.
[72] Ibid. 15.
[73] S.C. 2/208/6 mm. 13, 16.
[74] His (second) wife Maud died in 1449: *Wilts. Visitation Pedigrees*, 1623 (Harl. Soc.), 170.
[75] *W.A.M.* xxxvii. 19.
[76] Ibid. 33.
[77] Ibid. 35.
[78] Long MSS. Deed Sarah Martyn to Anthony Martyn, 7 Nov. 1650.
[79] C 142/517/104.
[80] See p. 217.
[81] W.R.O. Land Tax Assessments. For possible intermediate owners, see *W.N. & Q.* iii. 407 and Baker, *Northants.* i 495; see also p. 163.
[82] Long. MSS. Rental, 1844.
[83] E 326/4679.
[84] S.C. 2/208/6 m. 5.

[85] *Cal. Pat.* 1494–1509, 201.
[86] C 3/163/46; C 142/267/87; *Genealogist*, N.S. xiii. 24.
[87] Phillipps, *M.I. Wilts.*; P.C.C. 30 Pembroke; C 54/4922 no. 9.
[88] Long MSS. Rental, 1699.
[89] Phillipps, *M.I. Wilts.*
[90] Long MSS. Rental, 1844; ex inf. Mr. G. H. Stillman of Claremont, W. Australia.
[91] See p. 200.
[92] W.R.O. 212B, St. A. 1b.
[93] Ibid. 2.
[94] *Cal. Pat.* 1553, 164.
[95] *Wilts. Inq. p.m.* 1625–49 (Index Libr.), 273.
[96] Soc. Antiq. Jackson MSS.
[97] W.R.O. 212A, Deed Glover and Beach to Sturt.
[98] Soc. Antiq. Jackson MSS.; Aubrey, *Topog. Coll.* ed. Jackson, 354; W.R.O. Land Tax Assessments.
[99] See p. 202.
[1] *V.C.H. Wilts.* ii, p. 131.
[2] S.C. 12/699.
[3] S.C. 12/4/2.

granted away to Sir William Sharington,[4] but in 1775 rents amounting to over £18 were still being collected from free tenants.[5]

In 1086 40 villeins and 30 bordars held land for 20 ploughs. A rental and custumal of 1340[6] lists bond tenants of the abbess in all parts of the ancient manor except North Bradley, which was by this time reckoned a part of Edington manor.[7] Apart from cottagers and holders of a few acres, there were 71 bond tenants holding ½ virgate or more, few holdings being of more than one virgate. They held a total of 62½ virgates, of which 6½ lay in Southwick, 13 in West Ashton, 17 in Hinton, 8 in Littleton, 4½ in Semington, and 13½ in Steeple Ashton. In Steeple Ashton there were in addition 27 holders of ¼ virgates who were called acremen and who served the offices of oxherd, shepherd, and swineherd. The works demanded of the bond tenants for the demesne embraced the whole range of agricultural pursuits, and also carrying goods, and driving sheep to Romsey.

The demesne land of the manor appears to have been in Steeple Ashton only in 1340. The names or number of the common fields at this time have not survived, but furlong names such as Mudmead Furlong, Loppinger, Cranhill, and Morefurlong indicate that they probably lay north-west, south-west, and south-east of the village. Meadowland lay at Ashton Northmead, north of the present Dairyhouse Farm, and Daddlesmore, later Dodsmead, between the present Biss and Green Lane Woods.[8] Pasture for oxen lay at Albury, north of East Town, and Raydown, on the southern boundary of the parish.

The Biset property in West Ashton, which was later to be called the manor of Rood Ashton, had in 1307 a demesne of 80 a. arable, 3½ a. meadow, and 4 a. several pasture. Four customary tenants held ½ virgates and a number of others had smaller holdings.[9] In contrast to the main manor, the works of the ½-virgaters were completely commuted and those of the cottagers amounted only to being messengers for the lord four or five times a year and carrying hay a half-day a year. Deeds of the 13th century mention North, East, South, and Town fields in West Ashton.[10] Furlongs called 'Hameracrestyghele'[11] and 'la Smytheswell' indicate that Northfield lay near Stourton Hill, and 'la Witelond' and 'Cranhulle' that East Field lay south of East Town farm.[12] 'Upper Cranhulle' lay in South Field, which may have been between West Ashton and Dunge. It is possible that Town Field was one of the Steeple Ashton fields.

It is not easy to trace the course of agricultural change in Steeple Ashton in the later Middle Ages. There are a few indications of the increasing importance of sheep. In the early 1370's numbers of murrained sheep were presented at the manor court, and in 1374 William Trowbridge had overstocked the commons with sheep from outside.[13] By the end of the next century overstocking was constantly presented. In 1499 William Passion had 300 sheep at Hinton, and William Long of Trowbridge 1,000 at West Ashton where he had no common.[14] By 1414 many of the works of the customary tenants must have been commuted, for over £6 was received for them.[15] The demesne, however, was still in hand then. A mid-15th century rental[16] shows that a number of customary tenants held an acre or two of demesne arable or meadow, but it is not certain when the demesne entirely ceased to be farmed by the nuns; the first known lease of the site of the manor was in 1537 to Robert Temmes for 42 years.[17] Five tenants of Steeple Ashton were presented in 1493 for inclosing lands in the East Field, Moor Field and Standle Field with hedges and ditches.[18]

By the mid-16th century[19] a few of the principal inhabitants were each holding several small tenements on leases for long terms of years. Apart from these, a large number of small copyholders, mostly of a virgate or under, in all parts of the manor held their lands for lives by rents only. Some holdings had a few acres added to them, sometimes demesne land, but there is little evidence of any extensive consolidation of holdings, nor of much inclosure in any part of the manor except Southwick. A large proportion of the land was open-field arable; this was particularly preponderant in Steeple Ashton and Hinton, where little meadow or pasture and few inclosed grounds existed. Arable in Steeple Ashton lay in East Field, North Field, Standle Field, Loppinger Field, Windmill Field, and Moor Field. Of these, East Field and Moor Field lay east of the village near Spiers Piece Farm, Windmill Field probably near Mudmead Lane,[20] and Loppinger Field near the farm of that name. Standle Field probably lay west or south west of the village. The fields of Hinton were Middle Field, Crowcheyate Field, and Windmill Field. The latter lay west of the village north of Coldharbour.[21] At Semington there were Down Field, west of the village, Middle Field, and South Field between the Hilperton road and Hag Hill. At Littleton arable lay in Holbrook Field, Jacketts Field, East Field, and Down Field, and at West Ashton in Culverford Field, Cranhill Field, and Sandfield. Culverford Field lay near Stourton Hill and Cranhill Field south of East Town, corresponding to the North and East Fields of the 13th century.

The demesnes of Steeple Ashton were held in hand by Lord Seymour when he owned the manor. They consisted of the house, a close of 6 a., 66 a. of meadow at Ashton More, Northmead, and Dodsmead, 181½ a. of arable land in the common fields, and various rights of pasture.[22] After the demesnes

[4] See below.
[5] Long MSS. Estate Account Bk. 1775.
[6] S.C. 12/699.
[7] See p. 218.
[8] S.C. 2/208/9 m. 4.
[9] Wilts. Inq. p.m. 1242–1327 (Index Libr.), 334–6.
[10] W.A.M. xxxvii. 4.
[11] S.C. 12/699.
[12] W.R.O. Tithe Award gives field names Cranhill and Whitelands.
[13] S.C. 2/208/2 mm. 2d., 4d., 5d., 6.

[14] S.C. 2/208/6 mm. 8, 9.
[15] G. D. Liveing, Records of Romsey Abbey, 194.
[16] S.C. 12/16/65.
[17] S.C. 12/4/2. An (earlier) lease to 'one Addams' is mentioned in E 178/4697.
[18] S.C. 2/208/6 m. 3.
[19] This paragraph is mainly based on two surveys, S.C. 12/4/2 (c. 1540) and L.R. 2/191 (c. 1550).
[20] In 1841 Windmill Furlong lay east of Mudmead Lane near Stourton Plantation: W.R.O. Tithe Award.
[21] Windmill Fields: ibid.　　　[22] L.R. 2/191, f.156.

were alienated to the Marquess of Winchester in 1551, the common rights of the customary tenants in the meadows and the common pastures were the subject of protracted disputes. Eight tenants called 'neatholders' had winter pasture for oxen or sheep in Northmead, which contained 40 a., and all the tenants who held land there had winter common in the 60 a. of Dodsmead. The common pastures lay at Albury, Raydown, and Laydown, and contained in all over 200 a.[23] The rights of pasture which the various tenants and the farmer enjoyed in them for oxen and other beasts at various times of the year were governed by complex customs. Disputes were about such points as whether the owner of the demesnes had unlimited common, whether he could put cattle in instead of horses, and whether he could inclose any of the commons. In 1604 all the customary tenants prosecuted John Greenhill, the new owner of the farm, in the Exchequer, and alleged that their customs were necessary to their tillage, and that if Greenhill succeeded in putting them out of their commons, his farm would be £100 a year more valuable. When he was taxed with inclosing 12 a. out of Dodsmead, Greenhill retorted that the customary tenants had recently much improved their holdings by inclosures out of the common fields, and so wintered many more cattle than formerly. Another witness on his behalf estimated that 60 a. of meadow and 500 a. of arable had been inclosed in the past 50 years.[24]

Other disputes also occurred about the woods of the manor and the timber standing in the commons. These were evidently very valuable adjuncts of the manor. In 1604 it was estimated that the woods in West Ashton, Yarnbrook, and Broker's Wood in Southwick covered 450 a., and that there were almost 8,000 trees besides standing in the wastes.[25] The Marquess of Winchester claimed in 1574 that the woods belonged to the demesnes,[26] and ten years later claimed the strays found in the woods and commons.[27] These claims failed, for in 1583 the woods were let for 21 years to Edward Langford of Trowbridge and Richard Spencer of Steeple Ashton. They assigned the lease to the Brounckers of Erlestoke in 1585.[28] In 1596 it was assigned to Edmund Dowse and subsequently renewed to him.[29] By 1610 it had passed to Roger Martyn. Many trees had been felled and others spoilt by continuous lopping, but it was estimated that with careful restocking the woods would be worth £300 a year to the Crown.[30] They were, however, sold with the manor, and in 1636 Walter Long, the new lord, prosecuted Henry Martyn and Edward Martyn for waste in Broker's Wood.[31]

The process of consolidation of holdings and inclosure of the common fields, which had begun in the later 16th century, continued in the 17th. Leases refer continually to newly inclosed grounds and to several acres of arable lying together in the Steeple Ashton fields, although a considerable amount still lay dispersed.[32] Semington, too, was fairly extensively inclosed by the end of the 16th century.[33] The capital manor was by this time confined, except for woods and commons, to the tithings of Hinton and Steeple Ashton, the outlying copyhold lands having been granted separately by the Crown.[34] The process of consolidation of holdings into large farms was apparently slow, and there was no rack leasing in the 17th century. In 1699 106 copy and leaseholders in Steeple Ashton and Hinton produced a regular income which amounted to under £36 a year,[35] although large fines were no doubt paid at entry. In 1775 the copyhold and leasehold rents were just over £50, and two holdings let on rack leases produced £105 a year.[36] Some compact and fairly large inclosed farms not part of the manorial lands appear in the 17th and 18th centuries. In 1674 Dairyhouse Farm consisted of 60 a. of inclosed meadow and pasture and 15 a. of open-field arable, but the latter was disposed of by 1723, leaving a compact holding around the farmhouse.[37] Ashton Mill Farm consisted of about 45 a. of inclosed land in 1700.[38] Pasture land which had been inclosed at Crosswelldown by 1620[39] formed the nucleus of the farm of that name which in the 18th century was owned by the Ballard family.[40] At Littleton Nicholas Flower owned in 1632 a farm which contained 68 a. of inclosed land and only 7 a. in the open fields.[41] Paxcroft Farm, the property of the Duke of Kingston, was leased at a rent of £80 a year in 1731.[42] Of the 100 acres of the Beach property in West Ashton in 1763, all but 7 were inclosed.[43] Part of Hag Hill was inclosed by 1762.[44] Littleton Wood Farm consisted of over 60 acres, all inclosed, in 1788.[45]

Steeple Ashton was inclosed under an Act of Parliament passed in 1813.[46] The results of over two centuries of piecemeal inclosure, of which indications have been given above, are evident from the award maps. No common fields remained at Littleton, and at Semington only two small areas of open-field arable near the Hilperton road, and some common meadow near the Brook were left. Hinton too was almost fully inclosed, only a few acres of arable south of the village and Hinton Mead to the north remaining. In Steeple Ashton, however, considerable areas of the open fields remained uninclosed. Three of these then existed: High Field

---

[23] These were inclosed common pastures, which were 'hained' yearly, i.e. no stock was allowed in them while the grass grew, and afterwards numbers of animals and duration of pasture were regulated. They were distinct from the common, which was not hained and where grazing rights were unstinted.

[24] E 178/4697, which contains lengthy and detailed depositions. A court book of this period (Longleat MS. 10461) records a number of exchanges.

[25] E 178/4697.

[26] E 134/16 Eliz. I/Trin. 6.

[27] E 134/25 Eliz. I/Trin. 4.

[28] L.R. 14/612, 804; E 178/4599.

[29] E 178/4599; Cal. S.P. Dom. 1595–7, 445.

[30] B.M. Add. MS. 6027, f.130; E 178/4718.

[31] E 134/12 Chas. I/Trin. 5.

[32] W.R.O. 212A, Steeple Ashton Leases.

[33] W.R.O. 8, Deed Brouncker to Lowe, 1598.

[34] Cal. Pat. 1553, 164.

[35] Long MSS. Rental 1699.

[36] Ibid. Account Bk. 1775.

[37] W.R.O. 130, Deeds Seaman and others to Bisse, 1674; Blagden and others to Edwards, 1723; Map 1799.

[38] Long MSS. Deed Gilbert to Axford, 1700.

[39] C 142/379/71.

[40] W.N. & Q. iii. 530.

[41] Wilts. Inq. p.m. 1625–49 (Index Libr.), 197.

[42] Nottingham Univ. Libr., Manvers Coll., Rental 1731.

[43] W.R.O. 212A, Deed Glover and Beach to Sturt, 1763.

[44] W.R.O. 212A, Lease Long to Hancock, 1762.

[45] W.R.O. 248, Map 1788.

[46] 53 Geo. III, c. 96 (local and personal Act).

lay between Mudmead Lane and Sandpits Lane, Middle Field south of the village on both sides of Acreshort Lane, and Moor Field east of the Edington road. The common pastures of the Steeple Ashton tenants were also inclosed at this time, at Albury, Raydown, and Laydown,[47] and the remaining common meadow at Dodmsead. Finally Steeple Ashton, Hinton, and Littleton Wood Commons were inclosed. Steeple Ashton and Hinton Commons covered most of the low ground in the tithings of West Ashton, Steeple Ashton, and Hinton, extending from Kettle Lane on the Heywood boundary in a crescent shape to Stranger's Corner near Hinton. Only a little of this large expanse had been affected by earlier inclosure. Some meadow had been inclosed along the Biss and Paxcroft Brook, and encroachments extended from the higher ground to the lower at Armouracre and Snarlton. A number of inclosures had also been made on the southern slope of Hag Hill. Littleton Wood Common lay in the bend of the Semington Brook in the north-east corner of the parish. The southern part of Steeple Ashton Common was mainly woodland, estimated at over 500 acres in 1807.[48]

After inclosure farming in the parish began to assume its modern aspect. New farms were built in the inclosed lands at Spiers Piece, Newgrounds, Raydon, Brook, and Green Lane, and old farms were let on short leases at improved rents. By 1844 eight farms on the Long estate in the parish let for over £100 a year, the highest being Steeple Ashton Manor Farm at £670.[49] But some of the Long farms were still held on leases for lives at this time. The estate in 1841 comprised over 3,500 acres, somewhat more than half of the ancient parish. The next largest estates were the Ludlow's 650 acres in West Ashton,[50] the Duke of Somerset's 340 in Semington, and G. T. Chamberlaine's 150 in Littleton and Hinton. At this time arable totalled just over 30 per cent. of the total area of the parish, and pasture and meadow over 55 per cent. The former was most preponderant, as would be expected, on the higher ground, varying from about 42 per cent. in Steeple Ashton to only 16 per cent. at Semington.[51] By 1870 rents had risen considerably. Eight of the Long farms let for over £400 a year each, East Town making £910 a year and Spier's Piece £800. Their 13 largest farms in the parish produced over £5,400 a year.[52]

When Leland visited Steeple Ashton c. 1540 he remarked that 'it standithe muche by clothiars' and named two, Robert Long and Walter Lucas, who had assisted in the building of the parish church.[53] These two men flourished c. 1500, but no evidence has been found of any cloth industry at Steeple Ashton much before that time. Beside these two, the names of a few clothiers of the early and mid-

16th century are known. William Alcombe (d. c. 1513),[54] had been an associate of James Terumber, the rich Trowbridge clothier.[55] John Reynold held land in Steeple Ashton c. 1540,[56] and three members of the White family, George, Robert, and William, were fined for defective white cloths in 1561.[57] That Long and Lucas were prosperous men is shown by their works at the church and by Lucas's will,[58] and in 1545 Robert White, although not quite in the first rank of local clothiers, paid more tax than anyone else in the tithing.[59] But the period of prosperity was short, and apparently centred on a few men, who left no successors in a village which, with its lack of water power, offered no attractions to clothiers. Even before 1514 Walter Lucas had had to entice his son back from Bradford with a promise of his household goods.[60] Walter and Thomas, sons of Robert Long, moved to Trowbridge.[61] By 1576 only two men known to have been clothiers paid tax in Steeple Ashton, George White, who had apparently bought land, and William White, and neither was particularly prosperous.[62] Although spinning and weaving for the Trowbridge and Westbury clothiers no doubt continued there until the introduction of power machinery, the brief era of the clothiers of Steeple Ashton was practically over by 1600. After that date only two have been met with, Peter Crook (fl. c. 1633) and William Tipper (d. before 1700).[63]

The cloth industry's first known appearance at Littleton is also associated with Robert Long of Steeple Ashton, who in 1494 leased a fulling mill there of the Abbess of Romsey. The lease subsequently came into the possession of Anthony Passion, no doubt a member of a family that had held the mill before Long.[64] Although he held the mill, and leased or owned a good deal of land in Steeple Ashton and Littleton,[65] he too seems to have found it more convenient to carry on his business from Trowbridge,[66] where in 1545 he paid £7 in tax, a sum exceeded by only nine payers in the whole county.[67] In the 17th century the mill was occupied by successive clothiers of the Somner family of Littleton as a fulling mill.[68] Another clothier of Littleton in the early 17th century was Nicholas Flower,[69] who at his death in 1632 owned a considerable landed estate in Littleton and Melksham.[70] No evidence about the use of Littleton Mill for the cloth trade in the 18th century has been met with, although there is every probability that it was used as a fulling mill by clothiers from Trowbridge or Melksham. By about 1800 it was occupied by Francis Naish, a Trowbridge clothier. Soon afterwards, because he had introduced gig mills and shearing frames into it, the mill was destroyed by the Trowbridge shearmen.[71] There is no subsequent record of the cloth trade in Littleton.

47 See above, n. 23.
48 Long MSS. List of woods in hand, 1807.
49 Ibid. Rental, 1844.
50 Including the large farm at East Town, which belonged to the Longs by 1844.
51 W.R.O. Tithe Award.
52 Long MSS. Rental 1870.
53 Leland, *Itin.* ed. Toulmin Smith, i. 83.
54 C 1/881/13.
55 *W.A.M.* x. 247.
56 S.C. 12/4/2.
57 E 350/329.
58 *V.C.H. Wilts.* iv. 137.

59 *Taxation Lists* (W.A.S. Rec. Brch.), 34.
60 *V.C.H. Wilts.* iv. 137.
61 Ibid. vii. 137.
62 *Taxation Lists* (W.A.S. Rec. Brch.), 138.
63 *W.N. & Q.* vii. 37; W.R.O. 212A, Deed Tipper to Long, 1704.   64 C 3/168/64.
65 S.C. 12/4/2; *Cal. Pat.* 1553, 164.
66 *V.C.H. Wilts.* iv. 140.
67 *Taxation Lists* (W.A.S. Rec. Brch.), 33.
68 See p. 210.
69 *Genealogist*, N.S. xxvi. 232.
70 *Wilts. Inq. p.m.* 1625–49 (Index Libr.), 197–9.
71 *V.C.H. Wilts.* vii. 139.

Occasional references to clothiers at Semington have been found. William Witcom was fined for defective white cloth in 1562.[72] Daniel Somner (d. *c.* 1604) was a clothier of Semington,[73] and so was Henry Coulthurst (fl. *c.* 1710).[74] Here, too, spinning and weaving must have been carried on as a domestic occupation until the 19th century. Although no reference to the cloth trade in Great Hinton has been found, there is in the village a small factory building, dated 1815, adjoining the New Inn. It is of brick, of five bays and three stories with a mansard roof, and has the segmental-headed windows with stone mullions typical of mills in the neighbouring towns. It is named as a factory in 1841,[75] when it was owned and occupied by Stephen Sims, and the tradition that it was used for the making of cloth survives in the village.

Two limekilns once existed in Steeple Ashton. One lay near Mudmead Lane,[76] and the other south of the village east of the Edington road, where the quarries are still visible.[77]

MARKET AND FAIR. In 1266 Henry III granted to the nuns of Romsey a weekly market on Wednesday in their manor of Ashton, and a yearly fair there on 7, 8, and 9 September.[78] Two years later Richard de la Rokele complained that his market at Market Lavington, also held on Wednesday, had gone down £40 in value because of the abbess's market at Church Ashton. The abbess blandly replied that she had no vill of that name,[79] and the charter was confirmed by several kings, the last known confirmation being in 1537.[80] In 1410 two shops, several stalls and the tolls were held by William Whatden.[81] In the mid-15th century the tolls and stallage of the market were still farmed out; there was no certain return, but in the year to which the record referred, it was worth 8*d.*[82] A detailed rental of a century later[83] does not mention a market or fair. Aubrey attributed the decline of the market to a fire in the town, and said that the market at Lavington had prospered owing to the decay of Ashton.[84] Two attempts were made to revive the market in the 18th century. In 1756 it was announced that it was 'to be continued for ever for all sorts of corn, grain, cattle, meat, fowls and all sorts of provisions'. In 1766 the promoters reminded the public of the penalties against forestalling and ingrossing corn, and also assured it that the roads to Steeple Ashton were repaired, but all in vain.[85] The fair was still being held in 1625, when its suspension for that year was ordered to prevent the spread of plague.[86] In 1770 it

was held on 2 September for the sale of cheese,[87] and in 1831, when it was said to be inconsiderable, it was held on 18 September.[88]

The market 'cross' stands on the village green. It consists of a stepped base surmounted by a short circular column, which is crowned by a square stone block with a sundial on each face and a ball finial with wrought iron cross over. The date 1679 is carved on it and an inscription states that it was set up in 1071. The structure as it stands is probably of the late 17th century.[89]

MILLS. There were three mills within the manor of Steeple Ashton in 1086.[90] In 1340 there were also three,[91] at Bradley, Littleton, and 'La Lese'.[92] The mill at Littleton was a copyhold of the manor. It was held in 1340 by Thomas Shepherd and called Stikeberd's Mill from a former tenant.[93] A hundred years later the mill was held by Christine Passion.[94] In 1494 the abbess let the mill to Robert Long for 95 years, but he later assigned his lease to Anthony Passion. Anthony Passion settled it on his wife Edith, who married George Drinkwater as her second husband, and a succession of disputes followed between Drinkwater and William Passion, Anthony's son. After William's death the dispute was carried on by John Wychewell and Simon Sloper, successively husbands of his widow Marion.[95] Meanwhile the freehold of the mill, and of certain lands near it, had been granted away by the Crown in 1551 to Sir Thomas Wrothe.[96] By 1604 it belonged to Thomas Somner who at his death, in 1631, left the mills called Passion's Mills and various lands in Littleton to his brother Edward.[97] The mill was described as a fulling and grist mill in the 16th century,[98] and Thomas Somner as a clothier *c.* 1608.[99] In 1652 the mill, described as 2 fulling mills and a grist mill under one roof, and some 44 a. of land, were settled on Edward's son Thomas when he married Agnes Blagden. Thomas died *c.* 1668; in 1678 his son Thomas married Anne, daughter of Christopher Bennett of Steeple Ashton. At his death without issue in 1699 he left the mill and land to Thomas Somner Hippesley, son of his sister Joan by Robert Hippesley of Wanborough. Hippesley died without issue in 1731, leaving as heir Richard Goddard of Swindon, who only survived him a year. Leaving no issue, Goddard was succeeded by his brother Pleydell, who also died childless in 1742.[1] He is the last member of the family known to have held the mill; by 1780 it belonged to Ambrose Awdry of Seend, a member

[72] E 350/329.
[73] P.C.C. 24 Harte.
[74] *W.N. & Q.* vi. 8.
[75] W.R.O. Tithe Award.
[76] Ibid.
[77] O.S. Map 1/2,500 Wilts. XXXIX. 9, 10 (1st edn.).
[78] *Cal. Chart. R.* 1300–26, 128, an inspeximus of 1309: the original enrolment has not survived.
[79] J.I. 1/998 m. 10 d.
[80] C 66/675 m. 22.
[81] S.C. 2/208/3 m. 1.
[82] S.C. 12/16/65.
[83] L.R. 2/191.
[84] Aubrey, *Nat. Hist. Wilts.* ed. Britton, 115.
[85] *W.A.M.* xxxii. 184.
[86] *Acts of P.C.* 1625–6, 127.
[87] *Traveller's Pocket Book* (1770), 293.
[88] Lewis, *Topog. Dict. Eng.* (1831), i. 60.

[89] *W.A.M.* xxxii. 185.
[90] *V.C.H. Wilts.* ii, p. 131.
[91] S.C. 12/699.
[92] Two other mills, Baldham and Bulkington, both in Keevil parish, were later reckoned part of Ashton manor; they are dealt with at p. 258. For Bradley Mill, see p. 226.
[93] Thomas Stikeberd lived at Littleton in 1262: S.C. 2/208/1. By the mid-16th cent. the name had been corrupted to Sticklebridge: L.R. 2/191.
[94] *W.A.M.* xiii. 116.
[95] C 3/168/64; C 3/192/83; C 3/196/68.
[96] *Cal. Pat.* 1550–53, 189.
[97] *Wilts. Inq. p.m.* 1625–49 (Index Libr.), 177.
[98] C 3/168/64.
[99] *W.A.M.* xli. 13.
[1] Swindon Borough Libr. Goddard MSS. 623–59; *Genealogist*, N.S. xxvii, 105–12, and xxxv, 224; Burke, *Commoners*, iv. 327.

of a family closely related to the Goddards.[2] In 1790 it was thoroughly repaired at a cost of over £300; it was then called by its modern name of Littleton Wood Mill.[3] Shortly afterwards it passed to Thomas Naish, a Trowbridge clothier, whose introduction of shearing frames led to its destruction by a group of shearmen from Trowbridge in 1803.[4] By 1820 it had passed to the Kennet and Avon Canal Company, and was held on lease by Mrs. Freelove Noad.[5] Since then the mill has been occupied by successive members of the Noad family. Trading as J. and J. Noad, the firm uses this mill and others at Seend Head for the production of flour and compound feeds for farm stock. In 1961 water power was still used to drive the milling machinery by means of a turbine.[6]

In the mid-15th century John Tynny held a watermill and ⅓ virgate of land, which had formerly been held by Roger Tynny, as a copyhold of the manor of Steeple Ashton.[7] A century later the mill then called Tynny's Mill was held by Robert Hancock and Walter his brother.[8] The mill was variously called Hancock's Mill, Tynny's Mill, or Tinhead Mill in the early 17th century; it lay at the northern end of Ashton Normead and Tinhead Normead, in the position of the modern Ashton Mill Farm.[9] The freehold of the mill must have been granted by the Crown to the Brouncker family. In 1597 Martha Brouncker, widow, and Henry Brouncker conveyed it to Roger Blagden the younger,[10] and in 1606 he conveyed it to Edward Bromwich. In 1629 Bromwich's widow Margaret, who had remarried, claimed the reversion of the mill after the death of William Hancock.[11] By 1688 the freehold had passed to John Torksey, clerk, who then conveyed it to William Gilbert,[12] of Maddington. In 1700 Gilbert sold the mill and about 45 a. of land near it to John Axford of Erlestoke. At his death in 1704 Axford left it to his son, another John, who in 1762 sold the property to Gifford Warriner of Conock in Chirton. It descended in that family until it was sold to the Longs of Rood Ashton in 1834.[13] The building was demolished to make way for the airfield.[14]

There was a windmill in Steeple Ashton in 1371.[15] In the mid-16th century a cottage occupied its site, which was probably east of Mudmead Lane,[16] at the place called Windmill Furlong in 1841.[17] Another windmill no doubt existed in Hinton, giving a name to Windmill Fields west of the village,[18] but no mention of it has been found.

CHURCHES. A church at Steeple Ashton is first mentioned in 1252, in terms which imply that there had long been one in the village.[19] Semington has been a chapelry of Steeple Ashton since the Middle Ages; there was a chaplain there in 1370,[20] and the 15th-century chapel retains an inscribed stone which is probably of the 13th century. Another ancient chapel, which gave its name to Rood, formerly Chapel Ashton, existed in the parish, but nothing is known of any institutional relationship to the parish church.[21] West Ashton was made a separate ecclesiastical district in 1847.[22]

The rectory of Steeple Ashton had been appropriated by the Abbess of Romsey before 1252, by virtue of a papal grant.[23] The advowson had no doubt belonged to the nuns since before the Conquest. The first recorded presentation of a vicar was in 1338, and successive abbesses presented until the Dissolution with only two exceptions, when Sir Walter Hungerford in 1490, and Robert Foster in 1538, presented with their permission.[24] The advowson was alienated to Sir Thomas Seymour in the same way as the manor.[25] After his forfeiture it was retained by the Crown until the early 17th century. James I presented George Webb in 1605, but in 1609 Webb, dedicating a sermon to Sir James Ley, spoke of him as being 'lately seized with the patronage to which . . ., though unworthy, I owe myself and my service'.[26] In spite of this, Sir James did not hold the advowson at his death in 1629[27] and Charles I presented at the next vacancy in 1636.[28] Charles II presented in 1661,[29] but by 1663 the advowson had passed to Sir Samuel Jones, who presented in that year.[30] By 1676 it had passed to John Martyn, who presented then and in 1684 and 1688.[31] By 1697 it had been bought by Drue Drury of Riddlesworth Hall (Norf.), who at his death in the following year left the advowson and rectory to Magdalene College, Cambridge, to found a travelling fellowship for a 'gentleman's son of Norfolk'. The Martyn family evidently reserved the next presentation, for the vacancy which occurred in 1747 was filled by Samuel Martyn of Chippenham.[32] The advowson is still owned by Magdalene College.

In 1291 the church of Ashton was valued at £40, of which £13 6s. 8d. was the value of the vicarage.[33] In 1535 the gross value of the vicarage alone was £30 4s., but various payments, including £6 10s. for a chaplain at Semington, reduced its net value to £10 12s. 6d.[34] By 1698 it was estimated that the vicarage was worth £150 a year and the

[2] W.R.O. Land Tax Assessments; Burke, *Land. Gent.* (1846), 39.
[3] W.R.O. 78, Bundle of vouchers and letters.
[4] *V.C.H. Wilts.* vii. 139.
[5] W.R.O. Land Tax Assessments.
[6] *Wilts. Times*, 24 Feb. 1961.
[7] S.C. 12/16/65.
[8] S.C. 12/4/2; L.R. 2/191. They were probably descended in some way from the Tynny family, the name of Tynny *alias* Hancock being often found, e.g. in S.C. 2/208/6 m. 2d (1493).
[9] E 178/4697.
[10] C.P. 25(2)/242/39 Eliz. I Trin.
[11] C 3/414/100.
[12] C.P. 25(2)/803/3 Jas. II Hil.
[13] Long MSS. Title Deeds of Mill.
[14] See p. 199.
[15] S.C. 2/208/2 m. 3d.
[16] S.C. 12/4/2.
[17] W.R.O. Tithe Award.
[18] Ibid.
[19] B.M. Lansd. MS. 442, f. 33.
[20] S.C. 2/208/2 m. 1.
[21] See p. 203.
[22] *Retn. of Dist. Churches*, H.C. 433, p. 98 (1870), liv.
[23] B.M. Lansd MS. 442, f. 33. The papal grant has not been traced; it was made to Constance, Abbess 1247–60.
[24] Phillipps, *Wilts. Inst.* i, *passim*.
[25] See p. 202.
[26] *W.A.M.* xxv. 92.
[27] *Wilts. Inq. p.m.* 1625–49 (Index Libr.), 232–6.
[28] Phillipps, *Wilts. Inst.* ii. 18; this may have been because Webb was preferred to a bishopric: Phillimore, *Eccles. Law*, i. 52.
[29] Phillipps, op. cit. 24.
[30] P.R.O. Inst. Bks. s.a. 1663.
[31] Phillipps, *Wilts. Inst.* ii. 34, 39, 42.
[32] *W.N. & Q.* vi. 236, 278.
[33] *Tax. Eccl.* (Rec. Com.), 180.
[34] *Valor Eccl.* (Rec. Com.), 144.

rectorial tithes £100 a year.[35] In 1831 the average net income of the vicar was £852 a year, of which he paid £100 to the curate of Semington.[36]

Before 1252 all the great tithes had apparently been taken by Romsey Abbey, but then the great tithes of 'Gulde Ashton', Ashton Dunstanville, and West Ashton were awarded to the vicar.[37] It was probably the custom to lease out the rectorial tithes, at least of the outlying parts of the manor. In 1410 Thomas Flower of Littleton took a lease of the great tithes of Semington for ten years at an annual rent of 16 marks.[38] In 1538 the rectory and tithes of Steeple Ashton were leased to Peter Westbrook for 70 years at £13 6s. 8d. a year.[39] This lease may have been resumed, since c. 1550 Henry Long held the parsonage for £20 a year.[40] In 1561 the Crown leased the rectory to Nicholas Morgan for 21 years at the same rent,[41] and the lease to him was renewed for three lives in 1582.[42] It was settled on Morgan's widow, Christian, who had remarried Anthony Garnons, in 1589.[43] In 1588 a lease in reversion for 21 years was granted to Edward Bunyan.[44] In 1606 the rectory was granted by the Crown in fee to Sir John Ramsey.[45] After this its descent is not certain. The rectory and advowson were included in settlements of the Longs of Rood Ashton several times between 1615 and 1641,[46] but they never exercised the advowson, and neither was mentioned among the possessions of Gifford Long in 1635.[47] What probably happened was that the rectorial tithes became divided among several owners during this period, and that the Longs owned a part. In 1643 Edward Long and Thomas Long conveyed tithes in Semington and Steeple Ashton to George Keate, and in 1647 Keate conveyed them to Anthony and John Martyn.[48] In 1663 the tithes of Semington were settled on Anthony Martyn the younger.[49] Other tithes, in Semington and West Ashton, were in 1667 conveyed by George Lowe to Thomas Bythesea.[50] It is probable, however, that a large part of the rectorial tithes came to be concentrated in the Martyn family of Great Hinton, and that they sold the Steeple Ashton part of them with the advowson to Drue Drury (see above). They retained the great tithes of Hinton, however, which passed with Anne, daughter and sole heir of John Martyn of Hinton, on her marriage to Richard Long (d. 1760).[51] The great tithes of Semington may have passed to the Longs in the same way. But it is only when they were commuted in 1841 that the distribution of the great tithes becomes clear.

They were then mainly divided into three roughly equal parts. Magdalene College owned those of about 2,130 a., all in Steeple Ashton; Walter Long all the great tithes of Hinton and Semington and 35 a. in Steeple Ashton, about 1,920 a. in all; and the vicar almost all the great tithes of West Ashton and 283 a. in Steeple Ashton,[52] about 2,270 a. in all. The Magdalene tithes were commuted for £363 10s. and the Long tithes for £310; the vicar's were included with his small tithes (see below).[53] The great and small tithes of about 60 a. lying near Trowbridge were owned by the Rector of Trowbridge, and had been since at least the 17th century. It is probable that the customary payment of 4s. yearly paid by the rector to the Vicar of Steeple Ashton was a composition for these tithes.[54] This payment was imposed on the rectors of Trowbridge in 1252.[55]

In 1252 the whole of the glebe, with a house, which had formerly belonged to the rector, was assigned to the vicar, while the former vicar's glebe was all assigned to the abbess except for two acres.[56] In 1340 rectorial glebe, amounting to 7 houses and about 70 a., was held by seven bond tenants,[57] and it was still held by tenants in the mid-15th century[58] and c. 1540.[59] Its subsequent history or occupation is not known. In 1841 the glebe of Magdalene College amounted to only about 4 acres.[60]

In 1252 the vicar was allotted all the small tithes of the whole parish as well as the great tithes described above,[61] and continued to own them, except those belonging to the Rector of Trowbridge, until the 19th century. In 1841 the whole of the vicar's tithes were commuted for £920.[62] In 1604 the vicar's glebe consisted of an orchard and two gardens, a close containing 1½ a. and 2 a. in the common-field at Oathill, but in 1671 and 1704 only 1 a. in Oathill was mentioned.[63] In 1841 the vicar had about 16 a. of glebe.[64]

In 1252 it was ordered that the vicar should have two chaplains continually with him, to serve the church at his own expense.[65] In 1514 Walter Lucas left money to the three priests serving in the church of Ashton.[66] Probably one of these served the chapel at Semington where there was a chaplain by at least 1370.[67] In 1470 a dispute arose between the Vicar of Steeple Ashton and the inhabitants of Semington and Littleton about the cost of services there, and the bishop ordered that the vicar should, himself or by a suitable chaplain, celebrate mass and vespers every Sunday and feast day. For this

[35] W.N. & Q. vi. 236.
[36] Rep. Com. Eccl. Rev. H.C. 54, p. 840 (1835), xxii.
[37] B.M. Lansd. MS. 442, f. 33.
[38] S.C. 2/208/3 m. 1.
[39] S.C. 12/4/2. This presumably was the whole parish rather than the tithing, since no other leases are mentioned.
[40] L.R. 2/191, f. 155v.
[41] Cal. Pat. 1560-3, 216.
[42] C 66/1313 m. 26.
[43] C.P. (25)2/241/31 and 32 Eliz. I Mich.
[44] C 66/1313 m. 26.
[45] C 66/1698.
[46] C.P. 25(2)/371/13 Jas. I Mich. 372/20 Jas. I Mich., 510/11 Chas. I Trin., 511/17 Chas. I Hil.
[47] Wilts. Inq. p.m. 1625-49 (Index Libr.), 207-10.
[48] C.P. 25(2)/512/19 Chas. I Mich. and 23 Chas. I Mich.
[49] Long MSS. Release Martyn to Sheppard and Beach, 1663.

[50] C.P. 25(2)/745/18 and 19 Chas. II Hil.
[51] Soc. Antiq. Jackson MSS.
[52] These great tithes in Steeple Ashton were owned by the vicar in 1704: Sar. Dioc. R.O. Glebe Terrier; they may have formed part of the endowment of 1252.
[53] W.R.O. Tithe Award.
[54] W.A.M. xv. 229; see also V.C.H. Wilts. vii. 152.
[55] B.M. Lansd. MS. 442, f. 33.
[56] Ibid.
[57] S.C. 12/699.
[58] S.C. 12/16/65.
[59] S.C. 12/4/2.
[60] W.R.O. Tithe Award.
[61] B.M. Lansd. MS. 442, f. 33.
[62] W.R.O. Tithe Award.
[63] Sar. Dioc. R.O. Glebe Terriers.
[64] W.R.O. Tithe Award.
[65] B.M. Lansd. MS. 442, f.33.
[66] P.C.C. 31 Fetiplace.
[67] S.C. 2/208/2 m. 1.

the inhabitants were to pay 20s. a year over and above other dues, and to find all needful things except bread and wine.[68] Semington had its own churchwardens and managed its own affairs, probably at least from the date of this award, and certainly by the mid-16th century, and only paid the annual dues to the Vicar of Steeple Ashton.[69] The provision of a separate curate for Semington only ceased between the two World Wars.[70] John Carpenter, vicar 1428–9, a much beneficed clerk who later became Bishop of Worcester, is unlikely to have resided.[71] During the period covered by the early churchwardens' account book, 1543–1668, most vicars seem to have been resident.[72] George Webb, vicar 1605–36, held a cure at Bath from 1621, but was frequently at vestries in Steeple Ashton after that date. He was made Bishop of Limerick in 1634, and was the author of a number of sermons and theological works, the best known being *The Practice of Quietness*.[73] Henry Carpenter was vicar throughout the Interregnum, but his successor, Gabriel Sanger, was ejected in 1662, and became a presbyterian.[74] After 1698, when the advowson was obtained by Magdalene College, vicars had to be unmarried,[75] but the rule was relaxed after 1870, A. O. Hartley (1870–89) being the first married vicar.[76] In 1783 the vicar resided in Surrey because of ill-health. His curate lived in the village, but not in the vicarage itself. He performed Sunday services at Steeple Ashton morning and afternoon, and at Semington at 1.30 p.m., and also held extra services on saints' and red letter days and during Lent. From 30 to 50 people received the Sacrament four times a year.[77] Of Samuel Hey, vicar 1787–1828, it was said that 'the peculiarity of his dress and the simplicity of his manners had gained for him the title of The Hermit', and that he was 'a father to his parish'.[78]

The church of *ST. MARY THE VIRGIN* consists of a clerestoried nave, chancel, north and south aisles, square western tower, and north and south porches. Both aisles are extended to form chapels at either end, the western ones being the full width of the tower and the eastern ones corresponding to the first two bays of the chancel.[79] The dedication is first recorded in 1281.[80] The tower is thought to be of the early 15th century; it is of four stages, embattled, and decorated with crocketed pinnacles and gargoyles, and has a row of five niches on the second stage of the west front. It was formerly surmounted by a stone spire built *c.* 1480–1500 (see below),[81] which, when it was measured in 1606, was found to be 32 yards higher than the tower, making together the remarkable height of about 186ft. An inscription in the church records how the spire was struck by lightning in July 1670, and, just as repairs were being completed, struck again the following October. Two men working on

it were killed, and the body of the church severely damaged, so that no attempt to rebuild the spire was made. The parts of the aisles which flank the tower are also of the early 15th century, although their exteriors were remodelled when the rest of the church was rebuilt.

Another inscription in the church, copied from an earlier one, records that it was built between 1480 and 1500, the north aisle at the cost of Robert Long, the south aisle at the cost of Walter Lucas, and the rest of the church and steeple at the cost of the parishioners. This refers to a complete rebuilding of the nave and the two aisles east of the tower arch. The part played by Long and Lucas in building the aisles is also attested by Leland.[82] Long in his will of 1501 ordered that the works begun on the north side of the church should be completed at his expense.[83] Before his death he had agreed with Thomas Lovell of Trowbridge, freemason, to do the work for £80, but at Lovell's death £49 was still owing.[84] Long's widow's second husband, William Morgan, ordered in his will in 1508 that the works begun by Long should be completed.[85] The work done during these years is in an elaborate Perpendicular style with good proportions and unusually vigorous moulding and carving both internally and externally. The nave is of four bays, and has a lofty clerestory with large four-light transomed windows, and a five-light blocked window in the east gable above the chancel arch. The nave arcades are supported on composite piers with moulded capitals and high moulded bases. It was apparently intended to build a stone vault over the nave: stone springers rise from the capitals of the piers, and preparations were made outside to build flying buttresses, two pairs of which were completed, one at each end. The present roof, however, is of oak with plaster panels in a pattern of lierne vaulting; its four pendants and four bosses are elaborately carved. It may originally have been contemporary with the nave, but it is probable that it had either to be extensively repaired or rebuilt in 1670. The aisles and eastern chapels are vaulted in stone with elaborate bosses; the vaulting springs from canopied niches supported by vigorously carved figure corbels. Each bay has a four-light window. The bay to the west of the south porch was evidently damaged by the fall of the spire, and the rebuilt vaulting carries the initials of the churchwardens for 1670. A carving of the Assumption in the eastern chapel of the north aisle shows that it was the Lady Chapel. The south porch has a room above and a stone vaulted ceiling at the lower stage; the north porch is of one story only. The external parapets are embattled and decorated with crocketed pinnacles rising from the buttresses. Those on the aisles and south porch have octagonal panelled shafts; smaller pinnacles spring from the first offset of the

[68] B.M. Add. Ch. 5691.
[69] *W.N. & Q.* vi. 365f.
[70] *Crockford* (1926, 1935).
[71] Emden, *Biog. Reg. Oxon.* i. 360–1.
[72] *W.N. & Q.* vi and vii, *passim*.
[73] *W.A.M.* xxxvi. 350.
[74] A. G. Matthews, *Calamy Revised*, 427.
[75] Soc. Antiq. Jackson MSS.
[76] J. A. Venn, *Alumni Cantab.* 2nd ser. iii. 271.
[77] Sar. Dioc. R.O. Vis. Queries, 1783.
[78] C. Daubeny, *Guide to the Church* (1830), i, p. cxi.

[79] *W.A.M.* xxxii. 206, where is a full description of the church on which the following account is largely based.
[80] J.I. 1/1001 m. 22.
[81] Leland's statement that it was of stone, and the fact that it was pointed in 1606, seem conclusive, although Stukeley, who never saw it, said that it was of wood covered with lead.
[82] Leland, *Itin.* ed. Toulmin Smith, i. 83.
[83] P.C.C. 4 Blamyr.
[84] C 1/367/38.
[85] P.C.C. 6 Bennett.

buttresses. There is a fine display of grotesque gargoyles.

The chancel of the earlier church remained untouched in the late 15th century apart from the opening of the arches into the aisle chapels. It had a two-light window to the south and a steeply pitched roof which only just cleared the chapel arches. It was pulled down in 1853 and a higher and slightly longer chancel built to a design by Henry Clutton[86] in a style similar to the remainder of the church, the expense being borne by Magdalene College.[87]

The church retains considerable fragments of medieval glass. The tradition remains in the village that the glass was broken after the battle of Roundway in 1643, when Sir William Waller stabled his horses in the church, but it seems more likely that it was two years later, when Waller's army is known to have been in the district. In 1648 a heavy church rate was levied to repair the glass of the church.[88] There are many monuments, but none earlier than the 17th century. A small monument to Deborah Marks (d. 1730/1) in the north aisle has been made on the back of a copper plate for a Protestant engraving. This shows a Frenchman, a Pope, and the Devil outweighed in the balance by a Bible, with Queen Anne and others looking on. Only part of the design remains.[89]

The font, which stands in the chapel south of the tower at the west end of the south aisle, formerly called the Beach chapel, was given by Richard Crawley, vicar 1828–69, in memory of his mother.[90] It replaced a hexagonal font with quatrefoil panels.[91] A new pulpit was provided in 1605,[92] and remained in the church until the 19th century,[93] when it was replaced by one in memory of Richard Crawley. In 1514 Walter Lucas left money to buy organs for the church.[94] In 1589 the parish had 181 organ pipes in hand, although apparently dismantled, but in 1620 old pipes and fragments of the organs were sold.[95] In the early 19th century an orchestra played in a gallery at the west end of the church, but in 1835 a barrel organ was placed there. This organ was moved to the former Lady Chapel when the gallery was removed in 1868.[96] In 1877 it was replaced by the present organ, by Bryceson Bros. and Ellis, which was given by Charlotte Long. In 1883 a fund was set up to maintain the organ and to pay an organist.[97]

In 1543 the church had 5 great bells, a small bell, and a clock.[98] Three bells were recast by John Wallis of Salisbury in 1607, and he recast the tenor in 1616.[99] In 1666 Henry Long agreed to set up a sixth bell, for which he was given £18 and the sanctus bell.[1] Four bells were recast in the 18th century, another in 1889, and the only survivor of 1607, with one of 1772, were recast again in 1915. Another sanctus bell was provided in 1809.[2] Finally in 1959 the whole peal was recast.[3]

In 1495 Walter Lucas left a missal, a pair of vestments, and a chalice to the altar of St. John the Baptist in Steeple Ashton church.[4] In 1501 Robert Long left a chalice, a mass book of paper in print, and 2 chasubles.[5] In 1543 the church owned a chalice, 5 pairs of vestments, and 3 copes.[6] In 1553 the Commissioners left the chalice and took 4 oz. of silver.[7] In 1581 18s. was paid 'to exchange the chalice into a communion cup',[8] and this remodelled chalice still survives. By 1625 the parish owned a pewter flagon, and two more flagons were bought in 1636.[9] Amy Long left a second chalice to the church in 1649,[10] and this, hall-marked 1650, also still survives. Besides the two chalices, the plate now (1960) consists of a paten and alms dish of 1699, given by Henry Long, another paten of 1704, and a flagon of 1736.[11]

The parish registers begin in 1538 and are complete.[12] A volume of churchwardens' accounts covers the period 1543–1668, with some years missing.[13]

The vicarage stands somewhat away from the church. It appears to have been a stone-built hall house, probably of the 15th century, consisting of a one storied hall with a cross wing at its west end. The screens passage across the west end of the hall was entered by a moulded stone doorway with a two centred arch and a projecting porch, which still survive. The hall block retains much of its original roof of four bays, with three surviving arch-braced collar-beam trusses and some curved wind-braces. The division of the hall into two stories and the insertion of a staircase do not appear to have taken place until c. 1700, perhaps after the living had been acquired by Magdalene College. The west wing was also remodelled then. There is no indication of a corresponding wing to the east. A large extension was built there c. 1840, faced with ashlar masonry, the stone cut in pieces the size of bricks. Ellis Wright, vicar 1538–69, left 5 volumes of Chrysostom's works, printed at Basle in 1530, to his successors.[14] Samuel Hey, vicar 1787-1828, left 1,139 books and some articles of furniture for the use of future vicars.[15] Most of the volumes were

[86] Soc. Antiq. Jackson MSS.; cf. *W.A.M.* xxxii. 214, but Giles and Gane were more probably the builders.
[87] Drawings of the ch. by Buckler (1807) and Carter (1848) are in W.A.S. Libr., Devizes.
[88] P. C. Yerburgh, *The Story of the Church of ... Steeple Ashton*, Trowbridge, 1954. (Pamphlet on sale in church).
[89] *W.A.M.* xlii. 438–41.
[90] Ibid. xiii. 327.
[91] Soc. Antiq. Jackson MSS. Drawing of font.
[92] *W.N.& Q.* vi. 518.
[93] Print in church vestry.
[94] P.C.C. 31 Fetiplace.
[95] *W.N. & Q.* vi. 370, 427.
[96] P. C. Yerburgh, *Church of Steeple Ashton*.
[97] *Endowed Char. Wilts.* (1908), pp. 652–3.
[98] *W.N. & Q.* vi. 369.
[99] Ibid. 519, 568.

[1] Ibid. vii. 330.
[2] Walters, *Wilts. Bells*, 15.
[3] *Wilts. Times*, 27 Nov. 1959.
[4] P.C.C. 25 Vox.
[5] P.C.C. 4 Blamyr.
[6] *W.N. & Q.* vi. 369.
[7] Nightingale, *Wilts. Plate*, 119.
[8] *W.N. & Q.* vi. 425.
[9] Ibid. vii. 35, 73.
[10] Ibid. 187.
[11] Nightingale, *Wilts. Plate*, 119.
[12] Ex inf. Major C. J. Jacobs.
[13] *W.N. & Q.* vi. 364. The accounts are transcribed in this and the succeeding volume.
[14] *W.N. & Q.* vi. 371.
[15] Pamphlet issued at celebration service of 400th anniversary of consecration of church, 19 September 1900.

destroyed for salvage during the Second World War, but the works of Chrysostom and about 250 volumes of Hey's books survive.[16]

A church house is first mentioned *c.* 1550 when it was a copyhold estate of the manor[17] and expenditure for its repair occurs frequently in the early churchwardens' accounts. It was usually held from the church by two or three tenants on lease, and may have incorporated in it the shop for which the church received rent.[18] In 1662 Matthew Hancock gave his estate in it to the poor of the parish,[19] but by 1699 it had fallen down.[20]

The chapel of *ST. GEORGE* at Semington consists of nave, chancel, north porch, and south vestry. The dedication is first mentioned in 1470.[21] The nave and porch are of the 15th century, and the chancel of the first part of the 16th. It was perhaps in the 18th century that a thin square tower was built apparently resting on the roof of the chancel where it joins the nave.[22] This was removed in 1860, when the east and west walls were rebuilt, a small bell-turret built at the west gable, and the interior completely renewed. The new east and west windows are in the 14th century style. All the roofs were renewed, and a new font provided. The octagonal vestry was added in 1877.[23] Built into the porch is a stone with an incised inscription in old French offering pardon to whomever should pray for Philippa de Salcest (Sauser). Its date is probably the 13th century. There are several monuments including one in coloured marbles to the Blagden family by Ford of Bath.[24] The chapel had two bells in 1553; the present one, in a turret at the west end, was recast about 1850 from a pre-Reformation one,[25] which was traditionally said to have come from the chapel at Bulkington.[26] The plate consists of a chalice and paten of 1579, another paten of 1697, and a cruet-shaped flagon.[27] The registers of the chapelry begin in 1586. The organ is by Sweetland of Bath.

In 1597 Arthur Swayne and another conveyed a house and 8 a. of land in Semington to Edward Long and other feoffees, the profit to be used to maintain and repair the chapel, and to relieve the poor of the chapelry. It is not clear that Swayne was the donor and it seems more likely that the chapelry raised money and bought the land from him. The house was known as the church house. In 1704 a chamber in it was reserved for the use of the curate.[28] In 1833, described as an old thatched dwelling, it was let to the overseers. In 1859 it was given to be the site of the school. Part of the land was sold to the Kennet and Avon Canal Company

c. 1800 and the proceeds invested. The profits of the lands were devoted by successive feoffees to the maintenance of the chapel, and did away with the necessity for a church rate. After 1779 surpluses arose, which were used for various charitable purposes, such as apprenticing children and assisting emigrants. In 1861 some stock was sold to pay for the restoration of the chapel. In 1891 the vicar of Steeple Ashton and the chapelwardens of Semington were made trustees. In 1901 the property consisted of about 8 a. and £167 stock, producing an income of about £29.[29] The income was about the same in 1932.[30] In 1910 Frances E. Arden left £150 to the curate and churchwardens of Semington to keep her grave, and that of her parents, in repair, and to keep the churchyard grass tidy.[31]

There was a chapel at West Ashton by 1307, when the name Chapel Ashton for an estate there first occurs. In the later Middle Ages the more common form became the modern Rood Ashton, showing that it was noted for its rood.[32] This is supported by the only known reference to it, apart from its occurrence in the place name, when in 1533 Joan Try left to the chapel of Rood Ashton and to the rood there a pax of silver and two ells of cloth for the altar.[33] The chapel is traditionally said to have stood behind Rood Ashton house,[34] and the site was still called Church Hill in 1841.[35] Some remnants of a raised and levelled plot of ground, which was the probable site, can still be traced, although grown over with trees.

The church of *ST. JOHN THE EVANGELIST*, West Ashton, was built in 1846, chiefly at the cost of Walter Long.[36] It was designed by Wyatt and Brandon,[37] and consists of nave, chancel, and northern tower with small spire. It contains a number of 19th-century monuments, particularly of the Long family, for whom a vault was made in 1882.[38] The one bell is of the same date as the church, as is the chalice; the paten is an 18th-century piece presented later.[39] The original registers are still in use.[40]

In 1846 Walter Long gave a rent-charge of £100 payable out of lands in West Ashton to provide a stipend for the minister there. At the same time about £200 stock was bought with subscriptions to provide for the maintenance of the church and churchyard.[41] The Vicar of Steeple Ashton also set apart £100 from tithes to augment the stipend.[42] The advowson of the church belonged to the Long family until their estate was broken up in 1930, when it was bought by Canford School (Dors.).[43] About 1944 it passed to the Martyrs Memorial

[16] *The Parochial Libraries of the Church of England* (1959), 100. A book of hours which was among Hey's books is described in C. Wordsworth *Horae Eboracenses* (Surtees Soc. 1920), 161, where a vernacular metrical litany of the 15th century from it is printed.
[17] L.R. 2/191, f. 154.
[18] *W.N. & Q.* vi. 426.
[19] Ibid. vii.280.
[20] Long MSS. Rental 1699.
[21] B.M. Add. Ch. 5691.
[22] Soc. Antiq. Jackson MSS. Drawing of ch. by W. W. Wheatley.
[23] *W.A.M.* xxxii. 216, where is a full description of the church on which the following is based.
[24] *Genealogist*, N.S. vi. 116–9.
[25] Walters, *Wilts. Bells*, 195.
[26] *W.A.M.* xxxii. 218.

[27] Nightingale, *Wilts. Plate*, 121.
[28] Sar. Dioc. R.O. Glebe Terrier.
[29] *Endowed Char. Wilts.* (1908), pp. 657–8.
[30] Char Com. Accts. File.
[31] Ibid. File 91301.
[32] *P.N. Wilts.* (E.P.N.S.), 137.
[33] *W.N. & Q.* vi. 557.
[34] *W.A.M.* xiii. 332.
[35] W.R.O. Tithe Award.
[36] H.O. 129/10/259.
[37] Pevsner, *Wilts.* 497.
[38] Long MSS. Bill 1882.
[39] Nightingale, *Wilts. Plate*, 122.
[40] Ex inf. Major C. J. Jacobs.
[41] *Endowed Char. Wilts.* (1908), pp. 655–6.
[42] H.O. 129/10/259.
[43] Sar. Dioc. Regy. Patronage Reg.

Trust, which still held it in 1962.[44] Since 1962 the church has been held in plurality with that at Heywood.[45]

NONCONFORMITY. No return was made for Steeple Ashton to Bishop Compton's 'Census' in 1676; in Semington there were 207 conformists and 2 dissenters.[46] In 1704 the house and barn of James Smith were licensed as a meeting-house for Quakers, but the group does not seem to have survived.[47] A house at East Town was licensed for Independents in 1767, and between 1815 and 1817 houses at West Ashton, Steeple Ashton, and Hinton were all licensed for Independents by B. Kent, minister of the Tabernacle at Trowbridge; that at Steeple Ashton was described as a chapel.[48] No Independent meeting in the parish was mentioned in 1829.[49]

Baptist meetings were licensed in 1825 at West Ashton and Steeple Ashton, and another licence for Steeple Ashton was granted in 1828.[50] No Baptist congregation was mentioned either in 1829 or 1851,[51] but in 1864 a dwelling house facing the green was taken over as a station of the Baptist chapel at Bratton.[52] A Sunday school was started in 1874.[53] The chapel finally closed c. 1940, and its sale was authorised in 1947.[54] The building has since been reconverted into a dwelling house.

In 1783 a few Methodists were meeting in a labourer's house in Steeple Ashton; according to the curate their number had decreased by 'some hundreds' in the past few years.[55] Houses were licensed for Methodist meetings at Steeple Ashton and Semington in 1797, and one at West Ashton in 1798 may also have been for them.[56] In 1829 the Steeple Ashton Methodists were meeting in a farm house; there were 8 members and about 50 people attended.[57] In 1851 one room of a dwelling-house was used exclusively for worship. It afforded 120 sittings, and average congregations were about 100.[58] It was probably this group which built the Primitive Methodist Chapel at the north end of the village three years later. The plain brick building, dated 1854, can seat 130 worshippers,[59] and was in 1963 still in use.

In 1829 the Methodists at Semington had 27 members and an average congregation of 80.[60] The present chapel at Semington was built in 1884.[61] The Wesleyans had 9 members at West Ashton in 1829,[62] but no congregation survived in 1851.[63]

In 1814 and 1822 houses at Hinton were licensed.[64] They may have been for Methodists, for in 1829 a congregation with 5 members was meeting in the village.[65] By 1851 two congregations met in the village. The Wesleyan Methodists had a room used exclusively for worship, which could accommodate 100; the average congregation was about 20. Primitive Methodists met in an unoccupied cottage, with a congregation of similar size.[66] Both congregations subsequently built small chapels, the Wesleyans c. 1864, and the Primitive Methodists c. 1859.[67] In 1961 one remained in use.

In 1851 a congregation of Latter Day Saints met in a room of a house in Steeple Ashton, an average of about 50 attending the services.[68] The tradition of these meetings still remains in the village. Part of Nitt's Lane is nick-named God's Corner because they used to meet there in a house now called Old Chesils.[69]

PARISH GOVERNMENT. The earliest recorded meeting of the manor court of Steeple Ashton was in 1262.[70] In 1370 it met four times a year, and presentments were made by the homages of West Ashton, Southwick, Lovemead, Semington, Littleton, Hinton, and Steeple Ashton.[71] By the end of the 15th century it met only twice a year and Lovemead sent no homage.[72] The Abbess of Romsey's court for the hundred also commonly met in the village.[73]

There were two churchwardens for Steeple Ashton in 1543,[74] and this number has no doubt been general ever since. In 1570 the tithings of Steeple Ashton, Hinton, and West Ashton each had two collectors for the poor and two waymen.[75] Apart from a volume of churchwardens' accounts covering the period 1543–1668,[76] few parish records remain.

SCHOOLS. George Webb, vicar 1605–36, is said to have kept a school in Steeple Ashton.[77] In 1779 John Hicks left £5 a year toward paying a schoolmaster to teach poor children nominated by the vicar.[78] This was paid to a 'very ingenious and diligent man' who already kept a private school in the village. He taught reading, writing, arithmetic, and mathematics, which he had acquired 'merely by his own industry and application'.[79] In 1808 there were day schools for 76 children in the parish.[80] In 1815 John Togwell bequeathed an annuity of £50 to educate 30 boys and 20 girls of Steeple Ashton and West Ashton, but he died leaving insufficient estate to meet the charge. Finally only £17 a year was received from 1824

44 *Sar. Dioc. Kalendars.*
45 Order in Council, 11 May 1962.
46 *W.N. & Q.* iii. 537.
47 W.R.O. Certs. of Dissenters' Meeting Houses.
48 G.R.O. Retns. of Regns.
49 W.R.O. Retn. of Nonconformist Meetings, 1829.
50 G.R.O. Retns. of Regns.
51 W.R.O. Retn. of Nonconformist Meetings, 1829; H.O. 129/10/259.
52 Char. Com. File 101700.
53 *Kelly's Dir. Wilts.* (1931).
54 Char. Com. File 101700.
55 Sar. Dioc. R.O. Vis. Queries, 1783.
56 G.R.O. Retns. of Regns.
57 W.R.O. Retn. of Nonconformist Meetings, 1829.
58 H.O. 129/10/259.
59 Methodist Ch. Bldgs. Return, 1940.
60 W.R.O. Retn. of Nonconformist Meetings, 1829
61 *Kelly's Dir. Wilts.* (1931).
62 W.R.O. Retn. of Nonconformist Meetings, 1829.
63 H.O. 129/10/259.
64 G.R.O. Retns. of Regns.
65 W.R.O. Retn. of Nonconformist Meetings, 1829.
66 H.O. 129/10/259.
67 *Kelly's Dir. Wilts.* (1931).
68 H.O. 129/10/259.
69 Steeple Ashton W.I. village history.
70 S.C. 2/208/1.
71 S.C. 2/208/2.   72 S.C. 2/208/6.
73 See p. 197.
74 *W.N. & Q.* vi. 369. Semington had separate chapel wardens.
75 Ibid. 374.
76 Printed in *W.N. & Q.* vi–vii.
77 *D.N.B.*
78 *Endowed Char. Wilts.* (1908), p. 640.
79 Sar. Dioc. R.O. Vis. Queries, 1783.
80 Lambeth Palace Libr. MS. 1732.

onwards.[11] In 1819 the wife of the parish clerk with 'proper assistants' taught 40 children, 4 of whom were paid for by Hicks's charity and 16 paid for and partly clothed by the vicar. It was then thought that the poor had not sufficient means of education,[82] but in 1833 it was difficult to persuade the parents of children paid for by Hicks's bequest to keep them at school even for the year which was the normal period for receiving the charity. At that time a man and his wife taught the children under both charities, and took day scholars and boarders as well.[83]

In 1835 78 boys and 34 girls attended, of whom 22 were paid for by the charities and 7 by the vicar. There were also two small schools in the village where another 39 children were paid for by their parents.[84] They were probably the 'two dames' schools of a humble kind' which still taught about 30 younger children in 1859. By then the village school was accommodated in the present building, which had been built about twenty years previously. On the upper story 30 or 40 girls were taught by a certificated mistress; they were 'remarkably neat and cleanly' and 'very fairly instructed'. Below 40 boys under an uncertificated master were in less satisfactory accommodation.[85] The school had been affiliated to the National Society since at least 1846.[86] In 1899 the building and adjoining teacher's house were conveyed by Walter Long to the vicar and churchwardens. In 1903 about £16 10s. a year was being paid to the school from Hicks's and Togwell's charities.[87] Since 1941 senior children have gone to school in Trowbridge; the junior mixed and infants' school was given Aided status after the Act of 1947.

In 1699 Thomas Somner of Wellow (Som.) left £2 a year charged on lands at Littleton to provide for schooling of two poor boys from Semington.[88] By 1819 the number had increased to four boys, but it is not clear whether they were taught in the village.[89] By 1835, however, there were two schools in Semington, where 24 boys and 18 girls were taught, 8 of them at the cost of the vicar and curate.[90] One of these was no doubt that attended in 1833 by the charity children, again reduced to two in number.[91] In 1859 30 children were taught in a cottage room by an uncertificated mistress who had, however, received some training, and it was intended to build a new school in the coming Spring. Another 30 children attended two dames' schools.[92]

The village school built in 1859 near the chapel, on land given by the chapel trustees, was affiliated to the National Society by the terms of the gift.[93] In 1900 average attendance was 58.[94] The senior

children were taken away in 1941. Controlled status was granted to the school in 1949.

In 1819 there was a school in Steeple Ashton parish where about 16 poor girls were taught and partly clothed at the cost of the vicar, and a few others at the expense of Mrs. Long of Rood Ashton.[95] This school, no doubt, lay in West Ashton. It still existed in 1835, when 9 boys and 16 girls attended, and at another, begun in 1833, 6 girls were paid for by their parents.[96] In 1846 a new school was built on ground given by Walter Long, and affiliated to the National Society.[97] Within five years this school, under the guidance of the Revd. F. H. Wilkinson, had attained a remarkable position, and was held up by the government inspector as a model village school. In 1851 203 children attended the school, coming from the village and two or three miles around and from seven different parishes. Almost a quarter of these were over 12 years old, and they included 'a considerable number of females nearly grown up to womanhood, but sadly behind-hand in information'. Nineteen children lived in lodgings in the parish so that they could attend. 'Nothing unusual' was taught in the school and the inspector attributed its success to the intelligent manner in which the children were taught and to the personal influence of the vicar. 'It is a family', he wrote, 'and apparently a very happy one, with the clergyman at its head. ... his house is open to the children after school hours and his heart *always*'. He also noted the 'really remarkable' progress of the younger children, and their 'tone of cheerful obedience', which made children educated there in great request to be employed as servants.[98]

By 1859 success had overburdened the school so much that the pupils from outside the parish had been withdrawn to a new school instituted by Wilkinson in Trowbridge.[99] About 40 children remained at West Ashton, taught by an uncertificated mistress.[1] By 1899 average attendance was 58 children.[2] Senior children were withdrawn from the school in 1941.

In 1835 there was a day school at Hinton, begun in 1827, where 30 children were educated at the cost of their parents. It still existed in 1841, but nothing more is known of it.[3]

CHARITIES.[4] In 1643 Samuel Martyn left 2 a. of land to provide two coats and two gowns yearly for four poor people from West Ashton and Steeple Ashton. In the 19th century the rent was spent on coats and gowns, which were distributed in rotation to a list of beneficiaries.[5] In 1952 the income was £7, which was distributed in vouchers.[6]

[81] *Endowed Char. Wilts.* (1908), p. 642.
[82] *Digest of Returns to Cttee. on Educ. of Poor*, H.C. 224, p. 1038 (1819), ix (2).
[83] *Endowed Char. Wilts.* (1908), p. 640.
[84] *Educ. Enq. Abstract*, H.C. 62, p. 1027 (1835), xliii.
[85] *Acct. of Wilts. Schools*, H.C. 27, p. 4 (1859 Sess. 1), xxi (2).
[86] Nat. Soc. Sch. Enq. 1846.
[87] *Endowed Char. Wilts.* (1908), pp. 648-9.
[88] Ibid. p. 646.
[89] *Returns to Cttee. on Educ. of Poor* (1819), p. 1038.
[90] *Educ. Enq. Abstract* (1835), p. 1027.
[91] *Endowed Char. Wilts.* (1908), p. 646.
[92] *Acct. of Wilts. Schools* (1859), p. 4.
[93] *Endowed Char. Wilts.* (1908), p. 658.
[94] *Return of Schools*, 1899 [Cd. 315], p. 864, H.C.

(1900), lxv (2).
[95] *Returns to Cttee. on Educ. of Poor* (1819), p. 1038.
[96] *Educ. Enq. Abstract* (1835), p. 1027.
[97] *Endowed Char. Wilts.* (1908), p. 657.
[98] *Mins. of Educ. Cttee. of Council*, 1851–2, *vol. ii* [1480], pp. 7, 32, H.C. (1852), xl.
[99] This lay just across the parish boundary; it did not succeed, and closed a few years after Wilkinson's death in 1861.
[1] *Acct. of Wilts. Schools* (1859), p. 5.
[2] *Return of Schools*, 1899, p. 864.
[3] *Educ. Enq. Abstract* (1835), p. 1027; W.R.O. Tithe Award.
[4] Educational charities are dealt with above.
[5] *Endowed Char. Wilts.* (1908), pp. 641, 648.
[6] Char. Com. Accts. File.

In 1633 Peter Crook gave £2 a year charged on land at Tilshead to the poor of Steeple Ashton. In 1833 it had been the custom for many years to lay it out in shirts given annually to the second poor of the tithing.[7] By 1903 the rent charge was being spent with the income of Poor's Stock (see below).

By his will proved in 1720 John Brown left 4 a. of land in Steeple Ashton to trustees, who were to apply the profits for four poor honest Anglican men, living within 3 furlongs of Steeple Ashton Cross, over 45, and who had bred up families without aid from the parish. He also left £200 to acquire lands for the same purpose, which was used to buy 8 a. of land at Bowerhill in Melksham. In 1833 the four beneficiaries, who were appointed by the vicar, occupied the land in Steeple Ashton themselves, while a rent of £17 from the land at Bowerhill was divided between them. In 1903 the charity was still administered in the same way.[8] The lands were later let. In 1955 about £300 arising from the sale of timber on the Bowerhill estate was invested for the charity.[9] In 1952 the rent received was £27, of which about £24 was divided between the four beneficiaries.[10]

Several small sums given to the poor of Steeple Ashton in the 16th century and later were consolidated, and in 1729 £25 was paid to the overseers, the parish paying 25s. a year as interest. This sum, known as Poor's Stock, was spent on garments for the second poor until 1820, when it lapsed, but a payment of £1 a year was revived in 1833. This was disallowed by auditors in 1845, and a public subscription set on foot, from which £34 Consols was bought. Since that time it has produced 17s. a year, which has been spent with the income from Crook's charity in providing calico, and later vouchers for cloth.[11]

In 1671 Henry Long left £20 for the benefit of the poor of West Ashton, which was used in 1725 to buy 1 a. of meadow in Dodsmead. At inclosure the charity was allotted 3½ a. of land near West Ashton Hill, which in 1833 was being used as rent-free allotments by second poor. It was exchanged

for another piece in 1845. In 1903 it was still being used in the same way.[12]

In 1737 Elizabeth Martyn left a close of 3 a., part of East Town Farm, to provide linen cloth for poor women of East Town and West Ashton. The field was, however, still regarded as part of the farm, subject to a yearly charge of 40 ells of dowlas. This was supplied by the owner to the parish officers, who had it made into shirts for the second poor, the recipients being chosen by the owner. The charity was applied in this way until 1884, when the charge was redeemed for £150 Consols.[13] Since then the yearly income of £3 15s. has been laid out in linen which is distributed at Christmas.[14]

A sum of £42, given by an unknown donor, belonged to the parish officers of Hinton in 1786. It was afterwards used to buy a cottage at Coldharbour; when this was sold in 1812, £60 was invested in Consols. A further sum was invested in 1817, making a stock of £135. The income, just over £4 a year in 1833, was distributed among the second poor of the tithing.[15] In 1951 it was over £3, which was distributed among 7 old people.[16]

In 1852 George Tayler left £3,000 to found charities in Edington and three other parishes, of which Steeple Ashton was one. The provisions there for the distribution of bread, the preaching of a children's sermon, and the provision of buns for the Sunday School, were the same as those for Poulshot.[17] In 1906, when the whole charity was reorganized, the Steeple Ashton charity was made separate and allotted £469 stock.[18] In 1952 the income of over £12 was still being spent on the objects prescribed by the founder.[19]

By his will proved in 1857 Thomas Milsom left £100 for the benefit of Semington Sunday School and to supply coal to poor people there.[20] By his will proved in 1922 William Bruges of Semington left £100 for supplying coal to the poor of the village at Christmas.[21] A yearly sum of £1, whose donor is unknown, is charged on land called the Crofts at Semington. It is paid to the Vicar of Steeple Ashton for a sermon preached at Semington on Good Friday.[22]

NORTH BRADLEY

THE ancient parish of North Bradley included the modern civil parishes of North Bradley and Southwick, which lie south and south-west of Trowbridge and extend from the boundary of the urban district to the Somerset border.[1] The whole area was within the bounds of the manor of Steeple Ashton in Saxon times.[2] In the Middle Ages it was for a time reckoned part of the parish of Edington,[3] but from about the mid-14th century seems to have

been treated as an independent parish.[4] Southwick tithing relieved its poor separately from Bradley and so became a separate civil parish in the late 19th century. Detached parts of each parish were added to the other in 1885. After that the area of Bradley was 1,768 a., and of Southwick 2,473 a.[5] Southwick included the district of Rode Hill, adjoining the village of Rode (Som.), which became a district chapelry in 1852,[6] and subse-

[7] Endowed Char. Wilts. (1908), pp. 642, 649.
[8] Ibid., pp. 643, 650.
[9] Char. Com. File 19135.
[10] Ibid. Accts. File.
[11] Endowed Char. Wilts. (1908), pp. 643, 651.
[12] Ibid. pp. 644, 654.
[13] Ibid.
[14] Char. Com. File 1575.
[15] Endowed Char. Wilts. (1908), pp. 645, 657.
[16] Char. Com. Accts. File.
[17] See V.C.H. Wilts. vii. 125, and below, p. 250 n. 7.
[18] Char. Com. File 82647.   [19] Ibid. Accts. File.

[20] Endowed Char. Wilts. (1908), p. 658.
[21] Char. Com. File 101725.
[22] Endowed Char. Wilts. (1908), p. 660.
[1] The following maps were used: O.S. Maps 1/2,500 Wilts. XXXVIII. 9–16, XLVI. 2, 3, 6, 7; 1/25,000 ST 8£. Much of the preliminary work for this article was done by Margaret Morris.
[2] See p. 202.
[3] E 134/16 Eliz. I Trin./6.
[4] See p. 226.
[5] Census, 1891.
[6] See p. 226.

quently a separate ecclesiastical parish. The southern part of it was transferred to Somerset in 1937, thus reducing the area of Southwick to 2,255 a.[7]

The irregularly shaped ancient parish lies in the clay vale of west Wiltshire, stretching from the valley of the Biss on its eastern border to that of the Frome on its west. Each river forms the parish boundary for part of its course. The area between them is mostly drained by small streams which flow into the Biss, for the highest land lies on the western edge of the parish. It rises to about 275 ft. near Overcourt Farm and 250 ft. at Vagg's Hill, from which there is a steep drop down to the Frome. Most of the parish is given over to dairy farming. The only areas of woodland remaining are at Vagg's Hill in the west, around Brokerswood in the south, and at Picket Wood near Yarnbrook. In the Middle Ages there was probably much more woodland, and Bradley and Southwick both lay within the bounds of Selwood Forest until 1300.[8] In the 18th century the parish was remarkable for the extent of its commons. Bradley village was almost surrounded by Woodmarsh Common to the north, Bradley Common, which stretched almost to Southwick, and Little Common near the farm of that name. Drynham Common stretched along the Trowbridge boundary, and Yarnbrook Common lay between Yarnbrook and the Westbury boundary. Southwick itself was built round a large common green, and to the west the very large Rode Common divided the inclosed lands along the Frome from the remainder of the parish. Part of Rode Common was inclosed in 1792, and the other commons in the parish in 1805.[9]

There were formerly an earthwork and some barrows near Rode Hill, but they were destroyed in the early 19th century.[10] Roman remains have been found near Cutteridge Farm.[11] North Bradley and Southwick both appear as settlements in the early Middle Ages,[12] and were of moderate prosperity in the 14th century.[13] With the rise of the Wiltshire woollen industry they grew in importance as centres of domestic clothworking for clothiers from Trowbridge. The amount of common land in the parish may have attracted weavers who were able to build cottages and keep animals on it, and in the late 18th and early 19th centuries the parish reached a peak in population if not in prosperity. In 1821 there were over 2,600 inhabitants; although in succeeding years the extinction of the domestic industry led to a considerable decline, both villages have remained comparatively large,[14] and dependent upon Trowbridge for the employment of much of their population.

The village of North Bradley is built partly along the main road from Trowbridge to Westbury and partly round a minor road in the shape of a narrow horseshoe which lies south-west of the main road and encloses the church. The regular layout of this minor road only dates from the early 19th century. In 1773 the village consisted of a number of houses irregularly built along several lanes and paths and with pieces of common land in between.[15] The northern branch, now called Southwick Road, but formerly Pound Lane,[16] was straightened c. 1830, while the southern one, Church Lane, formerly ran slightly to the south of its present line.[17] A small village green, allotted in 1805 to the lord of the manor as a place to hold the fair,[18] lies north of the church. Facing it is the Daubeny Asylum,[19] and opposite is the Old Rectory, a brick house of c. 1790. The large mid-19th-century vicarage lies south-west of the church. Nearby stands a large block of malthouses, of brick with small stone-mullioned windows with segmental heads and keystones, and half-hipped roofs of slate with truncated gables; they are dated 1837. The village contains many brick cottages of the 18th and 19th centuries in which lived the clothworkers. A common feature is a dentilled string-course at first floor level. At the south end of the village is a pair of brick houses, each dated 1735 and bearing the initials of members of the Butcher family.[20] Other houses in Church Lane are dated 1734 and 1746.

A few more 18th- and early-19th-century cottages stand on the Westbury road, and here also are King's Farm, Pound Farm, and Manor Farm. King's Farm is a substantial L-shaped house, probably of the late 16th or early 17th century. The ground floor is largely of stone, and has mullioned windows with hood moulds. On the upper floor timber-framing has been obscured by plaster. The gable end of the cross-wing has shaped barge boards and a pendant. In 1963 the house was in very poor condition. Manor Farm was rebuilt in the 18th century,[21] and Pound Farm is a stone house of the early 19th century. The road towards Trowbridge has been affected by suburban development, which seems to have begun in the mid-19th century with Beach House and Broadleigh House and some pairs of smaller brick houses. Other terrace houses date from the early 20th century, and there are some more recent small houses and bungalows. The village hall was built in 1912,[22] and nearby is the Baptist chapel.

West of Bradley church are groups of cottages which in 1773 stretched along the edges of the common there.[23] That along a lane north of the Southwick road is called the Rank, while south of the road are groups called Scotland and Ireland. Encroachments on the common were made at Ireland in 1740.[24] The hamlet of Yarnbrook to the south of Bradley, where roads from Trowbridge and Melksham join and go south to West-

[7] Census, 1951.
[8] V.C.H. Wilts. iv. 415.
[9] W.R.O. Inclosure Awards made under 30 Geo. III c. 23 and 44 Geo. III c. 23.
[10] A.F[arquharson], History of North Bradley and Roadhill (Trowbridge, 1881), 48 (copy in Wilts. Tracts lxii).
[11] Ibid. 17; ex inf. Mr. L. H. Francis of Cutteridge Farm.
[12] P.N. Wilts. (E.P.N.S.), 138, 144.
[13] V.C.H. Wilts. iv. 302, 311.
[14] Ibid. 342, 357.
[15] Andrews and Dury, Map (W.A.S. Rec. Brch.), pl. 7.
[16] W.R.O. Inclosure Award.
[17] A.F., North Bradley, 6–7.
[18] W.R.O. Inclosure Award.
[19] See pl. facing p. 201.
[20] A.F., North Bradley, 23.
[21] See p. 221.
[22] Wilts. Times, 28 Sept. 1912.
[23] Andrews and Dury, Map (W.A.S. Rec. Brch.), pl. 7.
[24] W.R.O. 533, Disbursements on poor, 1738–46.

bury, contained only a few houses and Bradley Mill in 1773.[25] Several small terraces of cottages were built there soon after the common was inclosed, and between the world wars small houses were built on the Westbury road.

There were two public houses in Bradley c. 1800. One, called the 'Bell', stood in Church Lane, while the 'Axe and Cleaver' stood in the lane still called after it, leading west from Woodmarsh. It took its name from a butcher who kept it in the late 18th century. In 1803 the publican of the 'Axe and Cleaver' closed it and had the 'Long's Arms' at Yarnbrook built. Later in the century several more houses in Bradley were licensed.[26] The 'Old Ring of Bells' was part of the Winchester College estate, and was rebuilt in 1843,[27] and the 'Rising Sun' is a very similar building. The 'New Ring of Bells' was in the building now Malthouse Farm, a brick house dated 1703 on the gable and 1713 on the porch.[28] By 1881 there were also the 'Royal Oak' and the New Inn.[29] Of these only the 'Rising Sun' and the New Inn in the village are still licensed.

Westward from Bradley a road leads towards Southwick, and from it a winding minor road leads to the hamlet of Brokerswood at the southern extremity of the parish, and so on across the Somerset border. It passes Cutteridge Farm which stands near the site of a large house pulled down c. 1800.[30] Some of the other farms in this part can be traced from the 16th century or earlier.[31] Pole's Hole Farm is a timber-framed building with brick filling and three small gables, probably of the 17th century.

The main part of Southwick lies along the main road from Trowbridge to Frome. Many of the houses in it were originally built on roadside waste; in the later 18th century the Clutterbucks, lords of the manor, made a number of leases for 1,000 years of small plots on many of which cottages were already built.[32] More houses were subsequently built on some plots. Thus by 1818 one house and garden previously let for 1,000 years had had three more houses built on it.[33] Many of the houses on the north side of the village street date from that period. The Poplars is a small house of brick with stone dressings and hipped stone-tiled roof, probably of the late 17th century. On the south side the area from the 'Fleur de Lys' westward to Pound Farm was until 1805 a large village green of varying width, covering the sites now occupied by the church, Providence Chapel, and the council houses.[34] From it Wynsome Road leads south-eastwards towards Bradley. It was turnpiked in 1768.[35]

South and west of the village minor roads lead from the main road to the hamlets of Lamber's Marsh and Hoggington and to scattered farms. The loop of road on which Whitaker's Farm stands was

part of the main road in 1811, but a straight piece to cut it out had been built by 1841.[36] Whitaker's Farm is a 16th- or early-17th-century stone house, roofed with stone tiles and with three small timber-framed gables at the front. Manor Farm at Hoggington was in 1881 a labourer's cottage.[37] It is a 16th-century house of stone, with a symmetrical front of three gables with copings and finials and stone-mullioned windows. A later porch is dated 1673 and bears the initials of members of the Greenhill family, and the door bears the same initials and date in the ironwork surrounding the latch.

The roads in the western part of the parish were much altered at the inclosure of Rode Common, and some only date from that time. The one from Tellisford Bridge towards Southwick is, however, said to have been a pack-horse route from Bristol through the Somerset villages of Combe Hay, Wellow, and Norton St. Philip, and on by Bradley and Edington over the plain to Salisbury. It was still occasionally used by drovers in the 1880's.[38] Tellisford Bridge was rebuilt, partly at the expense of the parish, by John Ducey, a Tellisford mason, in 1692.[39] Vagg's Hill Farm is a stone house dated 1618, with a projecting semi-circular stair tower. Dillybrook, Romsey Oak, Chancefield, and Odessa Farms all date from after the inclosure of the parish.

MANORS. The land which later formed North Bradley parish lay within the boundaries of Ashton as King Edgar set them forth in 968, and passed to Romsey Abbey with that estate.[40] By the 14th century,[41] and possibly long before (it is not separately mentioned in Domesday Book), some freehold estates in North Bradley were held of the Abbess of Romsey's manor of Edington, although others, mainly in Southwick, still owed suit and rent to Steeple Ashton.[42] At the Dissolution the overlordship of these two groups divided and followed the descent of the manors to which they were annexed.[43] Freehold rents were still being paid to the lords of Edington in the early 17th century[44] and to the lords of Steeple Ashton in the 1870's.[45]

The largest of the estates held of the manor of Edington became known as the manor of *NORTH BRADLEY*. Humphrey of Bradley (fl. c. 1190)[46] was probably tenant of this manor. Three-quarters of a century later another Humphrey of Bradley held lands there;[47] the same Humphrey or else a descendant granted a lease of land in North Bradley in 1281, reserving rent and suit of court.[48] He was dead two years later.[49] The first certain tenant is Reynold of Bradley, who in the mid-14th century held an estate described as two carucates of land by a rent of £3 10s. 1½d.[50] What was clearly the same estate was held by Robert of Bradley in

[25] *Andrews and Dury, Map* (W.A.S. Rec. Brch.), pl. 7.
[26] A.F., *North Bradley*, 43–4.
[27] W.C.M. 4325.
[28] Ex inf. Mrs. Watts of Malthouse Farm.
[29] A.F., *North Bradley*, 44.
[30] See p. 223.
[31] See pp. 220–24, 225.
[32] W.R.O. 78, Bundle of Leases.
[33] Ibid. 137, Assignment Lucas to Lucas.
[34] W.R.O. Inclosure Award.
[35] 8 Geo. III, c. 49.
[36] O.S. Map 1″, sheet 14 (1st edn.); W.R.O. Tithe Award. [37] A.F., *North Bradley*, 23.

[38] Ibid. 53.
[39] W.R.O. 533, Contract.
[40] See p. 202.
[41] S.C. 11/706.
[42] S.C. 12/699.
[43] See pp. 202, 241.
[44] W.R.O. 436, Rental of Edington Romsey, 1625–6.
[45] Long MSS. Succession Duty Accts. of R. P. Long.
[46] Hist. MSS. Com. *Var. Coll.* i. 375; *Plac. Abbrev.* (Rec. Com.), 12.
[47] C.P. 25(1)/251/21/20.
[48] *Feet of F.* 1272–1327 (W.A.S. Rec. Brch.), 14.
[49] S.C. 6/1052/1. [50] S.C. 11/706.

1357.[51] By 1413 it had passed to Thomas Godfrey in right of his late wife Alice (or Joan), daughter and heir of Reynold of Bradley.[52] Thomas had a son, Geoffrey,[53] who may have died in his father's lifetime leaving either a daughter or no issue. All that seems clear is that an heiress of the Godfrey family named Margaret had by 1423 married Robert Long, and that Thomas Godfrey and another Margaret Godfrey in 1426 joined Robert and Margaret Long in conveying the estate to feoffees.[54] This Robert Long was the ancestor of the Long family of South Wraxall, and Bradley descended in the same way as Wraxall[55] to Sir Walter Long (d. 1610). In the settlement of the disputes which followed his division of his inheritance, Bradley was allotted to his younger son Walter, and descended in the Longs of Draycot Cerne[56] to Sir James Tylney-Long, who died a child in 1805. His estates devolved on his eldest sister Catharine, who married William Wellesley-Pole; after her death her husband succeeded to the earldom of Mornington. Their only son, the fifth earl, died unmarried in 1863 and left his estate to his relative, H. R. Wellesley, first Earl Cowley.[57] North Bradley was sold almost immediately to C. P. Moore, tenant of the Manor Farm, who in 1879 sold it to Walter Hume Long of Rood Ashton.[58] He retained it until the break-up of the Rood Ashton estates in the present century.[59] By the late 18th century the estate consisted only of the Manor Farm, of about 130 a.[60] The farmhouse was rebuilt after a fire in 1760; the previous house stood nearby, and many fine trees which grew about it were felled in the early 19th century.[61]

In the late 12th century the Abbess of Romsey granted to Walter Cheyney land in Cutteridge which Warin the Marshal had held there, and before him Thedulf.[62] It must have descended to another Walter Cheyney who held a carucate of land of the manor of Steeple Ashton c. 1340.[63] In 1351 John Cheyney sold all his land at Cutteridge to John of Edington.[64] As elsewhere, John of Edington was acting for his brother William, Bishop of Winchester, and the land was assigned for the endowment of his chantry in Edington, later the house of Bonhommes there.[65] It remained the property of

that house until the Dissolution.[66] In 1551 it was granted to the Warden and Scholars of Winchester College.[67] The estate was not large, but parts were held by copy of court roll and courts were held until the early 19th century.[68] In 1865 the College bought Church Farm, and in 1881 held 129 a. in the parish. Since then there have been further alterations in the estate, including the purchase of Organ Pool Farm in 1940.[69]

The manor of *SOUTHWICK* owed suit and rent to the manor of Steeple Ashton c. 1340,[70] although an estate which descended with it was held of the manor of Edington at about the same time.[71] Both rents were still paid in the 17th century.[72] The earliest known tenant of the estate was Adam de Grenville, who held land in Southwick in the reign of Richard I.[73] It was referred to as a manor in 1242, when this or another Adam de Grenville made an agreement with the Abbot of Keynsham, lord of Wingfield, about common rights.[74] Southwick descended in the Grenville family until the middle of the 14th century; holders included William de Grenville in 1274–5,[75] who may have had a son Adam,[76] another William and his wife Lucy in 1322,[77] and John de Grenville to whom Lucy released her dower in Southwick in 1338.[78] John was dead by 1349 leaving a daughter and heir Alice, whose wardship belonged to Humphrey de Bohun, Earl of Hereford.[79] John's widow, Margaret, released her dower to the Earl in 1352.[80]

Alice de Grenville married Humphrey, son of Sir John Stafford of Amelcote and Bromshull (Staffs.).[81] Their son Sir Humphrey Stafford (d. 1442) had three sons Richard, John, and William, each of whom married and left an only child. Each of these three children succeeded to the estate in turn, but none of them left any issue; the last, Sir Humphrey Stafford, Earl of Devon, was executed in 1469. The whole property then passed to the issue of his aunt Alice, only daughter of Sir Humphrey Stafford (d. 1442). She, by her two marriages, had left three daughters, and, the eldest dying without issue, the Stafford inheritance was divided between the other two.[82] Southwick passed through the elder of these, Alice's younger daughter by her

[51] C.P. 25(1)/255/49/27.
[52] S.C. 2/208/45 mm. 5d.–6.
[53] Ibid.
[54] S.C. 2/208/46 m. 2; C.P. 25(1)/290/60/48; in the 17th cent. Sir James Long believed that Robert Long had himself married Alice of Bradley: Kimber and Johnson, *Baronetage* (1771), ii. 266. Confusion of Margaret Godfrey with Robert Long's 2nd wife, Margaret Popham (see e.g. Wedgwood, *Hist. Parl.*, 1439–1509, *Biogs.* 551) has led to the erroneous assertion that the Longs derived their North Bradley estate from the Pophams (e.g. Burke, *Commoners*, iii. 212).
[55] See *V.C.H. Wilts.* vii. 22.
[56] Burke, *Commoners*, iii. 216–18; *Complete Baronetage*, iii. 257–9.
[57] *Complete Baronetage*, iii. 259; for their relationship see *Complete Peerage* s.v. Mornington and Cowley.
[58] A.F., *North Bradley*, 7–8.
[59] W.A.S. Libr. Devizes, Sale Cat.
[60] W.R.O. Land Tax Assessments and Tithe Award.
[61] A.F., *North Bradley*, 24.
[62] B.M. Lansd. MS. 442, f. 50; for the dating of this deed, by Abbess Juliana, see Liveing, *Records of Romsey Abbey*, 57. The grantee is described as Walt. 'de Quercu', but the later rubric calls him Cheyney; for this name's derivation, from 'oak grove', see Reaney, *Dict. British Surnames*, 67.

[63] S.C. 12/699.
[64] B.M. Lansd. MS. 422, f. 50d.
[65] *Cal. Pat.* 1350–54, 330; the rent by which the Cheyneys had held the estate was released by the abbess: ibid. 313.
[66] *Valor Eccl.* (Rec. Com.), ii. 141.
[67] *Cal. Pat.* 1550–53, 160.
[68] S.C. 6/Hen. VIII/3985 m. 42d.; W.C.M. 4315 and 4315A.
[69] A.F., *North Bradley*, 21; ex inf. the bursar of the College.
[70] S.C. 12/699.
[71] S.C. 11/706.
[72] Long MSS. Rent Roll 1699; W.R.O. 436, Rental of Edington Romsey, 1625–6.
[73] *Cur. Reg. R.* (P.R.S. xiv), 71–2.
[74] C.P. 25(1)/251/14/6.
[75] *Rot. Hund.* (Rec. Com.), ii. 278.
[76] See p. 229 n. 11.
[77] *Cal. Chart. R.* 1300–26, 446; *Cal. Pat.* 1327–30, 485.
[78] C.P. 25(1)/287/39/67.
[79] *Cal. Pat.* 1348–50, 322; the Grenvilles had held property of the earl in Somerset.
[80] C.P. 25(1)/255/48/18.
[81] W. H. H. Rogers, 'Stafford of Suthwyke', *W.N. &Q.* iii. 193–202, where full details of the family pedigree are given.
[82] Hutchins, *Hist. Dors.* ii (1863), 181.

first marriage, to Sir Edmund Cheyney of Brook in Westbury, and thence with Brook to the Willoughby family. It was held successively by Robert Lord Willoughby (d. 1502), and Robert his son (d. 1521).[83] The younger Robert sold it to Sir David Owen,[84] a bastard son of Owen Tudor, grandfather of Henry VII.

Sir David Owen died c. 1542 leaving an annuity of £22 out of Southwick to a chantry which he intended to found in the priory church of Easebourne (Suss.), which had, however, been dissolved since he made his will in 1529. The residue of the manor he left to the sons of his second marriage successively in tail male.[85] The eldest, Jasper, left no male issue; the second, Henry, possessed the estate,[86] but must also have left no male issue, for by 1547 it was in the hands of the youngest brother John.[87] In 1556 John Owen conveyed the manor to Christopher Bailey in return for an annuity of £42.[88] John Owen died in 1559 and the annuity passed to his son Henry,[89] who in 1573 sold it to Sir Wolstan Dixie, citizen and merchant of London. At his death in 1594 Dixie left the annuity to Christ's Hospital, London,[90] of which he was president.[91] It was paid until 1799, when the governors of the hospital sold it to Walter Long, then the lord, for £1,000.[92]

From Christopher Bailey, who had bought it in 1556, the manor passed to the Longs of Whaddon in the same way as the advowson of Wingfield,[93] and descended like Whaddon to Sir Philip Parker a Morley Long (d. 1741). Southwick was then divided; part remained with Sir Philip's daughter, who married John Thynne Howe, Lord Chedworth.[94] It was probably after his death in 1762 that his trustees sold the estate to Daniel and Lewis Clutterbuck of Bradford-on-Avon. At his death in 1769 Daniel left his share to Lewis.[95] Lewis, the ancestor of the Clutterbucks of Newark Park (Glos.), apparently sold Southwick to his nephew Daniel Clutterbuck (d. 1781), from whom descended the family of that name later seated at Hardenhuish.[96] The family still held some 500 a. in Southwick in 1881.[97]

The part of Southwick which remained with the Whaddon estates, descended in the Long family with that manor until the late 19th century.[98] It included Southwick Court, the capital messuage of the manor, but it is not known that any manorial rights were ever exercised. The house and farm were sold in the late 19th century, and have since changed hands several times.[99] The house stands at one side of an extensive moated site. It is an L-shaped building of stone with stone-tiled roof, of two stories and attics. The shorter wing bears two stones with the initials W.B. for Walter Bush, husband of Maud, formerly wife of Christopher Bailey, and the date 1567. It may have been added then to an older house in the same position as the longer wing of the present house. The south-west end of that wing is timber-framed, and the roof contains some smoke-blackened timbers, perhaps re-used from an earlier building. Other than that the wing seems to have been completely rebuilt in the late 17th century, and has the date 1693 cut on it. It has two-light stone-mullioned windows, and a central oval window on each floor of the north-west front. Several stone fireplaces and the staircase also probably date from the late 17th century. Attached to the north-east end of the longer wing is a two-storied gatehouse which may date from the mid-16th century; it is approached over the moat by a brick bridge, probably of the 18th century. The house was somewhat restored in the late 19th century; in particular the short wing has a large window of this period on the ground floor.

In 1241 William Blanchard held ½ virgate of land in Cutteridge which his father William had held before him; for it he paid a rent of 7s. to the Abbess of Romsey and owed suit to the manor of Steeple Ashton.[1] This estate, with others added to it later, formed the reputed manor of CUTTERIDGE, which remained in the Blanchard family until the mid-15th century. The exact descent is not clear, and the lands appear to have been sometimes divided between various members of the family. In 1304 William, son of Alexander Blanchard, assured the ½-virgate estate to another William Blanchard for his life.[2] Some 50 years later Thomas Blanchard held it.[3] John Blanchard, Archdeacon of Worcester, died in 1383 leaving a small property in Honeybridge to his brother, this or another Thomas, who held the main property.[4] Thomas died in 1387 leaving a son John,[5] who died c. 1395, when the wardship of his son John was granted to his wife's second husband.[6] Nicholas Blanchard was a suitor at the court of Steeple Ashton in 1413.[7] In the mid-15th century John Blanchard held the ½-virgate estate while Thomas Blanchard held a virgate which had once belonged to Hugh Beauservice; both properties had formerly been held by Nicholas.[8] A third estate which probably formed part of the family complex was that

[83] Complete Peerage; see above, p. 151.
[84] E 134/7 Jas. I/Mich. 13; Owen was connected by marriage to the Blount family to whom part of the Willoughby estates passed; in 1547 John Owen was at variance over Southwick with the heirs of another part: C 54/450 no. 25.
[85] W. H. Blaauw, 'On the effigy of Sir David Owen', Suss. Arch. Coll. vii. 22–43; Visitations of Sussex (Harl. Soc. liii), 95.
[86] S.C. 12/4/2; Longleat MS. 10462.
[87] C 54/450 no. 25; C 1/1148/40.
[88] Middx. Inq. p.m. ed. Fry, iii. 181.
[89] C 3/135/18.
[90] Middx. Inq. p.m. ed. Fry, iii, 181, 184.
[91] D.N.B.
[92] Endowed Char. London, H.C. 219, p. 100 (1840), xix.
[93] See V.C.H. Wilts. vii. 74.
[94] Complete Peerage.

[95] W.R.O. 78, Will of Danl. Clutterbuck; Jones, Bradford-on-Avon (1907), 132.
[96] A.F., North Bradley, 21; Burke, Land. Gent. (1937), 438.
[97] A.F., North Bradley, 21.
[98] Long MSS. Rentals, passim.
[99] Wilts. Times, 18 Aug., 27 Oct. 1961; Wilts. News, 27 Oct. 1961.
[1] C.P. 25(1)/251/13/43.
[2] Feet of F. Wilts. 1272–1327 (W.A.S. Rec. Brch.), 49.
[3] S.C. 12/699.
[4] Hoare, Mod. Wilts. Dunworth, 90–1; Cal. Pat. 1385–9, 51.
[5] C 136/49/10.
[6] Cal. Pat. 1399–1401, 97; ibid. 1401–5, 232, 367; ibid. 1405–8, 356.
[7] S.C. 2/208/4 m. 1d.
[8] S.C. 12/16/65; Beauservice had held a century before: S.C. 12/699.

held of the Abbess of Romsey of her manor of Edington by a family described as 'of Cutteridge'. The supposition is supported by the fact that there were tenants called Thomas (c. 1350),[9] and Nicholas (1420),[10] whose Christian names correspond with those of known members of the Blanchard family.

The Thomas Blanchard who lived in the mid-15th century married Agnes, daughter and coheir of William Mohun of Warminster,[11] and left an only daughter Alice who married Richard Kirton.[12] He did suit to the court of Steeple Ashton in 1498.[13] Alice was a widow by 1508.[14] Thomas Kirton held the manor in 1518[15] and Richard Kirton c. 1540.[16] In 1546 Richard and his son Christopher conveyed Cutteridge to Thomas Champneys,[17] no doubt a member of the family seated at Orchardleigh near Frome. Champneys sold it in 1558 to Richard Trenchard, a member of a Dorset family. Richard died two years later leaving an infant son William,[18] who died c. 1591. His son Francis died c. 1622, and was succeeded by a son Francis.[19] At his death in 1635 the younger Francis left only a daughter[20] who does not appear to have survived infancy, and Cutteridge passed to his younger brother Edward, who was a lunatic by 1655[21] and left no issue. The heir to the estate was his nephew William Trenchard, son of a third brother, John, who was already dead. William held the manor until his death in 1710. His son John was a barrister and M.P. for Taunton; he was a noted Whig pamphleteer, cooperating with Thomas Gordon in *The Independent Whig* and *Cato's Letters*.[22]

John Trenchard died childless in 1723, leaving his estates to his nephew Robert, second son of his sister Frances by John Hippesley of Stanton Fitzwarren. He assumed the name of Trenchard and held Cutteridge until he died in 1787. His only son John William died without issue in 1801, leaving his estates to his two nephews, children of his sister Ellen by her two husbands. Cutteridge passed to the elder, John Ashfordby, who assumed the name of Trenchard.[23] In 1807 he sold Cutteridge to John Whitaker whose widow Anna Maria held it in 1841.[24] Their grandson Frank Whitaker Bush held it in 1872,[25] and subsequently sold it to William Francis the tenant. He sold it immediately to Sir Roger Brown of Trowbridge,[26] after whose death in 1902 it passed to his heir W. H. Mann.[27]

A large house, traditionally said to have been second only to Longleat in size in the county, formerly stood near the site of Cutteridge Farm. The suggestion that it had not been built by

Leland's time, because he did not mention it when he visited Brook, is plausible, and it may have been built by the Trenchards in the late 16th or early 17th century. All that is known of it is that it was remarkable for the number and size of its windows and that it was roofed with copper. It was pulled down c. 1800.[28] The house appears to have stood in front of and slightly south-west of the present farmhouse. In 1773 it was surrounded by formal gardens and approached by avenues of trees;[29] two avenues of old limes still remain. The farm house probably formed a detached domestic building such as a brewhouse or kitchen. It is of stone with hipped stone-tiled roof and stone-mullioned windows of two lights. The ground floor was remodelled, and an extension added at the west end probably when the large house was pulled down.

The Grenvilles, lords of Southwick, held property in Langham by 1241.[30] The manor of *LANGHAM* probably included land subinfeudated by them, for a quit rent of 24s. was paid out of it to the manor of Southwick in the 16th century.[31] A quit rent of 6s. 8d. for another part of the manor was paid directly to the overlord, the Abbess of Romsey, and suit was performed at Steeple Ashton. The first known tenant of Langham was Philip de Welislegh who held it c. 1340[32] and died in 1348. His holding then consisted of a mill and a small quantity of land held of the manor of Southwick, and a toft, 30 a. of uncultivated land, and 6 a. of wood at 'the Frith', held of the abbess. His heirs were his daughter Joan, wife of Ralph of Tytherley, and William, the infant son of another daughter by William Bannister.[33] In 1351 the Tytherley moiety was sold to Sir Nicholas Seymour, lord of the adjoining manor of Rode.[34] Seymour held the whole manor before his death in 1361.[35] From him it descended in the same way as the manor of Wittenham in Wingfield to the Zouches, Lords Zouche.[36]

At the death of Richard, Lord Zouche, in 1552, the manor was apparently divided between his sons. One moiety descended with the title to his grandson Edward, Lord Zouche,[37] who sold it to Sir Walter Hungerford in 1578.[38] The other part belonged to Charles Zouche, probably the younger son of Richard, Lord Zouche,[39] who in 1570 assured it to John Walsh.[40] In the following year Walsh conveyed it to John Sturges the younger.[41] By 1586 it was in the hands of creditors of Sturges, who evidently attempted to sell it.[42] Some part of it appears to have passed to John Sadler in 1599;

[9] S.C. 11/706.
[10] S.C. 2/208/45 m. 11; see also ibid. m. 10, where other members of this family are mentioned.
[11] See p. 99.
[12] S.C. 2/208/6 m. 20.
[13] Ibid. m. 5.
[14] Ibid. m. 20.
[15] S.C. 2/208/8 m. 9.
[16] S.C. 12/4/2.
[17] C.P. 25(2)/46/324
[18] C 142/128/86.
[19] W.N. & Q. iv. 325–30.
[20] Ibid. 177, 283; C 142/477/167.
[21] C 142/778/151.
[22] Burke, *Commoners*, iv. 78–9; *D.N.B.*
[23] Burke, op. cit. iv. 79–80.
[24] W.R.O. Tithe Award; Hoare, *Mod. Wilts.* Westbury, 38–9.
[25] *W.A.M.* xiv. 34.
[26] W.R.O. 208.
[27] Information supplied to *V.C.H.* by the Vicar of Bradley, 1908.
[28] A.F., *North Bradley*, 15–17.
[29] *Andrews and Dury, Map.* (W.A.S. Rec. Brch.), pl. 7.
[30] C.P. 25(1)/251/12/8.
[31] E 134/7 Jas. I/Mich. 14.
[32] S.C. 12/699.
[33] *Cal. Inq. p.m.* ix. 391.
[34] C.P. 25(1)/255/48/11.
[35] Dugdale, *Baronage*, ii. 89.
[36] *V.C.H. Wilts.* vii. 72.
[37] *Complete Peerage.*
[38] C 54/1027; S.C. 2/200/14, p. 181.
[39] *Wilts. Visitation Pedigrees*, 1623 (Harl. Soc. cv–vi), 225.
[40] C.P. 25(2)/259/12 Eliz. I Trin.; C.P. 40/1286 rot. 141.
[41] C.P. 25(2)/259/13 Eliz. I Hil.; for his family see *Visitations of Somerset*, 1531, 1573, ed. Weaver, 81.
[42] C 2/Eliz. I/S4/25.

in 1601 he joined Sturges in conveying the whole of this moiety to Edward Hungerford, to whom the other moiety had descended.[43]

Langham descended in the Hungerford family of Farleigh Castle (Som.) until the break-up of their estates in the later 17th century. Like the castle itself and many other properties in the district, this manor seems to have been acquired by the Houlton family of Trowbridge. In 1737, however, Robert Houlton sold the lordship to John Andrews of Bristol,[44] retaining most of the land. Andrews died c. 1744, leaving Langham to his son Edward.[45] By 1792 it had passed to Edward's son, another Edward, of Mangotsfield (Glos.).[46] Four years later he sold it to Samuel Day of Hinton Charterhouse (Som.),[47] but no later mention of it has been found; it may have passed with Day's other property to the Pooll family of Rode.[48] Langham Farm was retained by the Houltons when they sold the lordship in 1737.[49] They sold it to T. W. Ledyard, a Rode clothier, in the early 19th century,[50] and his executors held it in 1841.[51] By the 1870's it belonged to Abraham Laverton of Westbury; it was sold in 1920 to Walter Greenhill of Hilperton Marsh.[52]

None of the lords of Langham is known to have lived on the manor, and nothing is known of any manor house. The house now called Langham House, formerly Rode Hill House, was probably built by T. W. Ledyard soon after 1800. It is of ashlar, of three stories and five bays. The windows on the ground floor have semi-circular heads, and the central door has a porch supported by pairs of columns. The house was rented by Samuel Kent, a factory inspector, in 1854, and here six years later his daughter, Constance, committed one of the most celebrated and puzzling crimes of the 19th century when she murdered her three-year-old step-brother.[53]

It is possible that the manor of *OVERCOURT* formed part of the lands of the Grenvilles, lords of Southwick, in the Middle Ages, and descended in the same way as Southwick to the Willoughbys of Brook in Westbury.[54] It was first described as a separate property in 1516 when it was held by Robert, Lord Willoughby.[55] It was retained when Southwick was sold, and descended in the same way as Brook to Charles Blount, Lord Mountjoy.[56] He sold it to Henry Long, lord of the manor of Southwick, in 1599.[57] In 1617 Long's widow and his son sold Overcourt to Francis Trenchard of Cutteridge. It then consisted of a demesne farm and land held by nine tenants; lands occupied by

William Druce were reserved out of the sale,[58] and as Druce's Farm descended in the same way as Southwick Court.[59] Overcourt remained part of the Trenchard estates until they were divided in the early 19th century, when it was allotted to Walter Long of Preshaw (Hants). He sold it to John Whitaker, the purchaser of Cutteridge, in 1807,[60] from whom it descended like Cutteridge until the present century.[61]

LESSER ESTATES. An estate in North Bradley which belonged to the Dukes of Bolton in the 18th century probably formed part of the Romsey Abbey property in the Middle Ages. If so, it descended in the same way as the manor of Edington Romsey, but was retained on the sale of the Edington property. It was let as a single farm in 1759,[62] called King's Farm by 1773.[63] In 1805 it was held by the widow of the last Duke of Bolton.[64] After her death it was divided between the issue of her husband's two daughters by separate marriages. They were George, Earl of Sandwich (d. 1818), and William, afterwards Duke of Cleveland (d. 1864).[65] In 1841 representatives of these families still held it.[66]

ECONOMIC HISTORY. Hardly any information has survived about the agriculture of the tithing of North Bradley in the Middle Ages. In the 12th century pasture which Alric had formerly inclosed lay near the church there,[67] and both arable land and inclosed crofts lay at Cutteridge in the 13th century.[68] In the 16th century a holding in Bradley included arable land in common fields called Little Field and Perry Field, and there was a common meadow called Hassage.[69] Little Field perhaps adjoined Little Common, north-east of the village, where ridge and furrow lands can still be seen. The inclosure of these fields probably took place piecemeal between the 16th and 18th centuries. Thus in 1625 the parish land, formerly described as ½ a. of arable, had become 'a ridge of pasture ground . . . lying in Mr. King's Leaze, the sixth ridge from the hithermost hedge',[70] and in 1703 two closes of pasture called the New Tyning lay near Drynham Common.[71] By 1788 the Trenchard property in Cutteridge, amounting to nearly 500 a., consisted entirely of inclosed land,[72] and by the time the parish was inclosed by Act of Parliament in 1807, no open arable land remained.[73]

In the mid-14th century some of the customary lands of the manor of Steeple Ashton lay in Southwick. They amounted to 6½ virgates held by 7

43 S.C. 2/200/14, pp. 200, 211; cf. C.P. 25(2)/385/6 Jas. I Mich., an assurance to Hungerford by Sadler and Lionel Duckett.
44 C 54/5598 no. 11.
45 C 54/5725 no. 3.
46 Collinson, *Somerset*, ii. 224; W.R.O. Rode and Langham Inclosure Award.
47 Som. R.O. Batten Pooll MSS.
48 Ex inf. Capt. A. H. Batten Pooll, V.C.
49 Houlton Settlement 5 Nov. 1774, *penes* Mr. F. C. Pitt of Trowbridge.
50 A. F., *North Bradley*, 49.
51 W.R.O. Tithe Award.
52 Ex inf. Mr. E. J. N. Cray of Rode.
53 J. W. Stapleton, *The Great Crime of 1860*; Y. Bridges, *Saint—with Red Hands?*
54 See p. 222.
55 C.P. 25(2)/51/361.
56 See p. 151.
57 C.P. 25(2)/257/41 Eliz. I Hil.
58 Wards 2/22C/72.
59 W.R.O. Land Tax Assessments and Tithe Award.
60 *W.A.M.* xiv. 34.
61 See p. 223.
62 B.M. Add. MS. 24831, f. 31.
63 *Andrews and Dury, Map* (W.A.S. Rec. Brch.), pl. 7.
64 W.R.O. 523, Valuation of N. Bradley, 1805.
65 *Complete Peerage*, s.v. Bolton, Cleveland, Sandwich.
66 W.R.O. Tithe Award.
67 B.M. Lansd. MS. 442, f. 61d.
68 Ibid. f. 70d.; C.P. 25(1)/251/13/43.
69 W.C.M. 4308.
70 W.R.O. 533, Chwdns'. Accts. 1625–42.
71 W.R.O. 130, Beach to Jones, 25 March 1703.
72 W.R.O. 212B, N.B. 10.
73 W.R.O. Inclosure Award.

tenants, who were obliged to perform works on the demesne land at Ashton.[74] These lands were still held of Steeple Ashton manor 200 years later; they then consisted chiefly of inclosed land, but also contained land in common fields called Carley Field, Copley Field, and Acre Field.[75] Arable land in Carley Field and Copley Field is regularly mentioned in the 17th and early 18th centuries;[76] it must have been inclosed piecemeal like the fields in Bradley tithing. Carley Field lay south of the village between Mutton Marsh and Overcourt Farm;[77] Copley Field perhaps lay in the north of the parish. References to land in Acrefield are more puzzling; they generally mention pasture land, meadow, and wood there,[78] and the ground seems to have been a common pasture partly cleared and divided between tenants rather than a conventional open arable field. It was unaffected by the inclosure of the parish, and in 1841 an area called Acrefield Wood still consisted of many small plots of different ownership, unfenced from one another, on the site of the present Park Farm.[79]

The common fields, then, seem from the 16th century at least, to have played only a minor and diminishing part in the agriculture of the parish. Even in the Middle Ages their extent may not have been great, for parts of the parish were clearly occupied by woodland which was gradually cleared into inclosed land. Thus in the north-east corner of the parish lay a 20-acre close of wood and pasture called Hookwoods, which formed part of the Edington monastery (later Winchester College) estate.[80] A close called Inwoods in Elizabeth's reign, with a grove of underwood adjoining it, had by 1655 been divided into 4 inclosures of pasture land.[81] In the early 17th century grounds 'anciently called Northleyes', then divided into 9 inclosures of some 97 a. in all, belonged to the manor farm of Southwick. They were distinct from the 'ingrounds' around Southwick Court, 7 closes amounting to 119 a.[82] Many of the farms in the parish become recognizable in the 17th and 18th centuries. Pound Farm was held by a family named Rogers in the 1630's;[83] as Rogers's Farm it was let at a rack rent by 1713.[84] Druce's Farm takes its name from a family holding land in Cutteridge of the manor of Southwick in Elizabeth's reign.[85] Blue Barn farmhouse bears the date 1637.[86] Norris's Farm was so called by 1746.[87] In 1788 the Trenchard estate consisted of Cutteridge and Overcourt Farms, each of some 150 a., and 8 smaller holdings of from 7 to 50 a.[88] Most of it consisted of pasture land. Against the Biss, west of Druce's Farm, is Barnfield, part of Cutteridge Farm, which in the

early 18th century had such a reputation at Smithfield that 'the name of Barnfield grazing produced an immediate sale', until all the cattle from the district were said to have been fattened there, and the deception was detected.[89] Yet although the clay land favoured this type of farming, some land was kept under the plough; in 1801 116 a. of wheat, 85 a. of oats, and small quantities of barley, potatoes, and beans were sown.[90]

A feature of the parish before the early 19th century was the extent of the common land in it. As early as 1242 Adam de Grenville, lord of Southwick, granted pasture for 240 sheep, 30 other beasts, and 30 pigs in his common to the Abbot of Keynsham, lord of Wingfield.[91] When they were inclosed, Rode Common in 1792, and the other commons in 1805, some 1,000 a. were added to the agricultural land of the parish.[92] Much of this land evidently went under the plough for in 1834 there were over 1,000 a. of arable land in the parish,[93] four times as much as in 1801. These were bad times for farming in the parish, however, largely due to the incidence of the poor rates, which were nearly £1 an acre in the worst years. The farmers complained c. 1830 of the 'poor, wet soil, requiring constant application of expensive labour', while the unemployed woollen workers for whom they were forced to find work were of little use to them.[94] In 1841 there were 923 a. of arable land and 2,751 a. of meadow and pasture. Few farms were of above 100 a.[95] After that time the proportion of grassland in the parish increased, especially with the growth of milk condensing in the district. By 1905 there were only about 200 a. of arable land,[96] and in 1963 most of the parish is permanent grass for dairying.

Although the villages of North Bradley and Southwick were from the 16th to the 19th centuries as much dependent upon the woollen manufacture of the district as upon agriculture, they were chiefly important as places where weavers and other workmen lived rather than as independent centres from which clothiers worked. Only a few clothiers are known to have carried on their businesses in the parish, and they were not very prosperous. Thus John Adams, who was active at Southwick in the reign of Henry VIII,[97] was only assessed at 8s. in 1545, a small sum compared with the clothiers of Trowbridge and Westbury.[98] Weavers and other clothworkers were clearly numerous in Bradley and Southwick from the 16th century until the mechanization of the industry in the 19th century.[99] In 1831 there were 250 families dependent on trade and manufacture com-

[74] S.C. 12/699.
[75] L.R. 2/191.
[72] S.C. 2/200/14; W.R.O. 78, Ct. Bks. of Southwick.
[77] W.R.O. Tithe Award.
[78] e.g. S.C. 2/200/14, pp. 201–2; L.R. 2/86, f. 8.
[79] W.R.O. Tithe Award.
[80] S.C. 6/Hen. VIII/3985 m. 42d; W.C.M. *passim.*
[81] S.C. 2/200/14, p. 198; W.R.O. 78, Survey 1655.
[82] S.C. 2/200/14, p. 243.
[83] W.R.O. Arch. Sar. Will Jn. Rogers, 1630; *Moulton's 1930 Catalogue*, 244.
[84] Long MSS. Calthrop Long's Accounts, 1713.
[85] S.C. 2/200/14, pp. 189, 191, 249.
[86] A.F., *North Bradley*, 23.
[87] W.R.O. 130, Mortgage by Wm. Hippesley.
[88] W.R.O. 212B, N.B. 10.

[89] J. Bodman, *History of Trowbridge* (Bristol, priv. printed, 1814), 22.
[90] H.O. 67/23.
[91] C.P. 25(1)/251/14/6.
[92] W.R.O. North Bradley and Rode and Langham Inclosure Awards. The total area affected was about 1,300 a., of which some 300 a. was woodland.
[93] *App. Rep. Com. Poor Law, Rural Queries*, H.L. 8c, p. 567a (1834), v.
[94] W.R.O. 533, Petition of Farmers of North Bradley.
[95] W.R.O. Tithe Award.
[96] Figures supplied by Bd. of Agric. 1905.
[97] E 134/7 Jas. I/Mich. 14.
[98] *Taxation Lists* (W.A.S. Rec. Brch.), 35.
[99] *Sess. Mins.* (W.A.S. Rec. Brch.), 21, 28, 109, 112, 148; *Q.S. and Ass. 1736* (W.A.S. Rec. Brch.), 28, 58, 83.

pared with 152 supported by agriculture.[1] When handloom weaving died out, many of the workers were able to obtain employment in the factories at Trowbridge and Westbury, to which they walked daily.[2]

A fair was held at Bradley in 1770 on the Monday after Holy Rood day (Sept. 14) for the sale of cattle and cheese.[3] It was still held then in 1866, and another was held on 13 May.[4] In 1881 the May fair has been discontinued but the ghost of the autumn fair, then held in October, remained. Only a few years before the village green had been covered with cattle and merchandize, but the fair was then entirely for pleasure.[5] It was given up about 1900.[6] A fair at Rode Hill, which had been held until a few years before 1881, was probably the same as that mentioned at Rode for the sale of cattle and cheese in 1770;[7] it was then held on the Monday after 29 August. In the later 19th century it was on the Monday after Rode Revel, held on or after 9 September, for the sale of cheese and for pleasure, but it was killed by the competition of the fair at Frome.[8]

MILLS. Isabel of Bradley held a water-mill in Bradley in the mid-14th century.[9] She was probably a member of the family which held the manor of Bradley, for the mill descended in the same way.[10] Thus Thomas Godfrey held it in 1411,[11] Henry Long at his death c. 1490,[12] and Sir Walter Long in 1604.[13] It was evidently separated from the manor in the 17th century, for in 1689 it was assured to John Greenhill the younger by Thomas Adams and others.[14] Grace Greenhill held it in 1697,[15] and another John Greenhill in 1724.[16] A mill at Bradley, presumably this one, was destroyed by rioters in 1766.[17] Since the late 18th century it has been owned by several families in succession.[18] Steam power was installed in the late 19th century, but water continued to be the main source of power until after the Second World War. The mill was in 1963 still used by Thomas Sloper & Sons for grinding animal foods. The large brick building is probably of the early 19th century; adjoining it is a stone house of about the same time.

There was a mill at Langham in 1241.[19] In 1348 it was ruinous.[20] It descended in the same way as the manor of Langham to Richard, Lord Zouche, who in 1551 confirmed an estate in it to Anthony Passion, a Trowbridge clothier.[21] It was then a

fulling mill. It is not clear whether Passion's interest was leasehold or freehold, though he certainly held freehold land at Langham which he acquired from James and Elizabeth Morris.[22] By 1600 Jeffery Whitaker, the Bratton clothier, had an interest in the mill, which was occupied by Edward Rutty.[23] In 1609 Walter Passion conveyed the mill to Edward Hungerford, lord of the manor of Langham.[24] At the break-up of the Hungerford estates toward the end of the century, the mill was sold separately from the rest of the manor to John George alias Edwards of Worton.[25] Elizabeth George held it in 1699,[26] and another John George in 1713.[27] By 1738 it had passed to Thomas Earle of Malmesbury, who made a lease of it in that year.[28] In the following year it was sold to the Houltons of Farleigh Castle (Som.), of whom it was held at a rack rent by William Pooll, millman, in 1771.[29] It was sold to T.W. Ledyard c. 1821,[30] and was still in use as a fulling mill in 1839.[31] It must have fallen out of use soon afterwards, and had disappeared by the end of the century.[32]

CHURCHES. A deed of the earlier 12th century mentions the *monasterium* of Bradley;[33] since nothing is known of any religious foundation there, it is probable that it refers to a chapel in the village. There was certainly a chapel by 1241,[34] when it was dependent on the church of Edington. It remained so until 1351, when the advowson passed to the newly-founded chantry, later house of Bonhommes at Edington; from that time it has been parochially independent. A chapel at Southwick Court was subordinate to the church of Bradley in the Middle Ages. In the 19th century daughter churches were founded at Rode Hill, Southwick, and Brokerswood. Rode Hill was made a district chapelry in 1852,[35] but the other two have remained chapels-of-ease to Bradley.

The church of Edington with Bradley chapel belonged to one of the three prebendaries in Romsey Abbey by 1241,[36] and he must have taken the great tithes and appointed vicars. Bradley was treated separately from Edington, for institutions of vicars to the chapel at the presentation of the prebendaries are recorded from 1316.[37] In 1317 a Trowbridge man was described as farmer of the chapel of Bradley;[38] he no doubt held the great tithes of the chapelry from the prebendary. In 1351 the chapel

[1] *Census*, 1831.
[2] A.F., *North Bradley*, 45.
[3] *The Traveller's Pocket Book*, 1770, 293.
[4] *Gilman's Devizes Public Register*, 1866, 49.
[5] A.F., *North Bradley*, 45.
[6] Local inf.
[7] *The Traveller's Pocket Book*, 1770, 283.
[8] A.F., *North Bradley*, 52.
[9] S.C. 12/699.
[10] See p. 220.
[11] S.C. 2/208/3 m. 3.
[12] S.C. 2/208/6 m. 1.
[13] Soc. Antiq. Jackson. MSS. Survey of Steeple Ashton, 1604.
[14] C.P. 25(2)/887/1 Wm. and Mary East.
[15] Long MSS. Rental 1699.
[16] C.P. 25(2)/1079/10 Geo. I Trin., which gives the name Greenway, probably in error.
[17] *W.N. &Q.* viii. 227.
[18] W.R.O. Land Tax Assessments, Tithe Award; ibid. 533, Valuations of parish, 1869, 1887.
[19] C.P. 25(1)/251/12/8.
[20] *Cal. Inq. p.m.* ix. 391; *Wilts. Inq. p.m.* 1327–77 (Index

Libr.), 219.
[21] C.P. 25(2)/65/532; for Passion see *V.C.H. Wilts.* iv. 140, 145 and above, p. 210.
[22] W.R.O. 490, List of deeds, 1651.
[23] *W.N. & Q.* i. 108.
[24] W.R.O. 490, List of deeds, 1651; for a pretended claim to the mill by former lords of ½ the manor of Langham, see *Cal. S.P. Dom.* 1611–8, 567.
[25] A.F., *North Bradley*, 49.
[26] Long MSS. Rental 1699.
[27] C.P. 25(2)/980/12 Anne Trin.
[28] W.R.O. 130, Lease Earle to Jenkins.
[29] Ibid. 212B, N.B. 8.
[30] A.F., *North Bradley*, 49.
[31] Robson, *Com. Dir.* (1939), Somerset section s.v. Frome.
[32] O.S. Map 1/2,500, Wilts. XXXVIII. 13.
[33] B.M. Lansd. MS. 442, f. 61v.
[34] H. G. D. Liveing, *Records of Romsey Abbey*, 72.
[35] *Lond. Gaz.* 1852, p. 1081.
[36] Liveing, *Records of Romsey Abbey*, 72, 126.
[37] Phillipps, *Wilts. Inst.* i. 14, 40, 41, 46.
[38] *Cal. Pat.* 1313–17, 609.

passed with Edington church from Romsey Abbey to the chantry, later house of Bonhommes, at Edington,[39] and licence to appropriate the great tithes was given in the same year.[40] The rector of the house presented vicars to Bradley until the Dissolution,[41] and then the king presented in 1543 and 1546.[42] In 1551 the advowson was granted with the rest of the Edington property in the parish to the Warden and Scholars of Winchester College,[43] by whom it was still held in 1963.

At the Dissolution the rectory was held by Ambrose Dauntsey by a lease for 23 years from 1538 at a rent of £9 1s. 4d.[44] The College let it to various tenants until 1639, when it was let to John Willis, Vicar of Bradley.[45] By 1646 Willis had left the parish and the lease had passed into other hands, for the inhabitants complained to the College that it was enjoyed by a stranger, and offered to pay the same rent for it, collect the tithes themselves, and hand the profit to the vicar.[46] It was probably as a result of this that the rectory was let to the new vicar, Matthew Buckett, in 1647, for his 'better livelihood and maintenance'.[47] For some reason this arrangement must have proved unsatisfactory, for Buckett surrendered his lease in 1651.[48] A new one was made to Robert Beach of West Ashton, charging the rectory with a yearly payment of £10 to the vicar.[49] This sum was still paid in the late 19th century.[50] In 1665 the rectory was worth £65 a year.[51] The Beach family of West Ashton held it until 1739. Tenants later in the 18th century included Avery Thompson, Vicar of Steeple Ashton, and his widow, who held it successively between 1743 and 1756. In 1795 it was let to Charles Daubeny, Vicar of Bradley,[52] who held it for the rest of his incumbency, and then to his successor, Harry Lee, who still held it in 1841.[53]

The early leases of the rectory included tithes of corn, grass, hay, wool and lambs, and all mortuaries,[54] but in 1641 it was said that mortuaries had always been paid to the vicar.[55] The lessee of the rectory was still disputing them with the vicar in 1704.[56] In 1841 the tithes of hay of about 600 a. were paid in small sums of money laid down by prescription.[57] It was probably these payments which William Pinniger, lessee in 1774, tried to increase, apparently without success.[58] The great tithes were commuted in 1841 for £460.[59]

A house and 2 a. of land belonged to the chapel of Bradley in 1351.[60] In 1538 4a. of arable land in Copley Field belonged to the rectory.[61] In 1581 a small tenement, formerly a copyhold, was added to the lease of the rectory and regularly let with it from that time.[62] It apparently only consisted of a house and 5 a. of pasture.[63] In 1642 the house, which contained a hall, a kitchen, a chamber, and a buttery, was much decayed.[64] The whole rectorial glebe in 1776 consisted of a house and some 11 a. of pasture.[65] Charles Daubeny rebuilt the house c. 1790 to provide accommodation for his curate,[66] and it still stands on the north side of the road opposite the village green. The inclosure of the parish increased the rectorial glebe to 22 a.[67]

The vicarage of Bradley was worth £10 18s. 9d. in 1535.[68] In 1646 its value was said to be so small that no 'well-deserving divine' would hold it.[69] Its augmentation by £10 a year charged on the rectory has been described above. When it was discharged from the payment of first fruits and tenths on the foundation of Queen Anne's Bounty, the vicarage was worth £33 a year.[70] There was a tradition in the 19th century that Edward Batten, vicar 1739–78, received only £20 a year, and that the congregation subscribed £5 a year to augment it.[71] Although £20 was probably an under-estimate, it is clear that the living was very poor. When Charles Daubeny was instituted in 1776, the income was about £50 and all was in such a state of decay that only a man of private means could have taken it.[72] It was augmented by the income from a bequest of £200 in 1778, and £200 was added from Queen Anne's Bounty.[73] By 1835 the income had risen to £400.[74]

In the 15th century the vicar had tithes of cows, calves, foals, pigs, geese, eggs, and gardens.[75] Matthew Buckett, vicar during the Interregnum, found that the sectaries who formed the greater part of his flock would not pay their tithes to him.[76] Some tithes were taken by composition in 1704.[77] During Charles Daubeny's incumbency the vicarial tithes were never worth more than £180 a year.[78] They were commuted for £640 in 1841.[79]

In the later 16th century the vicar's glebe consisted of a house, orchard, and garden, and two little closes. By 1608 a new house of 6 bays had replaced the old one of 2 bays. It was probably the same house that was described as a large, strong, tiled dwelling-house in 1704.[80] When Charles Daubeny went to Bradley the vicarage was a

[39] Ibid. 1350–54, 64.
[40] Cal. Pap. Let. iii. 539.
[41] Phillipps, Wilts. Inst. i, passim.
[42] Ibid. 210, 212.
[43] Cal. Pat. 1550–53, 160.
[44] S.C. 6/Hen. VIII/3985 m. 42d.
[45] W.C.M., U.M.R. Drawer 21.
[46] Ibid. 4299.
[47] Ibid. U.M.R. Drawer 21.
[48] Ibid. 4301.
[49] Ibid. U.M.R. Drawer 21.
[50] A.F., North Bradley, 34.
[51] W.C.M. 4303.
[52] Ibid. U.M.R. Drawer 21.
[53] W.R.O. Tithe Award.
[54] W.C.M., U.M.R. Drawer 21.　　[55] Ibid. 4300.
[56] Sar. Dioc. R.O. Glebe Terrier.
[57] W.R.O. Tithe Award.
[58] Ibid. 533 Disbursements on Poor, 1770–94.
[59] Ibid. Tithe Award.
[60] B.M. Lansd. MS. 442, f. 12.
[61] S.C. 6/Hen. VIII/3985 m. 42d.

[62] W.C.M., U.M.R. Drawer 21.
[63] Sar. Dioc. R.O. Undated Glebe Terrier; see also W.C.M. 4308, where it is the ten. of Nicholas Greenhill.
[64] W.C.M. 4304.
[65] Ibid. 4310.
[66] C. Daubeny, Guide to the Church (1830 edn.), i. p. xxiv.
[67] W.R.O. Tithe Award.
[68] Valor Eccl. (Rec. Com.), ii. 144.
[69] W.C.M. 4299.
[70] Ecton, Thesaurus (1763), 395.
[71] A.F., North Bradley, 31.
[72] Daubeny, Guide to the Church (1830), i, p. ix.
[73] Hodgson, Queen Anne's Bounty (1845), p. cccxxxv.
[74] Rep. Com. Eccl. Revenues, H.C. 54, pp. 826–7 (1835), xxii.
[75] B.M. Lansd. MS. 442, f. 237.
[76] W.C.M. 4302.
[77] Sar. Dioc. R.O. Glebe Terrier, 1704.
[78] Daubeny, Guide to the Church (1830), i, p. xi.
[79] W.R.O. Tithe Award.
[80] Sar. Dioc. R.O. Glebe Terriers.

'miserable hovel, scarcely habitable'. He largely rebuilt it and added to it,[81] so that in 1783 it contained 4 rooms downstairs, 6 bedrooms, and garrets He also inclosed the garden with a wall.[82] The present vicarage was built in 1841–3.[83]

Although Matthew Buckett was not presented to the church until 1645, he does not seem to have satisfied parishioners with radical tendencies, who refused to pay their tithes to him.[84] In 1654 they obtained licence for William Crabb to preach both on weekdays and Sunday afternoons at the church;[85] he was perhaps the preacher on whom the Anabaptists much relied and for whom they tried to get the living on Buckett's death.[86] Nathaniel Brewer, vicar 1720–7, held the living of Keevil as well,[87] and Edward Batten, 1739–77, was curate at Rode and Farleigh Hungerford.[88] By the end of Batten's incumbency the living was in 'a state of general dilapidation and disorder'. Service was performed only once on Sundays and was thinly attended, the parish was 'overrun with dissenters of the worst kind', and the population was 'wild and uncivilized'. Charles Daubeny, vicar 1777–1827, increased the services to twice on Sundays, began prayers on weekdays and holidays, and instituted monthly communions. He spent large sums of his own money on improving the church and the vicarage, instituting an asylum and a poorhouse, and building Christ Church at Rode Hill. By 1788 he had formed a Sunday school which met in the evening and to which his *Lectures on the Catechism* were originally delivered. Daubeny published many other works of theology and controversy, in which it has been said that he anticipated some of the views of the Oxford Movement. In spite of his very considerable charities, however, his spiritual success in his parish was limited. Rigid orthodoxy and lack of tact in attacking nonconformity cannot have been suitable for a parish with so strong a dissenting tradition, and his custom of spending the winter in Bath, leaving a curate in Bradley, was probably also a hindrance to him. Congregations remained small, and he saw three dissenting chapels built in the parish.[89] Daubeny's successor, Harry Lee, also held the living for over 50 years, but was non-resident and unpopular. Congregations did not increase;[90] in 1851 the average was 50 on Sunday morning and 100 in the afternoon, and there was a Sunday school of 35 children.[91]

The church of *ST. NICHOLAS* consists of clerestoried nave with north and south aisles, chancel, north and south chapels, south porch, and prominent western tower. A good deal of it was rebuilt in 1862,[92] but the previous building seems to have been carefully copied. The nave arcades of three bays were renewed then, but reproduce the round piers and capitals and doublechamfered arches of the 13th century ones they replaced. The south porch may also be part of an earlier

church, but all the rest of the building is in the style of the 15th century. The chancel and clerestory were rebuilt in 1862, but the two chapels, the outer walls of the aisles, and the tower were left undisturbed. The south chapel occupies the two eastern bays of the south aisle and one bay flanking the chancel. It formerly had glass in the east window which bore the arms of the Longs and related families,[93] and probably belonged to them as lords of the manor of Bradley. It was later used for burial by the Trenchards of Cutteridge, and was known in the 19th century as the Cutteridge chapel.[94]

The north chapel is of one bay only, to the north of the easternmost bay of the aisle. It was evidently built by the Stafford family of Southwick Court to hold the tomb of Emma (d. 1446) mother of John Stafford, Archbishop of Canterbury 1443–52. He was probably a bastard son of Sir Humphrey Stafford, lord of Southwick (d. 1413).[95] The chapel is richly decorated both inside and out. Outside is a two-tier frieze of quatrefoils above the base, and diagonal buttresses with two tiers of attached crocketed pinnacles. The upper pinnacles are decorated with faces, but the lower ones were built into position only roughed out, and the carving of the faces and crockets has never been completed. Inside, the square-headed north window is taken down as if to form a seat. The sides and back of the recess so formed are panelled to form a surround for the flat stone which bears the incised effigy of the archbishop's mother and an inscription to her. The chapel has a deep, panelled, timber ceiling, each panel being carved with hunting scenes.

The tall western tower is of three stages, and has an octagonal stair-turret carried up higher than the uppermost stage. The tower windows have tracery reminiscent of that at Keevil and Steeple Ashton. The tower and turret and the two chapels are embattled, and the nave and aisles have plain parapets.

Aubrey records that the windows of the church were 'extraordinary good' before the Civil War. For one window in the south aisle Westbury offered to pay £80 and glaze the window again. After the war the arms of the Staffords and Longs and families related to them remained in their chapels, and in the chancel could be seen those of Edington. In the south chapel were the remains of an inscription to Thomas Elme, Rector of Edington 1433–50, and the date 1527.[96] What fragments remained were destroyed at the restoration of 1862.[97]

When Charles Daubeny became vicar in 1777, the church was half in ruins.[98] In 1782 the parish agreed to spend one poor rate on it if the vicar gave an equal sum.[99] With this the vicar newly paved and repaired it throughout, re-roofed the chancel, and rebuilt the east window.[1] By 1861, however, it had again been in a bad state for many

81 Daubeny, *Guide to the Church* (1830), i, pp. ix, xi.
82 Sar. Dioc. R.O. Glebe Terrier, 1783.
83 A.F., *North Bradley*, 34.
84 W.C.M. 4302.
85 *Cal. S.P.Dom.* 1654, 32, 54.
86 W.C.M. 4302.
87 Foster, *Alumn. Oxon.* 1st ser. i. 177.
88 A.F., *North Bradley*, 31.
89 Daubeny, *Guide to the Church* (1830), i, pp. ix–xxiv; Sar. Dioc. R.O. Vis. Queries, 1783; *D.N.B.*; *Annual Biography and Obituary*, 1828, 56–65.

90 A.F., *North Bradley*, 35.
91 H.O. 129/10/259.
92 *Trowbridge Advertizer*, 6 April 1862.
93 Aubrey, *Topog. Coll.* ed. Jackson, 346.
94 A.F., *North Bradley*, 26.
95 *W.N. & Q.* iii. 195–6.
96 Aubrey, *Topog. Coll.* ed. Jackson, 345–9.
97 A.F., *North Bradley*, 27.
98 *Annual Biography and Obituary*, 1828, 61.
99 W.R.O. 533, Disbursements on Poor, 1770–94.
1 Daubeny, *Guide to the Church* (1830), p. xi.

years, and the fall of a large piece of the ceiling which nearly killed a farmer's wife made it clear that thorough restoration was needed.[2] Besides the rebuilding mentioned above, a west gallery was taken away, and a number of gravestones was destroyed. The churchyard was levelled and many stones there destroyed too.[3]

In the south chapel is a large baroque monument to William Trenchard of Cutteridge (d. 1710), and a tablet of coloured marble put up in 1756 to members of the Long family of Melksham, relatives of the Trenchards by marriage.[4] The font is a large one of the late 15th century, octagonal, and bearing on its panels symbols of the Passion and emblems of the evangelists.[5] On the south porch is a sundial inscribed *TEMPUS FUGIT* and *RAWLINGS, BOX, FECIT*, 1777.

There were 4 bells in the church in 1553. The oldest now remaining is by John Wallis of Salisbury, dated 1591. Five were cast by Thomas Bilbie of Chewstoke (Som.) in 1748,[6] and the peal was made up to 8 in 1950. In 1553 the Commissioners took 8½ oz. of silver for the king and left a chalice of 10 oz. In 1629 a silver chalice and a pewter flagon belonged to the church. In 1963 the plate consisted of a plated chalice, paten, and flagon, all dated 1818. They were probably provided by Charles Daubeny, who did not agree with the use of silver vessels. There are also preserved in the church a small pewter chalice and paten, believed to be of the 14th century, which were found in a coffin beneath the chancel at the restoration of 1862.[7]

In 1623 the churchwardens held ½ a. of land and a church house.[8] In 1657 they began to use the church house to keep poor people in, and a few years later it was in decay.[9] No more is heard of it. The ½ a. was effectively converted into a rent-charge of 6s. 8d. a year, which was redeemed in 1954.[10]

In the 13th century disputes between John of Romsey, Rector of Edington, and Adam de Grenville, lord of Southwick, were settled by an agreement which allowed Adam to have a perpetual chantry in his chapel of Southwick. The chaplains were to do fealty to successive rectors, only the Grenville family and their guests were to use the chapel, and careful provision was made about what offerings were to belong to the chantry chaplain and what to the chaplain of Bradley. Adam gave certain lands in free alms for the support of his chaplain, and promised to pay 2 lb. of wax to Bradley church each year.[11] The chapel was dedicated to St. John the Baptist.[12] In Henry

VIII's reign it was served by a morrow-mass priest, who was not allowed to say high mass. He lived in a small house adjoining the Trowbridge road, and was supported by the rents from several copyholds, which the lord of the manor kept in his own control and from which he took the entry fines. These rents amounted to a stipend of just over £6 a year, which was made up to about £11 by another gentleman of the parish. About 1544 the chantry priest, Hugh Lloyd, fled into sanctuary at Bradley to escape prosecution for incontinence and later went away. In the early 17th century several aged witnesses agreed that no service was performed in the chapel after Lloyd's departure, except that the vicar or curate of Bradley would read an epistle or a gospel there when they went in procession in Rogation week.[13] In spite of this, two more chantry priests were appointed after Lloyd's departure, for in 1545 John Owen, lord of the manor, presented Balthazar Leggat on the death of Percival Clough.[14] Leggat was still priest at the dissolution of chantries, but was 70 years old, feeble and lame. The lands of the chantry lay in Southwick, Steeple Ashton, and Keevil;[15] it was perhaps because they were never under the control of the chantry priest directly that they did not pass to the Crown.[16] Only the rent of £6 7s. was claimed; it was granted to John Shelbury and Philip Shute in 1606,[17] and they began a lawsuit against Henry Long to obtain it.[18] Its outcome is not known. The chapel building remained standing, used as a cow-house, until 1839.[19] Its site was apparently in the south-east part of the moated site of Southwick Court. Among the considerable fragments found there are two capitals, parts of the jambs of a door, and a piece of a Purbeck marble shaft, all indicative of a 13th-century building.

The building of a church at Rode Hill, the part of Rode within the parish of North Bradley, was first suggested by some of the inhabitants there in 1821. Archdeacon Daubeny was able to raise considerable subscriptions, and grants from Queen Anne's Bounty and the Church Building Society, amounting in all to over £8,000. The rest of the total building cost of over £12,000 he subscribed himself, and the church was begun in 1822 and opened in 1824.[20] Daubeny gave £1,000 to endow the living, and other benefactions and grants from Queen Anne's Bounty[21] made it possible to employ a stipendiary curate whose salary was £159 in 1835.[22] A house had by then been added to the living. In 1851 average attendance was 60 in the morning and 140 in the afternoon, and there was a

[2] *Trowbridge Advertizer*, 14 Dec. 1861.
[3] A.F., *North Bradley*, 27–8.
[4] Ibid. 19–20.
[5] *W.A.M.* liv. 193; A.F., *North Bradley*, 27.
[6] Walters, *Wilts. Bells*, 36; W.R.O. 533, Receipt from Bilbie.
[7] Nightingale, *Wilts. Plate*, 124–5; W.R.O. 533, Chwdns'. Accts. 1625–96.
[8] W.R.O. 533, Presentment of church lands.
[9] Sar. Dioc. R.O. Chwdns'. Pres. 1662.
[10] Char. Com. Files 71325, 114548.
[11] B.M. Lansd. MS. 442, f. 36. The deed is not precisely dateable; John of Romsey, Adam de Grenville, and R. Precentor of Sarum (a witness) all occur c. 1240 and also c. 1290. Adam is called son of William Grenville, and a William held Southwick in 1274, but not enough

is known of the family to say that the later date is preferable.
[12] C 138/234/41.
[13] E 134/7 Jas. I/Mich. 14; E 134/7 Jas. I/Hil. 1; E 178/2431; *Valor Eccl.* (Rec. Com.), ii. 144.
[14] Phillipps, *Wilts. Inst.* i. 211.
[15] E 301/58 no. 23.
[16] S.C. 2/200/14 and W.R.O. 78, Court Books of Southwick from 1591, in which the chantry lands are regularly mentioned with the other copyholds.
[17] E 308/4/35 no. 96.
[18] E 134/7 Jas. I/Mich. 14.
[19] A.F., *North Bradley*, 9.   [20] Ibid. 53–4.
[21] Hodgson, *Queen Anne's Bounty* (1845), p. cccxxxv.
[22] *Rep. Com. Eccl. Revenues*, H.C. 54, pp. 826–7 (1835), xxii.

Sunday school of 12 pupils.[23] Rode Hill was made a district chapelry in 1852 and about 500 a. of the ancient parish assigned to it.[24] Since 1933 the church has been held with that of Rode,[25] and the area it served forms part of the civil parish of Rode, Somerset.

CHRIST CHURCH stands on rising ground overlooking Rode village. It was designed by H.E. Goodridge of Bath in what a contemporary described as the 'purest Gothick style'.[26] 'It forms a feature', wrote another, 'on which the eye of the most fastidious critic may repose with transport'.[27] By the 1870's it was, however, described as 'hideously ugly',[28] and the historian of the parish felt obliged to defend it against those who had imbibed the ideas of architecture originated by Pugin.[29] Its latest critic speaks of its 'amazing exterior', with detail 'independent of Gothic precedent, wilful and entirely lacking in grace'.[30] It is a rectangular building of 5 bays, consisting of nave, shallow chancel, and lean-to aisles without windows. Flanking the chancel are a vestry on the north and an entrance porch opposite. The nave is lighted by tall, narrow clerestory windows, with geometrical tracery which was probably inserted later. The west front is flanked by two polygonal turrets surmounted by small spires. Many of the internal features were designed by Archdeacon Daubeny.[31] The sanctuary has its original gothic reredos, and the west gallery is also original. At a reseating in the 1890's the eastern part of the nave was included in the chancel, and there are other furnishings of that time. The sanctuary is flanked by elaborate monuments to members of the Daubeny family. That of the archdeacon has a communion table with a bible and a chalice standing on it, with full-size figures of Faith and Charity standing at the sides.

The one bell, by J. Rudhall, and the communion service of plated metal, are contemporary with the church. A barrel organ by Flight and Robson, which had formerly belonged to Frederick Augustus, Duke of York, was placed in the west gallery when the church was built. In 1876 the barrels were removed and the organ renovated and placed in the church.[32] It was replaced by a new organ by Prosser of Frome in 1897.

Daubeny House, the former vicarage, was built shortly after the completion of the church. It is a three-storied stone house with Gothic glazing bars to the windows and conservatory, and a gothic stone porch.

In 1851 the Revd. G. W. Daubeny, eldest son of the archdeacon, gave a small piece of land adjoining the vicarage so that it could be let to the incumbent, who was to pay £5 a year for it towards church repairs. Parts were subsequently sold to enlarge the burial ground of the church, and most of the remainder was sold with the vicarage. The proceeds of the sales have been invested for the same purpose.[33]

An iron mission church was built at Southwick in 1881, and destroyed by fire in 1897.[34] The present church of *ST. THOMAS* was built in 1903 to the design of C. E. Ponting. It is of hammer-dressed stone in the 14th-century style, and consists of nave with north aisle, chancel, and western tower surmounted by a shingled spire.[35] It contains a plain 14th-century font which was formerly at Chilton Foliat. At the west end of the church a tank is sunk into the floor for baptism by immersion, a concession to the strong tradition of Baptist principles in the village.[36]

A small iron mission church was built at Brokerswood in 1905, and is in 1963 still in use.[37]

PROTESTANT NONCONFORMITY. Southwick was one of the earliest and largest Baptist centres in Wiltshire.[38] Representatives from the congregation there were at the meeting of the Western Baptist Association in 1655,[39] and in 1661 it was said that the major part of the 'middle and inferior sort' of people in the parish were Anabaptists.[40] In the years after the first Act of Uniformity the congregation met at times in Witch Pit Wood, near Cutteridge House. The owner of the house, William Trenchard, was a justice, but was sympathetic and gave some protection;[41] it was perhaps because of this that a certain Major William King was able to build a meeting-house, which he called a barn, at which it was alleged that 800 or 1,000 people met.[42] This barn was at Pig Hill on the road from Bradley to Southwick where it stood until the 19th century. In 1669 meetings attracting 200 or 300 people were being held in it twice weekly, taught by a farmer, a brickmaker, and a tailor.[43] In 1670 two men were imprisoned for speaking treasonable words at the meeting,[44] and a year later it was said that as many as 2,000 people from this and surrounding parishes were meeting on Southwick Green and at Brokerswood.[45]

The importance of Southwick as a centre was clearly indicated at the first Declaration of Indulgence in 1672, when Thomas Collier, the great itinerant Baptist, was licensed to preach both there and at Bradley.[46] In 1676 a large part of the inhabitants, 340 out of 440, were obstinate separatists.[47] After the ending of the first period of toleration, the history of the congregation is obscure for

[23] H.O. 129/10/259.
[24] *Lond. Gaz.* 16 April 1852, p. 1081.
[25] *Crockford* (1935).
[26] Daubeny, *Guide to the Church* (1830), ii, app. p. lxxxvi.
[27] *Annual Biography and Obituary*, 1828, 60.
[28] *The Church Rambler in the Neighbourhood of Bath*, ii. 250.
[29] A.F., *North Bradley*, 54–5.
[30] N. Pevsner, *North Somerset and Bristol* (Buildings of Eng.), 251.
[31] Daubeny, *Guide to the Church* (1830), i, p. xliv.
[32] A.F., *North Bradley*, 55, 58–9.
[33] *Endowed Char. Wilts.* (1908), p. 71; Char. Com. File 23560.
[34] Wilts. Cuttings, ix. 42.

[35] Pevsner, *Wilts.* 425.
[36] *W.A.M.* liv. 192–3.
[37] *Kelly's Dir. Wilts.* (1939).
[38] The history of the Baptist cause in Southwick was extensively treated by W. Doel, *Twenty Golden Candlesticks!* (1890), on which much of this account is based. See also *V.C.H. Wilts.* iii. 103f.
[39] Doel, *Twenty Golden Candlesticks!*, 10–11.
[40] W.C.M. 4302.
[41] Doel, *Twenty Golden Candlesticks!*, 4–5, 17–18, 55–57.
[42] *Cal. S.P. Dom.* 1661–2, 212.
[43] Doel, *Twenty Golden Candlesticks!*, 55–57.
[44] *Cal. S.P. Dom.* 1660–70, 457.
[45] *V.C.H. Wilts.* iii. 109.
[46] *Cal. S.P. Dom.* 1672, 400, 401.
[47] Doel, *Twenty Golden Candlesticks!*, 56.

some years, though it evidently continued to exist.[48] During the period of persecution Southwick was a refuge for those unable to worship at Trowbridge. After 1689 they were free to worship in the town, but retained some association with the Southwick church for many years. John Davisson and John Lawes appear to have been ministers at both places in the early 18th century, and as late as 1714 the Conigre church at Trowbridge called itself the 'church usually meeting at Trowbridge and Southwick'.[49] This may, however, be misleading, for there appears to have been a split rather before then; a deed of 1704[50] assigned a small piece of land near Bradley Common to a number of trustees who included several prominent members of the Conigre congregation.[51] On this ground was built a chapel which was used for about a century by a congregation still connected with the Conigre church, but distinct from the Southwick Old Baptist chapel. Little is known of this chapel; after John Davisson's death in 1721 the members attempted to become independent, perhaps because of the new pastor's unorthodoxy, but were persuaded to remain. The cause dwindled in the later 18th century, and the chapel was taken down in 1800.[52]

The main part of the Southwick Baptists, however, had probably ended the connexion with Trowbridge before 1704. In 1706 four men were nominated for the ministry, and three years later a new chapel was built on land conveyed by one of them, John Miller, to James Taunton.[53] Taunton, a Trowbridge man, was the pastor; a few years later his congregation numbered 300, of whom ten were rich.[54] For much of the remainder of the 18th century little is known of the history of the meeting. The long pastorate of Thomas Sayer, from 1744 to 1785, seems to have been a period of decline, though it seems unlikely that Wilson's assertion that it actually became extinct is true.[55] Under Sayer's successor, William Norris, there was a notable revival, crowned in 1815 by the re-building of the chapel.[56] Two other successful pastorates followed;[57] in 1851 the Old Baptist chapel was the best-attended place of worship in the parish, with an average congregation of 370 on Sunday evenings; a Sunday School, which had been begun under Norris, numbered 120 pupils.[58] Under Henry Nightingale, 1856–61, arose the disputes in the congregation which led to the foundation of the Providence Chapel,[59] but the congregation did not fall off. The interior of the chapel was modernized in 1872, and the cause flourished during the pastorate of its historian, William Doel.[60]

Several small benefactions were made to the church in the 18th and 19th centuries. By his will dated 1787 Joshua Keates left 10s. a year to the

minister, but it was not paid after 1837. Another annuity of 30s. was left by Matthias Miller (d. 1730); £1 was to go to the minister and 10s. to poor members. This sum was still paid in 1963. Henry Usher (d. 1739) and Robert Keeping (d. 1756) left £30 and £50 respectively to the use of the ministry. The money was settled in trust in 1787, but appropriated to help to pay off the building debt in 1817, and never repaid. James Doel (d. 1876) left £100, the interest of which was to be divided equally between the Sunday School, poor members of the church, and choir expenses.[61] In 1939 Amelia Perry left £100 to provide for the upkeep of the chapel and graveyard.[62]

The chapel built in 1709 was a thatched building which stood on a site in front of the one which replaced it.[63] The chapel, of 1815, is of brick, with stone window and door surrounds and a hipped slate roof. The windows have segmental heads, keystones, and imposts, and the door has a flat stone hood on cut brackets.

Providence Chapel, Southwick, was founded when some twenty people, who did not approve of Henry Nightingale's dismissal from the pastorate of the Old Baptist Chapel in 1861, left with him to form a society of Strict Baptists. After meeting in a house for some months, they built a stone chapel in the village, to which a burial ground was later added. No settled pastor was appointed after Nightingale's death in 1877, and by 1890 the church was somewhat reduced in numbers, although there was a flourishing Sunday School with 60 pupils.[64]

Although the village of Bradley must have contained many Baptists from the 17th century, no organized congregation was founded there until 1768. Then a farmer, George Batchelor, began holding prayer meetings in his house,[65] at first under Wesleyan influence. He later arranged for Robert Marshman, pastor of the Baptist church at Westbury Leigh, to come and preach, and fitted up a room which would contain 100 people. A church was formally established in 1775 and a chapel was built in 1779. The congregation gradually increased; a gallery over the front entrance was built in 1796; in 1803 the chapel was lengthened at the back to take another gallery, and in 1831 it was widened along one side for a third. The space underneath the latter was left separated from the body of the church by the lower part of the old wall, and formed a room to accommodate the Sunday School begun in 1825.[66] In 1851 the average Sunday evening congregation was 240, and there were 135 Sunday School pupils.[67] A year later the interior was entirely remodelled, the schoolroom being thrown into the church and a new one built at the back. A new roof was built in 1887, and an

[48] Ibid. 26–28.
[49] Ibid. 29–34, 38.
[50] W.R.O. 212B, N.B. 4.
[51] Edw. Grant, Josh. and Robt. Houlton, Wm. Temple; for their connexion with Conigre, see *V.C.H. Wilts.* iii. 122–3 and vii. 158; Doel, *Twenty Golden Candlesticks!*, 101, 103.
[52] Doel, op. cit. 57, 104–5, 107; the site of the chapel may be identified on the Tithe Award, as it still belonged to the Conigre trustees.
[53] Doel, op. cit. 58.
[54] Dr. Williams's Libr. Evans MS., f. 125.
[55] Ibid. Wilson MS. I. 4, f. 320; Doel, *Twenty Golden Candlesticks!*, 62.

[56] Doel, op. cit. 62–3.
[57] Ibid. 83–8.
[58] H.O. 129/10/259; Doel, *Twenty Golden Candlesticks!*,
[59] See below.   [64.
[60] Doel, *Twenty Golden Candlesticks!*, 67–71.
[61] Ibid. 52–4; Keates made a similar bequest to the chapel connected with Conigre.
[62] Char. Com. File 65954.
[63] Doel, op. cit. 58-61.
[64] Ibid. 183–5.
[65] Probably King's Farm: W.R.O. Land Tax Assessments.
[66] Doel, *Twenty Golden Candlesticks!*, 186–91.
[67] H.O. 129/10/259.

organ by Mr. Prosser of Rode was installed.[68] In 1961, for a congregation of about 40, a new church was built on a site between the old chapel, which was then pulled down, and the main road.[69]

The congregation has benefited by several important gifts and bequests. George Batchelor at his death in 1814 left £200, of which the church received £180. This money was retained until 1869, when it was used to buy Lime Villa as a manse for the pastor. In 1903 Ann Greenhill left £50 to the church.[70] Three years later Clara Francis settled just over £350 in trust to pay £10 yearly for the maintenance of services; the rest of the interest was to accumulate to provide a new church. By 1948 the fund had reached nearly £4,000. In 1944 Harry Merritt, a native of the village, who had emigrated to the United States over 50 years before, left over 56,000 dollars for the same purpose.[71]

The old chapel was a plain brick building with stone quoins and a slated roof. It stood along a lane north-east of the Trowbridge-Westbury road facing what was, before the inclosure of the parish, Little Common. The new one was designed by T. W. Snailum in a mid-20th century style. It is of concrete framing and brick, with stone dressings and a low pitched roof covered with copper. The pulpit, dais rail, and some pews were brought from the old church; there is accommodation for 150 people. Behind are schoolroom, vestry, and kitchen.[72]

About 1850 a group of young men who were members of the North Bradley Baptist church began to hold prayer-meetings in a cottage at Yarnbrook. They soon moved to another house there, where they eventually fitted up a room at which regular services were held. Preachers generally came from Emmanuel Church at Trowbridge, and it was as a village station from there that a chapel was eventually built in 1874. A Sunday School began immediately, held at the lower end of the chapel. In 1890 there were 20 members and 70 Sunday School pupils.[73] In 1957 the chapel was sold; since then it has been used as an Independent Baptist chapel.[74] The chapel was designed and built by Noah Hobbs, a member of the original group of 1850; it is in the Gothic style and provides 120 seats.[75]

No group apart from the Baptists has made a permanent impression in the parish. Methodism came to Southwick in 1818 when a chapel was built in the lane to Poles Hole Farm.[76] In 1851 the congregation was about 40, and there was a Sunday School of about 50 pupils.[77] About 1870 the cause began to decline, and the chapel was closed in 1876 and subsequently pulled down.[78] Early in 1851

some 40 Methodists were meeting in a disused house at Bradley, but ceased to do so before the end of the year.[79]

Even more transient were a small group of Quakers in the village late in the 17th century,[80] Independents licensed to meet in a house in 1774,[81] and a 'Free Christian Church' registered at Yarnbrook in 1863.[82] The latter was begun by Charles Dunning in a room which was also used by the first Agricultural Labourers' Union in the county; the opposition of the farmers apparently extended to the meeting as well as the union, and both were given up.[83]

PARISH GOVERNMENT. One Overseer for each of the tithings of Bradley and Southwick was being appointed in the 1620's.[84] From that time until the end of the old poor law the poor of each tithing were relieved separately from rates raised within it, but the appointment and control of each overseer was carried out in one vestry for the whole parish.[85] The vestry was always open to all rate-payers;[86] in 1740 it was complained that the poor crowded in to the church at vestry meetings too.[87] A salaried assistant overseer was appointed in the early 19th century.[88]

In the 1640's and 1650's the amount expended on the poor was often between £40 and £60 a year for the whole parish.[89] Between then and the end of the century it rose gradually, so that c. 1700 each tithing was spending £70 or £80 a year on its poor. About half the money went in regular payments to some dozen recipients in each tithing, all aged people, widows with children, orphans, or infirm people. The remainder provided extra help for clothes, fuel, medicine, and rent both for the regular poor and for others when necessary.[90] The same system of payment was pursued throughout the 18th century, still with steadily rising expenditure. By 1740 the parish was spending almost £400 a year on its poor, and the rates were said to be daily increasing.[91] They were clearly proving a heavy burden at this time, for in 1734 the vestry agreed to build or buy a poor house, to withhold regular relief from those who refused to wear a parish badge, to require settlement certificates from strangers or else to enforce their removal, and to prosecute intruders on the commons.[92] The building of a workhouse was approved by Sir Philip Parker Long in 1737, but was evidently replaced by renting a house called Park Lane House. In 1739 it was agreed to rent more houses at Southwick and Rode, and ordered that in future no help was to be given with the payment of individuals' house rent. This order was soon disregarded, and

[68] Doel, op. cit. 190–1.
[69] Wilts. Times, 24 Nov. 1961. For old chapel, see pl. facing p. 181.   [70] Endowed Char. Wilts. (1908), p. 73.
[71] Wilts. Times, 24 Nov. 1961.
[72] Ibid. 20 Jan., 27 Oct., 24 Nov. 1961.
[73] Doel, Twenty Golden Candlesticks!, 158–60.
[74] Local inf.
[75] Doel, op. cit., 159.
[76] Ibid. 3.
[77] H.O. 129/10/259.
[78] Doel, Twenty Golden Candlesticks!, 3; G.R.O. Worship Reg., entry no 2303; A.F., North Bradley, 38.
[79] H.O. 129/10/259.
[80] V.C.H. Wilts. iii. 117.

[81] G.R.O. Retns. of Regns.
[82] Ibid. Worship Reg., entry no. 15632.
[83] A.F., North Bradley, 43.
[84] W.R.O. 533 Chwdns.' Acct. Bk. 1620–96.
[85] W.R.O. 533 passim.
[86] Ibid.; App. Rep. Com. Poor Law, Rural Queries, H.L. 8c–g, pp. 567a–e (1834), v–ix.
[87] W.R.O. 533, Letter from Sir P. P. Long.
[88] Poor Law, Rural Queries (1834), 567c.
[89] W.R.O. 533 Chwdns'. Acct. Bk. 1620–96.
[90] Ibid. Disbursements on poor, 1667–81, 1692–1707.
[91] Ibid. Disbursements on poor, 1707–46, and Letter from Sir P. P. Long.
[92] Ibid. Disbursements on poor, 1727–38.

the management of the poor seems to have carried on much as before.[93]

It may, however, have been the stricter application of the laws from the 1730's, coupled with improving times in the cloth industry,[94] which kept expenditure virtually stationary for about three decades. It was not until the 1770's that it regularly exceeded £400, and by c. 1790 it was exceeding £500. Then began the phenomenal rise in the poor rates characteristic of the greater part of England at this time. Within a few years expenditure doubled and doubled again: in 1796–7 each tithing spent over £500, in 1802–3 over £800, and in 1811–12 almost £1,000. In the worst years the £1,000 was well exceeded. In 1821 Southwick spent £1,404, and in 1831 Bradley £1,298.[95]

It is clear that, as elsewhere, the problem was caused by the necessity to relieve able-bodied labourers who could not obtain employment, but it was aggravated here by the large numbers whose employment in the woollen industry was only intermittent. The parish was able to do little except pay them enough to subsist on. No workhouse was ever built. In 1834 the parish still owned a number of cottages, in which there were 122 people, mainly brought in by removal orders. In addition it was usual to give out-relief to between 50 and 90 able-bodied workmen and their dependents, a total of over 200. Many woollen workers not regularly on the parish were helped to pay house-rent and loom-rent in attempts to keep them solvent. The roundsman system was tried in 1831, when labourers were allotted to farms in proportion to their poor-rate assessment, and wages were paid by the farmers according to a scale laid down by the parish. It proved extremely unpopular with the farmers and was discontinued. The provision of 35 a. of allotment land and of seed to sow it with failed, because, the farmers alleged, of the idleness of the paupers, who were unwilling to give up any of the parish allowance to which they had become accustomed. By 1834 it was generally agreed in the parish that the burden of the poor-rates was proving too much for the farmers to bear.[96]

SCHOOLS. There was a school at North Bradley church in Henry VIII's reign.[97] No more is known of a school there until Archdeacon Daubeny began one taught by the parish clerk in a house in Church Lane.[98] Daubeny subsequently incorporated a schoolroom in the Asylum which he built and endowed in 1808; it was intended for 30 day pupils and a Sunday School of 60.[99] In 1819 it was said education was a secondary consideration with most parents, who set their children to work at the clothing trade.[1] In 1833,

however, there were 60 day pupils at the Asylum School, which was conducted on Bell's system. All the children were taught to read, but could only learn to write if their parents supplied the necessary books. The schoolmistress had living quarters in the Asylum and £20 a year, and the resident curate supervised the school.[2] The school continued to educate some 60 pupils, all Anglicans, until 1880,[3] but at that time it had received no government aid, and neither the building nor the instruction met the requirements of the Education Act.[4] A School Board was set up compulsorily in that year,[5] but the new vicar, E. A. Were, quickly prevented the building of a non-sectarian school by offering to set apart a piece of the glebe and to build a school on it. The building, which included a teacher's house, was designed by Weaver and Adye of Bradford and opened in 1881.[6] Daubeny's school was closed, and a scheme of 1882 allotted £25 a year from the income of his charity to the new school.[7] It was placed in union with the National Society. In 1931 the senior children were removed to the Trowbridge schools, and since then it has been a junior mixed and infant school, which has controlled status under the 1944 Act.

There were 5 private day schools in Southwick in 1833.[8] In 1858 most of the children from the village attended the school at Upper Studley in Trowbridge parish.[9] Ten years later R.P. Long of Rood Ashton gave a piece of land, and a school and teacher's house were built by subscription. The building, of brick with stone dressings, was designed in a Tudor style by Lemuel Moody of Trowbridge.[10] It became a junior mixed and infant school in 1931 when the senior children were removed to the Trowbridge schools.

CHARITIES. By her will proved in 1781 Rachel Long, daughter of Sir James Long (d. 1729), lord of the manor of Bradley, left £3 a year charged on Manor Farm, to be divided among six deserving poor families. This charge was later increased to £4 and paid as directed to 8 families.[11]

In 1808–10 Charles Daubeny, Vicar of Bradley, built an Asylum near the church for the accommodation of 4 aged people 'of good character and rather above the *lowest* classes'.[12] The building also housed a school. In 1818 he built a row of three cottages to provide homes for 12 poor people who were maintained by the parish. At his death in 1827, he left £3,800 to the warden and scholars of Winchester College; out of the income they were to pay £30 a year to the minister of Christ Church, Rode Hill, to be divided equally between the maintenance of the church, the support of a Sunday School there, and the relief of regular attenders

[93] Ibid. 1738–46, and Letter from Sir P. P. Long.
[94] *V.C.H. Wilts.* iv. 160–1.
[95] W.R.O. 533 Disbursements on poor 1758–70, 1770–94, 1794–1804, 1812–17, 1820–35; *App. Rep. Sel. Cttee. on Poor Rate Retns.* H.C. 556, p. 190 (1822), v; ibid. H.C. 334, p. 230 (1825), iv.
[96] *Poor Law, Rural Queries* (1834), 567a–e; W.R.O. 533 Disbursements on poor, 1820–35 and Petition of farmers of parish c. 1831.
[97] E 134/7 Jas. I/Mich. 14.
[98] A.F., *North Bradley*, 44.
[99] Daubeny, *Guide to the Church* (1830), p. xxxii.
[1] *Digest of Returns to Cttee. on Educ. of Poor*, H.C. 224 (1819), ix (2).

[2] *Endowed Char. Wilts.* (1908), p. 68.
[3] Acct. of Wilts. Schools, H.C. 27 (1859 Sess. 1), xxi(2); A.F., *North Bradley*, 44.
[4] *Mins. of Educ. Cttee. of Council*, 1881–2, [C. 3312–I], p. 285 (1882), xxiii; Char. Com. File 7231.
[5] *Lond. Gaz.* 25 May 1880, p. 3173.
[6] A.F., *North Bradley*, 44.
[7] *Endowed Char. Wilts.* (1908), p. 68.
[8] *Educ. Enq. Abstract*, H.C. 62 (1835), xliii.
[9] *Acct. of Wilts. Schools* (1859 Sess. 1).
[10] A.F., *North Bradley*, 45.
[11] *Endowed Char. Wilts.* (1908), pp. 61, 64.; Burke, *Commoners*, iii. 218; Char. Com. Acct. File.
[12] C. Daubeny, *Guide to the Church* (1830), i, p. xxxii.

at the church. The remainder of the income was to support the Asylum, school, and poorhouses. The inmates of the asylum received 4s. a week each, the salary of the schoolmistress was £20 a year, and the rest was apparently given in occasional relief to the people in the poorhouses.

After the establishment of another school in Bradley in 1881, the school in the Asylum was closed and the whole charity regulated by a scheme. Winchester College was discharged from the trust, and £25 a year was assigned to the new school; it was provided that the old schoolroom in the Asylum should be let to the vicar for a parish room. The Rode Hill charity was allotted £1,000 of the stock to provide the £30 a year required for it. In 1903 the vicar's poorhouse was still occupied by people supported by the parish but there was little demand for admission. In 1959 the name of the poorhouse was changed to St. Nicholas's Cottages; only one

of the houses was occupied under the charity, the others being let. The Asylum only had two inmates and was in bad repair, and the whole future of the charity was doubtful.[13]

The Asylum stands facing the village green. The front is of ashlar, of two stories and seven bays, surmounted by a plain parapet with central pediment, containing the arms of Charles Daubeny and the date 1810. The rest of the building is of brick with stone dressings, and there is a hipped slated roof. It contains four two-storied and two-roomed houses, each with its own entrance. On the left of the central passage is the schoolroom, with teacher's quarters above.

By his will proved in 1868 Robert Nokes of Bradley Mill left £50 to provide small annual payments for six poor inhabitants of Yarnbrook; the income in 1963 was still laid out as directed.[14]

EAST COULSTON

East Coulston lies about 4½ miles east of Westbury. The parish is long and narrow, extending about 4½ miles from north to south, while its width before 1934 nowhere exceeded ½ mile.[1] In that year a strip of varying width running the whole length of the western boundary of the parish was transferred from Edington to East Coulston.[2] This more than doubled the size of the latter, from 875 to 1,988 a.[3] The northern part of the parish is flat and well watered, rising from below 175 ft. at the boundary with Bulkington to about 250 ft. near the village. It lies on the Kimmeridge clay belt of north-west Wiltshire, and is mainly meadow and pasture. The village stands on outcrops of Upper Greensand and Gault. South of the village the ground rises sharply up the northern edge of Salisbury Plain to over 700 ft. on Coulston Hill. The southern ⅔ of the parish is all chalk downland, between 500 and 700 ft. above sea level. There is a considerable area of arable land on the northern edge of the Plain, and more arable on the greensand near the village.[4] The southern part of the parish is included in the military training district centred on Imber.[5]

The secondary road from Westbury to West Lavington crosses the parish south of the village, which is connected to it by two minor roads. These unite in the village and continue north-westward to Marston. A road in this direction was in use in 1712[6] and still existed in 1773,[7] but seems to have fallen out of use by the 19th century. It was re-made in 1899.[8] There was a road northward to Keevil in the 16th century, but it was alleged in Mary's reign that Aldhelm Lambe had stopped it up.[9] The old slowcoach road from Bath to Salisbury

crosses the parish on Coulston Hill, but was not in 1959 passable except for farm vehicles.[10] The main railway line between Westbury and Lavington passes north of the village; the nearest station is Lavington, three miles to the east.

The village is built round irregular spurs of higher ground which project northward from the Plain. Before 1934 the western part lay in the tithing of West Coulston in Edington. The boundary passed through Baynton House, and for some way along the centre of the road in the village, so that the Bell Inn, the former school, and the Baptist Chapel were all in Edington parish. In the village the houses are well scattered. The part formerly known as West Coulston lies along the road from Westbury. The former Bell Inn, closed c. 1955, is a timber-framed building. A timber-framed house of the early 17th century with two gables to the front stands at the corner of the lane up to Baynton House. It has been converted into two cottages, of which one was derelict in 1963. Southward lies a road on which stand the former school and the former chapel. Manor Cottage is a timber-framed building with a thatched roof, probably of the 17th century. Another road leads eastward towards the church. On it stands Coulston House and the former rectory. Baynton House stands in extensive grounds between the church and the main road. There are isolated farms at Stokes Marsh and Brickfield in the north, and Coulston Hill, Baynton Hill, and Tinhead Hill on the downs.

In 1676 there were apparently 62 adults in the parish.[11] In 1783 it was said that it contained only nine houses, six of which were cottages.[12] The population of the parish increased from 90 in 1801

[13] Endowed Char. Wilts. (1908), pp. 61–3, 64–9; Char. Com. Files 35864, 57085, 7, 325, 141220.
[14] Endowed Char. Wilts. (1908), p. 72; Char. Com. File 82926.
[1] The following maps were used: O.S. Maps 1/2,500, Wilts. XXXIX. 15. XLV. 3 (1st and later edns.); 1/25,000, ST. 94, 95 (1958); 1″, sheet 14 (1st edn.).
[2] Wilts. Co. Review Order, 1934.
[3] Census, 1931, 1951.

[4] A. H. Fry, Land Utilization, Wilts., 157.
[5] Local inf.
[6] W.A.M. lvii, 226.
[7] Andrews and Dury, Map (W.A.S. Rec. Brch.), pl. 8.
[8] Wilts. Cuttings, xii. 304.
[9] Sta. Cha. 4/10/49.
[10] V.C.H. Wilts. vii. 82.
[11] W.N. & Q. iii. 82.
[12] Sar. Dioc. R.O. Vis. Queries, 1783.

to 133 in 1871, but thereafter decreased until it was 78 in 1931. In 1951, after the addition of territory from Edington, it was 155.[13]

Mary Delany (1700–1788), friend of Swift and Fanny Burney, was born at Coulston. She was the daughter of Bernard Granville, a younger brother of George Granville, Baron Lansdown (d. 1735), and her autobiography and correspondence have been published.[14]

MANORS. It has been suggested that when King Edgar gave Edington to Romsey Abbey in 968, the eastern boundary of the granted lands coincided with that of East Coulston rather than that of Edington, so that both parishes were included.[15] If this was so, part of the property must have passed out of the abbey's possession by 1086, for a five-hide manor in Coulston was then held by Brictric.[16] This manor, like the rest of Brictric's possessions, was in the hands of Edward of Salisbury by the early 12th century, and formed part of the lands later known as the honor of Trowbridge, given by Edward to Humphrey de Bohun (II). It descended in the Bohun family in the same way as Trowbridge[17] until 1229, when Humphrey de Bohun (V), Earl of Hereford, and Ela, Countess of Salisbury, agreed to a division of the honor. Coulston was still held in demesne, and was divided by this bargain; Humphrey took $\frac{2}{3}$, including the manor house, and Ela the remaining $\frac{1}{3}$ and the advowson.[18] Ela's $\frac{1}{3}$ descended as did Trowbridge to Henry of Bolingbroke,[19] son of John of Gaunt, who obtained possession of the other part of Coulston by his marriage to Mary, daughter and heir of Humphrey de Bohun (X), Earl of Hereford (d. 1373).[20] On Henry's accession to the throne in 1399 the overlordship merged in the Crown as parcel of the Duchy of Lancaster.

While the manor was divided, however, the overlords of each part created mesne estate which remained separate until they were united by the Lambe family in the 16th century. In 1236 William Longespée confirmed a previous grant from his mother, Countess Ela, to Ralph Long, of 'the land of Coulston' in fee.[21] The exact descent of this holding is not clear, but in 1329 another Ralph Long and Eleanor his wife conveyed property there to Nicholas Chamberlain.[22] By 1428 it was held by Thomas and Agnes Burton in right of Agnes,[23] formerly called Chamberlain,[24] who is also said to have brought her husband lands in Luckington.[25] She was a widow in 1431, and subsequently married Thomas Tropenell.[26] Her land in Coulston may have descended to Thomas Burton who was

lord of Luckington in 1442.[27] By the early 16th century this estate had apparently been divided between co-heirs; in 1523 Simon Kirkby of Norton Folgate (Mdx.) sold moieties of the manors of Coulston and Luckington to Sir William Compton of Compton Wynyates (Warws.).[28] His son Peter died in 1544 leaving a posthumous son Henry.[29] In 1556 Coulston was still held in dower by Peter's widow,[30] but Henry Compton did not hold it at his death in 1589.[31] There is little doubt that it had been sold to the Lambe family, for in 1615 John Lambe died seised of houses and lands called Burton's,[32] a name which must have referred to the 15th-century owners.

It is possible that some part of the property held of the Countess of Salisbury by the Longs in the 13th century had come to the Lambe family earlier than Burton's. In 1268 Peter Long and Maud his wife acknowledged that a mill and land in Coulston belonged to Nicholas Frankeleyn.[33] Peter Frankeleyn held land worth £10 there in 1401.[34] In the reign of Henry VII John Lambe had inherited what were probably the same lands from his kinsman Jenkin Frankeleyn.[35] Lambe died c. 1501 and was succeeded by his son John who died c. 1514; both were prosperous men.[36] The younger John's son, Aldhelm, was heavily rated in 1524 and 1545,[37] and soon afterwards acquired the larger part of the manor as it had been divided in 1229, which had descended as follows.

Humphrey de Bohun (V), who received it, gave it with his daughter Alice on her marriage to Roger, son of Ralph Tony.[38] Roger died c. 1277 leaving a son Ralph,[39] who exchanged Coulston with Walter Beauchamp of Alcester (Warws.) for lands elsewhere.[40] Beauchamp and his wife Alice, who was formerly called Tony, granted the manor to Simon Chamberlain and Elizabeth his wife for their lives in exchange for their manor of Mutton in East Knoyle.[41] Simon forfeited his land in 1325 because he adhered to Maurice of Berkeley the elder in his rebellion. He died in prison at Gloucester the same year, and the manor was immediately restored to his widow.[42] She still held it in 1338, when Sir William Beauchamp, second son of Walter and Alice, granted the reversion to Giles, his younger brother and eventual heir.[43] Giles died in 1361 and was succeeded by his son John, and the manor descended in the Beauchamp family to Richard, Lord Beauchamp of Powick, who died without male issue in 1503.[44] Before his death he had settled Coulston on his daughter Elizabeth, when she married Robert Willoughby, afterwards Lord Willoughby de Broke (d. 1521).[45] Elizabeth died

13 V.C.H. Wilts. iv. 345.
14 D.N.B..
15 Grundy, 'Saxon Land Charters of Wilts', Arch. Jnl. lxxvii. 80.
16 V.C.H. Wilts. ii, p. 160.
17 Ibid. pp. 108–10; vii. 128.
18 C.P. 25(1)/250/8/11.
19 V.C.H. Wilts. vii. 128–9.
20 Cal. Close, 1381–5, 514–5.
21 W.A.M. xxxv. 204.
22 C.P. 25(1)/252/26/34.
23 Feud. Aids. v. 276; C.P. 25(1)/257/61/33.
24 C 1/6/22.
25 W.N. &Q. vi. 93.
26 Tropenell Cart. ed. Davies, i. pp. xi, 122.
27 Collectanea (W.A.S. Rec. Brch.), 171.
28 Req. 2/12/145; C.P. 40/1035 rot. 531.

29 C 142/72/105.
30 S.C. 6/Ph. and M./502.
31 C 142/229/130.
32 C 142/355/93.
33 C.P. 25 (1)/251/21/47.
34 Feud. Aids, vi. 630.
35 Req. 2/6/57.
36 P.C.C. 13 Blamyr, 34 Fetiplace.
37 E 179/197/153; Taxation Lists (W.A.S. Rec. Brch.),
38 B.M. Add. MS. 28024, f. 187.   [35·
39 Dugdale, Baronage, i. 470.
40 B.M. Add. MS. 28024, f. 187.
41 Cal. Inq. Misc. ii, p. 201.
42 Cal. Close, 1323–7, 300.
43 C.P. 25(1)/254/43/37.
44 Complete Peerage, s.v. Beauchamp of Powick.
45 Cal. Inq. p.m. Hen. VII, ii, p. 503.

in the same year as her father, and after the death of Robert the property fell to the share of Blanche, one of his grand-daughters (children of his son Edward, who predeceased him).[46]

Blanche, who married Francis Dawtrey of Porchwood (Hants), died without issue, but the manor had been secured to her husband for life in 1539.[47] In 1545 he assigned his interest to Sir Thomas Moyle of Eastwell (Kent).[48] The reversion had passed to Blanche's sister Elizabeth, wife of Sir Fulk Greville, and in 1546 she and her husband sold Coulston to William Button of Alton Priors.[49] He was probably acting on behalf of his son-in-law Aldhelm Lambe, husband of his daughter Ruth,[50] in whose family it descended.

Aldhelm Lambe's eldest son John died c. 1546 in his father's lifetime,[51] and the estates passed to his son, another John. He died in 1615 holding three properties in East Coulston, one being the manor of 715 a., one called Burton's of 108 a., and one of 90 a.[52] It is possible that the largest of these was the Hereford or Beauchamp manor, and that the two smaller ones, having descended respectively through Burton and Frankeleyn, represented the share of the Countess of Salisbury in 1229. John Lambe's son, another John, was knighted before 1623, and died in 1659. Before his death he seems to have left Coulston,[53] and the estate was in the hands of his eldest son John by 1650. By then it was heavily encumbered by mortgages and John Lambe was forced by fraud, as he alleged, to sell parts of it to discharge them.[54] He sold the largest part with the manorial rights to his brother William, who had been bred up a merchant. He in turn sold part of the manor to his nephew Francis Godolphin, son of his sister Ruth; it consisted of three or four small copyholds, so that Godolphin could hold courts, and some other lands of small value. Lambe retained the manor house, and Godolphin built himself a new one, worth, as was alleged, only £200. Godolphin died in 1670 leaving his manor of East Coulston to his son William.[55]

Meanwhile, in 1669 William Lambe had sold the manor house of Coulston, over 100 a. of land, and four more copyholds to Sir Giles Hungerford of Corsham.[56] In 1678 Francis Godolphin, younger brother of William, sold most of his family's share of Coulston to Edward Hungerford,[57] from whom it passed like the rest of his estates to his uncle Sir Giles. The two chief parts of the manor were thus re-united. Sir Giles died in 1685, leaving Coulston to his widow Margaret (d. 1711) for her life and then to his daughter Margaret, who married Robert, Lord Lexinton of Aram.[58] In 1718 Lord Lexinton sold it to Sir Edward des

Bouverie of Longford. In 1723 Sir Edward sold it to Sir Jacob des Bouverie, who two years later sold the manor to George Heathcote, all except the manor house and one farm which were sold at the same time to Townsend Andrews. In 1737 Peter Delmé bought both parts,[59] and Coulston subsequently descended to the families of Smith and Watson-Taylor in the same way as the manor of Erlestoke.[60]

The manor house of Coulston was presumably that sold by William Lambe to Sir Giles Hungerford in 1669, and occupied in the 18th century by Townsend Andrews. It is said to have stood in a paddock called Lambe's Lawn at the west end of the churchyard.[61] Foundations have been uncovered there from time to time, and the tradition remains in the village that the Lambes and Godolphins lived very close together.[62] The house now called Coulston House was occupied by tenant farmers of the estate. It is of two stories and five bays, stuccoed and with a double hipped roof of slate, and dates from c. 1770. Behind is an extensive range of contemporary brick farm buildings.

Even the sale to Sir Giles Hungerford in 1669 left some property in Coulston in the hands of William Lambe, although it must have been small.[63] It descended in his family to Thomas Lambe, a great-grandson of Sir John, who died a young man in 1741. His heir was his sister Meliora, successively wife of Thomas Polden of Imber and Richard Long of Rood Ashton. It is said to have been sold by her or at her death.[64]

The Godolphins also retained some property when they sold their part of the manor. It was probably little more than the house which Francis Godolphin had built c. 1658. It was occupied by his daughter Elizabeth, who married her cousin Charles Godolphin. She died without issue in 1726, and by her will founded the Godolphin School at Salisbury.[65] Her heir was her nephew William Godolphin, who lived at Coulston until his death at a great age in 1781.[66] He bought a small property, which included Coulston Mill, from Peter Delmé in 1740.[67]

The house of the Godolphins evidently formed part of that now known as Baynton House. After William Godolphin's death in 1781 it was bought by William Evelyn, who is said to have enlarged what was previously a house 'of very small pretensions'.[68] In 1796 it was bought by William Long, whose manor house of Baynton in Edington had been destroyed by fire. He also altered it and renamed it Baynton House.[69] John Long, who inherited his property, lived in it in 1840,[70] but it subsequently passed to the Watson-Taylors of

[46] C 3/52/25.
[47] C.P. 25(2)/52/374/19.
[48] C 54/442.
[49] C.P. 25(2)/46/324/Hil. 37 Hen. VIII.
[50] Wilts. Visitation Pedigrees (Harl. Soc.), 106.
[51] W.R.O. Arch. Sar. Will of Jn. Lambe; Req. 2/47/13; Req. 2/146/98.
[52] C 142/355/93; P.C.C. 26 Rudd.
[53] W.A.M. iii. 105.
[54] C 6/7/139.
[55] F. G. Marsh, The Godolphins (priv. print. 1930), 30–35.
[56] C 6/184/52.
[57] C.P. 43/383 rot. 237.
[58] W.A.S. Libr. Devizes, Jackson's Hungerford MSS. Places, i. 283.

[59] W.R.O. 323, Title Deeds of Manor. For the origin of Townsend Andrews see Aubrey, Topog. Coll. ed. Jackson, 117.
[60] V.C.H. Wilts. vii. 84.
[61] W.A.M. iii. 105.
[62] Ex inf. Mr. R. H. Pearson.
[63] W.R.O. 212A, Release Lambe to Alexander, 1675; W.A.M. iii. 105.
[64] W.A.M. iii. 104.
[65] F.G. Marsh, The Godolphins, 37–9; V.C.H. Wilts. v. 362–3.
[66] Marsh, op. cit. 46–52.
[67] W.R.O. 323, Deed Delmé to Godolphin, 1740.
[68] Ibid. Land Tax Assessments; Soc. Antiq. Jackson MSS.
[69] Ibid.
[70] W.R.O. Tithe Award.

Erlestoke, from whom it was bought by G. S. H. Pearson c. 1915.[71] Parts of the house at the back probably date from the first building of c. 1658, and in the hall there is re-used panelling of the same time. The east front of the house was built in the late 18th century; it is of five bays and two stories with a central Doric porch. The south wing is a somewhat later addition.

LESSER ESTATES. After the Civil War John Lambe, who then controlled his father's estates in Coulston, decided to sell parts of them to try to clear mortgages on the rest. Although he tried to sell in the open market, he was forced, as he alleged, by the fraud of his attorney, Robert Beach of West Ashton, to sell to the mortgagers. One property, consisting of meadow and pasture land in the north of the parish, passed in this way to Walter Norborne of Calne.[72] In the early 18th century it was held by Norborne's daughters and coheirs, Elizabeth, Viscountess Hereford, and Susan, wife of Sir Ralph Hare. Their property then consisted of two houses and some 500 a. of land, much of which lay in West Coulston, and some of which may have once formed part of the manor of Baynton in Edington. In 1709 the tenant was William Tayler, and his family held it as leaseholders until 1797, when George Tayler bought it from the Marquess of Bath.[73] In 1840 the property in East Coulston consisted of Stokes Marsh Farm of 180 a.[74] Brickfield Farm was built on it later in the century, and both farms were sold by the Tayler family c. 1945.[75]

The other property sold by John Lambe consisted of arable land on the 'East Hill' of Coulston and a sheep sleight, amounting to 400 a. in all. It was mortgaged to John Bennett of Steeple Ashton, and was sold at his instance to his son Christopher.[76] By 1680 it had descended to Christopher's son Thomas.[77] This farm was probably that now called Coulston Hill Farm, which was called Lambe's Farm in 1773 and 1811.[78] By 1780 Edward Norris owned it. Richard Norris died c. 1827, and the farm was sold to G. Watson-Taylor.[79]

ECONOMIC HISTORY. In 1086 there was land for four ploughs at Coulston. Half of this was in demesne with 6 serfs, while 5 villeins and 3 bordars held the rest.[80] The ⅔ of the manor which were allotted to Humphrey de Bohun in 1229[81] consisted of a capital messuage, 4½ virgates, 6 cotlands, and 2½ a. of land held by villeins, and a demesne of 146 a. Common meadow lay at Nordmede and Linmede (later Inmead), and common pasture in the marsh (the low ground in the north

of the parish) and on the down.[82] In 1325 the same part of the manor, then leased to Simon Chamberlain, was in the king's hands for six weeks.[83] During that time pasture for 200 sheep was sold, and more pasture lay in the fallow lands. The pasture of the meadow and the marsh could not be sold because it was common in spring.[84] During Mary's reign 30 acres of meadow at Long Mead (on the parish boundary east of Brickfield Farm) were inclosed by Aldhelm Lambe, the lord of the manor. Before this the fields of Coulston and Erlestoke had not been separated, and the cattle of the two parishes had common over both fields.[85]

By the 17th century it is clear that almost all the lower part of the parish was inclosed, and that the only open-field arable lay on the down, with a sheep pasture beyond it to the south.[86] Stokes Marsh and Coulston Hill Farms both appear as separate freehold farms in the mid-17th century,[87] while in 1723 the part of Coulston manor which was sold by Sir Edward des Bouverie consisted of two farms, one of them the demesne farm, let at rack rents, and 17 cottages and other small holdings held by copies or leases for lives.[88] In 1783 dairy farming was the chief occupation of the inhabitants.[89] By 1800 the whole parish consisted chiefly of three farms. Inclosed meadow and pasture land in the north of the parish, with land in West Coulston, was owned and occupied by George Tayler.[90] In 1817 the farmhouse of this holding, named Coulston Dairy, lay in West Coulston, east of Baynton Dairy Farm,[91] but by 1840 it was being farmed from Stokes Marsh Farm.[92] In 1800 Richard Perret was tenant of the whole of Joshua Smith's estate in East Coulston and also land in West Coulston,[93] which in 1840 was farmed from the present Coulston House.[94] In the south of the parish Richard Norris owned and occupied Coulston Hill Farm.[95] By 1840 Jonathan Grant occupied both Perret's and Norris's farms, farming about 1100 acres in East and West Coulston; this included the whole of what had formerly been the open arable field of the manor on Coulston Hill.[96] When the Coulston estate was sold in 1914, Coulston Hill Farm was sold as one lot; it contained 334 acres, while only 85 acres were sold with Coulston House. Brickfield Farm was separated from Stokes Marsh Farm in 1919.[97]

A field east of Brickfield Farm was called Brickfield in 1840, but no workings are shown on the tithe map.[98] In 1867[99] and 1885[1] Robert Davis, brick and tile maker, worked in Coulston, no doubt on the same site.

There was a mill worth 10s. at Coulston in

[71] Ex inf. Mr. R. H. Pearson.
[72] C 6/7/139; C.P. 25(2)/512/22 Chas. I East.
[73] Longleat MSS. Title Deeds, Rentals, and Manor Bks.
[74] W.R.O. Tithe Award.
[75] Local inf.; in W.A.S. Libr., Devizes, is a Sale Cat. dated 1919, but presumably no sale was made.
[76] C 6/7/139.
[77] E 134/31–2 Chas. II/Hil. 13.
[78] Andrews and Dury, Map (W.A.S. Rec. Brch.), pl. 8; O.S. Map 1″, sheet 14 (1st edn.).
[79] W.R.O. Land Tax Assessments.
[80] V.C.H. Wilts. ii, p. 160.
[81] See p. 235.
[82] C.P. 25(1)/250/8/11.
[83] See p. 235.
[84] S.C. 6/1145/12.
[85] Sta. Cha. 4/10/49.

[86] C 6/7/139; C 6/184/52; Longleat MSS. Deed 1709.
[87] See p. 235.
[88] W.R.O. 323, Title Deeds of Manor.
[89] Sar. Dioc. R.O. Vis. Queries, 1783.
[90] W.R.O. Land Tax Assessments.
[91] O.S. Map 1″ 1st edn. sheet 14; but cf. Andrews and Dury, Map (W.A.S. Rec. Brch.), pl. 8 and Greenwood, Map of Wilts. 1820.
[92] W.R.O. Tithe Map.
[93] Ibid. Land Tax Assessments.
[94] Ibid. Tithe Map.
[95] Ibid. Land Tax Assessments.
[96] Ibid. Tithe Award.
[97] W.A.S. Libr. Devizes, Sale Cat.
[98] W.R.O. Tithe Award.
[99] P.O. Dir. Wilts. (1867).
[1] Kelly's Dir. Wilts. (1885).

1086.[2] A mill there belonged to Nicholas Frankeleyn in 1268,[3] and in 1325 a mill belonged to the part of the manor held by Simon Chamberlain.[4] A water corn-mill was sold by Peter Delmé to William Godolphin in 1740. It evidently lay above the church in what are now the grounds of Baynton House.[5] It was no doubt demolished by Godolphin or his successors, and its pond may be the origin of the ornamental lake now there. The late 18th-century farm buildings at Coulston House include a water mill, probably built to replace the old one.

CHURCH. A church at East Coulston is first mentioned in 1214,[6] but the doorway on the north side of the nave is probably of the late 12th century. At the division of the manor in 1229 the advowson was allotted to Countess Ela, and followed the descent of the overlordship of her part of the manor until it was merged in the Duchy of Lancaster in 1399.[7] It was then exercised by the sovereign or the Lord Chancellor[8] with a few exceptions. In 1472 Sir Gilbert Debenham presented and the benefice was described as a vicarage.[9] In 1565 the rectory and advowson were granted in fee to Roger Langesford and Christopher Marten;[10] for some reason this grant never took effect, for at the next vacancy in 1569 the queen was still patron. In 1602 she presented because of the minority of William Brouncker, and William himself presented at the next vacancy in 1626.[11] This was perhaps because the rectory was leased for a term of years. In 1934 the benefice was united to that of Erlestoke, and it was arranged that the Lord Chancellor and the executors of G. S. A. Watson-Taylor should present alternately.[12] In 1951 the Watson-Taylor turn was transferred to the Diocesan Board of Patronage,[13] and in 1960 the Lord Chancellor's turn was also transferred to the board in exchange for an alternate interest in the advowson of Hindon with Chicklade and Pertwood.[14]

The benefice was valued at £5 in 1291,[15] and at £8 2s. 8d. gross in 1535.[16] In 1835 the average net income was £168 a year.[17] In the early 17th century the tithes were let to Gawen Flower of Imber for five years.[18] They were commuted for £170 in 1840.[19] The earliest account of the glebe is in a terrier of 1672, when it was estimated at 30½ a.[20] In 1680 the rector claimed common for 30 sheep in the sheepsleight and fields of a farm on the downs; his sheep were to go with the farm flock and fold

the glebe land.[21] In 1887 there were 31 a. of glebe in Coulston and Steeple Ashton worth £93 a year.[22]

The church was served by a curate in 1685.[23] In 1783 the rector was also rector of Great Cheverell, and a curate, who served both churches for him, resided at Cheverell. He held a service at Coulston once each Sunday at about 2 p.m., which the parishioners found convenient because of their occupation with dairying. Most people attended, and the sacrament was administered three times a year.[24] In 1812 lateness and irregularity of services were complained of.[25] Since the benefice was united with Erlestoke the rector has lived at that village.

The church, now dedicated to *ST. THOMAS À BECKET*, was dedicated to St. Andrew at least as early as 1506.[26] It is last referred to as St. Andrew in 1763,[27] and first as St. Thomas in 1786.[28] It consists of a nave with chancel, and transeptal chapel on the north. On the south side of the nave is a blocked doorway of the late 12th century, and the heavily-restored chancel arch was probably of the same period. The chancel was built in the 14th century but rebuilt in 1868, parts of the south windows and the piscina being preserved. The large north chapel was added in the 14th century, and was no doubt the Lady Chapel to which John Lambe left money for repairs in 1501.[29] There is a piscina on the east jamb of the arch, and a blocked doorway with exterior stoup in the north wall of the chancel. The western door of the nave and most of its windows are of the 17th century.[30]

In 1501 John Lambe left money at the discretion of his executors to repair the Lady Chapel and the church.[31] In 1613 John Lambe left £4 for the repair of the church.[32] Elizabeth Godolphin (d. 1726) left £200 to be laid out in beautifying the chancel, and £80 to provide a yearly payment to a poor widow to keep the chancel clean.[33] The chancel was relaid with marble in 1728,[34] no doubt from this bequest, and in 1731 the rector received a velvet carpet for the communion table from Elizabeth Godolphin's executor.[35] The church was in bad condition in 1812,[36] and was restored in 1842.[37] The extent of the work is not known, but apparently included the removal of a transept on the south side which had been built by the Godolphin family to hold a seat.[38] Patches of brickwork on the exterior walls may date from this time, and the buttresses of the nave and the vestry on the north are probably of a later restoration. The roof of the nave was restored in

[2] *V.C.H. Wilts.* ii, p. 160.
[3] C.P. 25(1)/251/21/47.
[4] S.C. 6/1145/12.
[5] W.R.O. 323, Deed Delmé to Godolphin, 1740.
[6] *Cur. Reg. R.* vii. 51.
[7] See p. 235.
[8] Phillipps, *Wilts. Inst. passim*; *Rep. Com. Eccl. Revenues*, H.C. 54, p. 831 (1835), xxii; *Crockford*.
[9] Phillipps, op. cit. 161.
[10] *Cal. Pat.* 1563–6, 281.
[11] Phillipps, *Wilts. Inst.* ii. 2, 13.
[12] *Kelly's Dir. Wilts.* (1939).
[13] *St. Thomas à Becket, Coulston ... a short history* (pamphlet on sale in church).
[14] Order in Council, 3 Aug. 1960.
[15] *Tax. Eccl.* (Rec. Com.), 180.
[16] *Valor Eccl.* (Rec. Com.), 146.
[17] *Rep. Com. Eccl. Rev.* (1835), p. 831.
[18] E 134/31–32 Chas. II/Hil. 13.
[19] W.R.O. Tithe Award.
[20] Sar. Dioc. R.O. Glebe Terrier, 1672.

[21] E 134/31–32 Chas. II/Hil. 13.
[22] *Ret. Glebe Lands*, H.C. 307, p. 163 (1887), lxiv.
[23] P.C.C. 66 Cann.
[24] Sar. Dioc. R.O. Vis. Queries, 1783.
[25] *V.C.H. Wilts.* iii. 55.
[26] P.C.C. 34 Fetiplace.
[27] Ecton, *Thesaurus* (1763), 394; the rector mentioned this dedication *c.* 1705: W.R.O. 413, Answers to Parochial Queries *c.* 1705.
[28] Bacon, *Thesaurus* (1786), 893.
[29] P.C.C. 13 Blamyr.
[30] There are drawings of the ch. by Buckler in W.A.S. Libr. Devizes.
[31] P.C.C. 13 Blamyr.
[32] P.C.C. 26 Rudd.
[33] *Endowed Char. Wilts.* (1908), p. 132; the charity was extinct by 1833.
[34] *St. Thomas à Becket, Coulston*, (pamphlet in ch.).
[35] *W.A.M.* iii. 100.
[36] *V.C.H. Wilts.* iii. 54.
[37] *St. Thomas à Becket, Coulston.*   [38] *W.A.M.* iii. 97.

1935.[39] During the incumbency of C. W. Buckley, 1949–62, electric light was installed, the transept was restored and furnished as a chapel, and the church was practically re-roofed.[40]

Two brass coffin plates which were found in 1856 in a vault outside the south wall are fixed to the south wall inside the church.[41] Francis Saville Kent, who was murdered at Rode Hill, aged 3 years and 10 months, in 1860, is buried in the churchyard.[42]

The commissioners of Edward VI noted 2 bells at Coulston in 1553.[43] Only one, uninscribed, existed in 1959 on a bracket outside the west end of the nave.[44] No plate was mentioned in 1559.[45] In 1959 there was a large chalice with cover and paten, hall-marked 1683, given by Rebecca Bennett, and an almsdish hall-marked 1731 and engraved with the arms of Elizabeth Godolphin (d. 1726).[46] The registers are complete from 1714 except for a gap in baptisms from 1751 to 1754.[47]

NONCONFORMITY. In 1851 a congregation of about 30 Primitive Methodists met in a cottage in East Coulston, and about 40 Baptists in a cottage in West Coulston, where they had been meeting since 1831.[48] The Baptists were no doubt organized from the chapel at Bratton, of which they were certainly a station by 1868.[49] A small chapel was built in 1872, but closed in 1937.[50] In 1963 it was being converted to a private dwelling.

SCHOOLS. In 1808 about 10 very young children were taught by an old woman, who was paid 2d. a week for each child.[51] In 1819 there was a day school for 20 girls, but the curate considered that the poor were not desirous of education.[52] A school was built in West Coulston by Simon Watson-Taylor c. 1855. There was a master's house attached, and the schoolroom, which was described as large and well-ventilated, could be divided into two. In 1859 50–60 pupils of both sexes were taught by a respectable middle-aged master assisted by a sewing mistress.[53] In 1875 East Coulston and Edington were made a United District and a School Board was formed.[54] In 1893 average attendance was only 27. An endowment of £4. 3s. 9d. a year was received, but it is not known from whom.[55] By 1899 the school was closed,[56] and the children were sent to the one at Tinhead. In 1963 the schoolroom was used as the village hall, and the remainder was a dwelling house.

CHARITIES. Apart from the Godolphin charity referred to above,[57] no charities have been endowed in East Coulston.

EDINGTON

THE parish of Edington lies about 2 miles east of Westbury.[1] It is an irregular rectangle in shape, with a wedge-like projection to the west. Its length from north to south is about 6 miles; its greatest width is about 3 miles, but for most of its length it is only about a mile wide. In 1934 a strip of varying width running the whole length of the boundary between Edington and East Coulston was transferred to the civil parish of East Coulston.[2] The north of the parish lies on the Kimmeridge clay lands of mid-west Wilts; it is low and well watered, rising from about 150 ft. at the boundary with Keevil to about 250 ft. near Edington village, and is mainly permanent pasture. A stream, formerly called Milbourne,[3] rises at Luccombe Bottom, south of Bratton. It flows northward for some way, forming the parish boundary, and then north-eastward across Edington parish toward Keevil. South of the village the northern scarp of Salisbury Plain rises sharply to over 600 ft., and the southern part of the parish is all on the chalk, between 500 and 700 ft. high, reaching 739 ft. on Tinhead Hill. Between the Kimmeridge Clay and the chalk are outcrops of Upper Greensand and Gault, on which the villages of Edington and Tinhead, the chief centres of population in the parish, are built. Here there is some arable, and there is also a considerable area under the plough along the northern edge of the Plain.[4] The downland in the south is mainly included in the military training district centred on Imber. There is little woodland, but on the lower ground there are many trees in the hedgerows.

The secondary road from Westbury to West Lavington crosses the parish from west to east. Edington and Tinhead villages lie on this road and to the north of it, and from them minor roads lead north-westward to Steeple Ashton and Trowbridge. In 1773 a road to Bulkington existed,[5] but its course is now marked only by a lane and a footpath. The old slowcoach route from Bath to Salisbury ran from Steeple Ashton to Tinhead and up to the top of Coulston Down. Coaches ran on it in

[39] *St. Thomas à Becket, Coulston.*
[40] *Wilts. Times,* 19 Jan. 1962.
[41] *W.A.M.* iii. 97.
[42] See p. 224.
[43] *W.A.M.* xii. 366.
[44] Walters, *Wilts. Bells,* 66.
[45] *W.A.M.* xii. 366.
[46] Nightingale, *Wilts. Plate,* 102.
[47] Ex inf. Major C. J. Jacobs.
[48] H.O. 129/10/259. The entry about the Baptist chapel is under Edington parish, in which it stood until the boundary was changed.
[49] *Baptist Handbook,* 1868.
[50] Ex inf. Mrs. Reeves of Bratton.
[51] Lambeth Palace Libr. MS. 1732. For the account of the school, West Coulston, formerly in Edington parish, is considered with East Coulston.
[52] *Digest of Returns to Cttee. on Educ. of Poor,* H.C. 224, p. 1024 (1819), ix (2).
[53] *Account of Wilts. Schools,* H.C. 27, p. 17 (1859), xxi (2).
[54] *Lond. Gaz.* 1875, p. 5452.
[55] *Ret. of Schools,* 1893 [C 7529] p. 648, H.C. (1894), lxv.
[56] *Ret. of Schools,* 1899 [Cd. 315] H.C. (1900), lxv(2).
[57] See p. 235.
[1] The following maps were used: O.S. Maps 1/2,500 Wilts. XXXIX. 10, 11, 15, 15, XLV. 2, 3. (1st and later edns.); 1/25,000 ST 94, 95 (1958); 1″, sheet 14 (1st edn.).
[2] Wilts. Co. Review Order 1934.
[3] So called in 968: *P. N. Wilts.* (E.P.N.S.), 146.
[4] A. H. Fry, *Land Utilization, Wilts.* 157.
[5] *Andrews and Dury, Map* (W.A.S. Rec. Brch.), pl. 7.

1712,[6] and it was turnpiked as far as Tinhead Hill in 1751–2. It was not included in the renewing Act of 1767–8[7] and was last mentioned in coaching tables in 1780. Several milestones, one dated 1766, and a toll house near Ivymill Farm still remain.[8] None of the roads south of the Westbury-Lavington road is now (1959) passable except by farm vehicles. The main railway line from Westbury to Lavington passes north of the village. A station, known as Edington and Bratton, was opened when the line was built in 1900, but closed for passengers in 1952.[9] The station buildings have since been pulled down.

Edington village is built round spurs which extend northwards from the high chalk of the Plain. It has no obvious centre, and its houses are rather scattered and hidden from one another by groups of trees and the contour of the ground. Along the main road which forms the southern part of the village are several cottages and the 19th-century vicarage. To the south of the road at the east end of the village is a small group of cottages at the foot of a lane leading to the downs. It was called Little London in 1773 and 1811;[10] its present name of the City was in use by 1886.[11] The church and the site of the monastery lie slightly away from the village to the north-east.[12] Most houses lie along the minor road leading towards Trowbridge and lanes which lead from it to the north and south. They include several timber-framed houses. The house now called Old Manor Farmhouse consists of a principal timber-framed range which has been built up in stone at both gable ends to accommodate chimneys; there is a small projecting gabled wing to the front, and the whole house is thatched. Manor Farm nearby is a large house of brick built to replace a house which in 1842 stood near the present entrance to its drive.[13] Parsonage Farm is an L-shaped timber-framed house, probably of the 17th century, and there are several cottages of about the same period in different parts of the village. Of several brick houses of the 18th and 19th centuries, the Grange is a good example. It is of two stories with stone dressings, mullioned and transomed windows, and a central first floor window with twin arched lights. The date 1750 is scratched on the brickwork, and the back was probably added in 1773.[14]

Tinhead lies about ¼ mile east of Edington, and the villages have been joined by a small council housing scheme on a road north of, and parallel to, the main road which joins them. The Lamb Inn and the school lie on this main road, but most of the houses in Tinhead lie along a minor road leading northward towards Steeple Ashton and smaller roads and lanes which lead off it. The George Inn is an 18th-century building of brick, and was a stop for coaches

when they ran through the village.[15] Opposite, Shore House has a central part of timber-framed construction oversailing at first-floor level; it was added to and altered in the 18th century. Beckett's House appears originally to have consisted of a timber-framed range with a projection at the rear, perhaps of the mid-16th century. About 1600 a stone range was built at the rear enclosing the projecting timber-framed wing, and somewhat later both ranges were extended to the south. The house formerly contained some encaustic tiles, which were thought to have come from the monastic buildings at Edington, and some panelling with carved figures thought to be of c. 1600.[16] It still has a decorated plaster ceiling and some fireplaces of that period, and was evidently the home of a prosperous family, quite probably the Whitakers who were opulent clothiers in the village.[17]

The only other centre of population in the parish was the hamlet of West Coulston about a mile east of Tinhead; it is a part of East Coulston geographically, and was included in the area transferred to that parish in 1934.[18] The remainder of the parish contains only isolated farms. Upper Baynton Farm, near the site of the manor house of Baynton, is midway between Tinhead and Coulston. In the north of the parish are Lower Baynton, New Hurst, Ivymill, and Housecroft Farms, and on the Plain, West Down and South Down Farms. Baynton Hill (formerly East Down) and Tinhead Hill Farms were in the area transferred to East Coulston in 1934.[19]

The population of Edington parish was 834 in 1801, and had risen to 1,136 by 1841. From that time it declined gradually to 714 in 1931. In 1951 the civil parish, reduced in area since 1934, had 579 inhabitants.[20]

Edington is accepted by most modern scholars as the site of the battle of *Ethandun* in which Alfred defeated the Danes under Guthram in 878.[21] The Witan met there in 957.[22] In 1450, during Cade's rebellion, William Aiscough, Bishop of Salisbury, was taken from the church to the top of Edington Hill by a mob, and there murdered.[23] In 1838 and 1839 small Chartist meetings at Tinhead were addressed by William Carrier of Trowbridge.[24]

William of Edington, Bishop of Winchester from 1346 to 1366, holder of various offices in the royal household, and founder of the house of Bonhommes at Edington, was probably a younger son of the leading family of the village.[25] William Wey, who made two pilgrimages to Jerusalem in the 15th century, settled in the monastery at Edington to write an account of his travels.[26] Paul Bush, the last Rector of Edington monastery, was afterwards Bishop of Bristol from 1542 to 1554.[27]

MANORS AND LESSER ESTATES. Edington

[6] *W.A.M.* lvii. 226.
[7] *V.C.H. Wilts.* iv. 259.
[8] Ex inf. Miss I. M. Braidwood and Miss D. U. Seth-Smith.
[9] *V.C.H. Wilts.* iv. 289, 293.
[10] *Andrews and Dury, Map* (W.A.S. Rec. Brch.), pl. 7; O.S. Map 1″, sheet 14 (1st edn.).
[11] O.S. Map Wilts. 1/2,500 Wilts. XXXIX, 14.
[12] See p. 247.
[13] W.R.O. Tithe Award.
[14] Ex inf. Brig. A. C. Sykes.
[15] See above.
[16] *W.N. &Q.* vi. 1–3.

[17] See p. 245.
[18] See above.
[19] See above.
[20] *V.C.H. Wilts.* iv. 347–8.
[21] Ibid. ii, p. 6; for a discussion of the actual site, see *W.A.M.* liii. 405.
[22] *V.C.H. Wilts.* ii, p. 9.
[23] Ibid. iii. 323; *W.A.M.* i. 189.
[24] H.O. 40/48; *W.A.M.* liv. 171.
[25] *V.C.H. Wilts.* iii. 320.
[26] Ibid. 323.
[27] Ibid.

was part of the royal demesne in the 9th century, and was left by Alfred to his wife Ealhswith.[28] In 968 Edgar granted it to Romsey Abbey (Hants),[29] and the nuns held it in 1086. At that time they had three under-tenants, William, Osmund, and Hervey holding $4\frac{1}{2}$, 4, and 2 hides respectively, while some unnamed Englishmen held 5 hides and a virgate.[30] In addition, a small manor of 1 hide was held immediately of the king by Hervey of Wilton, a royal official and probably the same Hervey as the tenant of the nuns.[31] William, the holder of $4\frac{1}{2}$ hides, was William Scudet, the king's cook, who also held land in Westbury and Steeple Ashton. Henry I confirmed William's 'restoration and grant' to the nuns of the land he held of them.[32] Romsey Abbey retained the lordship of the capital manor until just before the Dissolution, but the foundation of the religious house at Edington in 1351[33] resulted in the creation of a mesne manor held by it of the abbess. This manor was later called *EDINGTON RECTOR* while the capital manor was known as *EDINGTON ROMSEY*.[34]

The endowment of the house of Edington was at first achieved by Bishop William of Edington acquiring small parcels of land in Edington either from the abbess or from her tenants. In 1351 for instance, John of Edington, probably acting for his brother William, bought of the abbess 2 houses and 2 virgates, a house and a virgate, which formerly belonged to Walter Nichol, and a house, 2 water mills, a virgate and certain meadow and pasture which formerly belonged to William of Sweltenham.[35] Other similar purchases were made in the following years,[36] and in this way the manor of Edington Rector was built up.

Tinhead is first mentioned incidentally as a personal name in 1190, when Philip 'de Tunhede' paid a forest fine.[37] In 1256 Michael of Tinhead bought land there of Asketil del Mareis,[38] and in 1275 John of Tinhead held 10 virgates there of the Abbess of Romsey.[39] In 1329 3 houses and 4 carucates of land there and in Semington were settled on another John of Tinhead, with remainder to his daughter Maud.[40] She had apparently succeeded him by *c.* 1355.[41] The estate, which was later known as *TINHEAD RECTOR*,[42] is first referred to as a manor in 1363, when Maud, widow of Robert Selyman, knight, and probably the same as the Maud referred to above, conveyed the reversion of the manor of Tinhead after her death and that of her son Robert, to John of Edington.[43] Part of the

manor was then said to be held of the king in chief by the service of an axe called *hache Daneys*. It had been so held since the Conquest by the ancestors of John of Tinhead, and probably represents the one-hide estate held by Hervey of Wilton in 1086. Of the remainder of the manor, a messuage and 17 acres were held of the abbess as of her manor of Edington, and a water mill of Richard Rous.[44] This manor of Tinhead was granted by John of Edington to his brother the bishop, and by him to the rector and brethren of Edington.[45] What had been the Romsey property in Tinhead was called *TINHEAD ROMSEY* after the Dissolution, although it had not been treated as a separate manor previously.[46]

In 1539 the Abbess of Romsey was given licence to alienate the nunnery's lands in Edington and Tinhead to Sir Thomas Seymour, afterwards Lord Seymour of Sudeley.[47] In the same year the monastery of Edington was surrendered,[48] and in 1541 its property in Edington and Tinhead was granted to Sir Thomas Seymour.[49] On the attainder and execution of Sir Thomas in 1549, the property there formerly belonging to both houses reverted to the Crown, and in the following year the whole was granted to William Paulet, Earl of Wiltshire.[50] The four manors of Edington Rector, Edington Romsey, Tinhead Rector, and Tinhead Romsey descended in the Paulet family, subsequently Marquesses of Winchester (1551) and Dukes of Bolton (1689), until 1768, when they were sold in pursuance of a decree in a chancery suit which followed the death of Charles, the fifth Duke (d. 1765). They were bought by Peter Delmé, but no conveyance was made to him. Accordingly in 1784 a private Act was obtained to enable Delmé to convey the estate to Joshua and Drummond Smith of Erlestoke Park.[51] The subsequent descent of all four manors is the same as that of Erlestoke manor.[52]

Before the Dissolution the manor farm of Edington Romsey had been leased to Meric ap Rice for 45 years from 1531.[53] He died *c.* 1544,[54] and was probably succeeded by his son Edward Merrick.[55] The Romsey manor farm is not heard of again. The Edington Rector farm was in hand when the monastery of Edington was dissolved.[56] In 1540 the farm and the site of the monastery were occupied by William Popeley.[57] In 1550 the site and demesnes were granted by the Crown for 41 years to Isabel, widow of Sir Henry Baynton of Bromham (d. 1544).[58] She married, as her second husband, Sir James Stumpe, and at his death in 1563 he left

[28] *Eng. Hist. Doc.* ed. F. E. Harmer, 18.
[29] *Cart. Sax.* ed. Birch, iii. 495; for an account of Romsey Abbey, see *V.C.H. Hants.* ii. 126.
[30] *V.C.H. Wilts.* ii, p. 131.
[31] Ibid. p. 165.
[32] Ibid. p. 73; J. H. Round, *King's Serjeants*, 11.
[33] For the history of the monastery, see *V.C.H. Wilts.* iii. 320
[34] See below n. 46.
[35] *Cal. Pat.* 1350–4, 110; *Cal. Close*, 1354–60, 104.
[36] C.P. 25 (1)/252/28/10; *Cal. Pat.* 1358–61, 25, 85, 302; 1361–4, 124, 184; 1370–74, 367; *Cal. Close*, 1354–60, 104–108, 330; *Cat. Anct. D.* ii, p. 436; *Wilts. Inq. p.m.* 1327–77 (Index Libr.), 223; *W.N. & Q.* iii. 75.
[37] *Pipe R.* 1190 (P.R.S. N.S. i), 123.
[38] *Cal. Feet of F. Wilts.* 1195–1272, ed. Fry, 50.
[39] *Rot. Hund.* (Rec. Com.), ii. 277.
[40] B.M. Lansd. MS. 442, f. 72.
[41] S.C. 11/706.
[42] See below, n. 46.   [43] *Cal. Pat.* 1361–4, 388.

[44] *Wilts. Inq. p.m.* 1327–77 (Index Libr.), 327.
[45] *Cal. Close*, 1364–8, 192.
[46] The name Tinhead Rector first occurs in 1494 (S.C. 2/208/7). The manors of Edington Romsey, Edington Rector and Tinhead Romsey are not so named until after the Dissolution: Edington Romsey and Tinhead Romsey in 1550 (*Cal. Pat.* 1549–51, 196) and Edington Rector about the same date (Longleat MS. 10462).
[47] *L. & P. Hen. VIII*, xiv(1), p. 75.
[48] *V.C.H. Wilts.* iii. 324.
[49] *L. & P. Hen. VIII*, xvi, p. 461.
[50] *Cal. Pat.* 1548–9, 376.
[51] Bolton Estate Act, 24 Geo. III, c. 9 (priv. act).
[52] See *V.C.H. Wilts.* vii. 84.
[53] *W.A.M.* xx. 285.
[54] P.C.C. 6 Pynnyng.
[55] *Taxation Lists* (W.A.S. Rec. Brch.), 34.
[56] *Valor Eccl.* (Rec. Com.), 240–2.
[57] S.C. 6/Hen. VIII/3985 m. 35.
[58] *Cal. Pat.* 1548–9, 376; Req. 2/178/49.

her the lease of the site of Edington and all his plate in the house there.[59] She died in 1573, and was succeeded by her son Henry Baynton, who greatly spoiled the house, so that, as the Marquess of Winchester alleged, £1,000 would not repair it.[60] By 1599 the house was occupied by William Jones of Keevil.[61] In the previous year, however, the Marquess of Winchester had leased the whole of his Edington and Tinhead property to two of his four illegitimate sons, for terms of 99 years. John was granted the manors of Edington Romsey and Tinhead Rector, and William the manors of Edington Rector and Tinhead Romsey.[62] William was living at Edington by 1603,[63] and evidently until his death in 1629, when his estate was assigned by his executors to Sir Edward Lewis of the Van (Glam.), for the remainder of the term.[64] Sir Edward was buried in Edington church in 1630, and his widow, Lady Anne Beauchamp (so-called from her earlier marriage to Sir Edward Seymour, Lord Beauchamp) lived at the house until her death in 1664. She was succeeded by her son Richard Lewis, who remained at Edington until c. 1694.[65] The manors of Edington Romsey and Tinhead Rector, which had been leased to John Paulet, were in Richard Lewis's hands by 1665,[66] and it is possible that the lease was purchased by his father at the same time as that of the other manors. In the 18th century, when the property had reverted to the main branch of the Paulet family, Lord Harry Paulet, later Duke of Bolton (d. 1759) lived at Edington.[67] The house, which had been of considerable size when Lady Anne Beauchamp occupied it,[68] was largely demolished by Joshua Smith in the late 18th century.[69] In 1798 the ruins of the house still stood in well-kept gardens.[70] The house now called the Priory must, however, have been a part of it, for two rooms contain decorated plaster ceilings of the 17th century. The exterior of the house has been much altered at various times, but some of the masonry may well date from the late Middle Ages. The heavy buttressed wall of the precinct, probably of the 14th century, also remains, as does the square fish pond to the north.

Tinhead Court was included in the lease granted to Isabel Baynton in 1550, for it was among the property damaged by her son.[71] It was occupied by Edward Carpenter in 1607,[72] and by Mrs. Wadman, a member of the Imber family, in 1712.[73] In 1774 it was held by John Price as a copyhold of the manor of Tinhead Romsey.[74] The house was demolished in the early 19th century; it was moated and had

what was described as an 'ecclesiastical barn'.[75]

The court of the lord of Baynton was mentioned in 1262.[76] In 1274 Maud Rous held two carucates of land at Baynton of the Abbess of Romsey.[77] In 1313 Sir John Rous renounced to the abbess certain rights of presenting nuns at Romsey, which his family had claimed on the grounds that it had given the abbey Baynton and 'Brawthorne'.[78] The manor of *BAYNTON*, first so called in 1735,[79] descended in the Rous family of Imber to Sir John Rous, who in 1414 settled it on his younger son John.[80] In 1444 this John granted it to the rector and brethren of Edington.[81] After the Dissolution Baynton was granted to Sir Thomas Seymour and forfeited on his attainder in the same was as Edington Rector. In 1557 it was granted by the Crown to Thomas Gratwicke of Seaford (Suss.), and Anselm Lambe of Coulston,[82] subject to a lease to three lives granted to Stephen Oriel in 1533.[83] Lambe died in 1559, apparently possessed of the whole manor, leaving two infant daughters. Agnes married Richard Burley of Potterne, and Joan married Henry Danvers, and they received livery of the manor in 1576.[84] In 1579 Henry Danvers and his wife granted a moiety of lands in Orcheston St. George, which were parcel of the manor,[85] to Richard Burley and his wife, receiving from them a grant of a moiety of the manor of Baynton.[86] The significance of this transaction is not clear, for Henry Danvers only held a moiety at his death in 1580,[87] and so did his eldest son John, an idiot from birth, when he died in 1626.[88] Joan, widow of Henry Danvers, who later married Hugh Jones, joined with her second son Charles, in granting a lease of part of the manor in 1620.[89] Charles succeeded his brother John, and died in 1626, holding both moieties. He had purchased one moiety and settled it on his wife Mary for life.[90] It is not clear from whom he obtained it, but it was perhaps from the Burleys; Richard Burley had some interest in the manor in 1594.[91] In 1673 John Danvers, grandson of Charles, sold the manor to John Long of Little Cheverell,[92] to whom it was already mortgaged.[93] Long died without issue in 1676, and left Baynton to his nephew William, eldest son of his younger brother William. The manor descended in the Long family to William, the last male member of the Baynton branch, who died without surviving issue in 1807. He left his estates at the disposal of his wife Mary, who died in 1822, leaving them to John Long of Monkton Farleigh, younger son of Richard Long of Rood Ashton, and a descendant of Thomas

[59] *W.N. & Q.* viii. 445.
[60] *W.A.M.* xx. 286–90. Canon Jackson confused Henry Baynton with his half-brother Andrew, who died in 1563.
[61] *W.N. & Q.* ii. 445.
[62] W.R.O. 436, Lease Winchester-Paulet, 10 June 1598.
[63] *W.A.M.* xx. 290.
[64] W.R.O. 436, Assignment Paulet-Lewis, 14 July 1629.
[65] *W.A.M.* xx. 291.
[66] C.P. 25 (2)/745/16 and 17 Chas. II Hil.
[67] *W.A.M.* xx. 292.
[68] W.R.O. 435, Inv. of Goods at Edington, 1664.
[69] *W.A.M.* xx. 293.
[70] *Univ. Brit. Dir.* (1798), iv. 737.
[71] E 134/33 Eliz. I/Hil. 22.
[72] W.A.S. Libr., Devizes, Transcript of Chwdns.' Accts.
[73] *W.A.M.* lvii. 226.
[74] W.R.O. 212A, Copy of Court Roll, 1774.
[75] *W.A.M.* xx. 261.   [76] S.C. 2/208/1 m. 2.

[77] *Rot. Hund.* (Rec. Com.), ii. 277.
[78] T. Madox, *Formulare Anglicanum*, 385.
[79] *Cal. Close*, 1374–7, 120.
[80] Hoare, *Mod. Wilts.* Heytesbury, 161.
[81] *Cal. Close*, 1441–7, 307; *Cal. Pat.* 1441–6, 206.
[82] *Cal. Pat.* 1557–8, 134.
[83] B.M. Harl. MS. 607, f. 25b.
[84] C 60/392.
[85] B.M. Harl. MS. 607, f. 25b.
[86] C 66/1197 m.14; C 66/1193 m. 13.
[87] C 142/193/49.
[88] *Wilts. Inq. p.m.* 1625–49 (Index Libr.), 48.
[89] W.R.O. 212A, Lease Jones and Danvers-Spinner, 2 April 1620.
[90] *Wilts. Inq. p.m.* 1625–49 (Index Libr.), 49.
[91] Req. 2/138/46.
[92] C.P. 25(2)/746/25 Chas. II Mich.
[93] W.R.O. 84, Bdle. 47.

Long of Little Cheverell, father of the original purchaser.[94] The manor still belonged to John Long in 1833,[95] but by 1842 the property in Baynton, and probably the manorial rights, had been sold to the Watson-Taylor family.[96] From the 16th century the manor was often called Baynton and West Coulston, but no evidence has been found of a separate manor of West Coulston.[97] The manor house of Baynton lay near the present Upper Baynton Farm, where a moat still exists. It was destroyed by fire in 1796, and its name was given to the house in Coulston to which the family removed.[98]

The Mompesson family held a property in Edington and Tinhead which was sometimes referred to as the manor of *TINHEAD MOMPESSON*. In 1499 Agnes Trye, widow of Drew Mompesson, held land there of the Abbess of Romsey, which was settled on her sons after her death.[99] Her son John Mompesson held it in 1511.[1] In 1579 Thomas Mompesson bought of William Brouncker of Erlestoke a capital messuage and farm in Tinhead, which had formerly been occupied by John Catcott.[2] This farm had belonged to Leonard Willoughby and was leased by him to Catcott.[3] Henry Brouncker had bought it of John Willoughby and others in 1563.[4] When Thomas Mompesson died in 1587 he left his lands in Edington and Tinhead to his executors to be sold,[5] and a conveyance of all his lands there to Jeffery Whitaker of Tinhead was made in 1588.[6] In spite of this, lands in Edington and Tinhead were among those settled on Thomas's son Giles Mompesson in 1607.[7] It may be that only the land acquired from Brouncker was in fact sold, for 'a barn called Catcutts' was owned by Henry Whitaker of Tinhead in 1672.[8] But by 1626 what had remained in the Mompesson family had also been sold, for Sir William Paulet then held land late Mompesson's of the manor of Edington Romsey.[9]

In c. 1355 John Forstal held a messuage and a carucate of land in Baynton of the Abbess of Romsey at a rent of 14s. 11d.[10] In 1394 Simon Best of 'Cannings' held an estate formerly occupied by Robert Forstal at the same rent,[11] and in 1519 the same estate, described as formerly occupied by John Best, was held by John Erley.[12] In 1603 Thomas Erneley died holding property in Coulston,[13] but by 1615 lands described in the same way were held by John Lambe.[14] In 1626 Sir John

Lambe paid the rent of 14s. 11d. for lands late Erneley's.[15]

ECONOMIC HISTORY. In 1086 Edington was assessed at 30 hides, of which 2 hides were in demesne and 15 hides and 3 virgates held by tenants. There was land for 35½ ploughs. Land for 7 ploughs was in demesne with 10 serfs, while 21 villeins, 23 bordars, and 10 coliberts held land for 15 ploughs. There was pasture 1 league long and ½ league broad, 100 acres of meadow, and woodland 10 furlongs long and 5 broad.[16]

By the 14th century much of the abbess's land had been granted to free tenants and their rents formed an important part of the receipts of the manor, amounting to over £24 in c.1350.[17] These rents were paid not only for holdings in Edington, Tinhead, Baynton, and Coulston, but also for lands in Imber, North Bradley, Corton in Boyton, and Wyke near Gillingham (Dors.). The total still remained at just over £24 in 1511.[18] A rental of the mid-14th century lists 28 bond tenants holding a virgate each, 25 holding half virgates, 11 mondaymen, each holding an acre or two, and 20 cottagers.[19] They paid rents, churchscot, and tallage amounting in all to about £10, beside certain customary payments of wheat and poultry.

The chief place in the demesne farming of the abbess's estate was occupied by sheep. In 1284 1,587 great fleeces and 365 lambs' fleeces were sold, and over 1,600 sheep remained at the end of the year.[20] In 1414 most of the clip was sent to Romsey to be sold; 1,918 sheep and 385 lambs had been sheared, and over 2,000 sheep remained.[21] In that year 129 sheep were sold, 88 of them to the royal household. In 1550 there were 1,051 wethers, 18 rams, 431 ewes, and 200 hoggets on the lands of Edington Romsey.[22] Compared with this, other livestock was unimportant. There were only 7 cows, 7 heifers, and 3 calves on the manor in 1284,[23] and in 1414 no dairy stock was mentioned. Quantities of butter and poultry were sent to Romsey in 1284.[24] The rabbit warren of the manor was at Luccombe.[25] It was leased to Peter Frankeleyn in 1396 at a rent of 6s. 8d. and four pairs of rabbits a year.[26]

In 1284 58 oxen were kept. It is probable that at this date some corn was sent to Romsey, for 170 horseshoes were provided for carthorses going there.[27] In 1417 the abbess's wheat growing on East Down was damaged by oxen belonging to the

94 Burke, *Commoners* (1833–38), iv. 70.
95 W.R.O. Land Tax Assessments.
96 W.R.O. Tithe Award.
97 The reference to the manor of West Coulston in C 142/193/49 as parcel of the possessions of Amesbury must arise from confusion with Choulston in Figheldean, which had also belonged to Anselm Lambe.
98 See p. 236.
99 *Cal. Inq. p.m. Hen. VII*, ii, p. 197.
1 S.C. 11/708.
2 W.R.O. 130, Bdle. 5b.
3 C 3/191/40.
4 *W.N. & Q.* v. 26.
5 Req. 2/153/26.
6 W.R.O. 130, Bdle. 5b.
7 C.P. 25(2)/369/6 Jas. I East.; *Wilts. Visitation Pedigrees*, 1623. (Harl. Soc. cv–vi), 133–4.
8 W.R.O. 130, Bdle. 5b.
9 W.R.O. 436, Paulet Rental, 1625–6.
10 S.C. 11/706.

11 S.C. 2/208/44.
12 S.C. 11/708.
13 C 142/289/54. He was probably a descendant of John Erley.
14 C 142/355/93.
15 W.R.O. 436, Paulet Rental, 1625–6.
16 *V.C.H. Wilts.* ii, p. 131.
17 S.C. 11/706 and 707. The following account of the Romsey property refers to the whole of the Abbess's estate in Edington; Tinhead was not treated as a separate manor before the Dissolution.
18 S.C. 11/708.
19 S.C. 11/706.
20 S.C. 6/1052/1.
21 S.C. 6/1052/2.
22 *Cal. Pat.* 1548–9, 376.
23 S.C. 6/1052/1.
24 Ibid.
25 S.C. 2/208/45 m. 5.
26 Ibid. m. 1.
27 S.C. 6/1052/1.

farmer of Imber.[28] In the earlier 15th century, the demesne arable was somewhat reduced, for two or three acres were often attached to small customary tenements.[29]

In 1284 there were at least two granges,[30] and in 1396 a south fold and an east fold are mentioned.[31] They may have been the same as the folds at South Down and 'Brawthorne', which the reeve was ordered to repair in 1413.[32] In 1502 there was a common animal house on Sheependown.[33] The common grazing for sheep lay on the downs in the south of the parish; in 1550 the lord was said to have common of pasture for 1,700 sheep on South Down and Brawthorne Down.[34] The abbess's tenants were often presented for overstocking. In 1429 Giles Serich and John Gouder had 480 sheep in the field of Edington, and Thomas Hayward 60,[35] and in 1502 the Rector of Edington had 300 sheep where he should only have had 160.[36] Some of the arable lay on the downs,[37] and some in 'the Clay', which was the lower ground between Edington and Bratton, near the present Fitzroy Farm.[38] East Field and West Field are mentioned in the late 13th century; references to strips in them near Woodbridge and Sweltenham Water indicate that they were on the low ground north of the village.[39] The abbess had several closes of land in the north of the parish, and autumn and winter pasture on other land there, and the first crop of hay of 40 acres of meadow in Normead and Inmead.[40] Normead, which is south-west of the present New Hurst Farm, was apparently shared with Steeple Ashton, for eight tenants of Steeple Ashton had winter pasture there in return for assistance at the sheep shearing at Edington.[41]

The manor of Edington Rector was valued at £21 7s. 10d. in 1535, including 76s. 4d. profits from the demesne.[42] A survey of c.1550[43] shows that parts of the demesne were let at over £16, but several closes of meadow and pasture and 241 a. arable were then in hand. The lord of the manor had common for 600 sheep on three several downs called Allondown, Sterte, and Talbots, and a common down, called Hysorton Down, and in the common fields, and for 140 ewes on Sheependown and Western Down. He had winter common on 50 a. in the north of the parish, and the first crop of hay of 28½ a. meadow in Normead and Inmead. The arable of the rector and the tenants lay dispersed and mixed with that of Edington Romsey in East Field and West Field and on Edington Hill. Some tenants also held arable in the fields of Tinhead and at Goldenham and Waddon there. The survey noted that the tenants of Edington and Tinhead had been forced by Sir Thomas Seymour to exchange certain of their arable land in the East Field for parts of the demesne arable

which were worth little or nothing. The tenants had stinted common for cattle in Sharpcroft and Sheepcroft, near the present Housecroft Farm, and in the common fields. Common for sheep lay on Sheependown and West Down, and common meadow in Normead, Inmead, and Dotsmead.

When the manor of Tinhead was granted to the Rector and Brethren of Edington in 1363, it consisted of buildings and a garden, a dovecote, 120 a. of arable, half of which lay fallow each year, 10 a. of meadow, several pasture for 24 oxen, and pasture for sheep. Free tenants paid 20s. and there were 4 bond half-virgaters. In addition, there was a house and a close of 16 a. at Feltham, near Ivymill Farm, which were held of the abbess, and a water mill held of Richard Rous.[44] At the Dissolution the manor of Tinhead Rector was valued at £21 6s. 11d.[45] In the survey of c. 1550[46] no demesne is listed separately for Tinhead, the whole of the demesne of the Bonhommes being listed with their Edington manor. There were twelve customary tenants, who had stinted common for cattle in Redyate, which lay near the present New Hurst Farm.[47]

There is little evidence for the state of agriculture in Edington in the 17th century. In 1686 the demesnes of all the Edington and Tinhead manors were leased out to tenants by Richard Lewis, the lessee under the Paulets. The future pattern of farming in the parish was already evolving, for several of the holdings must have been large. John Hooper rented South Down arable and sheepsleight, and other land at £268 10s. a year, Richard Browne certain lands at £225 a year, and East Down sheepsleight and arable were let for £180 a year. With the tithes, which were leased at £180, the total rental of the demesne came to over £1,400, while the customary rents ('olds rent') came to about £62.[48] The regular income which the copyhold lands provided was therefore negligible compared with the rents of the demesne, but they still no doubt yielded an intermittent return from fines paid for renewal of copies.

The arable of Edington continued in open fields until at least 1842.[49] In 1702 it was ordered that one field should be fallow every three years. The fields were then Edington Clay, Edington Hill, and Pixell, or Pigshill, or Pattenstone Piece Field.[50] The Clay was on the rising ground between the Bratton boundary and Edington Hill, near Fitzroy Farm. Pixell Field was near Patcombe Hill.[51] Some other arable which was to conform to the three-year course lay at the Byes and Behind Hayes. This may have been on the lower ground, perhaps near Woodbridge, where there was inclosed arable in 1774.[52] Customary tenants had common for their sheep with the common flock; one holding was

[28] S.C. 2/208/45 m. 7.
[29] Ibid.; S.C. 2/208/46.
[30] S.C. 6/1052/1; S.C. 2/208/46 m. 1.
[31] S.C. 2/208/45 m. 4.
[32] Ibid. m. 5.
[33] S.C. 2/208/49 m. 2.
[34] Cal. Pat. 1548–9, 376.
[35] S.C. 2/208/46 m. 6d.
[36] S.C. 2/208/48 m. 2.
[37] S.C. 2 /208/49 m. 7.
[38] S.C. 2/208/45 m. 13; W.R.O. Tithe Award.
[39] B.M. Lansd. MS. 442, ff. 55–6.
[40] Cal. Pat. 1548–9, 376.
[41] E 178/4697.
[42] Valor Eccl. (Rec. Com.), ii. 140.
[43] Longleat MS. 10462.
[44] Wilts. Inq. p.m. 1327–77 (Index Libr.), 327.
[45] Valor Eccl. (Rec. Com.), ii. 140.
[46] Longleat MS. 10462.
[47] W.R.O. Tithe Award.
[48] W.R.O. 84, Survey of Demesne, 1686.
[49] W.R.O. Tithe Award.
[50] Dorset R.O., D 45, Bolton Court Book.
[51] W.R.O. Tithe Award.
[52] W.R.O. 212A. Copies of Court Roll, 1774.

allowed 12 sheep one year and 24 the next, another 4 one year and 8 the next, and others in the same proportion.[53] In 1712 it was said that the parson, apparently meaning the lessee of the tithes, should provide a bull and a boar for the use of the parish.[54] The custom of the manor was copies for three lives, with the wife of each successive life holding for her widowhood.[55]

Tinhead arable in 1842 lay on the hill at Goldenham, which lay between Edington Hill and Long Hollow, and at Tinhead Clay, between Salisbury Hollow and the road to Coulston.[56] Tinhead Lowfield was mentioned in 1705, when some arable there had lately been inclosed.[57] Tenants of the two Tinhead manors had common in Tinhead Cowleaze in the proportion one cow to five sheep. Thus John Price's copyhold in 1755 had common there for 5 cows and 25 sheep, and Betty Rogers's for 4 beasts and 20 sheep in 1774.[58] In 1700 it was presented as the custom to have two bulls and a boar there, provided by the owner of the parsonage.[59]

In the 18th century the Bolton property included several large farms which were no doubt let at rack rents.[60] South Down Farm and sheepsleight which included a considerable amount of inclosed land about Edington village and the tithes arising from the farm were leased in 1702 for nine years at £400 a year.[61] In 1784 Hurst, South Down, Housecroft, Ivymill, Parsonage, Ballard's, Bartley's, Shores, and East Down farms were all of over 100 acres. The copyhold and lands let on long leases amounted to about 700 a. By 1835 no copyholds remained, and the Watson-Taylor property, called the manor of Edington, consisted chiefly of large farms held on yearly tenancies at rack rents. In that year 13 farms were let at over £100 a year each, including 5 over £400 and another 3 over £300. All rents, including cowleazes, cottages, and allotments, totalled over £4,750.[62] Further consolidation of holdings had taken place by 1851, when the decline in population of the parish was attributed to the 'incorporation' of several small farms.[63] The common fields were never inclosed by Act of Parliament. It was probably unnecessary to obtain one owing to the large proportion of the parish owned by the Watson-Taylor family, for in 1842 the family owned 4,819 a. out of a total of 5,709.[64] After the extinction of the copyholds the rights of pasture which had belonged to them were treated as separate pieces of property. In 1823 404 sheep leazes in Edington were occupied by 17 people, and 440 in Tinhead by 6 people. Sixty-five cowleazes in Tinhead Cowleaze were owned by 6 people; of these, Simon Watson-Taylor held 50, which he let to the poor.[65] Each cowleaze was let at 32s. a year

in 1835.[66] The Cowleaze was inclosed in 1865, when Simon Watson-Taylor owned 69 out of 70 leazes.[67]

The manor of Baynton was valued at £15 18s. 8d. in 1535.[68] Of this, 66s. 8d. was the value of two closes in the hands of the Bonhommes, and the rest was the tenants, rents. In 1557 the farm of the site of the manor and the lands belonging to it, which were leased on three lives, was worth £8 3s. 4d., rents of free and customary tenants 65s. 11d., and perquisites of courts 2s. 4d. A tenement in Orcheston St. George, which belonged to the manor, was leased for 60 years at 53s. 4d. a year.[69] A survey of c. 1673 shows that little of the manor was in hand except for 13 a. of woods and 20 a. of land sown with cinqfoil. The chief income of the manor came from the rack rents of three farms. Two of these, of 80 and 120 a. respectively, lay entirely in the low inclosed grounds around Baynton and north of it, while the third, of 120 a. included 90 a. of 'land to be sown yearly', which probably lay on the hill, and pasture for 850 sheep. The total of the rack rents of these farms and some smaller parcels was just over £400. Five small holdings were leased on lives. The timber on the estate was worth £1,000.[70] By the end of the 18th century the property consisted of three farms: Baynton, the present Upper Baynton Farm, of over 500 a.; Baynton Dairy, the present Lower Baynton Farm, of 140 a.; and Baynton Lower Dairy, which lay in the north of the parish near the present Stokes Marsh Farm.[71]

The woollen industry first came to Edington, as it did to neighbouring villages, to take advantage of the water power the Stradbrook afforded for the fulling of cloth. A tucking mill is first mentioned in Edington in the mid-14th century.[72] In 1427 Richard Tucker held a fulling mill of the Rector of Edington,[73] and in 1519 one Whitaker, a clothier of Westbury, had lately built a mill called New Mill.[74] These were no doubt the two fulling mills which belonged to Edington Rector manor c. 1550, one held by John Whitaker, and one by Andrew Michell and John Adlam.[75] Toward the end of the century the Whitakers were the most important clothiers in Edington. Jeffery Whitaker of Tinhead, 'clothman', left to his son, Nash, the business of his mill at Bratton, with New Mill in Edington and Langham Mill in North Bradley. His legacies totalled about £3,000.[76] Nash Whitaker, also of Tinhead, died in 1610, leaving his mill at Bratton and his best cloth-mark, called the yellow cross, to his son Jeffery.[77] This Jeffery was described as a clothier of Westbury in 1613, when he conveyed property at Edington to Sir William Paulet,[78] but as a gentleman at his death in 1625, when he left property in Edington and Steeple Ashton to his

[53] Ibid.
[54] Dorset R.O., D. 45, Bolton Court Book.
[55] Ibid.
[56] W.R.O. Tithe Award.
[57] Dorset R.O., D 45.
[58] W.R.O. 212A, Copy of Court Roll, 1775.
[59] Dorset R.O., D. 45.
[60] Bolton Estate Act, 24 Geo. III, c. 9 (priv. act).
[61] W.R.O. 334, Lease Bolton-Gilbert, 25 March 1702.
[62] W.R.O. 212A, Watson-Taylor Rental, 1835.
[63] V.C.H. Wilts. iv. 321.
[64] W.R.O. Tithe Award.
[65] W.A.S. Libr., Devizes, Abstract of Ch. Rate.
[66] W.R.O. 212A, Watson-Taylor Rental, 1835.

[67] W.R.O. Inclosure Award.
[68] Valor Eccl. (Rec. Com.) ii. 140.
[69] B.M. Harl. MS. 607, f. 25d.
[70] W.R.O. 84, Survey, c. 1673.
[71] W.R.O. Land Tax Assessments; W.A.S. Libr., Devizes, Abstract of Ch. Rate.
[72] S.C. 11/706, a Rental conjecturally dated c. 1355.
[73] S.C. 2/208/46, m. 5b.
[74] S.C. 2/208/49 m. 7d.
[75] Longleat MS. 10462.
[76] W.N. & Q. iv. 107.
[77] Ibid. 111.
[78] W.R.O. 436, Mortgage Paulet-Penyston, 24 May 1628.

uncle Jeffery.[79] Other clothiers in the late 16th century were Robert and William Blackborrow, who were both fined for defective white cloth, Robert in 1561 and William in 1563.[80] Robert, who was of Tinhead, died in 1578.[81] In that year Thomas Adlam, tucker, and Henry Noble, weaver, lived at Edington.[82] In the next century Stephen Gawen (fl. *c.* 1630), Abel Gawen (*c.* 1630), another Abel Gawen (*c.* 1664), and John Pryor (*c.* 1675) were all clothiers, the Gawens at Tinhead and Pryor at Edington.[83] Henry Spender of Baynton (d. *c.* 1621) was a weaver.[84] John Pryor took a copyhold estate in a fulling mill in 1703,[85] but no later reference to the industry in Edington has been found.

A limekiln stood at the top of Salisbury Hollow above Tinhead in 1817.[86] It was occupied by Mrs. Jane Boulter in 1857,[87] and was still standing in 1889, but had been demolished by 1901.[88]

MILLS. In 1086 there were two mills at Edington paying 19s.[89] By the mid-14th century there were at least four; two were held by Agatha and Sybil Palmer and two by William of Sweltenham. There was then a tucking mill in Edington, probably one of these four.[90] The two water mills of William of Sweltenham were acquired by William of Edington and granted to the Rector of Edington in 1351,[91] and a water mill which was charged with a payment of 10s. yearly to John Palmer was granted by Nicholas de Bonham and others to the rector in 1373.[92] Another water mill was granted to the rector with the manor of Tinhead in 1363. It was held of Richard Rous of Baynton, who was bound to supply timber for its repair, but it was then wholly in decay.[93] Rous's release to the rector indicates that it was near the Leaze in Tinhead.[94] In *c.* 1550 three mills were appurtenant to the manor of Edington Rector.[95] Of these, Sweltenham grist mill was no doubt one of the two conveyed to the rector in 1351, and an unnamed fulling mill was probably one of the others which had belonged to the manor since the 14th century. The third, a fulling mill called New Mill, was described as lately built in 1519.[96] There are indications that Sweltenham Mill lay on the site of the present Ivy Mill, which is first so named in 1720.[97] By the later part of the century Ivy Mill, or Mill Farm, had over 100 acres of land attached to it,[98] and has remained primarily a farm until the present time. In 1921 the three-stoned mill had been recently repaired at great expense,[99] and it remained in use until after the Second World War. The mill building is of three stories, the lowest of stone and the upper two timber-framed. It

appears to have been a dwelling house probably dating from the 15th century, which was later converted into a mill. It retains on the ground floor a pointed stone entrance doorway, and has three bays of an open timber roof which shows signs of smoke-blackening. It may have belonged to a first-floor hall. To provide sufficient power the small stream was turned into a banked-up mill pond which gave an eventual fall of 12ft. and turned an overshot wheel of 5 h.p. Much of the mill's machinery remained in 1963. The brick house adjoining the mill was rebuilt in the mid-19th century after a fire.[1]

The fulling mill of *c.* 1550, which was unnamed, probably stood on the site of the present Hudd's Mill. A grain and fulling mill called Mead Mill, which was parcel of the manor of Edington Rector, was occupied by William Hudd in 1711.[2] It was called Edington Mill in 1773[3] and continued to work as a corn mill until the late 19th century. The building, apparently of the 18th century, was in 1963 used as a farm building. It was powered by an overshot wheel of about 12 ft. diameter, fed from a pond into which the water ran through a high-banked leat. The extent of the earthworks needed to provide power both at Ivy Mill and Hudd's Mill, is remarkable.

New Mill stood on the upper side of Woodbridge on the road from Edington to West Ashton, where the outline of the mill pond can still be traced. It is last mentioned in the will of Jeffery Whitaker in 1601,[4] and no doubt fell into decay with the decline of the cloth industry in the district.

FAIR AND MARKET. A fair belonged to the manor of Edington Romsey *c.* 1550. It was held on Relic Sunday,[5] and the profit, which did not amount to 4d. a year, went to the reeve.[6] It was still held in the years before the First World War, on a Monday early in July, but was then entirely recreational. A feast was held on the previous day.[7] A market at Edington was being held in 1433, when a Warminster shoemaker took a life estate in an empty plot in the market of Edington next to the stall of Robert Letecombe.[8] Shambles are mentioned in 1511,[9] and in 1529 William Richards held one under the wall of the manor.[10] John Smyth *alias* Butcher held a shop called a shamble in 1539.[11] No reference to a market later than this has been found.

CHURCH. There was a parson of Edington in 1225[12] A church is first mentioned in 1241, when it was awarded to John of Romsey, Rector of

[79] *Wilts. Inq. p.m.* 1625–49 (Index Libr.), 42.
[80] E 350/329.
[81] P.C.C. 34 Arundell.
[82] *Sess. Mins.* (W.A.S. Rec. Brch.), 44.
[83] *Genealogist*, N.S. xxviii. 55; xxx. 127; xxxi. 181; xxxii. 206; *W.N. & Q.* vi. 258.
[84] P.C.C. 69 Dale.
[85] Dorset R.O., D. 45.
[86] O.S. Map 1″, sheet 14 (1st edn.)
[87] *P.O. Dir.* 1857.
[88] O.S. Map 1/2,500, Wilts. XLV. 2 (1st and 2nd edns.).
[89] *V.C.H. Wilts.* ii, p. 131.
[90] S.C. 11/706.
[91] *Cal. Close*, 1354–60, 104.
[92] *Cal. Pat.* 1370–4, 367.
[93] *Wilts. Inq. p.m.* 1327–77 (Index Libr.), 327.
[94] W.A.S. Libr. Devizes, Edington Cartulary Transcript, p. 206.

[95] Longleat MS. 10462.
[96] S.C. 2/208/49 m. 7d.
[97] Dorset R.O., D. 45.
[98] Bolton Estate Act, 24 Geo. III, c. 9 (priv. act).
[99] W.A.S. Libr., Devizes, Sale Cat.
[1] Ex. inf. Messrs. Tyler of Ivymill Farm.
[2] Dorset R.O., D. 45.
[3] *Andrews and Dury, Map* (W.A.S. Rec. Brch.), pl. 7.
[4] *W.N. & Q.* iv. 107.
[5] The third Sunday after Midsummer day.
[6] Longleat MS. 10462.
[7] Ex inf. Miss I. M. Braidwood and Miss D. U. Seth-Smith.
[8] S.C. 2/208/46 m. 7d.
[9] S.C. 11/708.
[10] S.C. 2/208/48.
[11] Ibid.
[12] *Cur. Reg. R.* xii. 305.

Edington, together with the chapel of Bradley, and tithes which had been disputed in Baynton, Tinhead, and Coulston.[13] There is little doubt that Romsey Abbey had held the church since before the Conquest, although no church is mentioned in Edgar's charter.[14] In 1241, and probably for many years previously, the church at Edington was a prebend of Romsey Abbey, and the rector acted, nominally, as a chaplain to the nuns, being represented at Edington by a vicar. When in 1351 William of Edington founded his chantry at Edington, the rector of the church resigned, and his place was taken by the first warden of the chantry. At the same time the abbess transferred the advowson to William of Edington, and agreed that the warden should be a canon of her house in place of the former rector. In 1358 the chantry was converted into a religious house, the head of which was called the rector.[15] From this time until the Dissolution the monastic church served as a parish church for Edington, and it was laid down in the foundation charter that two secular priests should minister to the parishioners in the nave.[16]

North Bradley was a chapelry of Edington at least as early as 1241.[17] The prebendaries of Edington appointed vicars to serve there, and after 1351, when the advowson of the chapel was granted to the chantry, the warden, and later the Rector of the Bonhommes of Edington, continued to do so until the Dissolution.[18] In the later Middle Ages North Bradley was usually referred to as a vicarage, and its subordination to the church of Edington was probably forgotten. After the Dissolution the advowson was granted separately from that of Edington, and North Bradley has since been regarded as a separate parish.[19] Baynton was also a chapelry of Edington, but the church there had fallen out of use by the 16th century (see below). Since 1939, when Imber was taken over by the War Department, the spiritualities of that parish have been served from Edington.[20]

The church of Edington was appropriated to the chantry at its foundation in 1351[21] and as the parish was served by priests from the monastery itself, both great and small tithes were presumably taken by the latter. After the Dissolution the rectory and church were granted with the monastery's property,[22] and descended in the same way until 1910, when the patronage of the living was transferred to the Bishop of Salisbury.[23] The tithes were wholly impropriate, and the cure was served by a perpetual curate appointed by the lay rector.[24]

In 1291 the rectory of Edington with its chapel of Bradley was assessed at £33 6s. 8d., and the vicar-age of Edington at a further £6 13s. 4d.[25] In 1341 the rector had a house and garden and a carucate of land in demesne, and tithes, offerings, and rents which amounted in all to £43 9s.[26] At the Dissolution the rectory was valued at £43 18d. 2d.[27] In 1561 it was charged with £7 6s. 8d., for the stipends of two curates.[28] In 1770 the curate was paid £30 a year out of the issues of the manor.[29] The benefice was augmented by Queen Anne's Bounty in 1809, 1813, and 1823,[30] and by 1831 the average net income was £87 with a house.[31] In 1842 the tithes were commuted for £1,300, the whole being allotted to the lay rector.[32] In 1882 the benefice was endowed with £48 a year, and a house provided for the vicar.[33]

Apart from William of Edington's chantry of 1351, which was afterwards converted into the house of Bonhommes, nothing is known of any chantries in the church. A chapel of St. Ethelfleda is mentioned in 1358, when the Abbess of Romsey received land near it from John of Edington,[34] but it seems likely that it was separate from the church. In 1413 the reeve of Edington gave two geese to the chaplain celebrating mass there on St. Ethelfleda's day.[35] Leland saw a chapel with a hermitage at the site of Bishop Aiscough's murder,[36] but nothing more is known about it.[37] A shop and a house belonged to the church in 1604.[38] The church house stood just north of the church in the field on the west of the road.[39]

The prebendaries who held the rectory of Edington before 1351 were nominally chaplains to the nuns at Romsey, but since several of them held other preferments,[40] it is almost certain that they did not reside either at Edington or Romsey. Little is known about the vicars whom they appointed, but in 1314 William, Vicar of Edington, promised to abstain from further connexion with Edith Harlot and four other women,[41] and in 1351 it was said that the church was neglected.[42] In 1428 six parishioners appeared before the bishop charged with having assembled at the cross at Tinhead and pledged themselves not to offer more than 1d. for weddings, churchings, and burials.[43] During the 18th century the curate is said to have acted as domestic chaplain to the lords of the manor, having a horse and servant found and table at the house.[44] In 1783, however, when the lords were absentees, the curate lived at Charlton beyond Devizes. He also held the curacy of Erlestoke, and held services at Edington once each Sunday, alternately morning and afternoon. As he wrote, the stipend was 'by no means a proper support for more duty'.[45] In 1812 lateness or irregularity of service was com-

13 H. G. D. Liveing, *Records of Romsey Abbey*, 72.
14 See p. 241.
15 *V.C.H. Wilts.* iii. 320.
16 *W.A.M.* xx. 257.
17 Liveing, *Romsey Records*, 72.
18 Phillipps, *Wilts. Inst. passim.*   19 See p. 226.
20 *W.A.M.* liv. 437.
21 *Cal. Papal Regs.* iii. 538.
22 *Cal. Pat.* 1548–9, 376.
23 Sar. Dioc. Regy. Patronage Reg.
24 *V.C.H. Wilts.* iii. 46.
25 *Tax. Eccl.* (Rec. Com.), 180.
26 *Inq. Non.* (Rec. Com.), 176.
27 *Valor Eccl.* (Rec. Com.), ii. 140.
28 *Cal. Pat.* 1560–63, 50.
29 Hants R.O. 11, M 49/121.
30 Hodgson, *Queen Anne's Bounty*, p. cccxxxv.

31 *Rep. Com. Eccl. Rev.* H.C. 54, p. 832 (1835), xxii.
32 W.R.O. Tithe Award.
33 *Lond. Gaz.* 3 Feb. 1882, 436.
34 *Wilts. Inq. p.m.* 1327–77 (Index Libr.), 253.
35 Liveing, *Romsey Records*, 192.
36 Leland, *Itin.* ed. Toulmin Smith, i. 268.
37 *W.A.M.* i. 189.
38 W.A.S. Libr., Devizes, Transcript of Chwdns.' Accts.
39 Ibid. Drawing by Jn. Britton.
40 See *e.g.* Liveing, *Romsey Records*, 127; *Cal. Pat.* 1321–24, 43.
41 *Reg. Simon de Gandavo* (Cant. and York Soc.), 549.
42 *Cal. Papal Regs.* iii. 538.
43 *V.C.H. Wilts.* iii. 25.
44 *W.A.M.* xx. 305.
45 Sar. Dioc. R.O. Vis. Queries, 1783.

plained of.[46] At that time the curate was William Roots, who had licence to reside at Warminster.[47]

The church of *ST. MARY THE VIRGIN, ST. KATHARINE AND ALL SAINTS*[48] was built at the foundation of the house of Bonhommes, and dedicated by the Bishop of Salisbury in 1361.[49] It replaced a church of which remains, of late Norman, character, of part of the south arcade, were found during the 19th-century restoration.[50] The present church consists of a clerestoried nave with aisles, north and south transepts, chancel, tower at the crossing, and south porch of three stories. Apart from the porch, which was added in the 15th century, the whole is of the mid-14th century, and is a good example of the transition from the Decorated to the Perpendicular style. This can be seen in the windows of the transepts and the side windows of the chancel, which have a form of reticulated tracery in which the vertical members have become straight instead of flowing. The east and west windows of the church show the same merging of the styles, but the west windows of the aisles and the tower windows only have Decorated tracery. Externally the church is embattled, but only the chancel and the east walls of the transepts are decorated with crocketed pinnacles. Inside, the chancel is richly decorated, with a pair of niches in the east wall flanking the window, a pair in the eastern corners, and a pair between the side windows. In two of them are headless figures. The carving of the niches, and of the corbels and other details thoughout the church, is exceptionally delicate and vigorous. The nave and transepts have ceilings of the 17th century, of pink and white plaster; that in the north transept is dated 1663. The chancel ceiling is of *c.* 1789, when it was built by Joshua Smith to replace the original one of stone.[51]

In the south transept is a large altar tomb with a recumbent figure of an ecclesiastic under a canopy. The whole is coloured and decorated with a rebus of a branch or sprig issuing from a barrel. The feet of the effigy rest on a barrel with the initials J.B. or T.B., but its identity has never been certainly established.[52] In one of the arches on the south side of the nave is a small chapel, consisting of a canopied altar tomb with space for a priest to kneel at one end. Brasses of a man and wife are missing, but the coats of arms of Cheyney and Pavely, and the Pavely badge of a rudder, make it probable that it commemorates Sir Ralph Cheyney (d. *c.* 1401) and his wife Joan, a coheir of Sir John Pavely of Brook.[53] On the south side of the chancel is a large marble and alabaster tomb with effigies of Sir Edward Lewis (d. 1630) and his wife Lady Anne Beauchamp (d. 1664). The kneeling children on this monument may have inspired the sculptor of a mural tablet to the Tayler family in the north

aisle, on which is a group of kneeling figures in 19th-century dress. On the north side of the chancel is a monument to Sir Simon Taylor (d. 1815) by Sir Francis Chantrey. There are many other monuments from the 17th century onwards.

The chancel screen or pulpitum is of the early 16th century, much restored. The spiked altar rails, pulpit with tester, and oak reredos in the north transept (furnished as a Lady Chapel) are all of the 17th century. The bowl of the black marble font dating from *c.* 1890 rests on a medieval stem. The wooden cover is dated 1626. In the south transept are the remains of a font probably of the 13th century.[54] There are considerable remains of medieval stained glass. In the north transept are a crucifixion and angels playing a lute and an organ; in the north aisle patterned glass with heraldic borders, and in the north clerestory windows are figures of saints. A Scudamore organ built by Nelson Hall of Warminster was placed in the church in 1860 in the hope that the congregation would join in the singing. It was replaced by the present organ, by Jones of Kensington, in 1901, and subsequently taken to Tilshead church.[55]

In the south aisle are two recumbent figures of the 14th century, a royal achievement of arms dated 1639, and a few fragments of old glass, all of which were removed from Imber church.[56]

There were four bells and a sanctus bell in 1553. There are now six bells and a sanctus bell; the earliest are the first, of 1640, and the fifth, of 1647.[57] The clock, which has no dial, is of the 16th century, though altered later. The commissioners of Edward VI left a chalice of 9 oz., and took away 15 oz. of silver. The present chalice, with paten on foot, is hall-marked 1738, and there is a pewter flagon and three plates.[58] The registers of burials begin in 1678, and of baptism and marriages in 1695. Baptisms and burials from 1789 to 1812 are missing.[59]

In 1812 it was said that the church was in good order,[60] but in 1857 it was described as a picture of decay and neglect. The floor was 'a chaotic plateau, with traces of stolen brasses and ruptured inscriptions,' the walls were 'green and dank', and 'a huge oven, similar to a brewing vat', heated the church.[61] It was restored in 1889–91 by C. E. Ponting.

A chapel at Baynton is first mentioned in 1225, when Walter of Baynton objected because the Abbot of Hyde had heard a case about the advowson in an ecclesiastical court.[62] The presentation went with the manor of Baynton, the first recorded patron being Sir John Rous in 1310.[63] The chapel was spoken of as a rectory and the incumbent claimed some tithes. In 1339 there was a dispute over tithes between the Rector of Baynton, backed by John Rous, and the Prebendary of Edington. There was an affray in Baynton Field in which a man was killed.[64] The sheriff was ordered to proclaim against

---

[46] *V.C.H. Wilts.* iii. 55.
[47] Parish Records, Licence.
[48] This dedication is mentioned in the foundation charter: Dugdale, *Mon.* vi. 536. The ch. was often spoken of as All Saints' in the 18th cent.
[49] *W.A.M.* xx. 295.
[50] Ibid. xxv. 210, where there is a full description of the church.   [51] Ibid. xx. 297.
[52] *W.N. & Q.* iii. 97–105, where Thomas Bulkington is suggested. This is the most plausible guess so far made, since Leland spoke of him as a benefactor of the Bonhommes, and he had an obit there (*Valor Eccl.* ii. 142).

[53] *W.A.M.* xx. 302.
[54] Ibid. lv. 378.
[55] Ex inf. Mr. Peter Madeley of Devizes.
[56] *W.A.M.* liv. 437.
[57] Walters, *Wilts. Bells*, 81.
[58] Nightingale, *Wilts. Plate*, 107.
[59] Ex inf. Major C. J. Jacobs.
[60] *V.C.H. Wilts.* iii. 54.
[61] *W.A.M.* iii. 51.
[62] *Cur. Reg. R.* xii. 305.
[63] Phillipps, *Wilts. Inst.* 10.
[64] W.A.S. Libr., Devizes, Simpson Notes on Imber.

EDINGTON CHURCH FROM THE SOUTH-EAST

Dedicated 1361

2

4

1

3

1. Steeple Ashton, with medieval cruck truss. 2. Keevil, early 17th century. 3. Warminster Common, probably 18th century. 4. Dilton Marsh, 19th century

EXAMPLES OF LOCAL COTTAGES OF DIFFERENT PERIODS

unlawful assemblies, and to allow the prebendary to collect the tithes belonging to him there. In the event, however, the sheriff took the rector's side, and imprisoned the prebendary's collectors, because, it was alleged, the under-sheriff was allied to the rector.[65] In 1351 Thomas, rector of the chapel, acknowledged that he had unjustly received the great tithes of two acres on 'Langehull' since 1341.[66] In 1361 the Bonhommes were awarded tithes worth 20 marks, and in return granted the Rector of Baynton an acre of meadow and all the rest of the tithes within the bounds of Baynton.[67] In 1363 Richard Rous gave 40s. yearly from his lands in Westbury Leigh for the maintenance of the rector and his successors.[68]

The advowson of Baynton was granted with the manor to the Bonhommes in 1444.[69] It seems that the chapel was allowed to decay, although a rector is mentioned as late as the reign of Edward IV.[70] In 1589 the decayed chapel of St. Katherine, or Our Lady, at Baynton was granted by the Crown to Charles Bagehott and Bartholomew Yardley,[71] but no further mention of it has been found. It is thought to have been near old Baynton House, in a field called Chapel Close. Near this site a copper signaculum, marked with the Virgin Mary and a chalice, was found in the 19th century.[72]

NONCONFORMITY. There were six Protestant nonconformists and one Papist at Edington in 1676.[73] Edward Froude of Edington, who was presented as an Anabaptist preacher in 1674, 1683, and 1686, was closely connected with the Baptist conventicle at Erlestoke,[74] but no organized dissenting church existed at Edington until over a century later. In 1794 a building at Tinhead, which had formerly been a malthouse, was registered as a place of worship.[75] No denomination was then stated, but from this congregation probably descended the Baptists who were meeting in the same building in 1851.[76] There is little doubt that they had been founded from the chapel at Bratton, for in later years the Tinhead chapel was a station of the Bratton one.[77] It closed c. 1897, when the lease of the building expired.[78]

Methodist meetings in Tinhead were being held in a cottage c. 1787.[79] James Rogers, minister of the Bradford Circuit, 1795–6, was probably the first travelling preacher to visit the village. In 1800 a coachhouse in 'Potters Barton' was made into a chapel and leased to the congregation, but in 1827 the lease of the building fell in, and, because of the hostility of the owner's steward, could not be renewed. Meetings were again held in a cottage, but

in 1828, through the efforts of Virtue Morgan and her husband, a chapel was built at the lower end of Coach Hollow in Tinhead. In the following year there were 26 members.[80] The chapel was enlarged in 1848 so that it contained 360 sittings,[81] and in 1851 the average Sunday evening congregation was 350.[82] In 1857 there were 38 members under 3 leaders,[83] and in 1898 the number was 41.[84] In 1904 the chapel was practically rebuilt.[85]

In 1893 James Newman left £100 to be invested to pay 10s. a year to augment the quarterly collection at the Methodist Chapel, 10s. a year for the Sunday School, and the rest of the income for the benefit of local preachers. Since most of the preachers then came from a distance, the fund was used towards their expenses in stabling their horses at the village inn and the refreshment of their drivers.[86]

A house in Tinhead was licensed for a congregation of Independents in 1791, but no other reference to it has been found.[87]

PARISH GOVERNMENT. In 1577 two churchwardens were chosen for Edington, and two churchmen for each of the tithings of Edington and Tinhead. Churchmen were last chosen in 1583; in the following year two assistant churchwardens and two collectors for the poor were chosen. The assistant churchwardens soon ceased to be appointed, but the collectors for the poor continued until 1611, when they were replaced by one overseer for each of the three tithings of Edington, Tinhead, and Baynton. During the period covered by the early churchwardens' account book (1577–1625), the parish had a stock of a few cattle and sheep which were let out at yearly rents. In 1604 the church shop and house were leased.[88] The parish bought two cottages in 1809, and also owned one in Tinhead; these were leased to tenants.[89]

Four volumes of overseers' accounts remain for the period 1806–34. It was the custom to appoint two overseers. In 1822 the vestry appointed a clerk to assist them with their accounts and in other ways, at a salary of £10 a year, which had increased to £20 by 1831. In that year the vestry ordered the overseers to call a vestry each month to hear the complaints of the poor, but no record of any such meetings remains. The average annual expenditure on the poor over five yearly periods rose from £685 in 1807–11, to £827 in 1822–6, while for the seven years 1827–34 it averaged £950.

Throughout the period covered by the books many of the weekly payments made were small sums in aid of wages, and it was a regular practice

[65] Cal. Close, 1339–41, 257, 263.
[66] B.M. Lansd. MS. 442, f. 11.
[67] Ibid. f. 23.
[68] Cal. Close, 1360–64, 439.
[69] Ibid. 1441–7, 307.
[70] W.A.M. xx. 274.
[71] C 66/1324 m. 15.
[73] W.N. & Q. iii. 536.
[74] V.C.H. Wilts. iii. 110.
[75] G.R.O. Retns. of Regns.
[76] H.O. 129/10/259.
[77] Baptist Handbook, 1868.
[78] Ex inf. Mrs. Reeves of Bratton.
[79] The following account is from T. R. Jones, The

[72] W.A.M. x. 258.

Departed Worthy, 127 f.
[80] W.R.O. Retns. of Nonconformist Meetings, 1829.
[81] T.R. Jones, The Departed Worthy, 127 f.
[82] H.O. 129/10/259.
[83] T.R. Jones, The Departed Worthy, 127 f.
[84] Melksham Circuit Quarterly Schedule, 1898.
[85] Document in custody of Revd. M. W. Powell of Chippenham, Superintendent Minister of Wilts. Mission (1951).
[86] Endowed Charities Wilts. (1908), p. 167.
[87] G.R.O. Retns. of Regns.
[88] W.A.S. Libr., Devizes, Transcript of Chwdns.' Accts. 1577–1625.
[89] Ibid. Abstract of Overseers' Accts. 1806–34.

to pay, or make an advance toward, rents and costs of clothing and bedding. Other payments were made to buy tools, to assist families to move away from the parish to obtain work, and for repairs to houses. Heavy unemployment in 1830 forced the parish to adopt the labour rate system. Two men were to be employed for every 50 a. of arable land and one for every 50 a. of pasture except on the downs. The remainder of the poor were to be employed on the parish roads. In 1833 the vestry ordered that the system was to apply each year from 29 November to 25 March.[90]

In 1577 two waymen were chosen for each of the three tithings of Edington, Tinhead, and Baynton and Coulston, but in later years only one was usually chosen for Baynton and Coulston.[91] In 1736 Edington and Tinhead were still maintaining their highways separately.[92] A highway account book for Edington tithing, 1809-27, is in the church chest.

SCHOOLS. In 1808 10 girls were educated and clothed at the expense of the lord of the manor, and about 30 more were paid for by their parents.[93] In 1819 there were two day schools, one for boys and one for girls, each containing about 20 pupils, and the curate stated that the poor were 'not in want of the means of education'.[94] In 1835 there were three infants' schools in the parish, providing education for 44 children of both sexes at the expense of their parents.[95] One of these may have been at West Coulston.[96] In 1859 40–50 girls were taught to read and sew, but not to write, in a cottage room 15 ft. square, by a mistress of doubtful competence. The Edington boys, and boys and girls from Tinhead, went to the schools at Bratton.[97] Edington and East Coulston were made a United District and a School Board formed in 1875,[98] and a school was built at Tinhead in 1877.[99] In 1894 there was accommodation for 124 pupils at the Board's mixed school and the average attendance

was 119.[1] By 1938 the school was used for junior-mixed and infants only, and average attendance had dropped to 49.[2]

CHARITIES. By his will proved in 1640 William Tubb left £50 to the poor of the parish.[3] The money was invested in land c. 1715. In 1833 the property lay in Steeple Ashton; at that time the rent of £3 15s. was accumulated for several years and then distributed equally among all the poor who had not been relieved by the parish during the last year.[4] The charity is still administered in much the same way; since 1894 recipients have been chosen by trustees appointed by the parish council.[5] Income in 1952 was £3.[6]

In 1852 George Tayler left £3,000 to be invested for charitable purposes, differing slightly from parish to parish, in Edington, Steeple Ashton, Keevil, and Poulshot. At Edington the provision of bread, the preaching of an annual childrens' sermon by the vicar, and the distribution of cakes to the children were the same as in Poulshot.[7] In addition, at Edington the Methodist minister was to have 10s. for a similar sermon, and his Sunday School was also to have cakes, and provision was made for the upkeep of the Tayler monuments in Edington church.[8] After the death of Tayler's administrator in 1906, the charity was divided into five parts, one for each parish and a separate educational foundation. The Edington charity was allotted £527 10s. stock, and with its proceeds the original objects of the charity are still carried out.[9] Income in 1951 was £14 16s.[10]

The Revd. Samuel Littlewood, curate of Edington, by his will proved in 1884, left £50 to be invested to supply Bibles and prayer books to poor parishioners who were over 50 years old and members of the Church of England.[11] The charity is still administered for this purpose.[12]

KEEVIL

KEEVIL lies about 5 miles east of Trowbridge and the same distance south of Melksham.[1] The ancient parish was about 3 miles long and 1½ wide, and roughly rectangular in shape. In the 1880's the eastern part, the tithing of Bulkington, became a separate civil parish, although ecclesiastically it remains part of Keevil.[2] It is 974 a. in area, and the civil parish of Keevil 2,063 a.[3] The western part of Keevil parish lies on the Corallian outcrop, described under Steeple Ashton,[4] which here gently declines from about 250 ft. on the parish boundary

down to the streams which water the eastern part of the parish at about 150 ft. The village lies on this slope. The remainder of the parish to the west, its northern fringes, and the whole of Bulkington lie in the clay vale. The land here is flat, about 150 ft. above sea level, and drained by a network of streams. The chief of these, Semington Brook, flows north-westward from the eastern boundary of Bulkington; passing to the south of that village, it forms the northern part of the Keevil-Bulkington boundary and then the north-eastern boundary of

[90] W.A.S. Libr. Devizes, Overseers' Accts.
[91] Ibid. Transcript of Chwdns.' Accts. 1577–1625.
[92] Q. Sess. and Ass. 1736 (W.A.S. Rec. Brch.), 73.
[93] Lambeth Palace Libr. MS. 1732.
[94] Digest of Returns to Cttee. on Educ. of Poor, H.C. 224, p. 1026 (1819), ix(2).
[95] Educ. Enq. Abstract, H.C. 62, p. 1037 (1835), xliii.
[96] For the school at West Coulston, see p. 239.
[97] Acct. of Wilts. Schools, H.C. 27, p. 22 (1859), xxi(2).
[98] Lond. Gaz. 1875, p. 5452.
[99] Date on building.
[1] Return of Schools, 1893 [C 7529], p. 648, H.C. (1894), lxv.
[2] Bd. of Educ. List. 21, 1938.
[3] P.C.C. 133 Coventry.

[4] Endowed Char. Wilts. (1908), p. 163.
[5] Char. Com. File 62082.
[6] Ibid. Accts. File.
[7] See V.C.H. Wilts. vii. 125; the £3,000 endowment is there incorrectly ascribed to Poulshot alone.
[8] Endowed Char. Wilts. (1908), pp. 164–6.
[9] Char. Com. File 82647.
[10] Ibid. Accts. File.
[11] Endowed Char. Wilts. (1908), pp. 166–7.
[12] Char. Com. File 40222.
[1] The following maps were used: O.S. Maps 1/2,500 Wilts. XXXIX. 2, 3, 5, 6, 7, 8 (all edns.); 1/25,000 ST. 95.
[2] See p. 259.
[3] Census, 1951.
[4] See p. 199.

Keevil. On the south it is joined by two streams flowing from East Coulston and Edington; the low ground between them was called Keevil Wick by the 13th century.[5] Another stream, called Summerham Brook, joins Semington Brook below Bulkington, having formed the northern boundary of the parish.

The main road from Trowbridge to Devizes runs for a short distance through the north of the parish. On it stands the hamlet now called the Strand; it was called Old Horse Shoe in 1773,[6] and subsequently Horseshoes.[7] This was presumably from the name of an inn, yet the inn there was called the 'Carpenters' Arms' in 1768.[8] It is now called the 'Lamb', and is an early 19th-century building of brick. A road or drove formerly led from it to the west end of Keevil village,[9] but it is now lost, and the quickest way is through Great Hinton. Further east another minor road leaves the main road and runs southward, and forks to join the road from Bulkington to Keevil at two points. The turnpike house, which stood at its northern end in 1773,[10] still stood, derelict, in 1963. The main road leaves the parish to the north-east by Baldham Bridge. There has been a bridge on the site since the 14th century;[11] the present one is of the 18th century, two-arched and built of ashlar. Nearby are Baldham Mill[12] and Baldham Farm, the latter an 18th-century stone house.

Keevil and Bulkington villages both stand on a minor road which winds across the parish from west to east, joining the Westbury-Melksham road to the road from Seend to West Lavington. Most of the houses in Keevil are built along this road, but branching to the south are Martin's Road and Pyatts, both of which contain houses of the 16th and 17th centuries. The church stands just south of Main Street at the end of a short lane. The large 16th-century manor house[13] is on the north side of Main Street, hidden from view by a high wall. Opposite is the high garden wall of Blagden House,[14] a somewhat smaller house of the 17th century. This stretch of road without visible houses, and with a high pavement on a grassy bank on the north side, divides the village into two parts hidden from one another by the curve of the road.

The western part of Keevil contains a notable group of timber-framed houses. Little Talboys[15] is a fine example of a cruck-framed house. It consists of four bays, of which the two centre ones formed a single-storied hall; the central open truss has an arch-braced collar beam with moulded timbers. The roof of the westernmost bay is unaltered, but the eaves of the other three were raised probably c. 1600, when a massive central chimney and a dividing floor in the open hall were inserted. The house has later brick infilling and a thatched roof. Cruck construction also survives in

the back wing of Manor Farm, which is of two bays, of which one has been raised to the east to form a small gable, now altered. The main part of the house is of stone, of two stories and attics; it probably dates from the early 17th century, but may be in origin an earlier timber-framed cross-wing which has been remodelled. Talboys, a large timber-framed house of c. 1500, is described below.[16] Opposite are two timber-framed and thatched houses, both of which have been divided into two cottages, but one is now used as one house again. They appear to be of the early 17th century, having small gables with shaped barge-boards and pendants and decorative timber-framing. It is possible, however, that the houses are older, and that these gables were added to give light to the upper floors of previously single-storied halls.

A similar house, now divided into two, stands in the lower part of the village in Pyatts. It has flanking gables, one of which has been raised, with a quadrant design in the apex, and a thatched roof. No. 22, formerly a shop, but recently converted into a house, and several cottages in Martin's Road, are also timber-framed buildings of the 16th and 17th centuries. In the 18th century brick came into use. Church Farm, and four cottages in Martin's Road show its use with thatched roofs; the cottages have the dentilled string-course at first-floor level which is common in the district. Beach House, formerly the 'Beach Arms', of brick with stone-mullioned windows, is of the earlier 18th century, and Longleaze Farm is dated 1790. The 'Rose and Crown' only dates from the early 19th century, but probably occupies the site of the 'Crown' which stood in the village in 1705.[17] In Martin's Road is a small estate of Council houses. The iron village hall there, built in 1892,[18] was in 1963 being replaced by a new one of brick. South of the village an airfield was built in the Second World War; in 1963 it was derelict.

East of the village and just south of the road to Bulkington is Pinkney Farm, originally a timber-framed building, which was remodelled in stone probably in the late 16th century. It has been considerably altered since then; there are dated stones of 1684 and 1785, and at the south end is an extension of the early 19th century. The road leads on to Keevil Wick, which was a settlement in the 13th century.[19] In 1773 there was a number of houses there built round a small green;[20] most have gone but there are two farms there and one or two cottages. The farms to the south, at Wick Leaze, Oxen Leaze, and Hurst, probably originated with the inclosure of old pasture land there in the 17th century.[21]

The road from Keevil to Bulkington crosses Semington Brook by the 18th-century Pantry Bridge. There was a bridge here in the 14th

5 P. N. Wilts. (E.P.N.S.), 143.
6 Andrews and Dury, Map (W.A.S. Rec. Brch.), pl. 10.
7 O.S. Map 1", sheet 167 (1934 edn.).
8 8 Geo. III, c. 49.
9 Andrews and Dury, Map (W.A.S. Rec. Brch.), pl. 10.
10 Ibid.
11 P.N. Wilts. (E.P.N.S.), 143.
12 See p. 258.
13 See p. 252.   14 See p. 255.

15 The name was given to the house by the Chamberlaine family; it was never the property of Thomas Talboys.
16 See p. 255.
17 E 134/4 Anne/Trin. 2.
18 Kelly's Dir. Wilts. (1911).
19 P.N. Wilts. (E.P.N.S.), 143.
20 Andrews and Dury, Map (W.A.S. Rec. Brch.), pl. 10.
21 See p. 257.

century.[22] In a ditch on the Bulkington side stands Turpin's Stone, which is said to have once had the inscription:

'Dick Turpin's dead and gone
'This stone's put here to think upon'

carved on it.[23] Almost all the houses in Bulkington village lie along the single curving street. The church and the London Co-operative Society creamery stand near the west end. A house, formerly the post office, is timber-framed with brick in-filling, and probably dates from the early 17th century. Otherwise the village consists chiefly of 18th- and 19th-century houses. On the south side of the street opposite Home Farm are several large brick cottages with a pattern of chequer work in vitrified headers, and stone-mullioned windows; one is dated 1720. Poplars Farm at the west end of the village is a stone house of c. 1770, with slated mansard roof; there are two pairs of coupled windows on each floor, and in the centre over the door is a single round-headed one. Withdean House, of brick with stone dressings, is dated 1802, and Manor Farm and Home Farm are of much the same time. In the centre of the village is the circular stepped base of a cross, of ancient masonry. It has been utilized to support the village war memorial, but nothing is known of its history.

Lanes lead southward from Bulkington to Mill Farm, and across Brasspan Bridge towards Oxen Leaze and Wick Leaze Farms. The latter, called Bulkington Drove, leads to Folly Green where a group of cottages stood in the early 19th century,[24] and thence to another green called Fullwood Green, which was inclosed in 1832.[25]

MANORS. Before the Conquest the manor of *KEEVIL* was held by Brixi, who held other manors in Somerset and Dorset.[26] It was granted after 1066 to Ernulf of Hesdin, one of William's chief followers, who held land in ten counties, and he held it in 1086.[27] It has been suggested[28] that he forfeited his lands because of his complicity in the rising of 1093; certainly a large part of his fief passed to Patrick de Chaworth, who is said to have married his daughter,[29] but Keevil, with some other manors, passed to a second Ernulf of Hesdin, son of the first,[30] who held it in 1130.[31] He was executed in 1138; a third Ernulf of Hesdin witnessed a charter in 1141, and quite possibly held Keevil in his turn. By 1160, however, 8½ fees in Wiltshire and Gloucestershire, including Keevil, were held by William

FitzAlan, whose father, Alan FitzFlaald, had married Aveline, sister of the second Ernulf.[32] These fees were later known as the honor of Keevil.[33] William FitzAlan's grandson, another William, died childless in 1215 and his estates passed to his brother John. In the same year he joined the rebels against King John, and the king granted Keevil to Robert of Samford.[34] After the king's death Henry III granted Keevil to John the Marshal,[35] but in 1217 John FitzAlan made his peace with the king and his lands were restored.[36] John married, as his first wife, Isabel, sister and coheir of Hugh, Earl of Arundel, and his issue by her became earls of Arundel.[37] In 1255 it was said that the manor of Keevil was held by payment of 20s. for the guard of Devizes Castle,[38] and this tenure is frequently mentioned from then on. Keevil descended in the FitzAlan family to Edmund, Earl of Arundel, who was executed in 1326 and subsequently attainted.[39] In the following year Edward III granted it to Edmund, Earl of Kent,[40] who was himself executed in 1330.[41] Keevil was granted to Geoffrey of Mortimer,[42] but in 1331 Richard FitzAlan, son of Edmund, was restored in blood and honours and Keevil passed back to his family. Richard's son Richard was executed in 1397,[43] and the king granted Keevil to Sir Henry Greene.[44] Thomas FitzAlan, son of the younger Richard, landed with Henry of Bolingbroke in 1399, and his estates were restored in 1400.[45] Thereafter Keevil descended in the FitzAlan family to Henry, Earl of Arundel (d. 1580), who in 1560 sold the manor to Richard Lambert, citizen and grocer of London.[46]

Richard Lambert's grandson, Edward, died in 1612 leaving two infant daughters,[47] who apparently died unmarried, for the manor passed to Thomas, Richard's younger brother.[48] His grandson, Thomas Lambert, sold Keevil to William Beach, son of William Beach of Brixton Deverill and Fittleton, in 1681.[49] It descended to his grandson William, who died in 1790 leaving an only surviving daughter and heir, Henrietta Maria.[50] She married Michael Hicks of Beverstone Castle (Glos.), who assumed the additional surname of Beach. Keevil passed to his second son William Beach, whose grandson W. A. Hicks Beach sold the property in lots in 1911.[51]

Keevil manor house is thought to have been built by one of the Lambert family c. 1580. It is a stone building of three stories with mullioned and transomed windows of six lights on the first two

[22] *P.N. Wilts.* (E.P.N.S.), 143.
[23] *W.A.M.* xxxix.102.
[24] O.S. Map 1″ sheet 14 (1st edn.); B.M. Add. MS. 42048, f. 238. This MS. is 'Annals of Keevil and Bulkington', by the Revd. A. T. Richardson, c. 1914; since this article was written, a copy has been acquired for W.A.S. Libr., Devizes.
[25] *Endowed Char. Wilts.* (1908), p. 252.
[26] *V.C.H. Wilts.* ii, p. 66.
[27] Ibid. p. 139.
[28] *Genealogist*, N.S. v. 211.
[29] *V.C.H. Wilts.* ii, p. 110.
[30] *Herald and Genealogist*, vi. 245; *Genealogist*, N.S. v. 209–13.
[31] *V.C.H. Wilts.* ii, p. 110.
[32] *Genealogist*, N.S. v. 210.
[33] *Wilts. Inq. p.m.* 1327–77 (Index Libr.), 57.
[34] R. W. Eyton, *Antiquities of Shropshire*, vii. 250; *Rot. Litt. Claus.* (Rec. Com.), 229.

[35] *Rot. Litt. Claus.* (Rec. Com.), 307.
[36] Eyton, *Shropshire*, vii. 251.
[37] *Complete Peerage.*
[38] *Rot. Hund.* (Rec. Com.), ii. 235.
[39] *Complete Peerage.*
[40] *Cal. Chart. R.* 1327–41, 4.
[41] *Complete Peerage.*
[42] *Cal. Chart. R.* 1327–41, 176.
[43] *Complete Peerage.*
[44] *Cal. Pat.* 1396–99, 198.
[45] *Complete Peerage.*
[46] *Cal. Pat.* 1560–63, 73.
[47] C 142/327/144.
[48] A pedigree of the Lambert family is in Hoare, *Mod. Wilts.* Heytesbury, 203.
[49] C.P. 25(2)/747/33 Chas. II East.
[50] W. Berry, *Hants Genealogies*, 256–7.
[51] Burke, *Land. Gent.* (1906), i. 99; Wilts. Cuttings, xiii. 236, xvi. 244.

floors and mullioned windows of three lights in the attics. The front has four symmetrical gables with stone copings and small square finials; the sides have three similar gables. In 1611 a two-storied porch was added at the centre of the front; it is decorated with Tuscan columns and inside has shell-headed niches similar to those on Edington church. In the garden is an archway of the same period which also contains a pair of these niches. Inside, the house contains many original features, notably the carved hall screen and some plaster ceilings. Some of the panelling is thought to be rather earlier than the house. In the garden are twelve clipped yew trees called the Twelve Apostles.

The Lambert family lived chiefly at their other manor of Boyton, although Edward Lambert, a younger son of the first purchaser of the manor, was described as of Keevil at his death c. 1586,[52] and may have been the builder of this house. The Beach family also seems only to have used the house as a second residence, for they were usually described as of Fittleton or Netheravon, or later of Oakley Hall near Basingstoke (Hants). In the later 19th century the house was occupied by Sir John Wallington, who had married a daughter of William Beach (d. 1856). He died at Keevil in 1910.[53] Maj.-Gen. J. B. B. Dickson bought the house in 1911;[54] he died in 1925,[55] and his widow was still living there in 1939.[56] It has since changed hands again.

In 1217 William Musard had lands in Bulkington, which he had forfeited because of his joining the rebels against John, restored to him.[57] William's widow, Joan de Bocland, held the estate in 1225,[58] but by 1242 another William Musard held 2 hides in Bulkington of John FitzAlan.[59] In 1244, when it was assigned in dower, to Amice his widow, the estate was first called the manor of *BULKING-TON*.[60] Another William Musard held it in 1302, when it was reckoned at ½ knight's fee,[61] and still in 1327, at ¼ and ⅛ fee.[62] In 1401 yet another William Musard held the two hides,[63] but by 1428 Richard Mayne held ½ knight's fee late of William Musard.[64] In 1440, however, Henry, Earl of Northumberland, and others had livery of a moiety of the manor of Bulkington called 'Mosardys'; they were apparently surviving trustees who had held the property on behalf of Beatrice, Countess of Arundel (d. 1439), for her life.[65] It is not clear why she held it, but it was said in 1441 that Richard and John Mayne had been taking the revenues since her death.[66] At least part of the estate, never subsequently referred to as a manor, passed to Richard Mayne's kinswoman and heir, Jane, wife of John Abbot.[67] By 1498 'Mayne's lands' belonged

to John Stokes of Seend, who then left them to his son, John, the younger.[68] By c. 1562 Thomas Baily of Baldham owned the property, for he then settled it on his son William when he married Edith, daughter of William Goddard.[69] William's son Thomas held it in 1571, when it was the subject of a lawsuit,[70] but the subsequent descent of the estate has not been traced.

Another part of Bulkington evidently remained with the FitzAlan family. In 1327 John of Keevil was a tenant of the Earl of Arundel,[71] and ten years later he settled 5 houses and 3 virgates of land on his son John.[72] In 1343 one of them paid a rent of over £45 for the land of Bulkington.[73] The younger John apparently became a priest, for in 1345 John of Keevil, clerk, held a moiety of the manor of Bulkington for life, with reversion to the Earl of Arundel.[74] He still held it in 1354,[75] but his property subsequently merged again in the FitzAlan inheritance and descended in the same way as Keevil. It was regularly mentioned as a moiety in the Middle Ages, but later simply as the manor of Bulkington, or else the whole estate was called the manor of Keevil and Bulkington.

In 1242 Peter of Bulkington held ½ knight's fee there.[76] Peter of Bulkington, who acquired land in Bulkington of William Sturdy in 1313, and William, son of Roger of Bulkington, who bought land of John of Aldrington there the following year, may have been descended from him.[77] Roger of Bulkington and John of Bulkington were both free tenants of the Earl of Arundel in 1327.[78] In 1428, however, Roger Coufold and Joan his wife held, for Joan's life, ½ knight's fee which formerly belonged to Peter of Bulkington. This life estate was held of Thomas 'Ereberd' and Agnes his wife, who held in right of Agnes.[79] Although the grant is unrecorded, there is little doubt that this was the property in Bulkington which passed to the house of Bonhommes at Edington. Leland mentioned Thomas Bulkington and Thomas Gereberd among benefactors who were remembered there;[80] the holder of the Bulkington property in 1428 must have been Thomas Gereberd of Odstock, whose widow Agnes was living in 1448.[81] It is possible that he gave Bulkington to the monastery, reserving a life estate for his wife, to found obits for himself and Thomas Bulkington, who was perhaps father of Agnes.

In 1560 the Edington manor, having passed to the Crown at the Dissolution, was granted to George Worth of Dauntsey.[82] He died the following year leaving an infant son George,[83] who held Bulkington for over 60 years. His only son Edward

[52] P.C.C. 1 Spencer.
[53] Burke, *Land. Gent.* (1937), 2351.
[54] *W.A.M.* xxxvii. 525.
[55] *Who was Who* 1916–28, 287.
[56] *Kelly's Dir. Wilts.* (1939).
[57] *Rot. Litt. Claus.* (Rec. Com.), 303.
[58] *Ex. e Rot. Fin.* (Rec. Com.), i. 133–4.
[59] *Bk. of Fees*, 718.
[60] *Close R.* 1242–47, 151.
[61] *Wilts. Inq. p.m.* 1242–1327 (Index Libr.), 288.
[62] Ibid. 449.
[63] *Feud. Aids*, vi. 529.
[64] Ibid. v. 265.
[65] *Cal. Close*, 1435–41, 327.   [66] C 139/98/28.
[67] C 1/114/69.
[68] *W.N. & Q.* v. 349; the testator had two sons called John.

[69] C 3/201/53.
[70] C 3/301/54; C 3/29/63.
[71] *Wilts. Inq. p.m.* 1242–1327 (Index Libr.), 449.
[72] C.P. 25(1)/254/43/23.
[73] W.R.O. 212A, Keevil Reeve's Acct. 1342–3
[74] *Cal. Pat.* 1343–45, 488.
[75] Ibid. 1354–58, 131.
[76] *Bk. of Fees*, 718, 731. In the first entry it is said to be held of Ralph of Wylliton, in the second of William de Lucy, both holding of John FitzAlan. The same estate is evidently referred to.
[77] *Feet of F. Wilts.* 1272–1327 (W.A.S. Rec. Brch.), 84.
[78] *Cal. Inq. p.m.* 1242–1327 (Index Libr.), 449.
[79] *Feud. Aids*, v. 265.
[80] *W.A.M.* xx. 279.
[81] Hoare, *Mod. Wilts.* Cawden, 19.
[82] *Cal. Pat.* 1558–60, 465.   [83] C 142/132/20.

died in his father's lifetime leaving five sisters to succeed to the property.[84] George Worth promised Robert Nicholas of Roundway, husband of his daughter Margaret, that she should have her share of it,[85] but in 1625 he settled the whole manor on the issue of his daughter Isabel when she married Francis Merewether of Market Lavington.[86] In spite of the opposition of at least one of the other sisters,[87] Merewether held Bulkington until 1649, when he sold the manor, except the capital house and demesnes, to Samuel Sheppard of Bisley (Glos.).[88] In 1657, and again in 1661, Sheppard sold parts of the manor in fee, reserving only quit-rents and suit of court.[89] By 1692 more land had been sold to Stephen Flower,[90] and a large part of the manor may have been disposed of in this way. The subsequent descent of what manorial rights remained has not been traced until, in the mid-18th century, they were claimed by the Mortimer family of Trowbridge, owners of Pinkney Farm in Keevil; they apparently consisted then only of quit-rents amounting to about £6.[91] In 1745, however, Edward Mortimer also held a farm of about 55 a. in Bulkington.[92] It passed to his daughter Mary, wife of Isaac Elton of Bristol. Their grandson sold his Bulkington property c. 1814, mostly to the Revd. Thomas Gaisford.[93]

The farm and demesnes of Bulkington, reserved out of the sale of the manor in 1649, were settled in 1660 on the vendor's son, Francis Merewether of Easterton.[94] In 1695 the farm, then called Worth's Farm, was again settled by Francis Merewether,[95] but no more is known of its history until 1773, when it was held by the Revd. William Long. From him it passed c. 1790 to Francis Long, and thence c. 1813 to the Revd. James Long who still held it in 1839.[96] It subsequently formed part of the Gaisford estate.

By 1771 the Beach family, lords of Keevil, owned no land in Bulkington, and it seems that much of it had passed to Thomas Gaisford,[97] a member of a family which had long been of note in the village. Thomas was succeeded by John Gaisford c. 1790.[98] John's son was Thomas Gaisford, Dean of Christ Church, Oxford, 1831–55, a noted Greek scholar.[99] He left a son Thomas Gaisford of Offington (Suss.), whose son J. C. Gaisford assumed the additional surname of St. Lawrence. He sold the estate in

1919, when it consisted chiefly of Home Farm, Lawn Farm, Bulkington Mill Farm, and Manor Farm. The 845 a. estate was bought in one lot by a syndicate of the tenants.[1]

The Baynton family of Bromham owned a manor in Bulkington, which, it was said in 1554, had belonged 50 years previously to Lord St. Amand.[2] It had therefore come to the Bayntons in the same way as their manor of Roches in Bromham.[3] In 1562 Andrew Baynton sold the manor to Roger Earth of Salisbury,[4] and from him it must have descended to his nephew William Earth, who, with his son Joseph, sold it to William Dodington in 1599.[5] It no doubt became merged in the property he already held in Bulkington (see below).

In 1587 property described as the manor of Bulkington was granted by the Crown to Sir Francis Walsingham and Francis Mylles.[6] No previous owner was mentioned; it is hard to see why the Crown held property in Bulkington, unless in fact it was another part of the Edington manor. In the same year Walsingham and Mylles sold the manor to William Dodington.[7] By 1613 his property in Bulkington, no doubt including that bought of William Earth (see above), had passed to Giles Tooker of Maddington, who then, with Edward Lambert and George Worth, owned manorial rights there.[8] Tooker died in 1623, holding the manor and was succeeded by Edward his son,[9] who in 1627 sold it to Thomas Lambert.[80] Lambert held it at his death in 1638,[11] and it no doubt became merged in his other manor of Bulkington (see above).

LESSER ESTATES. In 1558 John Jones of Keevil bought houses and lands there from Henry, Earl of Arundel.[12] Jones died in 1566[13] leaving an eldest son John, who in the following year sold land at Keevil Wick to Richard Lambert.[14] Thomas Jones, second son of the first John, also held land in Keevil, which he may have bought from his elder brother.[15] In 1585 he sold land to Roger Blagden, a Keevil clothier.[16] When he died in 1603 Blagden owned land at Wick Leaze and a cottage called 'Conscience alias Reades',[17] which had previously belonged to the Jones family.[18] His son Roger held this land at his death in 1630, and also more, probably of his own acquisition, which included a mansion house

[84] Wilts. Visitation Pedigrees, 1623 (Harl. Soc.), 218. The 5th sister, Mary, is named in W.R.O. 212A, Deed Worth and others to Danvers, 10 Oct. 1620.
[85] C 3/369/5.
[86] W.R.O. 212A, Deed Worth to Merewether, 17 Jan. 1624/5.
[87] C 3/369/5.
[88] W.R.O. 212A, Deed Merewether to Sheppard, 17 Jan. 1649.
[89] Ibid., Deeds Sheppard to Gaisford, 27 March 1657; Sheppard to Martyn, 10 Sept. 1661.
[90] Ibid. Flower Settlement, 22 Dec. 1692.
[91] Soc. Antiq. Jackson MSS. s.v. Bulkington.
[92] Bristol Univ. Hodge (Baker) MSS. D.M. 76/28–9.
[93] Burke, Land. Gent. (1937), s.v. Marwood-Elton; C.P. 25(2)/1234/29 Geo. II Mich.; C.P. 43/921 rot. 364; W.R.O. Land Tax Assessments.
[94] W.R.O. 212A, Deed Merewether to Sheppard and others, 24 March 1659/60.
[95] Ibid. Lease for year, Merewether to Sadleir and Long, 9 Oct. 1695.
[96] W.R.O. Land Tax Assessments and Tithe Award; W.A.S. Libr., Devizes, Maps of Bulkington, 1771.

[97] W.A.S. Libr., Devizes, Maps of Bulkington, 1771.
[98] W.R.O. Land Tax Assessments.
[99] D.N.B.
[1] W.A.S. Libr., Devizes, Wilts. Cuttings, xvi. 245, and Sale Cat.
[2] W.R.O. 48. Ct. Bk. of Baynton Estates, 1545–57.
[3] See V.C.H. Wilts. vii. 181.
[4] C 54/607 no. 24.
[5] C.P. 43/64 rot. 17; Wilts. Visitation Pedigrees, 1623 (Harl. Soc.), 53. Dodington was probably of Woodlands in Mere: Hoare, Mod. Wilts. Mere, 23.
[6] C 66/1289 m. 24.
[7] C.P. 43/19 rot. 19d.
[8] W.R.O. 288 Ct. Bk. 1602–26, April 1613.
[9] Wilts. Inq. p.m. 1625–49 (Index Libr.), 39.
[10] C.P. 25(2)/508/2 Chas. I Hil.
[11] Wilts. Inq. p.m. 1625–49 (Index Libr.), 331–5.
[12] W.N. &Q. iv. 311, 375; Req. 2/134/55.
[13] C 3/99/12.
[14] Req. 2/117/46; Req. 2/134/55.
[15] W.N. & Q. vii. 415.
[16] Req. 2/35/39.
[17] C 142/280/1.
[18] C 3/99/12; C 3/184/95.

called 'Stephen's Hold'.[19] This probably took its name from Lawrence Stephens, a prosperous clothier who died *c.* 1486.[20] The whole property remained in the Blagden family for several generations. Another Roger Blagden was living in 1668,[21] and an Edward Blagden in 1683. Another Edward died in 1730, and his son Edward died without issue in 1748. Anne and Eleanor Blagden, sisters of the last Edward, both died unmarried, in 1773 and 1785 respectively. The estate passed, probably by devise, to their cousin Ann Dare.[22] In 1793 it consisted of Blagden House, Church Farm, and Wick Leaze Farm.[23] At Ann Dare's death in 1807 the estate passed, probably again by devise, to John Chamberlaine, who died in 1812. His son the Revd. G. T. Chamberlaine held it until his death in 1858, and was succeeded by his daughter, who married W. H. Pooke, Vicar of Keevil, 1839–1902; he changed his name to Chamberlaine in 1872.[24] By 1863 Pinkney Farm and a farm at Keevil, Wick had been acquired.[25] The estates have been sold in the present century.[26]

Blagden House was probably built in the mid-17th century, but the back (west) wall is timber-framed, and it may be that the back part of the house contains some remains of 'Stephen's Hold' of the late 15th century. Otherwise the three-storied house is of brick, covered with stucco, standing on a stone plinth, and with a stone-tiled roof. The main front has three gables, and the sides two each; they have moulded copings and ball finials, and in them are two-light stone-mullioned attic windows. The lower parts of the house were remodelled in the early 18th century. An elaborately-decorated lead gutter joining rainwater heads between each gable is dated 1710. Sash windows in bolection-moulded stone surrounds were inserted, and there are many internal features, including a fine staircase, of this date. The pointed central doorway is probably of the later 18th century in the Gothic taste, and there is a two-storied extension of the same period to the north. A three-gabled stable block, of brick with stone quoins, having mullioned and transomed windows on the ground floor and oval windows above, probably dates from 1710. So too do the tall stone gate-piers crowned with carved vases and the garden wall of rubble with stone coping.

William Jones, third son of the John Jones who bought property of the Earl of Arundel, owned at his death in 1620 a house called Brent Place *alias* Barkesdale's, and certain lands belonging to it. This property was settled on his younger son Henry and his wife Abigail for life,[27] and Abigail claimed that she held it for life in 1644, although apparently as a leaseholder under Elizabeth Lambert, lady of the manor.[28] Whether it was freehold or leasehold, and its subsequent descent, have not been determined. It has been suggested more than once, however, that Jones lived in the house in Keevil now called Talboys.[29] Although unbacked by evidence, the suggestion is plausible. The house in which Jones lived took its name Brent Place *alias* Barkesdale's from William Brent (d. *c.* 1494) or from Thomas Barkesdale (fl. *c.* 1500–25), the most prosperous of all Keevil clothiers.[30] Either of these men may have been the builder of Talboys. Nothing is certainly known about the house, however, until the late 17th century, when it was held by Edward Berry, a maltster. A member of his family still held it in 1749,[31] but by 1765 it belonged to Thomas Talboys of Doughton in Tetbury (Glos.).[32] He died in that year leaving his property, including the house at Keevil, to his kinsman Thomas Talboys.[33] The younger Thomas still owned the house with about 35 a. of land in 1795,[34] but early in the 19th century it passed, no doubt by sale, to James Watts, and thence to the Chamberlaine family.[35] It was held of them by tenant farmers until the 1870's, when it was taken over and restored by Mrs. A. J. Kenrick, daughter of the Revd. G. T. Chamberlaine.[36]

Talboys is a timber-framed house dating from the late 15th or early 16th century, which originally consisted of a hall wing with a cross wing at the west end. In the restoration the inserted floor in the hall was removed to expose the roof, which has three tiers of curved wind-braces. The cross wing is jettied out at first-floor level, and has carved barge-boards. Its roof has arch-braced collar-beam trusses and one tier of wind-braces, and the lower room has a ceiling with moulded beams and bosses. In 1876 a similar cross wing was built at the east end of the hall block, which was lengthened, and a two storied porch was added at the centre to make a symmetrical façade. All the window tracery at the front was renewed then.[37]

Only one piece of monastic property apart from the manor of Bulkington has been traced in Keevil parish. In 1331 Ivychurch priory held some land in Bulkington of Ralph of Wilynton, under-tenant of the Earl of Arundel, paying the yearly rent of a rose. The priory had granted the land to John Wyght at a rent of a pound of cummin. Two of Wyght's tenants granted the land they held of him to the chapel at Bulkington.[38] This land so granted evidently became absorbed in the Rector of Edington's manor of Bulkington, for he was paying a yearly rent of 9*s.* 4*d.* for it to the Priory of Ivychurch in 1535.[39] Another rent, of 10*s.* 8*d.*, had

[19] *Wilts. Inq. p.m.* 1625–49 (Index Libr.), 92–3.
[20] P.C.C. 25 Logge.
[21] *Genealogist*, N.S. xxvii. 117.
[22] M.I.'s in Keevil and Semington churches.
[23] W.R.O. 84, Keevil Poor Rate, 1793.
[24] Ibid. Land Tax Assessments; M.I.'s Keevil church; Foster, *Alumn. Oxon.* 2nd ser. i. 234.
[25] W.R.O. Tithe Award.
[26] W.A.S. Libr., Devizes, Sale Cat. 1919.
[27] *Wilts. Inq. p.m.* 1625–49 (Index Libr.), 33.
[28] W.R.O. 288/2.
[29] *W.A.M.* xxxix. 100–2. The suggestions about the descent of Talboys through the Blagdens and the origin of the name are wrong.
[30] See p. 258.

[31] B.M. Add. MS. 42048, ff. 194, 249, 270.
[32] *Visitation of England and Wales*, ed. Crisp, xiv. 99–102; ibid. *Notes*, xi. 100–2. Talboys probably obtained the property by marriage. He was married at Trowbridge 15 Sept. 1735 to Sarah Woodcock: Trowbridge Par. Regs.
[33] C.P. 43/748 rot. 22.
[34] W.R.O. Inclosure Award.
[35] Ibid. Tithe Award and Land Tax Assessments.
[36] *W.A.M.* xxxii. 232.
[37] Pevsner, *Wilts.* 248–9. For similar houses at Steeple Ashton, see p. 200.
[38] *Wilts. Inq. p.m.* 1327–77 (Index Libr.), 79; see below p. 260.
[39] *Valor Eccl.* (Rec. Com.), ii. 96, 142.

once been received by the priory from Thomas Barkesdale, but had not been paid for many years.[40]

At least two chantries were endowed with land in Keevil. Among the property of Horton's chantry at Bradford[41] was a house and about 23 a. of land in Keevil, which in 1548 was held by Walter Lucas on a 40-year lease.[42] In the following year it was, like the rest of the chantry's property, granted by the Crown to the founder's nephew, Thomas Horton of Iford.[43] It evidently descended in his family to William Horton of Wolverton (Som.), who held it in 1605, but its subsequent descent has not been traced.[44] Grenville's chantry at North Bradley was endowed with a house and about 28 a. of land in Keevil.[45] It probably remained with the Long family in the same way as the other lands of the chantry.[46] In 1554 it was said that a rent out of a holding in Baynton's manor of Bulkington had formerly been paid to a chantry priest at Lavington,[47] but no further reference to this has been found.

Pinkney Farm belonged to Edward Mortimer of Trowbridge in 1745,[48] and remained the property of his family until 1812, when Edward Horlock Mortimer sold it to John Watts.[49] By 1850 it had passed to the Chamberlaines of Blagden House.[50] The farmhouse is described above.[51] The northernmost of the two farms at Keevil Wick also belonged to the Mortimers; Edward Mortimer the elder left it to his daughter Anne in 1743,[52] and she held it until the end of the century. It then passed to her relatives, the Eltons, and was later sold to the Chamberlaines.[53] The southern farm at Wick belonged to Daniel Capel in 1795, and to William Capel in 1850.[54] By 1863 it had passed to George Bartlett.[55] Oxen Leaze Farm was also the property of the Capel family between 1795 and 1863.[56]

ECONOMIC HISTORY. In 1086 Keevil was assessed at 16 hides and there was land for 16 ploughs; 7 hides and 6 ploughs, with 10 serfs, were in demesne, while 18 villeins and 14 bordars had 12 ploughs. A considerable amount of pasture and woodland belonged to the manor, which was worth £26 in all.[57] When Keevil was extended in 1284, the lord had in demesne a capital messuage; 80 a. of arable land, not measured by the 'reasonable' perch, but by the works of the tenants; certain parcels of meadow; several pasture; and the pasture, pannage, and underwood of a wood. Twenty bond tenants did small works in winter and Lent, and heavy ones in the hay and corn harvest, and there were 19 acremen and 11 Monday-men; the latter worked every Monday in the year except three. Rent received from free and bond tenants amounted to over £18.[58] The manor was leased to Robert Burnell, Bishop of Bath and Wells, for 12 years in 1292.[59] In 1302, when it was again extended, the demesne was reckoned at 400 a. arable, 40 a. meadow, a several pasture, and the pasture of West Wood. Free tenants, including holders of foreign fees at a distance, paid 23s. The bond tenants then comprised 3 whole-virgaters, 25 ½-virgaters, 13 ⅓-virgaters and 7 cottars; all except the cottars still did works.[60]

A third extent, made in 1327, shows a considerable change. The demesne had been reduced to 217 a. of arable and 41 a. of meadow; the lord had common for 60 cattle in Oxen Leaze and Cowenleaze, where the bond tenants also had pasture, and he had the pasture of a wood, also with the tenants. The number of bond tenants had increased considerably for there were then 3 whole-virgaters, 32 ½-virgaters, 20 ⅓-virgaters, 2 ¼-virgaters, and 26 cottars. The increase in their holdings had probably been achieved not only by reduction of the demesne, but also by extension of the cultivated area, for a rent was paid to the sheriff for assarted land. The works of the tenants were entirely commuted.[61] Four years later the demesne had been still further reduced to 116 a. arable and 13 a. meadow, and the large sum of £52 3s. was received for arable and meadow let at farm.[62] An account roll of 1343[63] shows that some of the demesne was still farmed, but apparently on an insignificant scale. Over £75 was received for land let at farm, beside over £45 for the manor of Bulkington held by John of Keevil,[64] giving a net return from the manor for that one year of about £150 in all. By 1394 demesne farming had entirely ended, and the demesnes were leased to Nicholas Frogg and William Webb.[65]

In the early 17th century a three-field course of husbandry was followed in Keevil, each field being successively sown with wheat and then beans, and then fallowed.[66] The fields were Cooplechurch Field between Keevil and Steeple Ashton, North Field north of the village, and Wick Field between the village and the stream west of Wick Farms. In 1613 the field for wheat was rid of stock on 9 October, and the last wheatfield broken the same day; the last beanfield was broken on 30 October, and the next field for beans rid on 25 March. In 1617 tenants were allowed to graze in the fields one cow or four sheep for every acre of arable they held, and double this allowance for meadow. These stints were varied in succeeding years by court orders. It was evidently the custom to sell pasture rights in the fields. In 1619 it was agreed that any men who could neither sell nor use their pasture should be compensated by a rate raised from the other com-

[40] *Valor Eccl.* (Rec. Com.), ii. 96.
[41] See *V.C.H. Wilts.* vii. 26.
[42] *W.N. & Q.* iv. 167.
[43] *Cal. Pat.* 1548–49, 249.
[44] C 3/285/29.
[45] E 301/58 no. 23; E 134/7 Jas. I/Mich. 14; S.C. 2/200/14.
[46] See p. 229.
[47] W.R.O. 48, Baynton Court Book, 1545–57.
[48] Bristol Univ., Hodge (Baker) MSS. D.M. 76/28–9.
[49] W.R.O. 130, Covt. to produce deeds, 1812.
[50] W.A.S. Libr., Devizes, Terrier of Keevil, 1850.
[51] See p. 251.
[52] Devon R.O. 281 M/T 832.
[53] W.R.O. Land Tax Assessments; W.A.S. Libr., Devizes, Terrier of Keevil, 1850.

[54] W.R.O. Inclosure Award; W.A.S. Libr., Devizes, Terrier of Keevil, 1850.
[55] W.R.O. Tithe Award.
[56] Ibid. Inclosure and Tithe Award.
[57] *V.C.H. Wilts.* ii, p. 139.
[58] *Wilts. Inq. p.m.* 1242–1327 (Index Libr.), 158.
[59] Ibid. 198; *Cal. Close,* 1288–96, 248.
[60] *Wilts. Inq. p.m.* 1242–1327 (Index Libr.), 288.
[61] Ibid. 448–51.
[62] Ibid. 1327–77, 57.
[63] W.R.O. 212A, Reeve's Acct. 1342–3.
[64] See p. 253.
[65] S.C. 2/209/9.
[66] The following account is based on W.R.O. 288, Court Bks. of Keevil and Bulkington, except where otherwise noted.

moners. In 1624 sheep were allowed in the wheat-field as long as they had a shepherd to keep them from the green corn. Much of the meadow of the tenants lay along the stream between Keevil and Keevil Wick, at Hitchingfield and Broadmead north of Pinkney Farm, and at Towmead near Wick Bridge. In 1608 it was agreed that the doles of meadow in Flipmead, Horslade, and Towmead should be measured, and every man's doles cast into one piece at one or other of them.

There seems to have been no open common in Keevil by 1600, but considerable commons, in which the tenants had stinted common rights at certain times of the year, lay to the north, west, and south-east of the village beyond the common fields. North Wood no doubt lay near Woodhouse Farm; in it 15 copyholders of Keevil and 2 free-holders had pasture for 3 beasts from April until December. In 1603 they agreed with the lord that it should be inclosed, every man having an acre for each beast leaze and the lord the remainder. Little Wood, in which 3 freeholders and 13 copy-holders had leazes in the autumn, was also inclosed then. By 1644 a number of closes in North Wood which had evidently fallen to the lord's share were held by tenants on lease, while considerable ex-changes between tenants of land in the Wood took place in the years following inclosure. West Wood lay on the Hinton boundary. Pasture rights were limited to such as were ancient commoners there, and were said in 1617 to be unlimited for all manner of cattle except sheep, which were only to winter there, and were to be limited to the number which could be pastured on each tenant's holding in the field then used for sheep. In the previous year, however, it had been ordered that West Wood should be measured, and the numbers of cattle that it would keep estimated. In 1621 overseers of the common to decide on the stints were appointed. In 1653 it was agreed that the West Wood should be hained from Lady Day to May Day yearly, and then fed with cattle until December, when sheep could go in. It is not known when the West Wood was inclosed. Oxen Leaze must have lain around the modern farm of that name; some tenants had stinted common for cattle and sheep in it. Forty seven acres of it, perhaps the lord of the manor's share, were bought and inclosed by Joseph Houlton of Trowbridge in the late 17th century; probably the whole was inclosed at this time.[67]

Some inclosure of open-field land had taken place in Keevil by the early 17th century. Most of the land which had belonged to Horton's chantry was inclosed by 1549,[68] and in 1603 Roger Blagden held 80 a. of inclosed land at Wick Meads and Wick Leaze.[69] A survey of the Lambert property in 1644[70] lists 54 copyholds, mainly ½ virgates and less, which were still largely open-field arable. About 50 leaseholds consisted chiefly of inclosed land; many of these holdings were small inclosures

from North Wood, but one or two leaseholders held somewhat larger inclosed farms, and John Harris had paid a fine of £650 for 40 a. of inclosed pasture at South Wick and Hurst Grounds. By the end of the century there is little doubt that all the land near the streams by Keevil Wick and Wick Leaze Farms was used exclusively for dairying and stock-raising. James Stokes held Wick Leaze from c. 1677 and stocked it with milch cows, fatting beasts and sheep, the farm being worth £112 a year.[71] Thomas Ellis kept 15 milch cows and 40 sheep on Oxenleaze Farm in 1706, and John Hayward kept 10 milch cows and 20 sheep.[72]

By the end of the 18th century the modern pattern of farming in Keevil had largely emerged. The common fields and meadows, of which only rem-nants remained, were inclosed by Act of Parliament in 1795.[73] Only 44 a. of the Beach property out of over 800 a. was still held by copyholders.[74] A large part of the rest had been consolidated from many small holdings into three farms. Westwood Farm consisted of 10, and Longleaze Farm of 13, former holdings, and Manor Farm had one smaller holding annexed to it. A fourth, Baldham, was probably a separate farm of long standing.[75] Other modern farms which had appeared as considerable holdings included Pinkney, Wick Leaze, Oxen Leaze, Church, Woodhouse, and Hurst Farms, and two farms at Keevil Wick.[76] In 1801 there were just over 400 a. of arable land in the ancient parish, mainly sown with wheat and beans.[77] By 1863, one new farm, Mere Farm, had been built. The largest farms in the parish, the four principal farms of the Beach estate, were all between 150 and 250 a., but most of the others were between 40 a. and 100 a.[78] By 1914 the parish was almost entirely given over to dairy farming.[79]

Nothing is known about agriculture in Bulking-ton before the 16th century. In 1555 three fields, called North, South, and East Fields were men-tioned.[80] A survey made in 1564 of the manor granted to George Worth shows that little of the land had been inclosed, except about a quarter of the demesnes, which were then held by John Somner on a 31-year lease. Tenants had stinted pasture in a common called Bulkington Leaze.[81] Although the land had been long inclosed, the names of the fields survived until the 19th century. North Field lay between Pantry Bridge and the road to Seend; East (or Little) Field between the village and Mill Farm; and South (or Great) Field between the stream past Mill Farm and the Erle-stoke boundary. Bulkington Leaze lay north-east of the village, between the North and East Fields.[82] A fourth field, called Hitching Field, is sometimes mentioned in the 17th century, although not all holdings included land in it. It lay apparently in the north-west corner of the tithing.[83] By 1644 at least part of Bulkington Leaze had been inclosed, and an inclosure of 30 a. had recently been made in

[67] E 134/4 Anne/Trin. 2.
[68] Cal. Pat. 1548–49, 249.
[69] C 142/280/1.
[70] W.R.O. 288/2, Court of Survey, 1644.
[71] E 134/6 Wm. & M./Trin. 3.
[72] E 134/4 Anne/Trin. 2.
[73] 34 Geo. III, c. 32 (priv. act).
[74] W.R.O. Inclosure Award.

[75] See p. 258.
[76] W.R.O. 84, Keevil Rate Books, 1793, 1796.
[77] H.O. 67/23.
[78] W.R.O. Tithe Award.
[79] B.M. Add. MS. 42048, f. 274.
[80] W.R.O. 48, Baynton Court Book, 1545–57.
[81] S.P. 15/12, f. 44.
[82] W.R.O. Tithe Award.   [83] W.R.O. 288, passim.

South Field.[84] Much inclosure had evidently taken place of the former Worth property in Bulkington. By 1660 the manor farm consisted of about 150 a. all inclosed,[85] and other parts of the manor included closes at Bulkington Leaze and Hitching Field.[86] The three fields still contained open arable land in 1738,[87] and the East and South Fields were still partly open in 1771.[88] No Inclosure Act was ever obtained and the inclosure of the tithing was probably complete before the end of the century. By 1839 the tithing was chiefly divided into 7 farms, of which 3 were over 100 a.[89]

As in other villages in the district, the earliest appearance of the cloth industry in Keevil was connected with the mills. Baldham Mill was used for fulling cloth by 1371,[90] when its racks were in decay, and Bulkington or Gayford Mill had been so used for some years before 1486.[91] Cloth was being made in Bulkington by three weavers in 1377,[92] and William Coterell was a weaver at Keevil in 1442.[93] Toward the end of the 15th century there were important clothiers in Keevil. Lawrence Stephens, who occupied Bulkington Mill, died a prosperous man in 1486, leaving the mill to his son,[94] who, dying soon after, was succeeded by Thomas Barkesdale in 1502.[95] Barkesdale was probably the most important of all Keevil clothiers. Transactions of his which are on record include the sale of cloth worth 400 marks to one buyer,[96] another sale of 20 broad cloths to a London merchant,[97] and a debt of £100 owed him by a London mercer.[98] He was more heavily assessed than any other man in the hundred in the subsidy of 1524.[99] His son, Robert Barkesdale, was also a clothier,[1] but Thomas was succeeded at Bulkington by William Baily, a member of the Trowbridge clothing family. Another branch of the Bailys had held Baldham Mill since at least 1502.[2] Other 16th century clothiers of Keevil included Roger Winslow (fl. c. 1546);[3] William Jones, who was fined for defective cloth in 1563;[4] Thomas Spire (fl. c. 1575);[5] and John Smith (fl. c. 1594),[6] who held Baldham Mill after the Bailys.[7] The most important clothier of the later 16th century at Keevil was Roger Blagden. He was heavily assessed

in the subsidy of 1576,[8] and before his death in 1603 had built up a considerable property.[9] A William Blagden, perhaps his grandson, was a clothier at Keevil in 1632.[10] By this time, however, few clothiers were left in the village.[11] What clothing trade remained after the mid-17th century was no doubt confined to the mills at Baldham and Bulkington. Nicholas Lyne was a fuller in 1652,[12] and Samuel Haynes, who held Bulkington Mill,[13] was described as a dyer in 1706.[14] Bulkington was still described as a tucking mill and gig mill in 1730, when it was held by a Devizes clothier.[15] The date when either mill ceased to work for the cloth trade has not been determined, but Bulkington probably survived until the 19th century, for in 1831 it was said that a cloth 'factory' there had recently closed.[16]

MILLS. There were two mills at Keevil in 1086.[17] These were probably the two mills which Ernulf of Hesdin, the first holder of that name, gave to the nuns of Romsey Abbey.[18] Nevertheless, two water mills, then ruinous, belonged to the manor of Keevil in 1327.[19] Over 30s. was spent on the repair of the mills of 'Wadeford' and Bulkington in 1343, and toll corn was received from the millers, although the rent of £6 13s. 4d. was in arrears.[20] One mill was in decay, owing to the neglect of John Gigull, in 1394,[21] but no further reference to any mills annexed to the manor of Keevil has been found.

The two mills granted to Romsey in the 11th century were those at Baldham and Gayford, near the site of the present Bulkington Mill Farm,[22] the only two mills in Keevil parish which survived into modern times. Baldham, the early connexion of which with the cloth trade has been outlined above,[23] was held by copyholders under the Abbess of Romsey in 1371,[24] in 1410, when the tenant forfeited it for waste,[25] and in the mid-15th century.[26] By 1502 it was held by William Baily.[27] He died in 1536[28] and his widow Marion took a 60-year lease of the mill, with lands belonging to it, in the following year.[29] After the death of their son Thomas, c. 1566, a dispute about the leasehold in-

---

[84] W.R.O. Court of Survey, 1644.
[85] Ibid. 212A, Deed Merewether to Sheppard and others, 24 March 1659/60.
[86] Ibid. Flower Settlement 1692; ibid. 130, Deeds Sheppard to Gaisford, 27 March 1657, Sheppard to Martin, 10 September 1661.
[87] Ibid., Deed Gaisford to Long and Thresher, 10 March 1737/8.
[88] W.A.S. Libr., Devizes, Maps of Bulkington, 1771.
[89] W.R.O. Bulkington Tithe Award.
[90] V.C.H. Wilts. iv. 121.
[91] P.C.C. 25 Logge.
[92] V.C.H. Wilts. iv. 122.
[93] Cal. Pat. 1441–46, 68.
[94] P.C.C. 25 Logge.
[95] S.C. 2/208/6 m. 13d.
[96] C 1/295/58.
[97] C 1/284/6.
[98] C 1/697/21.
[99] E 179/197/153.
[1] W.N. & Q. iv. 169.
[2] V.C.H. Wilts. iv. 143.
[3] L. & P. Hen. VIII, xxi (ii), p. 244.
[4] E 350/329.
[5] B. H. Cunnington, Devizes Borough Annals, ii. 127.
[6] W.N. & Q. v. 393.
[7] C 3/275/35.
[8] Taxation Lists (W.A.S. Rec. Brch.), 140.

[9] See p. 254.
[10] Genealogist N.S., xxviii, 243.
[11] William Harris (fl. c. 1631), ibid. 155, and Hugh Bullen (an old man in 1652), E 134/1651–2/Hil. 12, have been noted.
[12] E 134/1651–2/Hil. 12.
[13] W.R.O. 284, Deed Sutton to Goddard, 5 Feb. 1800.
[14] W.N. & Q. vi. 7.
[15] W.R.O. 284, Deed Sutton to Goddard, 5 Feb. 1800.
[16] V.C.H. Wilts. iv. 318.
[17] Ibid. ii, p. 139.
[18] Bracton's Note Bk. ed. Maitland, ii. 141.
[19] Wilts. Inq. p.m. 1242–1327, 448; these were evidently distinct from those given to Romsey, for there were 4 mills in the parish in 1341: Inq. Non. (Rec. Com.), 174.
[20] W.R.O. 212A, Reeve's Account, 1342–3.
[21] S.C. 2/209/9 m. 1.
[22] The name Gayford, and variants, was frequently used until the 16th century, but is now obsolete. It was probably more properly Gaysford, and must be the place from which the Gaisford family, of long standing in Bulkington, took its name.
[23] See above.
[24] S.C. 2/208/2 m. 2d.
[25] S.C. 2/208/3 m. 1d.
[26] S.C. 12/16/65.
[27] V.C.H. Wilts. iv. 143.
[28] P.C.C. 36 Hogen.
[29] S.C. 12/4/2.

terest arose between the widow of his son William and another son Nicholas.[30] Meanwhile the freehold of the mill, which had descended in the same way as the manor of Steeple Ashton,[31] was in 1553 granted by the Crown to Sir William Sharington.[32] The mill descended in the same way as the manor of Seend[33] to Sir Francis Fane, and Mary his wife, who in 1611 assured it to John and Mary Hardkyn and John Crook for their lives.[34] Hardkyn, who was a nephew of Sir Henry Sharington, had held the mill by lease since 1757.[35] The descent of the property in the 17th and 18th centuries has not been traced until 1795, when it was owned by Michael Hicks Beach;[36] its subsequent descent was the same as that of Keevil Manor.

The stone mill building dates from the 18th century. It is still in use as a flour mill by Messrs. J. & J. Noad and water power is in use.

In 1410 the Abbess of Romsey granted an estate for three lives in the house, mill and 13 a. of land 'in the close of Gayford' to Robert Coufold, who agreed to rebuild the house and mill.[37] In the late 15th and 16th centuries the mill was held by successive families of clothiers.[38] The freehold was granted to Sir William Sharington with Baldham Mill (see above), but he does not seem to have held it at his death in 1553.[39] In 1604 it was owned by George Collins[40] and in the early 18th century by Robert Purchas. By 1730 it belonged to James Sutton, a Devizes clothier, who then settled it on his son Prince. Prince's only surviving son, James, held the property in 1800, when it included two houses and a few acres of land.[41] By 1839 it belonged to the Revd. Charles Gaisford; the mill was held separately from the farm, which included 76 a. of land.[42]

The large three-storied mill is of brick, with flatheaded windows in stone surrounds and with a central stone mullion, and probably dates from the later 18th century. The massive construction of its floors was perhaps to bear the weight of clothworking machinery. It was powered by an undershot wheel. After it ceased to be used for the cloth trade it was used as a grist mill until early in the present century; since then it has been used as a farm building.[43]

CHURCHES. There was a church at Keevil by the late 11th century, for it was then granted to Shaftesbury Abbey. The institutional relationship of the chapel which existed at Bulkington in the Middle Ages to the church of Keevil is not known.[44] A new chapel was built at Bulkington in 1860; the Vicar of Keevil was patron, and the incumbent was designated a perpetual curate in 1883, but the tithing was never constituted a separate ecclesiastical parish.[45] Since 1905 the curacy has been continuously held with the vicarage of Keevil.[46]

Ernulf of Hesdin, the Domesday tenant of Keevil, gave the church, with its tithes and land, to the nuns of Shaftesbury when his daughter took the veil there, and his gift was confirmed by his son.[47] The abbess had apparently appropriated the rectory by 1222; there was then a perpetual vicar, Thomas, who paid a yearly stipend to the parson.[48] The benefice has remained a vicarage until the present time. The abbess's right to the advowson was questioned in 1222 by John FitzAlan, then lord of Keevil, who claimed that Henry II had presented the perpetual vicar 60 years before, when the FitzAlan barony was in the king's hands. The abbess produced William of Stokes, apparently the actual incumbent, and it was found that the benefice was not vacant.[49] The earliest recorded institutions, between 1301 and 1339, were at the presentation of abbesses, but in 1344 Richard, Earl of Arundel, presented.[50] Being challenged by the abbess, he claimed that after the previous dispute an agreement was reached between the parties that the lords of Keevil should present at every third vacancy, and that this was done for some time, but the abbess had presented at the last five vacancies by taking advantage of Richard's minority.[51] In particular, the earl claimed that his ancestor had presented one, Robert of Leicester; the abbess obtained a certificate from the bishop that a previous abbess had presented him,[52] and apparently won her case, for abbesses presented at the next four vacancies.[53] In 1393, however, the impropriate rectory and the advowson were, at the instance of John Bleobury, conveyed to the house of Bonhommes at Edington.[54] The rectors of Edington presented until the Dissolution.[55] In 1550 John Bush and William Hutton presented, apparently by virtue of a lease granted by the last rector,[56] for in 1541 the rectory and advowson had been granted to the Dean and Chapter of Winchester.[57] They have presented to the living ever since, but the endowment of the rectory passed to the Ecclesiastical Commissioners in the 19th century.[58]

The church of Keevil was worth £26 13s. 4d. c. 1291.[59] The clear value of the rectory in 1535 was

[30] C3/201/53-4.
[31] See p. 202.
[32] Cal. Pat. 1553, 164.
[33] See V.C.H. Wilts. vii. 100.
[34] C.P. 25(2)/370/9 Jas. I Trin.
[35] C3/275/35.
[36] W.R.O. Tithe Award.
[37] S.C. 2/208/3 m. 1d.
[38] See above.
[39] C 142/101/121.
[40] Soc. Antiq. Jackson MSS. s.v. Steeple Ashton.
[41] W.R.O. 248, Deed Sutton to Goddard, 15 Feb. 1800.
[42] W.R.O. Bulkington Tithe Award.
[43] P.O. and Kelly's Dirs. Wilts. to 1903; W.A.S. Libr., Devizes, Sale Cats.
[44] See p. 250.
[45] Endowed Char. Wilts. (1908), p. 253.
[46] Clergy List, 1905, and Crockford (various years).
[47] B.M. Lansd. MS. 442, f. 81; Rot. Chart. i. 150; a

confirmation by Henry I (Regesta Regum Anglo-Normannorum, ii, p. 347) refers to Gundreda as the donor, but in view of the clear statement made in 1222, this must be a scribal error in the copy, as Gundreda occurs in the following line.
[48] Bracton's Note Bk. ed. Maitland, ii 140-2.   [49] Ibid.
[50] Phillipps, Wilts. Inst. i. 3, 29, 35, 39.
[51] C.P. 40/346 rot. 63d.
[52] Cal. Pat. 1345-8, 224.
[53] Phillipps, Wilts. Inst. i. 50, 53.
[54] Cal. Pat. 1391-96, 336; B.M. Lansd. MS 442, ff. 81-4. Although Bleobury was William of Edington's executor, this was probably his own gift, for he was remembered at Edington as a benefactor.
[55] Phillipps, Wilts. Inst. i. passim.
[56] Ibid. 214.
[57] L. & P. Hen. VIII, xvi, p. 417.
[58] Probably under 3 and 4 Vic., c. 113.
[59] Tax. Eccl. (Rec. Com.), 180.

£18 11s. 4d.,[60] and in 1649 £260.[61] Although the great tithes in both Keevil and Bulkington belonged to the rectory, they were usually treated separately. The great tithes of Keevil had been held by William Baily before the Dissolution, but in 1538 they were leased to John Bodenham for 31 years at a rent of £14.[62] They were subsequently leased and assigned repeatedly, for in 1652 they had been held by at least eight tenants within living memory, some of whom had under-tenants.[63] In 1649 they were held on a 21-year lease at a rent of £17 a year,[64] and there is little doubt that leasing continued regularly throughout the 17th and 18th centuries. In 1795, when Sir William Heathcote was lessee,[65] the tithes of Keevil were commuted to a corn-rent, the rector being allotted £222 12s. a year.[66] This corn-rent was converted to a rent charge of £267 12s. in 1863, when the last lease, to Thomas Heathcote Tragett, had run out.[67] The rent charge on nearly 1,000 a. was assigned to the vicar in 1870 (see below).

The great tithes of Bulkington were leased to John Somner for 26 years in 1538 at an annual rent of £10.[68] They were evidently regularly leased in the 17th and 18th centuries. In 1649, when they were held on a lease for three lives granted in 1616, they were worth £80 a year.[69] Later holders included Joseph Houlton of Trowbridge, who held at his death in 1720,[70] and John Watts of Trowbridge, who mortgaged the tithes for £1,200 in 1774, when they were held on a 21-year lease at £10 rent.[71] In 1839, when the lessee was the Revd. Thomas Gaisford, the rectorial tithes of Bulkington were commuted for £145.[72]

In 1341 the rectorial glebe consisted of a virgate of land and 3 a. of meadow.[73] After the Dissolution it seems to have been invariably leased with the great tithes of Keevil. In 1649 it consisted of a thatched house of 4 rooms, a barn, and 36½ a. of land, worth in all £26 7s. 6d. a year,[74] and it was still reckoned at about the same area in 1795[75] and 1863.[76] The house was pulled down c. 1842; it stood on what was later the kitchen garden of the new vicarage built then.[77] There was no glebe in Bulkington tithing.

In 1222 a perpetual vicar paid 20s. 8d. a year to the actual incumbent.[78] In 1535 the vicarage was worth £12 6s. 11d. net.,[79] and in 1649 £40 a year.[80] In 1783 the vicar received a stipend of £25 a year from the dean and chapter beside his tithes.[81] In

1831 his average net income was £250.[82] The vicarage was endowed with £20 a year from the common fund in 1869; in the following year this was replaced by £133 14s. 6d. from the great tithes of the parish.[83] The vicar owned all the small tithes of Keevil and Bulkington,[84] which were usually taken by composition in the late 17th century. Richard Shrapnell rented the vicarial tithes c. 1700.[85] The vicar's tithes in Keevil were commuted to a corn rent of £135 6s. 7d. in 1795,[86] which was converted to a rent charge of £162 13s. 10d. in 1863.[87] His tithes in Bulkington were commuted for £101 in 1839.[88] In 1783 the vicar's glebe consisted only of a timber-framed house and a garden.[89] The house was considered unfit for residence in 1831,[90] and was pulled down in 1842, when a new vicarage was built nearby.[91] It stood on part of the rectorial glebe and was transferred to the vicar by the Ecclesiastical Commissioners in 1868.[92] After the Second World War it was sold, and a smaller vicarage built near the village street.

No chantries were founded in Keevil church. In 1483 there were lights of St. Leonard and Holy Cross there.[93] In 1332 Henry Thomas and John Gille were licensed to grant land in Bulkington to a chaplain to celebrate for their souls in the chapel there.[94] The endowment seems to have been absorbed into the property of the Bonhommes of Edington,[95] and nothing further is known of the chantry.

John Maundrell, one of the Marian martyrs, was a farmer at Bulkington. In the time of Henry VIII he was accused of speaking against certain ceremonies and did penance at Devizes. In Mary's reign he left the district for some time, but on his return went, with John Spicer and William Corberly,[96] to Keevil church and interrupted the vicar in his service. All three were subsequently taken to Salisbury, and burnt at Bemerton in 1556.[97] Further disturbances in church took place in the early 17th century. An injured party, Robert Blagden, declared that two of his opponents commonly disturbed the minister during service; one of them, William Jones, tore up briefs, and called the minister fool, ass, and knave. They in turn accused Blagden of publicly doubting whether the writings of the prophets and apostles were true.[98] Thomas Rutty, Vicar of Keevil, 1646- c. 1654, was afterwards ejected from Milston, and became a noted Presbyterian preacher in the Trowbridge and Melksham

60 *Valor Eccl.* (Rec. Com.), ii. 140.
61 *W.A.M.* xli. 38, 122.
62 S.C. 6/Hen. VIII/3985 m. 48.
63 E 134/1651-2/Hil. 12.
64 *W.A.M.* xli. 122.
65 W.R.O. 84, Keevil Rate Book, 1793.
66 W.R.O. Inclosure Award.
67 W.R.O. Tithe Award.
68 S.C. 6/Hen. VIII/3985 m. 48.
69 *W.A.M.* xli. 38.
70 *W.N. & Q.* vi. 212.
71 W.R.O. 130, Mortgage Watts to Cooper, 25 March 1774.
72 W.R.O. Bulkington Tithe Award.
73 *Inq. Non.* (Rec. Com.), 174.
74 *W.A.M.* xli. 123.
75 W.R.O. Inclosure Award.
76 W.R.O. Tithe Award.
77 B.M. Add. MS. 42048, f. 199.
78 *Bracton's Note Bk.* ii. 140-2.
79 *Valor Eccl.* (Rec. Com.), ii. 146.

80 *W.A.M.* xli. 124.
81 Sar. Dioc. R.O. Glebe Terrier.
82 *Rep. Com. Eccl. Rev.*, H.C. 54, p. 836 (1835), xxii.
83 *Lond. Gaz.* 1869, p. 4371; 1870, p. 3957.
84 Sar. Dioc. R.O. Glebe Terrier, 1783.
85 E 134/4 Anne/Trin. 2.
86 W.R.O. Inclosure Award.
87 W.R.O. Tithe Award.
88 W.R.O. Bulkington Tithe Award.
89 Sar. Dioc. R.O. Glebe Terrier.
90 *Rep. Com. Eccl. Rev.* (1835), 836.
91 B.M. Add. MS. 42048, f. 199.
92 *Lond. Gaz.* 1868, p. 2502.
93 P.C.C. 11 Logge.
94 *Cal. Pat.* 1330-34, 254.
95 See p. 255.
96 It is not clear whether they were local men or not.
97 J. Foxe, *Acts and Monuments*, ed. Cattley, 1839, viii, 102-5. For the site of the execution see *V.C.H. Wilts.* vi. 183.
98 Sta. Cha. 8/59/11.

districts.[99] James Garth, vicar 1670–1702, and Lancelot Docker, Lascelles Iremonger, W. D. Harrison, and Henry Richards, successively vicars between 1783 and 1839, were all non-residents.[1] In Docker's time his curate lived at Steeple Ashton, but performed services twice on Sunday, once with a sermon. He held extra services at the chief festivals, and administered the sacrament four times a year, generally to about six people.[2] Services were still held twice on Sundays in 1851; the congregation was about 50, and there was a Sunday School of 29 children.

The foundations of an early church were traditionally thought to lie in Cooplechurch Field, and were uncovered in 1913. The building was 56 ft. long, rectangular, and lay east and west. The base of a cross, now in the church, which had been found in the field previously, and two skeletons, found in 1913, indicate that it was a church, but no clue to its date was found.[3] It was perhaps an earlier parish church of Keevil.

The church of *ST. LEONARD* consists of nave, chancel, north and south transepts, south aisle, west tower, and north, west, and south porches. There are two single-light windows in the north and south walls of the chancel, probably of the 13th century. In the late 14th or early 15th century the church may have been rebuilt as a cruciform building, probably after the monks of Edington acquired the rectory in 1393. The tracery of the east window of the chancel has affinities with that at Edington, and the north porch is also probably unaltered from that time. In the early 16th century the church was remodelled in the style of the time, and a south aisle was added. The tower was also either added or rebuilt. Walter Lucas of Steeple Ashton left money to building works at Keevil in 1514,[4] and William Baily of Baldham in 1516 ordered 20s. to be spent on the building of the south aisle.[5]

The nave is of three bays, and has a low pitched roof resting on trusses with trefoil-headed panels above the tie beams. The ceiling panels are plastered here and in the south aisle, where the flat roof is also original. The south porch has a tunnel vault with traceried panels; it is now used as a vestry. The similar porch at the west end was rebuilt exactly like the previous one in 1873.[6] Externally the church is decorated with embattled parapets, pinnacles, and gargoyles. The tower is of three stages, with bell-openings with diagonal tracery reminiscent of Edington.

In 1807 the screen separating the chancel from the nave, apparently of the 16th century, was taken down; parts were found re-used as joists a century later. In 1814 the pews were renewed, and panelling 5 ft. high put round the church. A new pulpit and

reading desk were made, and an altar-piece put up.[7] A west gallery was removed in 1874, and the church was re-seated in 1909–10, when the present organ was built.[8] The font rests on a circular pedestal surrounded by four small shafts, perhaps of the 14th century; the octagonal bowl with quatrefoil panels was either remodelled or erected to replace a previous one in the early 16th century. In the early 19th century it was removed from the church, and a large octagonal stoup of the same period was used as a font instead. The old font was bought from a mason by the Vicar of Steeple Ashton and was for some time in the garden of the vicarage there. It was restored to the church later in the century.[9] The stoup is now in the vestry.

The church is rich in mural tablets of the 17th and 18th centuries. Notable are those to the Blagden family (c. 1785), James Richardson (1782), and Jane Talbot (1768), which all use coloured marbles; the Talbot one is by Ford of Bath. Under the tower is an achievment of the royal arms painted on wood, dated 1715. On the nave wall near the south transept is a decayed black letter inscription of a text, apparently of the 16th century.

There were four bells and a sanctus bell at Keevil in 1553. Of the present peal of six, two are by John Wallis of Salisbury (1609), two by Thomas Bilbie of Chewstoke (1761), one by James Wells of Aldbourne (1810), and one by Mears (1842). The sanctus bell mentioned in 1553 remains in a bellcot on the eastern gable of the nave. It is probably of the 13th century, and was not cast but turned on a lathe.[10] The plate consists of a chalice and cover of 1577, a chalice of 1784 bought for the parish in 1842, a paten of 1817, and a flagon of 1893.[11] The registers are complete from 1559.

It is possible that there were two chapels in Bulkington in the Middle Ages. In 1331 a chantry was founded in the chapel of St. Mary at Bulkington (see above). The lands with which it was endowed evidently became part of the property later acquired by the Bonhommes of Edington there, and they paid a rent for them at the Dissolution.[12] A 'house called the Chapel House' was in 1564 part of the demesnes of the manor they formerly held in Bulkington,[13] so that it seems that this chapel probably ceased to exist at the Dissolution of the monasteries; no record of its dissolution with the chantries exists. Nevertheless, in 1553 the Commissioners left a chalice and two bells for a chapel at Bulkington,[14] which would imply that it was a parochial chapel rather than a free chapel or chantry. In 1576 a chapel of St. Andrew in Bulkington was granted by the Crown to Andrew Palmer and others.[15] The only other references to chapels at Bulkington, bequests of money to the priest celebrating there in 1495,[16] and to the chapel

[99] A. G. Matthews, *Calamy Revised*, 421; *V.C.H. Wilts.* iii. 105, 108.
[1] B.M. Add. MS. 42048, f. 127.
[2] Sar. Dioc. R.O. Vis. Queries, 1783.
[3] *W.A.M.* xxxix. 101. Tradition also said that the church once served Keevil and Steeple Ashton parishes, and that the name of the field was derived from a church which 'coupled' the parishes. The field-name, however, may be derived from the fact that Keevil church is at its northern edge and Steeple Ashton church near its western boundary.
[4] P.C.C. 31 Fetiplace.

[5] P.C.C. 28 Holder.
[6] B.M. Add. MS. 42048, f. 115.
[7] Ibid. ff. 110–1, 155.
[8] Ibid. ff. 111, 115.
[9] Ibid. f. 109.
[10] Walters, *Wilts. Bells.* 109.
[11] Nightingale, *Wilts. Plate*, 107–8; B.M. Add. MS. 42048, ff. 107–8.
[12] See p. 253.
[13] S.P. 15/12, f. 44.
[14] Nightingale, *Wilts. Plate*, 101.
[15] C 66/1138 m. 30.   [16] P.C.C. 25 Vox.

in 1515,[17] both refer to 'the chapel of Bulkington' as though there were only one there. It may be that the Bonhommes appropriated the endowment of the chantry in St. Mary's chapel and transferred the masses to Edington in the 15th century, so that St. Andrew's chapel was the only one in the 16th century. Whether it was in fact a parochial chapel, and why it was abandoned between 1553 and 1576 is not known. No reference to any institutional relationship to Keevil parish church has been found.

The present church at Bulkington, *CHRIST CHURCH*, was built in 1860 to the design of T. Cundy.[18] It consists of a chancel, nave, and western bellcot with one bell; the window tracery is in the early Decorated style. The plate was presented when the church was founded.[19] The organ was bought from Yatesbury church.[20]

NONCONFORMITY. In spite of the early manifestation of dissent in Keevil by John Maundrell,[21] there were only seven nonconformists in the parish in 1676.[22] During the earlier 18th century three houses in Keevil were licensed for Protestant dissenters,[23] but nothing is known of the congregations that used them. The only sect which gained a permanent position in Keevil was the Methodist. In 1783 Methodists met monthly at the house of a labourer and were taught by a barber from Bradford.[24] A building was first licensed for Methodist worship in 1812;[25] this may have been in Bulkington, where the very small stone chapel with plastered front was built and licensed in 1816.[26] By 1829 there were congregations in both villages, with 40 members at Keevil and 50 or 60 at Bulkington.[27] A chapel was built and licensed at Keevil in 1833.[28] Both buildings were still in use in 1851; congregations at Keevil averaged between 70 and 80 and at Bulkington between 30 and 40. In addition, 40 or 50 Primitive Methodists were meeting in a cottage at Bulkington.[29] The licence for their room was cancelled in 1876.[30] Since then the two Wesleyan Methodist chapels have been the only nonconformist places of worship. A Sunday school was added to the Keevil chapel in 1901.[31]

SCHOOLS. In 1783 there was a school in Keevil for teaching children English and arithmetic.[32] There were two day schools in the parish in 1819. One of these received £5 a year out of a farm which belonged to Nicholas Hicks Beach, lord of the manor; this sum was thought to have been left by an ancestor, probably one of the Beach family, but no details of the bequest could be found. Be-

tween 8 and 12 poor boys were educated with this money, and about 20 other children at their parents' expense. A second school had about 20 pupils.[33] The school which received the charity still existed in 1835, with about the same number of pupils. The only other day school then in the parish was one at Bulkington, started in 1827, where 11 children were paid for by their parents.[34]

By 1859 the £5 endowment was no longer mentioned.[35] There was still a school in each of the villages, both housed in cottages. At Keevil an old man had 20 pupils, and at Bulkington the same number was taught by an elderly woman. Some children, however, went to Steeple Ashton and West Ashton.[36] A school at Keevil was built at the cost of Mrs. Chamberlaine[37] in 1868. Although it was recognized as a public elementary school, and began to receive a grant about ten years after its foundation, management remained largely in the hands of the Chamberlaine family. In 1871 it was found that the accommodation at the Keevil school would be insufficient for the children from Bulkington.[38] At that time 21 children attended a Church of England school there,[39] but places for 45 would be needed under the 1870 Act. Keevil people were unwilling to contribute to a school large enough to include the Bulkington children. A School Board was suggested, and discussion continued until 1880, when it was finally decided to keep the Bulkington children in a cottage there.[40]

By 1894, however, the children from both villages went to the Keevil school, average attendance being 68 and accommodation 91.[41] In 1906 the managers still held the school from the Chamberlaine family on a yearly tenancy, paying a £20 rent,[42] but a 21-year lease was granted in 1913. Finally the school was conveyed in trust to the Diocesan Board of Finance in 1925.[43] Senior children were removed to the Trowbridge schools in 1941. Controlled status was granted in 1950.[44]

CHARITIES. In 1723 Joan White left a yearly rent-charge of £2 on her lands to trustees to pay to poor people in the tithing of Bulkington. In 1833, and still in 1903, the £2 was divided equally among all the poor there over one year old, each share in 1903 being about 4½ d.[45] In 1959 it was distributed among a few elderly people.[46]

Keevil was one of four recipient parishes of a charity founded by George Tayler in 1852. The objects of the charity, in the distribution of bread, the preaching of a children's sermon, and the provision of buns for the Sunday School are the same

[17] P.C.C. 31 Fetiplace.
[18] Pevsner, *Wilts.* 138.
[19] Nightingale, *Wilts. Plate*, 101.
[20] B.M. Add. MS. 42048, f. 212.
[21] See p. 260; *V.C.H. Wilts.* iii. 99.
[22] *W.N. & Q.* iii. 536.
[23] W.R.O. Certs. of Dissenters' Meeting Houses, 1709, 1711, 1739.
[24] Sar. Dioc. R.O. Vis. Queries, 1783.
[25] G.R.O. Retns. of Regns.
[26] Char. Com. File 90817.
[27] W.R.O. Retns. of Nonconformist Meetings, 1829.
[28] W.R.O. Certs. of Dissenters' Meeting Houses.
[29] H.O. 129/10/259.
[30] G.R.O. Worship Reg.
[31] *Kelly's Dir. Wilts.* (1939).
[32] Sar. Dioc. R.O. Vis. Queries, 1783.
[33] *Digest of Returns to Cttee. on Educ. of Poor*, H.C. 224,

p. 1029 (1819), ix(2).
[34] *Educ. Enq. Abstract*, H.C. 62, p. 1040 (1835), xliii.
[35] In 1903 it had long been unpaid, and was regarded as lost: *Endowed Char. Wilts.* (1908), p. 253.
[36] *Acct. of Wilts. Schools*, H.C. 27, p. 28 (1859), xxi(2).C
[37] The then vicar's mother-in-law; see above, p. 255.
[38] M. of Educ. file P 46/156 pt. i.
[39] *Ret. relating to Elem. Educ.* H.C. 201, p. 424 (1871), lv.
[40] M. of Educ. file P. 46/156 pt. i.
[41] *Return of Schools*, 1893 [C 7529], p. 640, H.C. (1894), lxv.
[42] *Return of Non-Provided Schools*, H.C. 178, p. 846 (1906), lxxxviii.
[43] M. of Educ. file p 46/156 pt. i.
[44] Ex inf. L.E.A.
[45] *Endowed Char. Wilts.* (1908) pp. 250–1.
[46] Char. Com. Accts. File.

as at Poulshot.[47] When the charity was divided in 1906, Keevil was allotted £469 stock.[48] In 1954 the income of over £12 was being spent on the objects prescribed by the donor.[49]

In 1625 the inhabitants of Keevil obtained permission to build an almshouse, because many of the poor were forced to live in barns and out-houses;[50] nothing more is known of it.

[47] See *V.C.H. Wilts.* vii. 125, and above p. 250 n. 7.
[48] Char. Com. File 82647.

[49] Ibid. Accts. File.
[50] Hist. MSS. Com. *Var. Coll.* i. 95.

INDEX

NOTE: The following abbreviations have been used: adv., advowson; agric., agriculture; Alex., Alexander; And., Andrew; Ant., Anthony; abp., archbishop; Bart., Bartholomew; Ben., Benjamin; bp., bishop; Cast., Castle; Cath., Catherine; cath., cathedral; chant., chantry; chap., chapel; char., charities; Chas., Charles; Chris., Christopher; ch., church; Coll., College; Ctss., Countess; Dan., Daniel; D. and C., Dean and Chapter; d., died; Edm., Edmund; Edw., Edward; Eliz., Elizabeth; fam., family; fl., flourished; Fred., Frederick; Geof., Geoffrey; geol., geology; Geo., George; Gilb., Gilbert; govt., government; Hen., Henry; Herb., Herbert; hosp., hospital; ho., house; Humph., Humphrey; hund., hundred; inc., inclosure; ind., industry; Jas., James; Jos., Joseph; Kath., Katherine; Laur., Laurence; Lawr., Lawrence; Ld., Lord; man., manor; Marg., Margaret; m., married; Mat., Matthew; Mic., Michael; Nat., Nathaniel; Nic., Nicholas; nonconf., nonconformity; n., note; par., parish; Parl. rep., Parliamentary representation; Pet., Peter; Phil., Philip; pop., population; rly., railway; Ric., Richard; riv., river; Rob., Robert; Rog., Roger; Rom., Roman; Rom. Cath., Roman Catholicism; Sam., Samuel; sch., school; Sim., Simon; sta., station; Steph., Stephen; succ., succeeded; Thos., Thomas; U.D.C., Urban District Council; vct., viscount; vctss., viscountess; Wal., Walter; w., wife; Wm., William.

Abarrow, Edw., 17; fam., 17
Abath, Clement, 7, 134; Joshua, 55; Rob., 7, 10
Abbot, Jane, 253; John, 253
A Beckett Turner, see Turner
Abergavenny (Mon.), prior and priory of, 63, 79, 70; and see Richard
Abingdon, earls of, see Bertie
A' Court, John, 16; Pierce (later A' Court Ashe), 16
Acryse Park (Kent), 83
Adams, John, 225; Thos., 226
Adlam, Alice, m. Rob. Cogswell, 157; Edith, m. (1) John Lambe (2) John Westwell, 157; Geo., 168; Hen., 169; John (d. 1545), 157, 165, 168, 173, 177; John (fl. 1550), 174, 245; John (fl. 1599), 174; Rob., 168; Sam., 18, 20, 25; Sybil, 168; Thos., 246; Wm. (fl. 1602), 115; Wm. (fl. 1702), 69, 113 n; fam., 113, 126, 168
Admiralty Gunnery Equipment Depot, 26, 31
Aete, Wm. de, 152
Aethelbald, King, 76
Agard, Ambrose, 100; Steph., 100; fam., 100
Aiscough, Wm., bp. of Salisbury, 240, 247
Alcester (Warws.), 235
Alcombe, Wm., 209
Aldbourne, 82 n, 261
Aldridge, Mary, 135; Ralph, 179; fam., 113, 126
Aldrington, John of, 253
Alexander, Hon. Wal. Phil., 62, 65
Alfred, King, 62, 145, 240, 241
Alfric the cowherd (fl. 1170), 163
'Alleburne' (stream), 146
Allen, Hen., 114
Alric (fl. 11th cent.), 50, 172, 204, 224
Alton Barnes, 50
Alton Priors, 203, 236
Alvediston, 11
Alwold (fl. 11th cent.), 64
Amberlegh, John, 59
Amelcote (Staffs.), 221
Amesbury, 243 n
Ampney, see Down Ampney
Andover (Hants), 49
Andrews, Edw. (fl. 1744), 224; Edw. (fl. 1792), 224; Eliz., see Middleney; John (fl. c. 1410), 64; John (d. c. 1744), 224; Kath., 66; Nat., 125; Ric., 7, 17, 175; Thos., 66; Townsend, 236
Anne, Queen, 214
Ansty, preceptory of, 105
Antony (Antonius), Wm., 177
Aplin & Barrett, cheese manufacturers, 171

Applegate, Steph., 182
Appleguard, Steven, 169
Appuldurcombe, in Godshill (I.o.w.), 82
Arden, Frances E., 215
Arn Hill, 91
Arthur, Prince of Wales (d. 1502), 37
Arundel, earls of, 252; and see Aubigny, Fitz Alan
Arundel, Ric. de, 196
Arundell, Sir John (fl. 1470), 149; Sir John (fl. 1550), 150, 172; Kath., see Chidiock; Thos. (d. 1485), 150; Sir Thos. (d. 1552), 27, 29, 31
Ash (Ashe), Cecily, see Berkeley; Edw., 155; Jane, m. Wm. Bassett, 101; John (fl. 1550), 101, 102; John (fl. 1640), 155; Sam., 173; fam., 101, 155, 162
Ashby, Canons (Northants.), 66
Ashe, see Ash
Ashfordby, John (later Trenchard), 223
Ashlock, Thos. (fl. 1561), 69; Thos. (s. of Thos.), 69
Ashton, Sir Rob., 64, 66, 72
Ashton, Chapel, see Ashton, Rood
Ashton, Gulden (Gulde, Gyldene), see East Town
Ashton, Rood (Chapel Ashton), 65, 205, 206, 221; agric., 207; chap., 211, 215; man., 203; man. ho., 203–4; pk., 201, 203, 204
Ashton, Steeple, 99, 193, 194, 195, 196, **198-218**, 229, 238, 245, 250, 261; adv., 211, 212; agric., 206–9, 244; Ashton Ho., 200; bells, 214; boundaries, 198–9; char., 217–18; Chartism., 202; chs., 211-16; ch. ho., 215; cloth ind., 209; common, 200, 209; courts, 197, 199, 216; cross, 210; estates, 205–6; fair, 199, 210; fields, 207; fire, 199; geol., 199; houses, 199–200; ind., 207-9; limekilns, 210; local govt., 216; lock-up, 199; 'Long's Arms', 200; mans., 202-5, 220, 221, 222, 225; man.ho., 202-3; market, 199, 210; mills, 210-11; nonconf., 216; place-name, 198; Polish hostel, 199; pop., 199; roads, 199; schs., 216-17; 262; steeple, 213; tithes, 211-12; vicarage ho., 214; village, 199–200; woodland, 199, 208; work ho., 202; and see Blackball, East Town, Littleton, Lovemead, Paxcroft, Snarlton
Ashton, West, vicar of, 181
Ashton, West, 194, 195, 198, 199; adv., 215-16; agric., 207; char., 217; ch., 211, 215–16; estates, 205–6; fields, 207; inc., 208, 209;

man., 204; Manor Farm, 201; mineral well, 201; nonconf., 216; pop., 201; sch., 217, 262; tithes, 212; village, 201
Associated Portland Cement Manufacturers, 171
Astley, Francis Dugdale, 7, 8, 65, 66, 70, 103, 114; Sir John Dugdale, 7; Mary, see Buckler; fam., 7, 10, 51, 53, 55, 114, 115
Astor, Hon. J. J., 76
Aubigny, Hugh d', earl of Arundel (d. 1243), 252
Aubrey the Chamberlain (fl. 1086), 102
Aubrey, John, 58, 60, 116, 152, 178, 199, 210, 228
Aucombe, in Longbridge Deverill, 131
Audley, barons, see Tuchet
Audley, de, Eleanor, see Clare; Hugh, 102; Marg., m. Ralph, earl of Stafford, 102
Aure, de, Augusta, 148 n; John, 148 n
Austin, Thos., 184
Australia, Australians, 72, 206
Avenel, Mabel, see Malet; Nic. (d. by 1223), 100, 101, 118; Nic. (d. c. 1246), 101; Wm., 101
Avon, riv., 1, 79, 168, 193, 194, 201
Awdry, Ambrose (fl. 1780), 210; Ambrose (fl. 1838), 83; Pet., 83; fam., 211
Axford, John (d. 1704), 211; John (fl. 1762), 211; Wm., 169
Aylesbury, Thos., rector of Corsley, 22, 23
Azor (fl. 1086), 15

Babigton, Babinton, see Bapton
Bache, Joan, see St. Lo; John, 149
Bagehott, Chas., 249
Bailey (Baily), Chris., 222; Edith, see Goddard; Marion, 258; Maud, 222; Nic., 259; Thos. (d. c. 1566), 253, 258; Thos. (fl. 1571), 253; Wal., 27; Wm. (d. 1536), 258, 260, 261; Wm. (fl. 1571), 253, 259; Wm. (fl. 1641), 104, 110; fam., 258; see also Bayly
Ball fam., 112
Ballard, Hen., 165; John Aldridge, 165; Jonathan, 83, 163; Phil., 83 Timothy, 165; Wal., 206; Wm., 165; Wm. Aldridge, 151; fam., 145, 165, 208.
Ballon, de, Hamelin, 63, 69; John (fl. 1242), 63, 65; John (fl. 1274), 63; Reynold, 63; Thos., 63
Bamfield, Edw., 150; John, 150; Ric., 150
Bannister, John, 114; Wm. (I), 223; Wm. (II), 223

CORRIGENDA TO VOLUMES I-VII

Vol. I (1), page 165*g*, line 14 from end, *for* '1920' *read* '1900'

Vol. II, page 12, line 6 from end, *for* 'The estate . . . in Durnford.' *read* 'The name of the estate survives in Avon Farm in Stratford-sub-Castle.'

,, ,, 60, line 1, *for* 'Standen in Chute' *read* 'North Standen (in Hungerford, Berks.)'

,, ,, 92, line 3 from end, *for* 'Durnford' *read* 'Stratford-sub-Castle'

,, ,, 110, note 52, *for* 'Standen in Chute' *read* 'North Standen (in Hungerford, Berks.)'

,, ,, 124, *delete note 77*

,, ,, 139*b*, lines 23-24, *for* '[Standen in Chute]' *read* '[North Standen (in Hungerford, Berks.)]'

,, ,, 214, line 53, *for* 'Standen in Chute' *read* 'North Standen (in Hungerford, Berks.)'

,, ,, 230, *s.v.* Standen, *for* 'Standen (*Standone*) in Chute' *read* 'Standen, North (*Standone*) in Hungerford (Berks.)'

,, ,, 234, *s.v.* Avon, in Bremhill, *after* 'Avon' *insert* '(Aven)' *and delete* '124 *n*,'

,, ,, 234, *s.v.* Avon, in Christian Malford, *delete whole entry*

,, ,, 237, *s.v.* Durnford, *before* '13' *insert* '12,' *and delete* 'Avon Farm, 12, 92;'

,, ,, 242, *s.v.* Salisbury, earl(s) of, *delete* '124 *n*,'

,, ,, 242, *s.v.* Salisbury, Edward of, *delete* '124 *n*,'

,, ,, 242, *s.v.* Standen, *for* 'Standen, in Chute' *read* 'Standen, North, in Hungerford (Berks.)'

,, ,, 243, *s.v.* Stratford-sub-Castle, *after* '180' *add* '; Avon Farm, 12, 92'

Vol. III, page 43, line 19, *for* 'Ashton' *read* 'Langford'

,, ,, 219*b*, line 16 from end, *for* 'King John' *read* 'Henry III'

,, ,, 232*b*, line 4 from end, *for* 'Charlbury' *read* 'Chalbury'

,, ,, 233*a*, line 4, *for* 'Durnford' *read* 'Stratford-sub-Castle'

,, ,, 250*a*, line 17, *after* 'Barford,' *insert* 'Biddesden,'

,, ,, 274, note 32, *for* 'vii' *read* 'xii'

,, ,, 287*b*, line 3 from end, *for* 'William' *read* 'Thomas'

,, ,, 291*b*, line 20 from end, *for* " 'Muleford' " *read* 'Milford'

,, ,, 331*b*, line 21 from end, *for* 'FitzAnger' *read* 'FitzAuger'

,, ,, 334*a*, lines 4–6, *for* 'In April . . . Byrte.' *read* 'In February 1543 the site was granted to John Pye, of Chippenham, and Robert Were or Browne, the elder, of Marlborough.'

,, ,, 334, note 13, *for* 'xx(1), p. 299' *read* 'xviii(1), p. 132'

,, ,, 344*b*, line 29, *for* 'debilies' *read* 'debiles'

,, ,, 394*b*, 'The Priory of Corsham', last 2 lines, *for* 'by Queen Joan, . . . Cambridge.⁷' *read* 'by Queen Joan; it was given by Henry VI to King's College, Cambridge, but Edward IV gave it to Syon Abbey.⁷'

,, ,, 394, note 7, *after* '149' *add* '; *Cal. Pat.* 1461-7, 56–57, 177, 238; *Rot. Parl.* v. 456; *Valor Eccl.* (Rec. Com.), i. 426.'

,, ,, 400, *s.v.* Ashton, Steeple, *delete* '43,'

,, ,, 400, *s.v.* Avon, in Durnford, *for* 'Durnford' *read* 'Stratford-sub-Castle'

,, ,, 401, *s.v.* Biddesden, in Chute, *after* '246,' *insert* '250,'

,, ,, 402, *s.v.* Browne, *after* 'Rob., 177;' *insert* '(or Were), Rob., 334;'

,, ,, 403, *s.v.* Byrte, *delete* '334,'

,, ,, 403, *between* 'Chafyn-Grove' *and* 'Chalfield, Great' *insert* 'Chalbury (Dors.), 236'

,, ,, 404, *s.v.* Charlbury, *delete whole entry*

,, ,, 404, *s.v.* Chippenham, *after* '290' *insert* ', 334;'

,, ,, 407, *s.v.* Edward IV, *after* '323' *add* ', 394'

,, ,, 407, *s.v.* FitzAnger, *delete whole entry*

,, ,, 407, *s.v.* FitzAucher, *before* 'Ric.' *insert* '(FitzAuger), Hen., 331;'

,, ,, 410, *s.v.* Henry III, *after* '168,' *insert* '219,'

,, ,, 411, *s.v.* John, King, *delete* '219,'

,, ,, 412, *s.v.* Langford, Steeple, *after* '41,' *insert* '43,'

,, ,, 414, *s.v.* Milford, *after* '203,' *insert* '291'

,, ,, 414, *s.v.* 'Muleford', *delete whole entry*

,, ,, 416, *s.v.* Penne, Wm., *for* 'Wm.' *read* 'Thos.'

,, ,, 416, *s.v.* Pollard, *delete* '334,'

,, ,, 417, *s.v.* Pye, *before* 'Thos.' *insert* 'John, 334;'

,, ,, 420, *between* 'Synet' *and* 'Sypherwest' *insert* 'Syon (Mdx.), abbey, 394'

,, ,, 422, *s.v.* Were, *add* '; (or Browne), Rob., 334'

Vol. IV, page ix, *for* 'Canals . . . By C. HADFIELD' *read* 'Canals . . . By E. C. R. HADFIELD, C.M.G.'

,, ,, xiii, last line, *for* 'Sandall' *read* 'Sandell'

,, ,, 12, note 53, *for* '(in Chute)' *read* '(in Hungerford, Berks.)'

,, ,, 17, line 31, *for* 'Standen (in Chute)' *read* 'North Standen (in Hungerford, Berks.)'

,, ,, 21, note 77, *for* 'DL 29' *read* 'S.C. 6'

,, ,, 21, note 78, *for* 'DL 29' *read* 'S.C. 6' *and for* '1-29' *read* '1-19'

Vol. IV page 21, note 79, *for* 'DL 29' *read* 'S.C. 6'

,, ,, 22, note 4, *for* '1069' *read* '11069'

,, ,, 29, note 55, *for* 'Great Cheverell' *read* 'Little Cheverell'

,, ,, 38, line 2, *for* 'Steeple Ashton' *read* 'Market Lavington'

,, ,, 170, note 77, *for* '*Wilts. Times*' *read* 'W. H. Tucker's Diary'

,, ,, 300*b*, *s.v.* Standen, *for* 'Chute' *read* 'Hungerford'

,, ,, 302, note 80, *for* 'Underditch' *read* 'Alderbury'

,, ,, 309, *the entry relating to* Burton Hill *now placed under* Highworth Hundred *in col. 1 should be transferred to Malmesbury Hundred in col. 2*

,, ,, 358, last column, *s.v.* Stockton, *after* '268' *add* '(u)' *and at foot of page add new footnote* '(u) In 1934 part of Fisherton de la Mere C.P. (pop. 97 in 1931) was transferred to Stockton C.P.'

,, ,, 424, note 12, *for* 'In Chute.' *read* 'North Standen, in Hungerford (Berks.).'

,, ,, 462, *s.v.* Ashton, Steeple, *for* 'labour services, 37–38;' *read* 'labour services, 37;'

,, ,, 465, *s.v.* Bulkington, *for* 'road to, 361' *read* 'road to, 261'

,, ,, 466, *s.v.* Cheverell, Great, *delete* 'tenant holdings, 29 *n*'

,, ,, 466, *s.v.* Cheverell, Little, *after* 'tax., 301, 310' *add* '; tenant holdings, 29 *n*'

,, ,, 467*a*, [*s.v.* Chute], lines 3–4, *for* 'Standen, South, 12 *n*, 17, 300, 424–5;' *read* 'Standen, manor of, 425;'

,, ,, 470, *s.v.* Fisherton de la Mere, *after* 'pop., 348' *insert* ', 358;'

,, ,, 473, *s.v.* Hungerford (Berks.), *for* 'Standen, North, 300, 309, 418, 423' *read* 'Standen, North, 17, 300, 418, 423, 424; Standen, South, 12 *n*, 300, 418, 423'

,, ,, 474, *s.v.* Lavington, Market, *after* '*see* Lavington, West;' *insert* 'labour services, 38;'

,, ,, 478, *s.v.* Poulton, in Mildenhall, *for* '*see* Poulton' *read* '*see* Mildenhall'

,, ,, 481, *s.v.* Standen, South, *for* '*see* Chute' *read* '*see* Hungerford'

Vol. V, page xix, *s.v.* Chancery, *for* 'C 193 Patent Rolls, Protectorate' *read* 'C 193 Crown Office, Miscellaneous Books'

,, ,, xix, *s.v.* Chancery, *for* 'C 220 Patent Rolls, Chas. II' *read* 'C 220 Petty Bag Office, Books, Papers, etc., relating to Administration'

,, ,, 15, line 8, *for* 'who took office some time after 1256' *read* 'who was in office after 1256 (and possibly before)'

,, ,, 43, line 5 from end, *for* " 'Neckenvill' " *read* " 'Neckemull' "

,, ,, 43, note 24, *for* '1377–81, 50' *read* '1377–81, 50, where the reading is inaccurate'

,, ,, 50, line 12 from end, *for* 'Aûmale' *read* 'Aumale'

,, ,, 51, lines 25–26, *for* 'rental and survey . . . 1200 and 1212' *read* 'survey of church lands in Wiltshire dated *c.* 1210'

,, ,, 51, line 26, *for* 'is' *read* 'was'

,, ,, 51, line 27, *delete* 'bishop's'

,, ,, 51, line 27, *for* 'and demonstrates' *read* 'which belonged to Glastonbury Abbey and later became a detached part of the abbey's hundred of South Damerham. Thus we see'

,, ,, 59, line 3, *for* 'Aumâle' *read* 'Aumale'

,, ,, 64, note 96, *for* '*Select Pleas in Manorial Courts*, i (Selden Soc. 1888), 176 sqq.' *read* 'S.C. 2/208/1'

,, ,, 65, line 5, *for* 'Aumâle' *read* 'Aumale'

,, ,, 72, line 19, *before* 'Marlborough' *insert* 'Calne,'

,, ,, 72, line 3 from end, *for* '47' *read* '48'

,, ,, 72, note 2, *delete last sentence*

,, ,, 73, line 9, *for* 'ten' *read* 'eleven'

,, ,, 73, line 12, *for* '5' *read* '4.3'

,, ,, 73, line 13, *for* '11.7' *read* '11.6'

,, ,, 73, line 19, *delete* 'for the first' *and* 'and . . . 1369.'

,, ,, 73, line 20, *after* 'was' *insert* 'almost'

,, ,, 73, line 23, *for* '5.6' *read* '6.8'

,, ,, 73, line 17 from end, *for* 'with a single sitting in 1413,' *read* 'except in two Parliaments,'

,, ,, 73, line 15 from end, *for* 'thrice' *read* 'twice'

,, ,, 73, line 7 from end, *for* 'up' *read* 'from 1295'

,, ,, 73, line 5 from end, *for* '78' *read* '76'

,, ,, 73, line 5 from end, *for* '74' *read* '75'

,, ,, 73, notes 8 and 12, *after* 'survive' *delete full point and add* 'and for those for which there is a return only for New Salisbury.'

,, ,, 89, line 9 from end, *for* 'letter' *read* 'letters'

,, ,, 320, line 7 from end, *after* 'sold' *substitute full point for comma and for* 'it' *read* 'It'

,, ,, 369, *s.v.* Aûmale, *for* 'Aûmale' *read* 'Aumale'

,, ,, 374, *s.v.* Fortibus, *for* 'Aumâle' *read* 'Aumale'

,, ,, 378, *s.v.* 'Neckenvill', *for* " 'Neckenvill', in Cannings hund., 43' " *read* " 'Neckemull' in Bishop's Cannings, 43"

,, ,, 379, *s.v.* Quidhampton, *for* 'Quidhampton, in Wroughton, 75, 140' *read* 'Quidhampton, in Fuggleston St. Peter, 75' *and* 'Quidhampton, in Wroughton, 140'

Vol. V,   page 380, *s.v.* Salisbury (New), Parl. rep., *for* '204, 205' *read* '203–5'

,,   ,,   380, *s.v.* Salisbury hund., *delete whole entry*

Vol. VI,   page 65*b*, line 26, *for* 'Ethelreda' *read* 'Etheldreda'

,,   ,,   211*b*, line 19 from end, *for* 'Nesbit' *read* 'Nisbet'

,,   ,,   234, *s.v.* Nesbit, *delete whole entry*

,,   ,,   234, *between* 'Nimeguen' *and* 'Normandy' *insert* 'Nisbet, Josiah, 211'

Vol. VII, page   9*a*, lines 33–34, *delete* 'The Kennet and Avon Canal crosses the parish south of the river.'

,,   ,,   82*b*, line 13, *for* 'Terry' *read* 'Terry's'

,,   ,,   84*b*, last line—page 85*a*, line 3, *delete* 'In the north-east . . . families.[87]'

,,   ,,   85, *delete note 87*

,,   ,,   125*b*, last line, *for* 'Bridge at Beckington' *read* 'Bridge to Beckington'

,,   ,,   131*a*, line 3 from end, *for* 'Mary (Minshull)' *read* 'Mary (Chivers)'

,,   ,,   133*b*, lines 28 and 29, for 'Bellefield in Hilperton Road' *read* 'the Liberal Club in Frog Lane'

,,   ,,   133*b*, line 29, *delete* 'At Bellefield lived'

,,   ,,   133*b*, line 30, *after* 'day' *insert* ', lived at Bellefield in Hilperton Road.'

,,   ,,   137*a*, line 4 from end, *for* '*c.* 1484' *read* '1488 x 1491'

,,   ,,   151, note 34, *for* '*Wilts. Times*, 16 Feb. 1917' *read* 'Wilts. Cuttings, xiv, 70'

,,   ,,   152*a*, line 17, *before* 'to' *insert* 'lies'

,,   ,,   152*a*, lines 18–19, *for* ', originated in the purchase of 4½ acres' *read* '. Of this area 4½ acres were purchased'

,,   ,,   152*a*, lines 20–21, *for* 'that year' *read* '1884'

,,   ,,   152, note 55, *for* '*Wilts. Times*, 9 Febr. 1917' *read* 'Wilts. Cuttings, xiv, 70'

,,   ,,   152, note 60, *delete* '*W.A.M.* xliv, 482;' *and after* '12–13' *substitute semi-colon for full point and add* 'ex inf. Mr M. J. Lansdown.'

,,   ,,   155*b*, line 21, *for* '1483' *read* '1484'

,,   ,,   168*b*, line 35, *for* '1483' *read* '1484'

,,   ,,   168*b*, line 36, *for* '3*d.*' *read* '3*s.* 4*d.*' *and for* 'weekly' *read* 'quarterly'

,,   ,,   168, note 25, *for* '*Wilts. Times*, 16 Feb. 1917' *read* 'Wilts. Cuttings, xiv, 70'

,,   ,,   177, line 16, *for* 'Highway' *read* 'Clyffe Pypard'

,,   ,,   178, line 20, *delete* 'Bupton,'

,,   ,,   179*a*, lines 11–10 from end, *for* 'late 18th-century' *read* 'mid-18th-century'

,,   ,,   179*a*, line 8 from end, *after* 'cornice.' *insert* 'At the back is a timber-framed wing with exposed beams and stone fireplaces of the 16th or early 17th century.'

,,   ,,   180*a*, line 1, *for* 'early 18th-century cottage' *read* 'cottage of earlier date'

,,   ,,   180*a*, lines 4–7, *for* 'Cottage, was almost . . . of ashlar, and' *read* 'Cottage, was largely remodelled about 1700.[16a] Parts of a 16th- or early-17th-century house remain, including the base of one stone chimneypiece. The front is faced with ashlar and'

,,   ,,   180*a*, line 10, *after* 'at the angles.' *add* 'There have been additions at the south-west corner and on the east side of the house.'

,,   ,,   180*a*, lines 12–13, *for* 'a two-storied rectangular house that was entirely rebuilt' *read* 'a rectangular house of two and three stories, rebuilt'

,,   ,,   187, note 20, *for* 'Devises' *read* 'Devizes'

,,   ,,   191*a*, lines 26 and 28, *for* 'Swell' *read* 'Snell'

,,   ,,   194*a*, line 4, *for* 'Ida W. Gandy' *read* 'Ida Gandy'

,,   ,,   227, *s.v.* Bupton, *for* 'Highway' *read* 'Clyffe Pypard'

,,   ,,   228, *s.v.* Bythesea, *for* 'Minshull' *read* 'Chivers'

,,   ,,   228, *s.v.* Chivers, *before* 'Ric., 185;' *insert* 'Mary (mar. Bythesea), 131;'

,,   ,,   231, *s.v.* Gandy, *delete* 'W.'

,,   ,,   232, *s.v.* Hurst fam., *delete whole entry*

,,   ,,   233, *s.v.* Lavington, West, *after* 'mans., 199' *insert* ', 200, 205;'

,,   ,,   233, *between* 'Littlecote' *and* 'Littleton Pannell' *insert* 'Littleton Auncells (in West Lavington), man., 200, 205'

,,   ,,   235, *s.v.* Minshull, *delete* 'Mary (mar. Bythesea), 131;'

,,   ,,   238, *s.v.* Snell, *after* 'Jane, 183' *add* '; John, 191; Nich., 191'

,,   ,,   238, *s.v.* Swell, *delete whole entry*

,,   ,,   239, *s.v.* Townsend, *delete* '; fam., 85'

,,   ,,   239, *s.v.* Trowbridge, Liberal Club, *before* '146' *insert* '133,'

PRINTED IN THE NETHERLANDS
BY E. J. BRILL, LEIDEN